T4-AKY-081

Proc setinit;
run;
To configure what SAS program the computer has and expiration date.
(Read the log, there won't be output)

SAS® Programming 1: Essentials

Ted.Meleky@sas.com

Course Notes

Hana Demeke
Nov, 2016

SAS® Programming 1: Essentials Course Notes was developed by Charlot Bennett, Michele Ensor, and Kathy Passarella. Additional contributions were made by Davetta Dunlap, Susan Farmer, Ted Meleky, Linda Mitterling, and Theresa Stemler. Editing and production support was provided by the Curriculum Development and Support Department.

SAS and all other SAS Institute Inc. product or service names are registered trademarks or trademarks of SAS Institute Inc. in the USA and other countries. ® indicates USA registration. Other brand and product names are trademarks of their respective companies.

SAS® Programming 1: Essentials Course Notes

Copyright © 2016 SAS Institute Inc. Cary, NC, USA. All rights reserved. Printed in the United States of America. No part of this publication may be reproduced, stored in a retrieval system, or transmitted, in any form or by any means, electronic, mechanical, photocopying, or otherwise, without the prior written permission of the publisher, SAS Institute Inc.

Book code E70741, course code LWPG1/PG1, prepared date 24May2016. LWPG1_003

ISBN 978-1-62960-424-4

Table of Contents

Course Description

This course is for users who want to learn how to write SAS programs. It is the entry point to learning SAS programming and is a prerequisite to many other SAS courses. If you do not plan to write SAS programs and you prefer a point-and-click interface, you should attend the SAS® Enterprise Guide® 1: Querying and Reporting course.

To learn more…

For information about other courses in the curriculum, contact the SAS Education Division at 1-800-333-7660, or send e-mail to training@sas.com. You can also find this information on the web at http://support.sas.com/training/ as well as in the Training Course Catalog.

For a list of other SAS books that relate to the topics covered in this course notes, USA customers can contact the SAS Publishing Department at 1-800-727-3228 or send e-mail to sasbook@sas.com. Customers outside the USA, please contact your local SAS office.

Also, see the SAS Bookstore on the web at http://support.sas.com/publishing/ for a complete list of books and a convenient order form.

Prerequisites

Before attending this course, you should have experience using computer software. Specifically, you should be able to

- understand file structures and system commands on your operating systems
- access data files on your operating systems.

No prior SAS experience is needed. If you do not feel comfortable with the prerequisites or are new to programming and think that the pace of this course might be too demanding, you can take the SAS® Programming Introduction: Basic Concepts course before attending this course. SAS® Programming Introduction: Basic Concepts is designed to introduce you to computer programming and presents a portion of the SAS® Programming 1: Essentials material at a slower pace.

Chapter 1 Introduction

Copyright © 2016, SAS Institute Inc., Cary, North Carolina, USA. ALL RIGHTS RESERVED.

1.1 Overview

Objectives

- Define SAS.
- Describe the functionality of Base SAS.

3

What Is SAS?

SAS is a suite of business solutions and technologies to help organizations solve business problems.

4

- SAS is Computer Language
- Celebrating 40th birthday

Copyright © 2016, SAS Institute Inc., Cary, North Carolina, USA. ALL RIGHTS RESERVED.

Why Use SAS?

SAS enables you to do the following:

- access and manage data across multiple sources
- perform analyses and deliver information across your organization

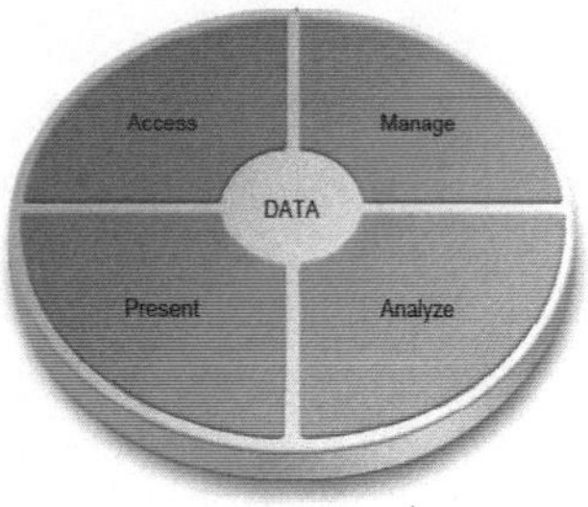

Base SAS is the primary focus of this course.

5

What Is Base SAS?

Base SAS is the foundation for all SAS software.

Base SAS provides the following:

- a highly flexible, highly extensible, fourth-generation programming language
- a rich library of encapsulated programming procedures
- a choice of programming interfaces

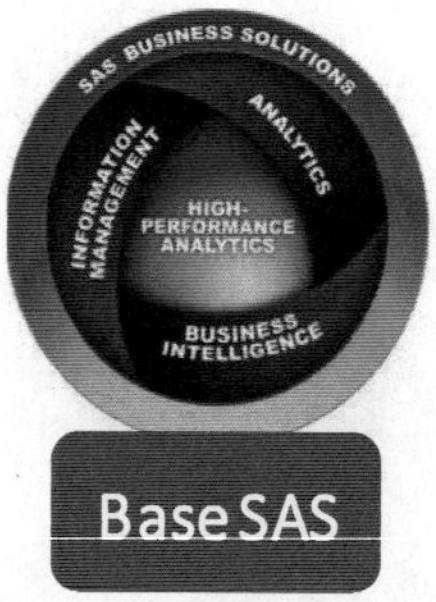

6

Copyright © 2016, SAS Institute Inc., Cary, North Carolina, USA. ALL RIGHTS RESERVED.

1.01 Multiple Choice Poll

What is your programming experience with SAS?

a. maintaining programs written by others
b. writing new programs
c. no experience
d. other

7

1.2 Course Logistics

Objectives

- Describe the data that is used in the course.
- Specify the naming convention that is used for the course files.
- Define the three levels of exercises.
- Explain the extended learning for this course.

10

Copyright © 2016, SAS Institute Inc., Cary, North Carolina, USA. ALL RIGHTS RESERVED.

Orion Star Sports & Outdoors

This course focuses on a fictitious global sports and outdoors retailer that has traditional stores, an online store, and a catalog business.

11

Orion Star Data

Large amounts of data are stored in various formats.

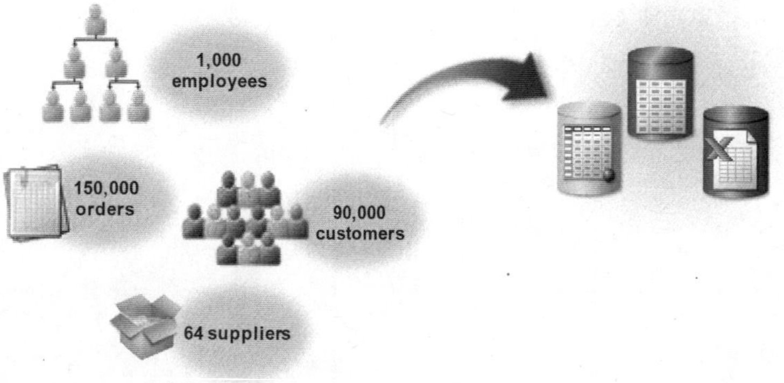

12

Copyright © 2016, SAS Institute Inc., Cary, North Carolina, USA. ALL RIGHTS RESERVED.

Program Naming Conventions

In this course, you use the structure below to retrieve and save SAS programs.

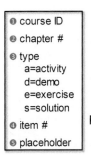

- ❶ course ID
- ❷ chapter #
- ❸ type
  - a=activity
  - d=demo
  - e=exercise
  - s=solution
- ❹ item #
- ❺ placeholder

p104d01x

❶ ❷ ❸ ❹ ❺

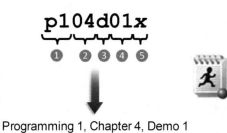

Programming 1, Chapter 4, Demo 1

13

Locating Data Files

In this course, macro variable references are used to give a more flexible approach for locating files.

```
%let path=s:\workshop;
```

```
infile "&path\sales.csv";
```

```
infile "&path\payroll.dat";
```

14

Copyright © 2016, SAS Institute Inc., Cary, North Carolina, USA. ALL RIGHTS RESERVED.

Three Levels of Exercises

The course is designed to have you complete only ***one*** set of exercises. Select the level that is most appropriate for your skill set.

Level 1	Provides step-by-step instructions.
Level 2	Provides less information and guidance.
Challenge	Provides minimal information and guidance. You might need to use SAS Help and documentation.

15

Extending Your Learning

After class, you have access to an extended learning page that was created for this course. The page includes the following:

- course data and program files
- a PDF file of the course notes
- other course-specific resources

EXTENDED LEARNING From SAS Education

16

Copyright © 2016, SAS Institute Inc., Cary, North Carolina, USA. ALL RIGHTS RESERVED.

Chapter 2 SAS® Programs

Copyright © 2016, SAS Institute Inc., Cary, North Carolina, USA. ALL RIGHTS RESERVED.

2.1 Introduction to SAS Programs

Objectives

- List the components of a SAS program.

3

SAS Programs

A *SAS program* is a sequence of one or more steps.

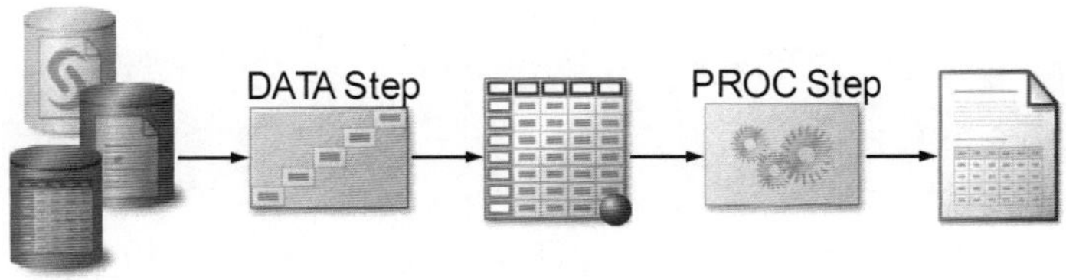

- *DATA steps* typically create SAS data sets.
- *PROC steps* typically process SAS data sets to generate reports and graphs, and to manage data.

4

Copyright © 2016, SAS Institute Inc., Cary, North Carolina, USA. ALL RIGHTS RESERVED.

SAS Program Steps

A *step* is a sequence of SAS statements. This program has a DATA step and a PROC step.

```
data work.newemps;
   infile "&path\newemps.csv" dlm=',';
   input First $ Last $ Title $ Salary;
run;

proc print data=work.newemps;
run;
```

5

Step Boundaries

SAS steps begin with either of the following:

- a DATA statement
- a PROC statement

SAS detects the end of a step when it encounters one of the following:

- a RUN statement (for most steps)
- a QUIT statement (for some procedures)
- the beginning of another step (DATA statement or PROC statement)

6

Copyright © 2016, SAS Institute Inc., Cary, North Carolina, USA. ALL RIGHTS RESERVED.

2.01 Short Answer Poll

How many steps are in program **p102d01**? 3

```
data work.newsalesemps;
   length First_Name $ 12
          Last_Name $ 18 Job_Title $ 25;
   infile "&path\newemps.csv" dlm=',';
   input First_Name $ Last_Name $
         Job_Title $ Salary;
run;

proc print data=work.newsalesemps;
run;

proc means data=work.newsalesemps;
   var Salary;
run;
```

data step

proc step

proc step

7 p102d01

SAS Program Example

This DATA step creates a temporary SAS data set named **work.newsalesemps** by reading four fields from a file.

```
data work.newsalesemps;
   length First_Name $ 12
          Last_Name $ 18 Job_Title $ 25;
   infile "&path\newemps.csv" dlm=',';
   input First_Name $ Last_Name $
         Job_Title $ Salary;
run;

proc print data=work.newsalesemps;
run;

proc means data=work.newsalesemps;
   var Salary;
run;
```

9 p102d01

Copyright © 2016, SAS Institute Inc., Cary, North Carolina, USA. ALL RIGHTS RESERVED.

SAS Program Example

This PROC PRINT step lists the **work.newsalesemps** data set.

```
data work.newsalesemps;
   length First_Name $ 12
          Last_Name $ 18 Job_Title $ 25;
   infile "&path\newemps.csv" dlm=',';
   input First_Name $ Last_Name $
         Job_Title $ Salary;
run;

proc print data=work.newsalesemps;
run;

proc means data=work.newsalesemps;
   var Salary;
run;
```

10 p102d01

SAS Program Example

This PROC MEANS step summarizes the **Salary** variable in the **work.newsalesemps** data set.

```
data work.newsalesemps;
   length First_Name $ 12
          Last_Name $ 18 Job_Title $ 25;
   infile "&path\newemps.csv" dlm=',';
   input First_Name $ Last_Name $
         Job_Title $ Salary;
run;

proc print data=work.newsalesemps;
run;

proc means data=work.newsalesemps;
   var Salary;
run;
```

11 p102d01

Copyright © 2016, SAS Institute Inc., Cary, North Carolina, USA. ALL RIGHTS RESERVED.

Idea Exchange

How does SAS detect the end of each step in this program?

```
data work.newsalesemps;
   length First_Name $ 12
          Last_Name $ 18 Job_Title $ 25;
   infile "&path\newemps.csv" dlm=',';
   input First_Name $ Last_Name $
         Job_Title $ Salary;
run;

proc print data=work.newsalesemps;

proc means data=work.newsalesemps;
   var Salary;
```

12

2.2 Submitting a SAS Program

Objectives

- Describe various processing modes and SAS interfaces.
- Define the three primary tabs or windows used within a SAS interface.
- Submit a SAS program to create the course data files.
- Submit the SAS program introduced in the previous section.

15

Copyright © 2016, SAS Institute Inc., Cary, North Carolina, USA. ALL RIGHTS RESERVED.

Processing Modes

The following are two possible processing modes for submitting a SAS program:

Interactive Mode	A SAS program is submitted within a SAS interface for foreground processing
Batch Mode	A SAS program is submitted to the operating environment for background processing

✎ In this course, interactive mode is used to process SAS programs.

16

- With foreground processing, the SAS interface coordinates all the work, so you cannot use your SAS interface to do other work while your program is running.
- With background processing, the operating environment coordinates all the work, so you can use your workstation session while your program is running.

SAS Interfaces

There are three possible SAS interfaces for processing a SAS program in interactive mode.

SAS Windowing Environment	SAS Enterprise Guide	SAS Studio

17

Copyright © 2016, SAS Institute Inc., Cary, North Carolina, USA. ALL RIGHTS RESERVED.

SAS Interfaces

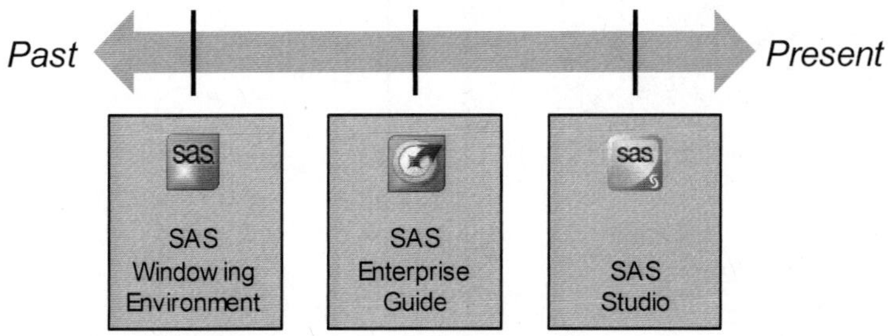

18

SAS Windowing Environment

The *SAS windowing environment* is an application that is accessed from different operating environments.

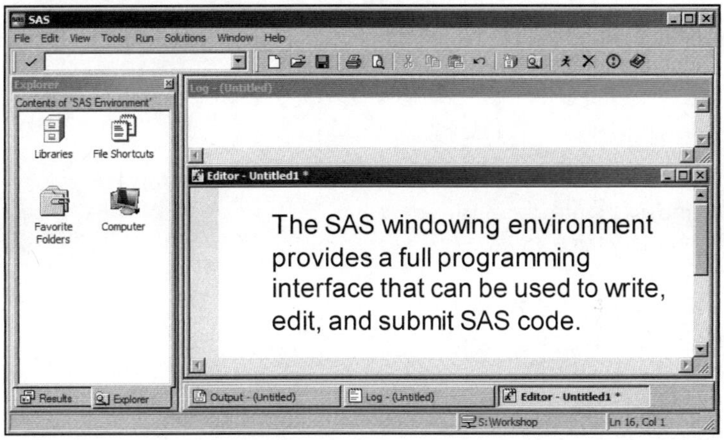

19

Copyright © 2016, SAS Institute Inc., Cary, North Carolina, USA. ALL RIGHTS RESERVED.

SAS Enterprise Guide

SAS Enterprise Guide is a client application that is accessed from the Windows operating environment.

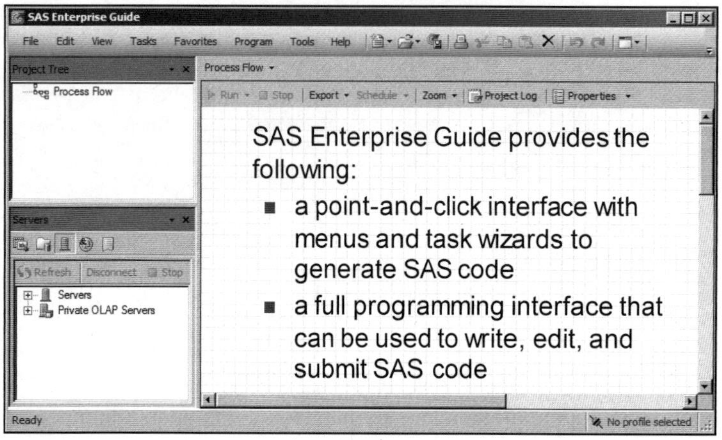

20

SAS Studio

SAS Studio is a web client that is accessed through an HTML5-compliant web browser.

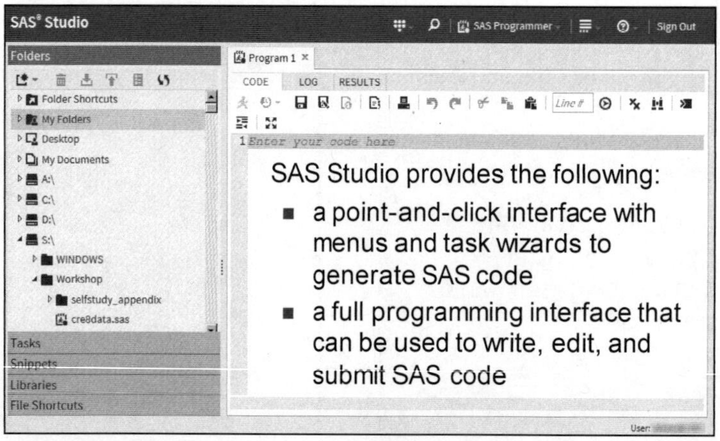

21

SAS Studio is the interface used in SAS University Edition. For more information about SAS University Edition, visit **http://www.sas.com/en_us/software/university-edition.html**.

Copyright © 2016, SAS Institute Inc., Cary, North Carolina, USA. ALL RIGHTS RESERVED.

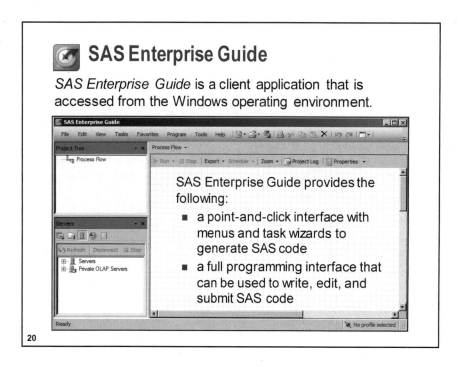

2.02 Multiple Choice Poll

Which interface will you use during this course?

a. SAS Studio
b. SAS Enterprise Guide
c. SAS windowing environment

22

SAS Interface Tabs or Windows

Regardless of the SAS interface that you choose to use, there are three primary tabs or windows.

Editor	Enter, edit, submit, and save a SAS program
Log	Browse notes, warnings, and errors relating to a submitted SAS program
Results	Browse output from reporting procedures

23

Copyright © 2016, SAS Institute Inc., Cary, North Carolina, USA. ALL RIGHTS RESERVED.

SAS Interface Tabs or Windows

Each interface uses specific terms to reference these three primary tabs or windows.

	SAS Studio (tabs)	SAS Enterprise Guide (tabs)	SAS Windowing Environment (windows)
Editor	Code	Program	Enhanced or Program Editor
Log	Log	Log	Log
Results	Results	Results	Results Viewer or Output

24

SAS Interface Tabs or Windows

The following is an example workflow of how a user might use the three primary tabs or windows:

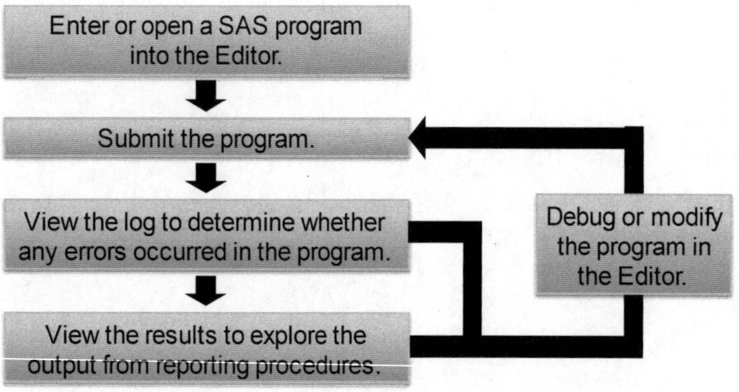

25

Copyright © 2016, SAS Institute Inc., Cary, North Carolina, USA. ALL RIGHTS RESERVED.

Business Scenario

In this section, the following actions are completed:

- Submit a SAS program to create the data files that are needed for the course.
- Submit the SAS program introduced in Section 2.1.

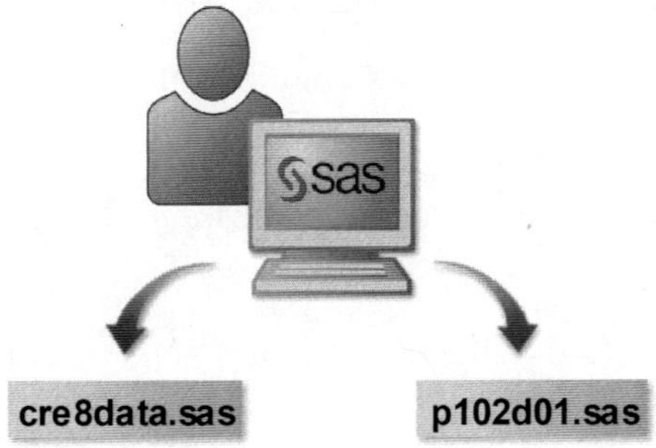

26

Copyright © 2016, SAS Institute Inc., Cary, North Carolina, USA. ALL RIGHTS RESERVED.

Submitting SAS Programs with SAS Studio

This demonstration is based on SAS Studio 3.3.

Submitting the cre8data Program

1. Start SAS Studio. The main window of SAS Studio consists of a navigation pane on the left and a work area on the right.
2. In the Folders section of the navigation pane, navigate in the file structure to find the **cre8data** program.
3. Double-click **cre8data** to open the program. Instead of double-clicking, you can drag the program into the work area.
4. On the CODE tab for the **cre8data** program, find the %LET statement.
5. If your data files are to be created at a location other than **s:\workshop**, change the value that is assigned to the **path** macro variable to reflect the location. If your data files are created in **s:\workshop**, then no change is needed.

   The **cre8data** program uses forward slashes for portability across operating environments. UNIX and Linux require forward slashes. Windows accepts forward slashes and might convert them to backslashes.
6. On the CODE tab, click (**Run**) or press F3 to submit the program.
7. On the RESULTS tab, verify that the output contains a list of data files.

Submitting the p102d01 Program

1. In the Folders section of the navigation pane, navigate in the file structure to find the **p102d01** program.
2. Double-click **p102d01** to open the program. Instead of double-clicking, you can drag the program into the work area.
3. On the CODE tab, click (**Run**) or press F3 to submit the program.
4. On the RESULTS tab, view the PROC PRINT and PROC MEANS output.
5. Click the **LOG** tab and verify that no errors or warnings appear.

End of Demonstration

Copyright © 2016, SAS Institute Inc., Cary, North Carolina, USA. ALL RIGHTS RESERVED.

Submitting SAS Programs with SAS Enterprise Guide

This demonstration is based on SAS Enterprise Guide 7.1.

Submitting the cre8data Program

1. Start SAS Enterprise Guide. Close the Welcome to SAS Enterprise Guide window by clicking the **X** in the right corner of the window. By default, SAS Enterprise Guide contains a Project Tree window and Servers window. They are docked on the left side. A Process Flow window is docked on the right side.
2. Select **File** ⇨ **Open** ⇨ **Program** or click (**Open**) ⇨ **Program**.
3. In the Open Program window, navigate in the file structure to find **cre8data** and click **Open**.
4. On the Program tab for the **cre8data** program, find the %LET statement.
5. If your data files are to be created at a location other than **s:\workshop**, change the value that is assigned to the **path** macro variable to reflect the location. If your data files are created in **s:\workshop**, then no change is needed.

   The **cre8data** program uses forward slashes for portability across operating environments. UNIX and Linux require forward slashes. Windows accepts forward slashes and might convert them to backslashes.

6. On the Program tab, click **Run** or press F3 to submit the program.
7. On the Results tab, verify that the output contains a list of data files.

Submitting the p102d01 Program

1. Select **File** ⇨ **Open** ⇨ **Program** or click (**Open**) ⇨ **Program**.
2. In the Open Program window, navigate in the file structure to find **p102d01** and click **Open**.
3. On the Program tab, click **Run** or press F3 to submit the program.
4. On the Results tab, view the PROC PRINT and PROC MEANS output.
5. Click the **Log** tab and verify that no errors or warnings appear.

End of Demonstration

Copyright © 2016, SAS Institute Inc., Cary, North Carolina, USA. ALL RIGHTS RESERVED.

Submitting SAS Programs in the SAS Windowing Environment

This demonstration is based on SAS 9.4M2.

Submitting the cre8data Program

1. Start the SAS windowing environment. If you see a pop-up window that references a change notice or getting started with SAS, click **Close**. By default, the SAS windowing environment consists of a left pane containing the Results and Explorer windows and a right pane containing the Output, Log, and Editor windows.
2. Click (**Open**) when the Editor window is the active window or select **File** ⇨ **Open Program**.
3. In the Open window, navigate in the file structure to find **cre8data** and click **Open**.
4. In the Editor window for the **cre8data** program, find the %LET statement.
5. If your data files are to be created at a location other than **s:\workshop**, change the value that is assigned to the **path** macro variable to reflect the location. If your data files are created in **s:\workshop**, then no change is needed.

   The **cre8data** program uses forward slashes for portability across operating environments. UNIX and Linux require forward slashes. Windows accepts forward slashes and might convert them to backslashes.

6. Click (**Submit**) or press F3 to submit the program.
7. In the Results Viewer window, verify that the output contains a list of data files.
8. Go to the Log window and click (**New**) or select **Edit** ⇨ **Clear All** to clear the Log window.

Submitting the p102d01 Program

1. Click (**Open**) when the Editor window is the active window or select **File** ⇨ **Open Program**.
2. In the Open window, navigate in the file structure to find **p102d01** and click **Open**.
3. Click (**Submit**) or press F3 to submit the program.
4. In the Results Viewer window, view the PROC PRINT and PROC MEANS output.
5. Go to the Log window and verify that no errors or warnings appear. Be sure to scroll up to see all messages.

End of Demonstration

Copyright © 2016, SAS Institute Inc., Cary, North Carolina, USA. ALL RIGHTS RESERVED.

Exercises

All of the exercises in this chapter are self-guided. No solutions are needed.

SAS Studio

You ***must*** complete this exercise to create the course data files. If you do not create the data files, the majority of programs in this course will fail.

1. Creating Course Data with SAS Studio

a. Start SAS Studio. The main window of SAS Studio consists of a navigation pane on the left and a work area on the right.

b. In the Folders section of the navigation pane, navigate in the file structure to find the **cre8data** program.

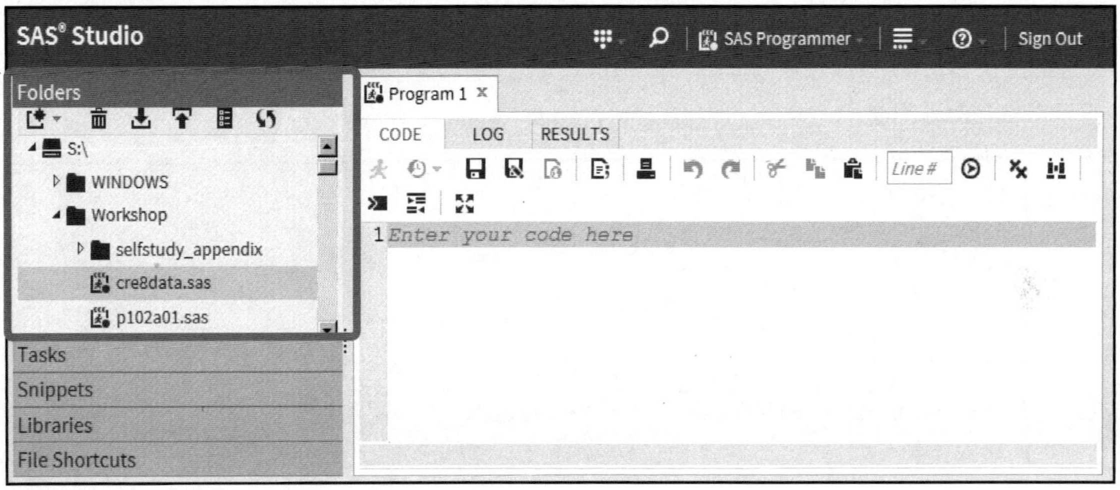

c. Double-click **cre8data** to open the program. Instead of double-clicking, you can drag the program into the work area.

d. On the CODE tab for the **cre8data** program, find the %LET statement shown below.

Copyright © 2016, SAS Institute Inc., Cary, North Carolina, USA. ALL RIGHTS RESERVED.

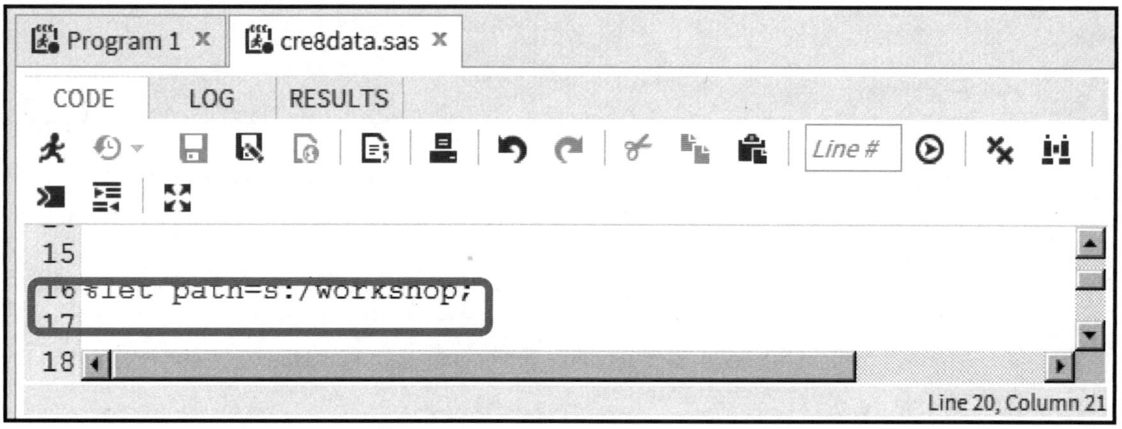

e. If your data files are to be created at a location other than **s:\workshop**, change the value that is assigned to the **path** macro variable to reflect the location. If your data files are created in **s:\workshop**, then no change is needed.

> ✎ The **cre8data** program uses forward slashes for portability across operating environments. UNIX and Linux require forward slashes. Windows accepts forward slashes and might convert them to backslashes.

f. On the CODE tab, click (**Run**) or press F3 to submit the program.

g. On the RESULTS tab, verify that the output contains a list of data files.

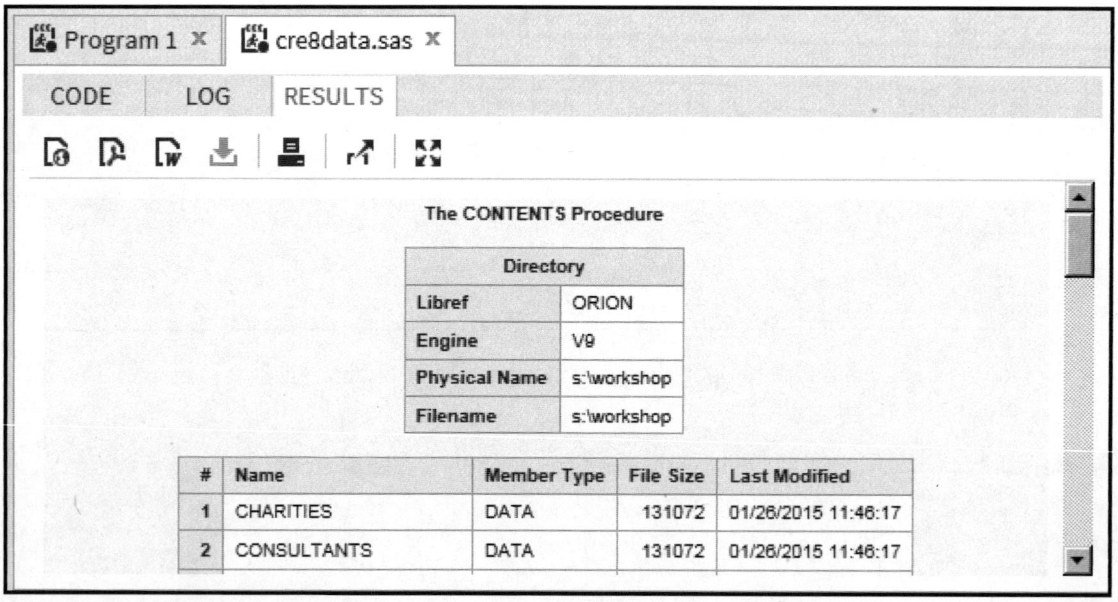

h. Close the program tab for **cre8data** by clicking the **X** next to the name.

2. Exploring SAS Studio

Using the Primary Interface Tabs

Copyright © 2016, SAS Institute Inc., Cary, North Carolina, USA. ALL RIGHTS RESERVED.

a. On the CODE tab of the Program 1 tab, enter the PROC PRINT step shown below.

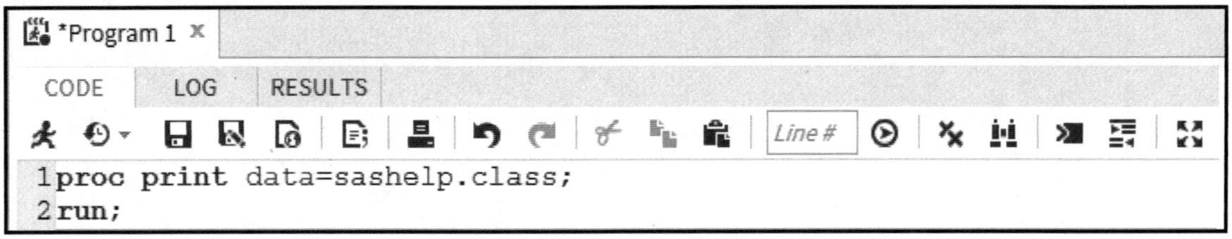

b. On the CODE tab, click (**Run**) or press F3 to submit the program. If the program runs successfully, the RESULTS tab automatically opens and shows the PROC PRINT output.

1) Click the **LOG** tab and check the log for the two notes below. If you see any warnings or errors, return to the CODE tab, fix any mistakes, and rerun the program.

```
NOTE: There were 19 observations read from the data set SASHELP.CLASS.
NOTE: PROCEDURE PRINT used (Total process time):
```

2) Click the **RESULTS** tab. Notice that the PROC PRINT output contains an **Obs** column.

Obs	Name	Sex	Age	Height	Weight
1	Alfred	M	14	69.0	112.5
2	Alice	F	13	56.5	84.0
3	Barbara	F	13	65.3	98.0
4	Carol	F	14	62.8	102.5
5	Henry	M	14	63.5	102.5

c. Click the **CODE** tab and add the NOOBS option to eliminate the **Obs** column.

```
proc print data=sashelp.class noobs;
run;
```

The NOOBS option is in the PROC PRINT statement before the semicolon.

1) On the CODE tab, click (**Run**) or press F3 to submit the program.

2) View the new information on the RESULTS tab and the LOG tab.

d. Create another program. In the Folders section of the navigation pane, click (**New**) ⇨ **SAS Program (F4)** or press F4.

Copyright © 2016, SAS Institute Inc., Cary, North Carolina, USA. ALL RIGHTS RESERVED.

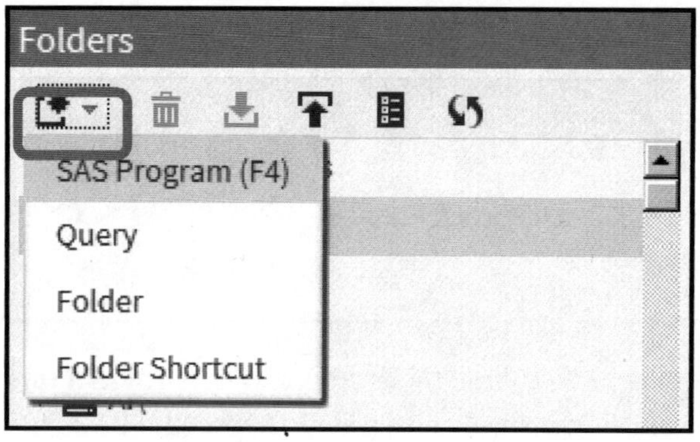

1) On the CODE tab of the Program 2 tab, enter the PROC PRINT step and the PROC MEANS step shown below.

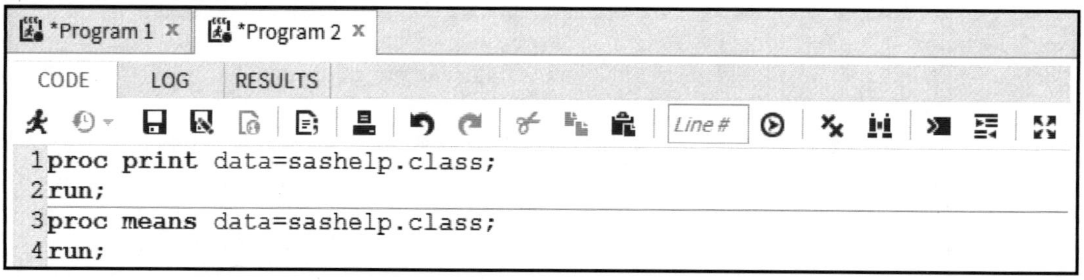

2) On the CODE tab, click (**Run**) or press F3 to submit the program. If the program runs successfully, the RESULTS tab automatically opens and shows the PROC PRINT and PROC MEANS output.

3) Click the **LOG** tab. Check the log for notes. If you see any warnings or errors, return to the CODE tab, fix any mistakes, and rerun the program.

4) Click the **CODE** tab and click (**Save As**) to save the program.

5) In the Save As window, choose a file location such as **s:\workshop**, name the file **MyProgram**, and click **Save**.

Copyright © 2016, SAS Institute Inc., Cary, North Carolina, USA. ALL RIGHTS RESERVED.

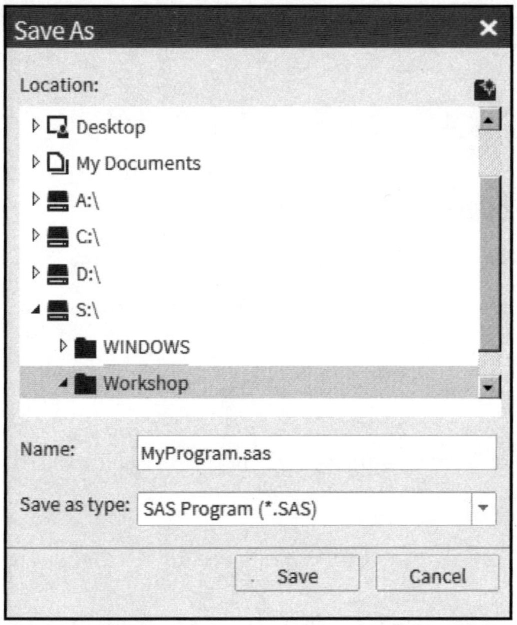

6) Notice that the Program 2 tab now appears with the program name. Close the program tab for **MyProgram** by clicking the **X** next to the name.

An asterisk (*) in front of a filename means that the program was not saved.

e. Open the program that you saved and closed. In the Folders section of the navigation pane, navigate to the file location for **MyProgram.sas**.

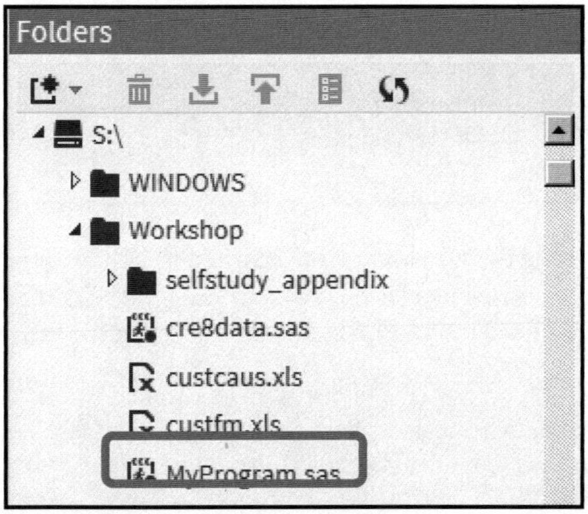

1) Double-click **MyProgram.sas** to open the program. Instead of double-clicking, you can drag the program into the work area.

2) Submit a portion of the program. On the CODE tab, highlight the PROC MEANS step (two lines of code) and click (**Run**) or press F3 to submit the highlighted code.

Copyright © 2016, SAS Institute Inc., Cary, North Carolina, USA. ALL RIGHTS RESERVED.

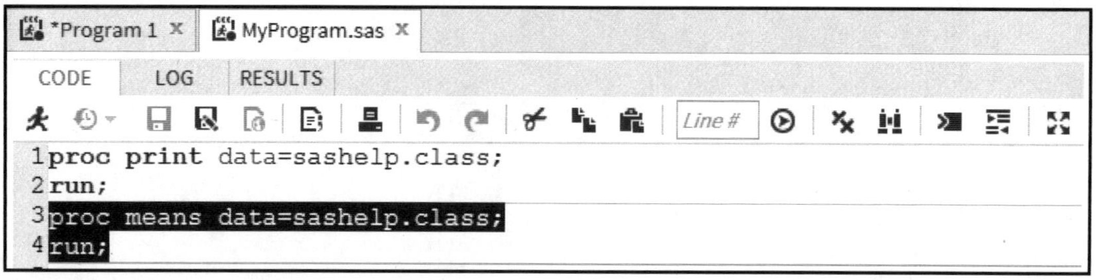

3) View the RESULTS tab and the LOG tab. Notice that the information on the tabs pertains only to the PROC MEANS step.

Using the CODE Tab Features

f. On the CODE toolbar, click (**Maximize View**) to maximize the work area and hide the navigation pane.

After you maximize the window, click (**Exit Maximize View**) to unhide the navigation pane.

g. In the Folders section of the navigation pane, click (**New**) ⇨ **SAS Program (F4)** or press F4 to start a new program.

1) On the CODE tab of Program 2, start to enter a PROC PRINT step. Notice the autocomplete feature as you type. The autocomplete feature gives you a window of possible keywords that might come next in your program. For example, after you enter **proc print**, a pop-up window appears. The window contains procedure options that pertain to the PRINT procedure.

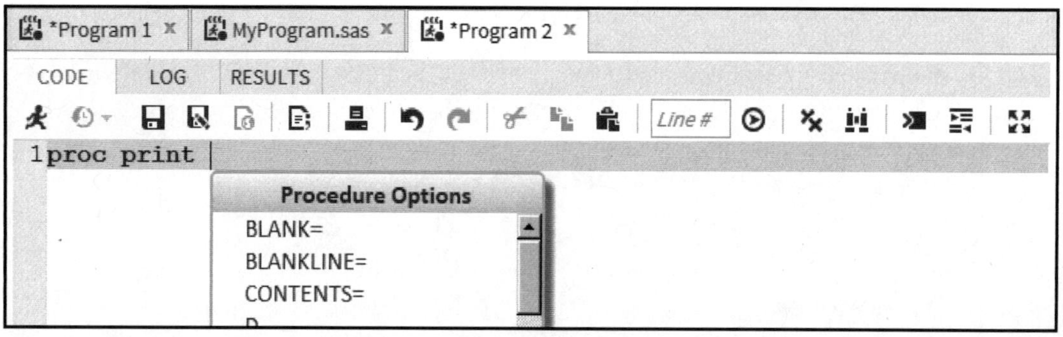

To navigate to the desired keyword in the window, scroll through the list by using the up and down arrow keys, the Page Up or Page Down keys, or drag the scroll bar with your mouse pointer. To add the keyword to your program, double-click the keyword or press the Enter key.

2) Start to enter the DATA= option. Syntax Help appears as you narrow the list of keywords. Syntax Help also appears if you right-click a keyword in the program and select **Syntax Help**.

Copyright © 2016, SAS Institute Inc., Cary, North Carolina, USA. ALL RIGHTS RESERVED.

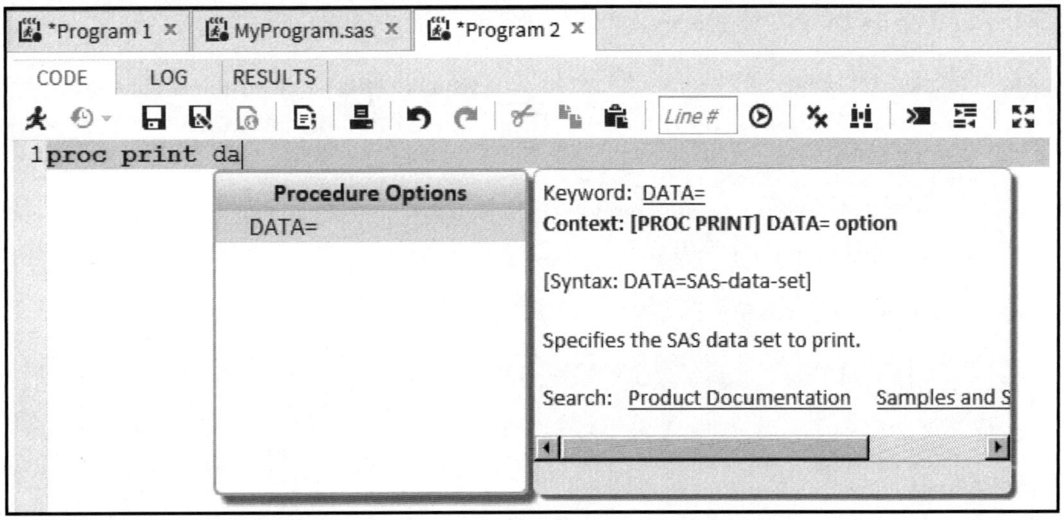

3) Complete the PROC PRINT step. Notice the autocomplete feature and Syntax Help as you type.

```
proc print data=sashelp.class;
run;
```

You can also access Syntax Help by positioning the mouse pointer on a valid keyword in your program, if you enable the feature in the editor preferences. To enable the option, click (**More Application Options**) on the main toolbar.

4) Select **Preferences** ⇨ **Editor** and notice the list of editor preferences.

5) Select the **Enable hint** check box and click **Save**.

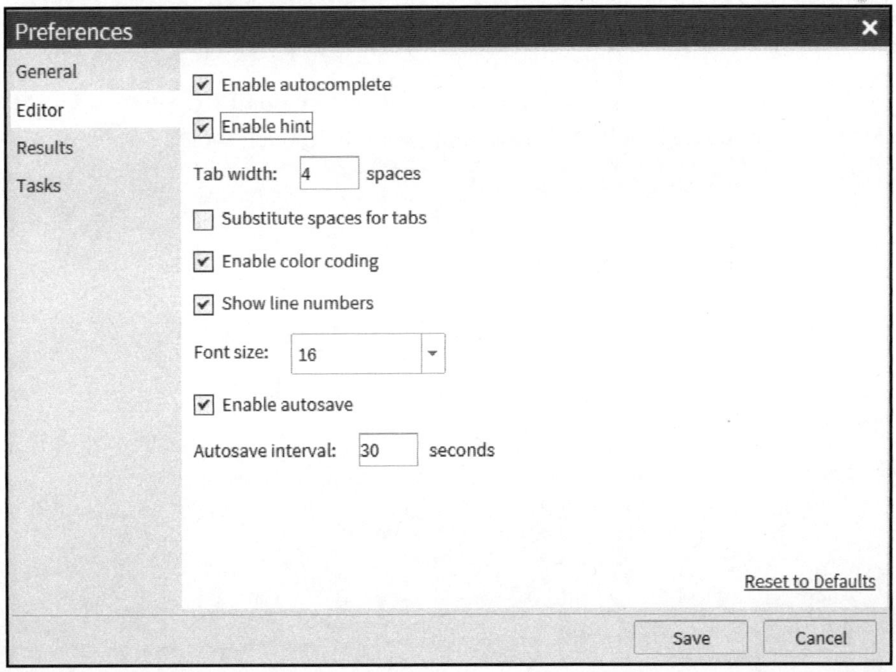

6) Position your mouse pointer on the word **print** in your program to see the Syntax Help.

Copyright © 2016, SAS Institute Inc., Cary, North Carolina, USA. ALL RIGHTS RESERVED.

Using RESULTS Tab Features

h. On the CODE tab of Program 2, click (**Run**) or press F3 to submit the PROC PRINT step. If the program runs successfully, the RESULTS tab automatically opens and shows the PROC PRINT output.

i. By default, the results created on the RESULTS tab are HTML5 output. On the RESULTS toolbar, click (**Open In A New Browser Tab**) to open the HTML5 output on another browser tab.

j. After viewing the output in the new browser tab, close the browser tab.

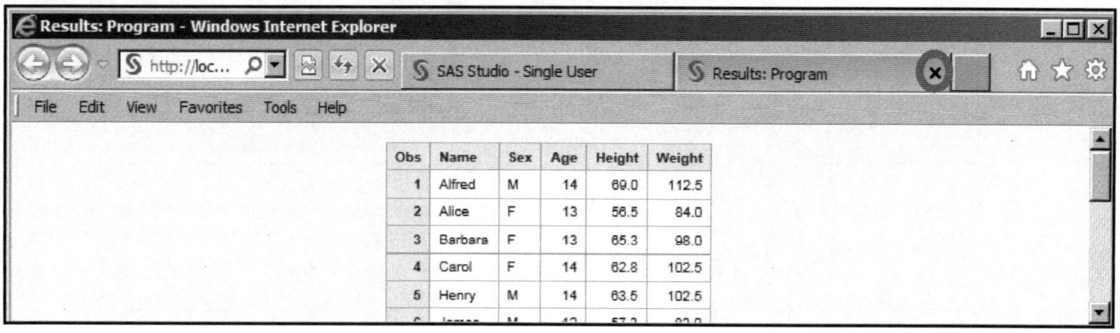

PDF output and RTF output are created by default in addition to HTML5 output. PDF output and RTF output are not displayed on the RESULTS tab. You can download the HTML5, PDF, and RTF output to a file by clicking the appropriate button.

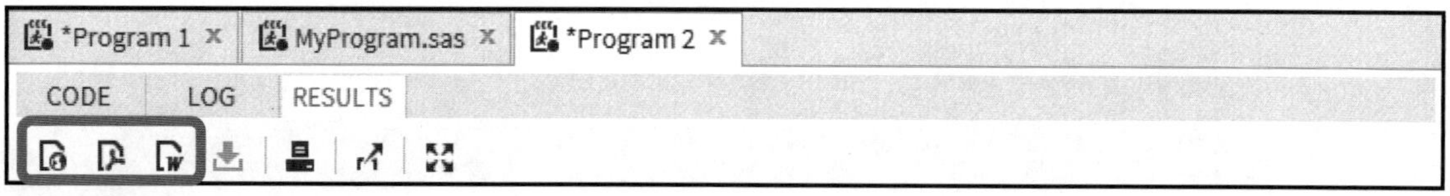

k. Click (**Download Results As A PDF File**) or (**Download Results As An RTF File**) to download the PDF or RTF output. Follow the prompts to open the file. After viewing the file, close the file.

l. You can change results preferences in the Preferences window. To access the results preferences, click (**More Application Options**).

1) Select **Preferences** ⇨ **Results** and notice the list of results preferences.

Copyright © 2016, SAS Institute Inc., Cary, North Carolina, USA. ALL RIGHTS RESERVED.

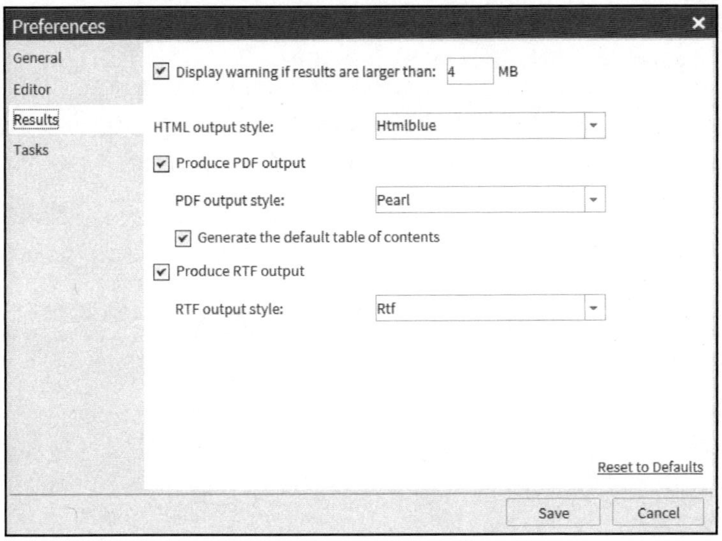

2) Click **Cancel** to close the Preferences window.

3. Accessing Help and Documentation

a. You can access SAS Help and documentation from the main toolbar.

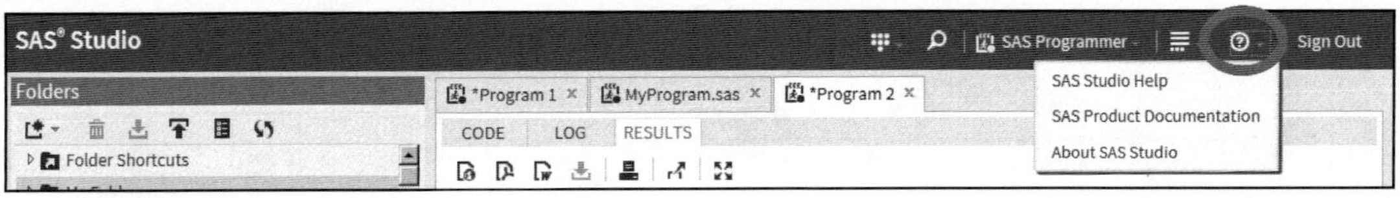

b. Click ⇨ **SAS Studio Help** to be directed to the SAS Studio documentation web page. This web page is useful for assistance with navigating the SAS Studio interface. After you view the web page, close the window.

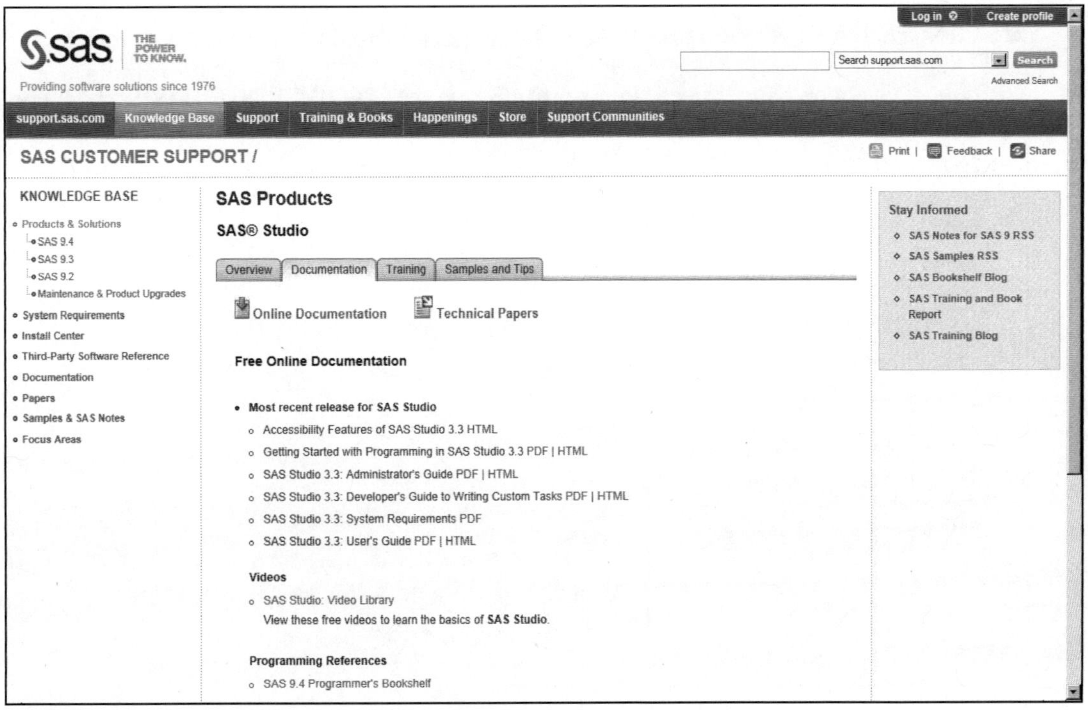

Copyright © 2016, SAS Institute Inc., Cary, North Carolina, USA. ALL RIGHTS RESERVED.

External address to the SAS Studio page: **http://support.sas.com/software/products/sasstudio/**

c. Click ⇨ **SAS Product Documentation** to be directed to the SAS Products & Solutions web page. This web page is useful for learning information about a SAS product.

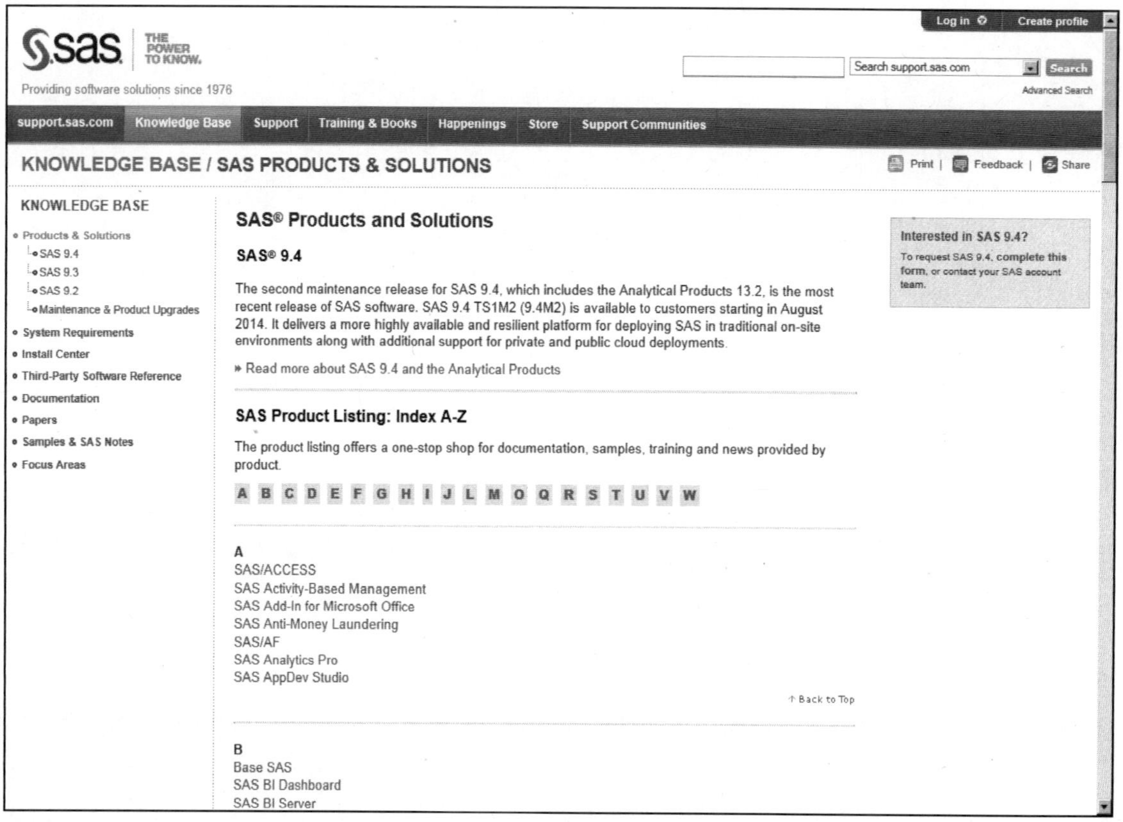

External address to the SAS Products page: **http://support.sas.com/software/**

d. From the above web page, select **Documentation** in the KNOWLEDGE BASE navigation pane.

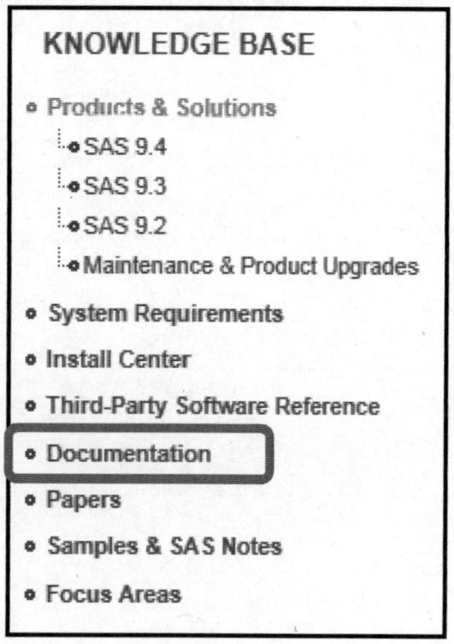

Copyright © 2016, SAS Institute Inc., Cary, North Carolina, USA. ALL RIGHTS RESERVED.

e. The SAS Product Documentation web page appears. This web page is useful for viewing the syntax documentation related to a SAS product.

External address to the SAS Product Documentation page: **http://support.sas.com/documentation/**

f. From this web page, select **Programmer's Bookshelf**. Then select the link for your version of SAS.

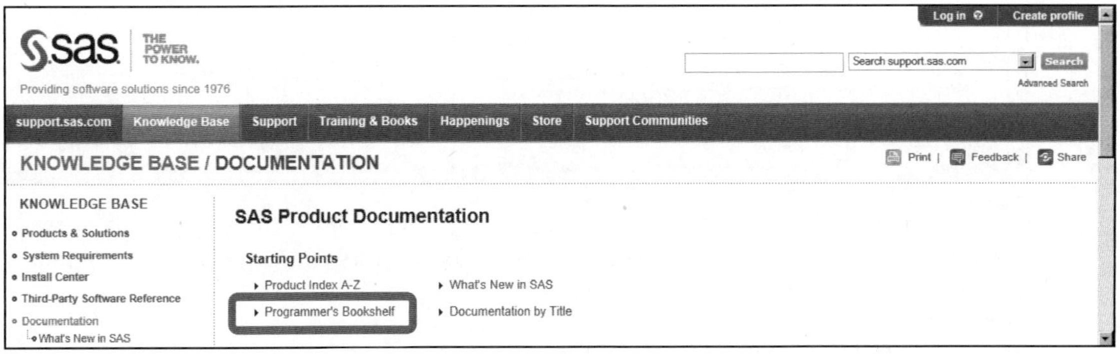

The Programmer's Bookshelf contains selected documentation for SAS products such as Base SAS.

g. Browse the Programmer's Bookshelf web page. Close the window when you are finished browsing.

SAS Enterprise Guide

You *must* complete this exercise to create the course data files. If you do not create the data files, the majority of programs in this course will fail.

4. Creating Course Data with SAS Enterprise Guide

a. Start SAS Enterprise Guide. Close the Welcome to SAS Enterprise Guide window by clicking the **X** in the right corner of the window. By default, SAS Enterprise Guide contains a Project Tree window and a Servers window. They are docked on the left side. The Process Flow window is docked on the right side.

b. Select **File** ⇨ **Open** ⇨ **Program** or click (**Open**) ⇨ **Program**.

c. In the Open Program window, navigate to the file location to find **cre8data** and click **Open**.

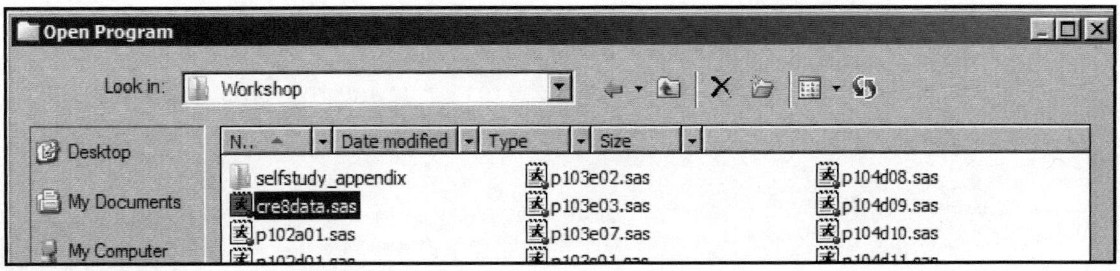

Copyright © 2016, SAS Institute Inc., Cary, North Carolina, USA. ALL RIGHTS RESERVED.

d. On the Program tab for the **cre8data** program, find the %LET statement shown below.

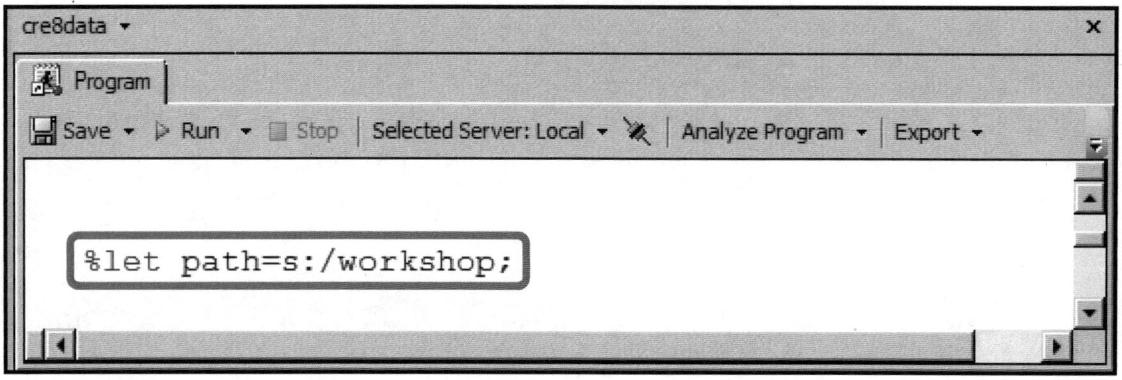

e. If your data files are to be created at a location other than **s:\workshop**, change the value that is assigned to the **path** macro variable to reflect the location. If your data files are created in **s:\workshop**, then no change is needed.

> The **cre8data** program uses forward slashes for portability across operating environments. UNIX and Linux require forward slashes. Windows accepts forward slashes and might convert them to backslashes.

1) On the Program tab, click **Run** or press F3 to submit the program.

2) On the Results tab, verify that the output contains a list of data files.

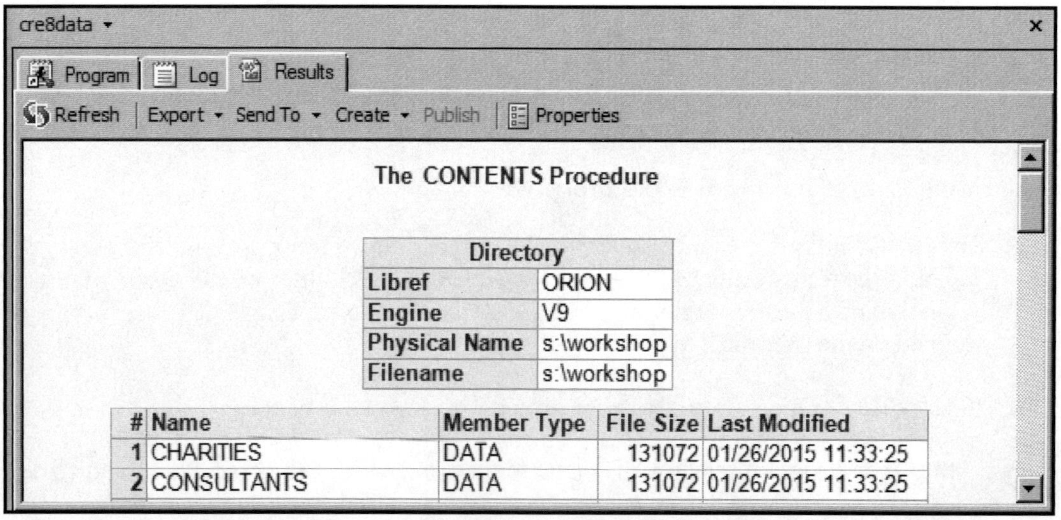

The CONTENTS Procedure

Directory	
Libref	ORION
Engine	V9
Physical Name	s:\workshop
Filename	s:\workshop

#	Name	Member Type	File Size	Last Modified
1	CHARITIES	DATA	131072	01/26/2015 11:33:25
2	CONSULTANTS	DATA	131072	01/26/2015 11:33:25

3) Remove **cre8data** from the project. Right-click **cre8data** in the Project Tree window and select **Delete**. Click **Yes** to delete all the items when you are prompted.

Copyright © 2016, SAS Institute Inc., Cary, North Carolina, USA. ALL RIGHTS RESERVED.

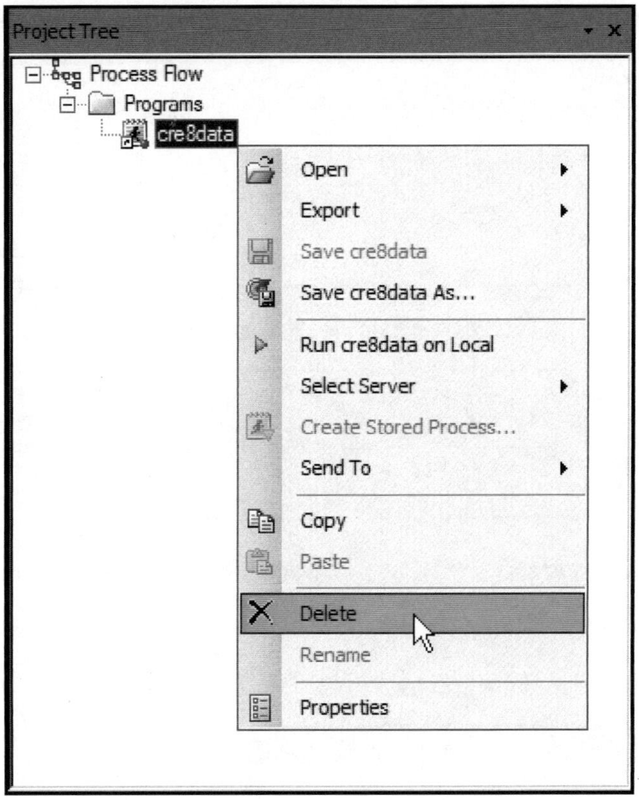

5. **Exploring SAS Enterprise Guide**

Using the Primary Interface Tabs

a. Start a new program by selecting **File** ⇨ **New** ⇨ **Program** or by clicking (**New**) ⇨ **Program**.

1) On the Program tab, enter the PROC PRINT step shown below.

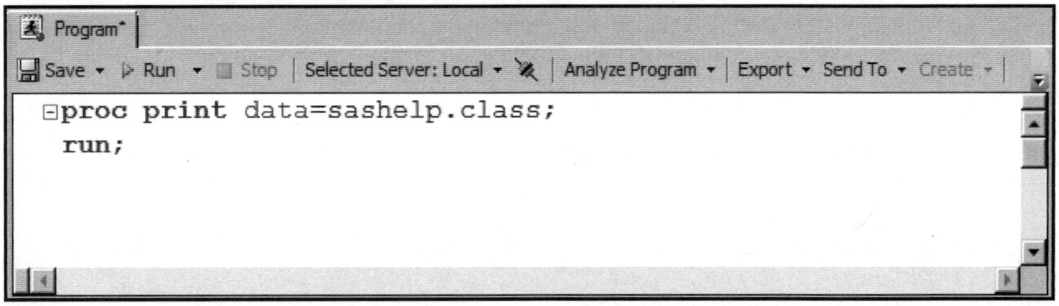

2) On the Program tab, click **Run** or press F3 to submit the program. If the program runs successfully, the Results tab automatically opens and shows the PROC PRINT output.

3) Click the **Log** tab and check the log for the two notes shown below. If you see any warnings or errors, return to the Program tab, fix any mistakes, and rerun the program.

```
NOTE: There were 19 observations read from the data set SASHELP.CLASS.
NOTE: PROCEDURE PRINT used (Total process time):
```

Copyright © 2016, SAS Institute Inc., Cary, North Carolina, USA. ALL RIGHTS RESERVED.

4) Click the **Results** tab. Notice that the PROC PRINT output contains an **Obs** column.

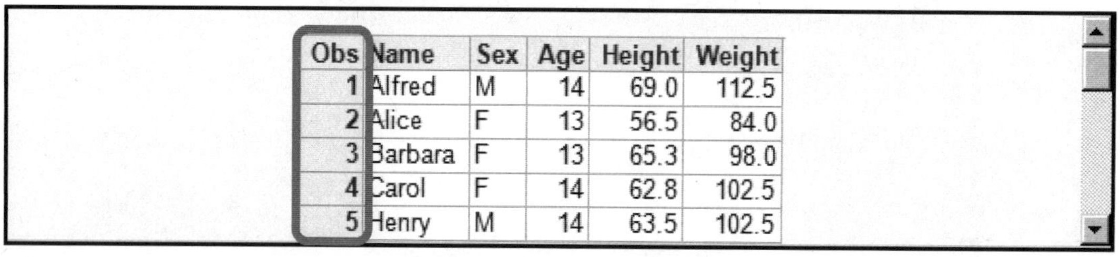

Obs	Name	Sex	Age	Height	Weight
1	Alfred	M	14	69.0	112.5
2	Alice	F	13	56.5	84.0
3	Barbara	F	13	65.3	98.0
4	Carol	F	14	62.8	102.5
5	Henry	M	14	63.5	102.5

5) Click the **Program** tab and add the NOOBS option to eliminate the **Obs** column.

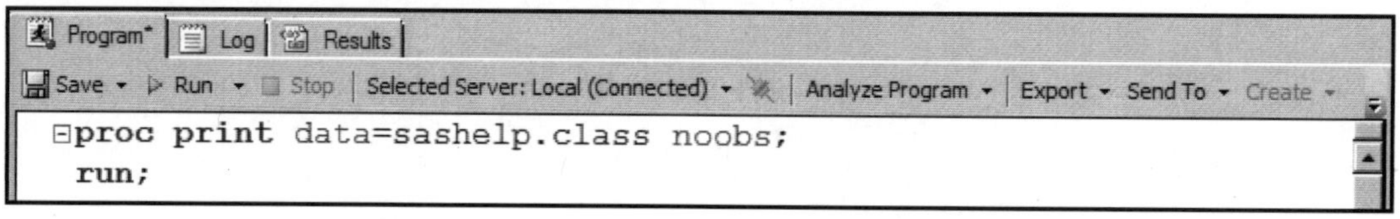


```
proc print data=sashelp.class noobs;
run;
```

The NOOBS option is in the PROC PRINT statement before the semicolon.

6) On the Program tab, click the **Run** button or press F3 to submit the program.

7) Click **Yes** to replace the results from the previous run.

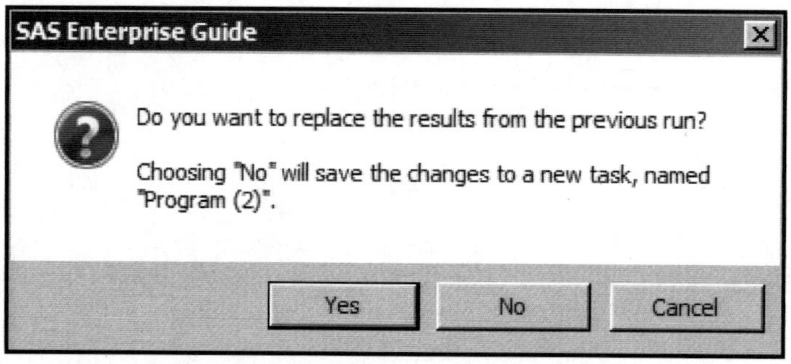

8) View the new information on the Results tab and the Log tab.

b. Create another program. Select **File** ⇨ **New** ⇨ **Program** or click (**New**) ⇨ **Program**.

1) On the new Program tab, enter the PROC PRINT step and the PROC MEANS step as shown.

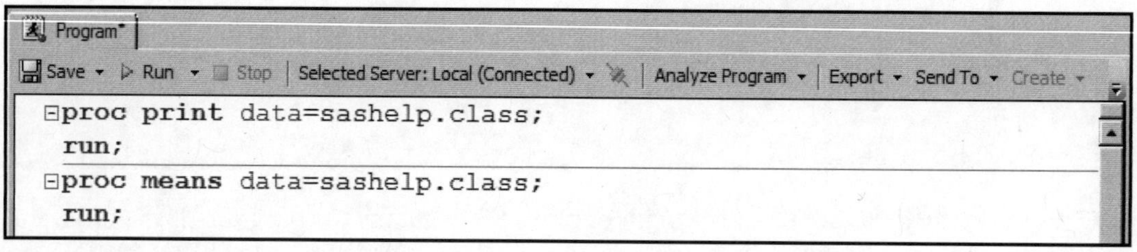


```
proc print data=sashelp.class;
run;
proc means data=sashelp.class;
run;
```

An asterisk (*) after the word **Program** on the Program tab means that the program was not saved.

2) On the Program tab, click the **Run** button or press F3 to submit the program. If the program runs successfully, the Results tab automatically opens and shows the PROC PRINT and PROC MEANS output.

Copyright © 2016, SAS Institute Inc., Cary, North Carolina, USA. ALL RIGHTS RESERVED.

3) Click the **Log** tab. Check the log for notes. If you see any warnings or errors, return to the Program tab, fix any mistakes, and rerun the program.

4) Click the **Program** tab. Select **File** ⇨ **Save Program (2) As** or click the **Save** button and then select **Save As** to save the program.

5) In the Save window, choose a file location such as **s:\workshop**, name the file **MyProgram**, and click **Save**.

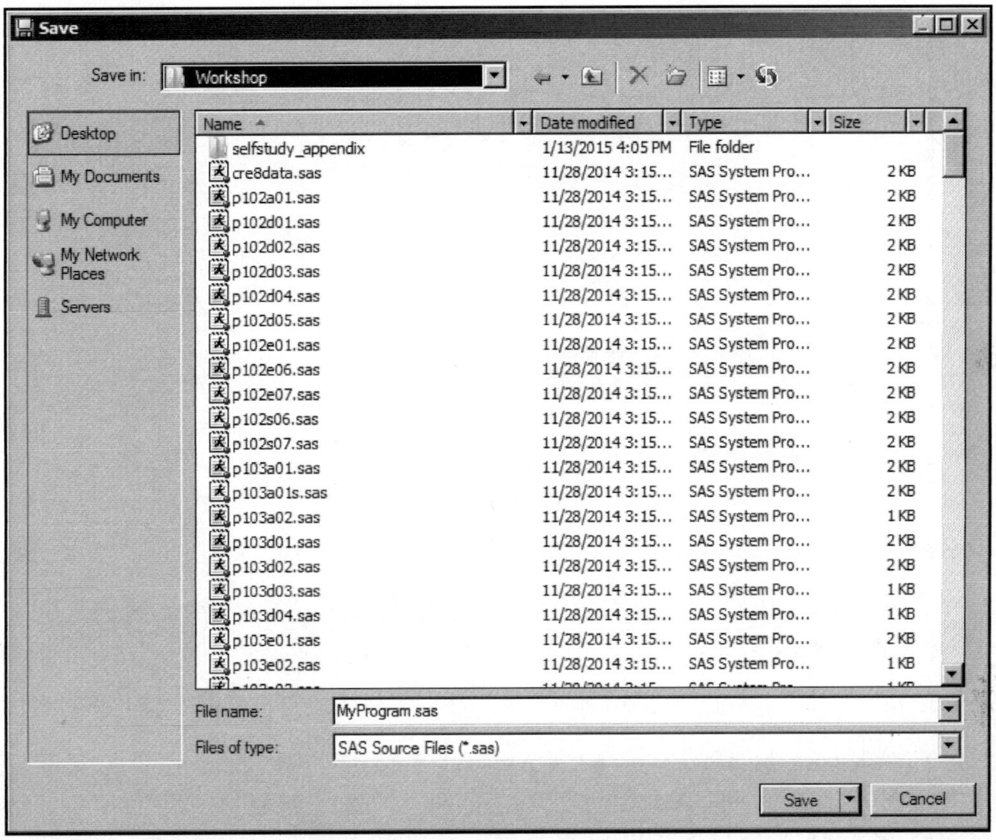

6) Notice that the workspace area contains the program name above the Program, Log, and Results tabs.

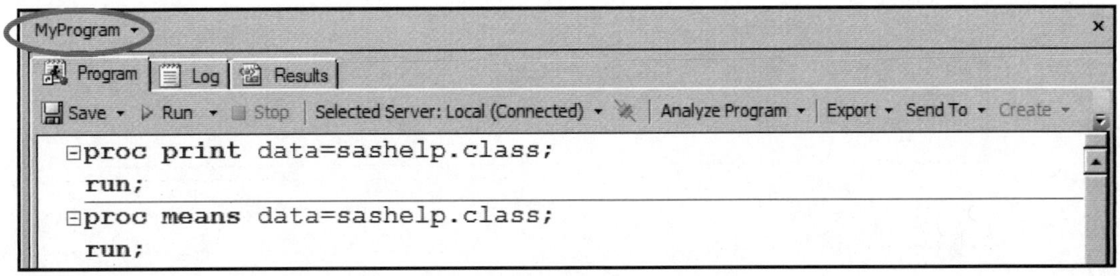

Copyright © 2016, SAS Institute Inc., Cary, North Carolina, USA. ALL RIGHTS RESERVED.

7) Remove **MyProgram** from the project. Right-click **MyProgram** in the Project Tree window and select **Delete**. Click **Yes** to delete all the items when you are prompted.

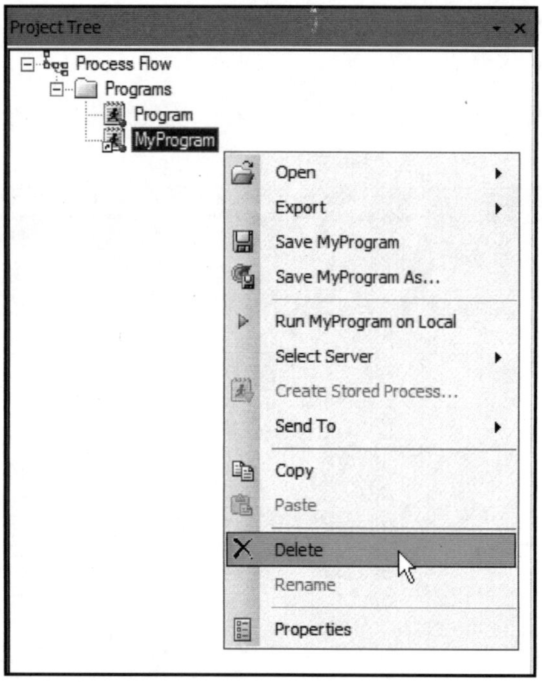

This action deletes the program from the project. However, the program still exists.

c. Open the program that you saved and removed. Select **File** ⇨ **Open** ⇨ **Program** or click (**Open**) ⇨ **Program**.

1) In the Open Program window, navigate to the file location to find **MyProgram**. Click **Open**.

2) Submit a portion of the program. On the Program tab, highlight the PROC MEANS step (two lines of code). Click the drop-down arrow next to the Run button and select **Run Selection** or press F3 to submit the highlighted code.

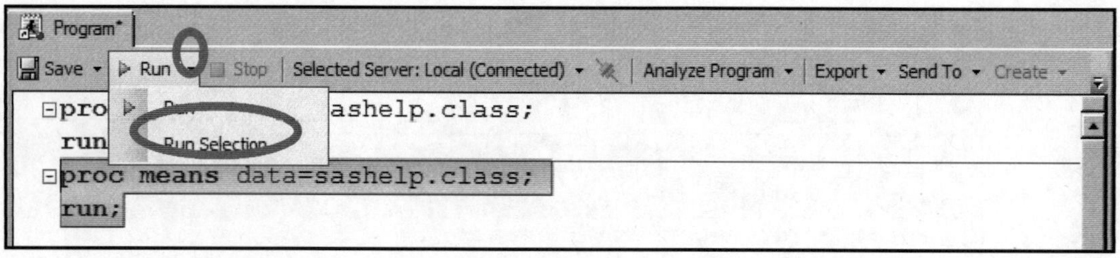

3) View the Results tab and the Log tab. Notice that the information on the tabs pertains only to the PROC MEANS step.

Using Program Tab Features

d. Select **View** ⇨ **Maximize Workspace** to maximize the Program window and hide the Project Tree and Servers windows.

To unhide the Project Tree and Servers windows, select **View** ⇨ **Maximize Workspace** again.

e. Click the **Program** tab for **MyProgram**.

Copyright © 2016, SAS Institute Inc., Cary, North Carolina, USA. ALL RIGHTS RESERVED.

1) The appearance and functionality of the Program tab can be customized. To customize it, select **Tools** ⇨ **Options** ⇨ **SAS Programs**. Then click **Editor Options**.

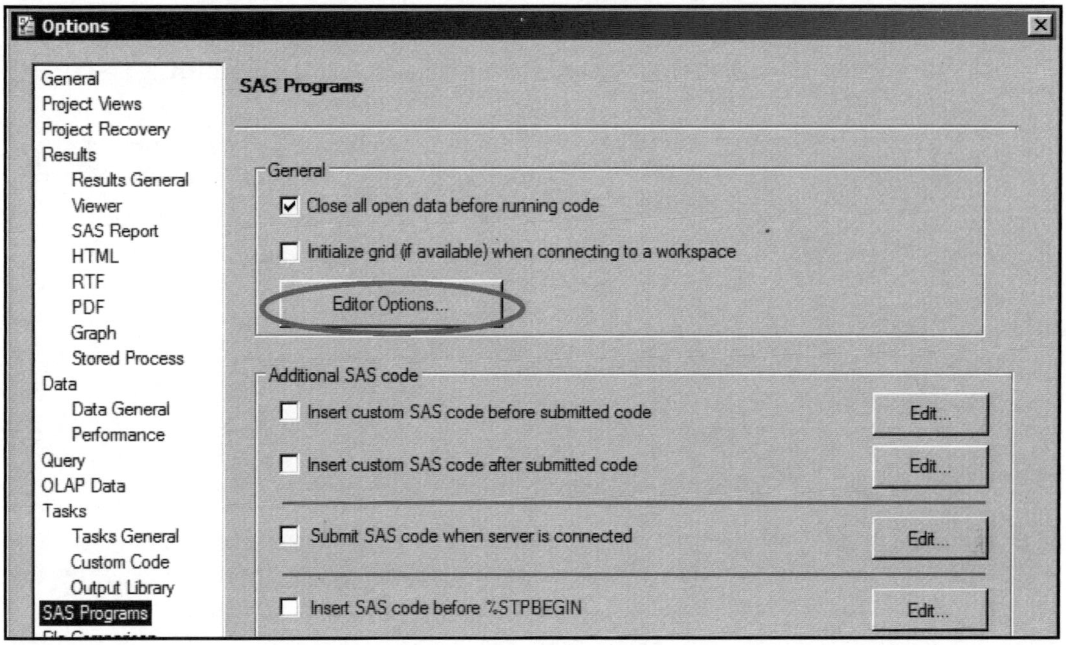

2) In the Enhanced Editor Options window, four tabs contain editor options. On the Appearance tab, increase the font size and click **OK**. Click **OK** to close the Options window. Notice the change in the text's font size on the Program tab.

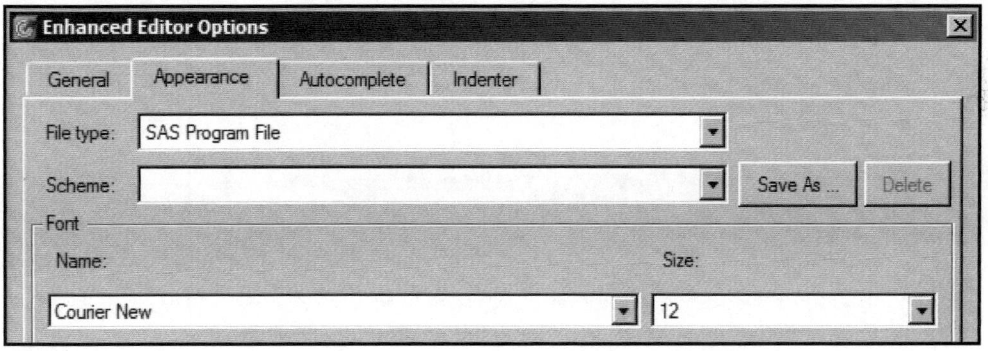

f. Start a new program. Select **File** ⇨ **New** ⇨ **Program** or click (**New**) ⇨ **Program**.

1) On the Program tab, start entering a PROC PRINT step. Notice the autocomplete feature as you type. The autocomplete feature gives you a window of possible keywords that can come next in your program. For example, after you enter **proc print**, a pop-up window appears with procedure options that pertain to the PRINT procedure.

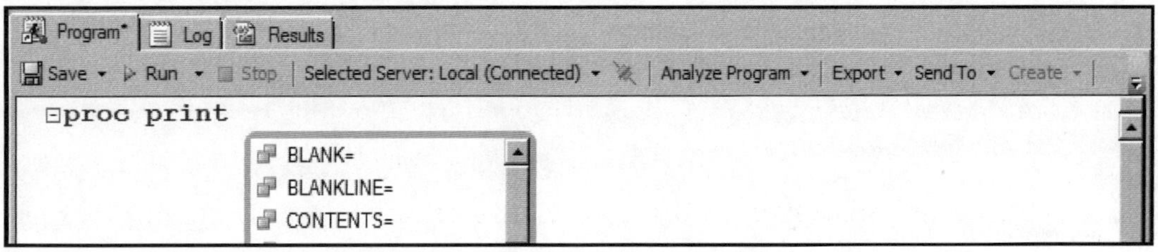

Copyright © 2016, SAS Institute Inc., Cary, North Carolina, USA. ALL RIGHTS RESERVED.

> ✎ To navigate to the desired keyword in the window, scroll through the list by using the up and down arrow keys, the Page Up or Page Down keys, or the scroll bar. To add a keyword to a program, double-click the keyword or press the Enter key or the spacebar.

2) In addition to displaying possible keywords, autocomplete can display libraries, data sets, and variables.

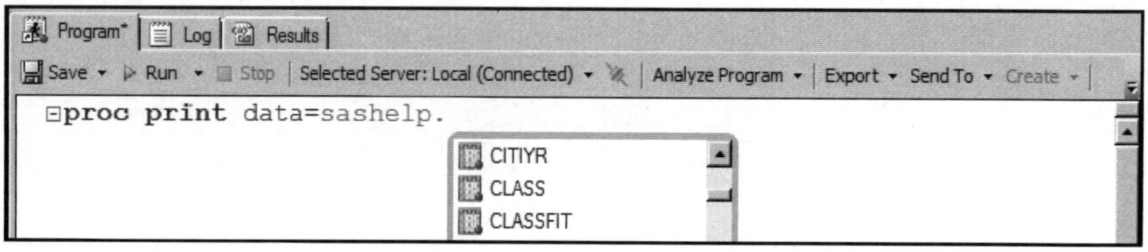

3) Complete the PROC PRINT step. Notice the autocomplete feature as you type.

```
proc print data=sashelp.class;
run;
```

g. You can access syntax Help by positioning the mouse pointer on a valid keyword in your program. Position your mouse pointer on the word **print** in the program to see the syntax Help.

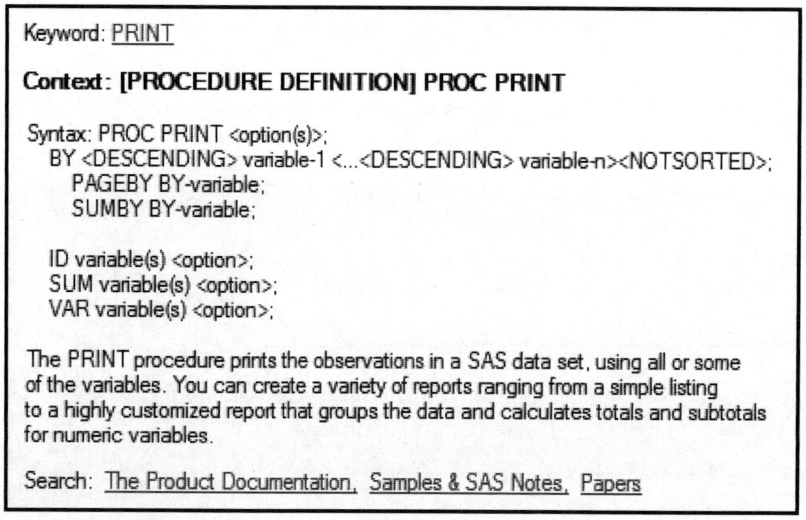

Keyword: PRINT

Context: [PROCEDURE DEFINITION] PROC PRINT

Syntax: PROC PRINT <option(s)>;
BY <DESCENDING> variable-1 <...<DESCENDING> variable-n><NOTSORTED>;
PAGEBY BY-variable;
SUMBY BY-variable;

ID variable(s) <option>;
SUM variable(s) <option>;
VAR variable(s) <option>;

The PRINT procedure prints the observations in a SAS data set, using all or some of the variables. You can create a variety of reports ranging from a simple listing to a highly customized report that groups the data and calculates totals and subtotals for numeric variables.

Search: The Product Documentation, Samples & SAS Notes, Papers

Customizing Results

h. On the Program tab, click the **Run** button or press F3 to submit the program. If the program runs successfully, the Results tab automatically opens and shows the PROC PRINT output.

1) By default, the results that are created on the Results tab are SAS Report output. SAS Report output is an XML file, which can be viewed within SAS applications.

2) In addition to creating SAS Report output, other output types can be created. Select **Tools** ⇨ **Options** ⇨ **Results General**.

Copyright © 2016, SAS Institute Inc., Cary, North Carolina, USA. ALL RIGHTS RESERVED.

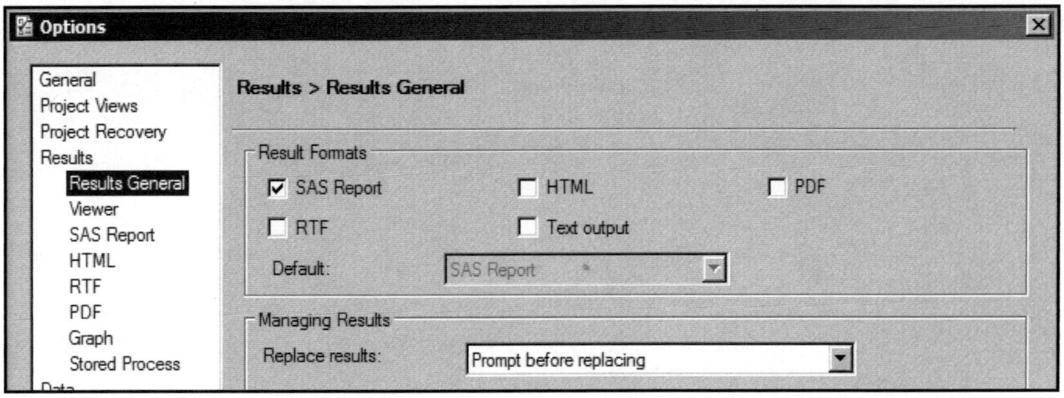

3) A check mark already appears in front of SAS Report. Select the **HTML**, **PDF**, **RTF**, and **Text output** check boxes. Click **OK**.

i. Submit the PROC PRINT step. Click **Yes** to replace the results from the previous run. Five Results tabs appear.

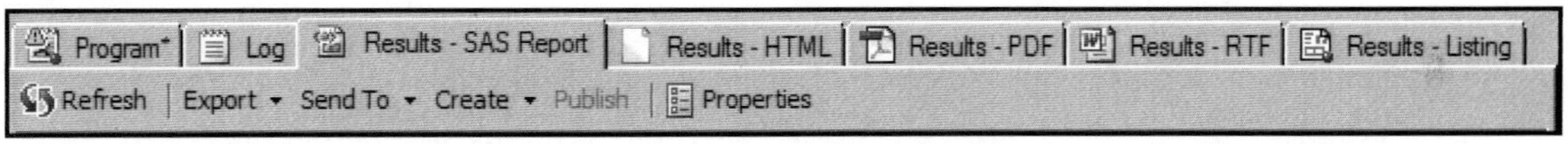

j. Click each tab to view the results. When you click the PDF tab, the PDF output opens in an Adobe product such as Adobe Reader. When you click the RTF tab, the RTF output opens in a word processing application such as Microsoft Word. After you click the PDF and RTF tabs, the tabs disappear because the files are opened outside of SAS. The Listing tab contains the text output.

k. Select **Tools** ⇨ **Options** ⇨ **Results General**. Clear the **HTML**, **PDF**, and **RTF** check boxes. Do ***not*** change the SAS Report and Text output check boxes. Click **OK**.

6. Accessing Help and Documentation

SAS Help and documentation can be accessed from the Help drop-down menu.

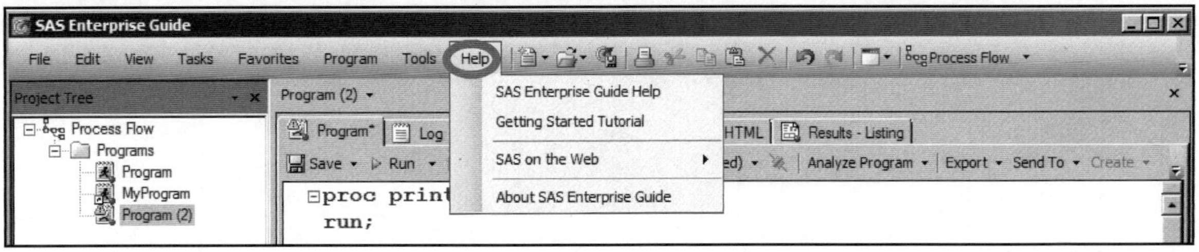

a. Select **Help** ⇨ **SAS Enterprise Guide Help** to be directed to a window that displays help for SAS Enterprise Guide. This window is useful for assistance with navigating the SAS Enterprise Guide interface. After you view the Help window, close the window

Copyright © 2016, SAS Institute Inc., Cary, North Carolina, USA. ALL RIGHTS RESERVED.

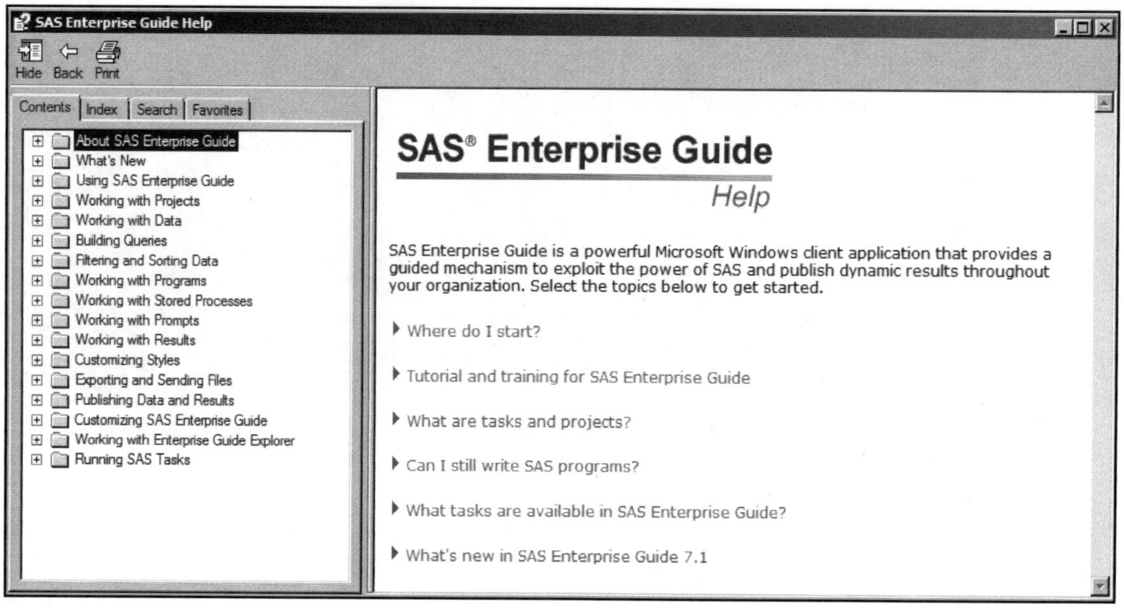

b. Select **Help** ⇨ **SAS on the Web** ⇨ **SAS Product Documentation** to be directed to the SAS Product Documentation web page. This web page is useful for viewing the syntax documentation related to a SAS product.

> External address to the SAS Product Documentation page:
> **http://support.sas.com/documentation/**

c. On this web page, select **Programmer's Bookshelf**. Then select the link for the appropriate SAS version.

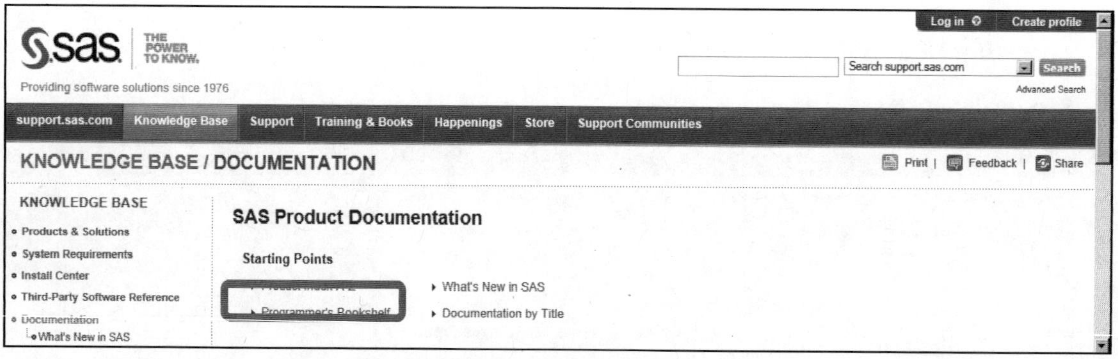

> The Programmer's Bookshelf contains selected documentation for SAS products such as Base SAS.

d. Browse the Programmer's Bookshelf web page. Close the window after browsing it.

SAS Windowing Environment

⚠ You *must* complete this exercise to create the course data files. If you do not create the data files, the majority of programs in this course will fail.

Copyright © 2016, SAS Institute Inc., Cary, North Carolina, USA. ALL RIGHTS RESERVED.

7. **Creating Course Data in the SAS Windowing Environment**

   a. Start the SAS windowing environment. If you see a pop-up window that references a change notice or getting started with SAS, click **Close**. By default, the SAS windowing environment consists of a left pane containing the Results and Explorer windows and a right pane containing the Output, Log, and Editor windows.

   b. Click (**Open**) when the Editor window is the active window or select **File** ⇨ **Open Program**.

   c. In the Open window, navigate to the file location to find **cre8data** and click **Open**.

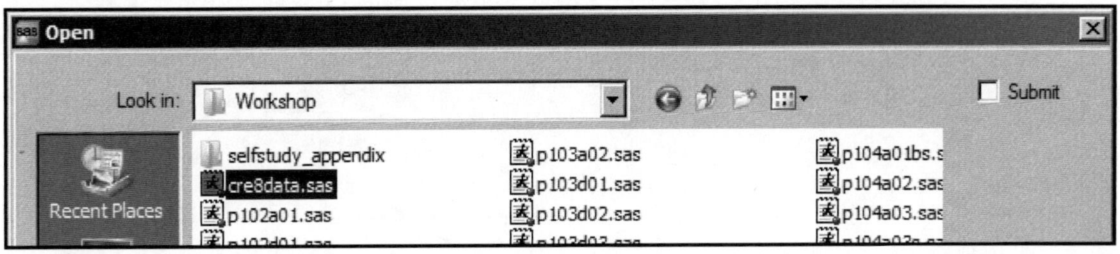

   d. In the Editor window for the **cre8data** program, find the %LET statement shown below.

   e. If your data files are to be created at a location other than **s:\workshop**, change the value that is assigned to the **path** macro variable to reflect the location. If your data files are created in **s:\workshop**, then no change is needed.

      The **cre8data** program uses forward slashes for portability across operating environments. UNIX and Linux require forward slashes. Windows accepts forward slashes and might convert them to backslashes.

   f. Click (**Submit**) or press F3 to submit the program.

   g. In the Results Viewer window, verify that the output contains a list of data files.

Copyright © 2016, SAS Institute Inc., Cary, North Carolina, USA. ALL RIGHTS RESERVED.

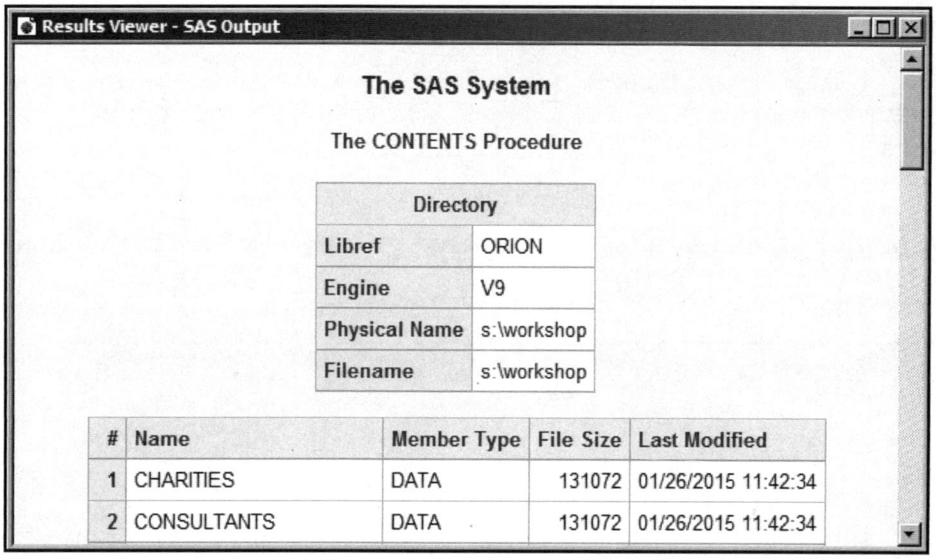

Directory	
Libref	ORION
Engine	V9
Physical Name	s:\workshop
Filename	s:\workshop

#	Name	Member Type	File Size	Last Modified
1	CHARITIES	DATA	131072	01/26/2015 11:42:34
2	CONSULTANTS	DATA	131072	01/26/2015 11:42:34

h. Go to the Log window and click (**New**) or select **Edit** ⇨ **Clear All** to clear the Log window.

i. Close the Editor window for **cre8data** by clicking the **X** in the right corner of the window.

8. Exploring the SAS Windowing Environment

Using the Primary Interface Windows

a. Select **View** ⇨ **Enhanced Editor** to open a new Editor window.

1) In the Editor window, enter the PROC PRINT step shown below.

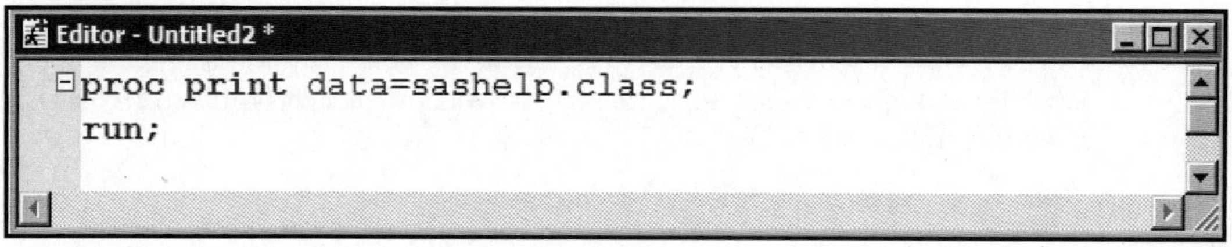


```
proc print data=sashelp.class;
run;
```

The Enhanced Editor is used when you use the Editor window.

2) Click (**Submit**) or press F3 to submit the program. If the program runs successfully, the Results Viewer window automatically appears and shows the PROC PRINT output.

3) Go to the Log window and check the log for the two notes below. If you see any warnings or errors, return to the Editor window, fix any mistakes, and rerun the program.

```
NOTE: There were 19 observations read from the data set SASHELP.CLASS.
NOTE: PROCEDURE PRINT used (Total process time):
```

Copyright © 2016, SAS Institute Inc., Cary, North Carolina, USA. ALL RIGHTS RESERVED.

4) Return to the Results Viewer window. Notice that the PROC PRINT output contains an **Obs** column.

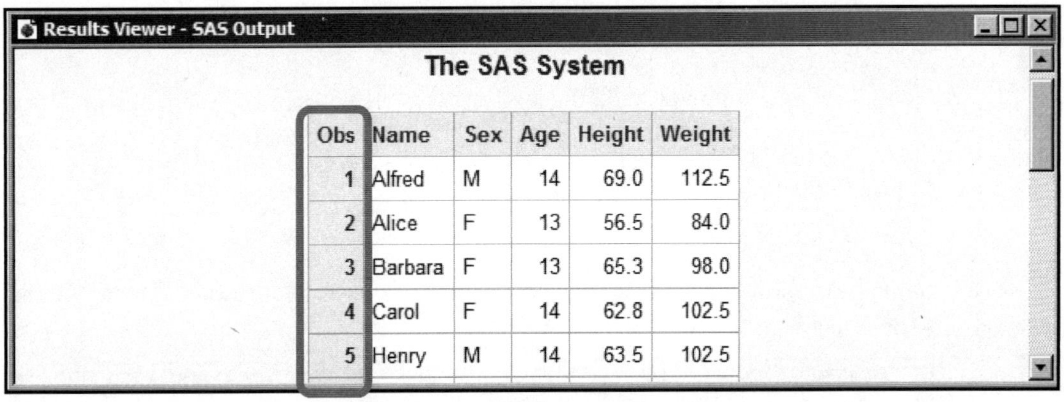

Obs	Name	Sex	Age	Height	Weight
1	Alfred	M	14	69.0	112.5
2	Alice	F	13	56.5	84.0
3	Barbara	F	13	65.3	98.0
4	Carol	F	14	62.8	102.5
5	Henry	M	14	63.5	102.5

5) Return to the Editor window and add the NOOBS option to eliminate the **Obs** column.

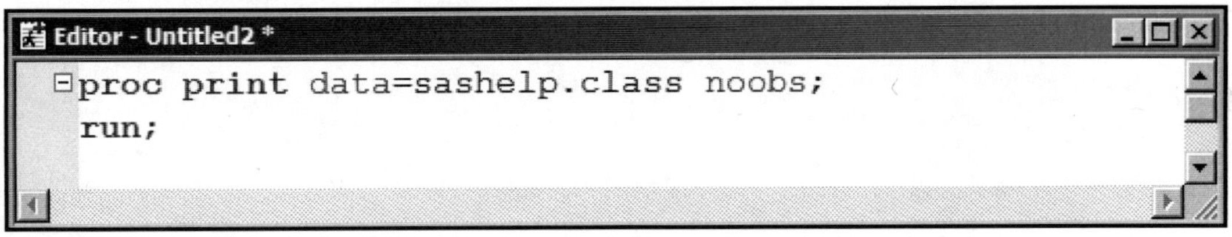


```
proc print data=sashelp.class noobs;
run;
```

The NOOBS option is in the PROC PRINT statement before the semicolon.

6) Click (**Submit**) or press F3 to submit the program.

7) View the information in the Results Viewer window and the Log window. Notice that the information in these windows is cumulative. The most recent information is added at the bottom.

8) Close the Log window by clicking the **X** in the right corner of the window. Select **View** ⇨ **Log** to reopen the log. The Log window still contains the information from the previous two submissions.

9) To clear the Log window, click (**New**) when the Log window is the active window. You can also select **Edit** ⇨ **Clear All** to clear the Log window.

b. Create another program. Click (**New**) from an existing Editor window or select **View** ⇨ **Enhanced Editor**.

1) In the new Editor window, enter the PROC PRINT step and PROC MEANS step shown below.

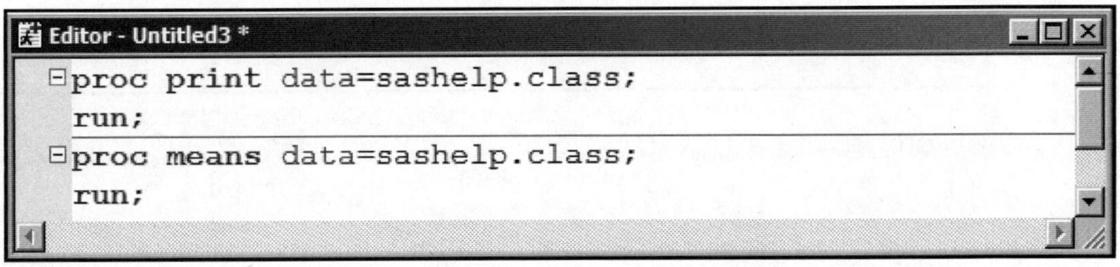


```
proc print data=sashelp.class;
run;
proc means data=sashelp.class;
run;
```

An asterisk (*) at the end of a filename means that the program was not saved.

Copyright © 2016, SAS Institute Inc., Cary, North Carolina, USA. ALL RIGHTS RESERVED.

2) Click (**Submit**) or press F3 to submit the program. If the program runs successfully, the Results Viewer window automatically appears and shows the PROC PRINT and PROC MEANS output. Do not forget that the Results Viewer is cumulative. The most recent information is added at the bottom.

3) Go to the Log window. Check the log for notes. If you see any warnings or errors, return to the Editor window, fix any mistakes, and rerun the program.

4) Return to the Editor – Untitled3 window. Click (**Save**) or select **File** ⇨ **Save As** to save the program.

5) In the Save As window, choose a file location such as **s:\workshop**, name the file **MyProgram**, and click **Save**.

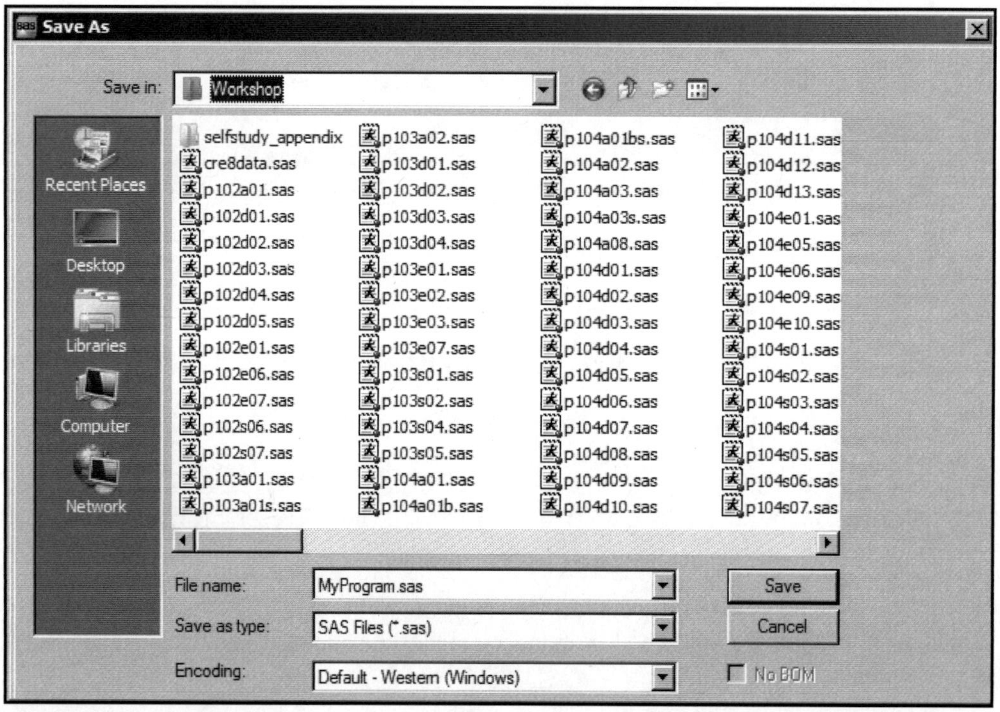

6) Notice that the Editor window now appears with the program name. Close the Editor window for **MyProgram** by clicking the **X** in the right corner of the window.

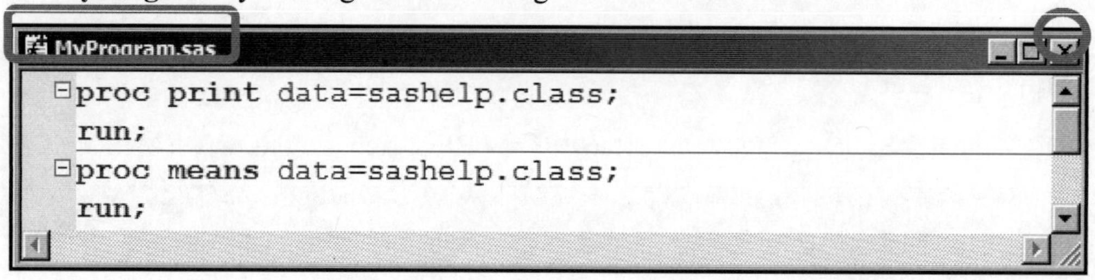

c. Open the program that you saved and closed. To open a program, click (**Open**) when the Editor window is the active window or select **File** ⇨ **Open Program**.

1) In the Open window, navigate to the file location to find **MyProgram** and click **Open**.

Copyright © 2016, SAS Institute Inc., Cary, North Carolina, USA. ALL RIGHTS RESERVED.

2) Submit a portion of the program. In the Editor window, highlight the PROC MEANS step (two lines of code). Click (**Submit**) or press F3 to submit the highlighted code.

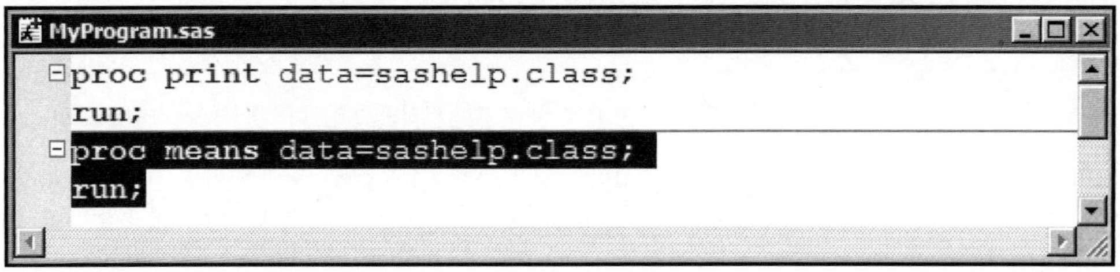

3) View the Results Viewer window and the Log window. Notice that the last submission submitted only the PROC MEANS step.

Customizing the Enhanced Editor

d. Return to the Editor window for **MyProgram**. If you want, click the **Maximize** button in the top right corner of the window to maximize the window.

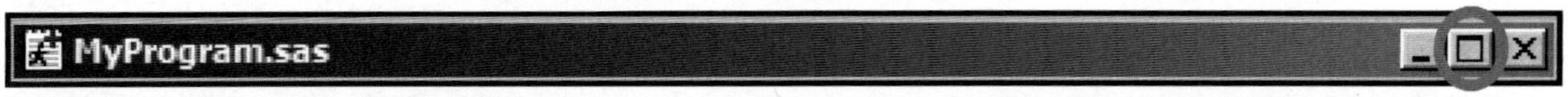

e. The appearance and functionality of the Enhanced Editor can be customized. To customize the Enhanced Editor, select **Tools** ⇨ **Options** ⇨ **Enhanced Editor** from the main toolbar.

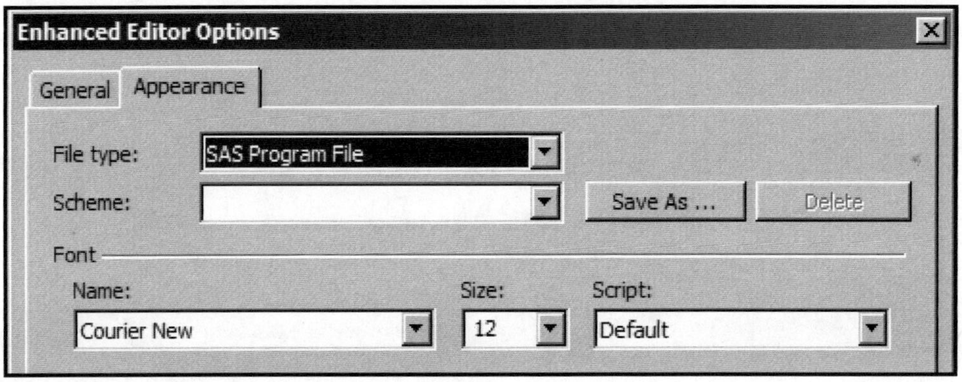

1) In the Enhanced Editor Options window, two tabs contain editor options. On the Appearance tab, increase the font size and click **OK**. Notice the change of the text's font size in the Editor window.

2) To browse a list of the function key definitions for the windowing environment, select **Tools** ⇨ **Options** ⇨ **Keys** to access the Keys window. Notice the following key definitions:

- F1 is help.
- F3 is end.
- F6 is log.
- F8 is zoom off and submit.

✎ The End command is an alias for the Submit command when it is initiated in the Editor window.

Copyright © 2016, SAS Institute Inc., Cary, North Carolina, USA. ALL RIGHTS RESERVED.

3) The function key definitions can be customized. For example, F12 can be set to clear the log and submit the program. This function key is used in an Editor window. Enter the following command in the Definition column for F12:

```
clear log; submit
```

4) Close the Keys window by clicking the **X** in the right corner of the window or by pressing F3.

f. Return to the Editor window for **MyProgram**. Press F12. Confirm that the Log window contains only the messages for the PROC PRINT and PROC MEANS steps that were submitted.

Customizing Results

g. By default, the results created in the Results Viewer window are cumulative HTML4 output. To clear the previous output, you can add ODS statements to the program to close the existing output and start new output. Add the following two ODS statements to the beginning of **MyProgram**:

```
ods html close; ods html;
```

h. Click (**Submit**) or press F3 to submit the modified program. Verify that the Results Viewer window contains only one PROC PRINT output and one PROC MEANS output.

i. In addition to creating HTML4 output in the Results Viewer window, you can create text output in the Output window.

1) Select **Tools** ⇨ **Options** ⇨ **Preferences** and click the **Results** tab. The Create HTML check box is already selected.

2) Select the **Create listing** check box to create text output. Click **OK**.

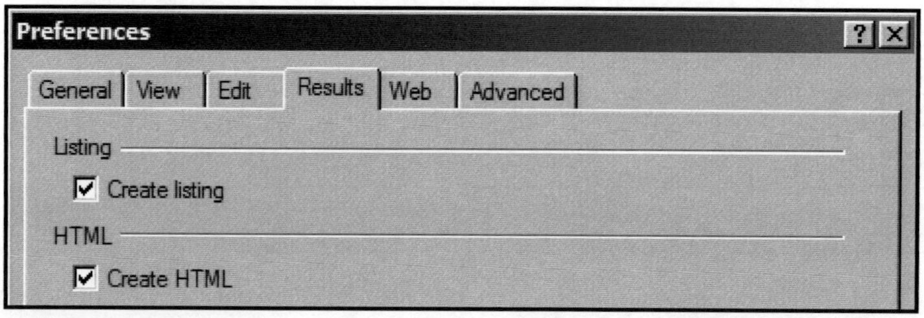

j. Submit the program.

1) Verify that the Results Viewer window contains PROC PRINT and PROC MEANS output. The Results Viewer window is not cumulative when you submit the two ODS statements.

2) In addition, verify that the PROC PRINT and PROC MEANS output is also visible in the Output window as text output. The Output window is cumulative. The most recent information is added at the bottom.

3) The Results window is used to navigate the results. The window contains bookmarks that you can expand and collapse.

Copyright © 2016, SAS Institute Inc., Cary, North Carolina, USA. ALL RIGHTS RESERVED.

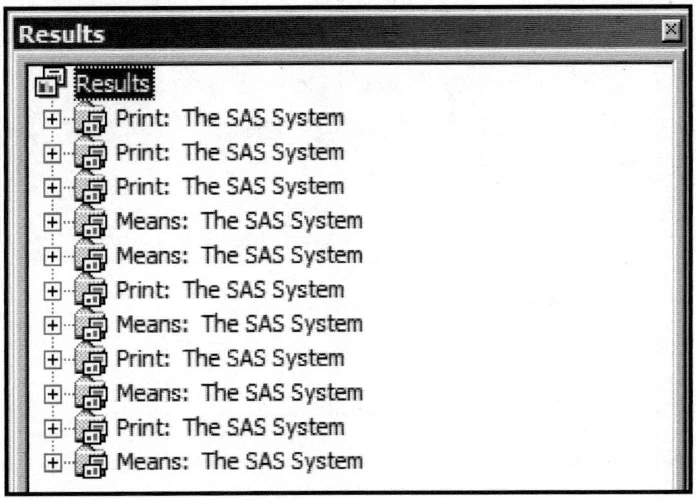

k. Select the last **Means** node in the Results window.

1) Click the plus sign in front of **Means** to expand the node.

2) Click the plus sign in front of **Summary statistics** to expand it. Each report bookmark contains an icon that indicates the file type, such as HTML or LISTING (text output).

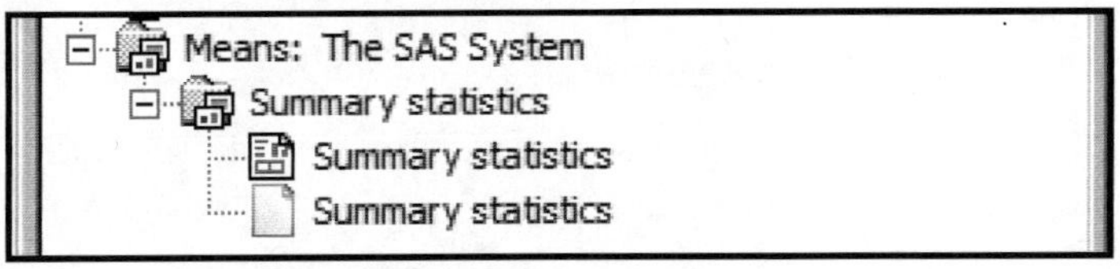

3) Double-click one of the report bookmarks to view the corresponding report in the appropriate window.

l. The previously defined F12 key can be modified to clear the Log window, clear the Output window, and clear the Results window.

1) To modify F12, select **Tools** ⇨ **Options** ⇨ **Keys** to access the Keys window.

2) Enter the following command in the Definition column for F12:

```
clear log; clear output; odsresults; clear;
```

3) Close the Keys window by clicking the **X** in the right corner of the window or by pressing F3.

4) Press F12. Confirm that the Log, Output, and Results windows are cleared.

m. Return to the Editor window for **MyProgram** and click (**Save**) or select **File** ⇨ **Save** to save the program.

n. Close the Editor window for **MyProgram** by clicking the **X** in the right corner of the window.

Copyright © 2016, SAS Institute Inc., Cary, North Carolina, USA. ALL RIGHTS RESERVED.

9. Accessing Help and Documentation

SAS Help and SAS documentation can be accessed from the **Help** drop-down menu.

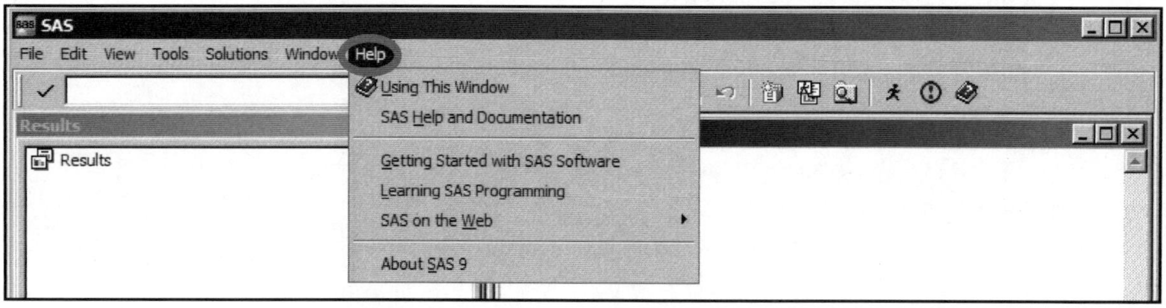

a. Click **Help** ⇨ **SAS Help and Documentation** to be directed to a window that displays SAS Help and documentation.

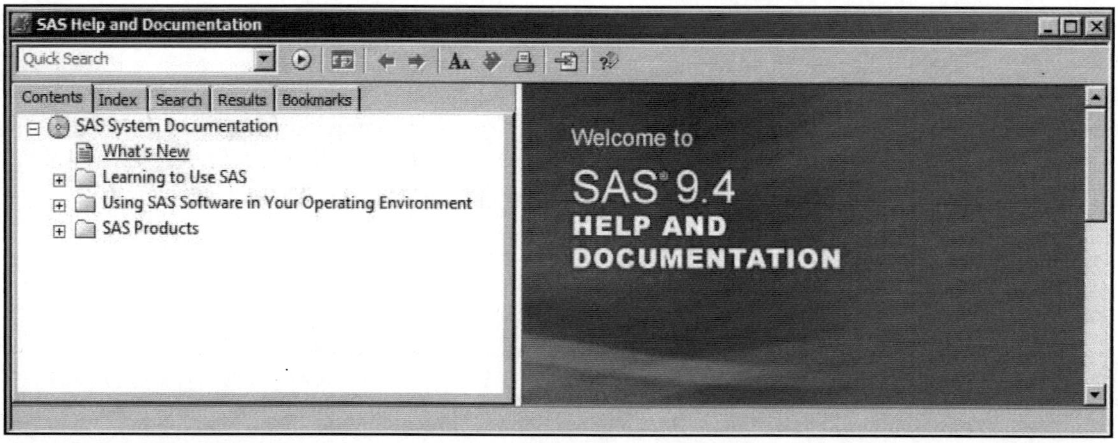

b. To view the syntax documentation for a specific product, expand **SAS Products** on the **Contents** tab. Choose the desired product, such as Base SAS, to view the product documentation. Close the window when you are finished browsing.

Copyright © 2016, SAS Institute Inc., Cary, North Carolina, USA. ALL RIGHTS RESERVED.

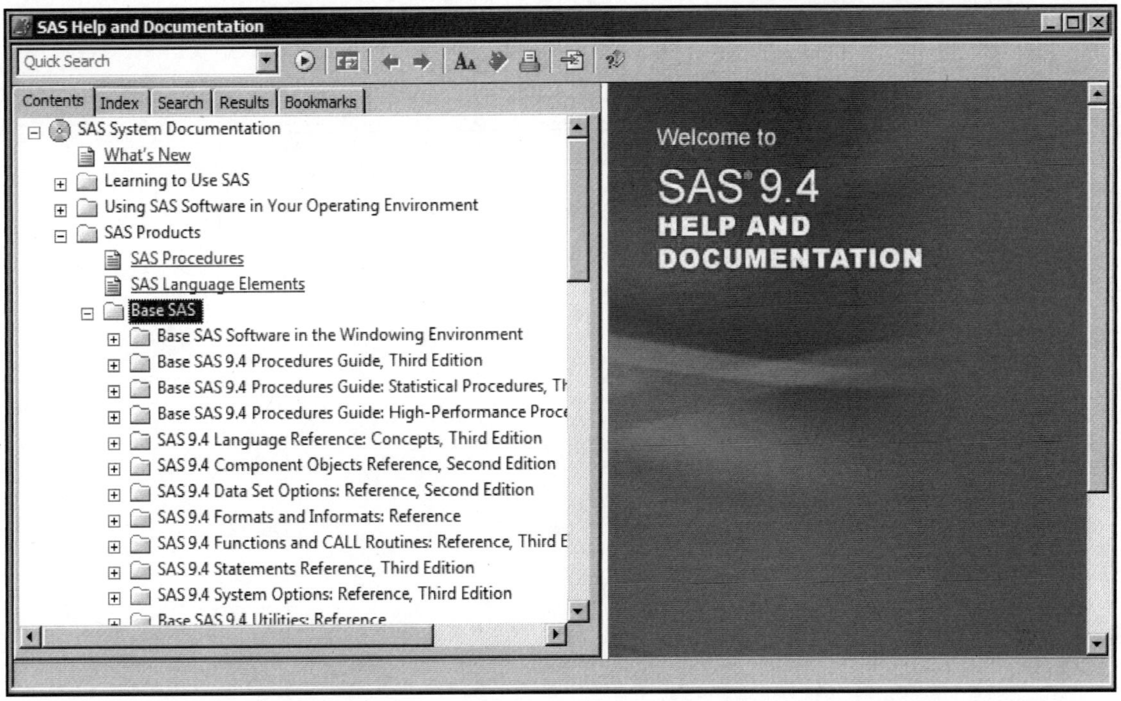

c. Alternatively, you can access the documentation for a SAS product directly from the following SAS Product Documentation web page: **http://support.sas.com/documentation/**.

d. From this web page, select **Programmer's Bookshelf**. Then choose the link for the appropriate version of SAS.

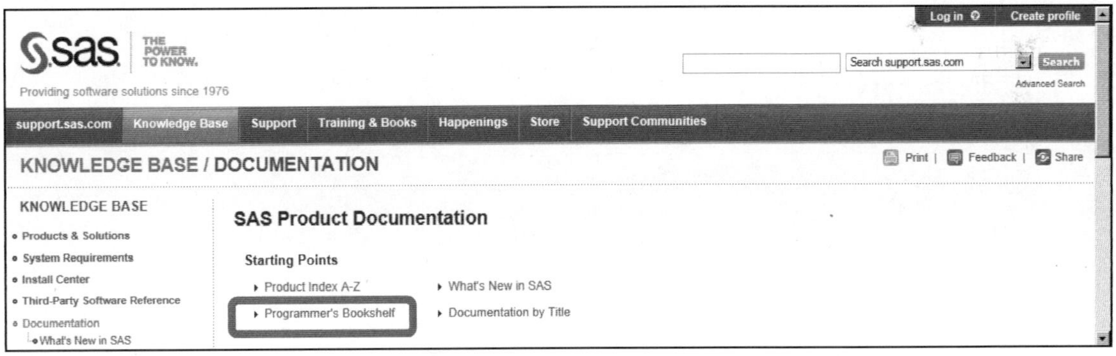

The Programmer's Bookshelf contains selected documentation for SAS products such as Base SAS.

e. Browse the Programmer's Bookshelf web page. Close the window after browsing it.

End of Exercises

Copyright © 2016, SAS Institute Inc., Cary, North Carolina, USA. ALL RIGHTS RESERVED.

2.3 SAS Program Syntax

Objectives

- Identify the characteristics of SAS statements.
- Define SAS syntax rules.
- Document a program using comments.
- Diagnose and correct a program with errors.

32

Business Scenario

Well-formatted, clearly documented SAS programs are an industry best practice.

33

Copyright © 2016, SAS Institute Inc., Cary, North Carolina, USA. ALL RIGHTS RESERVED.

SAS Syntax Rules: Statements

SAS statements

- usually begin with an ***identifying keyword***
- always end with a ***semicolon***.

```
data work.newsalesemps;
   length First_Name $ 12
          Last_Name $ 18 Job_Title $ 25;
   infile "&path\newemps.csv" dlm=',';
   input First_Name $ Last_Name $
         Job_Title $ Salary;
run;

proc print data=work.newsalesemps;
run;

proc means data=work.newsalesemps;
   var Salary;
run;
```

34

p102d01

2.03 Short Answer Poll

How many statements make up this DATA step?

```
data work.newsalesemps;
   length First_Name $ 12
          Last_Name $ 18 Job_Title $ 25;
   infile "&path\newemps.csv" dlm=',';
   input First_Name $ Last_Name $
         Job_Title $ Salary;
run;
```

5

This data step has 5 statments.

35

Copyright © 2016, SAS Institute Inc., Cary, North Carolina, USA. ALL RIGHTS RESERVED.

SAS Program Structure

SAS code is free format.

```
data work.newsalesemps;
length First_Name $ 12
Last_Name $ 18 Job_Title $ 25;
infile "&path\newemps.csv" dlm=',';
input First_Name $ Last_Name $
Job_Title $ Salary;run;
proc print data=work.newsalesemps; run;
   proc means data  =work.newsalesemps;
var Salary;run;
```

This program is syntactically correct but difficult to read.

37

p102d02

SAS Program Structure

Rules for SAS Statements

- Statements can begin and end in any column.
- A single statement can span multiple lines.
- Several statements can appear on the same line.
- Unquoted values can be lowercase, uppercase, or mixed case.

unconventional formatting

```
data work.newsalesEmps;
length First_Name $ 12
Last_Name $ 18 Job_Title $ 25;
infile "&path\newemps.csv" dlm=',';
input First_Name $ Last_Name $
Job_Title $ Salary;run;
proc print data=work.newsalesemps; run;
   proc means data  =work.newsalesemps;
var Salary;run;
```

38

Copyright © 2016, SAS Institute Inc., Cary, North Carolina, USA. ALL RIGHTS RESERVED.

Recommended Formatting

- Begin each statement on a new line.
- Use white space to separate words and steps.
- Indent statements within a step.
- Indent continued lines in multi-line statements.

```
data work.newsalesemps;
   length First_Name $ 12
          Last_Name $ 18 Job_Title $ 25;
   infile "&path\newemps.csv" dlm=',';
   input First_Name $ Last_Name $
         Job_Title $ Salary;
run;

proc print data=work.newsalesemps;
run;

proc means data=work.newsalesemps;
   var Salary;
run;
```

conventional formatting

39

White space can be blanks, tabs, and new lines. Add them to increase the readability of the code.

Program Documentation

You can embed comments in a program as explanatory text.

```
  /* create a temporary data set, newsalesemps */
  /* from the text file newemps.csv            */

data work.newsalesemps;
   length First_Name $ 12
          Last_Name $ 18 Job_Title $ 25;
   *read a comma delimited file;
   infile "&path\newemps.csv" dlm=',';
   input First_Name $ Last_Name $
         Job_Title $ Salary;
run;
```

/* comment */

* comment statement ;

SAS ignores comments during processing but writes them to the SAS log.

40

*** comment ;** These comments must be written as separate statements and cannot contain internal semicolons.

/* **comment** */ These comments can be any length and can contain semicolons. They cannot be nested.

Copyright © 2016, SAS Institute Inc., Cary, North Carolina, USA. ALL RIGHTS RESERVED.

SAS Comments

This program contains four comments.

```
*--------------------------------------*
|  This program creates and uses the   |   ❶
|  data set called work.newsalesemps.  |
*--------------------------------------*;
data work.newsalesemps;
   length First_Name $ 12 Last_Name $ 18
          Job_Title $ 25;
   infile "&path\newemps.csv" dlm=',';
   input First_Name $ Last_Name $
         Job_Title $ Salary /* numeric */;❷
run;
  /*
proc print data=work.newsalesemps;  ❸
run;
  */
proc means data=work.newsalesemps;
   * var Salary ;❹
run;
```

41 p102d03

- To comment out a block of code using the /* */ technique in the SAS interfaces, you can highlight the code and then press the Ctrl key and the / (forward slash) key simultaneously.
- To uncomment a block of code in SAS Studio, highlight the block and then press the Ctrl key and the / key simultaneously.
- To uncomment a block of code in SAS Enterprise Guide and the SAS windowing environment, highlight the block and then press the Ctrl key, the Shift key, and the / key simultaneously.

2.04 Short Answer Poll

Open and examine **p102a01**. Based on the comments, which steps do you think are executed and what output is generated?

Submit the program. Which steps were executed?

42

Copyright © 2016, SAS Institute Inc., Cary, North Carolina, USA. ALL RIGHTS RESERVED.

Business Scenario

Orion Star programmers must be able to identify and correct syntax errors in a SAS program.

45

Syntax Errors

A *syntax error* is an error in the spelling or grammar of a SAS statement. SAS finds syntax errors as it compiles each SAS statement, before execution begins.

Examples of syntax errors:

- misspelled keywords
- unmatched quotation marks
- missing semicolons
- invalid options

46

Copyright © 2016, SAS Institute Inc., Cary, North Carolina, USA. ALL RIGHTS RESERVED.

2.05 Short Answer Poll

This program includes three syntax errors. One is an invalid option. What are the other two syntax errors?

```
daat work.newsalesemps;
   length First_Name $ 12
          Last_Name $ 18 Job_Title $ 25;
   infile "&path\newemps.csv" dlm=',';
   input First_Name $ Last_Name $
         Job_Title $ Salary;
run;

proc print data=work.newsalesemps
run;

proc means data=work.newsalesemps average min;
   var Salary;
run;
```

invalid option

47 p102d04

Syntax Errors

Syntax errors in a SAS program can possibly be detected based on the color of the syntax on the Editor tab or in the window.

```
daat work.newsalesemps;
   length First_Name $ 12
          Last_Name $ 18 Job_Title $ 25;
   infile "&path\newemps.csv" dlm=',';
   input First_Name $ Last_Name $
         Job_Title $ Salary;
run;

proc print data=work.newsales
run;

proc means data=work.newsales
   var Salary;
run;
```

```
daat work.newsalesemps;
   length First_Name $ 12
          Last_Name $ 18 Job_Title $ 25;
   infile "&path\newemps.csv" dlm=',';
   input First_Name $ Last_Name $
         Job_Title $ Salary;
run;

proc print data=work.newsalesemps
run;

proc means data=work.newsalesemps average min;
   var Salary;
run;
```

49

Copyright © 2016, SAS Institute Inc., Cary, North Carolina, USA. ALL RIGHTS RESERVED.

Syntax Errors

When SAS encounters a syntax error, it writes a warning or error message to the log.

```
WARNING 14-169: Assuming the symbol DATA was misspelled as daat.
```

```
ERROR 22-322: Syntax error, expecting one of the following: ;, (,
              BLANKLINE, CONTENTS, DATA, DOUBLE, GRANDTOTAL_LABEL,
              GRANDTOT_LABEL, GRAND_LABEL, GTOTAL_LABEL,
              GTOT_LABEL, HEADING, LABEL, N, NOOBS, NOSUMLABEL,
              OBS, ROUND, ROWS, SPLIT, STYLE, SUMLABEL, UNIFORM,
              WIDTH.
```

⚠ You should always check the log to make sure that the program ran successfully, even if output is generated.

50

Copyright © 2016, SAS Institute Inc., Cary, North Carolina, USA. ALL RIGHTS RESERVED.

Diagnosing and Correcting Syntax Errors

p102d04

1. Open and submit **p102d04**.
2. Go to the log and view the notes, warnings, and errors.

Partial SAS Log

```
15    daat work.newsalesemps;
      ----
      14
WARNING 14-169: Assuming the symbol DATA was misspelled as daat.

16        length First_Name $ 12
17              Last_Name $ 18 Job_Title $ 25;
18        infile "&path\newemps.csv" dlm=',';
19        input First_Name $ Last_Name $
20             Job_Title $ Salary;
21    run;

NOTE: The infile "s:\workshop\newemps.csv" is:
      Filename=s:\workshop\newemps.csv,

NOTE: 71 records were read from the infile "s:\workshop\newemps.csv".
NOTE: The data set WORK.NEWSALESEMPS has 71 observations and 4 variables.

22
23    proc print data=work.newsalesemps
24    run;
      ---
      22
      202
ERROR 22-322: Syntax error, expecting one of the following: ;, (, BLANKLINE, CONTENTS, DATA,
              DOUBLE, GRANDTOTAL_LABEL, GRANDTOT_LABEL, GRAND_LABEL, GTOTAL_LABEL,
GTOT_LABEL,
              HEADING, LABEL, N, NOOBS, NOSUMLABEL, OBS, ROUND, ROWS, SPLIT, STYLE, SUMLABEL,
              UNIFORM, WIDTH.
ERROR 202-322: The option or parameter is not recognized and will be ignored.
25

NOTE: The SAS System stopped processing this step because of errors.

26    proc means data=work.newsalesemps average min;
                                        -------
                                        22
                                        202
```

Copyright © 2016, SAS Institute Inc., Cary, North Carolina, USA. ALL RIGHTS RESERVED.

```
ERROR 22-322: Syntax error, expecting one of the following: ;, (, ALPHA, CHARTYPE, CLASSDATA,
              CLM, COMPLETETYPES, CSS, CV, DATA, DESCEND, DESCENDING, DESCENDTYPES, EXCLNPWGT,
              EXCLNPWGTS, EXCLUSIVE, FW, IDMIN, KURTOSIS, LCLM, MAX, MAXDEC, MEAN, MEDIAN, MIN,
              MISSING, MODE, N, NDEC, NMISS, NOLABELS, NONOBS, NOPRINT, NOTHREADS, NOTRAP, NWAY,
              ORDER, P1, P10, P20, P25, P30, P40, P5, P50, P60, P70, P75, P80, P90, P95, P99,
              PCTLDEF, PRINT, PRINTALL, PRINTALLTYPES, PRINTIDS, PRINTIDVARS, PROBT, Q1, Q3,
              QMARKERS, QMETHOD, QNTLDEF, QRANGE, RANGE, SKEWNESS, STACKODS, STACKODSOUTPUT,
              STDDEV, STDERR, SUM, SUMSIZE, SUMWGT, T, THREADS, UCLM, USS, VAR, VARDEF.
ERROR 202-322: The option or parameter is not recognized and will be ignored.
27        var Salary;
28     run;

NOTE: The SAS System stopped processing this step because of errors.
NOTE: The SAS System stopped processing this step because of errors.
```

The log indicates that SAS did the following:

- assumed that the keyword DATA was misspelled, issued a warning, and executed the DATA step
- interpreted the word RUN as an option in the PROC PRINT statement (because of a missing semicolon), so the PROC PRINT step did not execute
- did not recognize the word AVERAGE as a valid option in the PROC MEANS statement, so the PROC MEANS step did not execute

3. Return to the program and edit the program.

   a. Correct the spelling of DATA.

   b. Put a semicolon at the end of the PROC PRINT statement.

   c. Change the word AVERAGE to MEAN in the PROC MEANS statement.

```
data work.newsalesemps;
   length First_Name $ 12
          Last_Name $ 18 Job_Title $ 25;
   infile "&path\newemps.csv" dlm=',';
   input First_Name $ Last_Name $
         Job_Title $ Salary;
run;

proc print data=work.newsalesemps;
run;

proc means data=work.newsalesemps mean min;
   var Salary;
run;
```

4. Submit the program. Verify that it executes without warnings or errors and produces results.

5. Save the corrected program.

End of Demonstration

Copyright © 2016, SAS Institute Inc., Cary, North Carolina, USA. ALL RIGHTS RESERVED.

2.06 Short Answer Poll

What is the syntax error in this program?

```
data work.newsalesemps;
   length First_Name $ 12
          Last_Name $ 18 Job_Title $ 25;
   infile "&path\newemps.csv" dlm=',';
   input First_Name $ Last_Name $
         Job_Title $ Salary;
run;

proc print data=work.newsalesemps
run;

proc means data=work.newsalesemps average min;
   var Salary;
run;
```

52

p102d05

Copyright © 2016, SAS Institute Inc., Cary, North Carolina, USA. ALL RIGHTS RESERVED.

Exercises

SAS Studio

10. Correcting Quotation Marks with SAS Studio

a. In SAS Studio, in the navigation pane, navigate in the file structure of the Folders section to find the **p102e10** program.

b. Double-click **p102e10** to open the program. Notice that the closing quotation mark for the DLM= option in the INFILE statement is missing.

c. On the CODE tab, click (**Run**) or press F3 to submit the program.

d. On the LOG tab, notice that there are no messages following each step in the log. The absence of messages often indicates unbalanced quotation marks.

Partial SAS Log

```
data work.newsalesemps;
   length First_Name $ 12
          Last_Name $ 18 Job_Title $ 25;
   infile "&path\\newemps.csv" dlm=',;
   input First_Name $ Last_Name $
         Job_Title $ Salary;
run;

proc print data=work.newsalesemps;
run;

proc means data=work.newsalesemps;
   var Salary;
run;
```

e. Return to the program. Add a closing quotation mark to the DLM= option in the INFILE statement to correct the program.

```
infile "&path\newemps.csv" dlm=',';
```

f. On the CODE tab, click (**Run**) or press F3 to submit the program.

g. On the RESULTS tab, view the PROC PRINT and PROC MEANS output.

h. On the LOG tab, verify that no errors or warnings appear.

i. On the CODE tab, click (**Save Program**) to save the program.

11. Diagnosing Errors with SAS Studio

a. In the Folders section of the navigation pane, click (**New**) ⇨ **SAS Program (F4)** or press F4 to start a new program.

b. On the CODE tab, enter the following program with the formatting as shown:

Copyright © 2016, SAS Institute Inc., Cary, North Carolina, USA. ALL RIGHTS RESERVED.

```
proc print data=  sashelp.class; run; proc  means
data=sashelp.class; run;
```

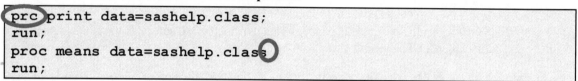

c. On the CODE toolbar, click **(Format Code)** to make your program easier to read. This button automatically formats your code by adding line breaks and indenting at appropriate nesting levels.

d. Add two mistakes to the program. Remove the letter **o** from the first PROC step and remove the semicolon after the last reference to **sashelp.class**.

```
prc print data=sashelp.class;
run;
proc means data=sashelp.class
run;
```

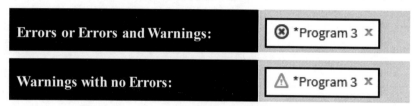

e. On the CODE tab, click **(Run)** or press F3 to submit the program. The Program tab shows an icon in front of the program name if the program contains errors, warnings, or both.

Errors or Errors and Warnings:

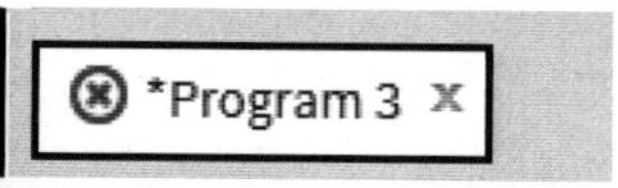

Warnings with no Errors:

f. On the RESULTS tab, notice that there is PROC PRINT output but no PROC MEANS output.

g. On the LOG tab, scroll through the log. Notes appear as blue text, warnings as green text, and errors as red text.

h. Expand the Errors, Warnings, and Notes sections to view the messages at the beginning of the Log window.

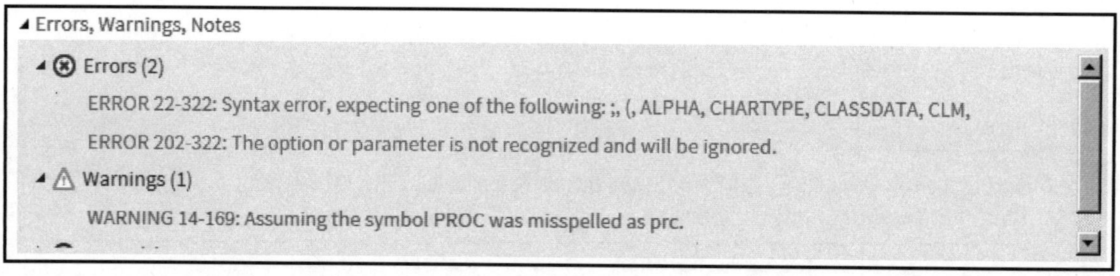

Errors, Warnings, Notes
Errors (2)
ERROR 22-322: Syntax error, expecting one of the following: ;, (, ALPHA, CHARTYPE, CLASSDATA, CLM,
ERROR 202-322: The option or parameter is not recognized and will be ignored.
Warnings (1)
WARNING 14-169: Assuming the symbol PROC was misspelled as prc.

i. Click on a message in an Errors, Warnings, or Notes section. The message is highlighted in the log farther down.

Copyright © 2016, SAS Institute Inc., Cary, North Carolina, USA. ALL RIGHTS RESERVED.

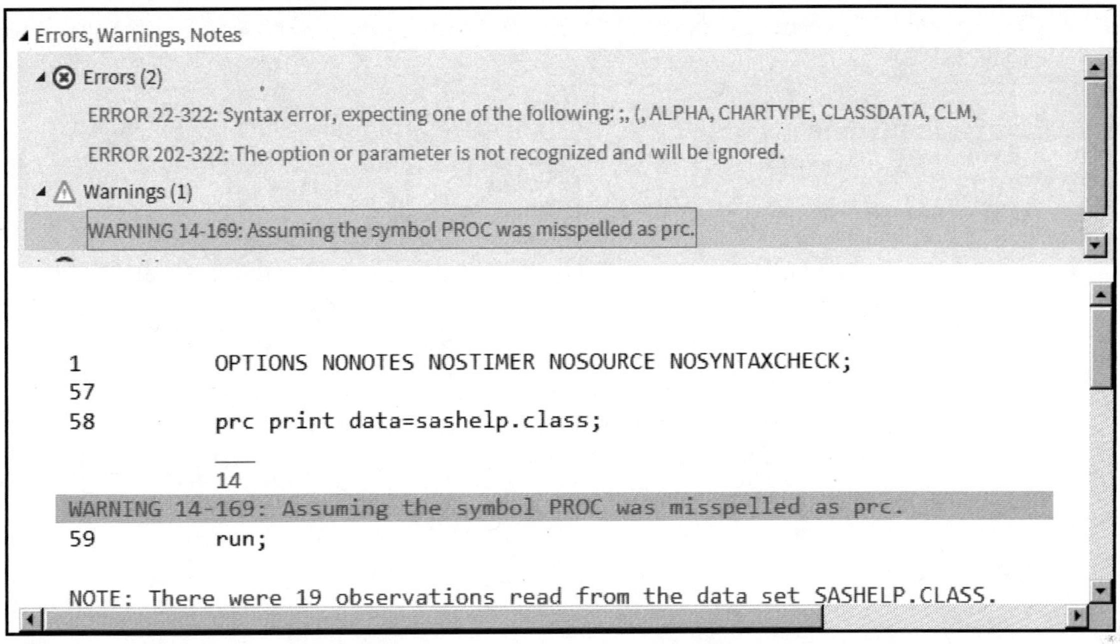

j. Return to the CODE tab and fix the two mistakes. Submit the program and verify that there are no errors or warnings in the log.

k. In the log, notice the OPTIONS statement at the beginning and ending of the program. SAS Studio automatically includes these statements before and after your program. In addition, SAS Studio includes supplemental code before and after your program. By default, this code is not visible in the log.

l. To view the complete program executed by SAS, including the generated code, click (**More Application Options**) ⇨ **Preferences** ⇨ **General**.

m. Select the **Show generated code in the SAS log** check box and click **Save**.

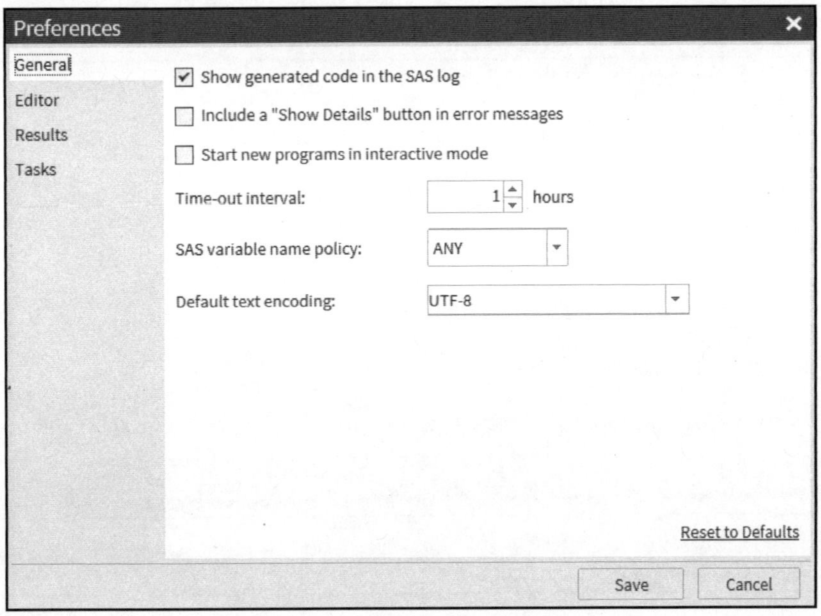

n. Submit the program and view the supplemental code in the log.

Copyright © 2016, SAS Institute Inc., Cary, North Carolina, USA. ALL RIGHTS RESERVED.

o. Return to the Preferences window and clear the **Show generated code in the SAS log** check box. Click **Save**.

SAS Enterprise Guide

12. Correcting Quotation Marks with SAS Enterprise Guide

a. In SAS Enterprise Guide, select **File** ⇨ **Open** ⇨ **Program** or click (**Open**) ⇨ **Program**.

b. In the Open Program window, navigate in the file structure to find **p102e12** and click **Open**. Notice that the closing quotation mark for the DLM= option in the INFILE statement is missing.

c. On the Program tab, click **Run** or press F3 to submit the program.

d. On the Log tab, notice that there are no messages following each step in the log. The absence of messages often indicates unbalanced quotation marks.

Partial SAS Log

```
data work.newsalesemps;
   length First_Name $ 12
          Last_Name $ 18 Job_Title $ 25;
   infile "&path\\newemps.csv" dlm=',;
   input First_Name $ Last_Name $
         Job_Title $ Salary;
run;

proc print data=work.newsalesemps;
run;

proc means data=work.newsalesemps;
   var Salary;
run;
```

e. Return to the program. Add a closing quotation mark to the DLM= option in the INFILE statement to correct the program.

```
   infile "&path\newemps.csv" dlm=',';
```

f. On the Program tab, click **Run** or press F3 to submit the program. Click **Yes** to replace the results.

g. On the Results tab, view the PROC PRINT and PROC MEANS output.

h. On the Log tab, verify that no errors or warnings appear.

i. On the Program tab, click **Save** to save the program.

13. Diagnosing Errors with SAS Enterprise Guide

a. Select **File** ⇨ **New** ⇨ **Program** or click (**New**) ⇨ **Program** to start a new program.

b. On the Program tab, enter the following program with the formatting as shown below.

```
proc print data=sashelp.class;
run; proc means data=sashelp.class;   run;
```

c. Click **Edit** ⇨ **Format Code** so that your program is easier to read. This selection automatically formats your code by adding line breaks and indenting at appropriate nesting levels.

Copyright © 2016, SAS Institute Inc., Cary, North Carolina, USA. ALL RIGHTS RESERVED.

d. Add two mistakes to the program. Remove the letter **o** from the first PROC step and remove the semicolon after the last reference to **sashelp.class**.

```
prc print data=sashelp.class;
run;
proc means data=sashelp.class
run;
```

e. On the Program tab, click the **Run** button or press F3 to submit the program. The Program tab shows a special icon in front of the program name if the program contains errors, warnings, or both.

Errors or Errors and Warnings:

Warnings with no Errors:

f. On the Results tab, notice that there is PROC PRINT output but no PROC MEANS output.

g. On the Log tab, scroll through the log. Notes appear as green text, warnings as light blue text, and errors as red text. Use the Up and Down arrows on the Log tab to find the previous or next warning or error.

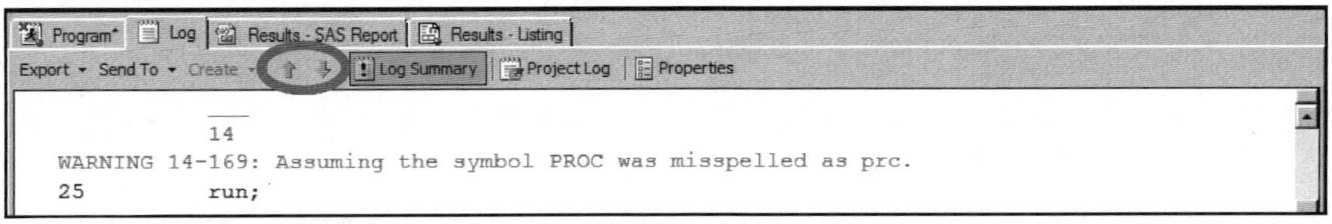

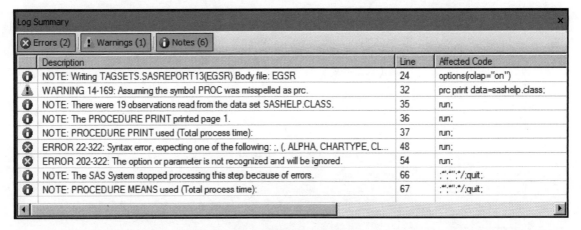

h. Go to the Log Summary window, which is located below the Log tab. The log summary lists all the errors, warnings, and notes that were generated when the program ran, as well as related line numbers and a sample of the affected code. By default, all types of messages are displayed. You can filter the messages by selecting or deselecting the tab for the type of message.

Log Summary

Errors (2) | Warnings (1) | Notes (6)

Description	Line	Affected Code
NOTE: Writing TAGSETS.SASREPORT13(EGSR) Body file: EGSR	24	options(rolap="on")
WARNING 14-169: Assuming the symbol PROC was misspelled as prc.	32	prc print data=sashelp.class;
NOTE: There were 19 observations read from the data set SASHELP.CLASS.	35	run;
NOTE: The PROCEDURE PRINT printed page 1.	36	run;
NOTE: PROCEDURE PRINT used (Total process time):	37	run;
ERROR 22-322: Syntax error, expecting one of the following: ;, (, ALPHA, CHARTYPE, CL...	48	run;
ERROR 202-322: The option or parameter is not recognized and will be ignored.	54	run;
NOTE: The SAS System stopped processing this step because of errors.	66	;*';*";*/;quit;
NOTE: PROCEDURE MEANS used (Total process time):	67	;*';*";*/;quit;

i. In the Log Summary window, click a message description and view the message on the Log tab.

Copyright © 2016, SAS Institute Inc., Cary, North Carolina, USA. ALL RIGHTS RESERVED.

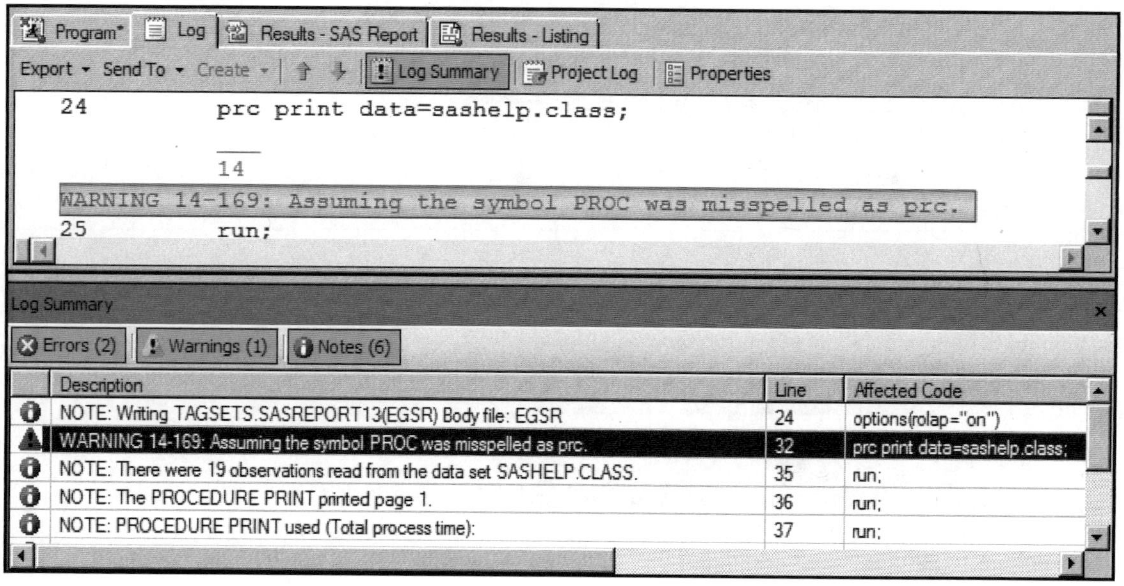

j. Click the **Program** tab and fix the two mistakes. Submit the program and click **Yes** to replace the results from the previous run. Verify that there are no errors or warnings in the log.

k. In the log, notice that SAS Enterprise Guide includes supplemental code before and after your program. This generated wrapper code is included in the log by default.

l. To hide the generated wrapper code in the log, select **Tools** ⇨ **Options** ⇨ **Results General**. Clear the **Show generated wrapper code in SAS log** check box and click **OK**.

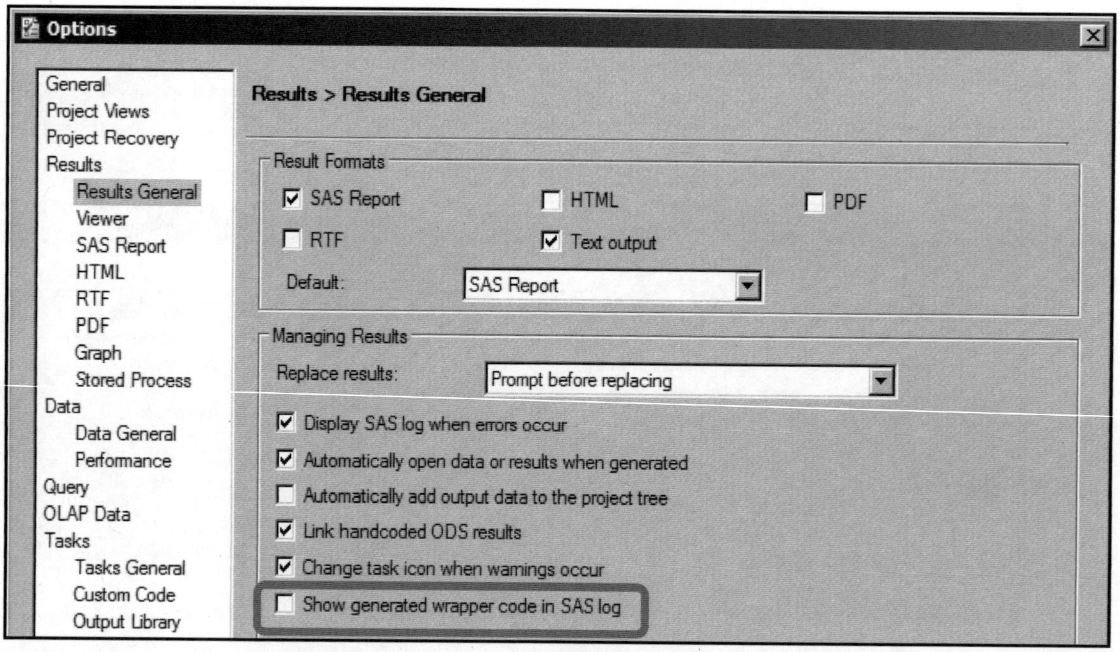

m. Submit the program and view the log. Notice that the majority of the generated wrapper code is hidden.

Copyright © 2016, SAS Institute Inc., Cary, North Carolina, USA. ALL RIGHTS RESERVED.

SAS Windowing Environment

14. Correcting Quotation Marks in the SAS Windowing Environment

a. In the SAS windowing environment, click (**Open**) when the Editor window is the active window or select **File** ⇨ **Open Program**.

b. In the Open window, navigate in the file structure to find **p102e14** and click **Open**. Notice that the closing quotation mark for the DLM= option in the INFILE statement is missing.

c. Click (**Submit**) or press F3 to submit the program.

d. In the Log window, notice that there are no messages following each step in the log. The absence of messages often indicates unbalanced quotation marks.

Partial SAS Log

```
data work.newsalesemps;
   length First_Name $ 12
          Last_Name $ 18 Job_Title $ 25;
   infile "&path\\newemps.csv" dlm=',;
   input First_Name $ Last_Name $
         Job_Title $ Salary;
run;

proc print data=work.newsalesemps;
run;

proc means data=work.newsalesemps;
   var Salary;
run;
```

e. In the Log window, click (**New**) or select **Edit** ⇨ **Clear All** to clear the Log window.

f. Return to the program. Notice the "DATA STEP running" message in the banner of the Editor window. This message appears because the RUN statement was viewed as part of the character literal and not as a step boundary.

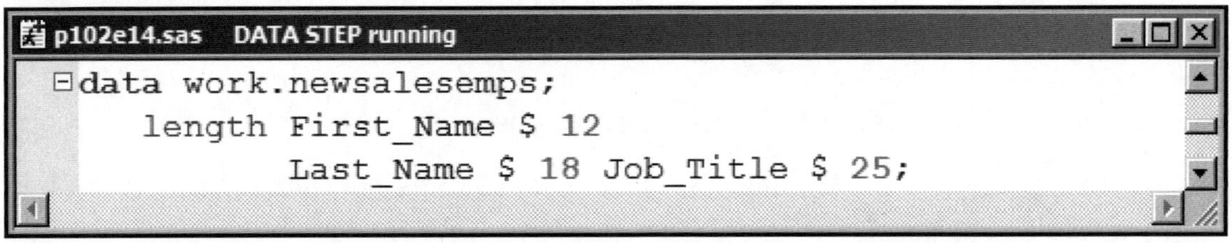
p102e14.sas DATA STEP running
data work.newsalesemps;
length First_Name $ 12
Last_Name $ 18 Job_Title $ 25;

g. To stop the DATA step from running, click (**Break**) or press the Ctrl and Break keys.

h. Select the **1. Cancel Submitted Statements** radio button in the Tasking Manager window. Click **OK**

Copyright © 2016, SAS Institute Inc., Cary, North Carolina, USA. ALL RIGHTS RESERVED.

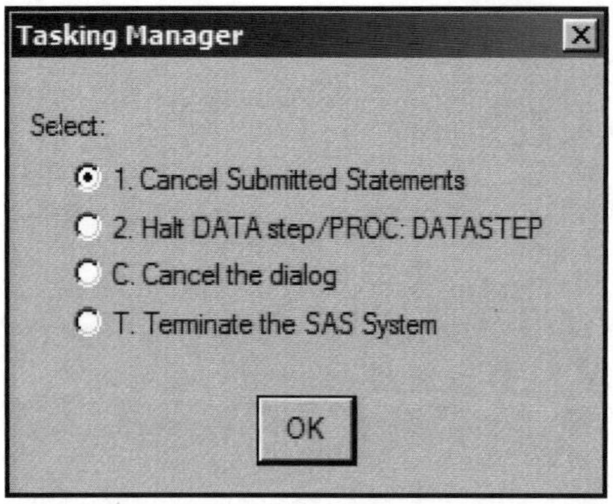

i. Select the **Y to Cancel submitted statements.** radio button. Click **OK**.

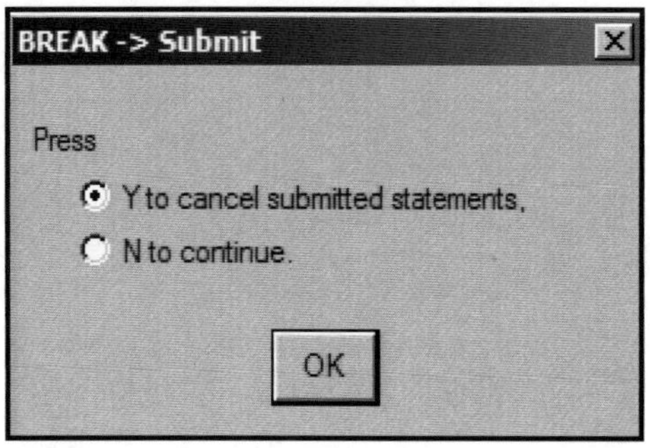

j. Add a closing quotation mark to the DLM= option in the INFILE statement to correct the program.

```
   infile "&path\newemps.csv" dlm=',';
```

k. Click (**Submit**) or press F3 to submit the program.

l. In the Results Viewer window, view the PROC PRINT and PROC MEANS output.

m. In the Log window, verify that no errors or warnings appear.

n. Click (**New**) or select **Edit** ⇨ **Clear All** to clear the Log window.

o. In the Editor window, click (**Save**) to save the program.

15. Diagnosing Errors in the SAS Windowing Environment

a. Click (**Open**) when the Editor window is the active window or select **File** ⇨ **Open Program** to open a program.

b. In the Open window, navigate in the file structure to find **MyProgram**. Click **Open**.

c. Add two mistakes to the program. Remove the letter **o** from the first PROC step and remove the semicolon after the last reference to **sashelp.class**.

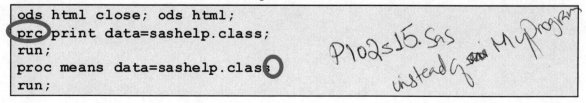

```
ods html close; ods html;
prc print data=sashelp.class;
run;
proc means data=sashelp.class
run;
```

P102s15.sas instead of MyProgram

Copyright © 2016, SAS Institute Inc., Cary, North Carolina, USA. ALL RIGHTS RESERVED.

d. Click (**Submit**) or press F3 to submit the program.

e. In the Results Viewer and Output windows, notice that there is PROC PRINT output, but no PROC MEANS output.

f. In the Log window, scroll through the log. Notes appear as blue text, warnings as green text, and errors as red text.

```
Log - (Untitled)
30     ods html close; ods html;
NOTE: Writing HTML Body file: sashtml6.htm
31     prc print data=sashelp.class;
       ---
       14
WARNING 14-169: Assuming the symbol PROC was misspelled as prc.
32     run;

NOTE: There were 19 observations read from the data set SASHELP.CLASS.
NOTE: PROCEDURE PRINT used (Total process time):
      real time           0.04 seconds
      cpu time            0.03 seconds


33     proc means data=sashelp.class
34     run;
       ---
       22
       202
ERROR 22-322: Syntax error, expecting one of the following: ;, (, ALPHA, CHARTYPE, CLASSDATA, CLM,
              COMPLETETYPES, CSS, CV, DATA, DESCEND, DESCENDING, DESCENDTYPES, EXCLNPWGT, EXCLNPWGTS,
              EXCLUSIVE, FW, IDMIN, KURTOSIS, LCLM, MAX, MAXDEC, MEAN, MEDIAN, MIN, MISSING, MODE, N,
              NDEC, NMISS, NOLABELS, NONOBS, NOPRINT, NOTHREADS, NOTRAP, NWAY, ORDER, P1, P10, P20,
              P25, P30, P40, P5, P50, P60, P70, P75, P80, P90, P95, P99, PCTLDEF, PRINT, PRINTALL,
              PRINTALLTYPES, PRINTIDS, PRINTIDVARS, PROBT, Q1, Q3, QMARKERS, QMETHOD, QNTLDEF,
              QRANGE, RANGE, SKEWNESS, STACKODS, STACKODSOUTPUT, STDDEV, STDERR, SUM, SUMSIZE,
              SUMWGT, T, THREADS, UCLM, USS, VAR, VARDEF.

ERROR 202-322: The option or parameter is not recognized and will be ignored.
```

g. Return to the Editor window. Notice the text on the title bar that states "PROC MEANS running."

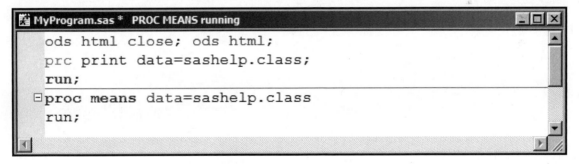

```
MyProgram.sas *  PROC MEANS running
ods html close; ods html;
prc print data=sashelp.class;
run;
proc means data=sashelp.class
run;
```

h. To stop the step from running, click (**Break**) or press the Ctrl and Break keys.

i. Select the **1. Cancel Submitted Statements** radio button in the Tasking Manager window. Click **OK**.

Copyright © 2016, SAS Institute Inc., Cary, North Carolina, USA. ALL RIGHTS RESERVED.

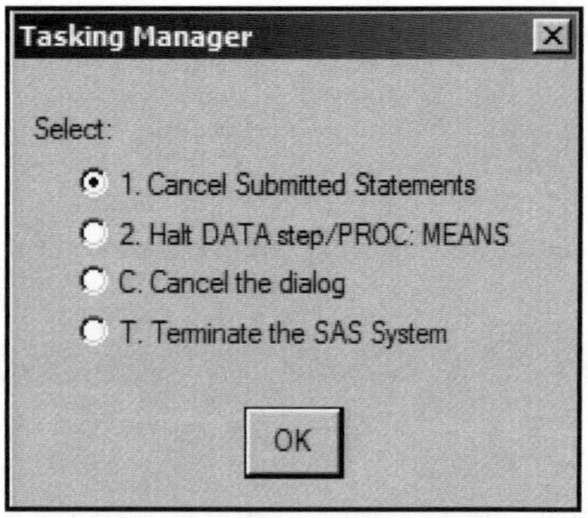

j. Select the **Y to cancel submitted statements.** radio button. Click **OK**.

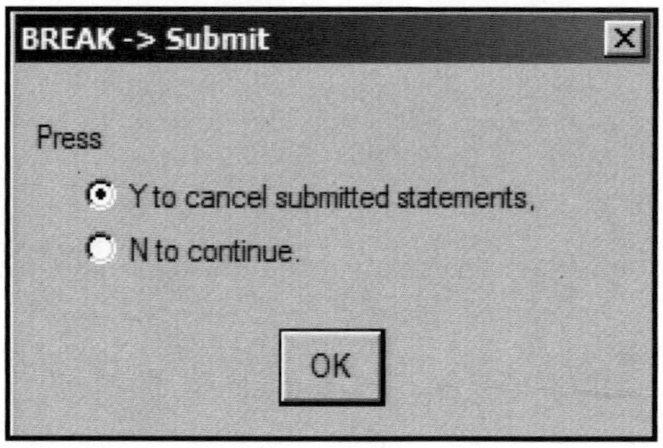

k. The program is no longer running, so fix the two mistakes. Clear the log, submit the program, and verify that there are no errors or warnings in the log.

End of Exercises

Copyright © 2016, SAS Institute Inc., Cary, North Carolina, USA. ALL RIGHTS RESERVED.

2.4 Solutions

Solutions to Student Activities (Polls/Quizzes)

2.01 Short Answer Poll – Correct Answer

How many steps are in program **p102d01**? **three**

```
data work.newsalesemps;
   length First_Name $ 12
          Last_Name $ 18 Job_Title $ 25;
   infile "&path\newemps.csv" dlm=',';
   input First_Name $ Last_Name $
         Job_Title $ Salary;
run;

proc print data=work.newsalesemps;
run;

proc means data=work.newsalesemps;
   var Salary;
run;
```

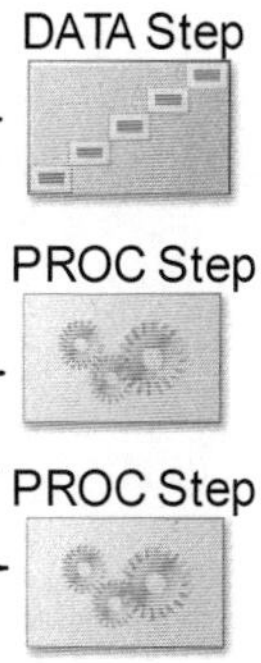

8 p102d01

2.03 Short Answer Poll – Correct Answer

How many statements make up this DATA step?

```
data work.newsalesemps;
   length First_Name $ 12
          Last_Name $ 18 Job_Title $ 25;
   infile "&path\newemps.csv" dlm=',';
   input First_Name $ Last_Name $
         Job_Title $ Salary;
run;
```

This DATA step has five statements.

36

Copyright © 2016, SAS Institute Inc., Cary, North Carolina, USA. ALL RIGHTS RESERVED.

2.04 Short Answer Poll – Correct Answer

Open and examine **p102a01**. Based on the comments, which steps do you think are executed and what output is generated?

Submit the program. Which steps were executed?

- **The DATA step executes and creates an output data set.**
- **The PROC PRINT step executes and produces a report.**
- **The PROC MEANS step is "commented out," and therefore, does not execute.**

43

2.05 Short Answer Poll – Correct Answer

This program includes three syntax errors. One is an invalid option. What are the other two syntax errors?

```
daat work         mps;
   lengt          e $ 12
           Last_Name $ 18 Job_Title $ 25;
   infile "&path\newemps.csv" dlm=',';
   input First_Name $ Last_Name $
         Job_Title $ Salary;
run;

proc print data=work.newsalesemps
run;

proc means data=work.newsalesemps average min;
   var Salary;
run;
```

misspelled keyword

missing semicolon

invalid option

48 p102d04

Copyright © 2016, SAS Institute Inc., Cary, North Carolina, USA. ALL RIGHTS RESERVED.

2.06 Short Answer Poll – Correct Answer

What is the syntax error in this program?

```
data work.newsalesemps;
   length First_Name $ 12
          Last_Name $ 18 Job_Title $ 25;
   infile "&path\newemps.csv" dlm=',;
   input First_Name $ Last_Name $
         Job_Title $ Salary;
run;

proc print data=work.newsalesemps
run;

proc means data=work.newsalesemps average min;
   var Salary;
run;
```

The program contains unbalanced quotation marks in the DLM= option in the INFILE statement.

53

p102d05

Copyright © 2016, SAS Institute Inc., Cary, North Carolina, USA. ALL RIGHTS RESERVED.

Copyright © 2016, SAS Institute Inc., Cary, North Carolina, USA. ALL RIGHTS RESERVED.

Chapter 3 Accessing Data

Copyright © 2016, SAS Institute Inc., Cary, North Carolina, USA. ALL RIGHTS RESERVED.

3.1 Examining SAS Data Sets

Objectives

- Define the components of a SAS data set.
- Use the CONTENTS procedure to browse the descriptor portion of a SAS data set.
- Use the PRINT procedure to browse the data portion of a SAS data set.
- Define a SAS variable.
- Define a missing value.
- Define a SAS date value.

3

Business Scenario

Many SAS data sets related to the Orion Star project already exist. The programmers need to know how to display the structure and contents of the data sets.

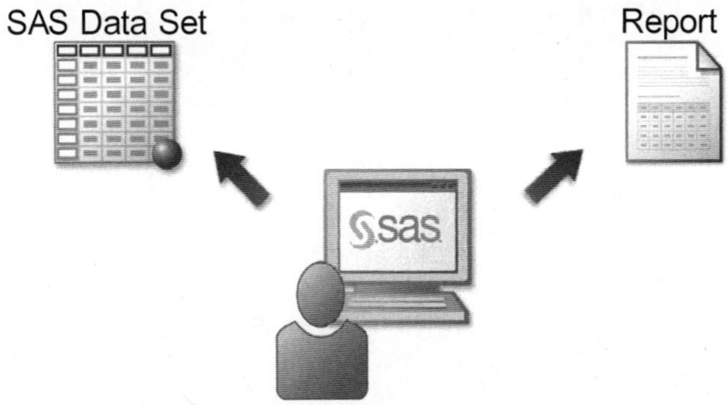

4

Copyright © 2016, SAS Institute Inc., Cary, North Carolina, USA. ALL RIGHTS RESERVED.

What Is a SAS Data Set?

A *SAS data set* is a specially structured data file that SAS creates and that only SAS can read. A SAS data set is a table that contains observations and variables.

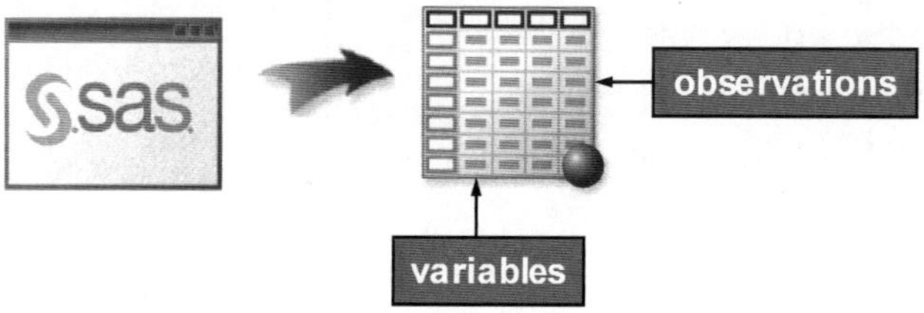

5

SAS Data Set Terminology

SAS Terminology		Database Terminology
SAS Data Set	⟷	Table
Observation	⟷	Row
Variable	⟷	Column

6

Copyright © 2016, SAS Institute Inc., Cary, North Carolina, USA. ALL RIGHTS RESERVED.

SAS Data Set Terminology

A SAS data set contains a descriptor portion and a data portion.

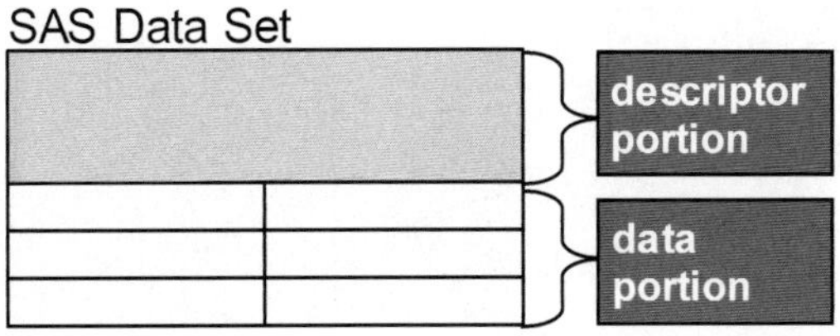

7

Descriptor Portion

The *descriptor portion* contains the following metadata:

- general properties (such as data set name and number of observations)
- variable properties (such as name, type, and length)

Partial **work.newsalesemps**

Data Set Name	**WORK.NEWSALESEMPS**
Engine	**V9**
Created	**Mon, Feb 27, 2012 01:28 PM**
Observations	**71**
Variables	**4**
...	

general properties

First_Name	**Last_Name**	**Job_Title**	**Salary**
$ 12	**$ 18**	**$ 25**	**N 8**

variable properties

8

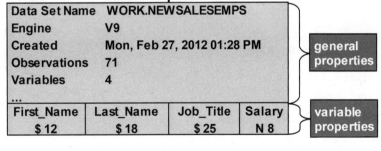

Copyright © 2016, SAS Institute Inc., Cary, North Carolina, USA. ALL RIGHTS RESERVED.

Browsing the Descriptor Portion

Use *PROC CONTENTS* to display the descriptor portion of a SAS data set.

```
proc contents data=work.newsalesemps;
run;
```

PROC CONTENTS DATA=*SAS-data-set***;**
RUN;

9 p103d01

Viewing the Output

Partial PROC CONTENTS Output

```
                          The CONTENTS Procedure

Data Set Name    WORK.NEWSALESEMPS                  Observations          71
Member Type      DATA                               Variables             4
Engine           V9                                 Indexes               0
Created          Mon, Feb 27, 2012 01:28:51 PM      Observation Length    64
Last Modified    Mon, Feb 27, 2012 01:28:51 PM      Deleted Observations  0
Protection                                          Compressed            NO
Data Set Type                                       Sorted                NO


                    Engine/Host Dependent Information
                                  ...


               Alphabetic List of Variables and Attributes

                    #    Variable      Type    Len

                    1    First_Name    Char     12
                    3    Job_Title     Char     25
                    2    Last_Name     Char     18
                    4    Salary        Num       8
```

10

The default PROC CONTENTS report has three parts:

- general data set properties
- engine/host information
- variable properties

Copyright © 2016, SAS Institute Inc., Cary, North Carolina, USA. ALL RIGHTS RESERVED.

3.01 Short Answer Poll

Open program **p103a01**. Add a PROC CONTENTS step after the DATA step to view **work.donations**. Submit the program and review the results. How many observations are in the data set **work.donations**?

11

Data Portion

The *data portion* of a SAS data set contains the data values, which are either character or numeric.

Partial **work.newsalesemps**

First_Name	Last_Name	Job_Title	Salary
Satyakam	Denny	Sales Rep. II	26780
Monica	Kletschkus	Sales Rep. IV	30890
Kevin	Lyon	Sales Rep. I	26955
Petrea	Soltau	Sales Rep. II	27440

variable names

data values

character values

numeric values

13

Variable names are part of the descriptor portion, not the data portion.

Copyright © 2016, SAS Institute Inc., Cary, North Carolina, USA. ALL RIGHTS RESERVED.

Browsing the Data Portion

Use *PROC PRINT* to display the data portion of a SAS data set.

```
proc print data=work.newsalesemps;
run;
```

PROC PRINT DATA=*SAS-data-set*;
RUN;

14 p103d02

Viewing the Output

Partial PROC PRINT Output

Obs	First_Name	Last_Name	Job_Title	Salary
1	Satyakam	Denny	Sales Rep. II	26780
2	Monica	Kletschkus	Sales Rep. IV	30890
3	Kevin	Lyon	Sales Rep. I	26955
4	Petrea	Soltau	Sales Rep. II	27440
5	Marina	Iyengar	Sales Rep. III	29715

15

Copyright © 2016, SAS Institute Inc., Cary, North Carolina, USA. ALL RIGHTS RESERVED.

SAS Variable Names

SAS variable names

- can be 1 to 32 characters long.
- must start with a letter or underscore. Subsequent characters can be letters, underscores, or numerals.
- can be uppercase, lowercase, or mixed case.
- are not case sensitive.

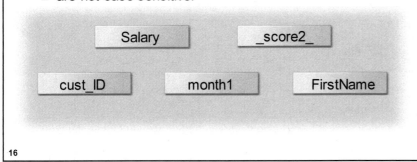

Salary _score2_

cust_ID month1 FirstName

16

The same naming rules apply to SAS data set names.

3.02 Multiple Answer Poll

Which variable names are invalid?

a. data5mon
b. 5monthsdata
c. data#5
d. five months data
e. five_months_data
f. FiveMonthsData
g. fivemonthsdata

17

A variable name can contain special characters if you place the name in quotation marks and immediately follow it with the letter N (for example, **'Flight#'n**). This is called a *SAS name literal*. In order to use SAS name literals as variable names, the VALIDVARNAME= option must be set to ANY.

```
options validvarname=any;
```

This setting is the default in SAS Enterprise Guide and SAS Studio.

Copyright © 2016, SAS Institute Inc., Cary, North Carolina, USA. ALL RIGHTS RESERVED.

Data Types

A SAS data set supports two types of variables.

Character variables

- can contain any value: letters, numerals, special characters, and blanks
- range from 1 to 32,767 characters in length
- have 1 byte per character.

Numeric variables

- store numeric values using floating point or binary representation
- have 8 bytes of storage by default
- can store 16 or 17 significant digits.

19

Missing Data Values

Missing values are valid values in a SAS data set.

Partial **work.newsalesemps**

First_Name	Last_Name	Job_Title	Salary
Monica	Kletschkus	Sales Rep. IV	.
Kevin	Lyon	Sales Rep. I	26955
Petrea	Soltau		27440

A blank represents a missing character value.

A period represents a missing numeric value.

✎ A value must exist for every variable in every observation.

20

By default, a period is printed for missing numeric values. This default can be altered with the MISSING= system option.

Copyright © 2016, SAS Institute Inc., Cary, North Carolina, USA. ALL RIGHTS RESERVED.

SAS Date Values

SAS stores calendar dates as numeric values.

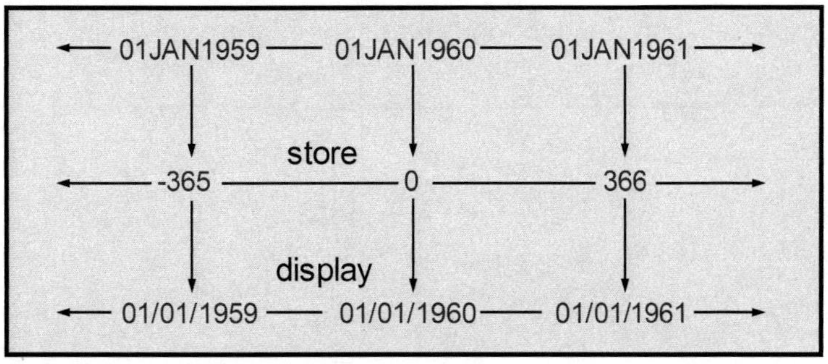

A *SAS date value* is stored as the number of days between January 1, 1960, and a specific date.

21

SAS can perform calculations on dates starting from 1582 A.D. SAS can read either two- or four-digit year values. If SAS encounters a two-digit year, the YEARCUTOFF= system option is used to specify to which 100-year span the two-digit year should be attributed. For example, by setting the YEARCUTOFF= option to 1950, the 100-year span from 1950 to 2049 is used for two-digit year values.

3.03 Short Answer Poll

Submit program **p103a02**. View the output to retrieve the current date as a SAS date value (that is, a numeric value referencing January 1, 1960). What is the numeric value for today's date?

22

Copyright © 2016, SAS Institute Inc., Cary, North Carolina, USA. ALL RIGHTS RESERVED.

Exercises

> If you restarted your SAS session since the last exercise, open and submit the **libname** program found in the data folder so that you can set the value of the macro variable, **path**.

Level 1

1. Examining the Data Portion of a SAS Data Set

a. Retrieve the starter program **p103e01**.

b. After the PROC CONTENTS step, add a PROC PRINT step to display all observations, all variables, and the Obs column for the data set named **work.donations**.

c. Submit the program to create the PROC PRINT report below. The results contain 124 observations.

Partial PROC PRINT Output

Obs	Employee_ ID	Qtr1	Qtr2	Qtr3	Qtr4	Total
1	120265	.	.	.	25	25
2	120267	15	15	15	15	60
3	120269	20	20	20	20	80
...						
123	121145	35	35	35	35	140
124	121147	10	10	10	10	40

Level 2

2. Examining the Descriptor and Data Portions of a SAS Data Set

a. Retrieve the starter program **p103e02**.

b. After the DATA step, add a PROC CONTENTS step to display the descriptor portion of **work.newpacks**.

c. Submit the program and answer the following questions:

How many observations are in the data set? 13

How many variables are in the data set? 3

What is the length (byte size) of the variable **Product_Name**? 43

d. After the PROC CONTENTS step, add a PROC PRINT to display the data portion of **work.newpacks**.

Copyright © 2016, SAS Institute Inc., Cary, North Carolina, USA. ALL RIGHTS RESERVED.

Submit the program to create the following PROC PRINT report:

```
                                 Supplier_
Obs    Supplier_Name              Country      Product_Name

  1    Top Sports                   DK         Black/Black
  2    Top Sports                   DK         X-Large Bottlegreen/Black
  3    Top Sports                   DK         Comanche Women's 6000 Q Backpack. Bark
...
 12    Luna sastreria S.A.          ES         Hammock Sports Bag
 13    Miller Trading Inc           US         Sioux Men's Backpack 26 Litre.
```

Challenge

3. Working with Times and Datetimes

a. Retrieve and submit the starter program **p103e03**.

b. Notice the values of **CurrentTime** and **CurrentDateTime** in the PROC PRINT output.

c. Use the SAS Help facility or product documentation to investigate how times and datetimes are stored in SAS.

d. Complete the following sentences:

(0 - 86400)

A SAS time value represents the number of seconds since midnight of the current day.

A SAS datetime value represents the number of seconds b/n Jan 1st, 1960, and an hr/minute/second within a specified date.

The remaining exercises in this chapter are self-guided, so no solutions are provided.

End of Exercises

Format date DDMMYY10.
Format time TimeAmPM.

Copyright © 2016, SAS Institute Inc., Cary, North Carolina, USA. ALL RIGHTS RESERVED.

3.2 Accessing SAS Libraries

Objectives

- Explain the concept of a SAS library.
- State the difference between a temporary library and a permanent library.
- Use a LIBNAME statement to assign a library reference name to a SAS library.
- Investigate a SAS library programmatically and interactively.

27

Business Scenario

Orion Star programmers need to access existing SAS data sets, so they need to understand how the data sets are stored in SAS.

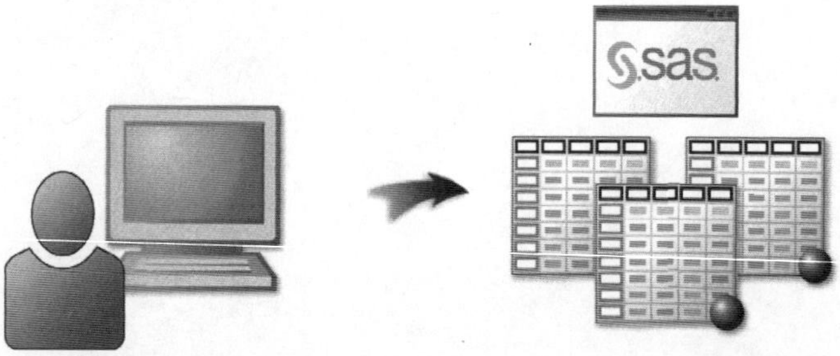

28

Copyright © 2016, SAS Institute Inc., Cary, North Carolina, USA. ALL RIGHTS RESERVED.

SAS Libraries

SAS data sets are stored in *SAS libraries*. A SAS library is a collection of SAS files that are referenced and stored as a unit.

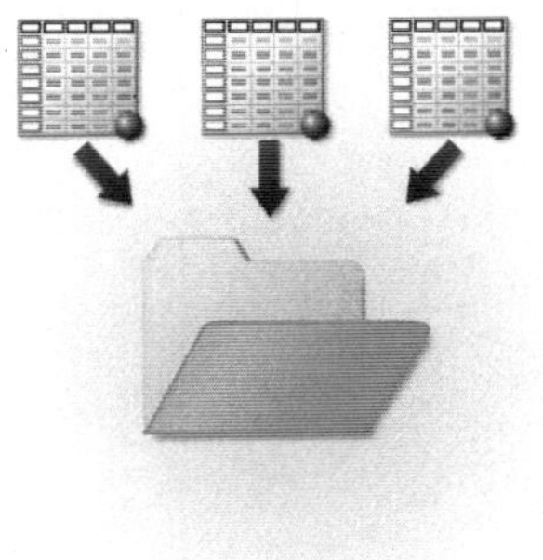

A file can be stored in a temporary or permanent library.

29

How SAS Libraries Are Defined

When a SAS session starts, SAS creates one temporary and at least one permanent SAS library. These libraries are open and ready to be used.

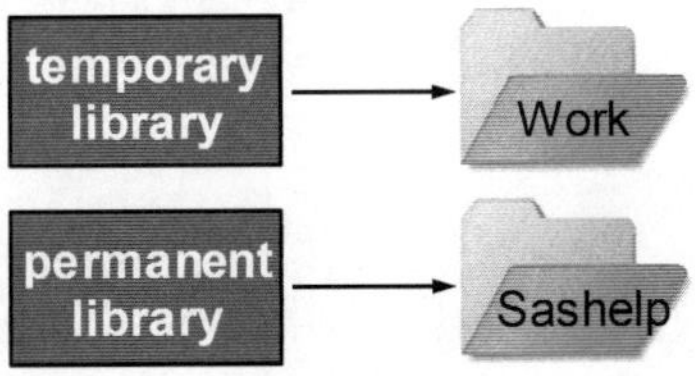

You refer to a SAS library by a logical name called a library reference name, or *libref*.

30

Copyright © 2016, SAS Institute Inc., Cary, North Carolina, USA. ALL RIGHTS RESERVED.

Temporary Library

Work is a temporary library where you can store and access SAS data sets for the duration of the SAS session. It is the default library.

⚠ SAS deletes the **Work** library and its contents when the session terminates.

31

Permanent Libraries

Sashelp is a permanent library that contains sample SAS data sets you can access during your SAS session.

32

Copyright © 2016, SAS Institute Inc., Cary, North Carolina, USA. ALL RIGHTS RESERVED.

Accessing SAS Data Sets

All SAS data sets have a two-level name that consists of the libref and the data set name, separated by a period.

libref | data set name

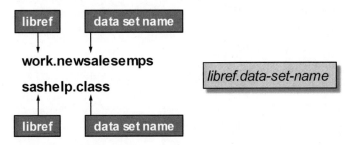

work.newsalesemps

sashelp.class

libref | data set name

libref.data-set-name

When a data set is in the temporary **Work** library, you can use a one-level name (for example, **newsalesemps**).

33

Business Scenario

Orion Star programmers need to access and view SAS data sets that are stored in a permanent user-defined library.

34

Copyright © 2016, SAS Institute Inc., Cary, North Carolina, USA. ALL RIGHTS RESERVED.

User-Defined Libraries

A user-defined library

- is created by the user.
- is permanent. Data sets are stored until the user deletes them.
- is not automatically available in a SAS session.
- is implemented within the operating environment's file system.

35

User-Defined Libraries

Operating Environment	A SAS library is...	Example
Microsoft Windows	a folder	s:\workshop
UNIX	a directory	~/workshop
z/OS (OS/390)	a sequential file	*userid*.workshop.sasdata

The user must submit a SAS LIBNAME statement to associate a libref with the physical location of the library.

36

Copyright © 2016, SAS Institute Inc., Cary, North Carolina, USA. ALL RIGHTS RESERVED.

LIBNAME Statement

The SAS LIBNAME statement is a *global* SAS statement.

```
libname orion "s:\workshop";
```

LIBNAME *libref "SAS-library" <options>*;

- It is not required to be in a DATA step or PROC step.
- It does not require a RUN statement.
- It executes immediately.
- It remains in effect until changed or canceled, or until the session ends.

⚠ Use the location of ***your*** course data in your LIBNAME statement.

37

- In the Microsoft Windows environment, an existing folder is used as a SAS library. The LIBNAME statement cannot create a new folder.
- In the UNIX environment, an existing directory is used as a SAS library. The LIBNAME statement cannot create a new directory.
- In the z/OS environment, a sequential file is used as a SAS library. z/OS (OS/390) users can use a SAS LIBNAME statement, a DD statement, or a TSO ALLOCATE command. These statements and commands can create a new library.

LIBNAME Statement

Partial SAS Log

```
47   libname orion "s:\workshop";
NOTE: Libref ORION was successfully assigned as follows:
      Engine:        V9
      Physical Name: s:\workshop
```

SAS files in **s:\workshop** are referenced using the **orion** libref.

orion.*data-set-name*

38

Copyright © 2016, SAS Institute Inc., Cary, North Carolina, USA. ALL RIGHTS RESERVED.

Changing or Canceling a Libref

A libref remains in effect until you change or cancel it, or until you end your SAS session.

To change a libref, submit a LIBNAME statement with the same libref but a different path.

```
libname orion "c:\myfiles";
```

To cancel a libref, submit a LIBNAME statement with the CLEAR option.

```
libname orion clear;
```

39

3.04 Multiple Choice Poll

Which of the following correctly assigns the libref **myfiles** to a SAS library in the **c:\mysasfiles** folder?

a. libname orion myfiles "c:\mysasfiles";
b. libname myfiles "c:\mysasfiles";
c. libref orion myfiles "c:\mysasfiles";
d. libref myfiles "c:\mysasfiles";

40

Copyright © 2016, SAS Institute Inc., Cary, North Carolina, USA. ALL RIGHTS RESERVED.

Browsing a Library

You can browse a library

- programmatically using the CONTENTS procedure
- interactively in SAS Studio, SAS Enterprise Guide, or the SAS windowing environment.

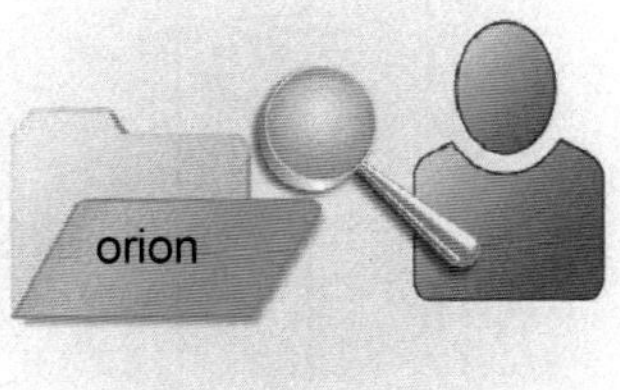

42

Browsing a Library Programmatically

Use PROC CONTENTS with the _ALL_ keyword to generate a list of all SAS files in a library.

```
proc contents data=orion._all_ nods;
run;
```

PROC CONTENTS DATA=*libref*._ALL_ NODS;
RUN;

- _ALL_ requests all the files in the library.
- The NODS option suppresses the individual data set descriptor information.
- NODS can be used only with the keyword _ALL_.

nods = No descriptor information (no details)

p103d03

43

Copyright © 2016, SAS Institute Inc., Cary, North Carolina, USA. ALL RIGHTS RESERVED.

Viewing the Output

Partial PROC CONTENTS Output

```
                        The CONTENTS Procedure

                              Directory

                        Libref         ORION
                        Engine         V9
                        Physical Name  S:\workshop
                        Filename       S:\workshop


                           Member     File
  #  Name                  Type       Size  Last Modified

  1  CHARITIES             DATA       9216  23Aug12:15:58:39
  2  CONSULTANTS           DATA       5120  23Aug12:15:58:39
  3  COUNTRY               DATA      17408  13Oct10:19:04:39
     COUNTRY               INDEX     17408  13Oct10:19:04:39
  4  CUSTOMER              DATA      33792  04Nov11:09:52:27
  5  CUSTOMER_DIM          DATA      33792  04Nov11:09:52:27
```

44

A member type of DATA indicates a standard SAS data set. The INDEX member type indicates a file that enables SAS to access observations in the SAS data set quickly and efficiently.

Copyright © 2016, SAS Institute Inc., Cary, North Carolina, USA. ALL RIGHTS RESERVED.

Browsing a SAS Library Programmatically

libname, p103d03

1. Open the **libname** program and add the LIBNAME statement shown below.

```
%let path=s:/workshop;
libname orion "s:/workshop";
```

The %LET statement creates a macro variable named **path** and assigns it a full path to the course data folder. The LIBNAME statement associates the libref, **orion**, with the same data location.

> The **libname** program is generated by the **cre8data** program. The code uses forward slashes for portability across operating environments. UNIX and Linux require forward slashes. Windows accepts forward slashes and can convert them to backslashes.

2. Submit the program.
3. Check the log to confirm that the **orion** libref was successfully assigned. The physical name reflects the location of your SAS data files and might differ from the name shown below.

```
43         %let path=s:/workshop;
44         libname orion "s:/workshop";
NOTE: Libref ORION was successfully assigned as follows:
      Engine:        V9
      Physical Name: s:\workshop
```

4. Save the **libname** program. This overwrites the previous version.

> When you work with the course data and programs, be sure to run the **libname** program at the start of every SAS session to set the **path** variable and assign the **orion** libref.

5. Use the CONTENTS procedure to explore the **orion** library programmatically. Open and submit the **p103d03** program to generate a list of library members. Partial output is shown below.

```
proc contents data=orion._all_ nods;
run;
```

Copyright © 2016, SAS Institute Inc., Cary, North Carolina, USA. ALL RIGHTS RESERVED.

```
                         The CONTENTS Procedure

                               Directory

                       Libref         ORION
                       Engine         V9
                       Physical Name  s:\workshop
                       Filename       s:\workshop

                          Member     File
  #  Name                 Type       Size  Last Modified

  1  CHARITIES            DATA       9216  23Aug12:15:58:39
  2  CONSULTANTS          DATA       5120  23Aug12:15:58:39
  3  COUNTRY              DATA      17408  13Oct10:19:04:39
     COUNTRY              INDEX     17408  13Oct10:19:04:39
  4  CUSTOMER             DATA      33792  04Nov11:09:52:27
```

6. Start a new program. Then enter and submit the following statement to clear the **orion** libref:

```
libname orion clear;
```

7. Check the log to verify that the **orion** libref was deassigned.

```
15         libname orion clear;
NOTE: Libref ORION has been deassigned.
```

End of Demonstration

Copyright © 2016, SAS Institute Inc., Cary, North Carolina, USA. ALL RIGHTS RESERVED.

Exercises

Using your preferred SAS interface, complete Exercise 4 and one additional exercise.
These exercises are self-guided, so no solutions are provided.

4. Assigning and Browsing a Library Programmatically

a. Open the **libname** program and add the LIBNAME statement shown below.

```
%let path=s:/workshop;
libname orion "s:/workshop";
```

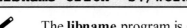

The **libname** program is generated by the **cre8data** program. The code uses forward slashes for portability across operating environments. UNIX and Linux require forward slashes. Windows accepts forward slashes and can convert them to backslashes.

b. Submit the program.

c. Check the log to confirm that the **orion** libref was successfully assigned. The physical name reflects the location of your SAS data files and might differ from the name shown below.

```
43         %let path=s:/workshop;
 44         libname orion "s:/workshop";
 NOTE: Libref ORION was successfully assigned as follows:
       Engine:        V9
       Physical Name: s:\workshop
```

d. Save the **libname** program. This overwrites the previous version.

e. Use the CONTENTS procedure to explore the **orion** library programmatically. Start a new program. Enter the following PROC CONTENTS step and a LIBNAME statement to clear the libref:

```
proc contents data=orion._all_ nods;
run;

libname orion clear;
```

f. Submit the program. Partial output is shown below.

```
                           The CONTENTS Procedure

                                 Directory

                         Libref          ORION
                         Engine          V9
                         Physical Name   s:\workshop
                         Filename        s:\workshop

                            Member      File
   #  Name                  Type        Size  Last Modified

   1  CHARITIES             DATA        9216  23Aug12:15:58:39
   2  CONSULTANTS           DATA        5120  23Aug12:15:58:39
   3  COUNTRY               DATA       17408  13Oct10:19:04:39
```

Copyright © 2016, SAS Institute Inc., Cary, North Carolina, USA. ALL RIGHTS RESERVED.

```
     COUNTRY              INDEX      17408   13Oct10:19:04:39
  4  CUSTOMER             DATA       33792   04Nov11:09:52:27
```

g. Check the log to verify that the **orion** libref was deassigned.

```
15         libname orion clear;
NOTE: Libref ORION has been deassigned.
```

When you work with the course data and programs, be sure to run the **libname** program at the start of every SAS session to set the **path** variable and assign the **orion** libref.

5. **Assigning and Browsing a Library Interactively with SAS Studio**

   a. In the Navigation pane, navigate to the **Libraries** section.

   b. Click the arrow in front of My Libraries to expand the folder. Observe the libraries that are assigned automatically in your SAS Studio session.

   c. Click (**New Library**) to assign a new library.

   d. In the New Library window, enter **orion** in the **Name** field, and enter s:**/workshop** or the path to your data folder in the **Path** field. Selecting the check box causes SAS to re-create the library at the start of each SAS Studio session. Click **OK**.

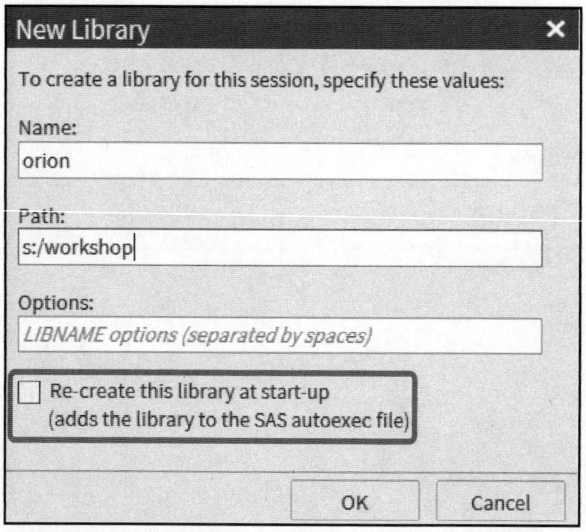

Copyright © 2016, SAS Institute Inc., Cary, North Carolina, USA. ALL RIGHTS RESERVED.

The **orion** library is displayed in the Libraries section.

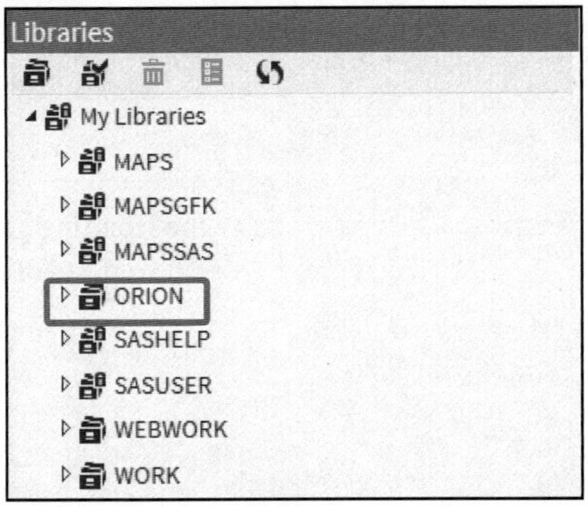

e. Expand **orion** to see the list of data sets that it contains.

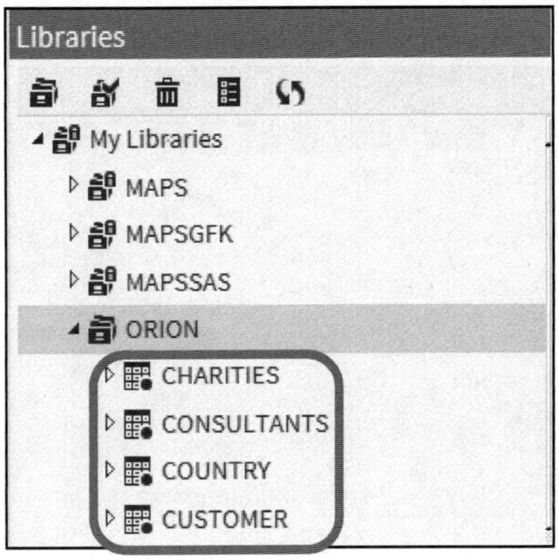

f. Double-click the **COUNTRY** data set to open it. The data is displayed in a data grid in the workspace. The columns are listed in the Columns section to the left of the data grid. All columns are selected by default.

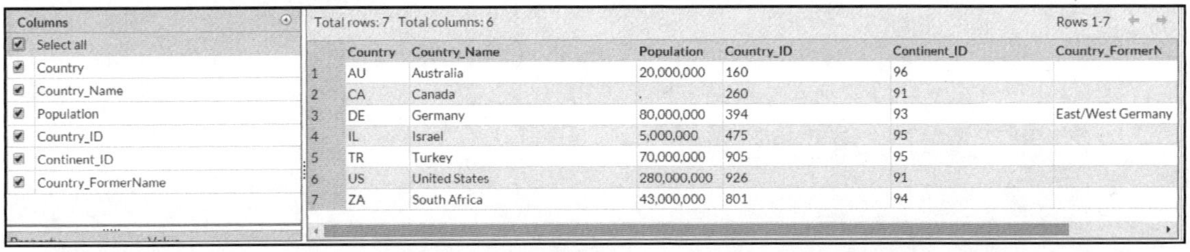

	Country	Country_Name	Population	Country_ID	Continent_ID	Country_FormerN
1	AU	Australia	20,000,000	160	96	
2	CA	Canada	.	260	91	
3	DE	Germany	80,000,000	394	93	East/West Germany
4	IL	Israel	5,000,000	475	95	
5	TR	Turkey	70,000,000	905	95	
6	US	United States	280,000,000	926	91	
7	ZA	South Africa	43,000,000	801	94	

g. Clear **Select all**, and then select the **Country_Name** check box. The column properties are displayed below the Columns list. Only the selected column appears in the data grid.

Copyright © 2016, SAS Institute Inc., Cary, North Carolina, USA. ALL RIGHTS RESERVED.

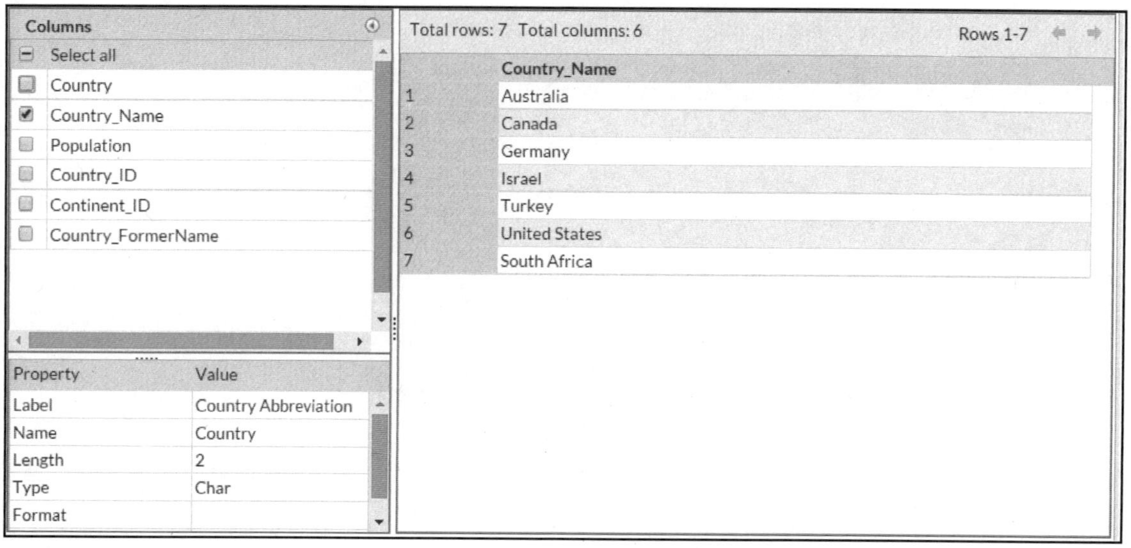

h. Click in the View toolbar to display the table properties. The SAS Table Properties dialog box lists the general properties. Click the **Columns** tab to display column properties.

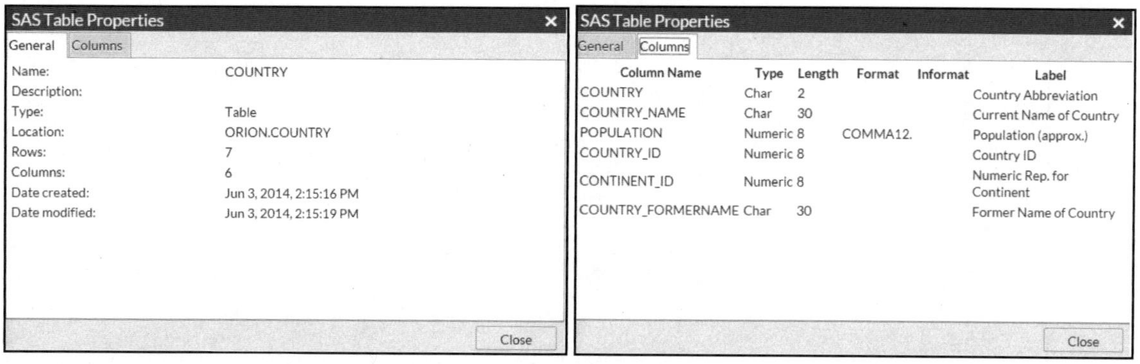

i. Click **Close** to close the SAS Table Properties dialog box.

j. Click on the **orion.country** tab to close the data grid.

6. **Assigning and Browsing a Library Interactively with SAS Enterprise Guide**

a. In the Servers pane, select **Servers** ⇨ **Local** ⇨ **Libraries**. Observe the libraries that are assigned automatically in your SAS Enterprise Guide session.

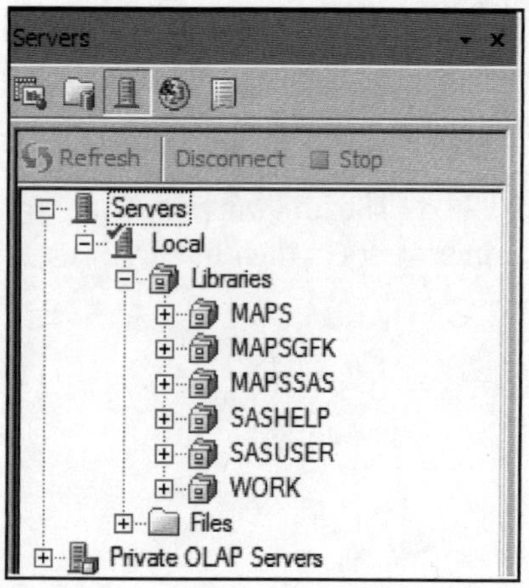

Copyright © 2016, SAS Institute Inc., Cary, North Carolina, USA. ALL RIGHTS RESERVED.

b. Select **Tools** ⇨ **Assign Project Library**.

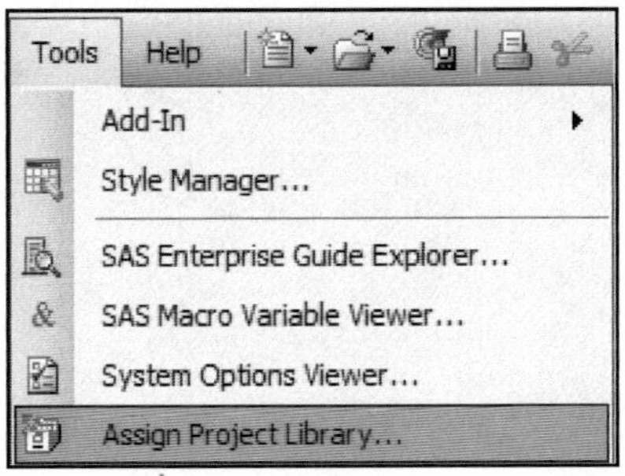

c. In the Assign Project Library Wizard, do the following:

- Step 1: Enter **orion** in the **Name** field, and click **Next**.
- Step 2: Accept the default engine and engine type. Click the **Browse** button and navigate to **s:\workshop**, or to the location of your data folder. Click **OK**. The path is displayed. Click **Next**.
- Step 3: Click **Next**.
- Step 4: Click **Finish**.

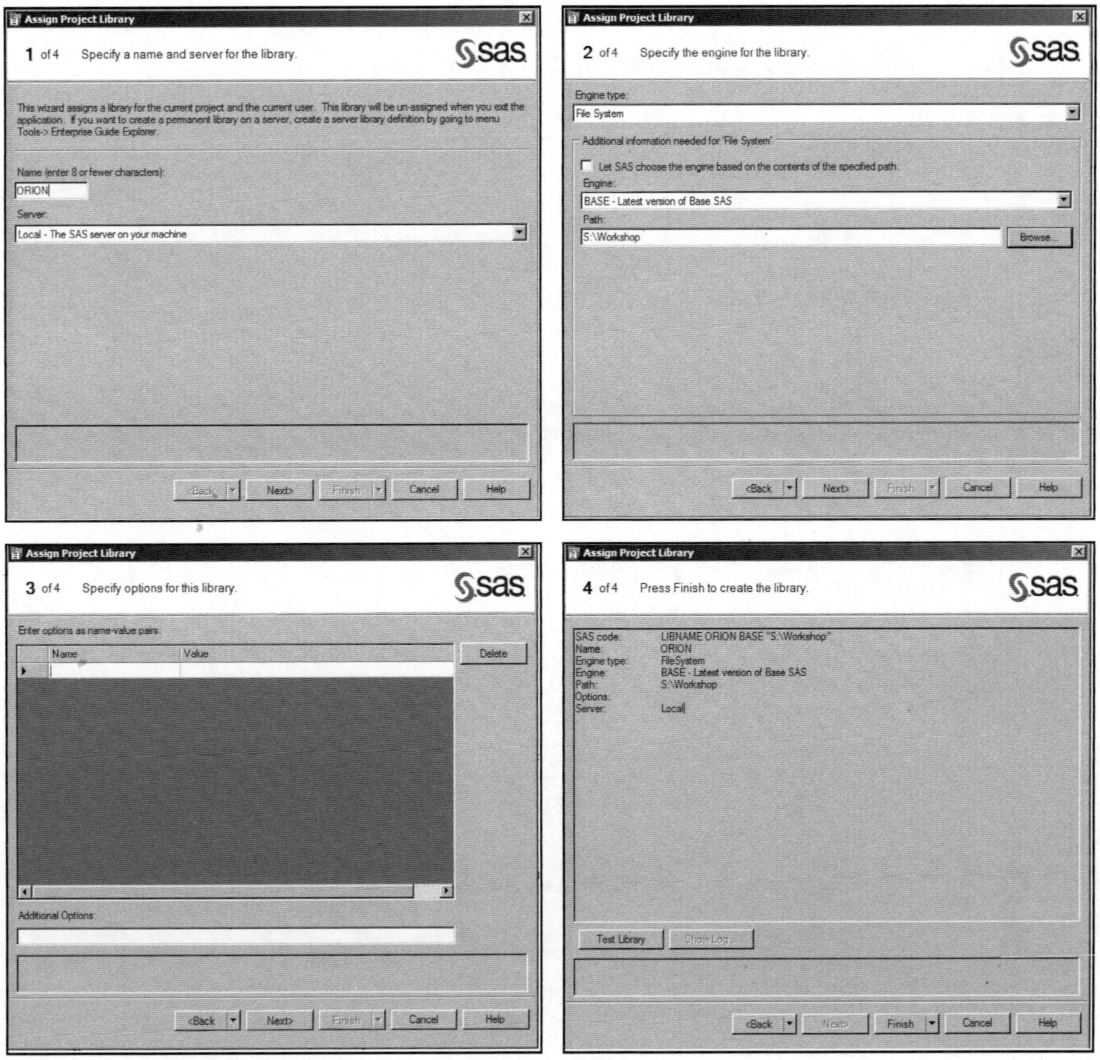

Copyright © 2016, SAS Institute Inc., Cary, North Carolina, USA. ALL RIGHTS RESERVED.

d. In the Servers pane, select **Libraries** and click **Refresh** or right-click **Libraries** and select **Refresh**.

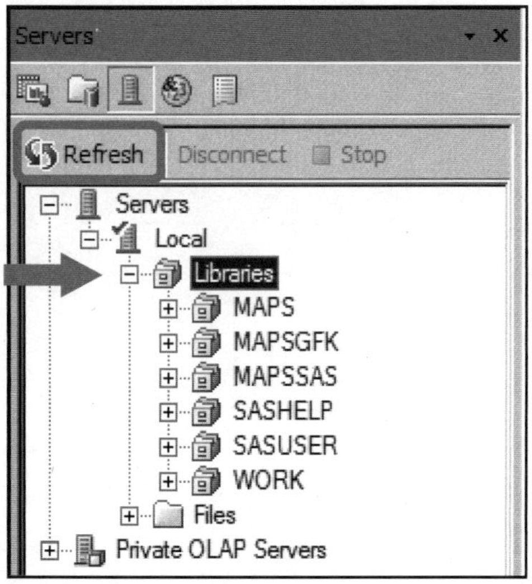

e. Verify that the **orion** library is displayed in the list of active libraries.

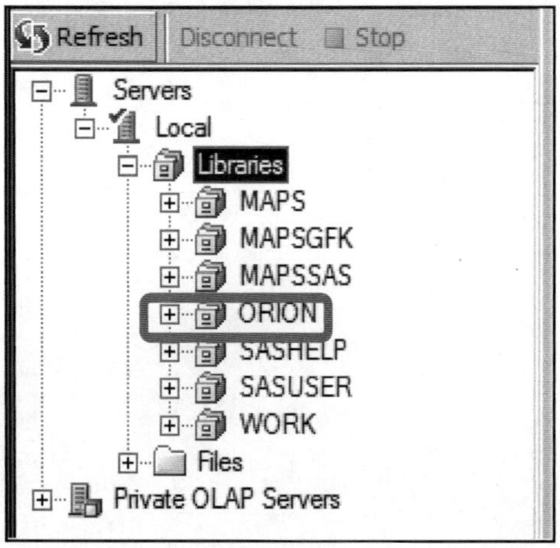

f. Expland the **orion** library.

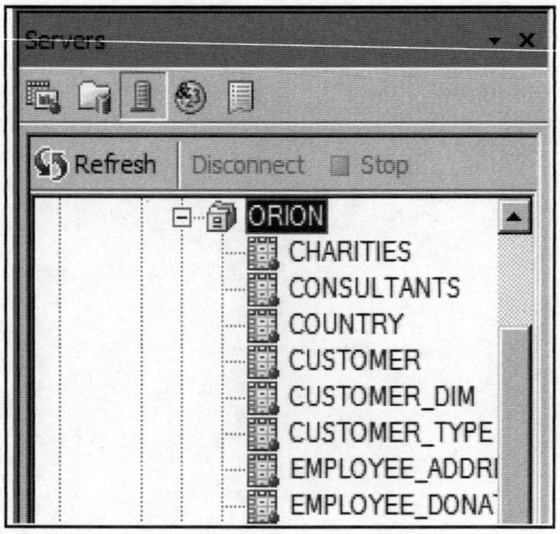

Copyright © 2016, SAS Institute Inc., Cary, North Carolina, USA. ALL RIGHTS RESERVED.

g. Double-click the **COUNTRY** data set in the **orion** library to open it. The data is displayed in a data grid in the workspace. Move the mouse pointer over a column name to see the column properties. Click × to close the data grid.

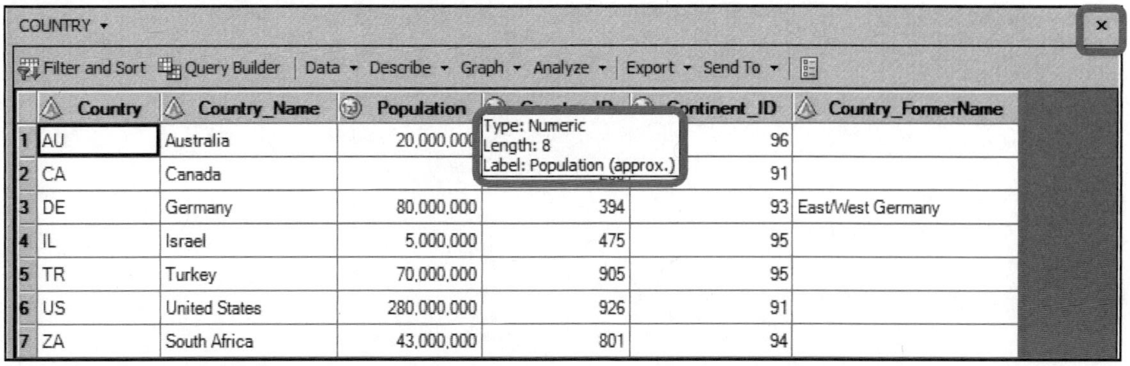

	Country	Country_Name	Population		Continent_ID	Country_FormerName
1	AU	Australia	20,000,000		96	
2	CA	Canada			91	
3	DE	Germany	80,000,000	394	93	East/West Germany
4	IL	Israel	5,000,000	475	95	
5	TR	Turkey	70,000,000	905	95	
6	US	United States	280,000,000	926	91	
7	ZA	South Africa	43,000,000	801	94	

h. Right-click the **COUNTRY** data set in the **orion** library to display the data set properties. The **General** tab is displayed by default. Click the **Columns** tab to see column properties. Click **Close** to close the COUNTRY Properties dialog box.

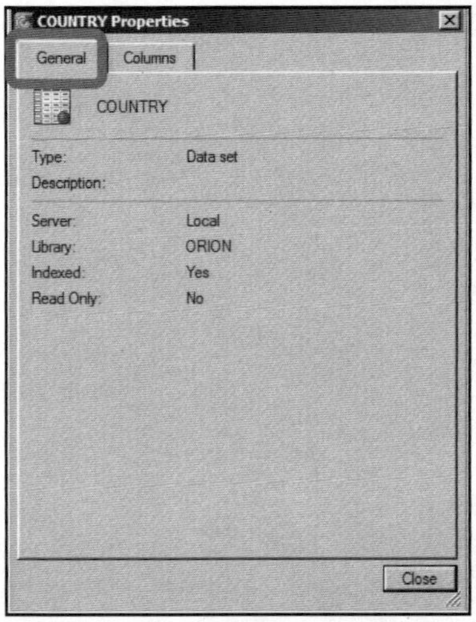

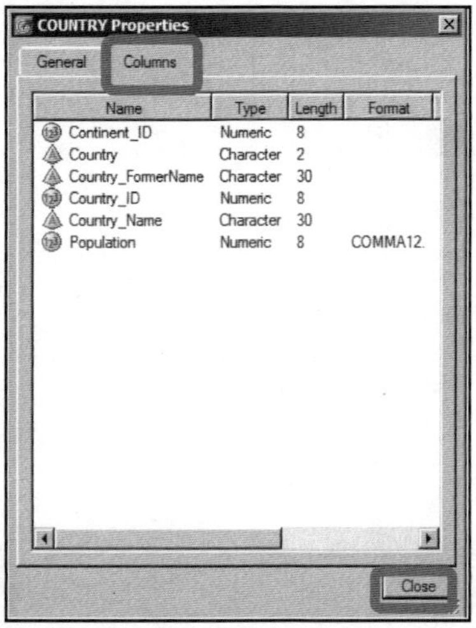

7. **Assigning and Browsing a Library Interactively in the SAS Windowing Environment**

a. Select **Tools** ⇨ **New Library**, or click (**Add New Library**). The New Library dialog box is displayed.

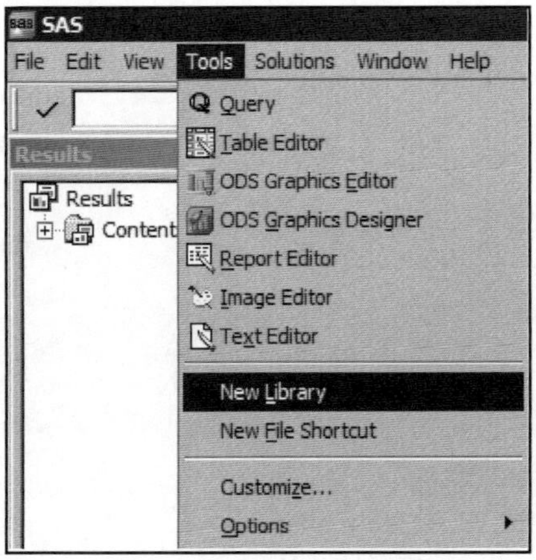

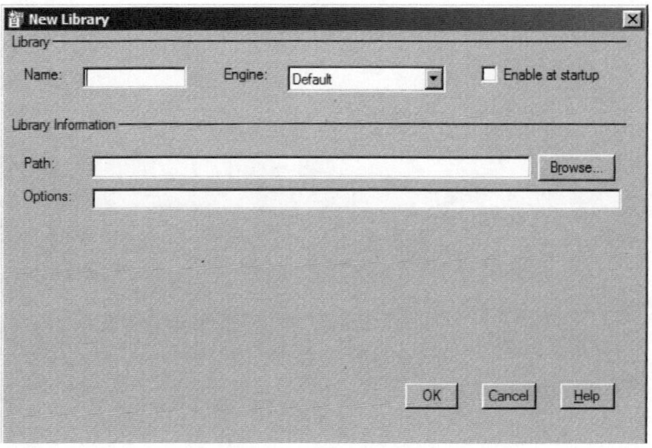

Copyright © 2016, SAS Institute Inc., Cary, North Carolina, USA. ALL RIGHTS RESERVED.

b. Enter **orion** in the **Name** field. Click **Browse** and navigate to **s:\workshop** or to the location of your data folder, and click **OK**. The path is displayed in the dialog box. Selecting the **Enable at startup** check box causes SAS to re-create the library at the start of each session.

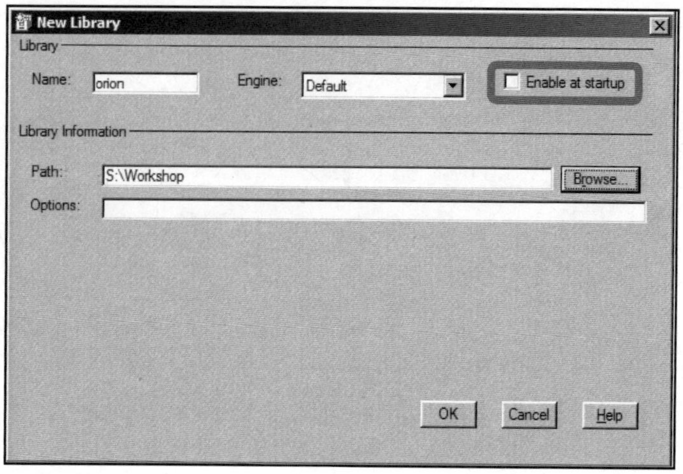

c. Click **OK**.

d. In the Explorer window, double-click **Libraries**.

e. Verify that the **Orion** library is displayed in the list of active libraries.

Copyright © 2016, SAS Institute Inc., Cary, North Carolina, USA. ALL RIGHTS RESERVED.

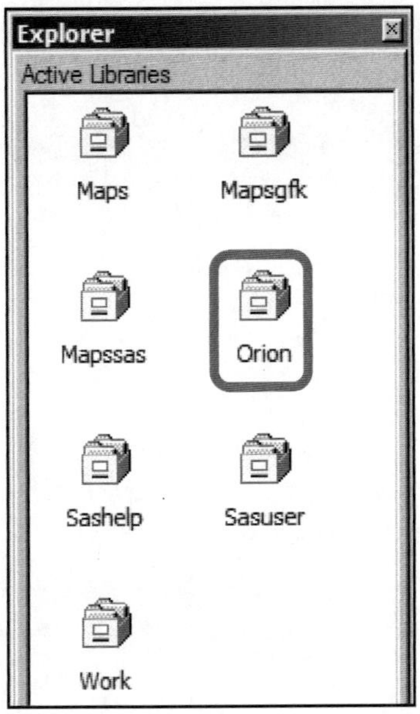

f. Double-click the **Orion** library. Verify that the data sets contained in the **Orion** library are displayed.

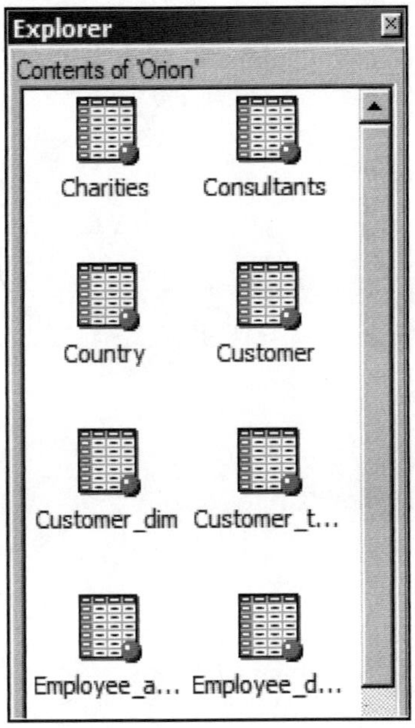

g. Double-click the **Country** data set in the **Orion** library to open it. The data is displayed in a viewtable. Column labels are displayed by default.

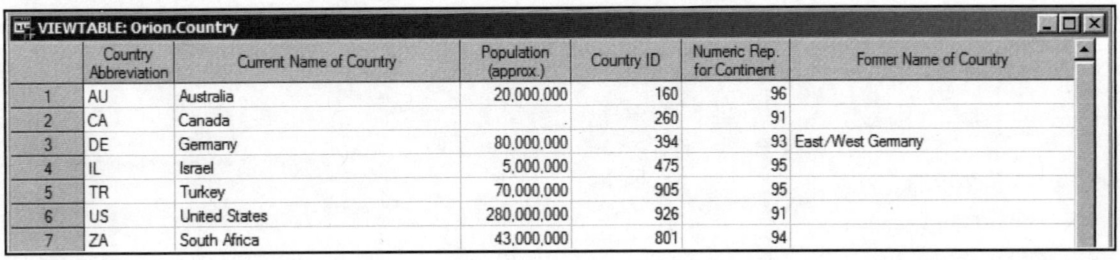
VIEWTABLE: Orion.Country

	Country Abbreviation	Current Name of Country	Population (approx.)	Country ID	Numeric Rep. for Continent	Former Name of Country
1	AU	Australia	20,000,000	160	96	
2	CA	Canada	.	260	91	
3	DE	Germany	80,000,000	394	93	East/West Germany
4	IL	Israel	5,000,000	475	95	
5	TR	Turkey	70,000,000	905	95	
6	US	United States	280,000,000	926	91	
7	ZA	South Africa	43,000,000	801	94	

Copyright © 2016, SAS Institute Inc., Cary, North Carolina, USA. ALL RIGHTS RESERVED.

h. Click **View** ⇨ **Column Names** on the toolbar to display column names instead of labels. Click [×] to close the viewtable.

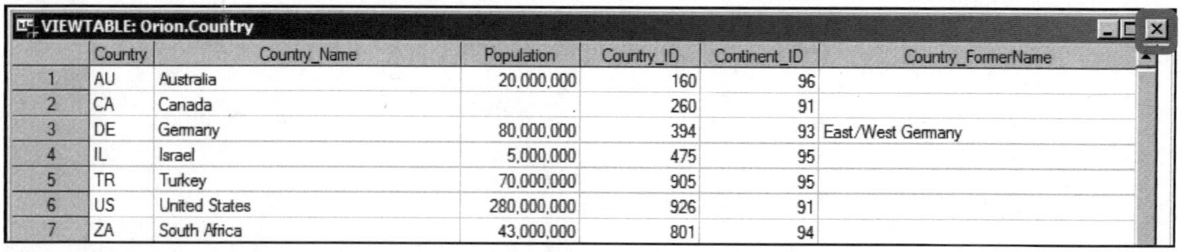

	Country	Country_Name	Population	Country_ID	Continent_ID	Country_FormerName
1	AU	Australia	20,000,000	160	96	
2	CA	Canada	.	260	91	
3	DE	Germany	80,000,000	394	93	East/West Germany
4	IL	Israel	5,000,000	475	95	
5	TR	Turkey	70,000,000	905	95	
6	US	United States	280,000,000	926	91	
7	ZA	South Africa	43,000,000	801	94	

i. Right click the **Country** data set in the **Orion** library, and select **Properties**. The data set properties are displayed with the **General** tab selected by default. Click the **Columns** tab to see column properties. Click [×] or **OK** to close the Orion.Country Properties dialog box.

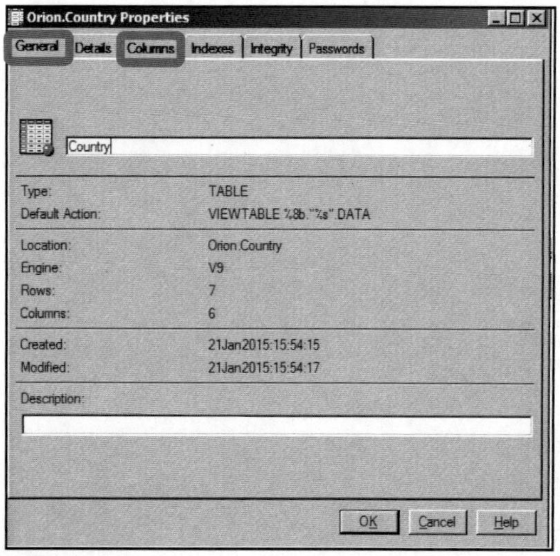

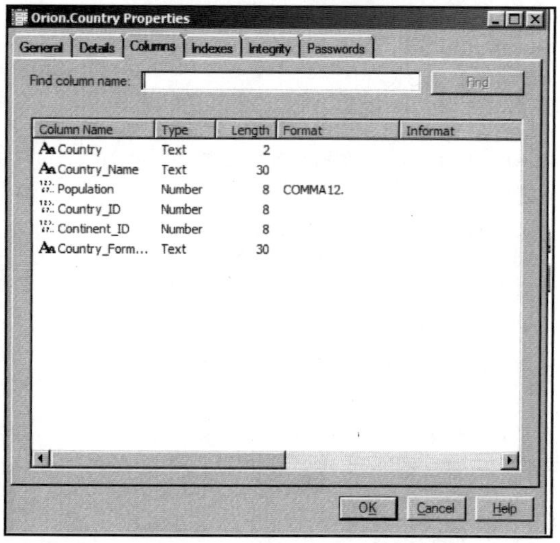

End of Exercises

Copyright © 2016, SAS Institute Inc., Cary, North Carolina, USA. ALL RIGHTS RESERVED.

3.3 Solutions

Solutions to Exercises

1. **Examining the Data Portion of a SAS Data Set**

```
data work.donations;
   infile "&path\donation.dat";
   input Employee_ID Qtr1 Qtr2 Qtr3 Qtr4;
   Total=sum(Qtr1,Qtr2,Qtr3,Qtr4);
run;

proc contents data=work.donations;
run;

proc print data=work.donations;
run;
```

2. **Examining the Descriptor and Data Portions of a SAS Data Set**

```
data work.newpacks;
   input Supplier_Name $ 1-20 Supplier_Country $ 23-24
         Product_Name $ 28-70;
   datalines;
Top Sports            DK   Black/Black
Top Sports            DK   X-Large Bottlegreen/Black
  ...
Miller Trading Inc    US   Sioux Men's Backpack 26 Litre.
;

proc contents data=work.newpacks;
run;

proc print data=work.newpacks noobs;
   var Product_Name Supplier_Name;
run;
```

- How many observations are in the data set? **13**
- How many variables are in the data set? **3**
- What is the length (byte size) of the variable **Product_Name**? **43**

3. **Working with Times and Datetimes**
   - A SAS time value represents the number of **seconds since midnight of the current day**.
   - A SAS datetime value represents the number of **seconds between midnight January 1, 1960, and an hour/minute/second within a specified date**.

End of Solutions

Copyright © 2016, SAS Institute Inc., Cary, North Carolina, USA. ALL RIGHTS RESERVED.

Solutions to Student Activities (Polls/Quizzes)

3.01 Short Answer Poll – Correct Answer

Open program **p103a01**. Add a PROC CONTENTS step after the DATA step to view **work.donations**. Submit the program and review the results. How many observations are in the data set **work.donations**? **124 observations**

```
data work.donations;
   infile "&path\donation.dat";
   input Employee_ID Qtr1 Qtr2 Qtr3 Qtr4;
   Total=sum(Qtr1,Qtr2,Qtr3,Qtr4);
run;

proc contents data=work.donations;
run;
```

12 p103a01s

3.02 Multiple Answer Poll – Correct Answer

Which variable names are invalid?

a. data5mon
b. 5monthsdata (circled)
c. data#5 (circled)
d. five months data (circled)
e. five_months_data
f. FiveMonthsData
g. fivemonthsdata

18

Copyright © 2016, SAS Institute Inc., Cary, North Carolina, USA. ALL RIGHTS RESERVED.

3.03 Short Answer Poll – Correct Answer

Submit program **p103a02**. View the output to retrieve the current date as a SAS date value (that is, a numeric value referencing January 1, 1960). What is the numeric value for today's date?

The answer depends on the current date.

Example: If the current date is February 27, 2012, the numeric value is 19050.

23

3.04 Multiple Choice Poll – Correct Answer

Which of the following correctly assigns the libref **myfiles** to a SAS library in the **c:\mysasfiles** folder?

a. libname orion myfiles "c:\mysasfiles";
b. libname myfiles "c:\mysasfiles";
c. libref orion myfiles "c:\mysasfiles";
d. libref myfiles "c:\mysasfiles";

41

Copyright © 2016, SAS Institute Inc., Cary, North Carolina, USA. ALL RIGHTS RESERVED.

Copyright © 2016, SAS Institute Inc., Cary, North Carolina, USA. ALL RIGHTS RESERVED.

Chapter 4 Producing Detail Reports

Copyright © 2016, SAS Institute Inc., Cary, North Carolina, USA. ALL RIGHTS RESERVED.

4.1 Subsetting Report Data

Objectives

- Create a default PROC PRINT report.
- Select variables with a VAR statement.
- Calculate totals with a SUM statement.
- Select observations with a WHERE statement.
- Define a date constant.
- Identify observations with an ID statement.

3

Business Scenario

Orion Star management wants a report that displays the names, salaries, and a salary total for all sales employees.

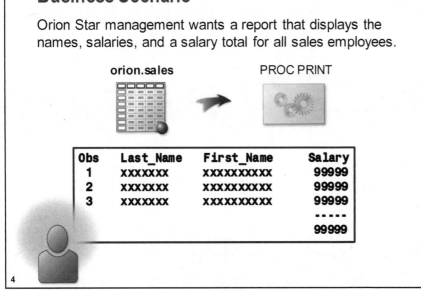

Obs	Last_Name	First_Name	Salary
1	xxxxxxx	xxxxxxxxxx	99999
2	xxxxxxx	xxxxxxxxxx	99999
3	xxxxxxx	xxxxxxxxxx	99999

			99999

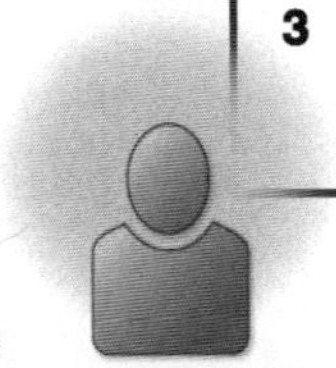

4

Copyright © 2016, SAS Institute Inc., Cary, North Carolina, USA. ALL RIGHTS RESERVED.

PRINT Procedure

By default, PROC PRINT displays all observations, all variables, and an Obs column on the left side.

```
proc print data=orion.sales;
run;
```

Partial PROC PRINT Output

Obs	Employee_ID	First_ Name	Last_Name	Gender	Salary	Job_Title	Country	Birth_ Date	Hire_ Date
1	120102	Tom	Zhou	M	108255	Sales Manager	AU	3510	10744
2	120103	Wilson	Dawes	M	87975	Sales Manager	AU	-3996	5114
3	120121	Irenie	Elvish	F	26600	Sales Rep. II	AU	-5630	5114
4	120122	Christina	Ngan	F	27475	Sales Rep. II	AU	-1984	6756
5	120123	Kimiko	Hotstone	F	26190	Sales Rep. I	AU	1732	9405

Statements and options can be added to the PRINT procedure to modify the default behavior.

5 p104d01

The columns are listed, left to right, in the order in which the variables are stored in the data set.

VAR Statement

The VAR statement selects variables to include in the report and specifies their order.

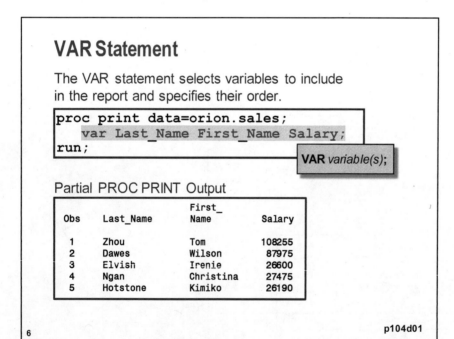

```
proc print data=orion.sales;
   var Last_Name First_Name Salary;
run;
```

VAR *variable(s)*;

Partial PROC PRINT Output

Obs	Last_Name	First_ Name	Salary
1	Zhou	Tom	108255
2	Dawes	Wilson	87975
3	Elvish	Irenie	26600
4	Ngan	Christina	27475
5	Hotstone	Kimiko	26190

6 p104d01

Copyright © 2016, SAS Institute Inc., Cary, North Carolina, USA. ALL RIGHTS RESERVED.

SUM Statement

The *SUM statement* calculates and displays report totals for the requested ***numeric*** variables.

```
proc print data=orion.sales;
   var Last_Name First_Name Salary;
   sum Salary;
run;
```

SUM *variable(s)*;

Partial PROC PRINT Output

```
                               First_
 Obs     Last_Name             Name            Salary

   1     Zhou                  Tom             108255
   2     Dawes                 Wilson           87975
   3     Elvish                Irenie           26600
         ...
 164     Capachietti           Renee            83505
 165     Lansberry             Dennis           84260
                                               ======
                                              5141420
```

7

p104d01

Viewing the Log

Partial SAS Log

```
84   proc print data=orion.sales;
85      var Last_Name First_Name Salary;
86      sum salary;
87   run;

NOTE: There were 165 observations read from the data set ORION.SALES.
```

✎ The order of statements in a SAS procedure is usually not important.

8

Copyright © 2016, SAS Institute Inc., Cary, North Carolina, USA. ALL RIGHTS RESERVED.

Business Scenario

Orion Star management wants a report that displays the names and salaries of the sales employees who earn less than $25,500. Suppress the Obs column.

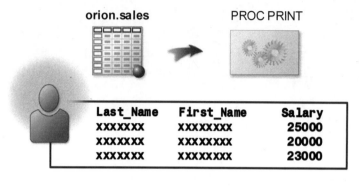

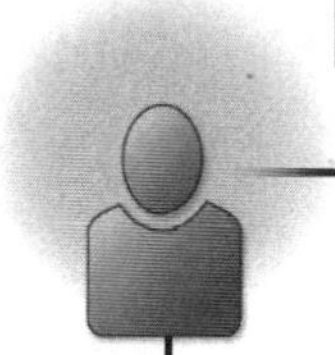

Last_Name	First_Name	Salary
xxxxxxx	xxxxxxxx	25000
xxxxxxx	xxxxxxxx	20000
xxxxxxx	xxxxxxxx	23000

9

WHERE Statement

The *WHERE statement* selects observations that meet the criteria specified in the WHERE expression.

```
proc print data=orion.sales;
   var Last_Name First_Name Salary;
   where Salary<25500;
run;
```

WHERE *WHERE-expression;*

10 p104d02

Copyright © 2016, SAS Institute Inc., Cary, North Carolina, USA. ALL RIGHTS RESERVED.

Viewing the Log

Only 7 of the 165 observations from **orion.sales** were selected by the WHERE statement.

```
295  proc print data=orion.sales;
296     var Last_Name First_Name Salary;
297     where Salary<25500;
298  run;

NOTE: There were 7 observations read from the data set ORION.SALES.
      WHERE Salary<25500;
```

11

Viewing the Output

PROC PRINT Output

Obs	Last_ Name	First_ Name	Salary
49	Tilley	Kimiko	25185
50	Barcoe	Selina	25275
85	Anstey	David	25285
104	Voron	Tachaun	25125
111	Polky	Asishana	25110
131	Ould	Tulsidas	22710
148	Buckner	Burnetta	25390

original observation numbers

12

Copyright © 2016, SAS Institute Inc., Cary, North Carolina, USA. ALL RIGHTS RESERVED.

Suppressing the Obs Column

Use the NOOBS option in the PROC PRINT statement to suppress the Obs column.

```
proc print data=orion.sales noobs;
   var Last_Name First_Name Salary;
   where Salary<25500;
run;
```

PROC PRINT DATA=*SAS-data-set* **NOOBS;**

PROC PRINT Output

Last_ Name	First_ Name	Salary
Tilley	Kimiko	25185
Barcoe	Selina	25275
Anstey	David	25285
Voron	Tachaun	25125
Polky	Asishana	25110
Ould	Tulsidas	22710
Buckner	Burnetta	25390

13 p104d02

WHERE Statement

The WHERE expression defines the condition (or conditions) for selecting observations.

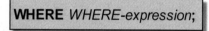

WHERE *WHERE-expression*;

Operands

- character constants
- numeric constants
- date constants
- character variables
- numeric variables

Operators

- symbols that represent a comparison, calculation, or logical operation

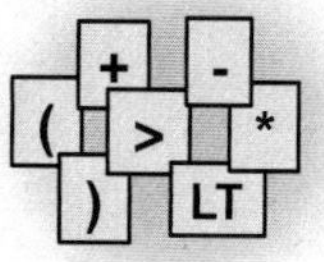

- SAS functions
- special WHERE operators

14

Copyright © 2016, SAS Institute Inc., Cary, North Carolina, USA. ALL RIGHTS RESERVED.

Operands

Constants are fixed values.

- Character values are enclosed in quotation marks and are case sensitive.
- Numeric values do not use quotation marks or special characters.

Variables must exist in the input data set.

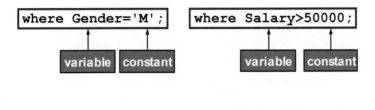

```
where Gender='M';
```

variable constant

```
where Salary>50000;
```

variable constant

15

SAS Date Constant

A *SAS date constant* is a date written in the following form: **'ddmmm<yy>yy'd**

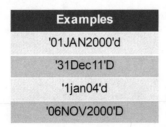

Examples
'01JAN2000'd
'31Dec11'D
'1jan04'd
'06NOV2000'D

SAS automatically converts a date constant to a SAS date value.

16

Copyright © 2016, SAS Institute Inc., Cary, North Carolina, USA. ALL RIGHTS RESERVED.

Comparison Operators

Comparison operators compare a variable with a value or with another variable.

Symbol	Mnemonic	Definition
=	EQ	Equal to
^= ¬= ~=	NE	Not equal to
>	GT	Greater than
<	LT	Less than
>=	GE	Greater than or equal
<=	LE	Less than or equal
	IN	Equal to one of a list

17

The caret (^), tilde (~), and the not sign (¬) indicate a logical *not*. Use the character available on your keyboard, or use the mnemonic equivalent.

Comparison Operators

Examples
`where Gender eq ' ';`
`where Salary ne .;`
`where Salary>=50000;`
`where Hire_Date<'01Jan2000'd;`
`where Country in ('AU','US');`
`where Country in ('AU' 'US');`
`where Order_Type in (1,2,3);`

The value list in the IN operator must be enclosed in parentheses and separated by either commas or blanks. Character values must be enclosed in quotation marks.

18

Copyright © 2016, SAS Institute Inc., Cary, North Carolina, USA. ALL RIGHTS RESERVED.

Setup for the Poll

Program **p104a01** contains two WHERE statements.
Open and submit the program.

19

4.01 Multiple Choice Poll

Which of the following is true?

a. The program executes, and applies both WHERE conditions successfully.
b. The program fails and an error message is written to the log.
c. The program executes, but only the first WHERE condition is applied.
d. The program executes, but only the second WHERE condition is applied.

20

Copyright © 2016, SAS Institute Inc., Cary, North Carolina, USA. ALL RIGHTS RESERVED.

Logical Operators

Logical operators combine or modify WHERE expressions.

```
proc print data=orion.sales;
   where Country='AU' and
         Salary<30000;
run;
```

WHERE *WHERE-expression-1* AND | OR *WHERE-expression-n*;

22 p104d03

Viewing the Log

Partial SAS Log

```
67   proc print data=orion.sales;
68      where Country='AU' and
69            Salary<30000;
70   run;

NOTE: There were 51 observations read from the data set ORION.SALES.
WHERE (Country='AU') and (Salary<30000);
```

23

Copyright © 2016, SAS Institute Inc., Cary, North Carolina, USA. ALL RIGHTS RESERVED.

Logical Operator Priority

The operators can be written as symbols or mnemonics, and parentheses can be added to modify the order of evaluation.

Symbol	Mnemonic	Priority
^ ¬ ~	NOT	I
&	AND	II
|	OR	III

The NOT operator modifies a condition by finding the complement of the specified criteria.

```
where City not in ('London','Rome','Paris');
```

24

- NOT modifies a condition by finding the complement of the specified criteria. Use the character that is available on your keyboard, or use the mnemonic equivalent.
- AND finds observations that satisfy both conditions.
- OR finds observations that satisfy one or both conditions.

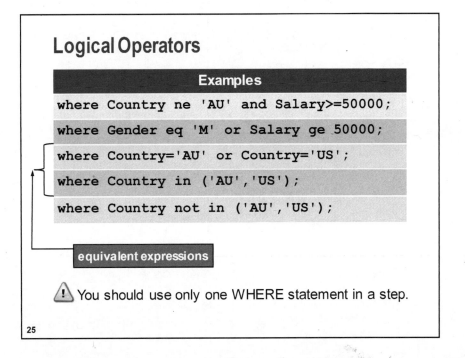

Logical Operators

Examples
`where Country ne 'AU' and Salary>=50000;`
`where Gender eq 'M' or Salary ge 50000;`
`where Country='AU' or Country='US';`
`where Country in ('AU','US');`
`where Country not in ('AU','US');`

equivalent expressions (the third and fourth examples)

⚠ You should use only one WHERE statement in a step.

25

Copyright © 2016, SAS Institute Inc., Cary, North Carolina, USA. ALL RIGHTS RESERVED.

4.02 Short Answer Poll

Which WHERE statement correctly subsets the numeric values for May, June, or July and missing character names?

a.
```
where Month in (5-7)
      and Names=.;
```

b.
```
where Month in (5,6,7)
      and Names=' ';
```

c.
```
where Month in ('5','6','7')
      and Names='.';
```

26

Business Scenario

Orion Star management wants a report that lists only the Australian sales representatives.

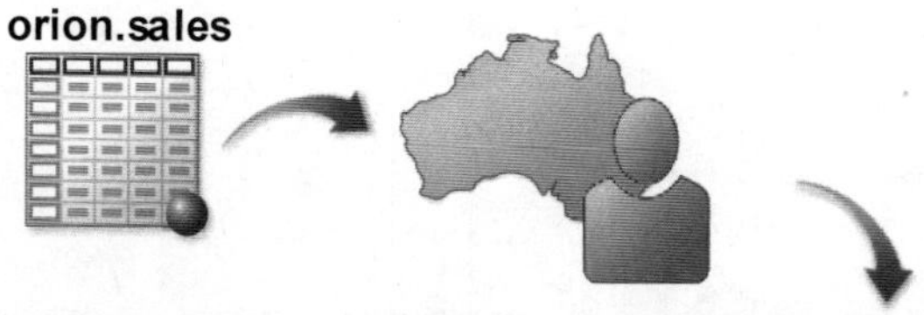

Last_Name	First_ Name	Country	Job_Title
xxxxxxxxxx	xxxxxxx	xx	xxxxxxxxxxxx
xxxxxxxxxx	xxxxxxx	xx	xxxxxxxxxxxx
xxxxxxxxxx	xxxxxxx	xx	xxxxxxxxxxxx
xxxxxxxxxx	xxxxxxx	xx	xxxxxxxxxxxx

28

Copyright © 2016, SAS Institute Inc., Cary, North Carolina, USA. ALL RIGHTS RESERVED.

Exploring the Data

```
proc print data=orion.sales noobs;
   var Last_Name First_Name Country
       Job_Title;
run;
```

Partial PROC PRINT Output

```
Plested       Billy       AU    Sales Rep. II
Wills         Matsuoka    AU    Sales Rep. III
George        Vino        AU    Sales Rep. II
Body          Meera       AU    Sales Rep. III
Highpoint     Harry       US    Chief Sales Officer
Magolan       Julienne    US    Sales Rep. II
Desanctis     Scott       US    Sales Rep. IV
Ridley        Cherda      US    Sales Rep. IV
```

29 p104d04

Subsetting in a PROC PRINT Step

Include a WHERE statement to subset by **Country** and **Job_Title**.

```
proc print data=orion.sales noobs;
   var Last_Name First_Name Country
       Job_Title;
   where Country='AU' and
         Job_Title contains 'Rep';
run;
```

CONTAINS is a special WHERE operator.

30 p104d04

Copyright © 2016, SAS Institute Inc., Cary, North Carolina, USA. ALL RIGHTS RESERVED.

CONTAINS Operator

The *CONTAINS operator* selects observations that include the specified substring.

Equivalent Statements
`where Job_Title contains 'Rep';`
`where Job_Title ? 'Rep';`

- ? can be used instead of the mnemonic.
- The position of the substring within the variable's values is not important.
- Comparisons made with the CONTAINS operator are case sensitive.

31

Viewing the Output

Partial PROC PRINT Output

Last_Name	First_ Name	Country	Job_Title
Elvish	Irenie	AU	Sales Rep. II
Ngan	Christina	AU	Sales Rep. II
Hotstone	Kimiko	AU	Sales Rep. I
Daymond	Lucian	AU	Sales Rep. I
Hofmeister	Fong	AU	Sales Rep. IV

32

Copyright © 2016, SAS Institute Inc., Cary, North Carolina, USA. ALL RIGHTS RESERVED.

Special WHERE Operators

Special WHERE operators are operators that can be used only in WHERE expressions.

Operator	Definition	Char	Num
CONTAINS	Includes a substring	x	
BETWEEN-AND	An inclusive range	x	x
WHERE SAME AND	Augment a WHERE expression	x	x
IS NULL	A missing value	x	x
IS MISSING	A missing value	x	x
LIKE	Matches a pattern	x	

33

Special WHERE operators cannot be used in IF-THEN or subsetting IF statements.

BETWEEN-AND Operator

The *BETWEEN-AND operator* selects observations in which the value of a variable falls within an inclusive range of values.

Examples
`where salary between 50000 and 100000;`
`where salary not between 50000 and 100000;`
`where Last_Name between 'A' and 'L';`
`where Last_Name between 'Baker' and 'Gomez';`

34

Copyright © 2016, SAS Institute Inc., Cary, North Carolina, USA. ALL RIGHTS RESERVED.

BETWEEN-AND Operator

Equivalent Statements
`where salary between 50000 and 100000;`
`where salary>=50000 and salary<=100000;`
`where 50000<=salary<=100000;`

35

WHERE SAME AND Operator

Use the *WHERE SAME AND operator* to add more conditions to an existing WHERE expression.

```
proc print data=orion.sales;
   where Country='AU' and Salary<30000;
   where same and Gender='F';
   var First_Name Last_Name Gender
       Salary Country;
run;
```

The WHERE SAME AND condition ***augments*** the original condition.

36 p104d05

Copyright © 2016, SAS Institute Inc., Cary, North Carolina, USA. ALL RIGHTS RESERVED.

Viewing the Log

Partial SAS Log

```
22   proc print data=orion.sales;
23       where Country='AU'  and Salary<30000;
24       where same and Gender='F';
NOTE: WHERE clause has been augmented.
25       var First_Name Last_Name Gender Salary Country;
26   run;

NOTE: There were 23 observations read from the data set ORION.SALES.
      WHERE (Country='AU') and (Gender='F') and (Salary<30000);
```

37

Viewing the Output

Partial PROC PRINT Output

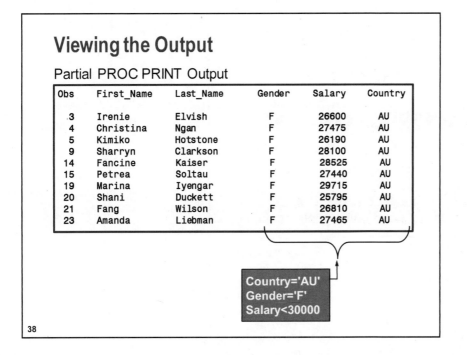

Obs	First_Name	Last_Name	Gender	Salary	Country
3	Irenie	Elvish	F	26600	AU
4	Christina	Ngan	F	27475	AU
5	Kimiko	Hotstone	F	26190	AU
9	Sharryn	Clarkson	F	28100	AU
14	Fancine	Kaiser	F	28525	AU
15	Petrea	Soltau	F	27440	AU
19	Marina	Iyengar	F	29715	AU
20	Shani	Duckett	F	25795	AU
21	Fang	Wilson	F	26810	AU
23	Amanda	Liebman	F	27465	AU

Country='AU'
Gender='F'
Salary<30000

38

Copyright © 2016, SAS Institute Inc., Cary, North Carolina, USA. ALL RIGHTS RESERVED.

4.03 Short Answer Poll

Open **p104a01b**. Change WHERE SAME AND to WHERE ALSO. Submit the program and view the log.

What message is written to the log?

39

IS NULL Operator

The *IS NULL operator* selects observations in which a variable has a missing value.

Examples
`where Employee_ID is null;`
`where Employee_ID is not null;`

IS NULL can be used for both character and numeric variables, and is equivalent to the following statements:

```
where employee_ID=' ';
```

```
where employee_ID=.;
```

41

Copyright © 2016, SAS Institute Inc., Cary, North Carolina, USA. ALL RIGHTS RESERVED.

IS MISSING Operator

The *IS MISSING operator* selects observations in which a variable has a missing value.

Examples
`where Employee_ID is missing;`
`where Employee_ID is not missing;`

IS MISSING can be used for both character and numeric variables, and is equivalent to the following statements:

```
where employee_ID=' ';
```

```
where employee_ID=.;
```

42

LIKE Operator

The *LIKE operator* selects observations by comparing character values to specified patterns. Two special characters are used to define a pattern.

- A percent sign (%) specifies that ***any number*** of characters can occupy that position.
- An underscore (_) specifies that ***exactly one*** character must occupy that position.

Examples
`where Name like '%N';`
`where Name like 'T_m';`
`where Name like 'T_m%';`

43

When you use the LIKE operator, be aware of the following:

- Consecutive underscores can be specified.
- A percent sign and an underscore can be specified in the same pattern.
- The operator is case sensitive.

Copyright © 2016, SAS Institute Inc., Cary, North Carolina, USA. ALL RIGHTS RESERVED.

4.04 Short Answer Poll

Which WHERE statement returns all the observations that have a first name starting with the letter M for the given values?

a.
```
where Name like '_, M_';
```

b.
```
where Name like '%, M%';
```

c.
```
where Name like '_, M%';
```

d.
```
where Name like '%, M_';
```

Name
Elvish, Irenie
Ngan, Christina
Hotstone, Kimiko
Daymond, Lucian
Hofmeister, Fong
Denny, Satyakam
Clarkson, Sharryn
Kletschkus, Monica

last name, first name

44

Business Scenario

The Sales Manager wants a report that includes only the customers who are 21 years old.

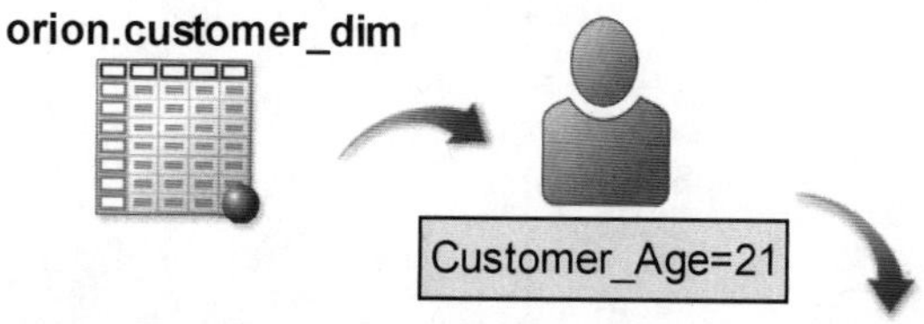

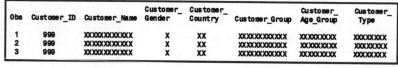

Obs	Customer_ID	Customer_Name	Customer_Gender	Customer_Country	Customer_Group	Customer_Age_Group	Customer_Type
1	999	XXXXXXXXXXXX	X	XX	XXXXXXXXXXXX	XXXXXXXXX	XXXXXXXX
2	999	XXXXXXXXXXXX	X	XX	XXXXXXXXXXXX	XXXXXXXXX	XXXXXXXX
3	999	XXXXXXXXXXXX	X	XX	XXXXXXXXXXXX	XXXXXXXXX	XXXXXXXX

47

Copyright © 2016, SAS Institute Inc., Cary, North Carolina, USA. ALL RIGHTS RESERVED.

Subsetting the Data Set

Display the required rows and variables.

```
proc print data=orion.customer_dim;
   where Customer_Age=21;
   var Customer_ID Customer_Name
       Customer_Gender Customer_Country
       Customer_Group Customer_Age_Group
       Customer_Type;
run;
```

✎ The subsetting variable does not need to be included in the report.

48 p104d06

Viewing the Output

In this output, two lines are used for each observation.

PROC PRINT Output

```
                                            Customer_   Customer_
Obs    Customer_ID   Customer_Name          Gender      Country        Customer_Group

 37             79   Najma Hicks            F           US             Orion Club members
 58          11171   Bill Cuddy             M           CA             Orion Club Gold members
 66          46966   Lauren Krasowski       F           CA             Orion Club members
...
 76          70210   Alex Santinello        M           CA             Orion Club members

       Customer_
Obs    Age_Group                Customer_Type

 37    15-30 years    Orion  Club members medium activity
 58    15-30 years    Orion Club Gold members low activity
 66    15-30 years    Orion  Club members high activity
...
 76    15-30 years    Orion  Club members medium activity
```

The Obs column helps identify observations that span multiple lines in a report.

49

Report width and wrapping depend on the LINESIZE system option, the ODS destination, or both.

Copyright © 2016, SAS Institute Inc., Cary, North Carolina, USA. ALL RIGHTS RESERVED.

ID Statement

The *ID statement* specifies the variable or variables to print at the beginning of each row instead of an observation number.

```
proc print data=orion.customer_dim;
   where Customer_Age=21;
   id Customer_ID;
   var Customer_Name Customer_Gender
       Customer_Country Customer_Group
       Customer_Age_Group Customer_Type;
run;
```

ID *variables;*

⚠ Choose ID variables that uniquely identify observations.

50 p104d07

Notice that the ID variable was removed from the VAR statement. If it were not removed, it would be displayed twice: once as the leftmost column and again in the position specified by the VAR statement.

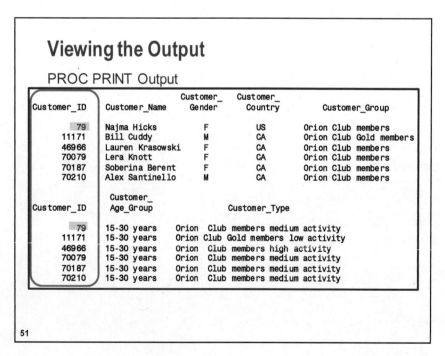

Viewing the Output

PROC PRINT Output

```
                            Customer_   Customer_
Customer_ID  Customer_Name   Gender      Country          Customer_Group

       79    Najma Hicks        F          US          Orion Club members
    11171    Bill Cuddy         M          CA          Orion Club Gold members
    46966    Lauren Krasowski   F          CA          Orion Club members
    70079    Lera Knott         F          CA          Orion Club members
    70187    Soberina Berent    F          CA          Orion Club members
    70210    Alex Santinello    M          CA          Orion Club members

              Customer_
Customer_ID   Age_Group               Customer_Type

       79    15-30 years    Orion  Club members medium activity
    11171    15-30 years    Orion Club Gold members low activity
    46966    15-30 years    Orion  Club members high activity
    70079    15-30 years    Orion  Club members medium activity
    70187    15-30 years    Orion  Club members medium activity
    70210    15-30 years    Orion  Club members medium activity
```

51

Copyright © 2016, SAS Institute Inc., Cary, North Carolina, USA. ALL RIGHTS RESERVED.

Exercises

> If you restarted your SAS session since the last exercise, open and submit the **libname.sas** program that can be found in the data folder.

Level 1

1. Displaying orion.order_fact with the PRINT Procedure

a. Retrieve the starter program **p104e01**. Run the program and view the output. Observe that there are 617 observations. Observations might be displayed over two lines, depending on output settings.

b. Add a SUM statement to display the sum of **Total_Retail_Price**. The last several lines of the report are shown below.

Obs	Order_ Type	Product_ID	Quantity	Total_Retail_ Price	CostPrice_ Per_Unit	Discount
610	1	240700100007	2	$45.70	$9.30	.
611	1	240700100017	2	$19.98	$11.40	40%
612	1	240700400003	2	$24.80	$5.60	.
613	1	240800100042	3	$760.80	$105.30	.
614	1	240500200016	3	$95.10	$14.50	.
615	1	240500200122	2	$48.20	$11.50	.
616	1	240700200018	4	$75.20	$10.30	.
617	1	220101400130	2	$33.80	$5.70	.
				=============		
				$100,077.46		

c. Add a WHERE statement to select only the observations with **Total_Retail_Price** more than 500. Submit the program. Verify that 35 observations are displayed.

What do you notice about the Obs column? start c̄ 22nd observation

Did the sum of **Total_Retail_Price** change to reflect only the subset? yes

d. Add an option to suppress the Obs column. Verify that there are 35 observations in the results.

How can you verify the number of observations in the results? Review log

e. Add an ID statement to use **Customer_ID** as the identifying variable. Submit the program. The results contain 35 observations.

How did the output change? Custome_ID is bold

f. Add a VAR statement to display **Customer_ID**, **Order_ID**, **Order_Type**, **Quantity**, and **Total_Retail_Price**.

What do you notice about **Customer_ID**? it showed up twice.

g. Modify the VAR statement to address the issue with **Customer_ID**.

Copyright © 2016, SAS Institute Inc., Cary, North Carolina, USA. ALL RIGHTS RESERVED.

Level 2

2. Displaying orion.customer_dim with the PRINT Procedure

a. Write a PRINT step to display **orion.customer_dim**.

b. Modify the program to display a subset of **orion.customer_dim** by selecting only the observations for customers between the ages of 30 and 40. Also, suppress the Obs column. The resulting report should contain 17 observations.

c. Add a statement to use **Customer_ID** instead of Obs as the identifying column. Submit the program and verify the results.

d. Add a statement to limit the variables to those shown in the report below.

```
                                      Customer_
Customer_ID     Customer_Name               Age       Customer_Type

          4     James Kvarniq                33       Orion Club members low activity
          9     Cornelia Krahl               33       Orion Club Gold members medium activity
         11     Elke Wallstab                33       Orion  Club members high activity
        ...     ...                         ...       ...
      54655     Lauren Marx                  38       Internet/Catalog Customers
      70201     Angel Borwick                38       Orion Club Gold members low activity
```

Challenge

3. Producing a Default Listing Report of orion.order_fact

This exercise assumes that you are creating LISTING output in the SAS windowing environment.

a. Produce a default listing report of **orion.order_fact**. The output might wrap onto a second line.

b. Investigate the use of the LINESIZE= SAS system option to adjust the width of the lines. What are the minimum and maximum values for the LINESIZE= option? ____________________

Submit an OPTIONS statement with LINESIZE= set to the highest allowed value. Resubmit the step, and observe the horizontal scroll bar, if it is displayed.

Reset the line size to 96 when you are finished.

c. Another way to create compact output is to request vertical headings. Investigate the HEADING= option in the PROC PRINT statement, and then experiment with it to generate vertical headings and then horizontal headings.

How do you specify vertical headings? ____________________

How do you specify horizontal headings? ____________________

4. Producing a Default Listing Report of orion.product_dim

This exercise assumes that you are creating LISTING output in the SAS windowing environment.

Copyright © 2016, SAS Institute Inc., Cary, North Carolina, USA. ALL RIGHTS RESERVED.

a. Produce a default listing report to display **orion.product_dim**. Notice that the column width varies from one page to the next, depending on the width of the values that are displayed on each page.

b. Investigate the WIDTH= option of the PROC PRINT statement, and modify the program to use this option with a value of UNIFORM.

How are the results different when you use the WIDTH=UNIFORM option? ________________

____

c. Why might the procedure run more slowly with this option? ____________________

____

d. How can you save computer resources and still display columns consistently across pages? _____

____

End of Exercises

Copyright © 2016, SAS Institute Inc., Cary, North Carolina, USA. ALL RIGHTS RESERVED.

4.2 Sorting and Grouping Report Data

Objectives

- Sort the observations in a SAS data set based on the values of one or more variables.
- Display the sorted observations.
- Display a data set with report totals and subtotals for each BY group.

55

Business Scenario

Display observations from **orion.sales** in ascending order by the variable **Salary**.

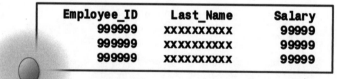

Employee_ID	Last_Name	Salary
999999	xxxxxxxxxx	99999
999999	xxxxxxxxxx	99999
999999	xxxxxxxxxx	99999

56

Copyright © 2016, SAS Institute Inc., Cary, North Carolina, USA. ALL RIGHTS RESERVED.

Creating a Sorted Report

Step 1 Use the SORT procedure to create a new data set, **work.sales**. Order the observations by the value of **Salary**.

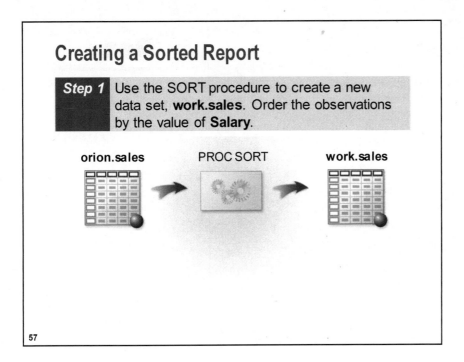

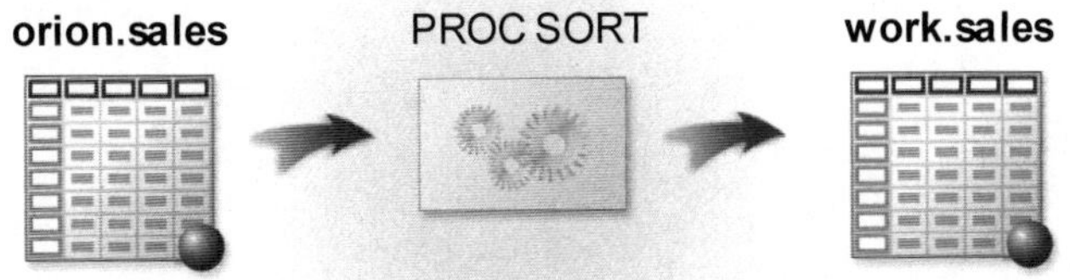

57

Creating a Sorted Report

Step 2 Use the PRINT procedure to display the sorted data set, **work.sales**.

58

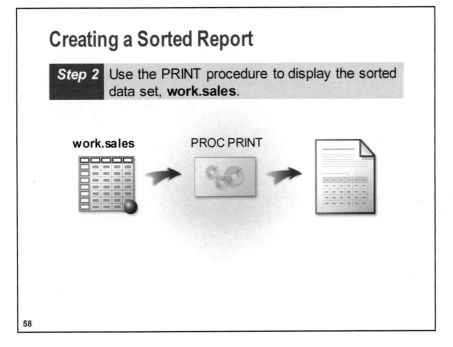

Copyright © 2016, SAS Institute Inc., Cary, North Carolina, USA. ALL RIGHTS RESERVED.

Step 1: SORT Procedure

The *SORT procedure* rearranges the observations in the input data set based on the values of the variable or variables listed in the BY statement.

```
proc sort data=orion.sales
          out=work.sales;
   by Salary;
run;
```

PROC SORT DATA=*input-SAS-data-set*
  <**OUT=***output-SAS-data-set*>;
  BY <**DESCENDING**> *variables*;
RUN;

The BY statement in a PROC SORT step specifies the sort variables, and if you indicate it, the sort order.

59 p104d08

Viewing the Log

The SORT procedure does not produce a report. Check the log for errors or warnings.

Partial SAS Log

```
34   proc sort data=orion.sales
35             out=work.sales;
36      by Salary;
37   run;

NOTE: There were 165 observations read from the data set
ORION.SALES.
NOTE: The data set WORK.SALES has 165 observations and 9
variables.
```

60

Copyright © 2016, SAS Institute Inc., Cary, North Carolina, USA. ALL RIGHTS RESERVED.

Step 2: Viewing the Output

```
proc print data=work.sales noobs;
   var Employee_ID Last_Name Salary;
run;
```

Partial PROC PRINT Output

Employee_ID	Last_Name	Salary
121084	Ould	22710
121064	Polky	25110
121057	Voron	25125
...		
121143	Favaron	95090
120102	Zhou	108255
120261	Highpoint	243190

61

p104d08

SORT Procedure

The SORT procedure

- replaces the original data set or creates a new one
- can sort on multiple variables
- sorts in ascending (default) or descending order
- does not generate printed output.

⚠ The input data set is overwritten unless the OUT= option is used to specify an output data set.

62

Copyright © 2016, SAS Institute Inc., Cary, North Carolina, USA. ALL RIGHTS RESERVED.

4.05 Short Answer Poll

Which step sorts the observations in a SAS data set and overwrites the same data set?

a.

```
proc sort data=work.EmpsAU
          out=work.sorted;
   by First;
run;
```

b.

```
proc sort data=orion.EmpsAU
          out=EmpsAU;
   by First;
run;
```

c.

```
proc sort data=work.EmpsAU;
   by First;
run;
```

63

Business Scenario

Produce a report that lists sales employees grouped by **Country**, in descending **Salary** order within country.

```
---------------------------Country=AU------------------------------

                First_  Last_                                 Birth_   Hire_
Employee_ID     Name    Name    Gender  Salary  Job_Title     Date     Date

    9999        xxxx    xxxxx     x     99999    xxxxxx       9999     9999
    9999        xxxx    xxxxx     x     99999    xxxxxx       9999     9999


---------------------------Country=US------------------------------

                First_  Last_                                 Birth_   Hire_
Employee_ID     Name    Name    Gender  Salary  Job_Title     Date     Date

    9999        xxxx    xxxxx     x     99999    xxxxxx       9999     9999
    9999        xxxx    xxxxx     x     99999    xxxxxx       9999     9999
    9999        xxxx    xxxxx     x     99999    xxxxxx       9999     9999
```

66

Copyright © 2016, SAS Institute Inc., Cary, North Carolina, USA. ALL RIGHTS RESERVED.

Creating a Grouped Report

Step 1 Use the SORT procedure to group data in a data set. This scenario requires two variables to be sorted:
- **Country**
- descending **Salary** within **Country**

Step 2 Use a BY statement in PROC PRINT to display the sorted observations grouped by **Country**.

67

Step 1: Sort the Data

Sort the data set to group the observations.

```
proc sort data=orion.sales
          out=work.sales;
   by Country descending Salary;
run;
```

BY <**DESCENDING**> *variables*;

68

p104d09

Copyright © 2016, SAS Institute Inc., Cary, North Carolina, USA. ALL RIGHTS RESERVED.

Specifying Sort Order

The *DESCENDING option* reverses the sort order for the variable that immediately follows it. The observations are sorted from the largest value to the smallest value.

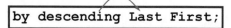

Examples:

```
by descending Last First;
```

```
by Last descending First;
```

```
by descending Last descending First;
```

69

Specifying Multiple BY Variables

- PROC SORT first arranges the data set by the values of the first BY variable.

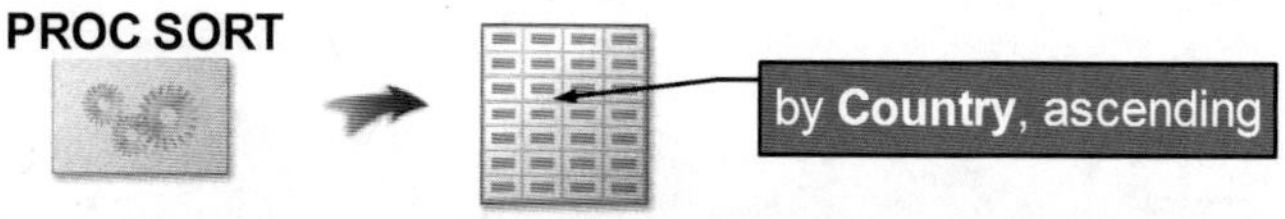

- PROC SORT then arranges any observations that have the same value as the first BY variable by the values of the second BY variable.

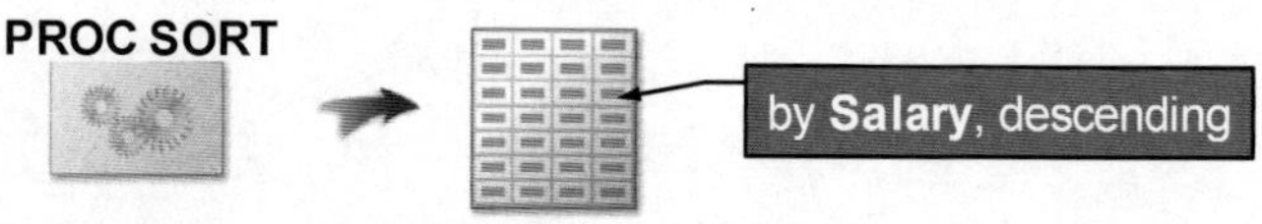

- This sorting continues for every specified BY variable.

70

Copyright © 2016, SAS Institute Inc., Cary, North Carolina, USA. ALL RIGHTS RESERVED.

Step 2: Specify Report Groupings

The BY statement in a PROC PRINT step specifies the variable or variables to use to form *BY groups*.

```
proc print data=work.sales noobs;
   by Country;
run;
```

BY <DESCENDING> *variables*;

- The variables in the BY statement are called *BY variables*.
- The observations in the data set ***must*** be in order according to the order of the BY variable (or variables).

71

p104d09

Viewing the Output

Partial PROC PRINT Output

```
--------------------------- Country=AU -------------------------

                                                               Hire_
Employee_ID   First_Name   Last_Name  Gender  Salary            Date

     120102   Tom          Zhou          M    108255           12205
     120103   Wilson       Dawes         M     87975   ...      6575
     120168   Selina       Barcoe        M     36605           18567

--------------------------- Country=US -------------------------

                                                               Hire_
Employee_ID   First_Name   Last_Name   Gender  Salary           Date

     120261   Harry        Highpoint     M     243190          11535
     121143   Louis        Favaron       M      95090   ...    15157
     121064   Asishana     Polky         M      84260          13027
```

72

Copyright © 2016, SAS Institute Inc., Cary, North Carolina, USA. ALL RIGHTS RESERVED.

4.06 Short Answer Poll

Open and submit **p104a02**. View the log. Why did the program fail?

73

Business Scenario

Modify the previous report to display selected variables, the salary subtotal for each country, and the salary grand total.

```
-------------------- Country=AU -------------------

First_Name    Last_Name      Gender        Salary

XXXX          XXXXXXX          X            99999
XXXX          XXXXXXX          X            99999
--------                                ---------
Country                                   999999

-------------------- Country=US -------------------

First_Name    Last_Name      Gender        Salary

XXXXXXX       XXXXXXX          X            99999
XXXXXXX       XXXXXXX          X            99999
--------                                ---------
Country                                   999999
                                        =========
                                          9999999
```

subtotals

grand total

75

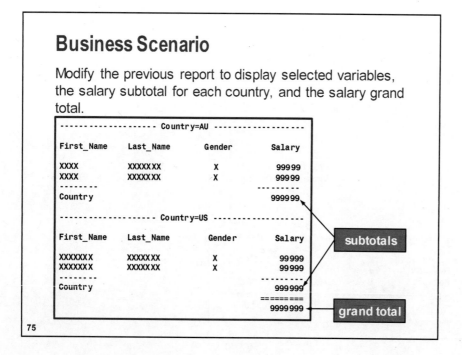

Copyright © 2016, SAS Institute Inc., Cary, North Carolina, USA. ALL RIGHTS RESERVED.

Generating Subtotals

Use a BY statement and a SUM statement in a PROC PRINT step.

```
proc sort data=orion.sales
          out=work.sales;
   by Country descending Salary;
run;

proc print data=work.sales noobs;
   by Country;
   sum Salary;
   var First_Name Last_Name Gender Salary;
run;
```

76 p104d10

Viewing the Output

```
----------------- Country=AU -----------------

First_Name    Last_Name       Gender    Salary

Tom           Zhou              M       108255
Wilson        Dawes             M        87975
Daniel        Pilgrim           M        36605
...
Kimiko        Tilley            F        25185
--------                               -------
Country                                1900015

------------------ Country=US ------------------

First_Name    Last_Name         Gender    Salary

Harry         Highpoint           M       243190
Louis         Favaron             M        95090
Dennis        Lansberry           M        84260
...
Tulsidas      Ould                M        22710
------------                             -------
Country                                  3241405
                                         =======
                                         5141420
```

subtotal for AU

subtotal for US

grand total

77

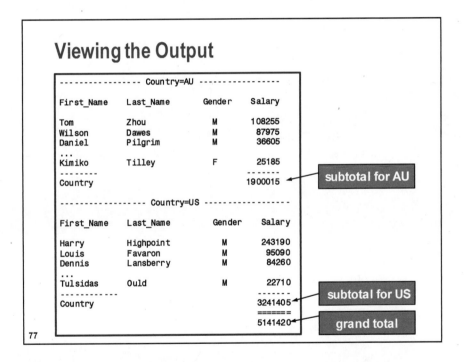

Copyright © 2016, SAS Institute Inc., Cary, North Carolina, USA. ALL RIGHTS RESERVED.

Setup for the Poll

Modify the previous report to display only employees earning less than 25,500. Which WHERE statement (or statements) results in the most efficient processing?

```
proc sort data=orion.sales
          out=work.sales;
   /* where Salary<25500; */
   by Country descending Salary;
run;
proc print data=work.sales noobs;
   by Country;
   sum Salary;
   /* where Salary<25500; */
   var First_Name Last_Name Gender Salary;
run;
```

78

p104a03

4.07 Multiple Choice Poll

Which WHERE statement (or statements) results in the most efficient processing?

a. The WHERE statement in the PROC SORT step.

b. The WHERE statement in the PROC PRINT step.

c. Both WHERE statements are needed.

d. The WHERE statements are equally efficient.

79

Copyright © 2016, SAS Institute Inc., Cary, North Carolina, USA. ALL RIGHTS RESERVED.

Exercises

If you restarted your SAS session since the last exercise, open and submit the **libname.sas** program that can be found in the data folder.

Level 1

5. Sorting orion.employee_payroll and Displaying the New Data Set

a. Open **p104e05**. Add a PROC SORT step before the PROC PRINT step to sort **orion.employee_payroll** by **Salary**. Place the sorted observations into a temporary data set named **sort_salary**.

b. Modify the PROC PRINT step to display the new data set. Verify that your output matches the report below.

Obs	Employee_ID	Employee_ Gender	Salary	Birth_ Date	Employee_ Hire_Date	Employee_ Term_Date	Marital_ Status	Dependents
1	121084	M	22710	3150	12784	.	M	3
2	120191	F	24015	1112	17167	17347	S	0
...								
422	120261	M	243190	4800	11535	.	O	1
423	120262	M	268455	5042	11932	.	M	2
424	120259	M	433800	2946	12297	.	M	1

6. Sorting orion.employee_payroll and Displaying Grouped Observations

a. Open **p104e06**. Add a PROC SORT step before the PROC PRINT step to sort **orion.employee_payroll** by **Employee_Gender**, and within gender, by **Salary** in descending order. Place the sorted observations into a temporary data set named **sort_salary2**.

b. Modify the PROC PRINT step to display the new data set with the observations grouped by **Employee_Gender**.

------------------------------------ Employee_Gender=F ------------------------------------

Obs	Employee_ID	Salary	Birth_ Date	Employee_ Hire_Date	Employee_ Term_Date	Marital_ Status	Dependents
1	120260	207885	3258	10532	.	M	2
2	120719	87420	4770	14641	.	M	1
3	120661	85495	-400	10227	17347	M	3
...							
190	120196	24025	10257	17167	17347	S	0
191	120191	24015	1112	17167	17347	S	0

------------------------------------ Employee_Gender=M ------------------------------------

Obs	Employee_ID	Salary	Birth_ Date	Employee_ Hire_Date	Employee_ Term_Date	Marital_ Status	Dependents
192	120259	433800	2946	12297	.	M	1

Copyright © 2016, SAS Institute Inc., Cary, North Carolina, USA. ALL RIGHTS RESERVED.

193	120262	268455	5042	11932	.	M	2
...							
423	120190	24100	10566	17837	18017	M	2
424	121084	22710	3150	12784	.	M	3

Level 2

7. Sorting orion.employee_payroll and Displaying a Subset of the New Data Set

a. Sort **orion.employee_payroll** by **Employee_Gender**, and by descending **Salary** within gender. Place the sorted observations into a temporary data set named **sort_sal**.

b. Print a subset of the **sort_sal** data set. Select only the observations for active employees (those without a value for **Employee_Term_Date**) who earn more than $65,000. Group the report by **Employee_Gender**, and include a total and subtotals for **Salary**. Suppress the Obs column. Display only **Employee_ID**, **Salary**, and **Marital_Status**. The results contain 18 observations.

```
---------------------------------- Employee_Gender=F ---------------------------------

                                                       Marital_
                              Employee_ID     Salary    Status

                                 120260       207885      M
                                 120719        87420      M
                                 ...
                                 120677        65555      M
                           ---------------    ------
                           Employee_Gender    605190


---------------------------------- Employee_Gender=M ---------------------------------

                                                       Marital_
                              Employee_ID     Salary    Status

                                 120259       433800      M
                                 120262       268455      M
                                 ...
                                 120268        76105      S
                           ---------------   -------
                           Employee_Gender   2072410
                                             =======
                                             2677600
```

Challenge

8. Retaining the First Observation of Each BY Group

a. Sort **orion.orders** by **Customer_ID**. Place the sorted observations in a temporary data set.

b. Display the sorted data set. The resulting report should contain 490 observations. **Customer_ID** is listed multiple times for customers that placed more than one order.

c. Investigate an option that causes PROC SORT to retain only the first observation in each BY group.

Copyright © 2016, SAS Institute Inc., Cary, North Carolina, USA. ALL RIGHTS RESERVED.

d. Add the appropriate option to the PROC SORT step to retain only the first observation in each BY group. The results contain 75 observations with no duplicate values for **Customer_ID**.

e. Explore the DUPOUT= option to write duplicate observations to a separate output data set.

End of Exercises

Copyright © 2016, SAS Institute Inc., Cary, North Carolina, USA. ALL RIGHTS RESERVED.

4.3 Enhancing Reports

Objectives

- Include titles and footnotes in a report.
- Use the LABEL statement to define descriptive column headings.
- Control the use of column headings with the LABEL and SPLIT= options.

84

Business Scenario

Enhance the payroll report by adding titles, footnotes, and descriptive column headings.

Obs	Employee_ID	Last_Name	Salary
1	9999	xxxxxxxxxx	99999
2	9999	xxxxxxxxxx	99999
3	9999	xxxxxxxxxx	99999

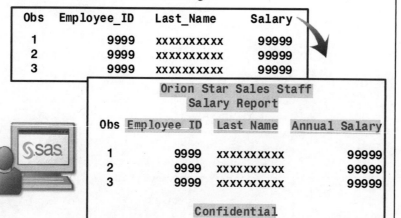

Orion Star Sales Staff
Salary Report

Obs	Employee ID	Last Name	Annual Salary
1	9999	xxxxxxxxxx	99999
2	9999	xxxxxxxxxx	99999
3	9999	xxxxxxxxxx	99999

Confidential

85

Copyright © 2016, SAS Institute Inc., Cary, North Carolina, USA. ALL RIGHTS RESERVED.

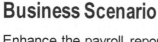

Displaying Titles and Footnotes

Use TITLE and FOOTNOTE statements to enhance the report.

```
title1 'Orion Star Sales Staff';
title2 'Salary Report';

footnote1 'Confidential';

proc print data=orion.sales;
   var Employee_ID Last_Name Salary;
run;

title;
footnote;
```

TITLE*n* *'text'*;

FOOTNOTE*n* *'text'*;

86 p104d11

Viewing the Output

Partial PROC PRINT Output

```
                 Orion Star Sales Staff
                     Salary Report

Obs    Employee_ID    Last_Name       Salary

  1      120102       Zhou            108255
  2      120103       Dawes            87975
  3      120121       Elvish           26600
...
164      121144       Capachietti      83505
165      121145       Lansberry        84260

                     Confidential
```

87

Copyright © 2016, SAS Institute Inc., Cary, North Carolina, USA. ALL RIGHTS RESERVED.

TITLE Statement

The global *TITLE statement* specifies title lines for SAS output.

```
TITLEn 'text';
```

- Titles appear at the top of the page.
- The default title is **The SAS System**.
- The value of ***n*** can be from 1 to 10.
- An unnumbered **TITLE** is equivalent to **TITLE1**.
- Titles remain in effect until they are changed, canceled, or you end your SAS session.

88

FOOTNOTE Statement

The global *FOOTNOTE statement* specifies footnote lines for SAS output.

```
FOOTNOTEn 'text';
```

- Footnotes appear at the bottom of the page.
- No footnote is printed unless one is specified.
- The value of ***n*** can be from 1 to 10.
- An unnumbered **FOOTNOTE** is equivalent to **FOOTNOTE1**.
- Footnotes remain in effect until they are changed, canceled, or you end your SAS session.

89

Copyright © 2016, SAS Institute Inc., Cary, North Carolina, USA. ALL RIGHTS RESERVED.

Changing Titles and Footnotes

To change a title line, submit a TITLE statement with the same number but different text.

- This replaces a previous title with the same number.
- It cancels all titles with higher numbers.

```
title1 'ABC Company';
title2 'Sales Division';
title3 'Salary Report';
```

```
title1 'Salary Report';
```

This statement changes title 1 and cancels titles 2 and 3.

Footnotes are changed the same way.

90

Canceling All Titles and Footnotes

- The null TITLE statement cancels all titles.

```
title;
```

- The null FOOTNOTE statement cancels all footnotes.

```
footnote;
```

91

Copyright © 2016, SAS Institute Inc., Cary, North Carolina, USA. ALL RIGHTS RESERVED.

Changing and Canceling Titles and Footnotes

PROC PRINT Code	Resultant Title(s)

`title1 'The First Line';`
`title2 'The Second Line';`
`proc print data=orion.sales;`
`run;`
	The First Line
	The Second Line

`title2 'The Next Line';`
`proc print data=orion.sales;`
`run;`
	The First Line
	The Next Line

`title 'The Top Line';`
`proc print data=orion.sales;`
`run;`
	The Top Line

`title3 'The Third Line';`
`proc print data=orion.sales;`
`run;`
	The Top Line
	
	The Third Line

`title;`
`proc print data=orion.sales;`
`run;`	

102

4.08 Short Answer Poll

Which footnote or footnotes appear in the second procedure output?

a.
```
Non Sales Employees
```

b.
```
Orion Star
Non Sales Employees
```

c.
```
Non Sales Employees
Confidential
```

d.
```
Orion Star
Non Sales Employees
Confidential
```

```
footnote1 'Orion Star';
footnote2 'Sales Employees';
footnote3 'Confidential';
proc print data=orion.sales;
run;

footnote2 'Non Sales Employees';
proc print data=orion.nonsales;
run;
```

103

Copyright © 2016, SAS Institute Inc., Cary, North Carolina, USA. ALL RIGHTS RESERVED.

Idea Exchange

Which of the following programs do you prefer and why?

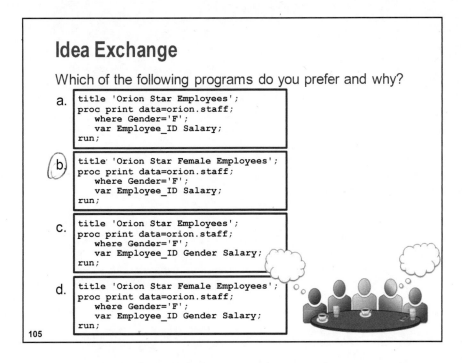

a.
```
title 'Orion Star Employees';
proc print data=orion.staff;
   where Gender='F';
   var Employee_ID Salary;
run;
```

b.
```
title 'Orion Star Female Employees';
proc print data=orion.staff;
   where Gender='F';
   var Employee_ID Salary;
run;
```

c.
```
title 'Orion Star Employees';
proc print data=orion.staff;
   where Gender='F';
   var Employee_ID Gender Salary;
run;
```

d.
```
title 'Orion Star Female Employees';
proc print data=orion.staff;
   where Gender='F';
   var Employee_ID Gender Salary;
run;
```

105

LABEL Statement and Option

Use a LABEL statement and the LABEL option to display descriptive column headings instead of variable names.

```
title1 'Orion Star Sales Staff';
title2 'Salary Report';
footnote1 'Confidential';

proc print data=orion.sales label;
   var Employee_ID Last_Name Salary;
   label Employee_ID='Sales ID'
         Last_Name='Last Name'
         Salary='Annual Salary';
run;

title;
footnote;
```

LABEL *variable-1*=*'label'*
...
variable-n=*'label'*;

p104d12

107

Copyright © 2016, SAS Institute Inc., Cary, North Carolina, USA. ALL RIGHTS RESERVED.

LABEL Statement

The LABEL statement assigns descriptive labels to variables.

- A label can be up to 256 characters and include any characters, including blanks.
- Labels are used automatically by many procedures.
- The PRINT procedure uses labels only when the LABEL or SPLIT= option is specified.

108

Viewing the Output

```
                  Orion Star Sales Staff
                      Salary Report

                                              Annual
Obs        Sales ID    Last Name              Salary

  1          120102    Zhou                   108255
  2          120103    Dawes                   87975
  3          120121    Elvish                  26600
...
164          121144    Capachietti             83505
165          121145    Lansberry               84260



                      Confidential
```

109

Copyright © 2016, SAS Institute Inc., Cary, North Carolina, USA. ALL RIGHTS RESERVED.

SPLIT= Option

The SPLIT= option in PROC PRINT specifies a split character to control line breaks in column headings.

```
proc print data=orion.sales split='*';
   var Employee_ID Last_Name Salary;
   label Employee_ID='Sales ID'
         Last_Name='Last*Name'
         Salary='Annual*Salary';
run;
```

SPLIT='*split-character*'

The SPLIT= option can be used instead of the LABEL option in a PROC PRINT step.

110 p104d13

Viewing the Output

Partial PROC PRINT Output

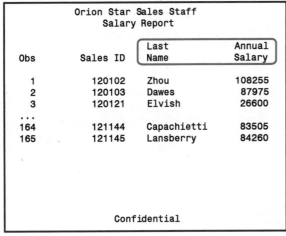

```
              Orion Star Sales Staff
                  Salary Report

                          Last                  Annual
Obs       Sales ID        Name                  Salary

  1         120102        Zhou                  108255
  2         120103        Dawes                  87975
  3         120121        Elvish                 26600
...
164         121144        Capachietti            83505
165         121145        Lansberry              84260



                   Confidential
```

111

Copyright © 2016, SAS Institute Inc., Cary, North Carolina, USA. ALL RIGHTS RESERVED.

Exercises

> If you restarted your SAS session since the last exercise, open and submit the **libname.sas** program that can be found in the data folder.

Level 1

9. Displaying Titles and Footnotes in a Detail Report

a. Open and submit **p104e09** to display all observations for Australian Sales Rep IVs

b. Add a VAR statement to display only the variables shown in the report below.

c. Add TITLE and FOOTNOTE statements to include the titles and footnotes shown in the report below.

d. Submit the program and verify the output. The results contain five observations as shown below.

e. Submit a null TITLE and null FOOTNOTE statement to clear all titles and footnotes.

```
                    Australian Sales Employees
                   Senior Sales Representatives

                              First_
 Obs     Employee_ID     Name          Last_Name         Gender     Salary

   7          120125     Fong          Hofmeister          M         32040
  10          120128     Monica        Kletschkus          F         30890
  17          120135     Alexei        Platts              M         32490
  41          120159     Lynelle       Phoumirath          F         30765
  48          120166     Fadi          Nowd                M         30660

                    Job_Title: Sales Rep. IV
```

10. Displaying Column Headings in a Detail Report

a. Open and submit **p104e10**. Modify the program to define and use the following labels:

Variable	Label
Employee_ID	Employee ID
First_Name	First Name
Last_Name	Last Name
Salary	Annual Salary

Submit the program and verify the output.

```
              Entry-level Sales Representatives

                                                   Annual
```

Copyright © 2016, SAS Institute Inc., Cary, North Carolina, USA. ALL RIGHTS RESERVED.

```
Employee ID     First Name       Last Name        Gender     Salary

     121023     Shawn            Fuller             M         26010
     121028     William          Smades             M         26585
     121029     Kuo-Chung        Mcelwee            M         27225
 ...
     121138     Hershell         Tolley             M         27265
     121140     Saunders         Briggi             M         26335

                 Job_Title: Sales Rep. I
```

b. Modify the program to use a blank space as the SPLIT= character to generate two-line column headings. Submit the modified program and verify that two-line column labels are displayed.

```
                     Entry-level Sales Representatives

          Employee    First          Last                      Annual
                ID    Name           Name            Gender    Salary

            121023    Shawn          Fuller            M        26010
            121028    William        Smades            M        26585
            121029    Kuo-Chung      Mcelwee           M        27225
             ...
            121138    Hershell       Tolley            M        27265
            121140    Saunders       Briggi            M        26335

                          Job_Title: Sales Rep. I
```

Level 2

11. Writing an Enhanced Detail Report

a. Write a program to display a subset of **orion.employee_addresses** as shown below. The program should sort the observations by **State**, **City**, and **Employee_Name** and then display the sorted observations grouped by **State**. The resulting report should contain 311 observations.

```
                              US Employees by State

          ------------------------------ State=CA --------------------------


               Employee                                                Zip
                  ID       Name                             City       Code

                120656     Amos, Salley                  San Diego    92116
                120759     Apr, Nishan                   San Diego    92071
                121017     Arizmendi, Gilbert            San Diego    91950
                121062     Armant, Debra                 San Diego    92025
                121049     Bataineh, Perrior             San Diego    92126
                 ...
```

End of Exercises

Copyright © 2016, SAS Institute Inc., Cary, North Carolina, USA. ALL RIGHTS RESERVED.

4.4 Solutions

Solutions to Exercises

1. **Displaying orion.order_fact with the PRINT Procedure**

```
proc print data=orion.order_fact noobs;
   where Total_Retail_Price>500;
   id Customer_ID;
   var Order_ID Order_Type Quantity Total_Retail_Price;
   sum Total_Retail_Price;
run;
```

a. Run the program and view the output.

b. Add a SUM statement and verify the resulting sum.

c. What do you notice about the Obs column? **The numbers are not sequential. The original observation numbers are displayed.**

Did the sum of **Total_Retail Price** change to reflect only the subset? **Yes**

d. If the Obs column is suppressed, how can you verify the number of observations in the results? **Check the log.**

e. When the ID statement was added, how did the output change? **Customer_ID is the leftmost column and is displayed on each line for an observation.**

f. When the VAR statement is added, what do you notice about **Customer_ID**? **There are two Customer_ID columns. The first column is the ID field, and a second one is included because Customer_ID is listed in the VAR statement.**

g. Remove the duplicate column by removing **Customer_ID** from the VAR statement.

2. **Displaying orion.customer_dim with the PRINT Procedure**

```
proc print data=orion.customer_dim noobs;
   where Customer_Age between 30 and 40;
   id Customer_ID;
   var Customer_Name Customer_Age Customer_Type;
run;
```

3. **Producing a Default Listing Report of orion.order_fact (SAS Windowing Environment)**

```
options ls=max;

proc print data=orion.order_fact;
run;

options ls=96;

proc print data=orion.order_fact headings=v;
run;
```

Copyright © 2016, SAS Institute Inc., Cary, North Carolina, USA. ALL RIGHTS RESERVED.

a. Submit a simple PROC PRINT step to produce a default listing report.

b. What are the minimum and maximum values for the LINESIZE= option? **The minimum value for LINESIZE= is 64 and the maximum size is MAX.**

When you are finished, use the following statement to reset the line size to 96:

```
options ls=96;
```

c. How do you specify vertical headings? **HEADINGS=V forces all column headings to be displayed vertically.**

How do you specify horizontal headings? **HEADINGS=H forces all column headings to be displayed horizontally.**

4. **Producing a Default Listing Report of orion.product_dim (SAS Windowing Environment)**

```
proc print data=orion.product_dim width=uniform;
run;
```

a. Submit a simple PROC PRINT step.

b. Add the WIDTH=UNIFORM option. How are the results different? **Each column has the same column width on each page.**

c. Why might the procedure run more slowly with this option? **With this option, PROC PRINT must read through the entire data set twice.**

d. How can you save computer resources and still display columns consistently across pages? **Use a format on every column to explicitly specify a field width so that PROC PRINT reads the data only once.**

5. **Sorting orion.employee_payroll and Displaying the New Data Set**

```
proc sort data=orion.employee_payroll out=work.sort_salary;
   by Salary;
run;

proc print data=work.sort_salary;
run;
```

6. **Sorting orion.employee_payroll and Displaying Grouped Observations**

```
proc sort data=orion.employee_payroll out=work.sort_salary2;
   by Employee_Gender descending Salary;
run;

proc print data=work.sort_salary2;
   by Employee_Gender;
run;
```

7. **Sorting orion.employee_payroll and Displaying a Subset of the New Data Set**

```
proc sort data=orion.employee_payroll out=work.sort_sal;
   by Employee_Gender descending Salary;
run;

proc print data=work.sort_sal noobs;
```

Copyright © 2016, SAS Institute Inc., Cary, North Carolina, USA. ALL RIGHTS RESERVED.

```
   by Employee_Gender;
   sum Salary;
   where Employee_Term_Date is missing and Salary>65000;
   var Employee_ID Salary Marital_Status;
run;
```

8. Retaining the First Observation of Each BY Group

```
proc sort data=orion.orders out=work.custorders nodupkey
          dupout=work.duplicates;
   by Customer_ID;
run;

title 'Unique Customers';
proc print data=work.custorders;
run;

title 'Duplicate Customer Observations';
proc print data=work.duplicates;
run;
title;
```

9. Displaying Titles and Footnotes in a Detail Report

```
title1 'Australian Sales Employees';
title2 'Senior Sales Representatives';
footnote1 'Job_Title: Sales Rep. IV';

proc print data=orion.sales;
   where Country='AU' and Job_Title contains 'Rep. IV';
   var Employee_ID First_Name Last_Name Gender Salary;
run;
title;
footnote;
```

10. Displaying Column Headings in a Detail Report

a.

```
title 'Entry-level Sales Representatives';
footnote 'Job_Title: Sales Rep. I';

proc print data=orion.sales noobs label;
   where Country='US' and Job_Title='Sales Rep. I';
   var Employee_ID First_Name Last_Name Gender Salary;
   label Employee_ID="Employee ID"
         First_Name="First Name"
         Last_Name="Last Name"
         Salary="Annual Salary";
run;

title;
footnote;
```

Copyright © 2016, SAS Institute Inc., Cary, North Carolina, USA. ALL RIGHTS RESERVED.

b.

```
title 'Entry-level Sales Representatives';
footnote 'Job_Title: Sales Rep. I';

proc print data=orion.sales noobs split=' ';
   where Country='US' and Job_Title='Sales Rep. I';
   var Employee_ID First_Name Last_Name Gender Salary;
   label Employee_ID="Employee ID"
         First_Name="First Name"
         Last_Name="Last Name"
         Salary="Annual Salary";
run;

title;
footnote;
```

11. Writing an Enhanced Detail Report

```
proc sort data=orion.employee_addresses out=work.address;
   where Country='US';
   by State City Employee_Name;
run;

title "US Employees by State";
proc print data=work.address noobs split=' ';
   var Employee_ID Employee_Name City Postal_Code;
   label Employee_ID='Employee ID'
         Employee_Name='Name'
         Postal_Code='Zip Code';
   by State;
run;
```

End of Solutions

Copyright © 2016, SAS Institute Inc., Cary, North Carolina, USA. ALL RIGHTS RESERVED.

Solutions to Student Activities (Polls/Quizzes)

4.01 Multiple Choice Poll – Correct Answer

Which of the following is true?

a. The program executes, and applies both WHERE conditions successfully.

b. The program fails and an error message is written to the log.

c. The program executes, but only the first WHERE condition is applied.

(d.) The program executes, but only the second WHERE condition is applied.

```
182  proc print data=orion.sales;
183     where Country='AU';
184     where Salary<30000;
NOTE: WHERE clause has been replaced.
185  run;

NOTE: There were 134 observations read from the data set ORION.SALES.
      WHERE Salary<30000;
```

21

4.02 Short Answer Poll – Correct Answer

Which WHERE statement correctly subsets the numeric values for May, June, or July and missing character names?

a.
```
where Month in (5-7)
      and Names=.;
```

(b.)
```
where Month in (5,6,7)
      and Names=' ';
```

c.
```
where Month in ('5','6','7')
      and Names='.';
```

27

Copyright © 2016, SAS Institute Inc., Cary, North Carolina, USA. ALL RIGHTS RESERVED.

4.03 Short Answer Poll – Correct Answer

Open **p104a01b**. Change WHERE SAME AND to WHERE ALSO. Submit the program and view the log. What message is written to the log?

```
27   proc print data=orion.sales;
28       where Country='AU'  and Salary<30000;
29       where also Gender='F';
NOTE: WHERE clause has been augmented.
30       var First_Name Last_Name Gender Salary Country;
31   run;

NOTE: There were 23 observations read from the data set ORION.SALES.
      WHERE (Country='AU') and (Gender='F') and (Salary<30000);
```

WHERE ALSO results in the same message:

WHERE clause has been augmented.

40

4.04 Short Answer Poll – Correct Answer

Which WHERE statement returns all the observations that have a first name starting with the letter M for the given values?

a. `where Name like '_, M_';`

(b.) `where Name like '%, M%';`

c. `where Name like '_, M%';`

d. `where Name like '%, M_';`

Name
Elvish, Irenie
Ngan, Christina
Hotstone, Kimiko
Daymond, Lucian
Hofmeister, Fong
Denny, Satyakam
Clarkson, Sharryn
Kletschkus, Monica

last name, first name

45

Copyright © 2016, SAS Institute Inc., Cary, North Carolina, USA. ALL RIGHTS RESERVED.

4.05 Short Answer Poll – Correct Answer

Which step sorts the observations in a SAS data set and overwrites the same data set?

a.

```
proc sort data=work.EmpsAU
          out=work.sorted;
   by First;
run;
```

b.

```
proc sort data=orion.EmpsAU
          out=EmpsAU;
   by First;
run;
```

(c.)

```
proc sort data=work.EmpsAU;
   by First;
run;
```

64

4.06 Short Answer Poll – Correct Answer

Open and submit **p104a02**. View the log. Why did the program fail?

The input data set was not sorted by Gender.

```
proc sort data=orion.sales
          out=work.sorted;
   by Country Gender;
run;

NOTE: There were 165 observations read from the data set ORION.SALES.
NOTE: The data set WORK.SORTED has 165 observations and 9 variables.


proc print data=work.sorted;
   by Gender;
run;

ERROR: Data set WORK.SORTED is not sorted in ascending sequence. The current
       BY group has Gender = M and the next BY group has Gender = F.
NOTE: The SAS System stopped processing this step because of errors.
NOTE: There were 64 observations read from the data set WORK.SORTED.
```

74

Copyright © 2016, SAS Institute Inc., Cary, North Carolina, USA. ALL RIGHTS RESERVED.

4.07 Multiple Choice Poll – Correct Answer

Which WHERE statement (or statements) results in the most efficient processing?

a. The WHERE statement in the PROC SORT step. (circled)
b. The WHERE statement in the PROC PRINT step.
c. Both WHERE statements are needed.
d. The WHERE statements are equally efficient.

Subsetting in PROC SORT is more efficient. It selects and sorts only the required observations.

⚠ **Be sure to use the OUT= option when you subset in PROC SORT or you will overwrite your original data set with the subset.**

80 p104a03s

4.08 Short Answer Poll – Correct Answer

Which footnote or footnotes appear in the second procedure output?

a.
```
Non Sales Employees
```

b. (circled)
```
Orion Star
Non Sales Employees
```

c.
```
Non Sales Employees
Confidential
```

d.
```
Orion Star
Non Sales Employees
Confidential
```

```
footnote1 'Orion Star';
footnote2 'Sales Employees';
footnote3 'Confidential';
proc print data=orion.sales;
run;

footnote2 'Non Sales Employees';
proc print data=orion.nonsales;
run;
```

104

Copyright © 2016, SAS Institute Inc., Cary, North Carolina, USA. ALL RIGHTS RESERVED.

Copyright © 2016, SAS Institute Inc., Cary, North Carolina, USA. ALL RIGHTS RESERVED.

Chapter 5 Formatting Data Values

Copyright © 2016, SAS Institute Inc., Cary, North Carolina, USA. ALL RIGHTS RESERVED.

5.1 Using SAS Formats

Objectives

- Describe SAS formats.
- Apply SAS formats with the FORMAT statement.

3

Business Scenario

Enhance the appearance of variable values in reports.

Last_Name	First_ Name	Country	Job_Title	Salary	Hire_ Date
Zhou	Tom	AU	Sales Manager	108255	12205
Dawes	Wilson	AU	Sales Manager	87975	6575
Elvish	Irenie	AU	Sales Rep. II	26600	6575

Last_Name	First_ Name	Country	Job_Title	Salary	Hire_Date
Zhou	Tom	AU	Sales Manager	$108,255	06/01/1993
Dawes	Wilson	AU	Sales Manager	$87,975	01/01/1978
Elvish	Irenie	AU	Sales Rep. II	$26,600	01/01/1978

4

Copyright © 2016, SAS Institute Inc., Cary, North Carolina, USA. ALL RIGHTS RESERVED.

SAS Formats

SAS formats can be used in a PROC step to change how values are displayed in a report.

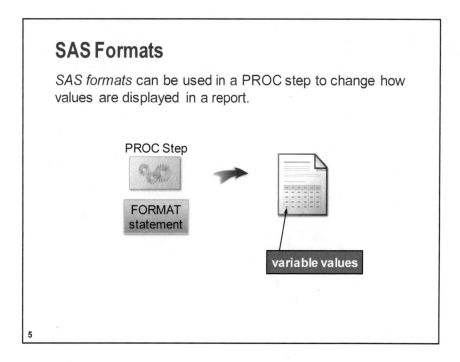

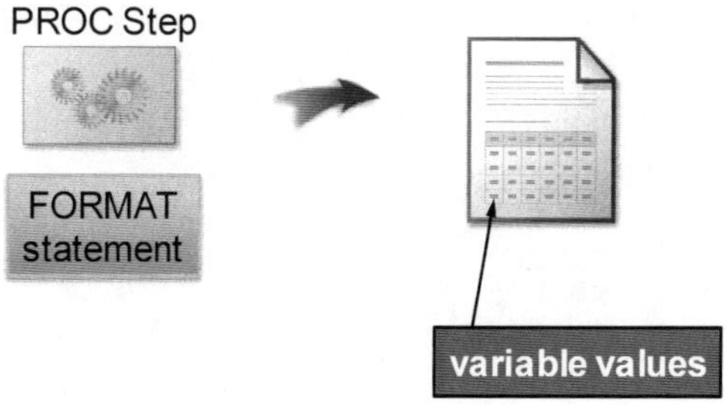

5

FORMAT Statement

The *FORMAT statement* associates a format with a variable.

```
proc print data=orion.sales noobs;
   format Salary dollar8. Hire_Date mmddyy10.;
   var Last_Name First_Name Country
       Job_Title Salary Hire_Date;
run;
```

FORMAT *variable(s) format ...*;

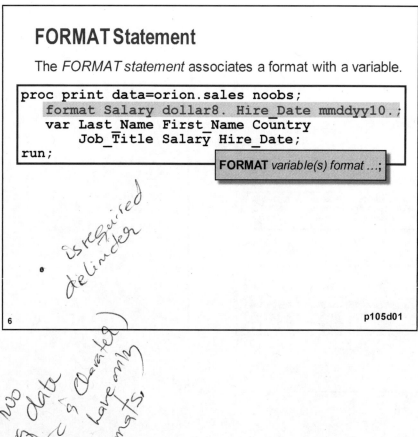

• is required delimiter

6 p105d01

As in two types of data (numeric & character) we also have only two formats.

Copyright © 2016, SAS Institute Inc., Cary, North Carolina, USA. ALL RIGHTS RESERVED.

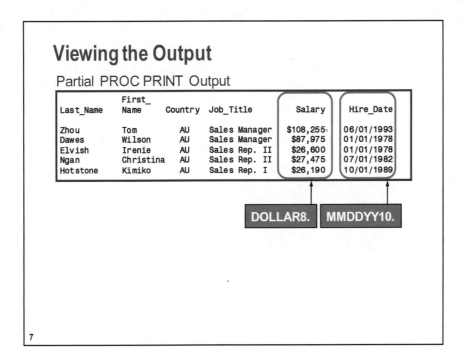

Viewing the Output

Partial PROC PRINT Output

Last_Name	First_ Name	Country	Job_Title	Salary	Hire_Date
Zhou	Tom	AU	Sales Manager	$108,255	06/01/1993
Dawes	Wilson	AU	Sales Manager	$87,975	01/01/1978
Elvish	Irenie	AU	Sales Rep. II	$26,600	01/01/1978
Ngan	Christina	AU	Sales Rep. II	$27,475	07/01/1982
Hotstone	Kimiko	AU	Sales Rep. I	$26,190	10/01/1989

DOLLAR8. MMDDYY10.

7

What Is a Format?

A *format* is an instruction to write data values.

- A format changes the appearance of a variable's value in a report.
- The values stored in the data set are ***not*** changed.

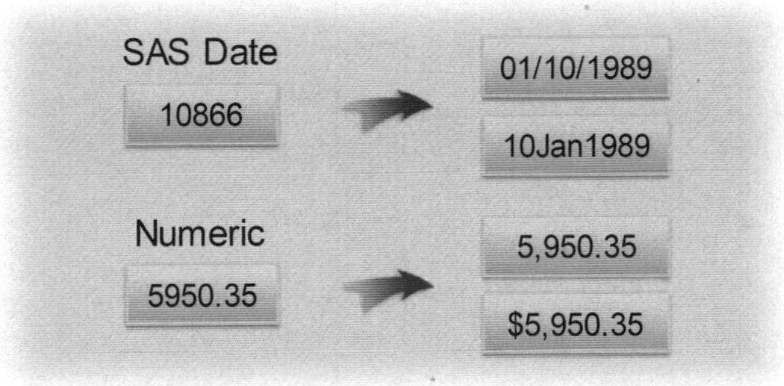

8

Copyright © 2016, SAS Institute Inc., Cary, North Carolina, USA. ALL RIGHTS RESERVED.

SAS Formats

SAS formats have the following form:

<$>format<w>.<d>

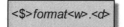

$	Indicates a character format.
format	Names the SAS format.
w	Specifies the total format width, including decimal places and special characters.
.	Is required syntax. Formats always contain a period (.) as part of the name.
d	Specifies the number of decimal places to display in numeric formats.

9

SAS Formats

Selected SAS formats:

Format	Definition
$*w.*	Writes standard character data.
w.D	Writes standard numeric data.
COMMA*w.d*	Writes numeric values with a comma that separates every three digits and a period that separates the decimal fraction.
DOLLAR*w.d*	Writes numeric values with a leading dollar sign, a comma that separates every three digits, and a period that separates the decimal fraction.
COMMAX*w.d*	Writes numeric values with a period that separates every three digits and a comma that separates the decimal fraction.
EUROX*w.d*	Writes numeric values with a leading euro symbol (€), a period that separates every three digits, and a comma that separates the decimal fraction.

10

Copyright © 2016, SAS Institute Inc., Cary, North Carolina, USA. ALL RIGHTS RESERVED.

SAS Format Examples

Selected SAS formats:

Format	Stored Value	Displayed Value
$4.	Programming	Prog
12.	27134.5864	27135
12.2	27134.5864	27134.59
COMMA12.2	27134.5864	27,134.59
DOLLAR12.2	27134.5864	$27,134.59
COMMAX12.2	27134.5864	27.134,59
EUROX12.2	27134.5864	€27.134,59

11

SAS Format Examples

If the format width is not large enough to accommodate a numeric value, the displayed value is automatically adjusted to fit the width.

Format	Stored Value	Displayed Value
DOLLAR12.2	27134.5864	$27,134.59
DOLLAR9.2	27134.5864	$27134.59
DOLLAR8.2	27134.5864	27134.59
DOLLAR5.2	27134.5864	27135
DOLLAR4.2	27134.5864	27E3

12

One aspect of the adjustment is rounding.

Copyright © 2016, SAS Institute Inc., Cary, North Carolina, USA. ALL RIGHTS RESERVED.

5.01 Short Answer Poll

Use SAS documentation or the SAS Help Facility to explore the *Zw.d* numeric format. What is it used for?

Hint: Search for *Zw.d* or explore “Formats by Category.”

The Zw.d format writes standard numeric data with leading zeros. It is similar to w.d.

13

SAS Date Format Examples

SAS date formats display SAS date values in standard date forms.

Format	Stored Value	Displayed Value
MMDDYY10.	0	01/01/1960
MMDDYY8.	0	01/01/60
MMDDYY6.	0	010160
DDMMYY10.	365	31/12/1960
DDMMYY8.	365	31/12/60
DDMMYY6.	365	311260

15

Copyright © 2016, SAS Institute Inc., Cary, North Carolina, USA. ALL RIGHTS RESERVED.

SAS Date Format Examples

Additional date formats:

Format	Stored Value	Displayed Value
DATE7.	-1	31DEC59
DATE9.	-1	31DEC1959
WORDDATE.	0	January 1, 1960
WEEKDATE.	0	Friday, January 1, 1960
MONYY7.	0	JAN1960
YEAR4.	0	1960

16

5.02 Short Answer Poll

Which FORMAT statement creates the output shown below?

a.
```
format Birth_Date Hire_Date mmddyy10.
       Term_Date monyy7.;
```

b.
```
format Birth_Date Hire_Date ddmmyyyy.
       Term_Date mmmyyyy.;
```

c.
```
format Birth_Date Hire_Date ddmmyy10.
       Term_Date monyy7.;
```

output

Birth_Date	Hire_Date	Term_Date
21/05/1969	15/10/1992	MAR2007

17

Copyright © 2016, SAS Institute Inc., Cary, North Carolina, USA. ALL RIGHTS RESERVED.

Format	Locale	Example
NLDATE*w.*	English_UnitedStates	`January 01, 1960`
	German_Germany	`01. Januar 1960`
NLDATEMN*w.*	English_UnitedStates	`January`
	German_Germany	`Januar`
NLDATEW*w.*	English_UnitedStates	`Fri, Jan 01, 60`
	German_Germany	`Fr, 01. Jan 60`
NLDATEWN*w.*	English_UnitedStates	`Friday`
	German_Germany	`Freitag`

National Language Support (NLS) enables a software product to function properly in every global market for which the product is targeted. SAS contains NLS features to ensure that SAS applications conform to local language conventions.

NLS date formats convert SAS date values to a locale-sensitive date string. The LOCALE= system option is used to specify the locale, which reflects the local conventions, language, and culture of a geographical region. For example, a locale value of *English_Canada* represents the country of Canada with a language of English. A locale value of *French_Canada* represents the country of Canada with a language of French.

The LOCALE= system option can be specified in a configuration file, at SAS invocation, or in the OPTIONS statement. For more information, refer to *SAS® 9.3 National Language Support Reference Guide* in the SAS documentation.

Copyright © 2016, SAS Institute Inc., Cary, North Carolina, USA. ALL RIGHTS RESERVED.

Exercises

If you restarted your SAS session since the last exercise, open and submit the **libname.sas** program, which can be found in the data folder.

Level 1

1. Displaying Formatted Values in a Detail Report

a. Open **p105e01** and submit it. Review the output.

b. Modify the PROC PRINT step to display only **Employee_ID**, **Salary**, **Birth_Date**, and **Employee_Hire_Date**.

c. Add a FORMAT statement to display **Salary** in a DOLLAR format, **Birth_Date** in the 01/31/2012 date style, and **Employee_Hire_Date** in the 01JAN2012 date style, as shown in the report below.

```
                                                    Employee_
Obs     Employee_ID          Salary     Birth_Date    Hire_Date

  1          120101     $163,040.00     08/18/1980    01JUL2007
  2          120102     $108,255.00     08/11/1973    01JUN1993
  3          120103      $87,975.00     01/22/1953    01JAN1978
...
423          121147      $29,145.00     05/28/1973    01SEP1991
424          121148      $52,930.00     01/01/1973    01JAN2002
```

Level 2

2. Displaying Formatted Values in a Detail Report

Write a PROC PRINT step to display the report below using **orion.sales** as input. Subset the observations and variables to produce the report. Include titles, labels, and formats. The results contain 13 observations.

```
                          US Sales Employees
                        Earning Under $26,000

                 First                                                Date
Employee_ID      Name         Last Name      Title          Salary     Hired

     121036      Teresa       Mesley        Sales Rep. I    $25,965    OCT2007
     121038      David        Anstey        Sales Rep. I    $25,285    AUG2010
     121044      Ray          Abbott        Sales Rep. I    $25,660    AUG1979
       ...
     121106      James        Hilburger     Sales Rep. I    $25,880    FEB2000
     121108      Libby        Levi          Sales Rep. I    $25,930    NOV2010
```

Copyright © 2016, SAS Institute Inc., Cary, North Carolina, USA. ALL RIGHTS RESERVED.

Challenge

3. Exploring Formats by Category

Display **orion.sales** as shown in the report below. Refer to SAS Help or product documentation to explore the **Dictionary of Formats** and investigate **Formats by Category**. Identify and use the character format that displays values in uppercase and a format that displays a character value in quotation marks. The results contain 165 observations.

```
                First_
Employee_ID     Name         Last_Name       Job_Title

     120102     TOM          ZHOU            "Sales Manager"
     120103     WILSON       DAWES           "Sales Manager"
     120121     IRENIE       ELVISH          "Sales Rep. II"
     ...
     121144     RENEE        CAPACHIETTI     "Sales Manager"
     121145     DENNIS       LANSBERRY       "Sales Manager"
```

End of Exercises

Copyright © 2016, SAS Institute Inc., Cary, North Carolina, USA. ALL RIGHTS RESERVED.

5.2 User-Defined Formats

Objectives

- Use the FORMAT procedure to create user-defined formats.
- Use a FORMAT statement to apply user-defined formats in a report.
- Use formats to recode data values.
- Use formats to collapse or aggregate data.

22

Business Scenario

Display country names instead of country codes in a report.

Current Report (partial output)

Obs	Employee_ID	Salary	Country	Birth_ Date	Hire_ Date
1	120102	$108,255	AU	AUG1973	JUN1993
2	120103	$87,975	AU	JAN1953	JAN1978
3	120121	$26,600	AU	AUG1948	JAN1978

Desired Report (partial output)

Obs	Employee_ID	Salary	Country	Birth_ Date	Hire_ Date
1	120102	$108,255	Australia	AUG1973	JUN1993
2	120103	$87,975	Australia	JAN1953	JAN1978
3	120121	$26,600	Australia	AUG1948	JAN1978

p105d02

23

Copyright © 2016, SAS Institute Inc., Cary, North Carolina, USA. ALL RIGHTS RESERVED.

User-Defined Formats: Part 1

Use PROC FORMAT to create a user-defined format.

```
proc format;
   value $ctryfmt  'AU'='Australia'
                   'US'='United States'
                  other='Miscoded';
run;
```

```
PROC FORMAT;
    VALUE format-name range1 = 'label '
                      range2 = 'label '
                       . . . ;
RUN;
```

24 p105d03

User-Defined Formats: Part 2

Use a FORMAT statement in the PROC PRINT step to apply the format to a specific variable.

```
proc print data=orion.sales;
   var Employee_ID Salary Country
       Birth_Date Hire_Date;
   format Salary dollar10.
          Birth_Date Hire_Date monyy7.
          Country $ctryfmt.;
run;
```

25 p105d03

Copyright © 2016, SAS Institute Inc., Cary, North Carolina, USA. ALL RIGHTS RESERVED.

Viewing the Output

Partial PROC PRINT Output

Obs	Employee_ID	Salary	Country	Birth_ Date	Hire_ Date
1	120102	$108,255	Australia	AUG1973	JUN1993
2	120103	$87,975	Australia	JAN1953	JAN1978
3	120121	$26,600	Australia	AUG1948	JAN1978
4	120122	$27,475	Australia	JUL1958	JUL1982
5	120123	$26,190	Australia	SEP1968	OCT1989

26

VALUE Statement

VALUE *format-name range1*='*label*'
range2='*label*'
. . . ;

A format name

- can be up to 32 characters in length
- for character formats, must begin with a dollar sign ($), followed by a letter or underscore
- for numeric formats, must begin with a letter or underscore
- cannot end in a number
- cannot be given the name of a SAS format
- cannot include a period in the VALUE statement.

27

Copyright © 2016, SAS Institute Inc., Cary, North Carolina, USA. ALL RIGHTS RESERVED.

VALUE Statement

VALUE *format-name range1='label'*
range2='label'
. . . ;

Each range can be

- a single value
- a range of values
- a list of values.

Labels

- can be up to 32,767 characters in length
- are enclosed in quotation marks.

28

Enclosing labels in quotation marks is a best practice, and it is required if a label contains internal blanks.

5.03 Multiple Answer Poll

Which names are invalid for user-defined formats?

a. $stfmt
b. $3levels
c. _4years
d. salranges
e. dollar

↳ Same as SAS supplied format

29

Copyright © 2016, SAS Institute Inc., Cary, North Carolina, USA. ALL RIGHTS RESERVED.

Defining a Character Format

character format name | discrete character values

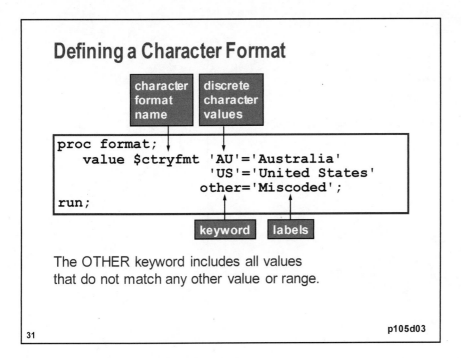

```
proc format;
   value $ctryfmt 'AU'='Australia'
                  'US'='United States'
                 other='Miscoded';
run;
```

keyword | labels

The OTHER keyword includes all values that do not match any other value or range.

31 p105d03

Applying a Format

User-defined and SAS formats can be applied in a single FORMAT statement.

```
proc print data=orion.sales label;
   var Employee_ID Salary Country
       Birth_Date Hire_Date;
   format Salary dollar10.
          Birth_Date Hire_Date monyy7.
          Country $ctryfmt.;
run;
```

✎ A period (for example, at the end of the $CTRYFMT format) is required when user-defined formats are used in a FORMAT statement.

32 p105d03

Copyright © 2016, SAS Institute Inc., Cary, North Carolina, USA. ALL RIGHTS RESERVED.

Idea Exchange

The formatting examples shown in this section are sometimes referred to as *translating values*.

Can you give an example of where this type of application might be useful?

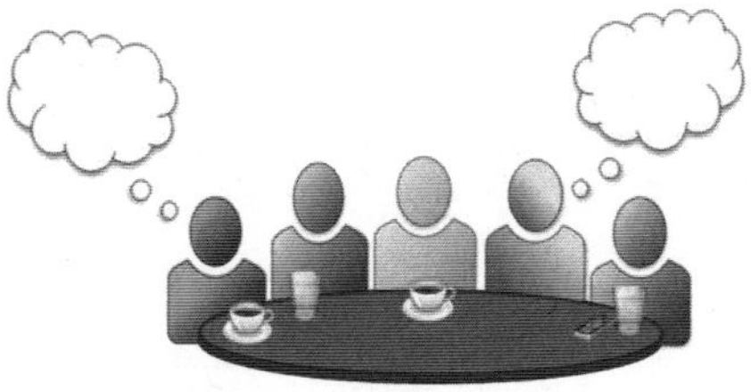

33

Business Scenario

An Orion Star manager wants a report that shows employee salaries collapsed into three user-defined groups or tiers.

Current Report

Obs	Employee_ID	Last_Name	Salary
1	120102	Zhou	108255
2	120103	Dawes	87975
3	120121	Elvish	26600
4	120122	Ngan	27475

Desired Report

Obs	Employee_ID	Last_Name	Salary
1	120102	Zhou	Tier 3
2	120103	Dawes	Tier 2
3	120121	Elvish	Tier 1
4	120122	Ngan	Tier 1

35

Copyright © 2016, SAS Institute Inc., Cary, North Carolina, USA. ALL RIGHTS RESERVED.

Specifying Ranges of Values

Use PROC FORMAT to specify the salary range for each tier.

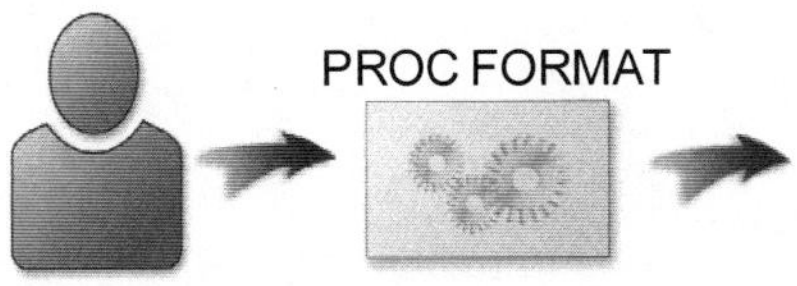

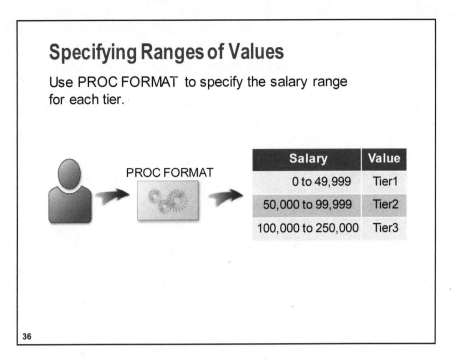

Salary	Value
0 to 49,999	Tier1
50,000 to 99,999	Tier2
100,000 to 250,000	Tier3

36

Defining a Numeric Format

numeric ranges

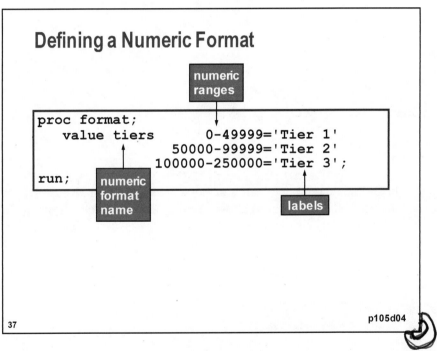

```
proc format;
   value tiers       0-49999='Tier 1'
                 50000-99999='Tier 2'
               100000-250000='Tier 3';
run;
```

numeric format name

labels

37 p105d04

Copyright © 2016, SAS Institute Inc., Cary, North Carolina, USA. ALL RIGHTS RESERVED.

Defining and Using a Numeric Format

p105d04

This demonstration illustrates the use of a user-defined numeric format.

```
proc format;
   value tiers      0-49999 ='Tier 1'
                50000-99999 ='Tier 2'
              100000-250000='Tier 3';
run;

data work.salaries;
   input Name $ Salary;
   Original_Salary=Salary;
   datalines;
Abi 50000
Mike 65000
Jose 50000.00
Joe 37000.50
Ursula 142000
Lu 49999.99
;

proc print data=work.salaries;
   format Salary tiers.;
run;
```

1. Program **p105d04** includes a PROC FORMAT step to create the TIERS format. The DATA step reads data lines within the program to create a data set that contains names and salaries. The PROC PRINT step displays the new data set, and applies the TIERS format. In the program, notice that **Salary** is assigned to **Original_Salary** so that both can be included in the report. (The assignment statement is discussed in a later chapter.)

2. Look at the data values and predict what label should be displayed when the TIERS format is applied to **Salary**. Lu's salary falls within a "gap."

Name	Salary	Coded Salary
Abi	50000	
Mike	65000	
Jose	50000.00	
Joe	37000.50	
Ursula	142000	
Lu	49999.99	

Copyright © 2016, SAS Institute Inc., Cary, North Carolina, USA. ALL RIGHTS RESERVED.

3. Submit the program. What **Salary** value is displayed for Lu? ______________________

   When a value does not match any of the ranges, PROC PRINT attempts to display the actual value. In this case, the column width was determined by the width of the formatted values, which is 6. As mentioned earlier, if the format width is not large enough to accommodate a numeric value, the displayed value is automatically adjusted to fit in the width. What can you do to correct this?

   ____

4. Specify a width of 8 in the TIERS format in the FORMAT statement and resubmit the program.

```
proc print data=work.salaries;
   format Salary tiers8.;
run;
```

   Now what **Salary** value is displayed for Lu? ______________________

End of Demonstration

Copyright © 2016, SAS Institute Inc., Cary, North Carolina, USA. ALL RIGHTS RESERVED.

Defining a Continuous Range

The less than (<) symbol excludes the endpoint from a range, which enables a continuous range.

- Put < after the starting value in a range to exclude it.
- Put < before the ending value in a range to exclude it.

Range	Starting Value	Ending Value
50000 - 100000	Includes 50000	Includes 100000
50000 - < 100000	Includes 50000	Excludes 100000
50000 < - 100000	Excludes 50000	Includes 100000
50000 < - < 100000	Excludes 50000	Excludes 100000

39

The < symbol is used to define an exclusive range. The > symbol is not permitted in a VALUE statement.

5.04 Short Answer Poll

How is a value of *50000* displayed if the TIERS format below is applied to the value?

a. Tier 1
b. Tier 2
c. 50000
d. a missing value

```
proc format;
   value tiers  20000-<50000 ='Tier 1'
                50000-<100000='Tier 2'
                100000-250000='Tier 3';
run;
```

40 p105d05

Copyright © 2016, SAS Institute Inc., Cary, North Carolina, USA. ALL RIGHTS RESERVED.

LOW and HIGH Keywords

the lowest possible value

```
proc format;
   value tiers     low-<50000 ='Tier 1'
                 50000-<100000='Tier 2'
                100000-high    ='Tier 3';
run;
```

the highest possible value

The LOW keyword

- includes missing values for character variables
- does not include missing values for numeric variables.

42 p105d06

Applying a Numeric Format

Part 1

```
proc format;
   value tiers     low-<50000 ='Tier 1'
                 50000-<100000='Tier 2'
                 100000-high  ='Tier 3';
run;
```

Part 2

```
proc print data=orion.sales;
   var Employee_ID Job_Title Salary
       Country Birth_Date Hire_Date;
   format Birth_Date Hire_Date monyy7.
          Salary tiers.;
run;
```

43 p105d06

Copyright © 2016, SAS Institute Inc., Cary, North Carolina, USA. ALL RIGHTS RESERVED.

Viewing the Output

Partial PROC PRINT Output

Obs	Employee_ID	Job_Title	Salary	Country	Birth_ Date	Hire_ Date
1	120102	Sales Manager	Tier 3	AU	AUG1973	JUN1993
2	120103	Sales Manager	Tier 2	AU	JAN1953	JAN1978
3	120121	Sales Rep. II	Tier 1	AU	AUG1948	JAN1978
4	120122	Sales Rep. II	Tier 1	AU	JUL1958	JUL1982
5	120123	Sales Rep. I	Tier 1	AU	SEP1968	OCT1989

44

User-Defined Format Example

Ranges can be specified using lists, ranges, discrete values, and keywords.

```
proc format;
   value mnthfmt 1,2,3='Qtr 1'
                   4-6='Qtr 2'
                   7-9='Qtr 3'
                 10-12='Qtr 4'
                     .='missing'
                 other='unknown';
run;
```

45

Copyright © 2016, SAS Institute Inc., Cary, North Carolina, USA. ALL RIGHTS RESERVED.

Multiple User-Defined Formats

Multiple VALUE statements can be included in a single PROC FORMAT step.

```
proc format;
   value $ctryfmt  'AU'='Australia'
                   'US'='United States'
                  other='Miscoded';

   value tiers      low-<50000 ='Tier 1'
                  50000-<100000='Tier 2'
                  100000-high  ='Tier 3';
run;
```

46 p105d07

Viewing the Output

```
proc print data=orion.sales;
   var Employee_ID Job_Title Salary
       Country Birth_Date Hire_Date;
   format Birth_Date Hire_Date monyy7.
          Country $ctryfmt.
          Salary tiers.;
run;
```

Partial PROC PRINT Output

Obs	Employee_ID	Job_Title	Salary	Country	Birth_ Date	Hire_ Date
1	120102	Sales Manager	Tier 3	Australia	AUG1973	JUN1993
2	120103	Sales Manager	Tier 2	Australia	JAN1953	JAN1978
3	120121	Sales Rep. II	Tier 1	Australia	AUG1948	JAN1978
4	120122	Sales Rep. II	Tier 1	Australia	JUL1958	JUL1982
5	120123	Sales Rep. I	Tier 1	Australia	SEP1968	OCT1989

47 p105d07

Copyright © 2016, SAS Institute Inc., Cary, North Carolina, USA. ALL RIGHTS RESERVED.

Exercises

If you restarted your SAS session since the last exercise, open and submit the **libname.sas** program, which can be found in the data folder.

Level 1

4. Creating User-Defined Formats

a. Retrieve the starter program **p105e04**.

b. Add a PROC FORMAT step following the DATA step to create a character format named $GENDER that displays gender codes as follows:

F	Female
M	Male

c. In the same PROC FORMAT step, create a numeric format named MNAME that displays month numbers as follows:

1	January
2	February
3	March

d. Add a PROC PRINT step following the PROC FORMAT step to display the **Q1Birthdays** data set. Apply the two user-defined formats to the **Employee_Gender** and **BirthMonth** variables, respectively. Include the title *Employees with Birthdays in Q1*, and clear the title at the end of the program.

e. Submit the program to produce the following report. The results contain 113 observations.

```
                    Employees with Birthdays in Q1

                                     Employee_     Birth
           Obs      Employee_ID       Gender       Month

             1         120103         Male         January
             2         120107         Female       January
             3         120108         Female       February
           ...
           112         121142         Male         February
           113         121148         Male         January
```

Level 2

5. Defining Ranges in User-Defined Formats

a. Retrieve the starter program **p105e05**.

Copyright © 2016, SAS Institute Inc., Cary, North Carolina, USA. ALL RIGHTS RESERVED.

b. Create a character format named $GENDER that displays gender codes as follows:

F	Female
M	Male
Any other value	**Invalid code**

c. Create a numeric format named SALRANGE that displays salary ranges as follows:

At least 20,000 but less than 100,000	Below $100,000
At least 100,000 and up to 500,000	$100,000 or more
missing	Missing salary
Any other value	Invalid salary

d. In the PROC PRINT step, apply these two user-defined formats to the **Gender** and **Salary** variables, respectively. Submit the program to produce the following report:

Partial PROC PRINT Output

```
                    Salary and Gender Values
                   for Non-Sales Employees

Obs    Employee_ID    Job_Title                      Salary            Gender

  1       120101      Director                       $100,000 or more  Male
  2       120104      Administration Manager         Below $100,000    Female
  3       120105      Secretary I                    Below $100,000    Female
  4       120106      Office Assistant II            Missing salary    Male
  5       120107      Office Assistant III           Below $100,000    Female
  6       120108      Warehouse Assistant II         Below $100,000    Female
  7       120108      Warehouse Assistant I          Below $100,000    Female
  8       120110      Warehouse Assistant III        Below $100,000    Male
  9       120111      Security Guard II              Below $100,000    Male
 10       120112                                     Below $100,000    Female
 11       120113      Security Guard II              Below $100,000    Female
 12       120114      Security Manager               Below $100,000    Invalid code
 13       120115      Service Assistant I            Invalid salary    Male
```

Challenge

6. Exploring Format Storage Options

User-defined formats are stored in the **formats** catalog in the **Work** library, **work.formats**. Use the SAS Help Facility or product documentation to explore permanent format catalogs in PROC FORMAT.

What option enables you to store the formats in a permanent library? ____________________

What option causes SAS to look for formats in permanent libraries? ____________________

End of Exercises

Copyright © 2016, SAS Institute Inc., Cary, North Carolina, USA. ALL RIGHTS RESERVED.

5.3 Solutions

Solutions to Exercises

1. **Displaying Formatted Values in a Detail Report**

```
proc print data=orion.employee_payroll;
   var Employee_ID Salary Birth_Date Employee_Hire_Date;
   format Salary dollar11.2 Birth_Date mmddyy10.
          Employee_Hire_Date date9.;
run;
```

2. **Displaying Formatted Values in a Detail Report**

```
title1 'US Sales Employees';
title2 'Earning Under $26,000';

proc print data=orion.sales label noobs;
   where Country='US' and Salary<26000;
   var Employee_ID First_Name Last_Name Job_Title Salary
Hire_Date;
   label First_Name='First Name'
         Last_Name='Last Name'
         Job_Title='Title'
         Hire_Date='Date Hired';
   format Salary dollar10. Hire_Date monyy7.;
run;
title;
footnote;
```

3. **Exploring Formats by Category**

```
proc print data=orion.sales noobs;
   var Employee_ID First_Name Last_Name Job_Title;
   format First_Name Last_Name $upcase. Job_Title $quote.;
run;
```

4. **Creating User-Defined Formats**

```
data Q1Birthdays;
   set orion.employee_payroll;
   BirthMonth=month(Birth_Date);
   if BirthMonth le 3;
run;

proc format;
   value $gender
      'F'='Female'
      'M'='Male';
   value mname
       1='January'
       2='February'
```

Copyright © 2016, SAS Institute Inc., Cary, North Carolina, USA. ALL RIGHTS RESERVED.

```
        3='March';
run;

title 'Employees with Birthdays in Q1';
proc print data=Q1Birthdays;
   var Employee_ID Employee_Gender BirthMonth;
   format Employee_Gender $gender.
          BirthMonth mname.;
run;
title;
```

5. **Defining Ranges in User-Defined Formats**

```
proc format;
   value $gender
        'F'='Female'
        'M'='Male'
      other='Invalid code';

   value salrange   .='Missing salary'
       20000-<100000='Below $100,000'
       100000-500000='$100,000 or more'
               other='Invalid salary';
run;

title1 'Salary and Gender Values';
title2 'for Non-Sales Employees';

proc print data=orion.nonsales;
   var Employee_ID Job_Title Salary Gender;
   format Salary salrange. Gender $gender.;
run;
title;
```

6. **Exploring Format Storage Options**

   What option enables you to store the formats in a permanent library? **LIBRARY=**

   What option causes SAS to look for formats in permanent libraries? **FMTSEARCH=**

End of Solutions

Copyright © 2016, SAS Institute Inc., Cary, North Carolina, USA. ALL RIGHTS RESERVED.

Solutions to Student Activities (Polls/Quizzes)

5.01 Short Answer Poll – Correct Answer

Use SAS documentation or the SAS Help Facility to explore the *Zw.d* numeric format. What is it used for?

Hint: Search for *Zw.d* or explore "Formats by Category."

The *Zw.d* format writes standard numeric data with leading zeros. It is similar to the *w.d* format except that *Zw.d* pads right-aligned output with zeros instead of blanks.

14

5.02 Short Answer Poll – Correct Answer

Which FORMAT statement creates the output shown below?

a.
```
format Birth_Date Hire_Date mmddyy10.
       Term_Date monyy7.;
```

b.
```
format Birth_Date Hire_Date ddmmyyyy.
       Term_Date mmmyyyy.;
```

(c.)
```
format Birth_Date Hire_Date ddmmyy10.
       Term_Date monyy7.;
```

output

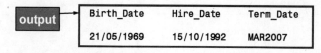

Birth_Date	Hire_Date	Term_Date
21/05/1969	15/10/1992	MAR2007

18

Copyright © 2016, SAS Institute Inc., Cary, North Carolina, USA. ALL RIGHTS RESERVED.

5.03 Multiple Answer Poll – Correct Answer

Which names are invalid for user-defined formats?

a. $stfmt
(b.) $3levels
c. _4years
d. salranges
(e.) dollar

Character formats must have a dollar sign as the first character and a letter or underscore as the second character.

User-defined formats cannot be given the name of a format provided by SAS.

30

5.04 Short Answer Poll – Correct Answer

How is a value of *50000* displayed if the TIERS format below is applied to the value?

a. Tier 1
(b.) Tier 2
c. 50000
d. a missing value

```
proc format;
   value tiers  20000-<50000 ='Tier 1'
                50000-<100000='Tier 2'
                100000-250000='Tier 3';
run;
```

41

p105d05

Copyright © 2016, SAS Institute Inc., Cary, North Carolina, USA. ALL RIGHTS RESERVED.

Copyright © 2016, SAS Institute Inc., Cary, North Carolina, USA. ALL RIGHTS RESERVED.

Chapter 6 Reading SAS® Data Sets

Copyright © 2016, SAS Institute Inc., Cary, North Carolina, USA. ALL RIGHTS RESERVED.

6.1 Reading a SAS Data Set

Objectives

- Define the business scenario that is used when you read from a data source to create a SAS data set.
- Use a DATA step to create a SAS data set from an existing SAS data set.
- Subset observations with a WHERE statement.
- Create a new variable with an assignment statement.

3

Business Scenario

Information about Orion Star sales employees resides in several input sources.

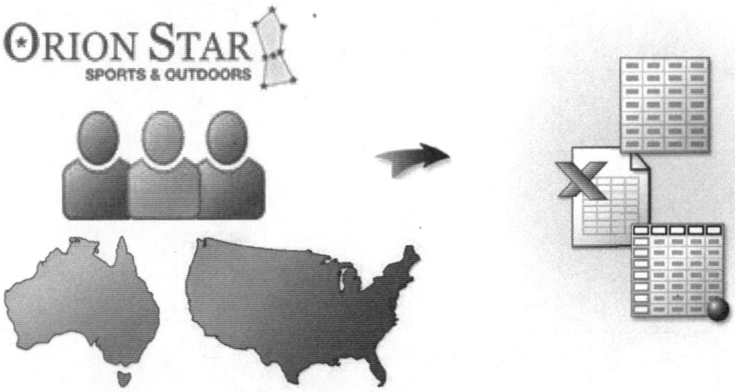

4

Copyright © 2016, SAS Institute Inc., Cary, North Carolina, USA. ALL RIGHTS RESERVED.

Considerations

Management wants a series of reports for Australian sales employees. You read data from various input sources to create a SAS data set that can be analyzed and presented.

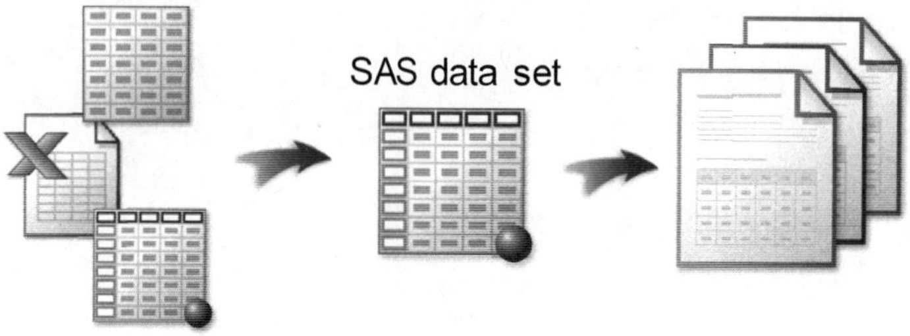

5

6.01 Multiple Answer Poll

Which types of files will you read into SAS?

a. SAS data sets
b. Excel worksheets
c. database tables
d. raw data files
e. other
f. not sure

6

Copyright © 2016, SAS Institute Inc., Cary, North Carolina, USA. ALL RIGHTS RESERVED.

Business Scenario: Part 1

Read an existing SAS data set to create a new data set. The new data set should include only the observations for the Australian sales representatives.

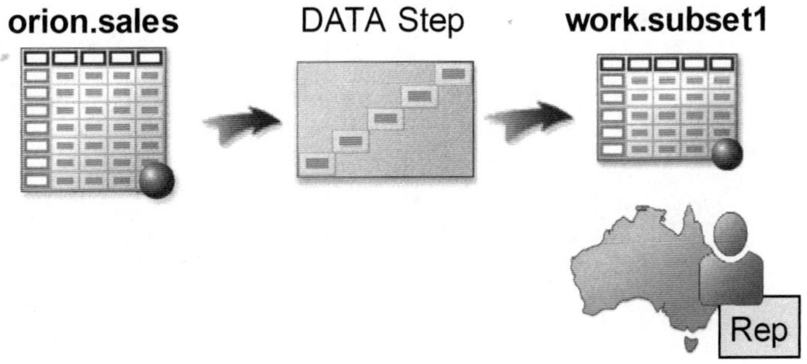

7

Using a SAS Data Set as Input

```
data work.subset1;
   set orion.sales;
   where Country='AU' and
         Job_Title contains 'Rep';
run;
```

DATA *output-SAS-data-set*;
    SET *input-SAS-data-set*;
    WHERE *WHERE-expression*;
RUN;

8 p106d01

Copyright © 2016, SAS Institute Inc., Cary, North Carolina, USA. ALL RIGHTS RESERVED.

DATA Statement

The *DATA statement* begins a DATA step and provides the name of the SAS data set to create.

```
data work.subset1;
   set orion.sales;
   where Country='AU' and
         Job_Title contains 'Rep';
run;
```

DATA *output-SAS-data-set*;

A DATA step can create temporary or permanent data sets.

✎ The rules for SAS variable names also apply to data set names.

9 p106d01

SET Statement

The *SET statement* reads observations from an existing SAS data set for further processing in the DATA step.

```
data work.subset1;
   set orion.sales;
   where Country='AU' and
         Job_Title contains 'Rep';
run;
```

SET *input-SAS-data-set*;

- The SET statement reads all observations and all variables from the input data set.
- Observations are read sequentially, one at a time.
- The SET statement can read temporary or permanent data sets.

10 p106d01

Copyright © 2016, SAS Institute Inc., Cary, North Carolina, USA. ALL RIGHTS RESERVED.

WHERE Statement

The *WHERE statement* selects observations from a SAS data set that meet a particular condition.

WHERE *WHERE-expression*;

```
data work.subset1;
   set orion.sales;
   where Country='AU' and
         Job_Title contains 'Rep';
run;
```

The variables named in the WHERE expression must exist in the input SAS data set.

p106d01

11

Using a WHERE statement might improve the efficiency of your SAS programs because SAS processes only the observations that meet the condition or conditions in the WHERE expression.

Viewing the Log

Partial SAS Log

```
42    data work.subset1;
43       set orion.sales;
44       where Country='AU' and
45             Job_Title contains 'Rep';
46    run;

NOTE: There were 61 observations read from the data set ORION.SALES.
      WHERE (Country='AU') and Job_Title contains 'Rep';
NOTE: The data set WORK.SUBSET1 has 61 observations and 9 variables.
```

SAS read 61 of the 165 observations.

12

Copyright © 2016, SAS Institute Inc., Cary, North Carolina, USA. ALL RIGHTS RESERVED.

Viewing the Output

```
proc print data=work.subset1 noobs;
run;
```

Partial PROC PRINT Output

Employee_ID	First_ Name	Last_Name	Gender	Salary	Job_Title	Country	Birth_ Date	Hire_ Date
120121	Irenie	Elvish	F	26600	Sales Rep. II	AU	-4169	6575
120122	Christina	Ngan	F	27475	Sales Rep. II	AU	-523	8217
120123	Kimiko	Hotstone	F	26190	Sales Rep. I	AU	3193	10866
120124	Lucian	Daymond	M	26480	Sales Rep. I	AU	1228	8460
120125	Fong	Hofmeister	M	32040	Sales Rep. IV	AU	-391	8460

13

p106d01

Setup for the Poll

Consider the DATA step below.

```
data us;
   set orion.sales;
   where Country='US';
run;
```

14

p106a01

Copyright © 2016, SAS Institute Inc., Cary, North Carolina, USA. ALL RIGHTS RESERVED.

6.02 Multiple Choice Poll

Considering this DATA step, which statement is true?

a. It reads a temporary data set and creates a permanent data set.
b. It reads a permanent data set and creates a temporary data set.
c. It contains a syntax error and does not execute.
d. It does not execute because you cannot work with permanent and temporary data sets in the same step.

15

Business Scenario: Part 2

Orion Star management wants to give a 10% bonus to each Australian Sales representative hired before January 1, 2000.

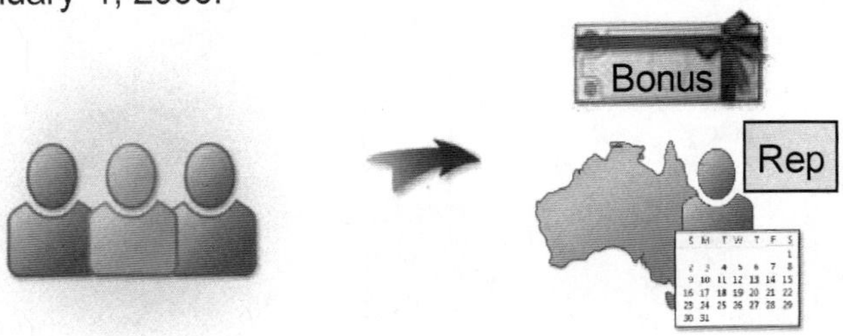

18

Copyright © 2016, SAS Institute Inc., Cary, North Carolina, USA. ALL RIGHTS RESERVED.

Considerations

Subsetting is based on **Hire_Date**, which contains a SAS date value. How can you compare a SAS date value to a calendar date?

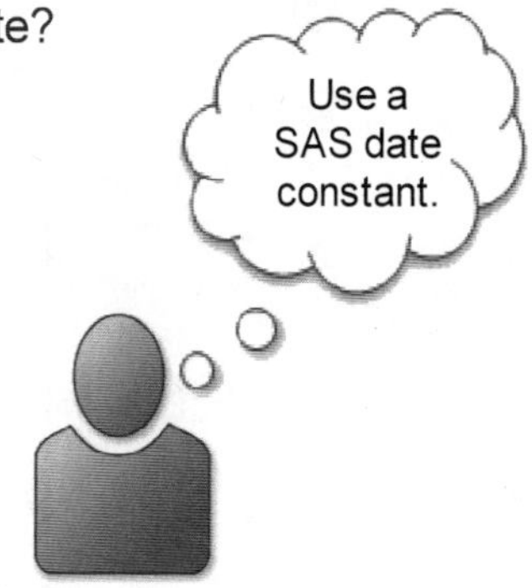

19

Date Constant

A date constant can be used in any SAS expression, including a WHERE expression.

```
data work.subset1;
   set orion.sales;
   where Country='AU' and
         Job_Title contains 'Rep' and
         Hire_Date<'01jan2000'd;
run;
```

A SAS date constant is a date written in the form **'ddmmm<yy>yy'd**.

20 p106d02

Copyright © 2016, SAS Institute Inc., Cary, North Carolina, USA. ALL RIGHTS RESERVED.

Considerations

Create a data set that includes the new variable, **Bonus**, which represents a 10% bonus.

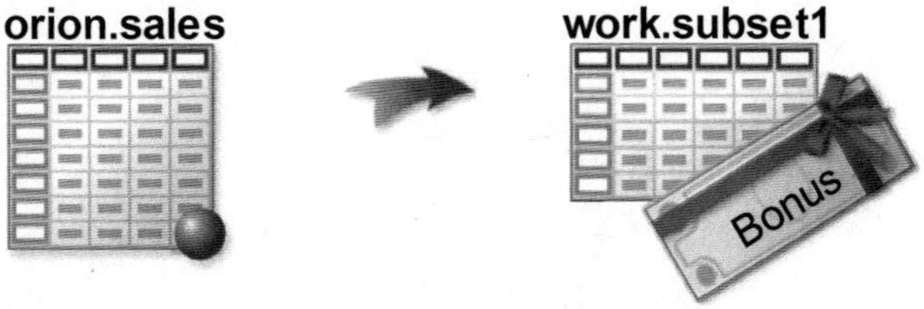

21

Assignment Statement

The *assignment statement* evaluates an expression and assigns the result to a new or existing variable.

```
data work.subset1;
   set orion.sales;
   where Country='AU' and
         Job_Title contains 'Rep' and
         Hire_Date<'01jan2000'd;
   Bonus=Salary*.10;
run;
```

variable=expression;

22 p106d02a

Copyright © 2016, SAS Institute Inc., Cary, North Carolina, USA. ALL RIGHTS RESERVED.

Assignment Statement

The *expression* consists of operands and operators.

variable=expression;

Operands

- character constants
- numeric constants
- date constants
- character variables
- numeric variables

Operators

- symbols that represent a calculation or manipulation

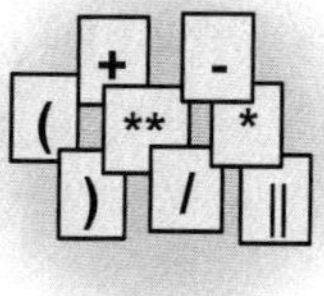

- SAS functions

23

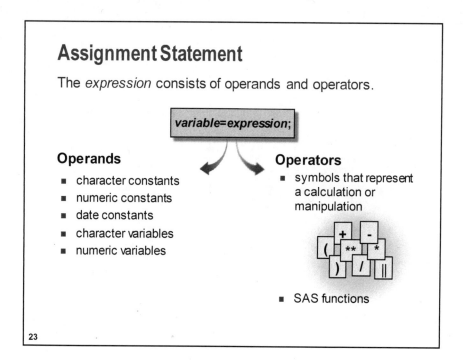

The operators can be character or arithmetic operators or SAS functions. A *function* is a routine that accepts arguments, performs a calculation or manipulation using the arguments, and returns a single value.

Sample Assignment Statements

Example	Type
`Salary=26960;`	Numeric constant
`Gender='F';`	Character constant
`Hire_Date='21JAN1995'd;`	Date constant
`BonusMonth=month(Hire_Date);`	SAS function
`Bonus=Salary*.10;`	Arithmetic expression

24

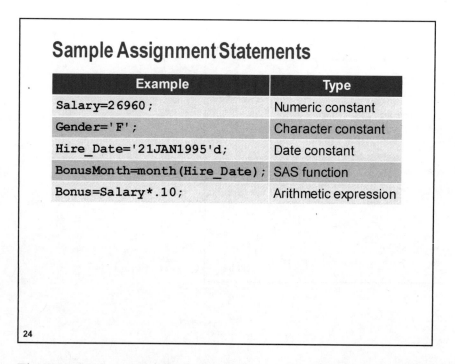

The MONTH function accepts a SAS date and returns the month portion of the date as an integer between 1 and 12. (You investigate this and other SAS functions in a later chapter.)

Copyright © 2016, SAS Institute Inc., Cary, North Carolina, USA. ALL RIGHTS RESERVED.

Arithmetic Operators

If any operand in an arithmetic expression has a missing value, the result is a missing value.

Symbol	Definition	Priority
**	Exponentiation	I
*	Multiplication	II
/	Division	II
+	Addition	III
-	Subtraction	III

Parentheses can be used to clarify or alter the order of operations in an arithmetic expression.

25

Viewing the Log

Partial SAS Log

```
data work.subset1;
   set orion.sales;
   where Country='AU' and
         Job_Title contains 'Rep' and
         Hire_Date<'01jan2000'd;
   Bonus=Salary*.10;
run;

NOTE: There were 29 observations read from the data set ORION.SALES.
      WHERE (Country='AU') and Job_Title contains 'Rep' and
      (Hire_Date<'01JAN2000'D);
NOTE: The data set WORK.SUBSET1 has 29 observations and 10 variables.
```

The input data set has 9 variables, and the new data set has 10 variables.

26

Copyright © 2016, SAS Institute Inc., Cary, North Carolina, USA. ALL RIGHTS RESERVED.

Viewing the Output

```
proc print data=work.subset1 noobs;
   var First_Name Last_Name Salary
       Job_Title Bonus Hire_Date;
   format Hire_Date date9.;
run;
```

Partial PROC PRINT Output

First_Name	Last_Name	Salary	Job_Title	Bonus	Hire_Date
Irenie	Elvish	26600	Sales Rep. II	2660.0	01JAN1978
Christina	Ngan	27475	Sales Rep. II	2747.5	01JUL1982
Kimiko	Hotstone	26190	Sales Rep. I	2619.0	01OCT1989
Lucian	Daymond	26480	Sales Rep. I	2648.0	01MAR1983
Fong	Hofmeister	32040	Sales Rep. IV	3204.0	01MAR1983

27 p106d02a

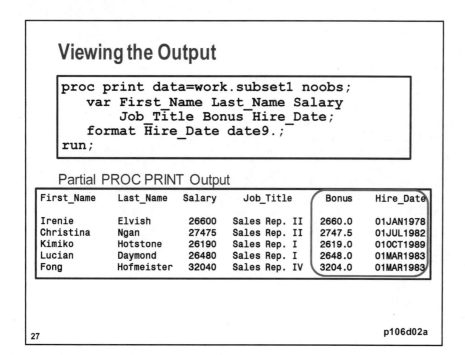

No format was specified for **Bonus**, so PROC PRINT uses a BEST*w.d* format. One decimal position is sufficient to display the values on this page.

6.03 Short Answer Poll

What are the values of **n1** and **n2** given the following variables and values?

x	y	z
.	4	10

a. `n1=y+z/2;`

b. `n2=x+z/2;`

28

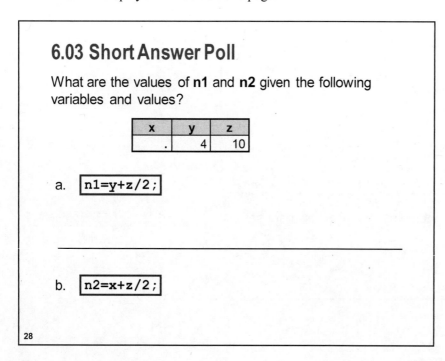

Copyright © 2016, SAS Institute Inc., Cary, North Carolina, USA. ALL RIGHTS RESERVED.

Exercises

> If you restarted your SAS session since the last exercise, open and submit the **libname.sas** program that can be found in the data folder.

Level 1

1. Creating a SAS Data Set

a. Retrieve and submit the starter program **p106e01**.

What is the name of the variable that contains gender values? Customer_Gender

What are the two observed gender values? M and F

b. Add a DATA step before the PROC PRINT step to create a new data set named **work.youngadult**. Use the data set **orion.customer_dim** as input. Include a WHERE statement to select only female customers.

Submit the program and confirm that **work.youngadult** was created with 30 observations and 11 variables.

c. Modify the program to select female customers whose ages are between 18 and 36. Submit the program and confirm that **work.youngadult** was created with 15 observations and 11 variables.

d. Modify the program to select 18- to 36-year-old female customers who have the word *Gold* in their **Customer_Group** values. Submit the program and confirm that **work.youngadult** was created with five observations and 11 variables.

e. Add an assignment statement to the DATA step to create a new variable, **Discount**, and assign it a value of *.25*.

f. Modify the PROC PRINT step to print the new data set as shown below. Use an ID statement to display **Customer_ID** instead of the Obs column. Results should contain five observations.

Customer_ID	Customer_Name	Customer_ Age	Customer_ Gender	Customer_Group	Discount
5	Sandrina Stephano	28	F	Orion Club Gold members	0.25
9	Cornelia Krahl	33	F	Orion Club Gold members	0.25
45	Dianne Patchin	28	F	Orion Club Gold members	0.25
49	Annmarie Leveille	23	F	Orion Club Gold members	0.25
2550	Sanelisiwe Collier	19	F	Orion Club Gold members	0.25

Level 2

2. Creating a SAS Data Set

a. Write a DATA step to create a new data set named **work.assistant**. Use the data set **orion.staff** as input.

Copyright © 2016, SAS Institute Inc., Cary, North Carolina, USA. ALL RIGHTS RESERVED.

b. The **work.assistant** data set should contain only the observations where **Job_Title** contains *Assistant* and **Salary** is less than *$26,000*.

c. Create two new variables, **Increase** and **New_Salary**.

- **Increase** is **Salary** multiplied by 0.10.
- **New_Salary** is **Salary** added to **Increase**.

d. Generate a detail listing report as shown below. Display **Employee_ID** as the identifier in place of the Obs column. The results should contain five observations.

Employee_ID	Job_Title	Salary	Increase	New_Salary
120685	Warehouse Assistant I	$25,130.00	$2,513.00	$27,643.00
120688	Warehouse Assistant I	$25,905.00	$2,590.50	$28,495.50
120690	Warehouse Assistant I	$25,185.00	$2,518.50	$27,703.50
121010	Service Assistant I	$25,195.00	$2,519.50	$27,714.50
121011	Service Assistant I	$25,735.00	$2,573.50	$28,308.50

Challenge

3. Using the SOUNDS-LIKE Operator to Select Observations

a. Write a DATA step to create a new data set named **work.tony**. Use **orion.customer_dim** as input.

b. Include a WHERE statement in the DATA step to select observations in which the **Customer_FirstName** value sounds like *Tony*.

> Documentation about the SOUNDS-LIKE operator can be found in the SAS Help Facility or product documentation by searching for "sounds-like operator."

c. Write a PROC PRINT step to create the following report:

Obs	Customer_ FirstName	Customer_ LastName
1	Tonie	Asmussen
2	Tommy	Mcdonald

End of Exercises

Copyright © 2016, SAS Institute Inc., Cary, North Carolina, USA. ALL RIGHTS RESERVED.

6.2 Customizing a SAS Data Set

Objectives

- Subset variables by using the DROP and KEEP statements.
- Explore the compilation and execution phases of the DATA step.
- Store labels and formats in the descriptor portion of a SAS data set.

33

Business Scenario: Part 3

All Australian sales representatives receive a bonus, regardless of hire date. The new data set should contain a subset of the variables from the input data set.

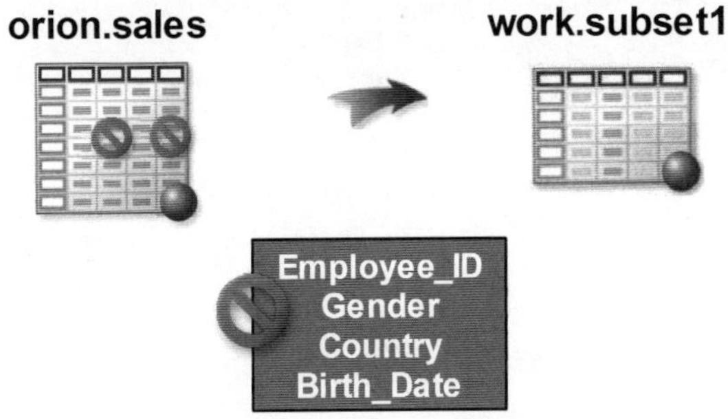

34

Copyright © 2016, SAS Institute Inc., Cary, North Carolina, USA. ALL RIGHTS RESERVED.

DROP Statement

The DROP statement specifies the variables to ***exclude*** from the output data set.

```
data work.subset1;
   set orion.sales;
   where Country='AU' and
         Job_Title contains 'Rep';
   Bonus=Salary*.10;
   drop Employee_ID Gender Country
        Birth_Date;
run;
```

DROP *variable-list*;

Partial SAS Log

```
NOTE: There were 61 observations read from the data set ORION.SALES.
      WHERE (Country='AU') and Job_Title contains 'Rep';
NOTE: The data set WORK.SUBSET1 has 61 observations and 6 variables.
```

35 p106d03

Viewing the Output

```
proc print data=work.subset1;
run;
```

Partial PROC PRINT Output

Obs	First_ Name	Last_Name	Salary	Job_Title	Hire_ Date	Bonus
1	Irenie	Elvish	26600	Sales Rep. II	6575	2660.0
2	Christina	Ngan	27475	Sales Rep. II	8217	2747.5
3	Kimiko	Hotstone	26190	Sales Rep. I	10866	2619.0
4	Lucian	Daymond	26480	Sales Rep. I	8460	2648.0
5	Fong	Hofmeister	32040	Sales Rep. IV	8460	3204.0

36 p106d03

Copyright © 2016, SAS Institute Inc., Cary, North Carolina, USA. ALL RIGHTS RESERVED.

KEEP Statement

The KEEP statement specifies all variables to ***include*** in the output data set.

```
data work.subset1;
   set orion.sales;
   where Country='AU' and
         Job_Title contains 'Rep';
   Bonus=Salary*.10;
   keep First_Name Last_Name Salary
        Job_Title Hire_Date Bonus;
run;
```

KEEP *variable-list*;

If a KEEP statement is used, it must include ***every*** variable to be written, including any new variables.

37 p106d03a

All new variables created has to be in keep statement if keep statement is used.

When you use a KEEP statement, be sure to name every variable to be written to the new SAS data set. Include any variables that are created within the step, such as **Bonus**.

Viewing the Log

Partial SAS Log

```
NOTE: There were 61 observations read from the data set ORION.SALES.
      WHERE (Country='AU') and Job_Title contains 'Rep';
NOTE: The data set WORK.SUBSET1 has 61 observations and 6 variables.
```

38

Copyright © 2016, SAS Institute Inc., Cary, North Carolina, USA. ALL RIGHTS RESERVED.

Viewing the Output

```
proc print data=work.subset1;
run;
```

Partial PROC PRINT Output

Obs	First_ Name	Last_Name	Salary	Job_Title	Hire_ Date	Bonus
1	Irenie	Elvish	26600	Sales Rep. II	6575	2660.0
2	Christina	Ngan	27475	Sales Rep. II	8217	2747.5
3	Kimiko	Hotstone	26190	Sales Rep. I	10866	2619.0
4	Lucian	Daymond	26480	Sales Rep. I	8460	2648.0
5	Fong	Hofmeister	32040	Sales Rep. IV	8460	3204.0

39 p106d03a

Business Scenario: Behind the Scenes

Orion Star programmers need to understand the internal processing that occurs when a DATA step is submitted.

41

Copyright © 2016, SAS Institute Inc., Cary, North Carolina, USA. ALL RIGHTS RESERVED.

DATA Step Processing

SAS processes the DATA step in two phases.

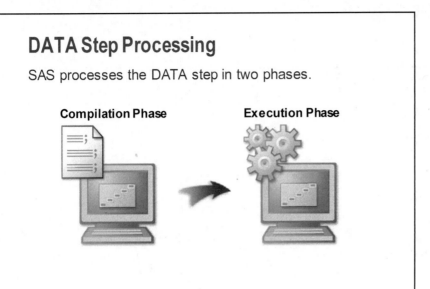

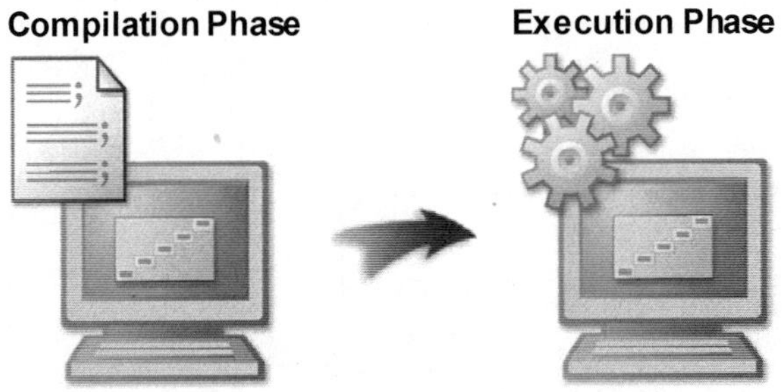

42

Compilation Phase

Scans the program for syntax errors; translates the program into machine language.

PDV

Name	Salary

Creates the *program data vector* (*PDV*) to hold one observation.

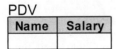

Creates the descriptor portion of the output data set.

43

Copyright © 2016, SAS Institute Inc., Cary, North Carolina, USA. ALL RIGHTS RESERVED.

Compilation

```
data work.subset1;
   set orion.sales;
   where Country='AU' and
         Job_Title contains 'Rep';
   Bonus=Salary*.10;
   drop Employee_ID Gender Country
        Birth_Date;
run;
```

44

p106d03

...

Compilation

```
data work.subset1;
   set orion.sales;
   where Country='AU' and
         Job_Title contains 'Rep';
   Bonus=Salary*.10;
   drop Employee_ID Gender Country
        Birth_Date;
run;
```

PDV

Employee_ID N 8	First_Name $ 12	Last_Name $ 18	Gender $ 1	Salary N 8	Job_Title $ 25

Country $ 2	Birth_Date N 8	Hire_Date N 8

45

...

Copyright © 2016, SAS Institute Inc., Cary, North Carolina, USA. ALL RIGHTS RESERVED.

Compilation

```
data work.subset1;
   set orion.sales;
   where Country='AU' and
         Job_Title contains 'Rep';
   Bonus=Salary*.10;
   drop Employee_ID Gender Country
        Birth_Date;
run;
```

PDV

Employee_ID N 8	First_Name $ 12	Last_Name $ 18	Gender $ 1	Salary N 8	Job_Title $ 25

Country $ 2	Birth_Date N 8	Hire_Date N 8	Bonus N 8

46 ...

Compilation

```
data work.subset1;
   set orion.sales;
   where Country='AU' and
         Job_Title contains 'Rep';
   Bonus=Salary*.10;
   drop Employee_ID Gender Country
        Birth_Date;
run;
```

PDV

Employee_ID (D) N 8	First_Name $ 12	Last_Name $ 18	Gender (D) $ 1	Salary N 8	Job_Title $ 25

Country (D) $ 2	Birth_Date (D) N 8	Hire_Date N 8	Bonus N 8

47 ...

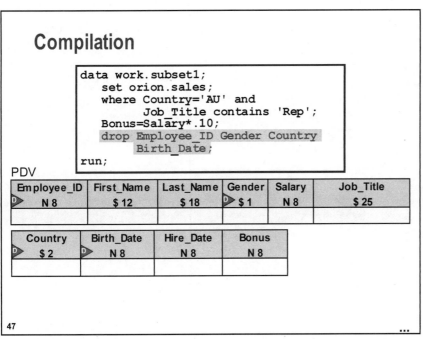

Copyright © 2016, SAS Institute Inc., Cary, North Carolina, USA. ALL RIGHTS RESERVED.

Compilation

```
data work.subset1;
   set orion.sales;
   where Country='AU' and
         Job_Title contains 'Rep';
   Bonus=Salary*.10;
   drop Employee_ID Gender Country
        Birth_Date;
run;
```

PDV

Employee_ID	First_Name	Last_Name	Gender	Salary	Job_Title
D N 8	$ 12	$ 18	D $ 1	N 8	$ 25

Country	Birth_Date	Hire_Date	Bonus
D $ 2	D N 8	N 8	N 8

Descriptor Portion of **work.subset1**

First_Name	Last_Name	Salary	Job_Title	Hire_Date	Bonus

48

Execution Phase

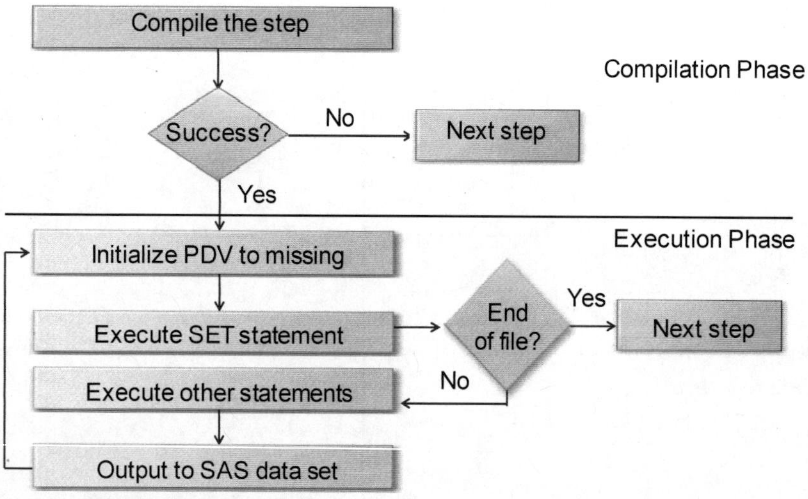

49

Copyright © 2016, SAS Institute Inc., Cary, North Carolina, USA. ALL RIGHTS RESERVED.

Execution

Partial **orion.sales**

Employee_ID	...	Hire_Date
120121		6575
120122	...	8217
120123		10866
120124		8460

Initialize PDV

```
data work.subset1;
   set orion.sales;
   where Country='AU' and
         Job_Title contains 'Rep';
   Bonus=Salary*.10;
   drop Employee_ID Gender Country
        Birth_Date;
run;
```

PDV

Employee_ID (D)	...	Salary	...	Country (D)	Birth_Date (D)	Hire_Date	Bonus
.		.			.	.	.

work.subset1

First_Name	Last_Name	Salary	Job_Title	Hire_Date	Bonus

50 ...

Execution

Partial **orion.sales**

Employee_ID	...	Hire_Date
120121		6575
120122	...	8217
120123		10866
120124		8460

```
data work.subset1;
   set orion.sales;
   where Country='AU' and
         Job_Title contains 'Rep';
   Bonus=Salary*.10;
   drop Employee_ID Gender Country
        Birth_Date;
run;
```

PDV

Employee_ID (D)	...	Salary	...	Country (D)	Birth_Date (D)	Hire_Date	Bonus
120121		26600		AU	-4169	6575	.

work.subset1

First_Name	Last_Name	Salary	Job_Title	Hire_Date	Bonus

51 ...

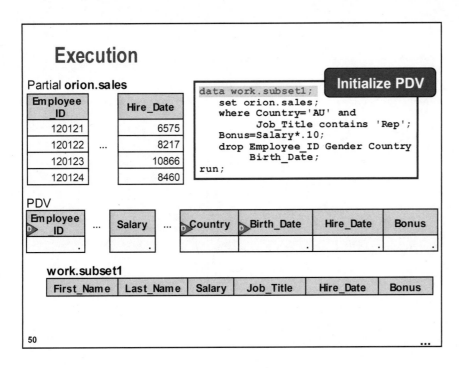

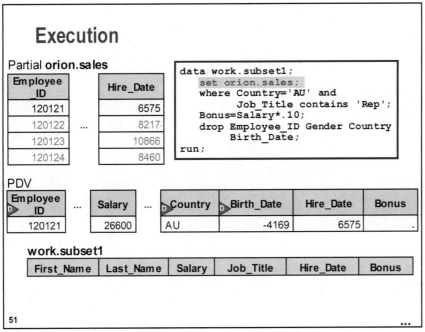

The WHERE statement is executed before the other executable statements.

Copyright © 2016, SAS Institute Inc., Cary, North Carolina, USA. ALL RIGHTS RESERVED.

Execution

Partial **orion.sales**

Employee _ID	...	Hire_Date
120121		6575
120122	...	8217
120123		10866
120124		8460

```
data work.subset1;
   set orion.sales;
   where Country='AU' and
         Job_Title contains 'Rep';
   Bonus=Salary*.10;
   drop Employee_ID Gender Country
        Birth_Date;
run;
```

PDV

Employee _ID (D)	...	Salary	...	Country (D)	Birth_Date (D)	Hire_Date	Bonus
120121		26600		AU	-4169	6575	2660

work.subset1

First_Name	Last_Name	Salary	Job_Title	Hire_Date	Bonus

52

Execution

Partial **orion.sales**

Employee _ID	...	Hire_Date
120121		6575
120122	...	8217
120123		10866
120124		8460

```
data work.subset1;
   set orion.sales;
   where Country='AU' and
         Job_Title contains 'Rep';
   Bonus=Salary*.10;
   drop Employee_ID Gender Country
        Birth_Date;
run;
```

Implicit OUTPUT;
Implicit RETURN;

PDV

Employee _ID (D)	...	Salary	...	Country (D)	Birth_Date (D)	Hire_Date	Bonus
120121		26600		AU	-4169	6575	2660

work.subset1

First_Name	Last_Name	Salary	Job_Title	Hire_Date	Bonus
Irenie	Elvish	26600	Sales Rep. II	6575	2660

53

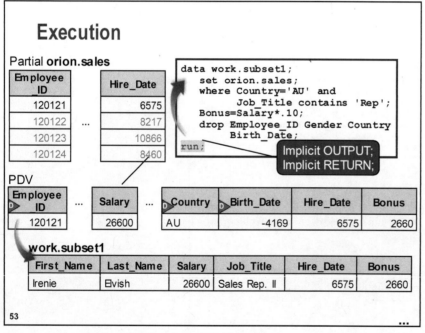

Copyright © 2016, SAS Institute Inc., Cary, North Carolina, USA. ALL RIGHTS RESERVED.

Execution

Partial **orion.sales**

Employee_ID	...	Hire_Date
120121		6575
120122		8217
120123		10866
120124		8460

Reinitialize PDV

```
data work.subset1;
   set orion.sales;
   where Country='AU' and
         Job_Title contains 'Rep';
   Bonus=Salary*.10;
   drop Employee_ID Gender Country
        Birth_Date;
run;
```

New variables are reinitialized.

PDV

Employee_ID (D)	...	Salary	...	Country (D)	Birth_Date (D)	Hire_Date	Bonus
120121		26600		AU	-4169	6575	.

work.subset1

First_Name	Last_Name	Salary	Job_Title	Hire_Date	Bonus
Irenie	Elvish	26600	Sales Rep. II	6575	2660

54 ...

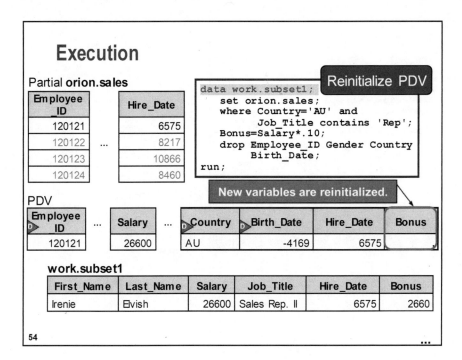

Only the new variables are reinitialized. The variables that come from the input data set are ***not*** reinitialized because they are overwritten when the next observation is read into the PDV. Values in the PDV are overwritten even if values in the next observation are missing.

Execution

Partial **orion.sales**

Employee_ID	...	Hire_Date
120121		6575
120122		8217
120123		10866
120124		8460

```
data work.subset1;
   set orion.sales;
   where Country='AU' and
         Job_Title contains 'Rep';
   Bonus=Salary*.10;
   drop Employee_ID Gender Country
        Birth_Date;
run;
```

PDV

Employee_ID (D)	...	Salary	...	Country (D)	Birth_Date (D)	Hire_Date	Bonus
120122		27475		AU	-523	8217	.

work.subset1

First_Name	Last_Name	Salary	Job_Title	Hire_Date	Bonus
Irenie	Elvish	26600	Sales Rep. II	6575	2660

55 ...

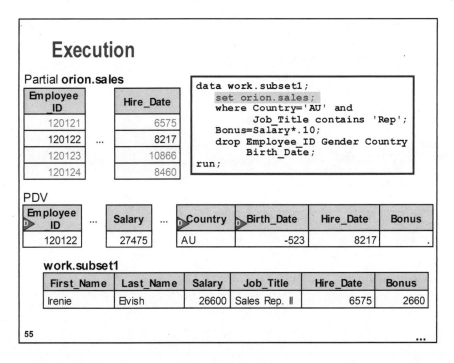

Copyright © 2016, SAS Institute Inc., Cary, North Carolina, USA. ALL RIGHTS RESERVED.

Execution

Partial **orion.sales**

Employee_ID	...	Hire_Date
120121		6575
120122	...	8217
120123		10866
120124		8460

```
data work.subset1;
   set orion.sales;
   where Country='AU' and
         Job_Title contains 'Rep';
   Bonus=Salary*.10;
   drop Employee_ID Gender Country
        Birth_Date;
run;
```

PDV

Employee_ID (D)	...	Salary	...	Country (D)	Birth_Date (D)	Hire_Date	Bonus
120122		27475		AU	-523	8217	2747.5

work.subset1

First_Name	Last_Name	Salary	Job_Title	Hire_Date	Bonus
Irenie	Elvish	26600	Sales Rep. II	6575	2660

56

...

Execution

Partial **orion.sales**

Employee_ID	...	Hire_Date
120121		6575
120122	...	8217
120123		10866
120124		8460

```
data work.subset1;
   set orion.sales;
   where Country='AU' and
         Job_Title contains 'Rep';
   Bonus=Salary*.10;
   drop Employee_ID Gender Country
        Birth_Date;
run;
```

Implicit OUTPUT;
Implicit RETURN;

PDV

Employee_ID (D)	...	Salary	...	Country (D)	Birth_Date (D)	Hire_Date	Bonus
120122		27475		AU	-523	8217	2747.5

work.subset1

First_Name	Last_Name	Salary	Job_Title	Hire_Date	Bonus
Irenie	Elvish	26600	Sales Rep. II	6575	2660.0
Christina	Ngan	27475	Sales Rep. II	8217	2747.5

57

...

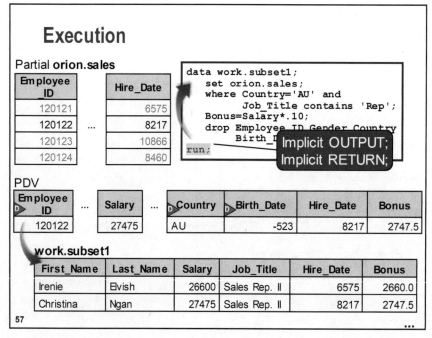

Copyright © 2016, SAS Institute Inc., Cary, North Carolina, USA. ALL RIGHTS RESERVED.

Execution

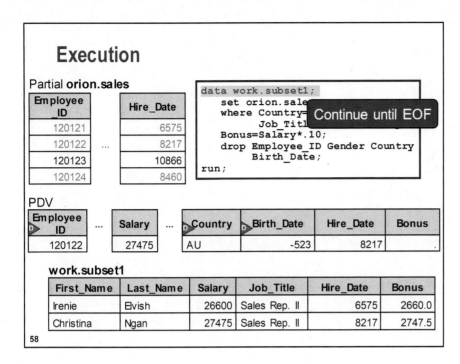

Partial **orion.sales**

Employee_ID		Hire_Date
120121	...	6575
120122		8217
120123		10866
120124		8460

```
data work.subset1;
   set orion.sale
   where Country=
         Job_Titl
   Bonus=Salary*.10;
   drop Employee_ID Gender Country
        Birth_Date;
run;
```

Continue until EOF

PDV

D Employee_ID	...	Salary	...	D Country	D Birth_Date	Hire_Date	Bonus
120122		27475		AU	-523	8217	.

work.subset1

First_Name	Last_Name	Salary	Job_Title	Hire_Date	Bonus
Irenie	Elvish	26600	Sales Rep. II	6575	2660.0
Christina	Ngan	27475	Sales Rep. II	8217	2747.5

58

Viewing the Output

```
proc print data=work.subset1;
run;
```

Partial PROC PRINT Output

Obs	First_Name	Last_Name	Salary	Job_Title	Hire_Date	Bonus
1	Irenie	Elvish	26600	Sales Rep. II	6575	2660.0
2	Christina	Ngan	27475	Sales Rep. II	8217	2747.5
3	Kimiko	Hotstone	26190	Sales Rep. I	10866	2619.0
4	Lucian	Daymond	26480	Sales Rep. I	8460	2648.0
5	Fong	Hofmeister	32040	Sales Rep. IV	8460	3204.0

59

p106d03

Copyright © 2016, SAS Institute Inc., Cary, North Carolina, USA. ALL RIGHTS RESERVED.

Business Scenario: Part 4

Create a data set that contains all Australian employees whose bonus is at least $3000.

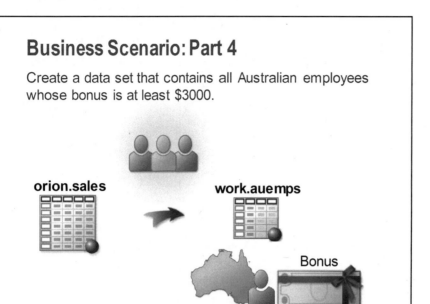

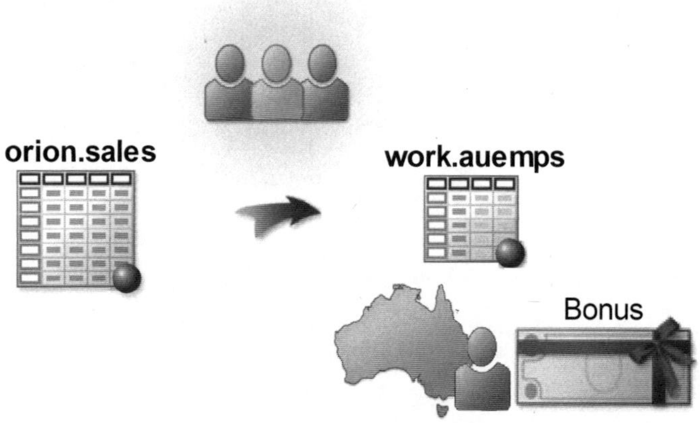

61

Selecting Observations

Subsetting is based on the new variable, **Bonus**, that is created with an assignment statement.

```
data work.auemps;
   set orion.sales;
   where Country='AU';
   Bonus=Salary*.10;
   drop Employee_ID Gender Country
        Birth_Date;
run;
```

A WHERE statement is used to subset observations when the selected variables exist in the ***input*** data set.

p106d04

62

Copyright © 2016, SAS Institute Inc., Cary, North Carolina, USA. ALL RIGHTS RESERVED.

6.04 Short Answer Poll

Open and submit **p106a03**. Is the output data set created successfully?

```
data work.usemps;
   set orion.sales;
   Bonus=Salary*.10;
   where Country='US' and Bonus>=3000;
run;
```

63 p106a03

Subsetting IF

The *subsetting IF* statement tests a condition to determine whether the DATA step should continue processing the current observation.

```
data work.auemps;
   set orion.sales;
   where Country='AU';
   Bonus=Salary*.10;
   if Bonus>=3000;
run;
```

IF *condition*;

In this program, processing reaches the bottom of the DATA step and outputs an observation only if the condition is true.

65 p106d05

Copyright © 2016, SAS Institute Inc., Cary, North Carolina, USA. ALL RIGHTS RESERVED.

Viewing the Log

Partial SAS Log

```
data work.auemps;
   set orion.sales;
   where Country='AU';
   Bonus=Salary*.10;
   if Bonus>=3000;
run;

NOTE: There were 63 observations read from the data set ORION.SALES.
      WHERE Country='AU';
NOTE: The data set WORK.AUEMPS has 12 observations and 10 variables.
```

Of the 165 observations in **orion.sales**, 63 were read into the PDV for processing, and only 12 were written to the new data set.

66

Viewing the Output

```
proc print data=work.auemps;
   var First_Name Last_Name Salary Bonus;
run;
```

PROC PRINT Output

Obs	First_ Name	Last_Name	Salary	Bonus
1	Tom	Zhou	108255	10825.5
2	Wilson	Dawes	87975	8797.5
3	Fong	Hofmeister	32040	3204.0
4	Monica	Kletschkus	30890	3089.0
5	Alvin	Roebuck	30070	3007.0
6	Alexei	Platts	32490	3249.0
7	Viney	Barbis	30265	3026.5
8	Caterina	Hayawardhana	30490	3049.0
9	Daniel	Pilgrim	36605	3660.5
10	Lynelle	Phoumirath	30765	3076.5
11	Rosette	Martines	30785	3078.5
12	Fadi	Nowd	30660	3066.0

67

Copyright © 2016, SAS Institute Inc., Cary, North Carolina, USA. ALL RIGHTS RESERVED.

Processing the Subsetting IF Statement

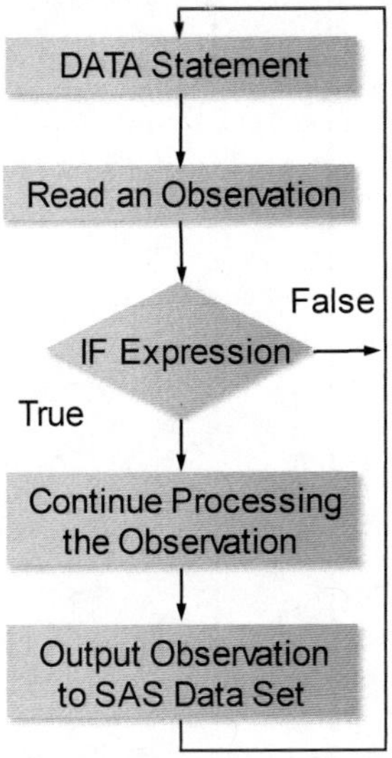

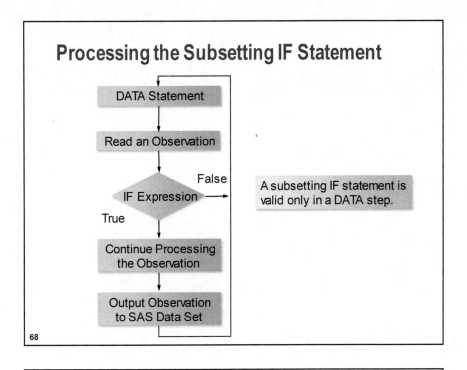

A subsetting IF statement is valid only in a DATA step.

68

Idea Exchange

File **p106a04** contains two versions of the previous program. Submit both programs and compare the output and number of observations read. What do you notice about the results?

```
data work.auemps;
   set orion.sales;
   Bonus=Salary*.10;
   if Country='AU' and Bonus>=3000;
run;
```

69

Copyright © 2016, SAS Institute Inc., Cary, North Carolina, USA. ALL RIGHTS RESERVED.

WHERE versus Subsetting IF Statement

Step and Usage	WHERE	IF
PROC step	Yes	No
DATA step (source of variable)		
SET statement	Yes	Yes
assignment statement	No	Yes

70

Business Scenario: Part 5

Define permanent labels and formats for some of the variables in the new data set.

72

Copyright © 2016, SAS Institute Inc., Cary, North Carolina, USA. ALL RIGHTS RESERVED.

LABEL Statement

The LABEL statement assigns descriptive labels to variables.

Sales Title **Date Hired**

work.subset1

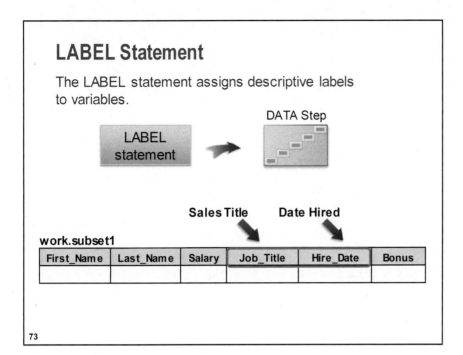

First_Name	Last_Name	Salary	Job_Title	Hire_Date	Bonus

73

Defining Permanent Labels

Use a LABEL statement in a DATA step to permanently assign labels to variables. The labels are stored in the descriptor portion of the data set.

```
data work.subset1;
   set orion.sales;
   where Country='AU' and
         Job_Title contains 'Rep';
   Bonus=Salary*.10;
   label Job_Title='Sales Title'
         Hire_Date='Date Hired';
   drop Employee_ID Gender Country
        Birth_Date;
run;
```

LABEL *variable='label '* <*variable='label '*...>;

74 **p106d06**

Copyright © 2016, SAS Institute Inc., Cary, North Carolina, USA. ALL RIGHTS RESERVED.

Viewing the Output

```
proc contents data=work.subset1;
run;
```

Partial PROC CONTENTS Output

Alphabetic List of Variables and Attributes

#	Variable	Type	Len	Label
6	Bonus	Num	8	
1	First_Name	Char	12	
5	Hire_Date	Num	8	Date Hired
4	Job_Title	Char	25	Sales Title
2	Last_Name	Char	18	
3	Salary	Num	8	

75 p106d06

Viewing the Output: Displaying Labels

To use labels in the PRINT procedure, use the LABEL option in the PROC PRINT statement.

```
proc print data=work.subset1 label;
run;
```

Partial PROC PRINT Output

Obs	First_ Name	Last_Name	Salary	Sales Title	Date Hired	Bonus
1	Irenie	Elvish	26600	Sales Rep. II	6575	2660.0
2	Christina	Ngan	27475	Sales Rep. II	8217	2747.5
3	Kimiko	Hotstone	26190	Sales Rep. I	10866	2619.0
4	Lucian	Daymond	26480	Sales Rep. I	8460	2648.0
5	Fong	Hofmeister	32040	Sales Rep. IV	8460	3204.0

76 p106d06

Copyright © 2016, SAS Institute Inc., Cary, North Carolina, USA. ALL RIGHTS RESERVED.

Viewing the Output: Splitting Labels

Use the PROC PRINT SPLIT= option to split labels across lines based on a split character.

```
proc print data=work.subset1 split=' ';
run;
```

Partial PROC PRINT Output

```
      First_                                    Sales          Date
Obs   Name         Last_Name     Salary         Title          Hired       Bonus

  1   Irenie       Elvish         26600    Sales Rep. II       6575     2660.0
  2   Christina    Ngan           27475    Sales Rep. II       8217     2747.5
  3   Kimiko       Hotstone       26190    Sales Rep. I       10866     2619.0
  4   Lucian       Daymond        26480    Sales Rep. I        8460     2648.0
  5   Fong         Hofmeister     32040    Sales Rep. IV       8460     3204.0
```

77 p106d06

PROC PRINT is the only SAS procedure that requires either the LABEL option or the SPLIT= option to use custom labels.

6.05 Short Answer Poll

What column heading is displayed for **Job_Title** in the program below?

```
data work.us;
   set orion.sales;
   where Country='US';
   Bonus=Salary*.10;
   label Job_Title='Sales Title';
   drop Employee_ID Gender Country
        Birth_Date;
run;
proc print data=work.us label;
   label Job_Title='Title';
run;
```

78 p106a05

Copyright © 2016, SAS Institute Inc., Cary, North Carolina, USA. ALL RIGHTS RESERVED.

FORMAT Statement

The FORMAT statement associates formats with variables.

commax8. ddmmyy10. commax8.2

work.subset1

First_Name	Last_Name	Salary	Job_Title	Hire_Date	Bonus
Irenie	Elvish	26600	Sales Rep. II	6575	2660.0

80

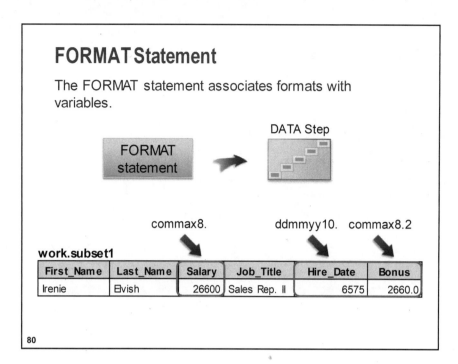

Defining Permanent Formats

Use a FORMAT statement in a DATA step to permanently associate formats with variables.

```
data work.subset1;
   set orion.sales;
   where Country='AU' and
         Job_Title contains 'Rep';
   Bonus=Salary*.10;
   label Job_Title='Sales Title'
         Hire_Date='Date Hired';
   format Salary commax8. Bonus commax8.2
          Hire_Date ddmmyy10.;
   drop Employee_ID Gender Country
        Birth_Date;
run;
```

FORMAT *variable(s) format ...;*

81 p106d07

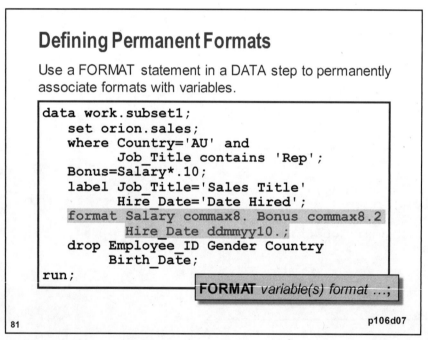

Copyright © 2016, SAS Institute Inc., Cary, North Carolina, USA. ALL RIGHTS RESERVED.

Viewing the Output

```
proc contents data=work.subset1;
run;
```

Partial PROC CONTENTS Output

Alphabetic List of Variables and Attributes

#	Variable	Type	Len	Format	Label
6	Bonus	Num	8	COMMAX8.2	
1	First_Name	Char	12		
5	Hire_Date	Num	8	DDMMYY10.	Date Hired
4	Job_Title	Char	25		Sales Title
2	Last_Name	Char	18		
3	Salary	Num	8	COMMAX8.	

82 p106d07

Viewing the Output

```
proc print data=work.subset1 label;
run;
```

Partial PROC PRINT Output

Obs	First_ Name	Last_Name	Salary	Sales Title	Date Hired	Bonus
1	Irenie	Elvish	26.600	Sales Rep. II	01/01/1978	2.660,00
2	Christina	Ngan	27.475	Sales Rep. II	01/07/1982	2.747,50
3	Kimiko	Hotstone	26.190	Sales Rep. I	01/10/1989	2.619,00
4	Lucian	Daymond	26.480	Sales Rep. I	01/03/1983	2.648,00
5	Fong	Hofmeister	32.040	Sales Rep. IV	01/03/1983	3.204,00

83 p106d07

Copyright © 2016, SAS Institute Inc., Cary, North Carolina, USA. ALL RIGHTS RESERVED.

Exercises

If you restarted your SAS session since the last exercise, open and submit the **libname.sas** program that can be found in the data folder.

Level 1

4. Subsetting Observations Based on Two Conditions

a. Retrieve the starter program **p106e04**.

b. Modify the DATA step to select only the observations with **Emp_Hire_Date** values on or after July 1, 2010. Subset the observations as they are being read into the program data vector.

c. In the DATA step, write another statement to select only the observations that have an increase greater than 3000.

d. The new data set should contain only the following variables: **Employee_ID**, **Emp_Hire_Date**, **Salary**, **Increase**, and **NewSalary**.

e. Add permanent labels for **Employee_ID**, **Emp_Hire_Date**, and **NewSalary** as shown in the report below.

f. Add permanent formats to display **Salary** and **NewSalary** with dollar signs, commas, and two decimal places, and **Increase** with commas and no decimal places.

g. Submit a PROC CONTENTS step to verify that the labels and formats are stored in the descriptor portion of the new data set, **work.increase**.

Partial PROC CONTENTS Output

Alphabetic List of Variables and Attributes

#	Variable	Type	Len	Format	Informat	Label
3	Emp_Hire_Date	Num	8	DATE9.	DATE9.	Hire Date
1	Employee_ID	Num	8	12.		Employee ID
4	Increase	Num	8	COMMA5.		
5	NewSalary	Num	8	DOLLAR10.2		New Annual Salary
2	Salary	Num	8	DOLLAR10.2		Employee Annual Salary

h. Some variables have labels and formats that were not defined in this program. How were these created? SAS default · descriptor orion.staff

i. Submit the program to create the PROC PRINT report below. Split the labels over multiple lines. Results should contain 10 observations.

Obs	Employee ID	Employee Annual Salary	Hire Date	Increase	New Annual Salary
1	120128	$30,890.00	01NOV2010	3,089	$33,979.00
2	120144	$30,265.00	01OCT2010	3,027	$33,291.50
3	120161	$30,785.00	01OCT2010	3,079	$33,863.50

Copyright © 2016, SAS Institute Inc., Cary, North Carolina, USA. ALL RIGHTS RESERVED.

```
...
 9          121085    $32,235.00    01JAN2011    3,224    $35,458.50
10          121107    $31,380.00    01JUL2010    3,138    $34,518.00
```

Level 2

5. Subsetting Observations Based on Three Conditions

a. Write a DATA step to create **work.delays**. Use **orion.orders** as input.

b. Create a new variable, **Order_Month**, and set it to the month of **Order_Date**.

   Hint: Use the MONTH function.

c. Use a WHERE statement and a subsetting IF statement to select only the observations that meet all of the following conditions:
   - **Delivery_Date** values that are more than four days beyond **Order_Date**
   - **Employee_ID** values that are equal to *99999999*
   - **Order_Month** values occurring in *August*

d. The new data set should include only **Employee_ID**, **Customer_ID**, **Order_Date**, **Delivery_Date**, and **Order_Month**.

e. Add permanent labels for **Order_Date**, **Delivery_Date**, and **Order_Month** as shown below.

f. Add permanent formats to display **Order_Date** and **Delivery_Date** as MM/DD/YYYY.

g. Add a PROC CONTENTS step to verify that the labels and formats were stored permanently.

Alphabetic List of Variables and Attributes

#	Variable	Type	Len	Format	Label
2	Customer_ID	Num	8	12.	Customer ID
4	Delivery_Date	Num	8	MMDDYY10.	Date Delivered
1	Employee_ID	Num	8	12.	Employee ID
3	Order_Date	Num	8	MMDDYY10.	Date Ordered
5	Order_Month	Num	8		Month Ordered

h. Write a PROC PRINT step to create the report below. Results should contain nine observations.

Obs	Employee_ID	Customer_ID	Order_Date	Delivery_ Date	Order_ Month
1	99999999	70187	08/13/2007	08/18/2007	8
2	99999999	52	08/20/2007	08/26/2007	8
3	99999999	16	08/27/2007	09/04/2007	8
4	99999999	61	08/29/2007	09/03/2007	8
5	99999999	2550	08/10/2008	08/15/2008	8
6	99999999	70201	08/15/2008	08/20/2008	8
7	99999999	9	08/10/2009	08/15/2009	8
8	99999999	71	08/30/2010	09/05/2010	8
9	99999999	70201	08/24/2011	08/29/2011	8

Copyright © 2016, SAS Institute Inc., Cary, North Carolina, USA. ALL RIGHTS RESERVED.

Challenge

6. Using an IF-THEN/DELETE Statement to Subset Observations

a. Write a DATA step to create **work.bigdonations**. Use **orion.employee_donations** as input.

b. Use the SUM function to create a new variable, **Total**, which holds the sum of the four quarterly donations.

c. Use the N function to create a new variable, **NumQtrs**, which holds the count of nonmissing values in **Qtr1**, **Qtr2**, **Qtr3**, and **Qtr4**. Explore the N function in the SAS Help Facility or online documentation.

d. The new data set should ***not*** include the charities or method of payment.

e. The final data set should contain only observations that meet the following two conditions:

- **Total** values greater than or equal to 50
- **NumQtrs** value equal to 4

Use an IF-THEN/DELETE statement to eliminate the observations where the conditions are not met. Explore the use of IF-THEN/DELETE in the SAS Help Facility or online documentation.

f. Store permanent labels in the new data set as shown in the report below.

g. Create the following report to verify that the labels were stored:

Alphabetic List of Variables and Attributes

#	Variable	Type	Len	Format	Label
1	Employee_ID	Num	8	12.	Employee ID
7	NumQtrs	Num	8		
2	Qtr1	Num	8		First Quarter
3	Qtr2	Num	8		Second Quarter
4	Qtr3	Num	8		Third Quarter
5	Qtr4	Num	8		Fourth Quarter
6	Total	Num	8		

h. Create the report below. The results should contain 50 observations.

Employee ID	First Quarter	Second Quarter	Third Quarter	Fourth Quarter	Total	Num Qtrs
120267	15	15	15	15	60	4
120269	20	20	20	20	80	4
120271	20	20	20	20	80	4
120275	15	15	15	15	60	4
120660	25	25	25	25	100	4

End of Exercises

Copyright © 2016, SAS Institute Inc., Cary, North Carolina, USA. ALL RIGHTS RESERVED.

6.3 Solutions

Solutions to Exercises

1. **Creating a SAS Data Set**

   What is the name of the variable that contains gender values? **Customer_Gender**

   What are the possible values of this variable? ***M* or *F***

```
data work.youngadult;
   set orion.customer_dim;
   where Customer_Gender='F' and
         Customer_Age between 18 and 36 and
         Customer_Group contains 'Gold';
   Discount=.25;
run;

proc print data=work.youngadult;
   var Customer_Name Customer_Age
       Customer_Gender Customer_Group Discount;
   id Customer_ID;
run;
```

2. **Creating a SAS Data Set**

```
data work.assistant;
   set orion.staff;
   where Job_Title contains 'Assistant' and
         Salary<26000;
   Increase=Salary*.10;
   New_Salary=Salary+Increase;
run;

proc print data=work.assistant;
   id Employee_ID;
   var Job_Title Salary Increase New_Salary;
   format Salary Increase New_Salary dollar10.2;
run;
```

3. **Using the SOUNDS-LIKE Operator to Select Observations**

```
data work.tony;
   set orion.customer_dim;
   where Customer_FirstName=* 'Tony';
run;

proc print data=work.tony;
   var Customer_FirstName Customer_LastName;
run;
```

4. **Subsetting Observations Based on Two Conditions**

Copyright © 2016, SAS Institute Inc., Cary, North Carolina, USA. ALL RIGHTS RESERVED.

```
data work.increase;
   set orion.staff;
   where Emp_Hire_Date>='01JUL2010'd;
   Increase=Salary*0.10;
   if Increase>3000;
   NewSalary=Salary+Increase;
   label Employee_ID='Employee ID'
         Salary='Annual Salary'
         Emp_Hire_Date='Hire Date'
         NewSalary='New Annual Salary';
   format Salary NewSalary dollar10.2 Increase comma5.;
   keep Employee_ID Emp_Hire_Date Salary Increase NewSalary;
run;

proc print data=work.increase split=' ';
run;
```

The existing labels and formats were inherited from the input data set.

5. **Subsetting Observations Based on Three Conditions**

```
data work.delays;
   set orion.orders;
   where Order_Date+4<Delivery_Date
         and Employee_ID=99999999;
   Order_Month=month(Order_Date);
   if Order_Month=8;
   label Order_Date='Date Ordered'
         Delivery_Date='Date Delivered'
         Order_Month='Month Ordered';
         format Order_Date Delivery_Date mmddyy10.;
   keep Employee_ID Customer_ID Order_Date Delivery_Date
        Order_Month;
run;

proc contents data=work.delays;
run;

proc print data=work.delays;
run;
```

6. **Using an IF-THEN/DELETE Statement to Subset Observations**

```
data work.bigdonations;
   set orion.employee_donations;
   Total=sum(Qtr1,Qtr2,Qtr3,Qtr4);
   NumQtrs=n(Qtr1,Qtr2,Qtr3,Qtr4);
   if Total<50 or NumQtrs<4 then delete;
   label Qtr1='First Quarter'
         Qtr2='Second Quarter'
         Qtr3='Third Quarter'
         Qtr4='Fourth Quarter';
```

Copyright © 2016, SAS Institute Inc., Cary, North Carolina, USA. ALL RIGHTS RESERVED.

```
   drop Recipients Paid_By;
run;

proc contents data=work.bigdonations;
run;

proc print data=work.bigdonations label noobs;
run;
```

End of Solutions

Copyright © 2016, SAS Institute Inc., Cary, North Carolina, USA. ALL RIGHTS RESERVED.

Solutions to Student Activities (Polls/Quizzes)

6.02 Multiple Choice Poll – Correct Answer

Considering this DATA step, which statement is true?

a. It reads a temporary data set and creates a permanent data set.

(b.) It reads a permanent data set and creates a temporary data set.

c. It contains a syntax error and does not execute.

d. It does not execute because you cannot work with permanent and temporary data sets in the same step.

```
data us;               /* Create a temporary data set */
   set orion.sales;   /* Read a permanent data set */
   where Country='US';
run;
```

16

6.03 Short Answer Poll – Correct Answer

What are the values of **n1** and **n2** given the following variables and values?

x	y	z
.	4	10

a. `n1=y+z/2;` → 4+10/2 → 4+5 → (9)

`n1=(y+z)/2;` → 14/2 → 7

b. `n2=x+z/2;` → .+10/2 → .+5 → (.)

29

Copyright © 2016, SAS Institute Inc., Cary, North Carolina, USA. ALL RIGHTS RESERVED.

6.04 Short Answer Poll – Correct Answer

Open and submit **p106a03**. Is the output data set created successfully?

```
data work.usemps;
   set orion.sales;
   Bonus=Salary*.10;
   where Country='US' and Bonus>=3000;
ERROR: Variable Bonus is not on file ORION.SALES.
run;

NOTE: The SAS System stopped processing this step because of
errors.
WARNING: The data set WORK.USEMPS may be incomplete.  When
this step was stopped there were 0 observations and 10
variables.
```

No. Bonus cannot be used in a WHERE statement because it is not in the input data set. It is a new variable that is created in this DATA step.

p106a03

64

6.05 Short Answer Poll – Correct Answer

What column heading is displayed for **Job_Title** in the program below?

```
data work.us;
   set orion.sales;
   where Country='US';
   Bonus=Salary*.10;
   label Job_Title='Sales Title';
   drop Employee_ID Gender Country
        Birth_Date;
run;
proc print data=work.us label;
   label Job_Title='Title';
run;
```

The column heading is Title. Labels and formats in PROC steps override permanent labels and formats.

p106a05

79

Copyright © 2016, SAS Institute Inc., Cary, North Carolina, USA. ALL RIGHTS RESERVED.

Copyright © 2016, SAS Institute Inc., Cary, North Carolina, USA. ALL RIGHTS RESERVED.

Chapter 7 Reading Spreadsheet and Database Data

Copyright © 2016, SAS Institute Inc., Cary, North Carolina, USA. ALL RIGHTS RESERVED.

7.1 Reading Spreadsheet Data

Objectives

- Use the VALIDVARNAME option to control special characters in column headings.
- Use SAS/ACCESS engines to access Microsoft Excel workbooks.
- Use the CONTENTS procedure to explore an Excel library.
- Use the PRINT procedure to display a worksheet.
- Create a SAS data set. Use a worksheet as input.

3

Business Scenario

The Sales Manager requested a report about Orion Star sales employees from Australia. The input data is in an Excel workbook.

4

Copyright © 2016, SAS Institute Inc., Cary, North Carolina, USA. ALL RIGHTS RESERVED.

Business Scenario

Use SAS/ACCESS Interface to PC Files to read the worksheet as if it were a SAS data set.

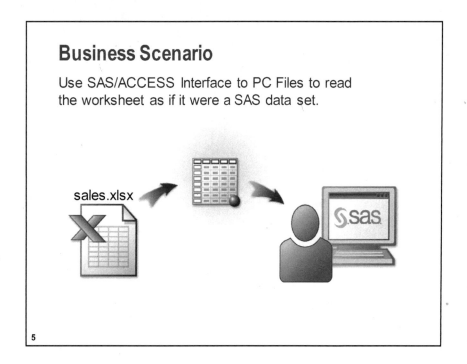

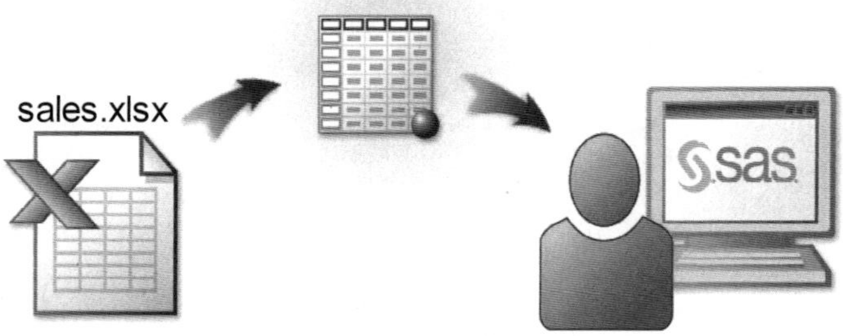

5

Examining sales.xlsx

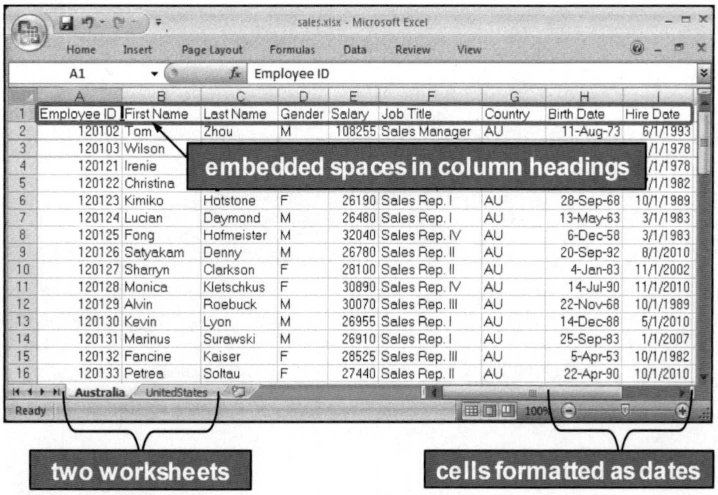

	A	B	C	D	E	F	G	H	I
1	Employee ID	First Name	Last Name	Gender	Salary	Job Title	Country	Birth Date	Hire Date
2	120102	Tom	Zhou	M	108255	Sales Manager	AU	11-Aug-73	6/1/1993
3	120103	Wilson							/1/1978
4	120121	Irenie							/1/1978
5	120122	Christina							/1/1982
6	120123	Kimiko	Hotstone	F	26190	Sales Rep. I	AU	28-Sep-68	10/1/1989
7	120124	Lucian	Daymond	M	26480	Sales Rep. I	AU	13-May-63	3/1/1983
8	120125	Fong	Hofmeister	M	32040	Sales Rep. IV	AU	6-Dec-58	3/1/1983
9	120126	Satyakam	Denny	M	26780	Sales Rep. II	AU	20-Sep-92	8/1/2010
10	120127	Sharryn	Clarkson	F	28100	Sales Rep. II	AU	4-Jan-83	11/1/2002
11	120128	Monica	Kletschkus	F	30890	Sales Rep. IV	AU	14-Jul-90	11/1/2010
12	120129	Alvin	Roebuck	M	30070	Sales Rep. III	AU	22-Nov-68	10/1/1989
13	120130	Kevin	Lyon	M	26955	Sales Rep. I	AU	14-Dec-88	5/1/2010
14	120131	Marinus	Surawski	M	26910	Sales Rep. I	AU	25-Sep-83	1/1/2007
15	120132	Fancine	Kaiser	F	28525	Sales Rep. III	AU	5-Apr-53	10/1/1982
16	120133	Petrea	Soltau	F	27440	Sales Rep. II	AU	22-Apr-90	10/1/2010

6

Copyright © 2016, SAS Institute Inc., Cary, North Carolina, USA. ALL RIGHTS RESERVED.

7.01 Poll

Based on material already discussed, does SAS allow embedded blanks and special characters in variable names?

- ❍ Yes
- ✔ No

7

SAS Variable Names

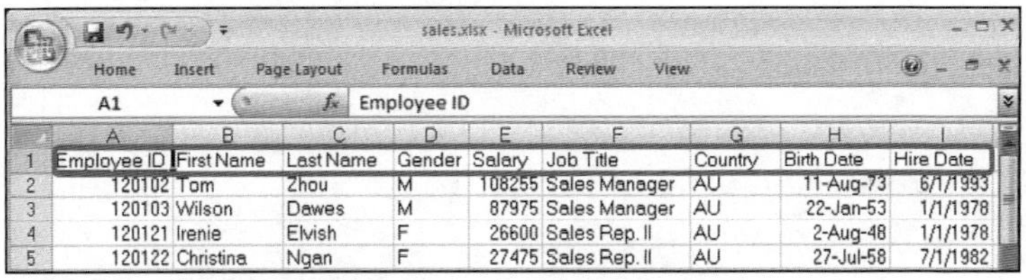

	A	B	C	D	E	F	G	H	I
1	Employee ID	First Name	Last Name	Gender	Salary	Job Title	Country	Birth Date	Hire Date
2	120102	Tom	Zhou	M	108255	Sales Manager	AU	11-Aug-73	6/1/1993
3	120103	Wilson	Dawes	M	87975	Sales Manager	AU	22-Jan-53	1/1/1978
4	120121	Irenie	Elvish	F	26600	Sales Rep. II	AU	2-Aug-48	1/1/1978
5	120122	Christina	Ngan	F	27475	Sales Rep. II	AU	27-Jul-58	7/1/1982

Excel column headings are used as variable names.

- The SAS windowing environment replaces blanks and special characters with underscores.
- By default, SAS Studio and SAS Enterprise Guide allow blanks and special characters in variable names.

9

- In the SAS windowing environment, the VALIDVARNAME= option is set to V7 by default. V7 does not allow variable names to contain special characters.
- In SAS Studio and SAS Enterprise Guide, the VALIDVARNAME= option is set to ANY by default. ANY enables variable names to contain special characters. If a variable name contains special characters, the variable name must be expressed as a SAS name literal.

Copyright © 2016, SAS Institute Inc., Cary, North Carolina, USA. ALL RIGHTS RESERVED.

SAS Name Literal

When a variable name contains embedded blanks or special characters, you must use a SAS name literal.

```
'Job Title'n
```

A *SAS name literal* is a string within quotation marks, followed by the upper or lowercase letter *n*.

10

VALIDVARNAME=Option

Set the VALIDVARNAME= option to **V7** to enforce SAS naming rules in SAS Studio and SAS Enterprise Guide.

```
options validvarname=V7;
```

- Up to 32 mixed-case alphanumeric characters are allowed.
- Names must begin with an alphabetic character or an underscore.
- Invalid characters are changed to underscores.
- Any column name that is not unique is made unique by appending a counter to the name.

11

Copyright © 2016, SAS Institute Inc., Cary, North Carolina, USA. ALL RIGHTS RESERVED.

SAS/ACCESS LIBNAME Statement

SAS/ACCESS has multiple LIBNAME engines that access Microsoft Excel workbooks.

```
libname orionx excel "&path\sales.xlsx";
```

```
libname orionx pcfiles path="&path\sales.xlsx";
```

```
libname orionx xlsx "&path\sales.xlsx";
```

The engine that you use depends on the operating environment of SAS and the bitness of SAS and Excel.

12

Both SAS and Microsoft Office offer 32-bit and 64-bit versions. The term *bitness* refers to the 32-bit and 64-bit versions of software. To determine the bitness of SAS and Microsoft Office, see the following usage notes:

- *Installing SAS® 9.3 PC Files Server and using it to convert 32-bit Microsoft Office files to SAS® 64-bit files* (**http://support.sas.com/kb/43/802.html**)
- *Summary of steps to install and use the SAS® 9.4 PC Files Server* (**http://support.sas.com/kb/54/413.html**)

SAS/ACCESS Engines

	EXCEL Engine	PCFILES Engine	XLSX Engine
SAS Operating Environment	Windows	Windows, Linux, and UNIX	Windows, Linux, and UNIX
Bitness	Same	Any combination	Any combination
Additional Software	Yes	Yes	No
Supported Excel File Types	.xls .xlsx	.xls .xlsx	.xlsx
Options	Yes	Yes	Limited

13

Copyright © 2016, SAS Institute Inc., Cary, North Carolina, USA. ALL RIGHTS RESERVED.

EXCEL Engine

LIBNAME *libref* <**EXCEL**> **"***workbook-name.ext***"** <*options*>**;**

- The engine name is optional if an Excel extension is specified.
- SAS must be located on Windows.
- The EXCEL engine is used when the bitness of SAS matches the bitness of Excel.
- This engine uses Microsoft ACE engine (Excel 2007 or later).
- It reads .xls and .xlsx file formats.
- It allows numerous LIBNAME and data set options.

14

- The Microsoft Jet (Joint Engine Technology) engine is used instead of the Microsoft ACE engine for versions prior to Excel 2007.
- The EXCEL engine can also read .xlsb and .xlsm files.

PCFILES Engine

LIBNAME *libref* **PCFILES PATH="***workbook-name.ext***"**
<**SERVER=***Windows server*> <*options*>**;**

- SAS can be located on Windows, Linux, or UNIX.
- The PCFILES engine is used with any bitness combination.
- This engine requires SERVER= when Linux or UNIX SAS is used.
- It uses the Microsoft ACE engine (Excel 2007 or later).
- The engine requires the SAS PC Files Server (Windows) in order to connect to the Excel file.
- It reads .xls and .xlsx file formats.
- It allows numerous LIBNAME and data set options.

15

- SERVER= specifies the name of the Windows computer that is running the SAS PC Files Server. This option is required for Linux and UNIX users to connect to the PC Files Server.
- Microsoft Jet (Joint Engine Technology) engine is used instead of Microsoft ACE engine for versions prior to Excel 2007.
- The PCFILES engine can also read .xlsb and .xlsm files.

Copyright © 2016, SAS Institute Inc., Cary, North Carolina, USA. ALL RIGHTS RESERVED.

XLSX Engine

LIBNAME *libref* **XLSX "***workbook-name.xlsx***"** <*options*>;

- The XLSX engine requires SAS 9.4M2 or later.
- SAS can be located on Windows, Linux, or UNIX.
- This engine is used with any bitness combination.
- It accesses the Excel file directly without using the Microsoft ACE engine.
- The Excel file must be accessible to Linux or UNIX when you use SAS that is not on Windows.
- The engine reads only .xlsx file formats (Excel 2007 or later).
- It can read more than 255 columns.
- It allows limited LIBNAME options.

16

A worksheet in a .xls file can have up to 256 columns and 65,536 rows. Excel 2007 and later files (.xlsx files) were enhanced to support 16,384 columns and 1,048,576 rows in a worksheet. Files that are created with Excel 2007 and later can have an .xlsx, .xlsb, or .xlsm extension. Due to how the Microsoft ACE driver and the Microsoft Jet driver work, the EXCEL and PCFILES engines are limited to 255 columns in an Excel file.

Documentation

For more information about the LIBNAME engines and PC Files Server, refer to the documentation.

http://support.sas.com/documentation/onlinedoc/access/

17

Copyright © 2016, SAS Institute Inc., Cary, North Carolina, USA. ALL RIGHTS RESERVED.

Exploring the Library

Regardless of the LIBNAME engine that is used, you can use the CONTENTS procedure to explore the library.

```
options validvarname=v7;
libname orionx pcfiles path="&path\sales.xlsx";

proc contents data=orionx._all_;
run;

libname orionx clear;
```

- When SAS has a libref that is assigned to an Excel workbook, the workbook cannot be opened in Excel.
- To disassociate the libref, use a LIBNAME statement with the CLEAR option.

p107d01a
p107d01b

18

Exploring the Library

Partial PROC CONTENTS Output

EXCEL and PCFILES engines

The CONTENTS Procedure

#	Name	Member Type	DBMS Member Type
1	Australia$	DATA	TABLE
2	UnitedStates$	DATA	TABLE

✎ For the EXCEL and PCFILES engines, worksheet names end with a dollar sign.

p107d01a

19

Copyright © 2016, SAS Institute Inc., Cary, North Carolina, USA. ALL RIGHTS RESERVED.

Exploring the Library

Partial PROC CONTENTS Output

XLSX engine

```
                 The CONTENTS Procedure


                                Member
          #  Name               Type

          1  AUSTRALIA          DATA
          2  UNITEDSTATES       DATA
```

✎ For the XLSX engine, worksheet names do ***not*** end with a dollar sign.

20 p107d01b

Exploring the Library

Additional PROC CONTENTS Output

```
#   Variable      Type  Len  Format   Informat   Label

8   Birth_Date    Num     8  DATE9.   DATE9.     Birth Date
7   Country       Char    2  $2.      $2.        Country
1   Employee_ID   Num     8                      Employee ID
2   First_Name    Char   10  $10.     $10.       First Name
4   Gender        Char    1  $1.      $1.        Gender
9   Hire_Date     Num     8  DATE9.   DATE9.     Hire Date
6   Job_Title     Char   14  $14.     $14.       Job Title
3   Last_Name     Char   12  $12.     $12.       Last Name
5   Salary        Num     8                      Salary
```

✎ Each engine supplies formats and labels for the Excel data.

21

Named Ranges

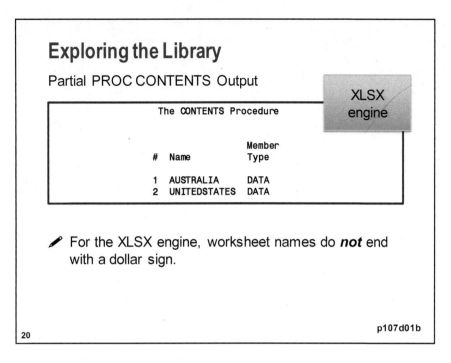

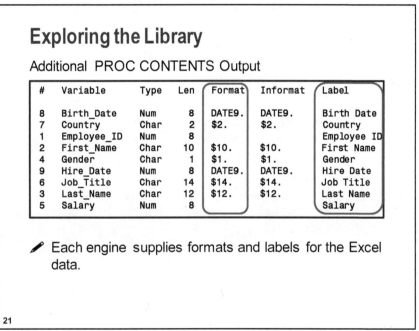

The SAS/ACCESS LIBNAME statement with the EXCEL, PCFILES, or XLSX engine is used to access worksheets within an Excel workbook. In addition, the statement can be used to access named ranges within an Excel workbook. A named range refers to a range of cells in a worksheet.

For example, the **sales.xls** file contains two worksheets (**Australia** and **UnitedStates**) and two named ranges (**AU** and **US**).

Copyright © 2016, SAS Institute Inc., Cary, North Carolina, USA. ALL RIGHTS RESERVED.

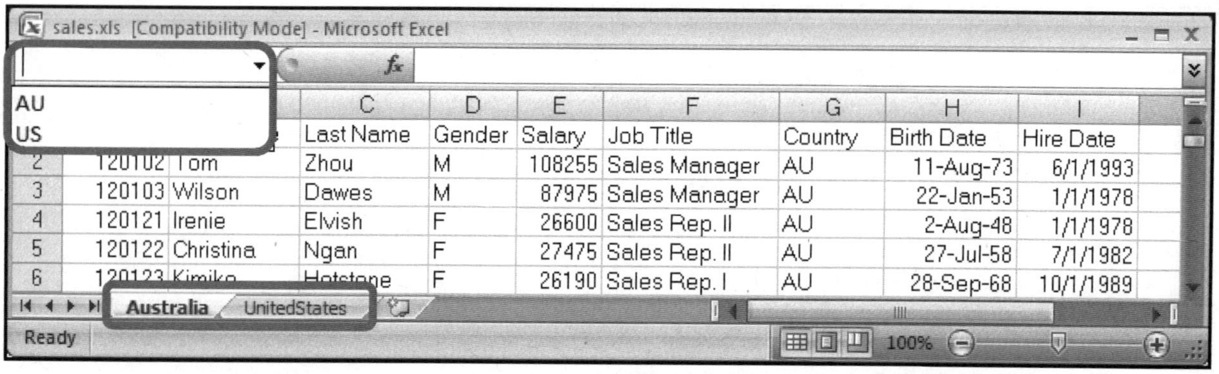

Given the following program:

```
options validvarname=v7;
libname orionx pcfiles path="&path\sales.xls";

proc contents data=orionx._all_;
run;

libname orionx clear;
```

The results of the CONTENTS procedure show the two worksheets and the two named ranges.

The CONTENTS Procedure

#	Name	Member Type	DBMS Member Type
1	AU	DATA	TABLE
2	Australia$	DATA	TABLE
3	US	DATA	TABLE
4	UnitedStates$	DATA	TABLE

- For the EXCEL and PCFILES engines, worksheet names end with a dollar sign and named ranges do ***not*** end with a dollar sign. Both worksheet names and named ranges are visible in PROC CONTENTS output.
- For the XLSX engine, worksheet names and named ranges do ***not*** end with a dollar sign. Worksheet names are visible in PROC CONTENTS output but named ranges are not.

Regardless of the engine that is used, the named range can be accessed with a two-level name. The following example shows the **AU** named range being used in a PROC step and DATA step:

```
proc print data=orionx.AU;
run;

data work.subset2;
   set orionx.AU;
run;
```

Copyright © 2016, SAS Institute Inc., Cary, North Carolina, USA. ALL RIGHTS RESERVED.

SAS Name Literal

Because the EXCEL and PCFILES engines refer to worksheets with dollar signs at the end of the names, use a SAS name literal to permit the special character in the worksheet name.

```
orionx.'Australia$'n
```

SAS name literal

The XLSX engine does not refer to worksheets with a dollar sign at the end of the name, so a SAS name literal is not needed.

```
orionx.Australia
```

22

Subsetting a Worksheet

Regardless of the LIBNAME engine used, the PRINT procedure can be used to display a subset of the worksheet.

```
proc print data=orionx.'Australia$'n noobs;
   where Job_Title contains 'IV';
   var Employee_ID Last_Name
       Job_Title Salary;
run;
```

EXCEL and PCFILES engines

```
proc print data=orionx.Australia noobs;
   where Job_Title contains 'IV';
   var Employee_ID Last_Name
       Job_Title Salary;
run;
```

XLSX engine

23

p107d02a
p107d02b

If the sheet name contains special characters or embedded blanks, a name literal must be used to refer to the sheet, even when you use the XLSX engine.

Copyright © 2016, SAS Institute Inc., Cary, North Carolina, USA. ALL RIGHTS RESERVED.

Subsetting a Worksheet

PROC PRINT Output

Employee_ ID	Last_Name	Job_Title	Salary
120125	Hofmeister	Sales Rep. IV	32040
120128	Kletschkus	Sales Rep. IV	30890
120135	Platts	Sales Rep. IV	32490
120159	Phoumirath	Sales Rep. IV	30765
120166	Nowd	Sales Rep. IV	30660

24

7.02 Short Answer Poll

You submit the statement below. Which step displays the UnitedStates worksheet?

```
libname xl excel 's:\workshop\custusau.xlsx';
```

a.
```
proc print data=xl.UnitedStates;
run;
```

b.
```
proc print data=xl.'UnitedStates';
run;
```

c.
```
proc print data=xl.'UnitedStates'n;
run;
```

d.
```
proc print data=xl.'UnitedStates$'n;
run;
```

25

Copyright © 2016, SAS Institute Inc., Cary, North Carolina, USA. ALL RIGHTS RESERVED.

Business Scenario

Create a SAS data set using a Microsoft Excel workbook as input.

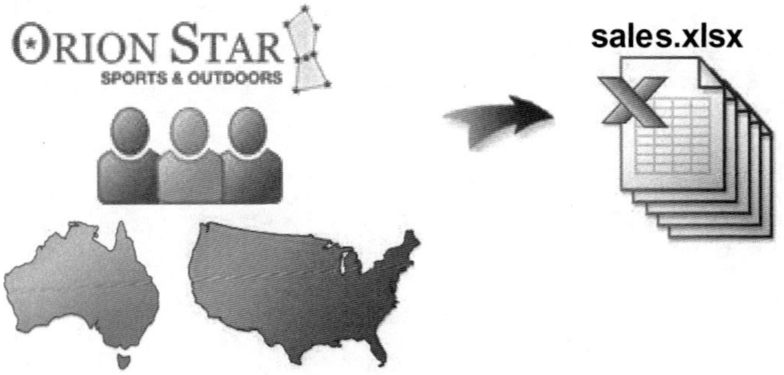

27

Considerations

Use the SAS/ACCESS LIBNAME engine to read the **Australia** worksheet and create a temporary data set.

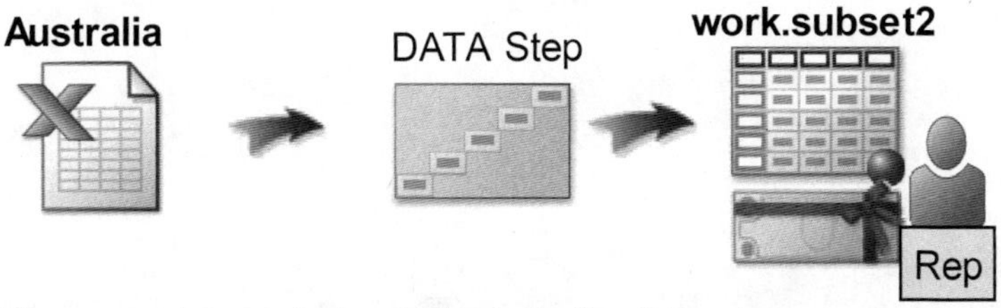

The new data set should include the following:

- only the employees with **Rep** in their job titles
- a **Bonus** variable that is 10% of **Salary**
- permanent labels and formats

28

Copyright © 2016, SAS Institute Inc., Cary, North Carolina, USA. ALL RIGHTS RESERVED.

Creating a SAS Data Set from an Excel Worksheet

p107d03a

This demonstration uses the SAS/ACCESS EXCEL or PCFILES engine to read an .xlsx file. An alternate version, **p107d03b**, uses the SAS/ACCESS XLSX engine to read the .xlsx file.

```
options validvarname=v7;
*libname xl excel "&path\sales.xlsx";
*libname xl pcfiles path="&path\sales.xlsx";

proc contents data=xl._all_;
run;

data work.subset2;
   set xl.'Australia$'n;
   where Job_Title contains 'Rep';
   Bonus=Salary*.10;
   keep First_Name Last_Name Salary Bonus
        Job_Title Hire_Date;
   label Job_Title='Sales Title'
         Hire_Date='Date Hired';
   format Salary comma10. Hire_Date mmddyy10.
          Bonus comma8.2;
run;

proc contents data=work.subset2;
run;

proc print data=work.subset2 label;
run;

libname xl clear;
```

1. Open **p107d03a** and uncomment the appropriate LIBNAME statement.
2. Submit the OPTIONS and LIBNAME statements, and the first PROC CONTENTS step.
3. Verify that the **xl** library contains the worksheets, **Australia$** and **UnitedStates$**.
4. Submit the DATA step to create a new data set, **work.subset2**.
5. Check the log. Verify that 61 observations were written to **work.subset2**.
6. Submit the second PROC CONTENTS step. Verify that the formats and labels were stored in the descriptor portion of **work.subset2**. Notice that all columns have labels, not only the columns that were assigned labels in the DATA step.

Copyright © 2016, SAS Institute Inc., Cary, North Carolina, USA. ALL RIGHTS RESERVED.

Partial PROC CONTENTS Output

Alphabetic List of Variables and Attributes

#	Variable	Type	Len	Format	Informat	Label
6	Bonus	Num	8	COMMA8.2		
1	First_Name	Char	10	$10.	$10.	First Name
5	Hire_Date	Num	8	MMDDYY10.	DATE9.	Date Hired
4	Job_Title	Char	14	$14.	$14.	Sales Title
2	Last_Name	Char	12	$12.	$12.	Last Name
3	Salary	Num	8	COMMA10.		Salary

7. Submit the PROC PRINT step. Verify that the results contain 61 observations and that the labels were displayed and formats were applied.

   Partial PROC PRINT Output

Obs	First Name	Last Name	Salary	Sales Title	Date Hired	Bonus
1	Irenie	Elvish	26,600	Sales Rep. II	01/01/1978	2,660.00
2	Christina	Ngan	27,475	Sales Rep. II	07/01/1982	2,747.50
3	Kimiko	Hotstone	26,190	Sales Rep. I	10/01/1989	2,619.00
4	Lucian	Daymond	26,480	Sales Rep. I	03/01/1983	2,648.00
5	Fong	Hofmeister	32,040	Sales Rep. IV	03/01/1983	3,204.00

8. Submit the LIBNAME statement to clear the resources.

9. Check the log for success.

End of Demonstration

Copyright © 2016, SAS Institute Inc., Cary, North Carolina, USA. ALL RIGHTS RESERVED.

Exercises

> If you restarted your SAS session since the last exercise, open and submit the **libname** program that can be found in the data folder.

Level 1

1. Accessing an Excel Worksheet

a. Retrieve the starter program **p107e01**.

b. Add an OPTIONS statement before the PROC CONTENTS step to set VALIDVARNAME to **V7**.

c. Add a LIBNAME statement after the OPTIONS statement to create a libref named **custfm** that references the Excel workbook, **custfm.xlsx**.

d. Submit the LIBNAME statement and the PROC CONTENTS step. Verify the output.

Partial PROC CONTENTS Output

```
                          The CONTENTS Procedure

                                          DBMS
                                  Member  Member
                    #  Name       Type    Type

                    1  Females$   DATA    TABLE
                    2  Males$     DATA    TABLE
```

e. Add a SET statement in the DATA step to read the worksheet that contains the data for males.

f. Add a KEEP statement in the DATA step to include only **First_Name**, **Last_Name**, and **Birth_Date** in the new data set.

g. Add a FORMAT statement in the DATA step to display **Birth_Date** as a four-digit year.

h. Add a LABEL statement in the DATA step to display **Birth Year** instead of **Birth_Date**.

i. Add a final LIBNAME statement to the program to clear the libref.

j. Submit the program to create the report below. Results should contain 47 observations.

Partial PROC PRINT Output

```
                                                    Birth
                 Obs    First Name    Last Name     Year

                   1    James         Kvarniq       1974
                   2    David         Black         1969
                   3    Markus        Sepke         1988
                   4    Ulrich        Heyde         1939
                   5    Jimmie        Evans         1954
```

Copyright © 2016, SAS Institute Inc., Cary, North Carolina, USA. ALL RIGHTS RESERVED.

Level 2

2. Accessing an Excel Worksheet

a. Open a new program and write an OPTIONS statement to set VALIDVARNAME to **V7**.

b. Write a LIBNAME statement to create a libref named **prod** that references the Excel workbook **products.xlsx**.

c. Write a PROC CONTENTS step to view all of the contents of **prod**.

d. Submit the program to determine the names of the four worksheets in **products.xlsx**.

e. Write a DATA step that reads the worksheet containing sports data and creates a new data set named **work.golf**.

f. The data set **work.golf** should have the following characteristics:
- include only the observations where **Category** is equal to *Golf*
- not include the **Category** variable
- include a label of **Golf Products** for the **Name** variable

f. Write a LIBNAME statement to clear the **prod** libref.

g. Write a PROC PRINT step to create the report below. Results should contain 56 observations.

Partial PROC PRINT Output

```
Obs    Golf Products

  1    Ball Bag
  2    Red/White/Black Staff 9 Bag
  3    Tee Holder
  4    Bb Softspikes - Xp 22-pack
  5    Bretagne Performance Tg Men's Golf Shoes L.
```

Challenge

3. Creating an Excel Worksheet

This program fails if the workbook already exists with a **salesemps** worksheet. Delete **employees.xls** from the data folder if it exists.

a. Open **p107e03**. Insert a LIBNAME statement to associate the libref **out** with the Excel workbook **employees.xls** in the default data folder.

b. Modify the program so that it creates a worksheet that is named **salesemps** in the **employees.xls** workbook.

Copyright © 2016, SAS Institute Inc., Cary, North Carolina, USA. ALL RIGHTS RESERVED.

c. Submit the SAS program and verify that it created the data set **out.salesemps** with 71 observations and four variables as shown in the partial SAS log below.

```
NOTE: 71 records were read from the infile "s:\workshop\newemps.csv".
NOTE: The data set OUT.salesemps has 71 observations and 4 variables.
```

d. Verify that the new Excel workbook **employees.xls** was created with one sheet, **salesemps**.

End of Exercises

Copyright © 2016, SAS Institute Inc., Cary, North Carolina, USA. ALL RIGHTS RESERVED.

7.2 Reading Database Data

Objectives

- Use a SAS/ACCESS engine to access an Oracle database.
- Use an Oracle table as input and create a SAS data set.

33

Business Scenario

The Northeast Sales Manager requested a report that lists supervisors from New York and New Jersey. The input data is in an Oracle database.

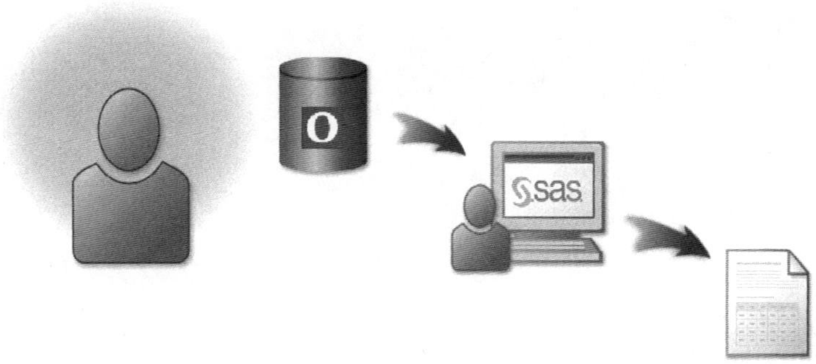

34

Copyright © 2016, SAS Institute Inc., Cary, North Carolina, USA. ALL RIGHTS RESERVED.

SAS/ACCESS LIBNAME Statement

The SAS/ACCESS LIBNAME statement assigns a libref to a relational database.

LIBNAME *libref engine <SAS/ACCESS options>*;

libref *engine name*

```
libname oa oracle user=edu001 pw=edu001
                  path=dbmssrv schema=educ;
```

options

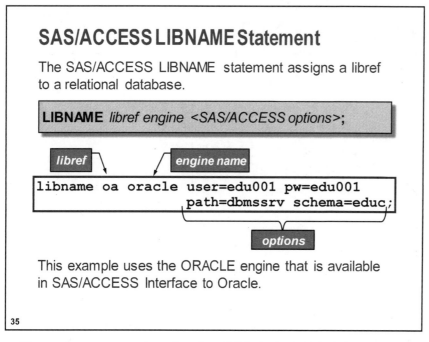

This example uses the ORACLE engine that is available in SAS/ACCESS Interface to Oracle.

35

- The engine name, such as Oracle or DB2, is the SAS/ACCESS component that reads and writes to your DBMS. The engine name is required.
- USER= specifies an optional Oracle user name. USER= must be used with PASSWORD=.
- PASSWORD= (or PW=) specifies an optional Oracle password associated with the Oracle user name.
- PATH= specifies the Oracle driver, node, and database. SAS/ACCESS uses the same Oracle path designation that you use to connect to Oracle directly.
- SCHEMA= enables you to read database objects, such as tables and views, in the specified schema. If this option is omitted, you connect to the default schema for your DBMS.

Accessing an Oracle Database

SAS treats the Oracle database as a library, and each table as a SAS data set. Use the CONTENTS procedure to explore the library.

```
libname oa oracle user=edu001 pw=edu001
                  path=dbmssrv schema=educ;

proc contents data=oa._all_;
run;

libname oa clear;
```

Submit a LIBNAME statement with the CLEAR option to release the database and associated resources.

36

Copyright © 2016, SAS Institute Inc., Cary, North Carolina, USA. ALL RIGHTS RESERVED.

Accessing an Oracle Table

Use a two-level name to reference any table in this Oracle database.

```
libname oa oracle user=edu001 pw=edu001
                  path=dbmssrv schema=educ;

proc print data=oa.supervisors;
   where state in ('NY' 'NJ');
run;

data work.nysup;
   set oa.supervisors;
   where state='NY';
run;

libname oa clear;
```

37

Viewing the Output

PROC PRINT Output

Obs	EMPID	STATE	JOBCATEGORY
1	1834	NY	BC
2	1433	NJ	FA
3	1983	NY	FA
4	1420	NJ	ME
5	1882	NY	ME

38

Copyright © 2016, SAS Institute Inc., Cary, North Carolina, USA. ALL RIGHTS RESERVED.

Documentation

Refer to the documentation for information relating to a specific relational database.

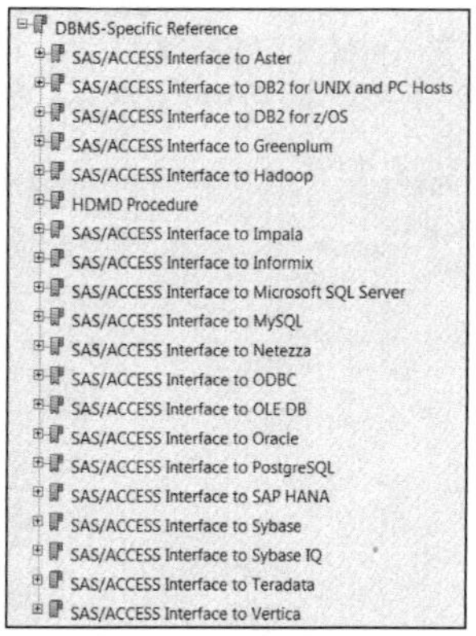

http://support.sas.com/documentation/onlinedoc/access/

39

Copyright © 2016, SAS Institute Inc., Cary, North Carolina, USA. ALL RIGHTS RESERVED.

7.3 Solutions

Solutions to Exercises

1. **Accessing an Excel Worksheet**

```
options validvarname=v7;
*libname custfm excel "&path/custfm.xlsx";
*libname custfm pcfiles path="&path/custfm.xlsx";
proc contents data=custfm._all_;
run;

data work.males;
   set custfm.'Males$'n;
   keep First_Name Last_Name Birth_Date;
   format Birth_Date year4.;
   label Birth_Date='Birth Year';
run;

proc print data=work.males label;
run;

libname custfm clear;

/* Alternate solution */

options validvarname=v7;
libname custfm xlsx "&path/custfm.xlsx";

proc contents data=custfm._all_;
run;

data work.males;
   set custfm.Males;
   keep First_Name Last_Name Birth_Date;
   format Birth_Date year4.;
   label Birth_Date='Birth Year';
run;

proc print data=work.males label;
run;

libname custfm clear;
```

2. **Accessing an Excel Worksheet**

```
options validvarname=v7;
*libname prod excel "&path\products.xlsx";
*libname prod pcfiles path="&path\products.xlsx";
```

Copyright © 2016, SAS Institute Inc., Cary, North Carolina, USA. ALL RIGHTS RESERVED.

```
proc contents data=prod._all_;
run;

data work.golf;
   set prod.'sports$'n;
   where Category='Golf';
   drop Category;
   label Name='Golf Products';
run;

libname prod clear;
proc print data=work.golf label;
run;

/* Alternate solution */

options validvarname=v7;
libname prod xlsx "&path\products.xlsx";

proc contents data=prod._all_;
run;

data work.golf;
   set prod.sports;
   where Category='Golf';
   drop Category;
   label Name='Golf Products';
run;

libname prod clear;

proc print data=work.golf label;
run;
```

3. **Creating an Excel Worksheet**

```
options validvarname=v7;
*libname out excel "&path\employees.xls";
*libname out pcfiles path="&path\employees.xls";

data out.salesemps;
   length First_Name $ 12 Last_Name $ 18
          Job_Title $ 25;
   infile "&path\newemps.csv" dlm=',';
   input First_Name $ Last_Name $
         Job_Title $ Salary;
run;

libname out clear;
```

Copyright © 2016, SAS Institute Inc., Cary, North Carolina, USA. ALL RIGHTS RESERVED.

End of Solutions

Solutions to Student Activities (Polls/Quizzes)

7.01 Poll – Correct Answer

Based on material already discussed, does SAS allow embedded blanks and special characters in variable names?

❍ Yes
(❍) No

SAS variable names

- can be 1 to 32 characters long.
- must start with a letter or underscore. Subsequent characters can be letters, underscores, or numerals.
- can be uppercase, lowercase, or mixed case.
- are not case sensitive.

8

7.02 Short Answer Poll – Correct Answer

You submit the statement below. Which step displays the UnitedStates worksheet?

```
libname xl excel 's:\workshop\custusau.xlsx';
```

a.
```
proc print data=xl.UnitedStates;
run;
```

b.
```
proc print data=xl.'UnitedStates';
run;
```

c.
```
proc print data=xl.'UnitedStates'n;
run;
```

(d.)
```
proc print data=xl.'UnitedStates$'n;
run;
```

26

Copyright © 2016, SAS Institute Inc., Cary, North Carolina, USA. ALL RIGHTS RESERVED.

Copyright © 2016, SAS Institute Inc., Cary, North Carolina, USA. ALL RIGHTS RESERVED.

Chapter 8 Reading Raw Data Files

Copyright © 2016, SAS Institute Inc., Cary, North Carolina, USA. ALL RIGHTS RESERVED.

8.1 Introduction to Reading Raw Data Files

Objectives

- Identify the types of raw data files and input styles.
- Define the terms *standard* and *nonstandard* data.

3

Business Scenario

Information about Orion Star sales employees from Australia and the United States is stored in a raw data file.

Programmers need to be able to identify the layout and type of information in the raw data file.

4

Copyright © 2016, SAS Institute Inc., Cary, North Carolina, USA. ALL RIGHTS RESERVED.

Raw Data Files

A raw data file is also known as a *flat file.*

- They are text files that contain one record per line.
- A record typically contains multiple fields.
- Flat files do not have internal metadata.
- External documentation, known as a *record layout*, should exist.
- A record layout describes the fields and locations within each record.

5

Raw Data Files

Fields in a raw data file can be delimited or arranged in fixed columns.

Delimited File

```
120102,Tom,Zhou,M,108255,Sales Manager,AU,11AUG1973,06/01/1993
120103,Wilson,Dawes,M,87975,Sales Manager,AU,22JAN1953,01/01/1978
120121,Irenie,Elvish,F,26600,Sales Rep. II,AU,02AUG1948,01/01/1978
120122,Christina,Ngan,F,27475,Sales Rep. II,AU,27JUL1958,07/01/1982
```

Fixed Column File

```
         1    1    2    2    3    3    4    4    5    5    6
1---5----0----5----0----5----0----5----0----5----0----5----0--
120102Tom          Zhou           Sales Manager        108255AU
120103Wilson       Dawes          Sales Manager         87975AU
120121Irenie       Elvish         Sales Rep. II         26600AU
120122Christina    Ngan           Sales Rep. II         27475AU
```

6

Copyright © 2016, SAS Institute Inc., Cary, North Carolina, USA. ALL RIGHTS RESERVED.

Fields in Raw Data Files

In order for SAS to read a raw data file, you must specify the following information about each field:

- the location of the data value in the record
- the name of the SAS variable in which to store the data
- the type of the SAS variable

7

Reading Raw Data Files

There are different techniques, or *input styles*, for reading raw data files in SAS.

Input Style	Used for Reading
Column Input	Standard data in fixed columns
Formatted Input	Standard and nonstandard data in fixed columns
List Input	Standard and nonstandard data separated by blanks or some other delimiter

8

Copyright © 2016, SAS Institute Inc., Cary, North Carolina, USA. ALL RIGHTS RESERVED.

Standard and Nonstandard Data

Standard data is data that SAS can read without any additional instruction.

- Character data is always standard.
- Some numeric values are standard and some are not.

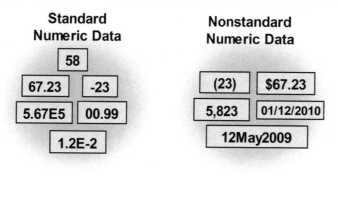

Standard Numeric Data	Nonstandard Numeric Data
58	(23)
67.23	$67.23
-23	5,823
5.67E5	01/12/2010
00.99	12May2009
1.2E-2	

9

8.01 Multiple Answer Poll

What type of raw data files do you read?

a. delimited
b. fixed column
c. both delimited and fixed column
d. I do not read raw data files.

10

Copyright © 2016, SAS Institute Inc., Cary, North Carolina, USA. ALL RIGHTS RESERVED.

8.2 Reading Standard Delimited Data

Objectives

- Use list input to create a SAS data set from a delimited raw data file.
- Examine the compilation and execution phases of the DATA step when you read a raw data file.
- Explicitly define the length of a variable.
- Examine behavior when a data error is encountered.

12

Business Scenario

Information about Orion Star sales employees is stored in a comma-delimited raw data file. The file contains both standard and nonstandard data fields.

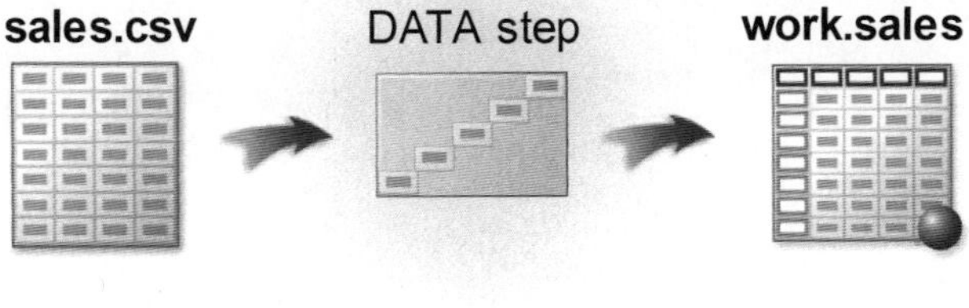

13

Copyright © 2016, SAS Institute Inc., Cary, North Carolina, USA. ALL RIGHTS RESERVED.

List Input

Use list input to read **delimited** raw data files.

Partial **sales.csv**

```
120102,Tom,Zhou,M,108255,Sales Manager,AU,11AUG1973,06/01/1993
120103,Wilson,Dawes,M,87975,Sales Manager,AU,22JAN1953,01/01/1978
120121,Irenie,Elvish,F,26600,Sales Rep. II,AU,02AUG1948,01/01/1978
120122,Christina,Ngan,F,27475,Sales Rep. II,AU,27JUL1958,07/01/1982
120123,Kimiko,Hotstone,F,26190,Sales Rep. I,AU,28SEP1968,10/01/1989
```

- SAS considers a space (blank) to be the default delimiter.
- Both standard and nonstandard data can be read.
- Fields must be read sequentially, left to right.

14

8.02 Short Answer Poll

Which fields in this file can be read as standard numeric values?

Partial **sales.csv**

```
120102,Tom,Zhou,M,108255,Sales Manager,AU,11AUG1973,06/01/1993
120103,Wilson,Dawes,M,87975,Sales Manager,AU,22JAN1953,01/01/1978
120121,Irenie,Elvish,F,26600,Sales Rep. II,AU,02AUG1948,01/01/1978
120122,Christina,Ngan,F,27475,Sales Rep. II,AU,27JUL1958,07/01/1982
120123,Kimiko,Hotstone,F,26190,Sales Rep. I,AU,28SEP1968,10/01/1989
```

15

Copyright © 2016, SAS Institute Inc., Cary, North Carolina, USA. ALL RIGHTS RESERVED.

Reading a Delimited Raw Data File

Use *INFILE* and *INPUT statements* in a DATA step to read a raw data file.

```
data work.subset;
   infile "&path\sales.csv" dlm=',';
   input Employee_ID First_Name $
         Last_Name $ Gender $ Salary
         Job_Title $ Country $;
run;
```

DATA *output-data-set*;
  INFILE "*raw-data-file***"** <**DLM='***delimiter***'**>;
  INPUT *variable* <**$**> *variable* <**$**> ... ;
RUN;

17 p108d01

DLM= is an alias for DELIMITER=*delimiter(s)*. It is used to specify an alternate delimiter (other than a blank) to be used for list input. *Delimiter(s)* is one or more characters enclosed in quotation marks. If more than one delimiter is specified, each is treated as a delimiter. The delimiter is case sensitive.

- To specify a tab delimiter on Windows or UNIX, enter **dlm='09'x**.
- To specify a tab delimiter on z/OS (OS/390), enter **dlm='05'x**.

INFILE Statement

The INFILE statement identifies the raw data file to be read.

```
infile "&path\sales.csv" dlm=',';
```

INFILE "*raw-data-file***"** <**DLM='***delimiter***'**>;

- A full path is recommended.
- Using the **&path** macro variable reference makes the program more flexible.
- The DLM= option specifies alternate delimiters.

⚠ Be sure to use double quotation marks when you reference a macro variable within a quoted string.

18

A %LET statement was submitted in the **libname.sas** program to create the user-defined macro variable, **path**. The INFILE statement references the value of the macro variable by placing an ampersand before its name. The macro variable exists for the duration of the SAS session unless it is changed or deleted.

Copyright © 2016, SAS Institute Inc., Cary, North Carolina, USA. ALL RIGHTS RESERVED.

INPUT Statement

The INPUT statement reads the data fields sequentially, left to right. Standard data fields require only a variable name and type.

Partial **sales.csv**

```
120102,Tom,Zhou,M,108255,Sales Manager,AU,11AUG1969,06/01/1989
120103,Wilson,Dawes,M,87975,Sales Manager,AU,22JAN1949,01/01/1974
120121,Irenie,Elvish,F,26600,Sales Rep. II,AU,02AUG1944,01/01/1974
```

```
input Employee_ID First_Name $ Last_Name $
      Gender $ Salary Job_Title $ Country $;
```

INPUT *variable* <$> *variable* <$> ...;

- The dollar sign indicates a character variable.
- Default length for ***all*** variables is eight bytes, regardless of type.

19

Viewing the Log

Partial SAS Log

```
249  data work.subset;
250     infile "&path\sales.csv" dlm=',';
251     input Employee_ID First_Name $ Last_Name $
252           Gender $ Salary Job_Title $ Country $;
253  run;

NOTE: The infile "s:\workshop\sales.csv" is:
      Filename=s:\workshop\sales.csv,
      RECFM=V,LRECL=256,File Size (bytes)=11340

NOTE: 165 records were read from the infile "s:\workshop\sales.csv".
      The minimum record length was 61.
      The maximum record length was 80.
NOTE: The data set WORK.SUBSET has 165 observations and 7 variables.
```

20 p108d01

Copyright © 2016, SAS Institute Inc., Cary, North Carolina, USA. ALL RIGHTS RESERVED.

Viewing the Output

```
proc print data=work.subset noobs;
run;
```

Partial PROC PRINT Output

Employee_ ID	First_ Name	Last_ Name	Gender	Salary	Job_ Title	Country
120102	Tom	Zhou	M	108255	Sales Ma	AU
120103	Wilson	Dawes	M	87975	Sales Ma	AU
120121	Irenie	Elvish	F	26600	Sales Re	AU
120122	Christin	Ngan	F	27475	Sales Re	AU
120123	Kimiko	Hotstone	F	26190	Sales Re	AU

Some character values are truncated.

21

p108d01

Business Scenario

It is important to understand the processing that occurs when a DATA step reads a raw data file.

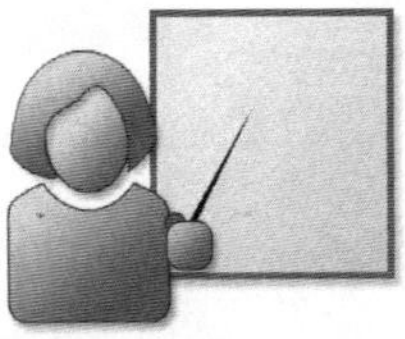

22

Copyright © 2016, SAS Institute Inc., Cary, North Carolina, USA. ALL RIGHTS RESERVED.

Compilation Phase

During compilation, SAS does the following:

- scans the step for syntax errors
- translates each statement into machine language
- creates an *input buffer* to hold one record at a time from the raw data file

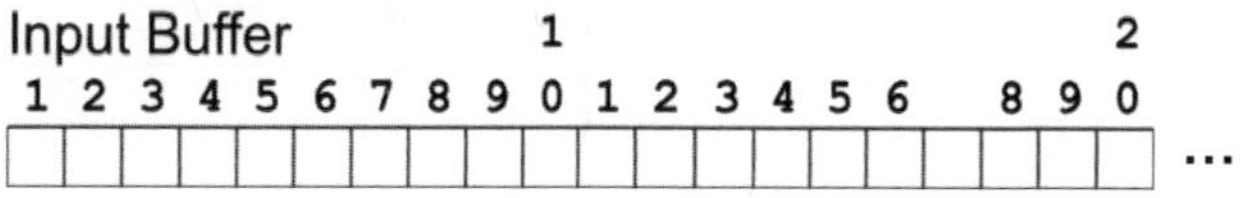

- creates the program data vector (PDV) to hold one observation
- creates the descriptor portion of the output data set

23

Compilation

```
data work.subset;
   infile "&path\sales.csv" dlm=',';
   input Employee_ID First_Name $ Last_Name $
         Gender $ Salary Job_Title $ Country $;
run;
```

24 p108d01

...

Copyright © 2016, SAS Institute Inc., Cary, North Carolina, USA. ALL RIGHTS RESERVED.

Compilation

```
data work.subset;
   infile "&path\sales.csv" dlm=',';
   input Employee_ID First_Name $ Last_Name $
         Gender $ Salary Job_Title $ Country $;
run;
```

Input Buffer

1 2 3 4 5 6 7 8 9 0 1 2 3 4 5 6 7 8 9 0 1 2 3 4 5

25 ...

The default length of the input buffer depends on the operating system. You can use the LRECL= option in the INFILE statement to modify it.

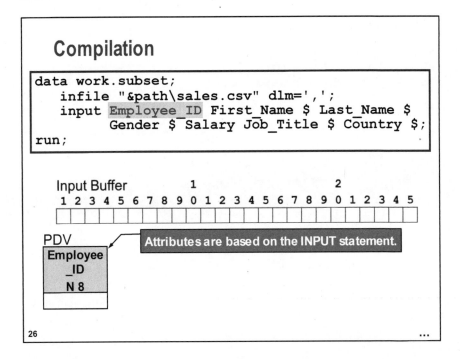

Compilation

```
data work.subset;
   infile "&path\sales.csv" dlm=',';
   input Employee_ID First_Name $ Last_Name $
         Gender $ Salary Job_Title $ Country $;
run;
```

Input Buffer

1 2 3 4 5 6 7 8 9 0 1 2 3 4 5 6 7 8 9 0 1 2 3 4 5

PDV

Employee _ID N 8

Attributes are based on the INPUT statement.

26 ...

Copyright © 2016, SAS Institute Inc., Cary, North Carolina, USA. ALL RIGHTS RESERVED.

Compilation

```
data work.subset;
   infile "&path\sales.csv" dlm=',';
   input Employee_ID First_Name $ Last_Name $
         Gender $ Salary Job_Title $ Country $;
run;
```

Input Buffer

1	2	3	4	5	6	7	8	9	10	1	2	3	4	5	6	7	8	9	20	1	2	3	4	5

PDV

Employee_ID N 8	First_Name $ 8

With list input, the default length for character variables is eight bytes.

27 ...

Compilation

```
data work.subset;
   infile "&path\sales.csv" dlm=',';
   input Employee_ID First_Name $ Last_Name $
         Gender $ Salary Job_Title $ Country $;
run;
```

Input Buffer

1	2	3	4	5	6	7	8	9	10	1	2	3	4	5	6	7	8	9	20	1	2	3	4	5

PDV

Employee_ID N 8	First_Name $ 8	Last_Name $ 8	Gender $ 8	Salary N 8	Job_Title $ 8	Country $ 8

28 ...

Copyright © 2016, SAS Institute Inc., Cary, North Carolina, USA. ALL RIGHTS RESERVED.

Compilation

```
data work.subset;
   infile "&path\sales.csv" dlm=',';
   input Employee_ID First_Name $ Last_Name $
         Gender $ Salary Job_Title $ Country $;
run;
```

PDV

Employee_ID N 8	First_Name $ 8	Last_Name $ 8	Gender $ 8	Salary N 8	Job_Title $ 8	Country $ 8

Descriptor Portion of **work.subset**

Employee_ID N 8	First_Name $ 8	Last_Name $ 8	Gender $ 8	Salary N 8	Job_Title $ 8	Country $ 8

29 ...

8.03 Multiple Choice Poll

Which statement is true?

a. An input buffer is created only if you are reading data from a raw data file.

b. The PDV at compile time holds the variable name, type, byte size, and initial value.

c. The descriptor portion is the first item that is created at compile time.

30

Copyright © 2016, SAS Institute Inc., Cary, North Carolina, USA. ALL RIGHTS RESERVED.

DATA Step Processing

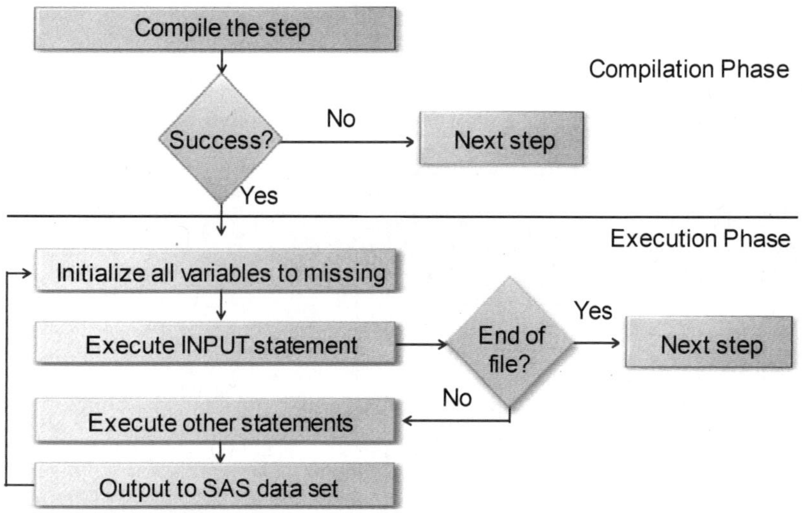

32

Execution

Partial **sales.csv**

```
120102,Tom,Zhou, ...
120103,Wilson,Dawes, ...
120121,Irenie,Elvish, ...
120122,Christina,Ngan, ...
120123,Kimiko,Hotstone, ...
120124,Lucian,Daymond, ...
120125,Fong,Hofmeister, ...
```

Initialize PDV

```
data work.subset;
   infile "&path\sales.csv"
          dlm=',';
   input Employee_ID First_Name $
         Last_Name $ Gender $
         Salary Job_Title $
         Country $;
run;
```

Input Buffer

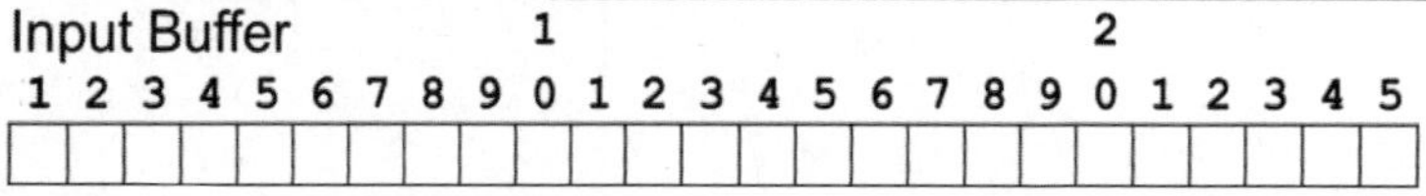

PDV

Employee _ID N 8	First _Name $ 8	Last _Name $ 8	Gender $ 8	Salary N 8	Job _Title $ 8	Country $ 8
.				.		

33 ...

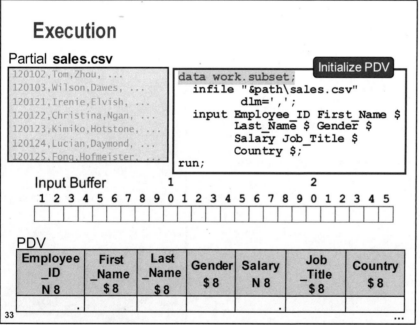

Copyright © 2016, SAS Institute Inc., Cary, North Carolina, USA. ALL RIGHTS RESERVED.

Execution

Partial **sales.csv**

```
120102,Tom,Zhou, ...
120103,Wilson,Dawes, ...
120121,Irenie,Elvish, ...
120122,Christina,Ngan, ...
120123,Kimiko,Hotstone, ...
120124,Lucian,Daymond, ...
120125,Fong,Hofmeister, ...
```

```
data work.subset;
  infile "&path\sales.csv"
         dlm=',';
  input Employee_ID First_Name $
        Last_Name $ Gender $
        Salary Job_Title $
        Country $;
run;
```

Input Buffer

1	2	3	4	5	6	7	8	9	10	1	2	3	4	5	6	7	8	9	20	1	2	3	4	5

PDV

Employee _ID N 8	First _Name $ 8	Last _Name $ 8	Gender $ 8	Salary N 8	Job _Title $ 8	Country $ 8
.				.		

34 ...

Execution

Partial **sales.csv**

```
120102,Tom,Zhou, ...
120103,Wilson,Dawes, ...
120121,Irenie,Elvish, ...
120122,Christina,Ngan, ...
120123,Kimiko,Hotstone, ...
120124,Lucian,Daymond, ...
120125,Fong,Hofmeister, ...
```

```
data work.subset;
  infile "&path\sales.csv"
         dlm=',';
  input Employee_ID First_Name $
        Last_Name $ Gender $
        Salary Job_Title $
        Country $;
run;
```

SAS reads a record into the input buffer.

Input Buffer

1	2	3	4	5	6	7	8	9	10	1	2	3	4	5	6	7	8	9	20	1	2	3	4	5
1	2	0	1	0	2	,	T	o	m	,	Z	h	o	u	,	M	,	1	0	8	2	5	5	,

PDV

Employee _ID N 8	First _Name $ 8	Last _Name $ 8	Gender $ 8	Salary N 8	Job _Title $ 8	Country $ 8
.				.		

35 ...

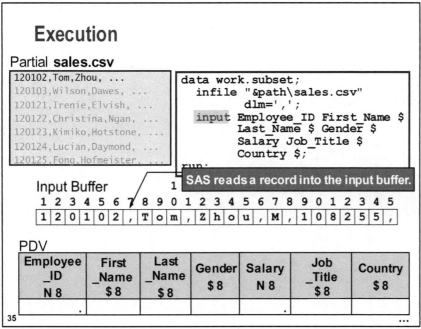

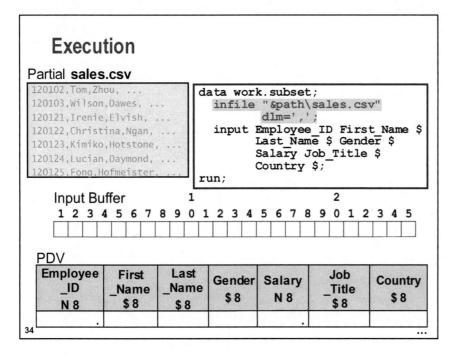

Copyright © 2016, SAS Institute Inc., Cary, North Carolina, USA. ALL RIGHTS RESERVED.

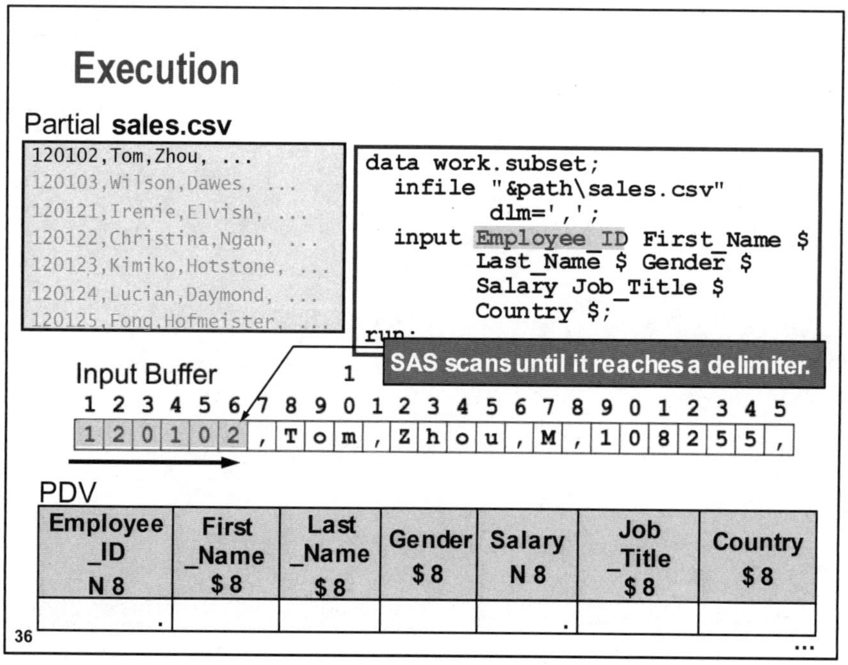

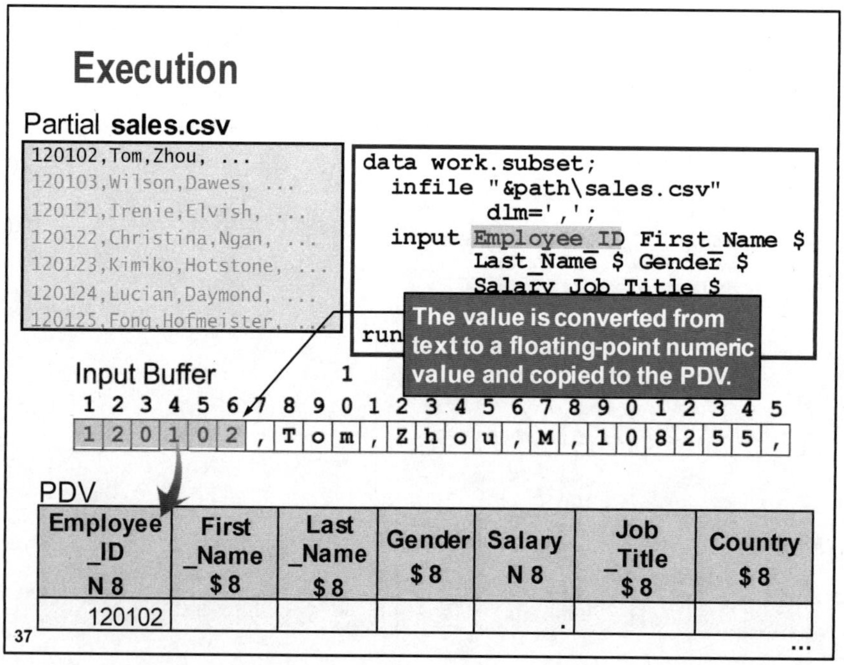

Copyright © 2016, SAS Institute Inc., Cary, North Carolina, USA. ALL RIGHTS RESERVED.

Execution

Partial **sales.csv**

```
120102,Tom,Zhou, ...
120103,Wilson,Dawes, ...
120121,Irenie,Elvish, ...
120122,Christina,Ngan, ...
120123,Kimiko,Hotstone, ...
120124,Lucian,Daymond, ...
120125,Fong,Hofmeister, ...
```

```
data work.subset;
  infile "&path\sales.csv"
         dlm=',';
  input Employee_ID First_Name $
        Last_Name $ Gender $
        Salary Job_Title $
        Country $;
run;
```

SAS skips the delimiter and scans to the next delimiter.

Input Buffer

```
                  1                   2
1 2 3 4 5 6 7 8 9 0 1 2 3 4 5 6 7 8 9 0 1 2 3 4 5
1 2 0 1 0 2 , T o m , Z h o u , M , 1 0 8 2 5 5 ,
```

PDV

Employee _ID N 8	First _Name $ 8	Last _Name $ 8	Gender $ 8	Salary N 8	Job _Title $ 8	Country $ 8
120102				.		

38 ...

Execution

Partial **sales.csv**

```
120102,Tom,Zhou, ...
120103,Wilson,Dawes, ...
120121,Irenie,Elvish, ...
120122,Christina,Ngan, ...
120123,Kimiko,Hotstone, ...
120124,Lucian,Daymond, ...
120125,Fong,Hofmeister, ...
```

```
data work.subset;
  infile "&path\sales.csv"
         dlm=',';
  input Employee_ID First_Name $
        Last_Name $ Gender $
        Salary Job_Title $
        Country $;
run;
```

The text value is copied to the PDV without conversion.

Input Buffer

```
                  1                   2
1 2 3 4 5 6 7 8 9 0 1 2 3 4 5 6 7 8 9 0 1 2 3 4 5
1 2 0 1 0 2 , T o m , Z h o u , M , 1 0 8 2 5 5 ,
```

PDV

Employee _ID N 8	First _Name $ 8	Last _Name $ 8	Gender $ 8	Salary N 8	Job _Title $ 8	Country $ 8
120102	Tom			.		

39 ...

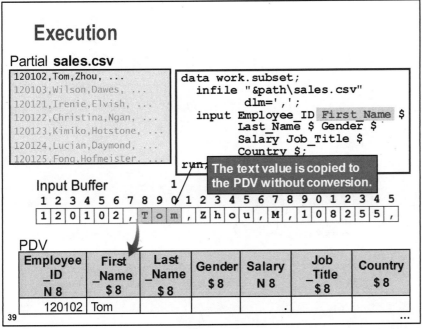

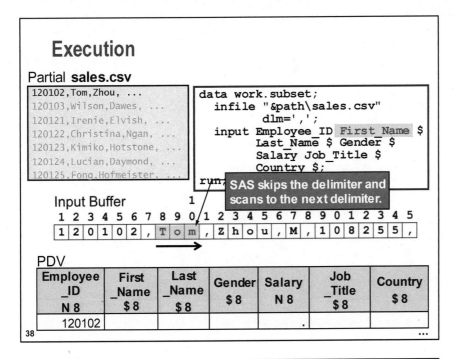

Copyright © 2016, SAS Institute Inc., Cary, North Carolina, USA. ALL RIGHTS RESERVED.

Execution

Partial **sales.csv**

```
120102,Tom,Zhou, ...
120103,Wilson,Dawes, ...
120121,Irenie,Elvish, ...
120122,Christina,Ngan, ...
120123,Kimiko,Hotstone, ...
120124,Lucian,Daymond, ...
120125,Fong,Hofmeister, ...
```

```
data work.subset;
  infile "&path\sales.csv"
         dlm=',';
  input Employee_ID First_Name $
        Last_Name $ Gender $
        Salary Job_Title $
        Country $;
run;
```

These actions continue for all variables in the INPUT statement.

Input Buffer

1	2	3	4	5	6	7	8	9	10	11	12	13	14	15	16	17	18	19	20	21	22	23	24	25
1	2	0	1	0	2	,	T	o	m	,	Z	h	o	u	,	M	,	1	0	8	2	5	5	,

PDV

Employee _ID N 8	First _Name $ 8	Last _Name $ 8	Gender $ 8	Salary N 8	Job _Title $ 8	Country $ 8
120102	Tom	Zhou	M	108255	Sales Ma	AU

40 ...

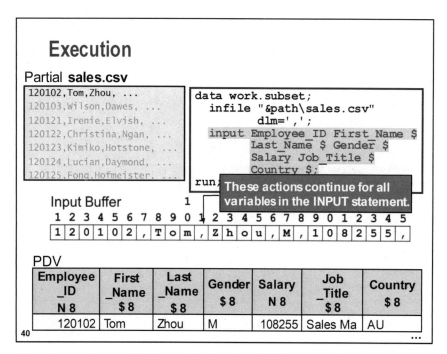

There is usually no delimiter after the last field in a record, so SAS stops reading when it encounters an end-of-record marker.

Execution

Partial **sales.csv**

```
120102,Tom,Zhou, ...
120103,Wilson,Dawes, ...
120121,Irenie,Elvish, ...
120122,Christina,Ngan, ...
120123,Kimiko,Hotstone, ...
120124,Lucian,Daymond, ...
120125,Fong,Hofmeister, ...
```

```
data work.subset;
  infile "&path\sales.csv"
         dlm=',';
  input Employee_ID First_Name $
        Last_Name $ Gender $
        Salary Job_Title $
        Country $;
run;
```

Implicit OUTPUT;
Implicit RETURN;

Input Buffer

1	2	3	4	5	6	7	8	9	10	11	12	13	14	15	16	17	18	19	20	21	22	23	24	25
1	2	0	1	0	2	,	T	o	m	,	Z	h	o	u	,	M	,	1	0	8	2	5	5	,

PDV

Employee _ID N 8	First _Name $ 8	Last _Name $ 8	Gender $ 8	Salary N 8	Job _Title $ 8	Country $ 8
120102	Tom	Zhou	M	108255	Sales Ma	AU

41 ...

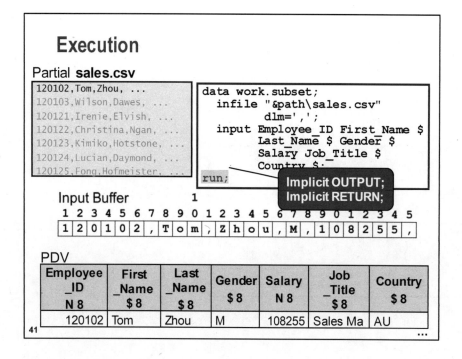

Copyright © 2016, SAS Institute Inc., Cary, North Carolina, USA. ALL RIGHTS RESERVED.

Execution

Here is the output data set after the first iteration of the DATA step.

work.subset

Employee _ID	First _Name	Last _Name	Gender	Salary	Job _Title	Country
120102	Tom	Zhou	M	108255	Sales Ma	AU

42 ...

Execution

Partial **sales.csv**

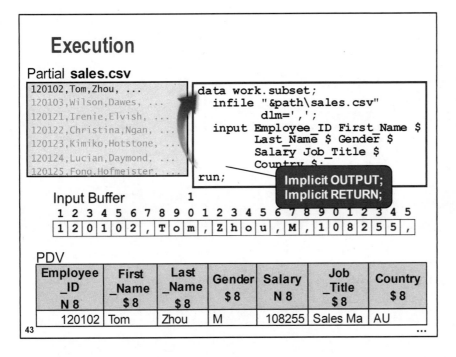

```
120102,Tom,Zhou, ...
120103,Wilson,Dawes, ...
120121,Irenie,Elvish, ...
120122,Christina,Ngan, ...
120123,Kimiko,Hotstone, ...
120124,Lucian,Daymond, ...
120125,Fong,Hofmeister, ...
```

```
data work.subset;
  infile "&path\sales.csv"
         dlm=',';
  input Employee_ID First_Name $
        Last_Name $ Gender $
        Salary Job_Title $
        Country $;
run;
```

Implicit OUTPUT;
Implicit RETURN;

Input Buffer

1	2	3	4	5	6	7	8	9	10	1	2	3	4	5	6	7	8	9	0	1	2	3	4	5
1	2	0	1	0	2	,	T	o	m	,	Z	h	o	u	,	M	,	1	0	8	2	5	5	,

PDV

Employee _ID N 8	First _Name $ 8	Last _Name $ 8	Gender $ 8	Salary N 8	Job _Title $ 8	Country $ 8
120102	Tom	Zhou	M	108255	Sales Ma	AU

43 ...

Copyright © 2016, SAS Institute Inc., Cary, North Carolina, USA. ALL RIGHTS RESERVED.

Execution

Partial **sales.csv**

```
120102,Tom,Zhou, ...
120103,Wilson,Dawes, ...
120121,Irenie,Elvish, ...
120122,Christina,Ngan, ...
120123,Kimiko,Hotstone, ...
120124,Lucian,Daymond, ...
120125,Fong,Hofmeister, ...
```

Reinitialize PDV

```
data work.subset;
   infile "&path\sales.csv"
          dlm=',';
   input Employee_ID First_Name $
         Last_Name $ Gender $
         Salary Job_Title $
         Country $;
run;
```

Input Buffer

1	2	3	4	5	6	7	8	9	10	1	2	3	4	5	6	7	8	9	20	1	2	3	4	5
1	2	0	1	0	2	,	T	o	m	,	Z	h	o	u	,	M	,	1	0	8	2	5	5	,

All variables in the PDV are reinitialized.

PDV

Employee_ID N 8	First_Name $ 8	Last_Name $ 8	Gender $ 8	Salary N 8	Job_Title $ 8	Country $ 8
.				.		

44 ...

Execution

Partial **sales.csv**

```
120102,Tom,Zhou, ...
120103,Wilson,Dawes, ...
120121,Irenie,Elvish, ...
120122,Christina,Ngan, ...
120123,Kimiko,Hotstone, ...
120124,Lucian,Daymond, ...
120125,Fong,Hofmeister, ...
```

```
data work.subset;
   infile "&path\sales.csv"
          dlm=',';
   input Employee_ID First_Name $
         Last_Name $ Gender $
         Salary Job_Title $
         Country $;
run;
```

Input Buffer

1	2	3	4	5	6	7	8	9	10	1	2	3	4	5	6	7	8	9	20	1	2	3	4	5
1	2	0	1	0	2	,	T	o	m	,	Z	h	o	u	,	M	,	1	0	8	2	5	5	,

PDV

Employee_ID N 8	First_Name $ 8	Last_Name $ 8	Gender $ 8	Salary N 8	Job_Title $ 8	Country $ 8
.				.		

45 ...

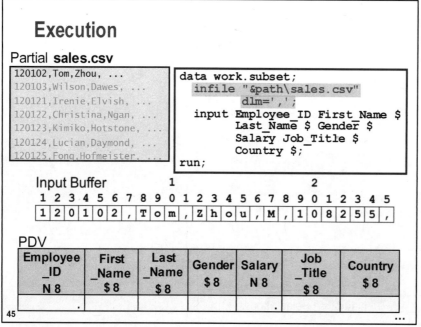

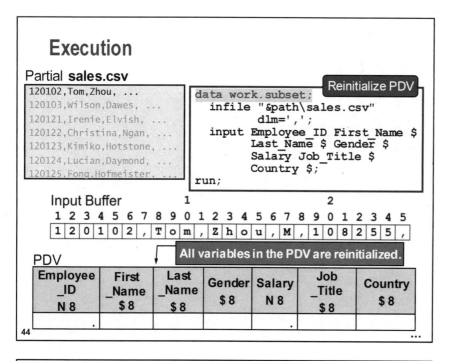

Copyright © 2016, SAS Institute Inc., Cary, North Carolina, USA. ALL RIGHTS RESERVED.

Execution

Partial **sales.csv**

```
120102,Tom,Zhou, ...
120103,Wilson,Dawes, ...
120121,Irenie,Elvish, ...
120122,Christina,Ngan, ...
120123,Kimiko,Hotstone, ...
120124,Lucian,Daymond, ...
120125,Fong,Hofmeister, ...
```

```
data work.subset;
  infile "&path\sales.csv"
         dlm=',';
  input Employee_ID First_Name $
        Last_Name $ Gender $
        Salary Job_Title $
        Country $;
run;
```

Input Buffer

1	2	3	4	5	6	7	8	9	10	1	2	3	4	5	6	7	8	9	20	1	2	3	4	5
1	2	0	1	0	3	,	W	i	l	s	o	n	,	D	a	w	e	s	,	M	,	8	7	9

PDV

Employee_ID N 8	First_Name $ 8	Last_Name $ 8	Gender $ 8	Salary N 8	Job_Title $ 8	Country $ 8
.				.		

46 ...

Execution

Partial **sales.csv**

```
120102,Tom,Zhou, ...
120103,Wilson,Dawes, ...
120121,Irenie,Elvish, ...
120122,Christina,Ngan, ...
120123,Kimiko,Hotstone, ...
120124,Lucian,Daymond, ...
120125,Fong,Hofmeister, ...
```

```
data work.subset;
  infile "&path\sales.csv"
         dlm=',';
  input Employee_ID First_Name $
        Last_Name $ Gender $
        Salary Job_Title $
        Country $;
run;
```

Input Buffer

1	2	3	4	5	6	7	8	9	10	1	2	3	4	5	6	7	8	9	20	1	2	3	4	5
1	2	0	1	0	3	,	W	i	l	s	o	n	,	D	a	w	e	s	,	M	,	8	7	9

PDV

Employee_ID N 8	First_Name $ 8	Last_Name $ 8	Gender $ 8	Salary N 8	Job_Title $ 8	Country $ 8
120103	Wilson	Dawes	M	87975	Sales Ma	AU

47 ...

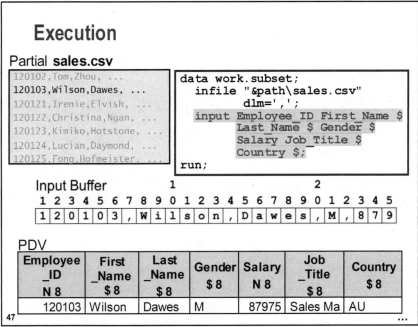

Copyright © 2016, SAS Institute Inc., Cary, North Carolina, USA. ALL RIGHTS RESERVED.

Execution

Partial **sales.csv**

```
120102,Tom,Zhou, ...
120103,Wilson,Dawes, ...
120121,Irenie,Elvish, ...
120122,Christina,Ngan, ...
120123,Kimiko,Hotstone, ...
120124,Lucian,Daymond, ...
120125,Fong,Hofmeister, ...
```

```
data work.subset;
   infile "&path\sales.csv"
          dlm=',';
   input Employee_ID First_Name $
         Last_Name $ Gender $
         Salary Job_Title $
         Country $;
run;
```

Implicit OUTPUT;
Implicit RETURN;

Input Buffer

1	2	3	4	5	6	7	8	9	10	11	12	13	14	15	16	17	18	19	20	21	22	23	24	25
1	2	0	1	0	3	,	W	i	l	s	o	n	,	D	a	w	e	s	,	M	,	8	7	9

work.subset

Employee _ID	First _Name	Last _Name	Gender	Salary	Job _Title	County
120102	Tom	Zhou	M	108255	Sales Ma	AU
120103	Wilson	Dawes	M	87975	Sales Ma	AU

48 ...

Execution

Partial **sales.csv**

```
120102,Tom,Zhou, ...
120103,Wilson,Dawes, ...
120121,Irenie,Elvish, ...
120122,Christina,Ngan, ...
120123,Kimiko,Hotstone, ...
120124,Lucian,Daymond, ...
120125,Fong,Hofmeister, ...
```

```
data work.subset;
   infile "&path\sales.csv"
   input Employee_ID First_Name $
         Last_Name $ Gender $
         Salary Job_Title $
         Country $;
run;
```

Continue until EOF

Input Buffer

1	2	3	4	5	6	7	8	9	10	11	12	13	14	15	16	17	18	19	20	21	22	23	24	25
1	2	0	1	0	3	,	W	i	l	s	o	n	,	D	a	w	e	s	,	M	,	8	7	9

PDV

Employee _ID N 8	First _Name $ 8	Last _Name $ 8	Gender $ 8	Salary N 8	Job _Title $ 8	Country $ 8
.				.		

49

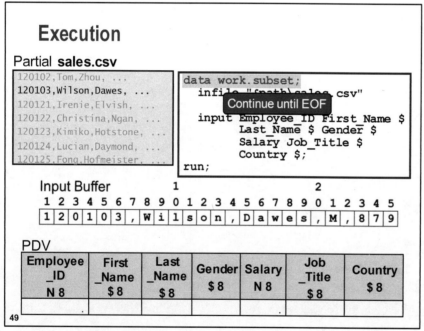

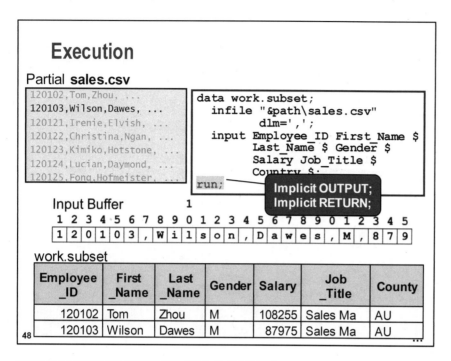

Copyright © 2016, SAS Institute Inc., Cary, North Carolina, USA. ALL RIGHTS RESERVED.

Viewing the Output

```
proc print data=work.subset noobs;
run;
```

Partial PROC PRINT Output

Employee_ ID	First_ Name	Last_ Name	Gender	Salary	Job_ Title	Country
120102	Tom	Zhou	M	108255	Sales Ma	AU
120103	Wilson	Dawes	M	87975	Sales Ma	AU
120121	Irenie	Elvish	F	26600	Sales Re	AU
120122	Christin	Ngan	F	27475	Sales Re	AU
120123	Kimiko	Hotstone	F	26190	Sales Re	AU
120124	Lucian	Daymond	M	26480	Sales Re	AU
120125	Fong	Hofmeist	M	32040	Sales Re	AU

Some character values are truncated.

50 p108d01

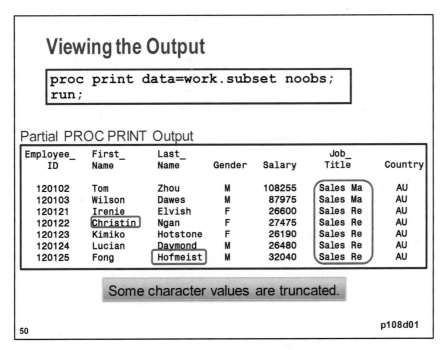

Some character values contain unnecessary trailing blanks, although this is not obvious in a PROC PRINT report.

LENGTH Statement

The *LENGTH statement* defines the type and length of a variable.

LENGTH *variable(s)* <$> *length* ...;

```
data work.subset;
   length First_Name $ 12 Last_Name $ 18
          Gender $ 1 Job_Title $ 25
          Country $ 2;
   infile "&path\sales.csv" dlm=',';
   input Employee_ID First_Name $ Last_Name $
         Gender $ Salary Job_Title $ Country $;
run;
```

Put the LENGTH statement before the INPUT statement.

51 p108d02

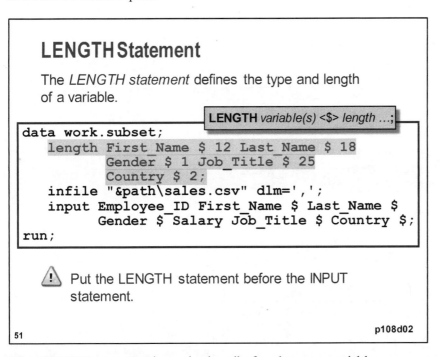

The LENGTH statement is used primarily for character variables.

Copyright © 2016, SAS Institute Inc., Cary, North Carolina, USA. ALL RIGHTS RESERVED.

Compilation

```
data work.subset;
   length First_Name $ 12 Last_Name $ 18
          Gender $ 1 Job_Title $ 25
          Country $ 2;
   infile "&path\sales.csv" dlm=',';
   input Employee_ID First_Name $ Last_Name $
         Gender $ Salary Job_Title $ Country $;
run;
```

Attributes are based on the LENGTH statement.

PDV

First_ Name $ 12	Last _Name $ 18	Gender $ 1	Job_Title $ 25	Country $ 2

52 ...

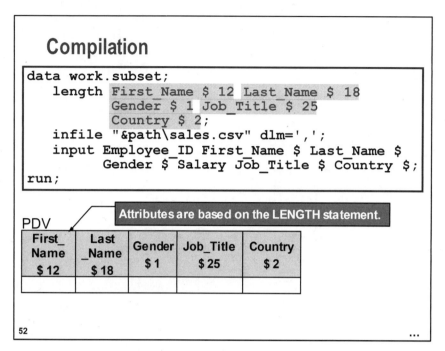

The name, type, and length of a variable are determined at the variable's first use. These specifications can be in a LENGTH statement or the INPUT statement, whichever appears first in the DATA step. The name is used exactly as specified at first use, including the case.

Compilation

```
data work.subset;
   length First_Name $ 12 Last_Name $ 18
          Gender $ 1 Job_Title $ 25
          Country $ 2;
   infile "&path\sales.csv" dlm=',';
   input Employee_ID First_Name $ Last_Name $
         Gender $ Salary Job_Title $ Country $;
run;
```

PDV

First_ Name $ 12	Last _Name $ 18	Gender $ 1	Job_Title $ 25	Country $ 2	Employee_ ID N 8	Salary N 8

53

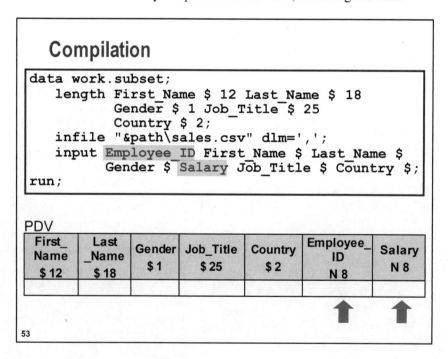

Copyright © 2016, SAS Institute Inc., Cary, North Carolina, USA. ALL RIGHTS RESERVED.

Viewing the Output

```
proc print data=work.subset noobs;
run;
```

Partial PROC PRINT Output

First_ Name	Last_Name	Gender	Job_Title	Country	Employee_ ID	Salary
Tom	Zhou	M	Sales Manager	AU	120102	108255
Wilson	Dawes	M	Sales Manager	AU	120103	87975
Irenie	Elvish	F	Sales Rep. II	AU	120121	26600
Christina	Ngan	F	Sales Rep. II	AU	120122	27475
Kimiko	Hotstone	F	Sales Rep. I	AU	120123	26190

The character values are no longer truncated, but the order of the variables changed.

p108d02

54

8.04 Short Answer Poll

Suppose you want the order of the variables to match the order of the fields. You can include the numeric variables in the LENGTH statement. Which of the following produces the correct results?

a.

```
length Employee_ID First_Name $ 12
       Last_Name $ 18 Gender $ 1
       Salary Job_Title $ 25
       Country $ 2;
```

b.

```
length Employee_ID 8 First_Name $ 12
       Last_Name $ 18 Gender $ 1
       Salary 8 Job_Title $ 25
       Country $ 2;
```

55

Copyright © 2016, SAS Institute Inc., Cary, North Carolina, USA. ALL RIGHTS RESERVED.

Using a LENGTH Statement

The LENGTH statement identifies the character variables, so dollar signs can be omitted from the INPUT statement.

```
data work.subset;
   length Employee_ID 8 First_Name $ 12
          Last_Name $ 18 Gender $ 1
          Salary 8 Job_Title $ 25
          Country $ 2;
   infile "&path\sales.csv" dlm=',';
   input Employee_ID First_Name Last_Name
         Gender Salary Job_Title Country;
run;
```

57

p108d03

Viewing the Output

Display the variables in creation order.

```
proc contents data=work.subset varnum;
run;
```

Partial PROC CONTENTS Output

Variables in Creation Order

#	Variable	Type	Len
1	Employee_ID	Num	8
2	First_Name	Char	12
3	Last_Name	Char	18
4	Gender	Char	1
5	Salary	Num	8
6	Job_Title	Char	25
7	Country	Char	2

58

Copyright © 2016, SAS Institute Inc., Cary, North Carolina, USA. ALL RIGHTS RESERVED.

Viewing the Output

Partial PROC PRINT Output

Employee_ ID	First_ Name	Last_Name	Gender	Salary	Job_Title	Country
120102	Tom	Zhou	M	108255	Sales Manager	AU
120103	Wilson	Dawes	M	87975	Sales Manager	AU
120121	Irenie	Elvish	F	26600	Sales Rep. II	AU
120122	Christina	Ngan	F	27475	Sales Rep. II	AU
120123	Kimiko	Hotstone	F	26190	Sales Rep. I	AU
120124	Lucian	Daymond	M	26480	Sales Rep. I	AU
120125	Fong	Hofmeister	M	32040	Sales Rep. IV	AU

59

Business Scenario

A raw data file contains information about Orion Star sales employees. It includes some invalid data values.

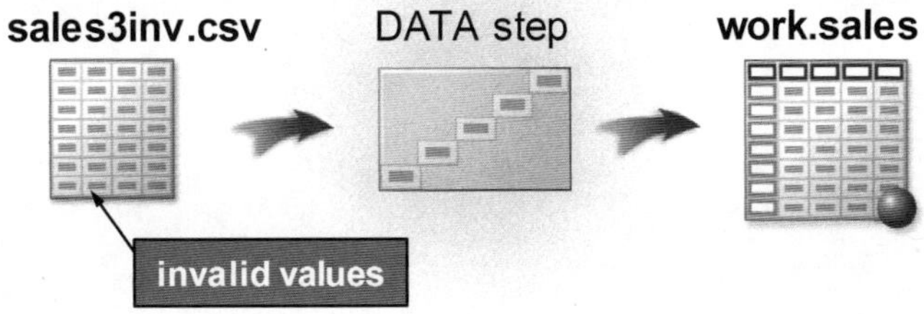

61

Copyright © 2016, SAS Institute Inc., Cary, North Carolina, USA. ALL RIGHTS RESERVED.

8.05 Short Answer Poll

What problems do you see with the data values for the last two data fields, **Salary** and **Country**?

Partial **sales3inv.csv**

```
120102,Tom,Zhou,Manager,108255,AU
120103,Wilson,Dawes,Manager,87975,AU
120121,Irenie,Elvish,Rep. II,26600,AU
120122,Christina,Ngan,Rep. II,n/a,AU
120123,Kimiko,Hotstone,Rep. I,26190,AU
120124,Lucian,Daymond,Rep. I,26480,12
120125,Fong,Hofmeister,Rep. IV,32040,AU
```

62

Reading a Raw Data File with Data Errors

```
data work.sales;
   infile "&path\sales3inv.csv" dlm=',';
   input Employee_ID First $ Last $
         Job_Title $ Salary Country $;
run;

proc print data=work.sales;
run;
```

Salary is defined as numeric and **Country** as character.

64

p108d04

Copyright © 2016, SAS Institute Inc., Cary, North Carolina, USA. ALL RIGHTS RESERVED.

Viewing the Output

Partial PROC PRINT Output

Obs	Employee_ ID	First	Last	Job_ Title	Salary	Country
1	120102	Tom	Zhou	Manager	108255	AU
2	120103	Wilson	Dawes	Manager	87975	AU
3	120121	Irenie	Elvish	Rep. II	26600	AU
4	120122	Christin	Ngan	Rep. II	.	AU
5	120123	Kimiko	Hotstone	Rep. I	26190	AU
6	120124	Lucian	Daymond	Rep. I	26480	12
7	120125	Fong	Hofmeist	Rep. IV	32040	AU

- A missing value was stored in **Salary** for the input value *n/a*.
- The value *12* was successfully stored in **Country**.
- A data error occurred on observation 4, but not on observation 6.

65

Data Errors

A data error occurs when a data value does not match the field specification. The following information is written to the SAS log:

- a note describing the error
- a column ruler
- the input record
- the contents of the PDV

```
NOTE: Invalid data for Salary in line 4 31-33.
RULE:      ----+----1----+----2----+----3----+----4----+----5-
4          120122,Christina,Ngan,Rep. II,n/a,AU 36
Employee_ID=120122 First=Christin Last=Ngan Job_Title=Rep. II Salary=..
Country=AU _ERROR_=1 _N_=4
```

A missing value is assigned to the corresponding variable, and execution continues.

66

Even though these are referred to as *data errors*, they generate notes, not error messages. Syntax errors stop the DATA step, whereas data errors enable processing to continue.

Copyright © 2016, SAS Institute Inc., Cary, North Carolina, USA. ALL RIGHTS RESERVED.

Data Errors

Two temporary variables are created during the processing of every DATA step.

- **_N_** is the DATA step iteration counter.
- **_ERROR_** indicates data error status.
  - *0* indicates that no data error occurred on that record.
  - *1* indicates that one or more data errors occurred on that record.

```
NOTE: Invalid data for Salary in line 4 31-33.
RULE:      ----+----1----+----2----+----3----+----4----+----5-
4          120122,Christina,Ngan,Rep. II,n/a,AU 36
Employee_ID=120122 First=Christin Last=Ngan Job_Title=Rep. II Salary=.
Country=AU _ERROR_=1 _N_=4
```

67

ERROR is reset to *0*, and _N_ is incremented by 1 at the beginning of each iteration.

Copyright © 2016, SAS Institute Inc., Cary, North Carolina, USA. ALL RIGHTS RESERVED.

Examining Data Errors

p108d04

```
data work.sales;
   infile "&path\sales3inv.csv" dlm=',';
   input Employee_ID First $ Last $
         Job_Title $ Salary Country $;
run;

proc print data=work.sales;
run;
```

1. Open the raw data file **sales3inv.csv**.

   In SAS Enterprise Guide, select **File** ⇨ **Open** ⇨ **Data**. Navigate to your data folder.

   In the SAS windowing environment, select **File** ⇨ **Open Program**. Select **All Files (*.*)** from the File of type menu.

   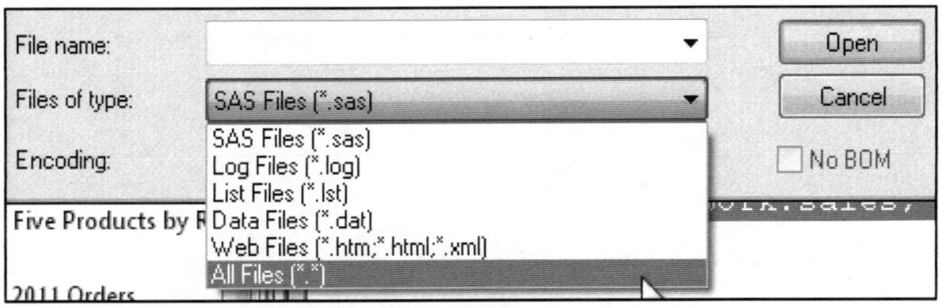

   Select **sales3inv.csv** from the list of files.

2. View the **Salary** values. There are three invalid values and one missing value.
3. Open and submit **p108d04**.
4. Examine the log. The DATA step creates an output data set, **work.sales**, with 50 observations. The three invalid **Salary** values were identified in the log, and the corresponding observations have a missing value for **Salary**. The missing **Salary** value was not reported as a data error because *missing* is a valid value in SAS.
5. Examine the output. Notice that there are four observations with missing **Salary** values.

End of Demonstration

Copyright © 2016, SAS Institute Inc., Cary, North Carolina, USA. ALL RIGHTS RESERVED.

8.06 Multiple Choice Poll

Submit program **p108a01** and examine the log.

Which statement best describes the reason for the error?

a. The data in the raw data file is invalid.
b. The programmer incorrectly read the data.

69

Use the SAS system option, ERRORS=*n*, to specify the maximum number of observations for which error messages about data input errors are printed.

```
options errors=5;
```

Copyright © 2016, SAS Institute Inc., Cary, North Carolina, USA. ALL RIGHTS RESERVED.

Exercises

> If you restarted your SAS session since the last exercise, open and submit the **libname.sas** program that can be found in the data folder.

Level 1

1. **Reading a Comma-Delimited Raw Data File**

   a. Open **p108e01**. Add the appropriate LENGTH, INFILE, and INPUT statements to read the comma-delimited raw data file, which can be named as follows:

Windows	**"&path\newemps.csv"**
UNIX	**"&path/newemps.csv"**
z/OS (OS/390)	**"&path..rawdata(newemps)"**

Partial Raw Data File

```
Satyakam,Denny,Sales Rep. II,26780
Monica,Kletschkus,Sales Rep. IV,30890
Kevin,Lyon,Sales Rep. I,26955
Petrea,Soltau,Sales Rep. II,27440
Marina,Iyengar,Sales Rep. III,29715
```

   b. Read the following fields from the raw data file:

Name	Type	Length
First	Character	12
Last	Character	18
Title	Character	25
Salary	Numeric	8

   c. Submit the program to create the report below. The results should contain 71 observations.

Partial PROC PRINT Output

```
          Obs    First       Last                  Title               Salary

            1    Satyakam    Denny                 Sales Rep. II        26780
            2    Monica      Kletschkus            Sales Rep. IV        30890
            3    Kevin       Lyon                  Sales Rep. I         26955
            4    Petrea      Soltau                Sales Rep. II        27440
            5    Marina      Iyengar               Sales Rep. III       29715
```

Copyright © 2016, SAS Institute Inc., Cary, North Carolina, USA. ALL RIGHTS RESERVED.

Level 2

2. Reading a Space-Delimited Raw Data File

a. Write a DATA step to create a new data set named **work.qtrdonation**. Read the space-delimited raw data file, which can be named as follows:

Windows	**"&path\donation.dat"**
UNIX	**"&path/donation.dat"**
z/OS (OS/390)	**"&path..rawdata(donation)"**

Partial Raw Data File

```
120265 . . . 25
120267 15 15 15 15
120269 20 20 20 20
120270 20 10 5 .
120271 20 20 20 20
```

b. Read the following fields from the raw data file:

Name	Type	Length
IDNum	Character	6
Qtr1	Numeric	8
Qtr2	Numeric	8
Qtr3	Numeric	8
Qtr4	Numeric	8

c. Write a PROC PRINT step to create the report below. The results contain 124 observations.

Partial PROC PRINT Output

```
Obs    IDNum     Qtr1    Qtr2    Qtr3    Qtr4

  1    120265      .       .       .      25
  2    120267     15      15      15      15
  3    120269     20      20      20      20
  4    120270     20      10       5       .
  5    120271     20      20      20      20
```

Copyright © 2016, SAS Institute Inc., Cary, North Carolina, USA. ALL RIGHTS RESERVED.

Challenge

3. Reading a Tab-Delimited Raw Data File

a. Create a temporary data set, **managers2**. Use the tab-delimited raw data file, which can be named as follows:

Windows	**"&path\managers2.dat"**
UNIX	**"&path/ managers2.dat"**
z/OS (OS/390)	**"&path..rawdata(managers2)"**

Raw Data File

```
120102 Tom    Zhou    M        108255  Sales Manager
120103 Wilson Dawes   M        87975   Sales Manager
120261 Harry  Highpoint        M       243190  Chief Sales Officer
121143 Louis  Favaron M        95090   Senior Sales Manager
121144 Renee  Capachietti      F       83505   Sales Manager
121145 Dennis Lansberry        M       84260   Sales Manager
```

b. Read the following fields from the raw data file:

Name	Type
ID	Numeric
First	Character
Last	Character
Gender	Character
Salary	Numeric
Title	Character

c. The new data set should contain only **First**, **Last**, and **Title**.

d. Generate the report below. The results should contain six observations.

```
Obs    First     Last          Title

  1    Tom       Zhou          Sales Manager
  2    Wilson    Dawes         Sales Manager
  3    Harry     Highpoint     Chief Sales Officer
  4    Louis     Favaron       Senior Sales Manager
  5    Renee     Capachietti   Sales Manager
  6    Dennis    Lansberry     Sales Manager
```

End of Exercises

Copyright © 2016, SAS Institute Inc., Cary, North Carolina, USA. ALL RIGHTS RESERVED.

8.3 Using Informats to Read Delimited Data

Objectives

- Use informats to read character data.
- Use informats to read nonstandard data.
- Subset observations and add permanent attributes.

74

Business Scenario

Create a temporary SAS data set by reading both standard and nonstandard values from a comma-delimited raw data file.

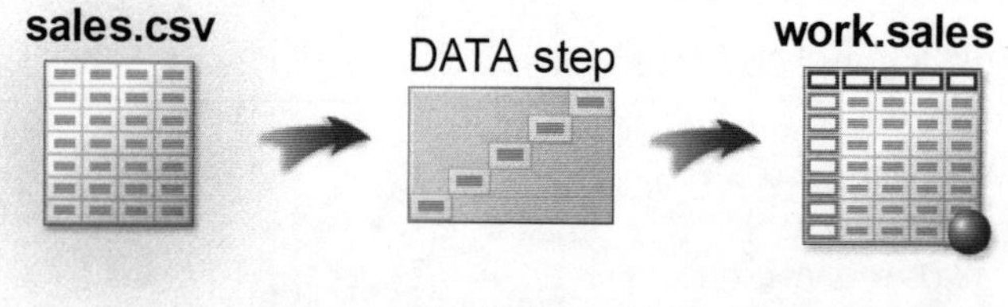

The new data set should contain a subset of the input data and include permanent attributes.

75

Copyright © 2016, SAS Institute Inc., Cary, North Carolina, USA. ALL RIGHTS RESERVED.

Considerations

Use modified list input to read all the fields from **sales.csv**. Store the date fields as SAS dates.

Partial **sales.csv**

```
120102,Tom,Zhou,M,108255,Sales Manager,AU,11AUG1973,06/01/1993
120103,Wilson,Dawes,M,87975,Sales Manager,AU,22JAN1953,01/01/1978
120121,Irenie,Elvish,F,26600,Sales Rep. II,AU,02AUG1948,01/01/1978
120122,Christina,Ngan,F,27475,Sales Rep. II,AU,27JUL1958,07/01/1982
120123,Kimiko,Hotstone,F,26190,Sales Rep. I,AU,28SEP1968,10/01/1989
```

76

Modified List Input

This DATA step uses *modified list input.* Instead of a LENGTH statement, an informat specifies the length for each character variable.

input *variable* <*:informat.*> *...;*

```
data work.subset;
   infile "&path\sales.csv" dlm=',';
   input Employee_ID First_Name :$12.
         Last_Name :$18. Gender :$1. Salary
         Job_Title :$25. Country :$2.;
run;
```

- The **$12.** informat defines a length of 12 for **First_Name** and enables up to 12 characters to be read.
- The : format modifier tells SAS to read until it encounters a delimiter.

77

p108d05

Copyright © 2016, SAS Institute Inc., Cary, North Carolina, USA. ALL RIGHTS RESERVED.

Modified List Input

⚠ Omitting the colon modifier causes unexpected results.

Partial **sales.csv** — reads 12 characters

```
120102,Tom,Zhou,M,108255,Sales Manager,AU,11AUG1973,06/01/1993
```

```
input Employee_ID First_Name $12.
      Last_Name :$18. Gender :$1. Salary
      Job_Title :$25. Country :$2.;
```

PDV

Employee_ID N 8	First_Name $ 12	Last_Name $ 18	Gender $ 1
120102	Tom,Zhou,M,1	08255	S

Salary N 8	Job_Title $ 25	Country $ 2
.	11AUG1973	06

78

Reading Nonstandard Data

An informat is ***required*** to read nonstandard numeric data.

Partial **sales.csv**

```
120102,Tom,Zhou,M,108255,Sales Manager,AU,11AUG1973,06/01/1993
120103,Wilson,Dawes,M,87975,Sales Manager,AU,22JAN1953,01/01/1978
120121,Irenie,Elvish,F,26600,Sales Rep. II,AU,02AUG1948,01/01/1978
120122,Christina,Ngan,F,27475,Sales Rep. II,AU,27JUL1958,07/01/1982
120123,Kimiko,Hotstone,F,26190,Sales Rep. I,AU,28SEP1968,10/01/1989
```

In this example, informats are needed to specify the style of the date fields so that they can be read and converted to SAS dates.

79

Copyright © 2016, SAS Institute Inc., Cary, North Carolina, USA. ALL RIGHTS RESERVED.

8.07 Short Answer Poll

A *format* is an instruction that tells SAS how to display data values. What formats could you specify to display a SAS date in the styles shown below?

a) 01JAN2000

b) 01/16/2000

80

Informats for Nonstandard Data

An *informat* is an instruction that SAS uses to ***read*** data values into a variable.

Partial **sales.csv**

```
120102,Tom,Zhou,M,108255,Sales Manager,AU,11AUG1973,06/01/1993
120103,Wilson,Dawes,M,87975,Sales Manager,AU,22JAN1953,01/01/1978
120121,Irenie,Elvish,F,26600,Sales Rep. II,AU,02AUG1948,01/01/1978
120122,Christina,Ngan,F,27475,Sales Rep. II,AU,27JUL1958,07/01/1982
120123,Kimiko,Hotstone,F,26190,Sales Rep. I,AU,28SEP1968,10/01/1989
```

DATE. MMDDYY.

The informat describes the data value and tells SAS how to convert it.

82

Copyright © 2016, SAS Institute Inc., Cary, North Carolina, USA. ALL RIGHTS RESERVED.

SAS Informats

SAS informats have the following form:

```
<$><informat><w>.
```

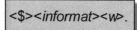

$	Indicates a character informat.
informat	Names the SAS informat or user-defined informat.
w	Specifies the width or number of columns to read or specifies the length of a character variable.
.	Is required syntax.

✎ The width is typically not used with list input because SAS reads each field until it encounters a delimiter.

83

SAS Informats

Selected SAS Informats

Informat	Definition
COMMA. DOLLAR.	Reads nonstandard numeric data and removes embedded commas, blanks, dollar signs, percent signs, and dashes.
COMMAX. DOLLARX.	Reads nonstandard numeric data and removes embedded non-numeric characters; reverses the roles of the decimal point and the comma.
EUROX.	Reads nonstandard numeric data and removes embedded non-numeric characters in European currency.
$CHAR.	Reads character values and preserves leading blanks.
$UPCASE.	Reads character values and converts them to uppercase.

84

Copyright © 2016, SAS Institute Inc., Cary, North Carolina, USA. ALL RIGHTS RESERVED.

SAS Informats

Informats are used to read and convert raw data.

Informat	Raw Data Value	SAS Data Value
COMMA. DOLLAR.	*$12,345*	*12345*
COMMAX. DOLLARX.	*$12.345*	*12345*
EUROX.	*€12.345*	*12345*
$CHAR.	*##Australia*	*##Australia*
$UPCASE.	*au*	*AU*

The character # represents a blank space.

85

SAS Informats

Use date informats to read and convert dates to SAS date values.

Informat	Raw Data Value	SAS Data Value
MMDDYY.	*010160* *01/01/60* *01/01/1960* *1/1/1960*	*0*
DDMMYY.	*311260* *31/12/60* *31/12/1960*	*365*
DATE.	*31DEC59* *31DEC1959*	*-1*

86

Copyright © 2016, SAS Institute Inc., Cary, North Carolina, USA. ALL RIGHTS RESERVED.

8.08 Short Answer Poll

Use the SAS Help Facility or documentation to investigate the **DATE*w*.** informat and answer the following questions:

a) What does the ***w*** represent?

b) What is the default width of this informat?

87

Using Informats to Read Nonstandard Data

```
120102,Tom,Zhou,M,108255,Sales Manager,AU,11AUG1973,6/1/1993
120103,Wilson,Dawes,M,87975,Sales Manager,AU,7JAN1953,1/10/1978
```

DATE.
Default: 7

MMDDYY.
Default: 6

- An informat is needed to read a nonstandard value.
- The width is optional when you use list input.
- If the width and the colon format modifier are omitted, the default width for that informat is used.

89

Copyright © 2016, SAS Institute Inc., Cary, North Carolina, USA. ALL RIGHTS RESERVED.

Modified List Input

The colon format modifier (:) tells SAS to read until it encounters a delimiter.

```
input Employee_ID First_Name :$12.
      Last_Name :$18. Gender :$1.
      Salary Job_Title :$25. Country :$2.
      Birth_Date :date. Hire_Date :mmddyy.;
```

INPUT *variable* <$> *variable* <*:informat*> *...*;

colon format modifier

90

p108d06

Viewing the Log

```
data work.sales;
   infile "&path\sales.csv" dlm=',';
   input Employee_ID First_Name :$12. Last_Name :$18.
         Gender :$1. Salary Job_Title :$25. Country :$2.
         Birth_Date :date. Hire_Date :mmddyy.;
run;

NOTE: The infile "s:\workshop\sales.csv" is:
      Filename=s:\workshop\sales.csv,
      RECFM=V,LRECL=256,File Size (bytes)=11340,

NOTE: 165 records were read from the infile "s:\workshop\sales.csv".
NOTE: The data set WORK.SALES has 165 observations and 9 variables.
```

91

p108d06

Copyright © 2016, SAS Institute Inc., Cary, North Carolina, USA. ALL RIGHTS RESERVED.

Viewing the Output

```
proc print data=work.sales;
run;
```

Partial PROC PRINT Output

Obs	First_ Name	Last_Name	Gender	Job_Title	Country	Employee_ ID	Salary	Birth_ Date	Hire_ Date
1	Tom	Zhou	M	Sales Manager	AU	120102	108255	4971	12205
2	Wilson	Dawes	M	Sales Manager	AU	120103	87975	-2535	6575
3	Irenie	Elvish	F	Sales Rep. II	AU	120121	26600	-4169	6575
4	Christina	Ngan	F	Sales Rep. II	AU	120122	27475	-523	8217
5	Kimiko	Hotstone	F	Sales Rep. I	AU	120123	26190	3193	10866

92 p108d06

Additional SAS Statements

Additional SAS statements can be added to perform further processing in the DATA step.

```
data work.sales;
   infile "&path\sales.csv" dlm=',';
   input Employee_ID First_Name :$12. Last_Name :$18.
         Gender :$1. Salary Job_Title :$25. Country :$2.
         Birth_Date :date. Hire_Date :mmddyy.;
   if Country='AU';
   keep First_Name Last_Name Salary
        Job_Title Hire_Date;
   label Job_Title='Sales Title'
         Hire_Date='Date Hired';
   format Salary dollar12. Hire_Date monyy7.;
run;
```

A subsetting IF statement is used to subset observations when SAS reads from a raw data file.

93 p108d07

Copyright © 2016, SAS Institute Inc., Cary, North Carolina, USA. ALL RIGHTS RESERVED.

Viewing the Output

```
proc print data=work.sales label;
run;
```

Partial PROC PRINT Output

Obs	First_ Name	Last_Name	Sales Title	Salary	Date Hired
1	Tom	Zhou	Sales Manager	$108,255	JUN1993
2	Wilson	Dawes	Sales Manager	$87,975	JAN1978
3	Irenie	Elvish	Sales Rep. II	$26,600	JAN1978
4	Christina	Ngan	Sales Rep. II	$27,475	JUL1982
5	Kimiko	Hotstone	Sales Rep. I	$26,190	OCT1989

94

p108d07

WHERE versus Subsetting IF Statement

Step and Usage	WHERE	IF
PROC step	Yes	No
DATA step (source of variable)		
SET statement	Yes	Yes
assignment statement	No	Yes
➡ INPUT statement	No	Yes

95

Copyright © 2016, SAS Institute Inc., Cary, North Carolina, USA. ALL RIGHTS RESERVED.

Idea Exchange

What factors need to be considered when SAS reads **salary.dat**, which is shown below?

Partial **salary.dat**

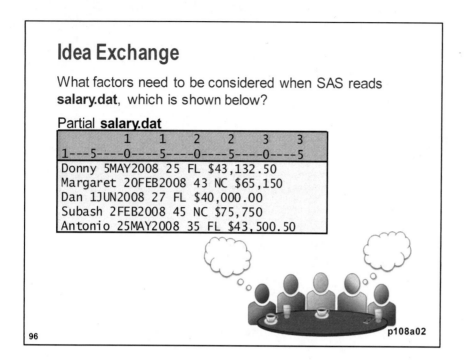

```
         1    1    2    2    3    3
1---5----0----5----0----5----0----5
Donny 5MAY2008 25 FL $43,132.50
Margaret 20FEB2008 43 NC $65,150
Dan 1JUN2008 27 FL $40,000.00
Subash 2FEB2008 45 NC $75,750
Antonio 25MAY2008 35 FL $43,500.50
```

96

p108a02

Copyright © 2016, SAS Institute Inc., Cary, North Carolina, USA. ALL RIGHTS RESERVED.

Using List Input: Importance of Colon Format Modifier

p108a02

1. Open **p108a02** and examine the INPUT statement.
   - The INFILE statement does not contain DLM= because the file is space delimited.
   - **HireDate** and **Salary** are nonstandard numeric fields, so an informat is needed.
2. In the SAS windowing environment, select **File** ⇨ **Open Program**, change the value for **Files of type** to **Data Files (*.dat)**, and select **salary.dat**.

   Files with a .dat extension can be imported in SAS Enterprise Guide but not viewed in an editor.

   Partial **salary.dat**

```
Donny 5MAY2008 25 FL $43,132.50
Margaret 20FEB2008 43 NC 65,150
Dan 1JUN2008 27 FL $40,000.00
Subash 2FEB2008 45 NC 75,750
Antonio 25MAY2008 35 FL $43,500.50
```

3. Submit Part 1 and view the log and output. The expected output is shown below.

```
   /* Part 1 - using colon format modifiers*/
data work.salaries;
   infile "&path\salary.dat";
   input Name $ HireDate :date. Age State $ Salary :comma.;
run;

proc print data=work.salaries;
run;
```

   Partial PROC PRINT Output

```
                   Hire
Obs    Name        Date    Age    State     Salary

 1     Donny      17657     25     FL      43132.5
 2     Margaret   17582     43     NC      65150.0
 3     Dan        17684     27     FL      40000.0
 4     Subash     17564     45     NC      75750.0
 5     Antonio    17677     35     FL      43500.5
```

4. Observe what happens when a colon format modifier is omitted from **Salary**. Submit Part 2.

```
  /* Part 2 - omit the colon format modifier for Salary */
data work.salaries;
   infile "&path\salary.dat";
   input Name $ HireDate :date. Age State $ Salary comma.;
run;

proc print data=work.salaries;
run;
```

Copyright © 2016, SAS Institute Inc., Cary, North Carolina, USA. ALL RIGHTS RESERVED.

5. Examine the log. There are no errors or warnings.

```
923     /* Part 2 ╥ omit the colon format modifier for Salary */
924   data work.salaries;
925       infile "&path\salary.dat";
926       input Name $ HireDate :date. Age State $ Salary comma.;
927   run;

NOTE: The infile "s:\workshop\salary.dat" is:
      Filename=s:\workshop\salary.dat,
NOTE: 8 records were read from the infile "s:\workshop\salary.dat".
NOTE: The data set WORK.SALARIES has 8 observations and 5 variables.
```

6. Examine the output.

Obs	Name	Date	Age	State	Salary
1	Donny	17657	25	FL	.
2	Margaret	17582	43	NC	6
3	Dan	17684	27	FL	.
4	Subash	17564	45	NC	7
5	Antonio	17677	35	FL	.

The **Salary** values are incorrect. Why are the values either missing or only one digit in length?

- The COMMA. informat has a default width of 1, so SAS reads one column from the input file. This reads the first character of the **Salary** value.
- When the first column contains a dollar sign, a missing value is assigned to the numeric variable. This does not cause a data error because the COMMA. informat removes non-numeric characters, including the dollar sign. When the first column contains a digit, that digit becomes the value of the variable.

⚠ In some cases, omitting a colon results in missing or invalid values. In other cases, it results in data errors.

End of Demonstration

Copyright © 2016, SAS Institute Inc., Cary, North Carolina, USA. ALL RIGHTS RESERVED.

Business Scenario

You are working on a new project, but the raw data file is not created yet. You can include in-stream data in a DATA step.

98

DATALINES Statement

The DATALINES statement supplies data within a program.

```
data work.newemps;
   input First_Name :$12. Last_Name :$18.
         Job_Title :$15. Salary :dollar.;
datalines;
Steven Worton Auditor $40,450
Marta-Lyn Bamberger Manager $32,000
Merle Hieds Trainee $24,025
;
```

```
DATALINES;
...
;
```

- DATALINES is the last statement in the DATA step and immediately precedes the first data line.
- A null statement (a single semicolon) indicates the end of the input data.

99 p108d08

To take advantage of INFILE statement options, you can use an INFILE statement with DATALINES.

```
data work.newemps;
   infile datalines dsd;
   length First_Name Last_Name $ 15 Job_Title $ 25;
   input First_Name $ Last_Name $  Job_Title $ Salary :dollar.;
datalines;
Mary Ann,Worthman,Internal Auditor,"$87,500"
Alena M.,Moody,Sales Trainee,"$20,000"
Edwin,Comber,Sales Rep. III,"$45,500"
;
```

Copyright © 2016, SAS Institute Inc., Cary, North Carolina, USA. ALL RIGHTS RESERVED.

Viewing the Output

```
proc print data=work.newemps;
run;
```

PROC PRINT Output

Obs	First_ Name	Last_Name	Job_ Title	Salary
1	Steven	Worton	Auditor	40450
2	Marta-Lyn	Bamberger	Manager	32000
3	Merle	Hieds	Trainee	24025

100 p108d08

Copyright © 2016, SAS Institute Inc., Cary, North Carolina, USA. ALL RIGHTS RESERVED.

Exercises

> If you restarted your SAS session since the last exercise, open and submit the **libname.sas** program that can be found in the data folder.

Level 1

4. Reading Nonstandard Data from a Comma-Delimited Raw Data File

a. Open **p108e04**. Add the appropriate LENGTH, INFILE, and INPUT statements to read the comma-delimited raw data file, which can be named as follows:

Windows	**"&path\custca.csv"**
UNIX	**"&path/custca.csv"**
z/OS (OS/390)	**"&path..rawdata(custca)"**

Partial Raw Data File

```
Bill,Cuddy,11171,M,16/10/1986,21,15-30 years
Susan,Krasowski,17023,F,09/07/1959,48,46-60 years
Andreas,Rennie,26148,M,18/07/1934,73,61-75 years
Lauren,Krasowski,46966,F,24/10/1986,21,15-30 years
Lauren,Marx,54655,F,18/08/1969,38,31-45 years
```

Read the following fields:

Name	Type	Length
First	Character	20
Last	Character	20
ID	Numeric	8
Gender	Character	1
BirthDate	Numeric	8
Age	Numeric	8
AgeGroup	Character	12

Copyright © 2016, SAS Institute Inc., Cary, North Carolina, USA. ALL RIGHTS RESERVED.

b. Use FORMAT and DROP statements in the DATA step to create a data set that results in the report below when it is displayed with a PROC PRINT step. Include an appropriate title. The results should contain 15 observations.

Partial PROC PRINT Output

```
                         Canadian Customers

                                                              Birth
Obs   First     Last        Gender   AgeGroup              Date

  1   Bill      Cuddy         M      15-30 years        OCT1986
  2   Susan     Krasowski     F      46-60 years        JUL1959
  3   Andreas   Rennie        M      61-75 years        JUL1934
  4   Lauren    Krasowski     F      15-30 years        OCT1986
  5   Lauren    Marx          F      31-45 years        AUG1969
```

Level 2

5. Reading a Delimited Raw Data File with Nonstandard Data Values

a. Write a DATA step to create a temporary data set, **prices**. Read the delimited raw data file named as follows:

Windows	**"&path\pricing.dat"**
UNIX	**"&path/ pricing.dat"**
z/OS (OS/390)	**"&path..rawdata(pricing)"**

All data fields are numeric.

Partial Raw Data File

```
210200100009*09JUN2011*31DEC9999*$15.50*$34.70
210200100017*24JAN2011*31DEC9999*$17.80*22.80
210200200023*04JUL2011*31DEC9999*$8.25*$19.80
210200600067*27OCT2011*31DEC9999*$28.90*47.00
210200600085*28AUG2011*31DEC9999*$17.85*$39.40
```

b. Generate the report below. The results should contain 16 observations.

Partial PROC PRINT Output

```
                              2011 Pricing

                                                                 Sales
Obs      ProductID     StartDate       EndDate       Cost       Price

  1   210200100009    06/09/2011    12/31/9999      15.50       34.70
  2   210200100017    01/24/2011    12/31/9999      17.80       22.80
  3   210200200023    07/04/2011    12/31/9999       8.25       19.80
  4   210200600067    10/27/2011    12/31/9999      28.90       47.00
  5   210200600085    08/28/2011    12/31/9999      17.85       39.40
```

Copyright © 2016, SAS Institute Inc., Cary, North Carolina, USA. ALL RIGHTS RESERVED.

Challenge

6. Reading In-Stream Delimited Data

a. Open **p108e06**. Write a DATA step to read the delimited in-stream data shown below.

> ✎ An INFILE statement is required. Use SAS Help or online documentation to explore the use of DATALINES as a file specification in an INFILE statement.

```
120102/Tom/Zhou/M/108,255/Sales Manager/01Jun1993
120103/Wilson/Dawes/M/87,975/Sales Manager/01Jan1978
120261/Harry/Highpoint/M/243,190/Chief Sales Officer/01Aug1991
121143/Louis/Favaron/M/95,090/Senior Sales Manager/01Jul2001
121144/Renee/Capachietti/F/83,505/Sales Manager/01Nov1995
121145/Dennis/Lansberry/M/84,260/Sales Manager/01Apr1980
```

b. Generate the report below.

Orion Star Management Team

First	Last	Title	ID	Gender	Salary	HireDate
Tom	Zhou	Sales Manager	120102	M	108255	06/01/1993
Wilson	Dawes	Sales Manager	120103	M	87975	01/01/1978
Harry	Highpoint	Chief Sales Officer	120261	M	243190	08/01/1991
Louis	Favaron	Senior Sales Manager	121143	M	95090	07/01/2001
Renee	Capachietti	Sales Manager	121144	F	83505	11/01/1995
Dennis	Lansberry	Sales Manager	121145	M	84260	04/01/1980

End of Exercises

Copyright © 2016, SAS Institute Inc., Cary, North Carolina, USA. ALL RIGHTS RESERVED.

8.4 Handling Missing Data

Objectives

- Use the DSD option to read consecutive delimiters as missing values.
- Use the MISSOVER option to recognize missing values at the end of a record.

104

Business Scenario

Orion Star programmers discovered that some files have records with missing data in one or more fields.

105

Copyright © 2016, SAS Institute Inc., Cary, North Carolina, USA. ALL RIGHTS RESERVED.

Missing Values in the Middle of the Record

The records in **phone2.csv** have a contact name, phone number, and a mobile number. The phone number is missing from some of the records.

Missing data is indicated by consecutive delimiters.

phone2.csv

```
         1    1    2    2    3    3    4    4
1---5----0----5----0----5----0----5----0----5
James Kvarniq,(704) 293-8126,(701) 281-8923
Sandrina Stephano,,(919) 271-4592
Cornelia Krahl,(212) 891-3241,(212) 233-5413
Karen Ballinger,,(714) 644-9090
Elke Wallstab,(910) 763-5561,(910) 545-3421
```

106

Consecutive Delimiters in List Input

List input treats two or more consecutive delimiters as a single delimiter and not as a missing value.

Partial phone2.csv

```
         1    1    2    2    3    3    4    4
1---5----0----5----0----5----0----5----0----5
Sandrina Stephano,,(919) 271-4592
Cornelia Krahl,(212) 891-3241,(212) 233-5413
```

When there is missing data in a record, SAS does the following:

- loads the next record to finish the observation
- writes a note to the log

107

Copyright © 2016, SAS Institute Inc., Cary, North Carolina, USA. ALL RIGHTS RESERVED.

8.09 Short Answer Poll

Submit **p108a03 and e**xamine the log and output.

How many input records were read and how many observations were created?

Does the output look correct?

```
data work.contacts;
   length Name $ 20 Phone Mobile $ 14;
   infile "&path\phone2.csv" dlm=',';
   input Name $ Phone $ Mobile $;
run;

proc print data=work.contacts noobs;
run;
```

108 **p108a03**

DSD Option

Use the DSD option to correctly read **phone2.csv**.

```
data work.contacts;
   length Name $ 20 Phone Mobile $ 14;
   infile "&path\phone2.csv" dsd;
   input Name $ Phone $ Mobile $;
run;
```

INFILE "*raw-data-file*" <DLM=> DSD;

The DSD option does the following:

- sets the default delimiter to a comma
- treats consecutive delimiters as missing values
- enables SAS to read values with embedded delimiters if the value is enclosed in quotation marks

110 **p108d09**

The DLM= option can be used with the DSD option, but it is not needed for comma-delimited files.

Copyright © 2016, SAS Institute Inc., Cary, North Carolina, USA. ALL RIGHTS RESERVED.

Viewing the Output

Adding the DSD option gives the correct results.

PROC PRINT Output

Name	Phone	Mobile
James Kvarniq	(704) 293-8126	(701) 281-8923
Sandrina Stephano		(919) 271-4592
Cornelia Krahl	(212) 891-3241	(212) 233-5413
Karen Ballinger		(714) 644-9090
Elke Wallstab	(910) 763-5561	(910) 545-3421

Partial SAS Log

```
NOTE: 5 records were read from the infile "S:\workshop\phone2.csv".
      The minimum record length was 31.
      The maximum record length was 44.
NOTE: The data set WORK.CONTACTS has 5 observations and 3
variables.
```

111

Business Scenario

Orion Star programmers discovered that some files have observations with missing data at the end of the record. As a result, there are fewer fields in the record than specified in the INPUT statement.

113

Copyright © 2016, SAS Institute Inc., Cary, North Carolina, USA. ALL RIGHTS RESERVED.

Missing Values at the End of a Record

The raw data file **phone.csv** contains missing values at the end of some records.

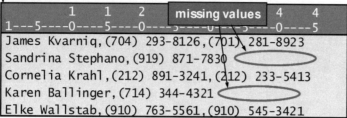

phone.csv

missing values

```
James Kvarniq,(704) 293-8126,(701) 281-8923
Sandrina Stephano,(919) 871-7830
Cornelia Krahl,(212) 891-3241,(212) 233-5413
Karen Ballinger,(714) 344-4321
Elke Wallstab,(910) 763-5561,(910) 545-3421
```

The DSD option is not appropriate because the missing data is not marked by consecutive delimiters.

114

MISSOVER Option

The *MISSOVER option* prevents SAS from loading a new record when the end of the current record is reached.

```
data contacts;
   length Name $ 20 Phone Mobile $ 14;
   infile "&path\phone.csv" dlm=',' missover;
   input Name $ Phone $ Mobile $;
run;

proc print data=contacts noobs;
run;
```

INFILE "*raw-data-file*" <DLM=> MISSOVER;

If SAS reaches the end of a record without finding values for all fields, variables without values are set to missing.

115 p108d10

Copyright © 2016, SAS Institute Inc., Cary, North Carolina, USA. ALL RIGHTS RESERVED.

Viewing the Output

Partial SAS Log

```
NOTE: 5 records were read from the infile "S:\workshop\phone.csv".
      The minimum record length was 31.
      The maximum record length was 44.
NOTE: The data set WORK.CONTACTS has 5 observations and 3
variables.
```

PROC PRINT Output

```
        Name                    Phone             Mobile

  James Kvarniq          (704) 293-8126    (701) 281-8923
  Sandrina Stephano      (919) 871-7830
  Cornelia Krahl         (212) 891-3241    (212) 233-5413
  Karen Ballinger        (714) 344-4321
  Elke Wallstab          (910) 763-5561    (910) 545-3421
```

116

INFILE Options

INFILE "*raw-data-file*" <DLM=> <DSD> <MISSOVER>;

Option	Description
DLM=	Specifies an alternate delimiter.
DSD	Sets the default delimiter to a comma, treats consecutive delimiters as missing values, and allows embedded delimiters when the data value is enclosed in quotation marks.
MISSOVER	Sets variables to missing if the end of the record is reached before finding values for all fields.

117

Copyright © 2016, SAS Institute Inc., Cary, North Carolina, USA. ALL RIGHTS RESERVED.

Exercises

If you restarted your SAS session since the last exercise, open and submit the **libname.sas** program that can be found in the data folder.

Level 1

7. Reading a Comma-Delimited File with Missing Values

a. Open **p108e07**. Insert INFILE and INPUT statements to read the comma-delimited raw data, which can be named as follows:

Windows	**"&path\donation.csv"**
UNIX	**"&path/donation.csv"**
z/OS (OS/390)	**"&path..rawdata(donation)"**

Partial Raw Data File

```
120265,,,,25
120267,15,15,15,15
120269,20,20,20,20
120270,20,10,5
120271,20,20,20,20
```

b. There might be missing data in the middle or at the end of a record. Read the following fields from the raw data file:

Name	Type
EmpID	Numeric
Q1	Numeric
Q2	Numeric
Q3	Numeric
Q4	Numeric

c. Submit the PROC PRINT step to generate the report below. The results should include 124 observations.

```
Obs    EmpID    Q1    Q2    Q3    Q4

 1    120265     .     .     .    25
 2    120267    15    15    15    15
 3    120269    20    20    20    20
 4    120270    20    10     5     .
 5    120271    20    20    20    20
```

Copyright © 2016, SAS Institute Inc., Cary, North Carolina, USA. ALL RIGHTS RESERVED.

Level 2

8. Reading a Delimited File with Missing Values

a. Write a DATA step to create a temporary data set, **prices**. Use the asterisk-delimited raw data file, which can be named as follows:

Windows	**"&path\prices.dat"**
UNIX	**"&path/prices.dat"**
z/OS (OS/390)	**"&path..rawdata(prices)"**

Partial Raw Data File

```
210200100009*09JUN2007*31DEC9999*$15.50*$34.70
210200100017*24JAN2007*31DEC9999*$17.80
210200200023*04JUL2007*31DEC9999*$8.25*$19.80
210200600067*27OCT2007*31DEC9999*$28.90
210200600085*28AUG2007*31DEC9999*$17.85*$39.40
```

There might be missing data at the end of some records. Read the following fields from the raw data file:

Name	Type	Length
ProductID	Numeric	8
StartDate	Numeric	8
EndDate	Numeric	8
UnitCostPrice	Numeric	8
UnitSalesPrice	Numeric	8

b. Define labels and formats in the DATA step to create a data set that generates the following output when they are used in the PROC PRINT step. The results should contain 259 observations.

Partial PROC PRINT Output

```
                                2007 Prices

                                                                  Sales
                        Start of       End of       Cost Price    Price per
Obs     Product ID      Date Range     Date Range    per Unit      Unit

  1    210200100009    06/09/2007     12/31/9999       15.50       34.70
  2    210200100017    01/24/2007     12/31/9999       17.80         .
  3    210200200023    07/04/2007     12/31/9999        8.25       19.80
  4    210200600067    10/27/2007     12/31/9999       28.90         .
  5    210200600085    08/28/2007     12/31/9999       17.85       39.40
```

Copyright © 2016, SAS Institute Inc., Cary, North Carolina, USA. ALL RIGHTS RESERVED.

Challenge

9. Reading a Delimited File with Missing Values and Embedded Delimiters

a. Write a DATA step to create a temporary data set, **salesmgmt**. Use the raw data file, which can be named as follows:

Windows	**"&path\managers.dat"**
UNIX	**"&path/managers.dat"**
z/OS (OS/390)	**"&path..rawdata(managers)"**

Partial Raw Data File

```
120102/Tom/Zhou/M//Sales Manager/AU/11AUG1969/'06/01/1989'
120103/Wilson/Dawes/M/87975/Sales Manager/AU/22JAN1949/'01/01/1974'
120261/Harry/Highpoint/M/243190//US/21FEB1969/'08/01/1987'
121143/Louis/Favaron/M/95090/Senior Sales Manager/US/26NOV1969/'07/01/1997'
121144/Renee/Capachietti/F/83505/Sales Manager/US/28JUN1964
121145/Dennis/Lansberry/M/84260/Sales Manager/US/22NOV1949/'04/01/1976'
```

b. **ID** is a numeric value. The **salesmgmt** data set should contain only the variables shown in the report below.

c. Write a PROC PRINT step to generate the report below. The results should contain six observations.

PROC PRINT Output

```
                                 Orion Star Managers

Obs      ID       Last           Title                     HireDate     Salary

  1    120102     Zhou           Sales Manager            01JUN1989          .
  2    120103     Dawes          Sales Manager            01JAN1974      87975
  3    120261     Highpoint                               01AUG1987     243190
  4    121143     Favaron        Senior Sales Manager     01JUL1997      95090
  5    121144     Capachietti    Sales Manager                    .      83505
  6    121145     Lansberry      Sales Manager            01APR1976      84260
```

End of Exercises

Copyright © 2016, SAS Institute Inc., Cary, North Carolina, USA. ALL RIGHTS RESERVED.

8.5 Solutions

Solutions to Exercises

1. **Reading a Comma-Delimited Raw Data File**

```
data work.newemployees;
   length First $ 12 Last $ 18 Title $ 25;
   infile "&path\newemps.csv" dlm=',';
   input First $ Last $ Title $ Salary;
run;

proc print data=work.newemployees;
run;
```

2. **Reading a Space-Delimited Raw Data File**

```
data work.qtrdonation;
   length IDNum $ 6;
   infile "&path\donation.dat";
   input IDNum $ Qtr1 Qtr2 Qtr3 Qtr4;
run;

proc print data=work.qtrdonation;
run;
```

3. **Reading a Tab-Delimited Raw Data File**

```
data work.managers2;
   length First Last $ 12 Title $ 25;
   infile "&path\managers2.dat" dlm='09'x;
   input ID First $ Last $ Gender $ Salary Title $;
   keep First Last Title;
run;

proc print data=work.managers2;
run;
```

4. **Reading Nonstandard Data from a Comma-Delimited Raw Data File**

```
data work.canada_customers;
   length First Last $ 20 Gender $ 1 AgeGroup $ 12;
   infile "&path\custca.csv" dlm=',';
   input First $ Last $ ID Gender $
         BirthDate :ddmmyy. Age AgeGroup $;
   format BirthDate monyy7.;
   drop ID Age;
run;

title 'Canadian Customers';
proc print data=work.canada_customers;
run;
```

Copyright © 2016, SAS Institute Inc., Cary, North Carolina, USA. ALL RIGHTS RESERVED.

```
title;
  /* Alternate solution using informats */
data work.canada_customers;
   infile "&path\custca.csv" dlm=',';
   input First :$20. Last :$20. ID Gender :$1.
         BirthDate :ddmmyy. Age AgeGroup :$12.;
   format BirthDate monyy7.;
   drop ID Age;
run;

title 'Canadian Customers';
proc print data=work.canada_customers;
run;
title;
```

5. **Reading a Delimited Raw Data File with Nonstandard Values**

```
data work.prices;
   infile "&path\pricing.dat" dlm='*';
   input ProductID StartDate :date. EndDate :date.
         Cost :dollar. SalesPrice :dollar.;
   format StartDate EndDate mmddyy10.
          Cost SalesPrice 8.2;
run;

title '2011 Pricing';
proc print data=work.prices;
run;
title;
```

6. **Reading In-Stream Delimited Data**

```
data work.managers;
   infile datalines dlm='/';
   input ID First :$12. Last :$12. Gender $ Salary :comma.
            Title :$25. HireDate :date.;
   datalines;
120102/Tom/Zhou/M/108,255/Sales Manager/01Jun1993
120103/Wilson/Dawes/M/87,975/Sales Manager/01Jan1978
120261/Harry/Highpoint/M/243,190/Chief Sales Officer/01Aug1991
121143/Louis/Favaron/M/95,090/Senior Sales Manager/01Jul2001
121144/Renee/Capachietti/F/83,505/Sales Manager/01Nov1995
121145/Dennis/Lansberry/M/84,260/Sales Manager/01Apr1980
;

title 'Orion Star Management Team';
proc print data=work.managers noobs;
   format HireDate mmddyy10.;
run;
title;
```

Copyright © 2016, SAS Institute Inc., Cary, North Carolina, USA. ALL RIGHTS RESERVED.

7. **Reading a Comma-Delimited File with Missing Values**

```
data work.donations;
   infile "&path\donation.csv" dsd missover;
   input EmpID Q1 Q2 Q3 Q4;
run;

proc print data=work.donations;
run;
```

8. **Reading a Delimited File with Missing Values**

```
data work.prices;
   infile "&path\prices.dat" dlm='*' missover;
   input ProductID StartDate :date. EndDate :date.
         UnitCostPrice :dollar. UnitSalesPrice :dollar.;
   label ProductID='Product ID'
         StartDate='Start of Date Range'
         EndDate='End of Date Range'
         UnitCostPrice='Cost Price per Unit'
         UnitSalesPrice='Sales Price per Unit';
   format StartDate EndDate mmddyy10.
          UnitCostPrice UnitSalesPrice 8.2;
run;

title '2007 Prices';
proc print data=work.prices label;
run;
title;
```

9. **Reading a Delimited File with Missing Values and Embedded Delimiters**

```
data work.salesmgmt;
   length First Last $ 12 Gender $ 1 Title $ 25 Country $ 2;
   format BirthDate HireDate date9.;
   infile "&path\managers.dat" dsd dlm='/' missover;
   input ID First Last Gender Salary Title Country
         BirthDate :date. HireDate :mmddyy.;
run;

title 'Orion Star Managers';
proc print data=work.salesmgmt;
   var ID Last Title HireDate Salary;
run;
title;

  /* Alternate solution using informats */
data work.salesmgmt;
   format BirthDate HireDate date9.;
   infile "&path\managers.dat" dsd dlm='/' missover;
   input ID First :$12. Last :$12. Gender :$1. Salary Title :$25.
         Country :$2. BirthDate :date. HireDate :mmddyy.;
```

Copyright © 2016, SAS Institute Inc., Cary, North Carolina, USA. ALL RIGHTS RESERVED.

```
run;

title 'Orion Star Managers';
proc print data=work.salesmgmt;
   var ID Last Title HireDate Salary;
run;
title;
```

End of Solutions

Copyright © 2016, SAS Institute Inc., Cary, North Carolina, USA. ALL RIGHTS RESERVED.

Solutions to Student Activities (Polls/Quizzes)

8.02 Short Answer Poll – Correct Answer

Which fields in this file can be read as standard numeric values?

The employee ID and salary. The date fields are nonstandard and require special processing.

Partial **sales.csv**

```
120102,Tom,Zhou,M,108255,Sales Manager,AU,11AUG1973,06/01/1993
120103,Wilson,Dawes,M,87975,Sales Manager,AU,22JAN1953,01/01/1978
120121,Irenie,Elvish,F,26600,Sales Rep. II,AU,02AUG1948,01/01/1978
120122,Christina,Ngan,F,27475,Sales Rep. II,AU,27JUL1958,07/01/1982
120123,Kimiko,Hotstone,F,26190,Sales Rep. I,AU,28SEP1968,10/01/1989
```

16

8.03 Multiple Choice Poll – Correct Answer

Which statement is true?

a. An input buffer is created only if you are reading data from a raw data file.
b. The PDV at compile time holds the variable name, type, byte size, and initial value.
c. The descriptor portion is the first item that is created at compile time.

31

Copyright © 2016, SAS Institute Inc., Cary, North Carolina, USA. ALL RIGHTS RESERVED.

8.04 Short Answer Poll – Correct Answer

Suppose you want the order of the variables to match the order of the fields. You can include the numeric variables in the LENGTH statement. Which of the following produces the correct results?

a.
```
length Employee_ID First_Name $ 12
       Last_Name $ 18 Gender $ 1
       Salary Job_Title $ 25
       Country $ 2;
```

(b.)
```
length Employee_ID 8 First_Name $ 12
       Last_Name $ 18 Gender $ 1
       Salary 8 Job_Title $ 25
       Country $ 2;
```

56

8.05 Short Answer Poll – Correct Answer

What problems do you see with the data values for the last two data fields, **Salary** and **Country**?

Partial **sales3inv.csv**

```
120102,Tom,Zhou,Manager,108255,AU
120103,Wilson,Dawes,Manager,87975,AU
120121,Irenie,Elvish,Rep. II,26600,AU
120122,Christina,Ngan,Rep. II,n/a,AU
120123,Kimiko,Hotstone,Rep. I,26190,AU
120124,Lucian,Daymond,Rep. I,26480,12
120125,Fong,Hofmeister,Rep. IV,32040,AU
```

63

Copyright © 2016, SAS Institute Inc., Cary, North Carolina, USA. ALL RIGHTS RESERVED.

8.06 Multiple Choice Poll – Correct Answer

Which statement best describes the reason for the error?

a. The data in the raw data file is invalid.
b. The programmer incorrectly read the data.

Partial SAS Log

Last was read as numeric but needs to be read as character.

```
404      input Employee_ID First $ Last;
405   run;

NOTE: Invalid data for Last in line 1 16-17.
RULE:      ----+----1----+----2----+----3----+----4----+----5----+----6
1          120101,Patrick,Lu,M,163040,Director,AU,18AUG1976,01JUL2003 58
Employee_ID=120101 First=Patrick Last=. _ERROR_=1 _N_=1
NOTE: Invalid data for Last in line 2 15-24.
2          120104,Kareen,Billington,F,46230,Administration Manager,au,1
      61   1MAY1954,01JAN1981 78
Employee_ID=120104 First=Kareen Last=. _ERROR_=1 _N_=2
```

70

8.07 Short Answer Poll – Correct Answer

A *format* is an instruction that tells SAS how to display data values. What formats could you specify to display a SAS date in the styles shown below?

a) 01JAN2000 ⇨ **DATE9.**

b) 01/16/2000 ⇨ **MMDDYY10.**

81

Copyright © 2016, SAS Institute Inc., Cary, North Carolina, USA. ALL RIGHTS RESERVED.

8.08 Short Answer Poll – Correct Answer

Use the SAS Help Facility or documentation to investigate the **DATE*w*.** informat and answer the following questions:

a) What does the ***w*** represent?
   the width of the input field

b) What is the default width of this informat?
   The default width is 7.

88

8.09 Short Answer Poll – Correct Answer

Submit **p108a03 and** examine the log and output.

How many input records were read and how many observations were created? **five read, three created**

Does the output look correct? **no**

```
NOTE: 5 records were read from the infile "S:\workshop\phone2.csv".
      The minimum record length was 31.
      The maximum record length was 44.
NOTE: SAS went to a new line when INPUT statement reached past the
end of a line.
NOTE: The data set WORK.CONTACTS has 3 observations and 3 variables.
```

Name	Phone	Mobile
James Kvarniq	(704) 293-8126	(701) 281-8923
Sandrina Stephano	(919) 871-7830	Cornelia Krahl
Karen Ballinger	(714) 344-4321	Elke Wallstab

109

Copyright © 2016, SAS Institute Inc., Cary, North Carolina, USA. ALL RIGHTS RESERVED.

Chapter 9 Manipulating Data

Copyright © 2016, SAS Institute Inc., Cary, North Carolina, USA. ALL RIGHTS RESERVED.

9.1 Using SAS Functions

Objectives

- Use SAS functions to create data values.

3

Business Scenario

Orion Star management plans to give a $500 bonus to each employee in his or her hire month.

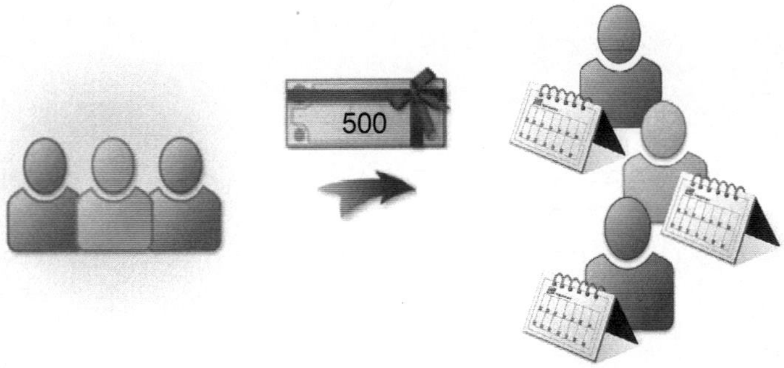

4

Copyright © 2016, SAS Institute Inc., Cary, North Carolina, USA. ALL RIGHTS RESERVED.

Considerations

Create a new data set with three new variables.

- **Bonus**, which is a constant 500
- **Compensation**, which is the sum of **Salary** and **Bonus**
- **BonusMonth**, which is the month in which the employee was hired

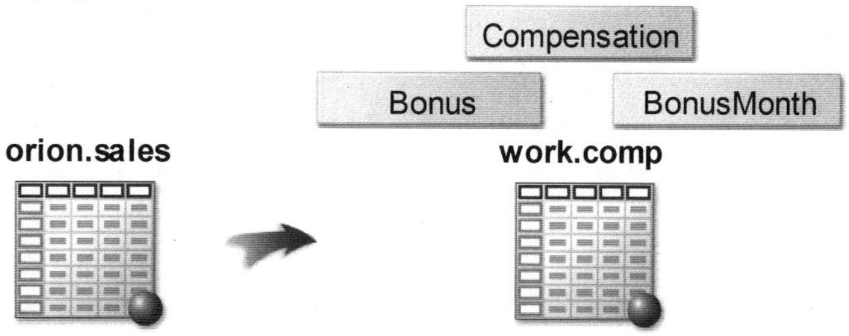

5

Considerations

Partial **orion.sales**

Employee_ID	First_Name	Last_Name	Gender	Salary	Job_Title	Country	Birth_Date	Hire_Date
120102	Tom	Zhou	M	108255	Sales Manager	AU	3510	10744
120103	Wilson	Dawes	M	87975	Sales Manager	AU	-3996	5114
120121	Irenie	Elvish	F	26600	Sales Rep. II	AU	-5630	5114

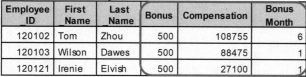

Partial **work.comp**

Employee_ID	First_Name	Last_Name	Bonus	Compensation	Bonus Month
120102	Tom	Zhou	500	108755	6
120103	Wilson	Dawes	500	88475	1
120121	Irenie	Elvish	500	27100	1

Drop **Gender**, **Salary**, **Job_Title**, **Country**, **Birth_Date**, and **Hire_Date** from **work.comp**.

6

Copyright © 2016, SAS Institute Inc., Cary, North Carolina, USA. ALL RIGHTS RESERVED.

9.01 Multiple Choice Poll

Which of the following statements creates a numeric variable, **Bonus**, with a value of 500?

a. Bonus=$500;
b. Bonus=500;
c. label Bonus='500';
d. format Bonus 500.;

Partial **work.comp**

Bonus	Compensation	Bonus Month
500	108755	6
500	88475	1
500	27100	1

7

SAS Functions

SAS functions can be used in an assignment statement. A *function* is a routine that accepts arguments and returns a value.

```
variable=function-name(argument1, argument2, ...);
```

Some functions manipulate character values, compute descriptive statistics, or manipulate SAS date values.

- Arguments are enclosed in parentheses and separated by commas.
- A function can return a numeric or character result.

9

Copyright © 2016, SAS Institute Inc., Cary, North Carolina, USA. ALL RIGHTS RESERVED.

SUM Function

Use the *SUM function* to create **Compensation**. The SUM function is a descriptive statistics function that returns the sum of its arguments.

```
Compensation=sum(Salary,Bonus);
```

SUM(*argument1,argument2, ...***)**

- The arguments must be numeric.
- Missing values are ignored by SUM and other descriptive statistics functions.

10

MONTH Function

Use the *MONTH function* to extract the month of hire from **Hire_Date**.

```
BonusMonth=month(Hire_Date);
```

MONTH(*SAS-date***)**

Other date functions can do the following:

- extract information from SAS date values
- create SAS date values

11

Copyright © 2016, SAS Institute Inc., Cary, North Carolina, USA. ALL RIGHTS RESERVED.

Date Functions: Extracting Values

Syntax	Description
YEAR(*SAS-date*)	Extracts the year from a SAS date and returns a four-digit year.
QTR(*SAS-date*)	Extracts the calendar quarter from a SAS date and returns a number from 1 to 4.
MONTH(*SAS-date*)	Extracts the month from a SAS date and returns a number from 1 to 12.
DAY(*SAS-date*)	Extracts the day of the month from a SAS date and returns a number from 1 to 31.
WEEKDAY(*SAS-date*)	Extracts the day of the week from a SAS date and returns a number from 1 to 7, where 1 represents Sunday.

12

Date Functions: Creating SAS Dates

Syntax	Description
TODAY() DATE()	Returns the current date as a SAS date value.
MDY(*month,day,year*)	Returns a SAS date value from numeric month, day, and year values.

Examples
CurrentDate=today();
y2k=mdy(01,1,2000);
NewYear=mdy(Mon,Day,2013);

13

Copyright © 2016, SAS Institute Inc., Cary, North Carolina, USA. ALL RIGHTS RESERVED.

Using SAS Functions

A function call can be used alone in an assignment statement.

```
BonusMonth=month(Hire_Date);
AnnivBonus=mdy(BonusMonth,15,2008);
```

A function call can be part of any SAS expression.

```
if month(Hire_Date)=12;
```

A function call can be an argument to another function.

```
AnnivBonus=mdy(month(Hire_Date),15,2012);
```

14

Using SAS Functions

Create **Bonus**, **Compensation**, and **BonusMonth**.

```
data work.comp;
   set orion.sales;
   Bonus=500;
   Compensation=sum(Salary,Bonus);
   BonusMonth=month(Hire_Date);
run;
```

```
data work.comp;
   set orion.sales;
   Bonus=500;
   Compensation=sum(Salary,Bonus);
   BonusMonth=month(Hire_Date);
run;

NOTE: There were 165 observations read from the data set ORION.SALES.
NOTE: The data set WORK.COMP has 165 observations and 12 variables.
```

orion.sales has nine variables.

15 p109d01

Copyright © 2016, SAS Institute Inc., Cary, North Carolina, USA. ALL RIGHTS RESERVED.

Viewing the Output

```
proc print data=work.comp noobs;
   var Employee_ID First_Name Last_Name
       Bonus Compensation BonusMonth;
run;
```

Partial PROC PRINT Output

Employee_ID	First_ Name	Last_Name	Bonus	Compensation	Bonus Month
120102	Tom	Zhou	500	108755	6
120103	Wilson	Dawes	500	88475	1
120121	Irenie	Elvish	500	27100	1
120122	Christina	Ngan	500	27975	7
120123	Kimiko	Hotstone	500	26690	10

16

p109d01

9.02 Short Answer Poll

A DROP statement was added to this DATA step. Can the program calculate **Compensation** and **BonusMonth** correctly?

```
data work.comp;
   set orion.sales;
   drop Gender Salary Job_Title Country
        Birth_Date Hire_Date;
   Bonus=500;
   Compensation=sum(Salary,Bonus);
   BonusMonth=month(Hire_Date);
run;
```

17

p109a01

Copyright © 2016, SAS Institute Inc., Cary, North Carolina, USA. ALL RIGHTS RESERVED.

Viewing the Output

```
proc print data=work.comp noobs;
run;
```

Partial PROC PRINT Output

Employee_ID	First_ Name	Last_Name	Bonus	Compensation	Bonus Month
120102	Tom	Zhou	500	108755	6
120103	Wilson	Dawes	500	88475	1
120121	Irenie	Elvish	500	27100	1
120122	Christina	Ngan	500	27975	7
120123	Kimiko	Hotstone	500	26690	10

19

p109a01

Copyright © 2016, SAS Institute Inc., Cary, North Carolina, USA. ALL RIGHTS RESERVED.

Exercises

> If you restarted your SAS session since the last exercise, open and submit the **libname.sas** program that can be found in the data folder.

Level 1

1. Creating New Variables

a. Retrieve the starter program **p109e01**.

b. In the DATA step, create three new variables:
   - **Increase**, which is **Salary** multiplied by 0.10
   - **NewSalary**, which is **Salary** added to **Increase**
   - **BdayQtr**, which is the quarter in which the employee was born

c. The new data set should include only **Employee_ID**, **Salary**, **Birth_Date**, and the three new variables.

d. Store permanent formats to display **Salary**, **Increase**, and **NewSalary** with commas.

e. Modify the program to create the report below, including labels. The results should contain 424 observations.

Partial PROC PRINT Output

```
                              Employee
                               Annual     Employee                                  Bday
Obs      Employee ID           Salary     Birth Date      Increase      NewSalary    Qtr

  1           120101          163,040     18AUG1980         16,304        179,344      3
  2           120102          108,255     11AUG1973         10,826        119,081      3
  3           120103           87,975     22JAN1953          8,798         96,773      1
  4           120104           46,230     11MAY1958          4,623         50,853      2
  5           120105           27,110     21DEC1978          2,711         29,821      4
```

Level 2

2. Creating New Variables

a. Write a DATA step that reads **orion.customer** to create **work.birthday**.

b. In the DATA step, create three new variables: **Bday2012**, **BdayDOW2012**, and **Age2012**.
   - **Bday2012** is the combination of the month of **Birth_Date**, the day of **Birth_Date**, and the constant of **2012** in the MDY function.
   - **BdayDOW2012** is the day of the week of **Bday2012**.
   - **Age2012** is the age of the customer in 2012. Subtract **Birth_Date** from **Bday2012** and divide the result by 365.25.

Copyright © 2016, SAS Institute Inc., Cary, North Carolina, USA. ALL RIGHTS RESERVED.

c. Include only the following variables in the new data set: **Customer_Name**, **Birth_Date**, **Bday2012**, **BdayDOW2012**, and **Age2012**.

d. Format **Bday2012** to appear in the form 01Jan2012. **Age2012** should be formatted to appear with no decimal places.

e. Write a PROC PRINT step to create the report below. The results should contain 77 observations.

Partial PROC PRINT Output

Obs	Customer_Name	Birth_ Date	Bday2012	Bday DOW2012	Age2012
1	James Kvarniq	27JUN1978	27JUN2012	4	34
2	Sandrina Stephano	09JUL1983	09JUL2012	2	29
3	Cornelia Krahl	27FEB1978	27FEB2012	2	34
4	Karen Ballinger	18OCT1988	18OCT2012	5	24
5	Elke Wallstab	16AUG1978	16AUG2012	5	34

Challenge

3. Using the CATX and INTCK Functions to Create Variables

a. Write a DATA step that reads **orion.sales** to create **work.employees**.

In the DATA step, create a new variable, **FullName**. This variable is the combination of **First_Name**, a space, and **Last_Name**. Use the CATX function. You can find documentation about CATX in the SAS Help Facility or in the online documentation.

In the DATA step, create a new variable, **Yrs2012**. This variable is the number of years between January 1, 2012, and **Hire_Date**. Use the INTCK function. Documentation about INTCK can be found in the SAS Help Facility or in the online documentation.

b. Format **Hire_Date** to appear in the form 31/01/2012.

c. Give **Yrs2012** a label of **Years of Employment as of 2012**.

d. Create the report shown below. The results should contain 165 observations.

Partial PROC PRINT Output

Obs	FullName	Hire_Date	Years of Employment as of 2012
1	Tom Zhou	01/06/1993	19
2	Wilson Dawes	01/01/1978	34
3	Irenie Elvish	01/01/1978	34
4	Christina Ngan	01/07/1982	30
5	Kimiko Hotstone	01/10/1989	23

End of Exercises

Copyright © 2016, SAS Institute Inc., Cary, North Carolina, USA. ALL RIGHTS RESERVED.

9.2 Conditional Processing

Objectives

- Use IF-THEN/ELSE statements to process data conditionally.
- Use DO and END statements to execute multiple statements conditionally.
- Use the LENGTH statement to control the length of character variables.

23

Business Scenario

Orion Star management plans to give each sales employee a bonus based on his or her job title.

24

Copyright © 2016, SAS Institute Inc., Cary, North Carolina, USA. ALL RIGHTS RESERVED.

Considerations

Create a new data set, **work.comp**. Use **orion.sales** as input. Include a new variable, **Bonus**, with a value that is based on **Job_Title**.

Job_Title	Bonus
Sales Rep. IV	1000
Sales Manager	1500
Senior Sales Manager	2000
Chief Sales Officer	2500

25

IF-THEN Statements

The IF-THEN statement executes a SAS statement for observations that meet a specific condition.

```
data work.comp;
   set orion.sales;
   if Job_Title='Sales Rep. IV' then
      Bonus=1000;
   ...
run;
```

IF *expression* **THEN** *statement*;

- *expression* defines a condition.
- *statement* can be any executable SAS statement.
- If *expression* is true, then *statement* executes.

26

Copyright © 2016, SAS Institute Inc., Cary, North Carolina, USA. ALL RIGHTS RESERVED.

Conditional Processing

The value assigned to **Bonus** is determined by testing for various values of **Job_Title**.

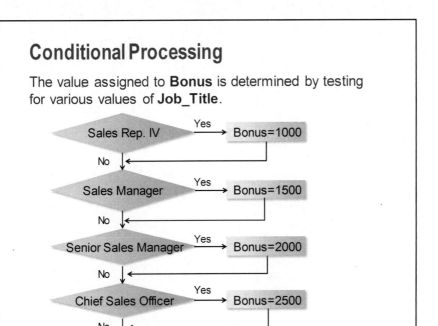

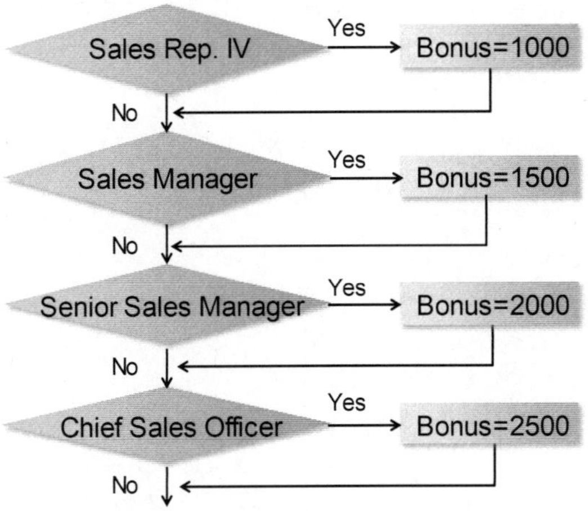

27

Conditional Processing

```
data work.comp;
   set orion.sales;
   if Job_Title='Sales Rep. IV' then
      Bonus=1000;
   if Job_Title='Sales Manager' then
      Bonus=1500;
   if Job_Title='Senior Sales Manager'
      then Bonus=2000;
   if Job_Title='Chief Sales Officer'
      then Bonus=2500;
run;
```

PDV

Employee_ID	Last_Name	...	Job_Title	Bonus
120102	Zhou	...	Sales Manager	.

p109d02

28

Copyright © 2016, SAS Institute Inc., Cary, North Carolina, USA. ALL RIGHTS RESERVED.

Conditional Processing

```
data work.comp;
   set orion.sales;
   if Job_Title='Sales Rep. IV' then
      Bonus=1000;
   if Job_Title='Sales Manager' then
      Bonus=1500;
   if Job_Title='Senior Sales Manager'
      then Bonus=2000;
   if Job_Title='Chief Sales Officer'
      then Bonus=2500;
run;
```

false

PDV

Employee_ID	Last_Name	...	Job_Title	Bonus
120102	Zhou	...	Sales Manager	.

29 ...

Conditional Processing

```
data work.comp;
   set orion.sales;
   if Job_Title='Sales Rep. IV' then
      Bonus=1000;
   if Job_Title='Sales Manager' then
      Bonus=1500;
   if Job_Title='Senior Sales Manager'
      then Bonus=2000;
   if Job_Title='Chief Sales Officer'
      then Bonus=2500;
run;
```

true

PDV

Employee_ID	Last_Name	...	Job_Title	Bonus
120102	Zhou	...	Sales Manager	.

30 ...

Copyright © 2016, SAS Institute Inc., Cary, North Carolina, USA. ALL RIGHTS RESERVED.

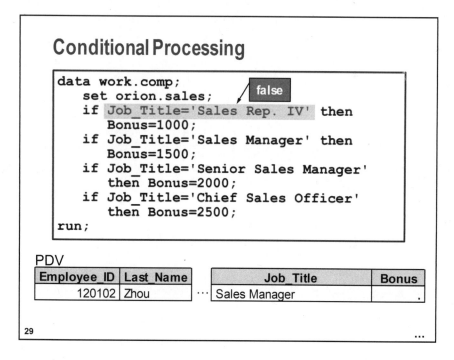

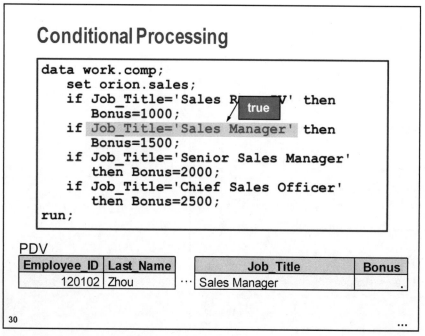

Conditional Processing

```
data work.comp;
   set orion.sales;
   if Job_Title='Sales Rep. IV' then
      Bonus=1000;
   if Job_Title='Sales Manager' then
      Bonus=1500;
   if Job_Title='Senior Sales Manager'
      then Bonus=2000;
   if Job_Title='Chief Sales Officer'
      then Bonus=2500;
run;
```

PDV

Employee_ID	Last_Name	...	Job_Title	Bonus
120102	Zhou	...	Sales Manager	1500

31 ...

Conditional Processing

```
data work.comp;
   set orion.sales;
   if Job_Title='Sales Rep. IV' then
      Bonus=1000;
   if Job_Title='Sales Manager' then
      Bonus=1500;
   if Job_Title='Senior Sales Manager'
      then Bonus=2000;
   if Job_Title='Chief Sales Officer'
      then Bonus=2500;
run;
```

false

PDV

Employee_ID	Last_Name	...	Job_Title	Bonus
120102	Zhou	...	Sales Manager	1500

32 ...

Copyright © 2016, SAS Institute Inc., Cary, North Carolina, USA. ALL RIGHTS RESERVED.

Conditional Processing

```
data work.comp;
   set orion.sales;
   if Job_Title='Sales Rep. IV' then
      Bonus=1000;
   if Job_Title='Sales Manager' then
      Bonus=1500;
   if Job_Title='Senior Sales Manager'
      then Bonus=2000;
   if Job_Title='Chief Sales Officer'
      then Bonus=2500;
run;
```

false

PDV

Employee_ID	Last_Name		Job_Title	Bonus
120102	Zhou	...	Sales Manager	1500

33 ...

Conditional Processing

```
data work.comp;
   set orion.sales;
   if Job_Title='Sales Rep. IV' then
      Bonus=1000;
   if Job_Title='Sales Manager' then
      Bonus=1500;
   if Job_Title='Senior Sales Manager'
      then Bonus=2000;
   if Job_Title='Chief Sales Officer'
      then Bonus=2500;
run;
```

Implicit OUTPUT;
Implicit RETURN;

PDV

Employee_ID	Last_Name		Job_Title	Bonus
120102	Zhou	...	Sales Manager	1500

34

Copyright © 2016, SAS Institute Inc., Cary, North Carolina, USA. ALL RIGHTS RESERVED.

Conditional Processing

```
data work.comp;
   set orion.sales;
   if Job_Title='Sales Rep. IV' then
      Bonus=1000;
   if Job_Title='Sales Manager' then
      Bonus=1500;
   if Job_Title='Senior Sales Manager'
      then Bonus=2000;
   if Job_Title='Chief Sales Officer'
      then Bonus=2500;
run;
```

Continue until EOF

PDV

Employee_ID	Last_Name	...	Job_Title	Bonus
120102	Zhou	...	Sales Manager	1500

35

Viewing the Output

```
proc print data=work.comp;
   var Last_Name Job_Title Bonus;
run;
```

Partial PROC PRINT Output

```
Obs    Last_Name      Job_Title           Bonus

  1    Zhou           Sales Manager        1500
  2    Dawes          Sales Manager        1500
  3    Elvish         Sales Rep. II           .
  4    Ngan           Sales Rep. II           .
  5    Hotstone       Sales Rep. I            .
  6    Daymond        Sales Rep. I            .
  7    Hofmeister     Sales Rep. IV        1000
  8    Denny          Sales Rep. II           .
  9    Clarkson       Sales Rep. II           .
 10    Kletschkus     Sales Rep. IV        1000
 11    Roebuck        Sales Rep. III          .
 12    Lyon           Sales Rep. I            .
```

p109d02

36

Copyright © 2016, SAS Institute Inc., Cary, North Carolina, USA. ALL RIGHTS RESERVED.

9.03 Multiple Choice Poll

In the previous program, is it possible for more than one condition to be true for a single observation?

a. Yes, more than one condition can be true.

b. No, the conditions are mutually exclusive, so only one condition can be true.

37

Using the ELSE Statement

Use the *ELSE statement* when you test mutually exclusive conditions.

```
data work.comp;
   set orion.sales;
   if Job_Title='Sales Rep. IV'
      then Bonus=1000;
   else if Job_Title='Sales Manager'
      then Bonus=1500;
   else if Job_Title='Senior Sales Manager'
      then Bonus=2000;
   else if Job_Title='Chief Sales Officer'
      then Bonus=2500;
run;
```

IF *expression* **THEN** *statement*;
<ELSE IF *expression* **THEN** *statement*;**>**
<ELSE IF *expression* **THEN** *statement*;**>**

39 p109d03

Copyright © 2016, SAS Institute Inc., Cary, North Carolina, USA. ALL RIGHTS RESERVED.

Conditional Processing

When an expression is true, the associated statement is executed and subsequent ELSE statements are skipped.

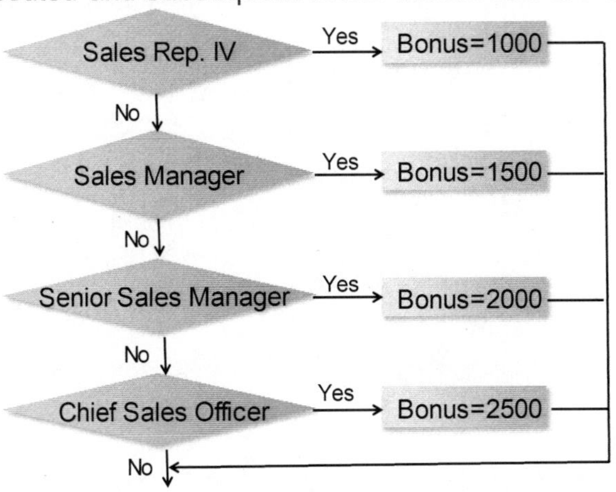

40

IF-THEN Statements

```
data work.comp;
   set orion.sales;
   if Job_Title='Sales Rep. IV' then
      Bonus=1000;
   else if Job_Title='Sales Manager' then
      Bonus=1500;
   else if Job_Title='Senior Sales Manager'
      then Bonus=2000;
   else if Job_Title='Chief Sales Officer'
      then Bonus=2500;
run;
```

PDV

Employee_ID	Last_Name	...	Job_Title	Bonus
120102	Zhou	...	Sales Manager	.

p109d03

41 ...

Copyright © 2016, SAS Institute Inc., Cary, North Carolina, USA. ALL RIGHTS RESERVED.

IF-THEN Statements

```
data work.comp;
   set orion.sales;
   if Job_Title='Sales Rep. IV' then
      Bonus=1000;
   else if Job_Title='Sales Manager' then
      Bonus=1500;
   else if Job_Title='Senior Sales Manager'
      then Bonus=2000;
   else if Job_Title='Chief Sales Officer'
      then Bonus=2500;
run;
```

false

PDV

Employee_ID	Last_Name	...	Job_Title	Bonus
120102	Zhou		Sales Manager	.

42 ...

IF-THEN Statements

```
data work.comp;
   set orion.sales;
   if Job_Title='Sales Rep. IV' then
      Bonus=1000;
   else if Job_Title='Sales Manager' then
      Bonus=1500;
   else if Job_Title='Senior Sales Manager'
      then Bonus=2000;
   else if Job_Title='Chief Sales Officer'
      then Bonus=2500;
run;
```

true

PDV

Employee_ID	Last_Name	...	Job_Title	Bonus
120102	Zhou		Sales Manager	.

43 ...

Copyright © 2016, SAS Institute Inc., Cary, North Carolina, USA. ALL RIGHTS RESERVED.

IF-THEN Statements

```
data work.comp;
   set orion.sales;
   if Job_Title='Sales Rep. IV' then
      Bonus=1000;
   else if Job_Title='Sales Manager' then
      Bonus=1500;
   else if Job_Title='Senior Sales Manager'
      then Bonus=2000;
   else if Job_Title='Chief Sales Officer'
      then Bonus=2500;
run;
```

PDV

Employee_ID	Last_Name	…	Job_Title	Bonus
120102	Zhou	…	Sales Manager	1500

44 ...

IF-THEN Statements

```
data work.comp;
   set orion.sales;
   if Job_Title='Sales Rep. IV' then
      Bonus=1000;
   else if Job_Title='Sales Manager' then
      Bonus=1500;
   else if Job_Title='Senior Sales Manager'
      then Bonus=2000;
   else if Job_Title='Chief Sales Officer'
      then Bonus=2500;
run;
```

Implicit OUTPUT;
Implicit RETURN;

PDV

Employee_ID	Last_Name	…	Job_Title	Bonus
120102	Zhou	…	Sales Manager	1500

45

Copyright © 2016, SAS Institute Inc., Cary, North Carolina, USA. ALL RIGHTS RESERVED.

IF-THEN Statements

```
data work.comp;
   Continue until EOF es;
   if Job_Title='Sales Rep. IV' then
      Bonus=1000;
   else if Job_Title='Sales Manager' then
      Bonus=1500;
   else if Job_Title='Senior Sales Manager'
      then Bonus=2000;
   else if Job_Title='Chief Sales Officer'
      then Bonus=2500;
run;
```

PDV

Employee_ID	Last_Name	...	Job_Title	Bonus
120102	Zhou	...	Sales Manager	1500

46

Viewing the Output

```
proc print data=work.comp;
   var Last_Name Job_Title Bonus;
run;
```

Partial PROC PRINT Output

Obs	Last_Name	Job_Title	Bonus
1	Zhou	Sales Manager	1500
2	Dawes	Sales Manager	1500
3	Elvish	Sales Rep. II	.
4	Ngan	Sales Rep. II	.
5	Hotstone	Sales Rep. I	.
6	Daymond	Sales Rep. I	.
7	Hofmeister	Sales Rep. IV	1000
8	Denny	Sales Rep. II	.
9	Clarkson	Sales Rep. II	.
10	Kletschkus	Sales Rep. IV	1000

47 p109d03

Copyright © 2016, SAS Institute Inc., Cary, North Carolina, USA. ALL RIGHTS RESERVED.

Business Scenario: Part 2

Orion Star management wants to modify the bonus plan as defined below.

Job_Title	Bonus
Sales Rep. III	1000
Sales Rep. IV	1000
Sales Manager	1500
Senior Sales Manager	2000
Chief Sales Officer	2500
All other titles	500

48

Using Conditional Processing

```
data work.comp;
   set orion.sales;
   if Job_Title='Sales Rep. III' or
      Job_Title='Sales Rep. IV' then
         Bonus=1000;
   else if Job_Title='Sales Manager' then
      Bonus=1500;
   else if Job_Title='Senior Sales Manager'
      then Bonus=2000;
   else if Job_Title='Chief Sales Officer'
      then Bonus=2500;
   else Bonus=500;
run;
```

compound condition

IF *expression* **THEN** *statement*;
<ELSE IF *expression* **THEN** *statement*;**>**
<...>
<**ELSE** *statement*;>

p109d04

49

Copyright © 2016, SAS Institute Inc., Cary, North Carolina, USA. ALL RIGHTS RESERVED.

Conditional Processing

An optional final ELSE statement gives an alternative action if none of the conditions are true.

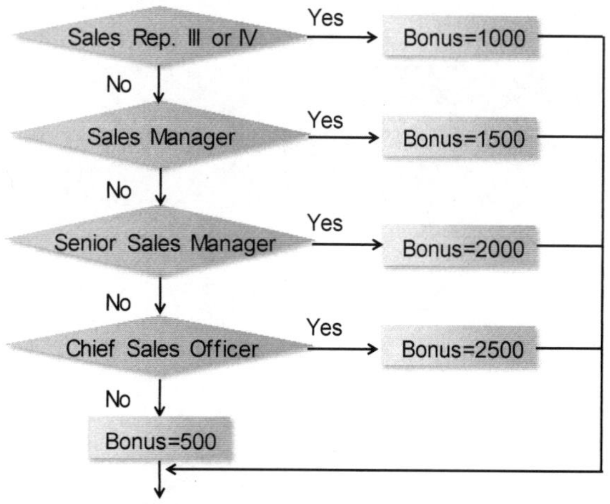

50

Viewing the Output

```
proc print data=work.comp;
   var Last_Name Job_Title Bonus;
run;
```

Partial PROC PRINT Output

Obs	Last_Name	Job_Title	Bonus
1	Zhou	Sales Manager	1500
2	Dawes	Sales Manager	1500
3	Elvish	Sales Rep. II	500
4	Ngan	Sales Rep. II	500
5	Hotstone	Sales Rep. I	500
6	Daymond	Sales Rep. I	500
7	Hofmeister	Sales Rep. IV	1000
8	Denny	Sales Rep. II	500
9	Clarkson	Sales Rep. II	500
10	Kletschkus	Sales Rep. IV	1000

51 p109d04

Copyright © 2016, SAS Institute Inc., Cary, North Carolina, USA. ALL RIGHTS RESERVED.

Business Scenario

Orion Star managers are considering a country-based bonus. Create a new SAS data set named **work.bonus**. Use **orion.sales** as input. The value of the new variable, **Bonus**, is based on **Country**.

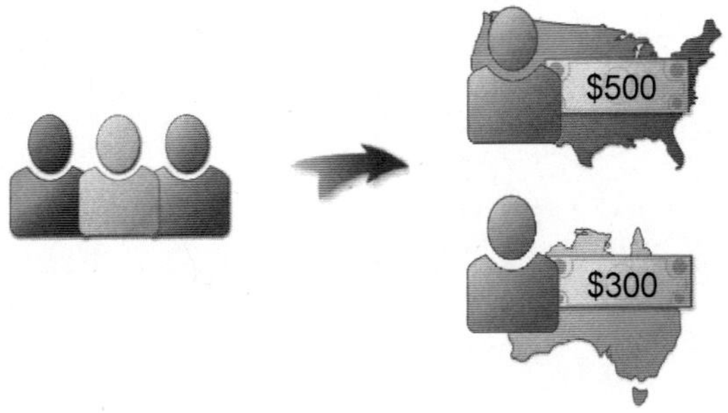

52

IF-THEN/ELSE Statements

If **orion.sales** is validated and includes ***only*** the **Country** values *US* and *AU*, the conditional clause can be omitted from the ELSE statement.

```
data work.bonus;
   set orion.sales;
   if Country='US' then Bonus=500;
   else Bonus=300;
run;
```

IF *expression* **THEN** *statement*;
ELSE *statement*;

⚠ All observations not equal to *US* are assigned a bonus of 300.

53 p109d05

You should use this technique only when you know that the final ELSE statement must be executed for all other observations.

Copyright © 2016, SAS Institute Inc., Cary, North Carolina, USA. ALL RIGHTS RESERVED.

Viewing the Output

```
proc print data=work.bonus;
   var First_Name Last_Name Country Bonus;
run;
```

Partial PROC PRINT Output

Obs	First_Name	Last_Name	Country	Bonus
60	Billy	Plested	AU	300
61	Matsuoka	Wills	AU	300
62	Vino	George	AU	300
63	Meera	Body	AU	300
64	Harry	Highpoint	US	500
65	Julienne	Magolan	US	500
66	Scott	Desanctis	US	500
67	Cherda	Ridley	US	500
68	Priscilla	Farren	US	500
69	Robert	Stevens	US	500

54 p109d05

9.04 Short Answer Poll

Program **p109a02** reads **orion.nonsales**, a non-validated data set. Open and submit the program and review the results. Why is **Bonus** set to 300 in observations 125, 197, and 200?

```
data work.bonus;
   set orion.nonsales;
   if Country='US' then Bonus=500;
   else Bonus=300;
run;
```

55

Copyright © 2016, SAS Institute Inc., Cary, North Carolina, USA. ALL RIGHTS RESERVED.

Testing for Invalid Data

You can test for multiple values of **Country**.

```
data work.bonus;
   set orion.nonsales;
   if Country in ('US','us')
      then Bonus=500;
   else Bonus=300;
run;
```

You can use the UPCASE function in the expression.

```
data work.bonus;
   set orion.nonsales;
   if upcase(Country)='US'
      then Bonus=500;
   else Bonus=300;
run;
```

57

p109a02s

Cleaning Invalid Data

You can clean the data before checking the value.

```
data work.bonus;
   set orion.nonsales;
   Country=upcase(Country);
   if Country='US'
      then Bonus=500;
   else Bonus=300;
run;
```

✎ It is a best practice to clean the data at the source, but in some cases, that is not possible. With this method, you are creating a clean data set.

58

p109d06

Copyright © 2016, SAS Institute Inc., Cary, North Carolina, USA. ALL RIGHTS RESERVED.

Business Scenario

Orion Star employees receive a bonus once or twice a year. In addition to **Bonus**, add a new variable, **Freq**, that is equal to the following:

- *Once a Year* for United States employees
- *Twice a Year* for Australian employees

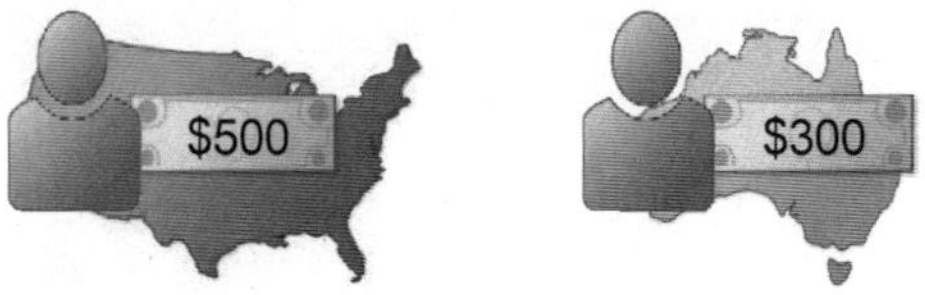

Once a Year Twice a Year

60

IF-THEN/ELSE Statements

Only ***one*** executable statement is allowed in IF-THEN and ELSE statements.

IF *expression* **THEN** *statement*;
ELSE IF *expression* **THEN** *statement*;
ELSE *statement*;

For this business scenario, ***two*** statements must be executed for each true expression.

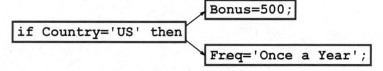

```
if Country='US' then
    Bonus=500;
    Freq='Once a Year';
```

61

Copyright © 2016, SAS Institute Inc., Cary, North Carolina, USA. ALL RIGHTS RESERVED.

DO Group

Multiple statements are permitted in a *DO group*.

```
data work.bonus;
   set orion.sales;
   if Country='US' then do;
      Bonus=500;
      Freq='Once a Year';
   end;
   else if Country='AU' then do;
      Bonus=300;
      Freq='Twice a Year';
   end;
run;
```

DO group

Each DO group ends with an END statement.

62

p109d07

IF-THEN DO/ELSE DO Statements

Multiple statements are also permitted in an ELSE DO group.

IF *expression* **THEN DO;**
   executable statements
END;
ELSE IF *expression* **THEN DO;**
   executable statements
END;
ELSE DO;
   executable statements
END;

DO group

DO group

DO group

63

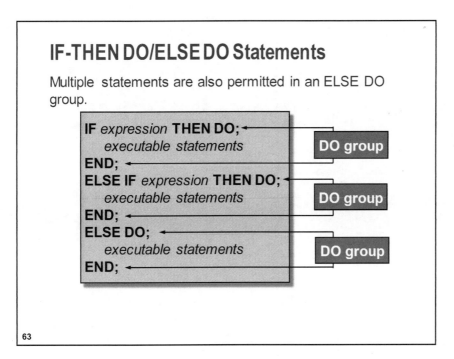

Copyright © 2016, SAS Institute Inc., Cary, North Carolina, USA. ALL RIGHTS RESERVED.

Viewing the Output

```
proc print data=work.bonus;
   var First_Name Last_Name Country Bonus
       Freq;
run;
```

Partial PROC PRINT Output

Obs	First_Name	Last_Name	Country	Bonus	Freq
60	Billy	Plested	AU	300	Twice a Yea
61	Matsuoka	Wills	AU	300	Twice a Yea
62	Vino	George	AU	300	Twice a Yea
63	Meera	Body	AU	300	Twice a Yea
64	Harry	Highpoint	US	500	Once a Year
65	Julienne	Magolan	US	500	Once a Year
66	Scott	Desanctis	US	500	Once a Year
67	Cherda	Ridley	US	500	Once a Year
68	Priscilla	Farren	US	500	Once a Year
69	Robert	Stevens	US	500	Once a Year

truncation

64

p109d07

Compilation

```
data work.bonus;
   set orion.sales;
   if Country='US' then do;
      Bonus=500;
      Freq='Once a Year';
   end;
   else if Country='AU' then do;
      Bonus=300;
      Freq='Twice a Year';
   end;
run;
```

PDV

Employee_ID N 8	First_Name $ 12	...	Hire_Date N 8

65

p109d07

...

Copyright © 2016, SAS Institute Inc., Cary, North Carolina, USA. ALL RIGHTS RESERVED.

Compilation

```
data work.bonus;
   set orion.sales;
   if Country='US' then do;
      Bonus=500;
      Freq='Once a Year';
   end;
   else if Country='AU' then do;
      Bonus=300;
      Freq='Twice a Year';
   end;
run;
```

PDV

Employee_ID N 8	First_Name $ 12	...	Hire_Date N 8	Bonus N 8

66 ...

Compilation

```
data work.bonus;
   set orion.sales;
   if Country='US' then do;
      Bonus=500;
      Freq='Once a Year';
   end;
   else if Country='AU' then do;
      Bonus=300;
      Freq='Twice a Year';
   end;
run;
```

11 characters

PDV

Employee_ID N 8	First_Name $ 12	...	Hire_Date N 8	Bonus N 8	Freq $ 11

67 ...

Copyright © 2016, SAS Institute Inc., Cary, North Carolina, USA. ALL RIGHTS RESERVED.

Compilation

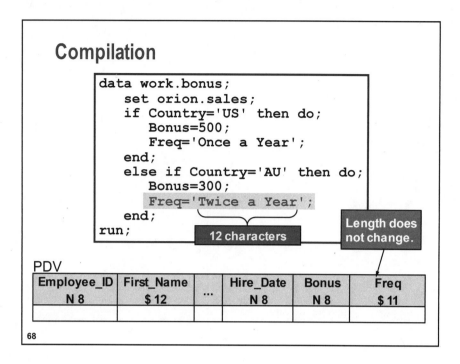

```
data work.bonus;
   set orion.sales;
   if Country='US' then do;
      Bonus=500;
      Freq='Once a Year';
   end;
   else if Country='AU' then do;
      Bonus=300;
      Freq='Twice a Year';
   end;
run;
```

12 characters

Length does not change.

PDV

Employee_ID	First_Name	...	Hire_Date	Bonus	Freq
N 8	$ 12		N 8	N 8	$ 11

68

9.05 Short Answer Poll

How would you prevent **Freq** from being truncated?

69

Copyright © 2016, SAS Institute Inc., Cary, North Carolina, USA. ALL RIGHTS RESERVED.

Defining Character Variables

Set the length of the variable **Freq** to avoid truncation.

```
data work.bonus;
   set orion.sales;
   length Freq $ 12;
   if Country='US' then do;
      Bonus=500;
      Freq='Once a Year';
   end;
   else if Country='AU' then do;
      Bonus=300;
      Freq='Twice a Year';
   end;
run;
```

LENGTH *variable(s)* <$> *length*;

It is a good practice to use a LENGTH statement anytime that you create a new character variable.

71 p109d08

The LENGTH statement is usually placed at or near the top of the DATA step.

Compilation

```
data work.bonus;
   set orion.sales;
   length Freq $ 12;
   if Country='US' then do;
      Bonus=500;
      Freq='Once a Year';
   end;
   else if Country='AU' then do;
      Bonus=300;
      Freq='Twice a Year';
   end;
run;
```

PDV

Employee_ID	First_Name	...	Hire_Date
N 8	$ 12		N 8

72 p109d08 ...

Copyright © 2016, SAS Institute Inc., Cary, North Carolina, USA. ALL RIGHTS RESERVED.

Compilation

```
data work.bonus;
   set orion.sales;
   length Freq $ 12;
   if Country='US' then do;
      Bonus=500;
      Freq='Once a Year';
   end;
   else if Country='AU' then do;
      Bonus=300;
      Freq='Twice a Year';
   end;
run;
```

PDV

Employee_ID N 8	First_Name $ 12	...	Hire_Date N 8	Freq $ 12

73 ...

Compilation

```
data work.bonus;
   set orion.sales;
   length Freq $ 12;
   if Country='US' then do;
      Bonus=500;
      Freq='Once a Year';
   end;
   else if Country='AU' then do;
      Bonus=300;
      Freq='Twice a Year';
   end;
run;
```

PDV

Employee_ID N 8	First_Name $ 12	...	Hire_Date N 8	Freq $ 12	Bonus N 8

74 ...

Copyright © 2016, SAS Institute Inc., Cary, North Carolina, USA. ALL RIGHTS RESERVED.

Compilation

```
data work.bonus;
   set orion.sales;
   length Freq $ 12;
   if Country='US' then do;
      Bonus=500;
      Freq='Once a Year';
   end;
   else if Country='AU' then do;
      Bonus=300;
      Freq='Twice a Year';
   end;
run;
```

Length does not change.

PDV

Employee_ID N 8	First_Name $ 12	...	Hire_Date N 8	Freq $ 12	Bonus N 8

75

Viewing the Output

```
proc print data=work.bonus;
   var First_Name Last_Name Country
       Bonus Freq;
run;
```

Partial PROC PRINT Output

Obs	First_Name	Last_Name	Country	Bonus	Freq
60	Billy	Plested	AU	300	Twice a Year
61	Matsuoka	Wills	AU	300	Twice a Year
62	Vino	George	AU	300	Twice a Year
63	Meera	Body	AU	300	Twice a Year
64	Harry	Highpoint	US	500	Once a Year
65	Julienne	Magolan	US	500	Once a Year
66	Scott	Desanctis	US	500	Once a Year
67	Cherda	Ridley	US	500	Once a Year
68	Priscilla	Farren	US	500	Once a Year
69	Robert	Stevens	US	500	Once a Year

no truncation

76 p109d08

Copyright © 2016, SAS Institute Inc., Cary, North Carolina, USA. ALL RIGHTS RESERVED.

Exercises

If you restarted your SAS session since the last exercise, open and submit the **libname.sas** program that can be found in the data folder.

Level 1

4. Using Conditional Processing

a. Retrieve the starter program **p109e04**.

b. In the DATA step, create a new variable, **Method**, and assign a value based on **Order_Type**.

If **Order_Type** is equal to 1, then **Method** equals *Retail.*

If **Order_Type** is equal to 2, then **Method** equals *Catalog.*

If **Order_Type** is equal to 3, then **Method** equals *Internet.*

For any other values of **Order_Type**, **Method** equals *Unknown.*

c. Modify the PROC PRINT step to display the report below. The results should contain 490 observations.

Partial PROC PRINT Output

```
                          Order_
Obs         Order_ID       Type       Method

  1       1230058123        1       Retail
  2       1230080101        2       Catalog
  3       1230106883        2       Catalog
  4       1230147441        1       Retail
  5       1230315085        1       Retail
```

5. Using Conditional Processing with DO Groups

a. Retrieve the starter program **p109e05**.

b. Modify the DATA step to create three new variables: **Discount**, **DiscountType**, and **Region**. Assign values to the new variables based on **Country**.

If **Country** is equal to *CA* or *US*, then the listed variables equal the following values:
Discount is equal to 0.10.
DiscountType is equal to *Required.*
Region is equal to *North America.*

If **Country** is equal to any other value, then the listed variables equal the following values:
Discount is equal to 0.05.
DiscountType is equal to *Optional.*
Region is equal to *Not North America.*

Copyright © 2016, SAS Institute Inc., Cary, North Carolina, USA. ALL RIGHTS RESERVED.

c. The new data set should include only **Supplier_Name**, **Country**, **Discount**, **DiscountType**, and **Region**.

d. Submit the program to create the report below. The results should contain 52 observations.

Partial PROC PRINT Output

Obs	Supplier_Name	Country	Region	Discount	Discount Type
1	Scandinavian Clothing A/S	NO	Not North America	0.05	Optional
2	Petterson AB	SE	Not North America	0.05	Optional
3	Prime Sports Ltd	GB	Not North America	0.05	Optional
4	Top Sports	DK	Not North America	0.05	Optional
5	AllSeasons Outdoor Clothing	US	North America	0.10	Required

Level 2

6. Creating Multiple Variables in Conditional Processing

a. Write a DATA step that reads **orion.customer_dim** to create **work.season**.

b. Create two new variables: **Promo** and **Promo2**.

The value of **Promo** is based on the quarter in which the customer was born.

- If the customer was born in the first quarter, then **Promo** is equal to *Winter*.
- If the customer was born in the second quarter, then **Promo** is equal to *Spring*.
- If the customer was born in the third quarter, then **Promo** is equal to *Summer*.
- If the customer was born in the fourth quarter, then **Promo** is equal to *Fall*.

The value of **Promo2** is based on the customer's age.

- For young adults, whose age is between 18 and 25, set **Promo2** equal to *YA*.
- For seniors, aged 65 or older, set **Promo2** equal to *Senior*.

Promo2 should have a missing value for all other customers.

c. The new data set should include only **Customer_FirstName**, **Customer_LastName**, **Customer_BirthDate**, **Customer_Age**, **Promo**, and **Promo2**.

d. Create the report below. The results should include 77 observations.

Partial PROC PRINT Output

Obs	Customer_ FirstName	Customer_ LastName	Customer_ BirthDate	Promo	Customer_ Age	Promo2
1	James	Kvarniq	27JUN1978	Spring	33	
2	Sandrina	Stephano	09JUL1983	Summer	28	
3	Cornelia	Krahl	27FEB1978	Winter	33	
4	Karen	Ballinger	18OCT1988	Fall	23	YA
5	Elke	Wallstab	16AUG1978	Summer	33	
6	David	Black	12APR1973	Spring	38	
7	Markus	Sepke	21JUL1992	Summer	19	YA
8	Ulrich	Heyde	16JAN1943	Winter	68	Senior

Copyright © 2016, SAS Institute Inc., Cary, North Carolina, USA. ALL RIGHTS RESERVED.

7. Creating Variables Unconditionally and Conditionally

a. Write a DATA step that reads **orion.orders** to create **work.ordertype**.

b. Create a new variable, **DayOfWeek**, that is equal to the weekday of **Order_Date**.

c. Create the new variable **Type**, which is equal to the following:
- *Retail Sale* if **Order_Type** is equal to *1*
- *Catalog Sale* if **Order_Type** is equal to *2*
- *Internet Sale* if **Order_Type** is equal to *3*.

d. Create the new variable **SaleAds**, which is equal to the following:
- *Mail* if **Order_Type** is equal to *2*
- *Email* if **Order_Type** is equal to *3*.

e. Do not include **Order_Type**, **Employee_ID**, and **Customer_ID** in the new data set.

f. Create the report below. The results should contain 490 observations.

Partial PROC PRINT Output

Obs	Order_ID	Order_ Date	Delivery_ Date	Type	Sale Ads	Day Of Week
1	1230058123	11JAN2007	11JAN2007	Retail Sale		5
2	1230080101	15JAN2007	19JAN2007	Catalog Sale	Mail	2
3	1230106883	20JAN2007	22JAN2007	Catalog Sale	Mail	7
4	1230147441	28JAN2007	28JAN2007	Retail Sale		1
5	1230315085	27FEB2007	27FEB2007	Retail Sale		3

Challenge

8. Using WHEN Statements in a SELECT Group to Create Variables Conditionally

a. Write a DATA step that reads **orion.nonsales** to create **work.gifts**.

b. Create two new variables, **Gift1** and **Gift2**. Use a SELECT group with WHEN statements. You can find documentation about the SELECT group with WHEN statements in the SAS Help Facility or in the online documentation.

If **Gender** is equal to *F*, then the listed variables equal the following values:

Gift1 is equal to *Scarf*.

Gift2 is equal to *Pedometer*.

If **Gender** is equal to *M*, then the listed variables equal the following values:

Gift1 is equal to *Gloves*.

Gift2 is equal to *Money Clip*.

If **Gender** is not equal to *F* or *M*, then the listed variables equal the following values:

Gift1 is equal to *Coffee*.

Gift2 is equal to *Calendar*.

Copyright © 2016, SAS Institute Inc., Cary, North Carolina, USA. ALL RIGHTS RESERVED.

c. The new data set should include only **Employee_ID**, **First**, **Last**, **Gender**, **Gift1**, and **Gift2**.

d. Create the report below. The results should contain 235 observations.

Partial PROC PRINT Output

Employee_ID	First	Last	Gender	Gift1	Gift2
120101	Patrick	Lu	M	Gloves	Money Clip
120104	Kareen	Billington	F	Scarf	Pedometer
120105	Liz	Povey	F	Scarf	Pedometer
120106	John	Hornsey	M	Gloves	Money Clip
120107	Sherie	Sheedy	F	Scarf	Pedometer

End of Exercises

Copyright © 2016, SAS Institute Inc., Cary, North Carolina, USA. ALL RIGHTS RESERVED.

9.3 Solutions

Solutions to Exercises

1. **Creating New Variables**

```
data work.increase;
   set orion.staff;
   Increase=Salary*0.10;
   NewSalary=sum(Salary,Increase);
  /* alternate statement is */
  /* NewSalary=Salary+Increase; */
   BdayQtr=qtr(Birth_Date);
   keep Employee_ID Birth_Date Salary Increase NewSalary BdayQtr;
   format Salary Increase NewSalary comma8.;
run;

proc print data=work.increase label;
run;
```

2. **Creating New Variables**

```
data work.birthday;
   set orion.customer;
   Bday2012=mdy(month(Birth_Date),day(Birth_Date),2012);
   BdayDOW2012=weekday(Bday2012);
   Age2012=(Bday2012-Birth_Date)/365.25;
   keep Customer_Name Birth_Date Bday2012 BdayDOW2012 Age2012;
   format Bday2012 date9. Age2012 3.;
run;

proc print data=work.birthday;
run;
```

3. **Using the CATX and INTCK Functions to Create Variables**

```
data work.employees;
   set orion.sales;
   FullName=catx(' ',First_Name,Last_Name);
   Yrs2012=intck('year',Hire_Date,'01JAN2012'd);
   format Hire_Date ddmmyy10.;
   label Yrs2012='Years of Employment in 2012';
run;

proc print data=work.employees label;
   var FullName Hire_Date Yrs2012;
run;
```

Copyright © 2016, SAS Institute Inc., Cary, North Carolina, USA. ALL RIGHTS RESERVED.

4. **Using Conditional Processing**

```
data work.ordertype;
   set orion.orders;
   length Method $ 8;
   if Order_Type=1 then Method='Retail';
   else if Order_Type=2 then Method='Catalog';
   else if Order_type=3 then Method='Internet';
   else Method='Unknown';
run;

proc print data=work.ordertype;
   var Order_ID Order_Type Method;
run;
```

5. **Using Conditional Processing with DO Groups**

```
data work.region;
   set orion.supplier;
   length Region $ 17;
   if Country in ('CA','US') then do;
      Discount=0.10;
      DiscountType='Required';
      Region='North America';
   end;
   else do;
      Discount=0.05;
      DiscountType='Optional';
      Region='Not North America';
   end;
   keep Supplier_Name Country
        Discount DiscountType Region;
run;

proc print data=work.region;
run;
```

6. **Creating Multiple Variables in Conditional Processing**

```
data work.season;
   set orion.customer_dim;
   length Promo2 $ 6;
   Quarter=qtr(Customer_BirthDate);
   if Quarter=1 then Promo='Winter';
   else if Quarter=2 then Promo='Spring';
   else if Quarter=3 then Promo='Summer';
   else if Quarter=4 then Promo='Fall';
   if Customer_Age>=18 and Customer_Age<=25 then  Promo2='YA';
   else if Customer_Age>=65 then  Promo2='Senior';
   keep Customer_FirstName Customer_LastName Customer_BirthDate
        Customer_Age Promo Promo2;
run;
```

Copyright © 2016, SAS Institute Inc., Cary, North Carolina, USA. ALL RIGHTS RESERVED.

```
proc print data=work.season;
   var Customer_FirstName Customer_LastName Customer_BirthDate
Promo
       Customer_Age Promo2;
run;
```

7. **Creating Variables Unconditionally and Conditionally**

```
data work.ordertype;
   set orion.orders;
   length Type $ 13 SaleAds $ 5;
   DayOfWeek=weekday(Order_Date);
   if Order_Type=1 then
      Type='Retail Sale';
   else if Order_Type=2 then do;
      Type='Catalog Sale';
      SaleAds='Mail';
   end;
   else if Order_Type=3 then do;
      Type='Internet Sale';
      SaleAds='Email';
   end;
   drop Order_Type Employee_ID Customer_ID;
run;

proc print data=work.ordertype;
run;
```

8. **Using WHEN Statements in a SELECT Group to Create Variables Conditionally**

```
data work.gifts;
   set orion.nonsales;
   length Gift1 $ 6 Gift2 $ 10;
   select(Gender);
      when('F') do;
         Gift1='Scarf';
         Gift2='Pedometer';
      end;
      when('M') do;
         Gift1='Gloves';
         Gift2='Money Clip';
      end;
      otherwise do;
         Gift1='Coffee';
         Gift2='Calendar';
      end;
      end;
      keep Employee_ID First Last Gender Gift1 Gift2;
run;
```

Copyright © 2016, SAS Institute Inc., Cary, North Carolina, USA. ALL RIGHTS RESERVED.

```
proc print data=work.gifts noobs;
run;
```

End of Solutions

Solutions to Student Activities (Polls/Quizzes)

9.01 Multiple Choice Poll – Correct Answer

Which of the following statements creates a numeric variable, **Bonus**, with a value of 500?

a. Bonus=$500;
(b.) Bonus=500;
c. label Bonus='500';
d. format Bonus 500.;

Partial **work.comp**

Bonus	Compensation	Bonus Month
500	108755	6
500	88475	1
500	27100	1

You use an assignment statement to set the value of the variable, Bonus, equal to 500. Numeric constants do not include commas or currency symbols.

8

9.02 Short Answer Poll – Correct Answer

A DROP statement was added to this DATA step. Can the program calculate **Compensation** and **BonusMonth** correctly?

```
data work.comp;
   set orion.sales;
   drop Gender Salary Job_Title Country
        Birth_Date Hire_Date;
   Bonus=500;
   Compensation=sum(Salary,Bonus);
   BonusMonth=month(Hire_Date);
run;
NOTE: There were 165 observations read from the data set ORION.SALES.
NOTE: The data set WORK.COMP has 165 observations and 6 variables.
```

Yes. A drop flag is set for the dropped variables, but the variables are in the PDV and therefore available for processing. DROP is a compile-time only statement.

18

Copyright © 2016, SAS Institute Inc., Cary, North Carolina, USA. ALL RIGHTS RESERVED.

9.03 Multiple Choice Poll – Correct Answer

In the previous program, is it possible for more than one condition to be true for a single observation?

a. Yes, more than one condition can be true.

(b.) No, the conditions are mutually exclusive, so only one condition can be true.

For each observation, there is only one value for Job_Title. If that value matches one of the conditions, then it cannot match any other condition.

38

9.04 Short Answer Poll – Correct Answer

Program **p109a02** reads **orion.nonsales**, a non-validated data set. Open and submit the program and review the results. Why is **Bonus** set to 300 in observations 125, 197, and 200?

```
data work.bonus;
   set orion.nonsales;
   if Country='US' then Bonus=500;
   else Bonus=300;
run;
```

The Country variable has some mixed case values in orion.nonsales. Observations with a country value of *US* are assigned 500. All others are assigned 300, including *us*.

56

Copyright © 2016, SAS Institute Inc., Cary, North Carolina, USA. ALL RIGHTS RESERVED.

9.05 Short Answer Poll – Correct Answer

How would you prevent **Freq** from being truncated?

Possible solutions:

- **Pad the first occurrence of the Freq value with blanks to be the length of the longest possible value.**
- **Switch conditional statements to place the longest value of Freq in the first conditional statement.**
- **Add a LENGTH statement to declare the byte size of the variable up front.**

70

Copyright © 2016, SAS Institute Inc., Cary, North Carolina, USA. ALL RIGHTS RESERVED.

Copyright © 2016, SAS Institute Inc., Cary, North Carolina, USA. ALL RIGHTS RESERVED.

Chapter 10 Combining Data Sets

Copyright © 2016, SAS Institute Inc., Cary, North Carolina, USA. ALL RIGHTS RESERVED.

10.1 Concatenating Data Sets

Objectives

- Concatenate two or more SAS data sets. Use the SET statement in a DATA step.
- Change the names of variables. Use the RENAME= data set option.

3

Business Scenario

You were asked to combine the data sets that contain information about Orion Star employees from Denmark and France into a new data set.

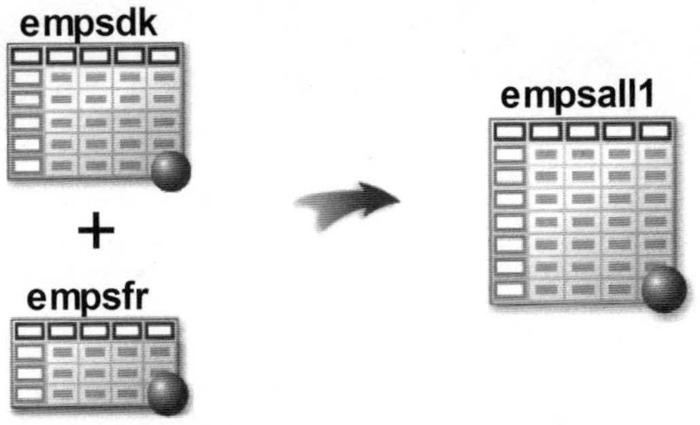

4

Copyright © 2016, SAS Institute Inc., Cary, North Carolina, USA. ALL RIGHTS RESERVED.

Considerations

Concatenate like-structured data sets, **empsdk** and **empsfr**, to create a new data set named **empsall1**.

empsdk

First	Gender	Country
Lars	M	Denmark
Kari	F	Denmark
Jonas	M	Denmark

empsfr

First	Gender	Country
Pierre	M	France
Sophie	F	France

empsall1

First	Gender	Country
Lars	M	Denmark
Kari	F	Denmark
Jonas	M	Denmark
Pierre	M	France
Sophie	F	France

Both data sets contain the same variables.

5

Using a DATA Step

Use a DATA step to concatenate the data sets.
List the data sets in the SET statement.

```
data empsall1;
   set empsdk empsfr;
run;
```

SET *SAS-data-set1 SAS-data-set2 . . .;*

- The SET statement reads observations from each data set in the order in which they are listed.
- Any number of data sets can be included in the SET statement.

6 **p110d01**

Copyright © 2016, SAS Institute Inc., Cary, North Carolina, USA. ALL RIGHTS RESERVED.

Compilation

empsdk

First	Gender	Country
Lars	M	Denmark
Kari	F	Denmark
Jonas	M	Denmark

empsfr

First	Gender	Country
Pierre	M	France
Sophie	F	France

```
data empsall1;
   set empsdk empsfr;
run;
```

PDV

First	Gender	Country

empsall1

First	Gender	Country

7

p110d01

...

Execution

empsdk

First	Gender	Country
Lars	M	Denmark
Kari	F	Denmark
Jonas	M	Denmark

empsfr

First	Gender	Country
Pierre	M	France
Sophie	F	France

Initialize PDV

```
data empsall1;
   set empsdk empsfr;
run;
```

PDV

First	Gender	Country

empsall1

First	Gender	Country

8

...

Copyright © 2016, SAS Institute Inc., Cary, North Carolina, USA. ALL RIGHTS RESERVED.

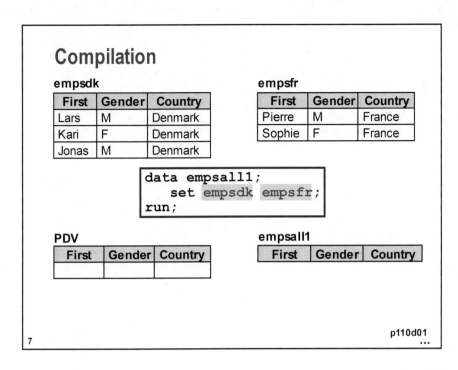

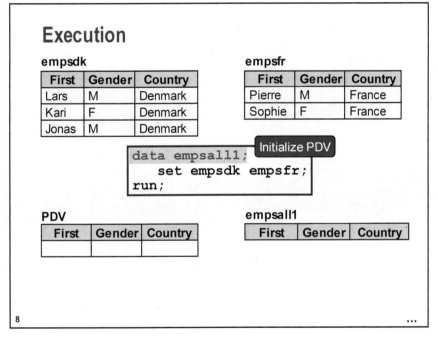

Execution

empsdk

First	Gender	Country
Lars	M	Denmark
Kari	F	Denmark
Jonas	M	Denmark

empsfr

First	Gender	Country
Pierre	M	France
Sophie	F	France

```
data empsall1;
   set empsdk empsfr;
run;
```

PDV

First	Gender	Country
Lars	M	Denmark

empsall1

First	Gender	Country

9 ...

Execution

empsdk

First	Gender	Country
Lars	M	Denmark
Kari	F	Denmark
Jonas	M	Denmark

empsfr

First	Gender	Country
Pierre	M	France
Sophie	F	France

```
data empsall1;
   set emps
run;
```

Implicit OUTPUT;
Implicit RETURN;

PDV

First	Gender	Country
Lars	M	Denmark

empsall1

First	Gender	Country
Lars	M	Denmark

10 ...

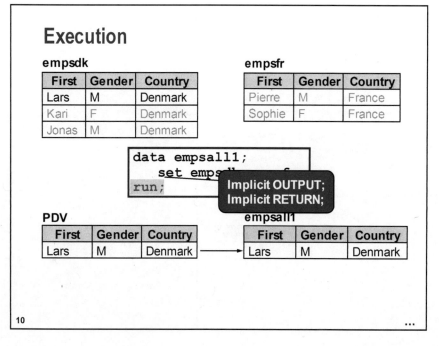

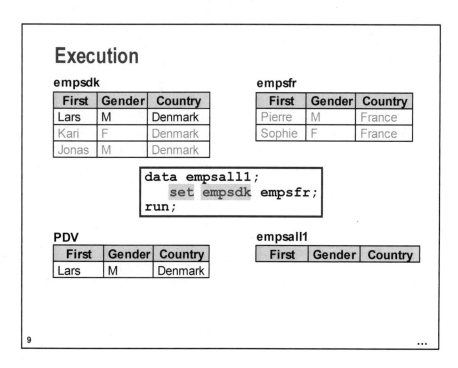

Copyright © 2016, SAS Institute Inc., Cary, North Carolina, USA. ALL RIGHTS RESERVED.

Execution

empsdk

First	Gender	Country
Lars	M	Denmark
Kari	F	Denmark
Jonas	M	Denmark

empsfr

First	Gender	Country
Pierre	M	France
Sophie	F	France

```
data empsall1;
   set empsdk empsfr;
run;
```

PDV

First	Gender	Country
Lars	M	Denmark

empsall1

First	Gender	Country
Lars	M	Denmark

Data set variables are not reinitialized.

11 ...

Execution

empsdk

First	Gender	Country
Lars	M	Denmark
Kari	F	Denmark
Jonas	M	Denmark

empsfr

First	Gender	Country
Pierre	M	France
Sophie	F	France

```
data empsall1;
   set empsdk empsfr;
run;
```

PDV

First	Gender	Country
Kari	F	Denmark

empsall1

First	Gender	Country
Lars	M	Denmark

12 ...

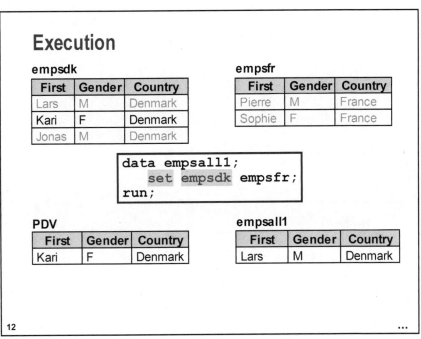

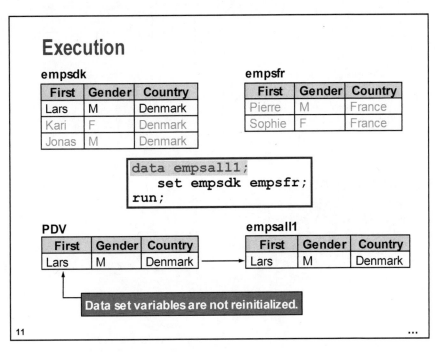

Copyright © 2016, SAS Institute Inc., Cary, North Carolina, USA. ALL RIGHTS RESERVED.

Execution

empsdk

First	Gender	Country
Lars	M	Denmark
Kari	F	Denmark
Jonas	M	Denmark

empsfr

First	Gender	Country
Pierre	M	France
Sophie	F	France

```
data empsall1;
   set emps
run;
```

Implicit OUTPUT;
Implicit RETURN;

PDV

First	Gender	Country
Kari	F	Denmark

empsall1

First	Gender	Country
Lars	M	Denmark
Kari	F	Denmark

13 ...

Execution

empsdk

First	Gender	Country
Lars	M	Denmark
Kari	F	Denmark
Jonas	M	Denmark

empsfr

First	Gender	Country
Pierre	M	France
Sophie	F	France

```
data empsall1;
   set empsdk empsfr;
run;
```

PDV

First	Gender	Country
Kari	F	Denmark

PDV is not reinitialized.

empsall1

First	Gender	Country
Lars	M	Denmark
Kari	F	Denmark

14 ...

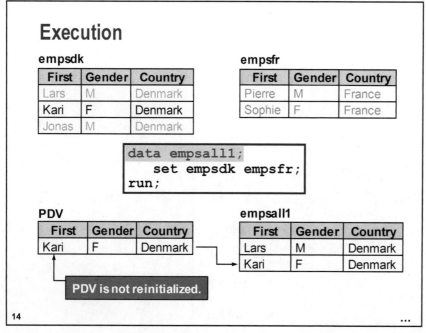

Copyright © 2016, SAS Institute Inc., Cary, North Carolina, USA. ALL RIGHTS RESERVED.

Execution

empsdk

First	Gender	Country
Lars	M	Denmark
Kari	F	Denmark
Jonas	M	Denmark

empsfr

First	Gender	Country
Pierre	M	France
Sophie	F	France

```
data empsall1;
   set empsdk empsfr;
run;
```

PDV

First	Gender	Country
Jonas	M	Denmark

empsall1

First	Gender	Country
Lars	M	Denmark
Kari	F	Denmark

15 ...

Execution

empsdk

First	Gender	Country
Lars	M	Denmark
Kari	F	Denmark
Jonas	M	Denmark

empsfr

First	Gender	Country
Pierre	M	France
Sophie	F	France

```
data empsall1;
   set emps
run;
```

Implicit OUTPUT;
Implicit RETURN;

PDV

First	Gender	Country
Jonas	M	Denmark

empsall1

First	Gender	Country
Lars	M	Denmark
Kari	F	Denmark
Jonas	M	Denmark

16 ...

Copyright © 2016, SAS Institute Inc., Cary, North Carolina, USA. ALL RIGHTS RESERVED.

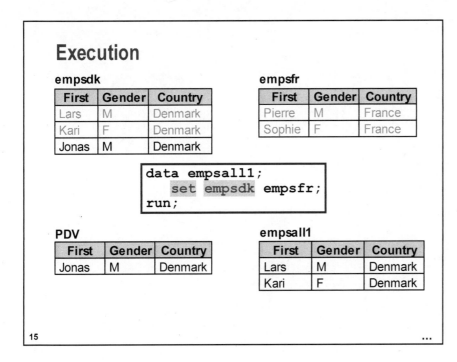

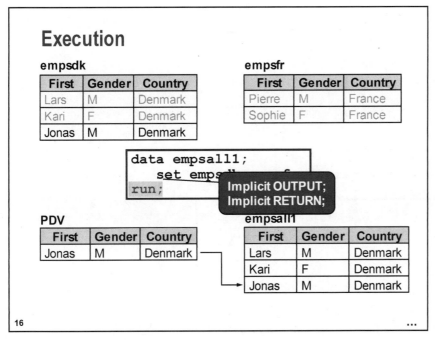

Execution

empsdk

First	Gender	Country
Lars	M	Denmark
Kari	F	Denmark
Jonas	M	Denmark

empsfr

First	Gender	Country
Pierre	M	France
Sophie	F	France

```
data empsall1;
   set empsdk empsfr;
run;
```

PDV

First	Gender	Country
Jonas	M	Denmark

PDV is not reinitialized.

empsall1

First	Gender	Country
Lars	M	Denmark
Kari	F	Denmark
Jonas	M	Denmark

17 ...

Execution

empsdk

First	Gender	Country
Lars	M	Denmark
Kari	F	Denmark
Jonas	M	Denmark

EOF

empsfr

First	Gender	Country
Pierre	M	France
Sophie	F	France

```
data empsall1;
   set empsdk empsfr;
run;
```

PDV

First	Gender	Country
Jonas	M	Denmark

empsall1

First	Gender	Country
Lars	M	Denmark
Kari	F	Denmark
Jonas	M	Denmark

18 ...

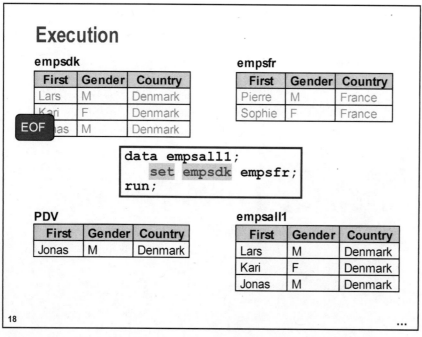

Copyright © 2016, SAS Institute Inc., Cary, North Carolina, USA. ALL RIGHTS RESERVED.

Execution

empsdk

First	Gender	Country
Lars	M	Denmark
Kari	F	Denmark
Jonas	M	Denmark

empsfr

First	Gender	Country
Pierre	M	France
Sophie	F	France

```
data empsall1;
   set empsdk empsfr;
run;
```

Reinitialize PDV

PDV

First	Gender	Country

PDV is reinitialized before processing the next data set.

empsall1

First	Gender	Country
Lars	M	Denmark
Kari	F	Denmark
Jonas	M	Denmark

19 ...

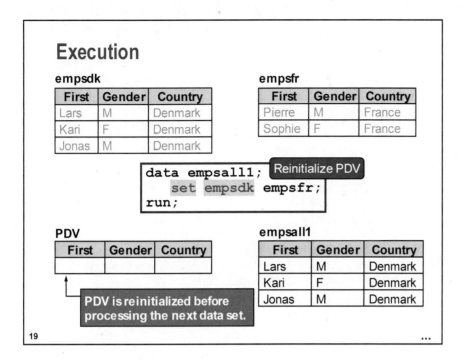

When concatenating data sets, SAS reinitializes the entire PDV before it begins reading the next data set that is listed in the SET statement.

Execution

empsdk

First	Gender	Country
Lars	M	Denmark
Kari	F	Denmark
Jonas	M	Denmark

empsfr

First	Gender	Country
Pierre	M	France
Sophie	F	France

```
data empsall1;
   set empsdk empsfr;
run;
```

PDV

First	Gender	Country
Pierre	M	France

empsall1

First	Gender	Country
Lars	M	Denmark
Kari	F	Denmark
Jonas	M	Denmark

20 ...

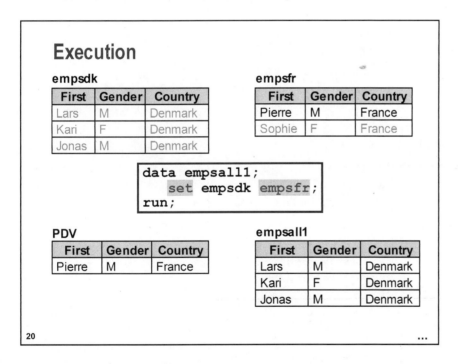

Copyright © 2016, SAS Institute Inc., Cary, North Carolina, USA. ALL RIGHTS RESERVED.

Execution

empsdk

First	Gender	Country
Lars	M	Denmark
Kari	F	Denmark
Jonas	M	Denmark

empsfr

First	Gender	Country
Pierre	M	France
Sophie	F	France

```
data empsall1;
   set emps
run;
```

Implicit OUTPUT;
Implicit RETURN;

PDV

First	Gender	Country
Pierre	M	France

empsall1

First	Gender	Country
Lars	M	Denmark
Kari	F	Denmark
Jonas	M	Denmark
Pierre	M	France

21 ...

Execution

empsdk

First	Gender	Country
Lars	M	Denmark
Kari	F	Denmark
Jonas	M	Denmark

empsfr

First	Gender	Country
Pierre	M	France
Sophie	F	France

```
data empsall1;
   set empsdk empsfr;
run;
```

PDV

First	Gender	Country
Pierre	M	France

PDV is not reinitialized.

empsall1

First	Gender	Country
Lars	M	Denmark
Kari	F	Denmark
Jonas	M	Denmark
Pierre	M	France

22 ...

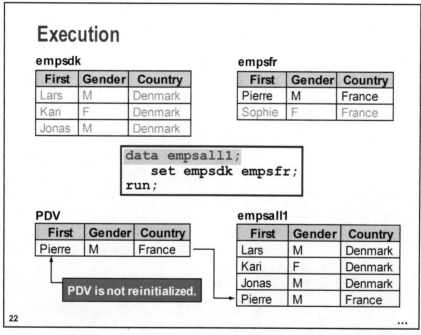

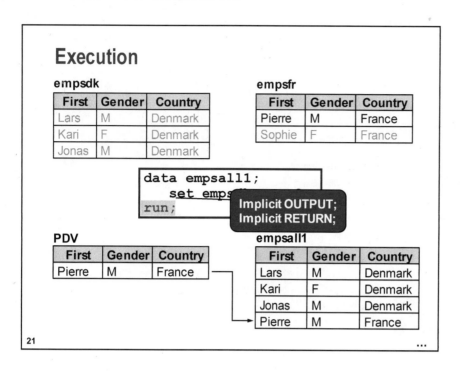

Copyright © 2016, SAS Institute Inc., Cary, North Carolina, USA. ALL RIGHTS RESERVED.

Execution

empsdk

First	Gender	Country
Lars	M	Denmark
Kari	F	Denmark
Jonas	M	Denmark

empsfr

First	Gender	Country
Pierre	M	France
Sophie	F	France

```
data empsall1;
   set empsdk empsfr;
run;
```

PDV

First	Gender	Country
Sophie	F	France

empsall1

First	Gender	Country
Lars	M	Denmark
Kari	F	Denmark
Jonas	M	Denmark
Pierre	M	France

23 ...

Execution

empsdk

First	Gender	Country
Lars	M	Denmark
Kari	F	Denmark
Jonas	M	Denmark

empsfr

First	Gender	Country
Pierre	M	France
Sophie	F	France

```
data empsall1;
   set emps
run;
```

Implicit OUTPUT;
Implicit RETURN;

PDV

First	Gender	Country
Sophie	F	France

empsall1

First	Gender	Country
Lars	M	Denmark
Kari	F	Denmark
Jonas	M	Denmark
Pierre	M	France
Sophie	F	France

24 ...

Copyright © 2016, SAS Institute Inc., Cary, North Carolina, USA. ALL RIGHTS RESERVED.

Execution

empsdk

First	Gender	Country
Lars	M	Denmark
Kari	F	Denmark
Jonas	M	Denmark

empsfr

First	Gender	Country
Pierre	M	France
Sophie	F	France

```
data empsall1;
   set empsdk empsfr;
run;
```

PDV

First	Gender	Country
Sophie	F	France

PDV is not reinitialized.

empsall1

First	Gender	Country
Lars	M	Denmark
Kari	F	Denmark
Jonas	M	Denmark
Pierre	M	France
Sophie	F	France

25

Execution

empsdk

First	Gender	Country
Lars	M	Denmark
Kari	F	Denmark
Jonas	M	Denmark

empsfr

First	Gender	Country
Pierre	M	France
Sophie	F	France

EOF

```
data empsall1;
   set empsdk empsfr;
run;
```

PDV

First	Gender	Country
Sophie	F	France

empsall1

First	Gender	Country
Lars	M	Denmark
Kari	F	Denmark
Jonas	M	Denmark
Pierre	M	France
Sophie	F	France

26

Copyright © 2016, SAS Institute Inc., Cary, North Carolina, USA. ALL RIGHTS RESERVED.

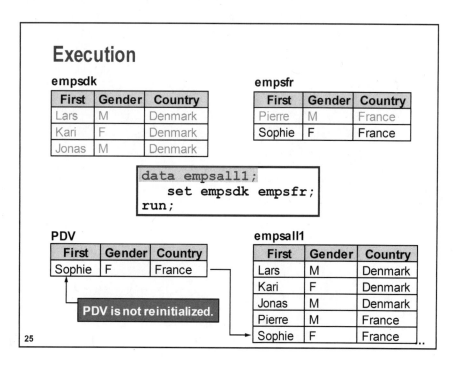

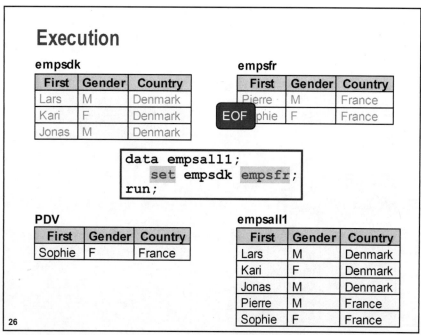

Viewing the Log

Partial SAS Log

```
145  data empsall1;
146     set empsdk empsfr;
147  run;

NOTE: There were 3 observations read from the data set WORK.EMPSDK.
NOTE: There were 2 observations read from the data set WORK.EMPSFR.
NOTE: The data set WORK.EMPSALL1 has 5 observations and 3
variables.
```

27

Unlike-Structured Data Sets

Concatenate **empscn** and **empsjp** to create a new data set named **empsall2**.

empscn

First	Gender	Country
Chang	M	China
Li	M	China
Ming	F	China

empsjp

First	Gender	Region
Cho	F	Japan
Tomi	M	Japan

The data sets do not contain the same variables.

```
data empsall2;
   set empscn empsjp;
run;
```

28 **p110d02**

Copyright © 2016, SAS Institute Inc., Cary, North Carolina, USA. ALL RIGHTS RESERVED.

10.01 Short Answer Poll

How many variables will be in **empsall2** after concatenating **empscn** and **empsjp**?

empscn

First	Gender	Country
Chang	M	China
Li	M	China
Ming	F	China

empsjp

First	Gender	Region
Cho	F	Japan
Tomi	M	Japan

```
data empsall2;
   set empscn empsjp;
run;
```

29

Compilation

empscn

First	Gender	Country
Chang	M	China
Li	M	China
Ming	F	China

empsjp

First	Gender	Region
Cho	F	Japan
Tomi	M	Japan

```
data empsall2;
   set empscn empsjp;
run;
```

PDV

First	Gender	Country

31

p110d02

...

Copyright © 2016, SAS Institute Inc., Cary, North Carolina, USA. ALL RIGHTS RESERVED.

Compilation

empscn

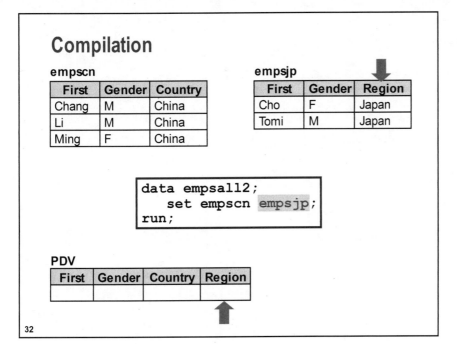

First	Gender	Country
Chang	M	China
Li	M	China
Ming	F	China

empsjp

First	Gender	Region
Cho	F	Japan
Tomi	M	Japan

```
data empsall2;
   set empscn empsjp;
run;
```

PDV

First	Gender	Country	Region

32

Final Results

empsall2

First	Gender	Country	Region
Chang	M	China	
Li	M	China	
Ming	F	China	
Cho	F		Japan
Tomi	M		Japan

- **Region** has missing values due to PDV initialization.
- **Country** has missing values due to PDV reinitialization before processing the second data set.

33

Copyright © 2016, SAS Institute Inc., Cary, North Carolina, USA. ALL RIGHTS RESERVED.

Business Scenario

Rename variables in one or more data sets to align columns.

empscn

First	Gender	Country
Chang	M	China
Li	M	China
Ming	F	China

empsjp

First	Gender	Region
Cho	F	Japan
Tomi	M	Japan

Rename **Region** to **Country**.

34

RENAME= Data Set Option

The *RENAME= data set option* changes the name of a variable.

```
data empsall2;
   set empscn empsjp(rename=(Region=Country));
run;
```

SAS-data-set **(RENAME=(***old-name-1***=***new-name-1*
*old-name-2***=***new-name-2*
...
*old-name-n***=***new-name-n***))**

- The RENAME= option must be specified in parentheses immediately after the appropriate SAS data set name.
- The name change affects the PDV and the output data set. It has no effect on the input data set.

35

Copyright © 2016, SAS Institute Inc., Cary, North Carolina, USA. ALL RIGHTS RESERVED.

RENAME= Data Set Option

Multiples variables can be renamed in one or more data sets.

```
set empscn(rename=(Country=Region))
    empsjp;
```

```
set empscn(rename=(First=Fname
                   Country=Region))
    empsjp(rename=(First=Fname));
```

```
set empscn
    empsjp(rename=(Region=Country));
```

36

10.02 Short Answer Poll

Which statement has correct syntax?

a.

```
set empscn(rename(Country=Location))
    empsjp(rename(Region=Location));
```

b.

```
set empscn(rename=(Country=Location))
    empsjp(rename=(Region=Location));
```

c.

```
set empscn rename=(Country=Location)
    empsjp rename=(Region=Location);
```

37

Copyright © 2016, SAS Institute Inc., Cary, North Carolina, USA. ALL RIGHTS RESERVED.

Compilation

empscn

First	Gender	Country
Chang	M	China
Li	M	China
Ming	F	China

empsjp

First	Gender	Region
Cho	F	Japan
Tomi	M	Japan

```
data empsall2;
   set empscn empsjp(rename=(Region=Country));
run;
```

PDV

First	Gender	Country

39 p110d03

...

Compilation

empscn

First	Gender	Country
Chang	M	China
Li	M	China
Ming	F	China

empsjp

First	Gender	Region
Cho	F	Japan
Tomi	M	Japan

```
data empsall2;
   set empscn empsjp(rename=(Region=Country));
run;
```

PDV

First	Gender	Country

40

...

Copyright © 2016, SAS Institute Inc., Cary, North Carolina, USA. ALL RIGHTS RESERVED.

Compilation

empscn

First	Gender	Country
Chang	M	China
Li	M	China
Ming	F	China

empsjp

First	Gender	Region
Cho	F	Japan
Tomi	M	Japan

```
data empsall2;
   set empscn empsjp(rename=(Region=Country));
run;
```

PDV

First	Gender	Country

41 ...

Compilation

empscn

First	Gender	Country
Chang	M	China
Li	M	China
Ming	F	China

empsjp

First	Gender	Region
Cho	F	Japan
Tomi	M	Japan

```
data empsall2;
   set empscn empsjp(rename=(Region=Country));
run;
```

PDV

First	Gender	Country

42 ...

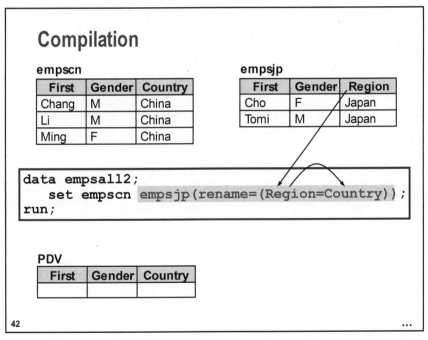

Copyright © 2016, SAS Institute Inc., Cary, North Carolina, USA. ALL RIGHTS RESERVED.

Compilation

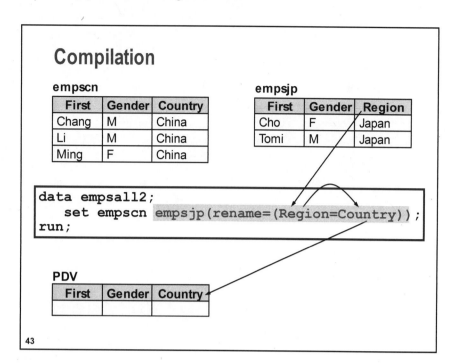

empscn

First	Gender	Country
Chang	M	China
Li	M	China
Ming	F	China

empsjp

First	Gender	Region
Cho	F	Japan
Tomi	M	Japan

```
data empsall2;
   set empscn empsjp(rename=(Region=Country));
run;
```

PDV

First	Gender	Country

43

Final Results

The **Region** values are stored in **Country**.

empsall2

First	Gender	Country
Chang	M	China
Li	M	China
Ming	F	China
Cho	F	Japan
Tomi	M	Japan

44

Copyright © 2016, SAS Institute Inc., Cary, North Carolina, USA. ALL RIGHTS RESERVED.

Exercises

> If you restarted your SAS session since the last exercise, open and submit the **libname.sas** program that can be found in the data folder.

Level 1

1. Concatenating Like-Structured Data Sets

a. Write and submit a DATA step to concatenate **orion.mnth7_2011**, **orion.mnth8_2011**, and **orion.mnth9_2011** to create a new data set, **work.thirdqtr**.

How many observations in **work.thirdqtr** are from **orion.mnth7_2011**? ____________________

How many observations in **work.thirdqtr** are from **orion.mnth8_2011**? ____________________

How many observations in **work.thirdqtr** are from **orion.mnth9_2011**? ____________________

b. Write a PROC PRINT step to create the report below. The results should contain 32 observations.

Partial PROC PRINT Output

Obs	Order_ID	Order_ Type	Employee_ID	Customer_ID	Order_ Date	Delivery_ Date
1	1242691897	2	99999999	90	02JUL2011	04JUL2011
2	1242736731	1	121107	10	07JUL2011	07JUL2011
3	1242773202	3	99999999	24	11JUL2011	14JUL2011
4	1242782701	3	99999999	27	12JUL2011	17JUL2011
5	1242827683	1	121105	10	17JUL2011	17JUL2011

2. Concatenating Unlike-Structured Data Sets

Open **p110e02**. Submit the two PROC CONTENTS steps or explore the data sets interactively to compare the variables in the two data sets. What are the names of the two variables that are different in the two data sets?

orion.sales	orion.nonsales

a. Add a DATA step after the PROC CONTENTS steps to concatenate **orion.sales** and **orion.nonsales** to create a new data set, **work.allemployees**.

Use a RENAME= data set option to change the names of the different variables in **orion.nonsales**.

The new data set should include only **Employee_ID**, **First_Name**, **Last_Name**, **Job_Title**, and **Salary**.

Copyright © 2016, SAS Institute Inc., Cary, North Carolina, USA. ALL RIGHTS RESERVED.

b. Add a PROC PRINT step to create the report below. The results should contain 400 observations.

Partial PROC PRINT Output

```
                                  First_
      Obs    Employee_ID    Name          Last_Name    Salary     Job_Title

        1       120102      Tom           Zhou          108255    Sales Manager
        2       120103      Wilson        Dawes          87975    Sales Manager
        3       120121      Irenie        Elvish         26600    Sales Rep. II
        4       120122      Christina     Ngan           27475    Sales Rep. II
        5       120123      Kimiko        Hotstone       26190    Sales Rep. I
```

Level 2

3. Concatenating Data Sets with Variables of Different Lengths and Types

a. Open **p110e03**. Submit the PROC CONTENTS steps or explore the data sets interactively to complete the table below. Fill in attribute information for each variable in each data set.

	Code		Company		ContactType	
	Type	Length	Type	Length	Type	Length
orion.charities						
orion.us_suppliers						
orion.consultants						

b. Write a DATA step to concatenate **orion.charities** and **orion.us_suppliers** and create a temporary data set, **contacts**.

c. Submit a PROC CONTENTS step to examine **work.contacts**. From which input data set were the variable attributes assigned? ______________________

d. Write a DATA step to concatenate **orion.us_suppliers** and **orion.charities** and create a temporary data set, **contacts2**. Notice that these are the same data sets as in the previous program, but they are in reverse order.

e. Submit a PROC CONTENTS step to examine **work.contacts2**. From which input data set were the variable attributes assigned? ______________________

f. Write a DATA step to concatenate **orion.us_suppliers** and **orion.consultants** and create a temporary data set, **contacts3**.

Why did the DATA step fail? ______________________

End of Exercises

Copyright © 2016, SAS Institute Inc., Cary, North Carolina, USA. ALL RIGHTS RESERVED.

10.2 Merging Data Sets One-to-One

Objectives

- Prepare data sets for merging. Use the SORT procedure.
- Merge SAS data sets one-to-one based on a common variable.

48

Match-Merging

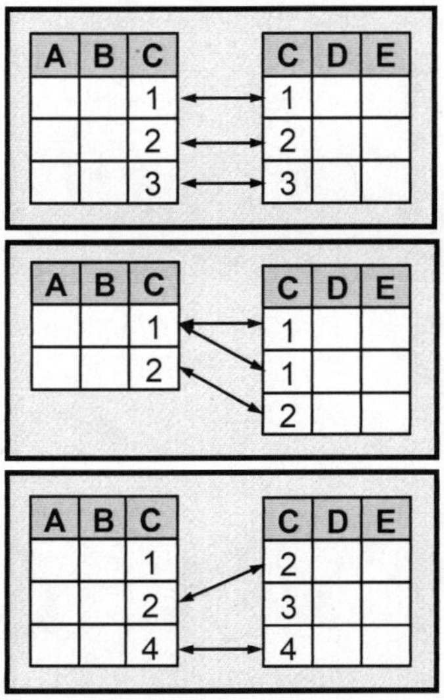

One-to-One

A single observation in one data set is related to exactly one observation in another data set based on the values of one or more selected variables.

One-to-Many

A single observation in one data set is related to more than one observation in another data set based on the values of one or more selected variables.

Nonmatches

At least one observation in one data set is unrelated to any observation in another data set based on the values of one or more selected variables.

49

Copyright © 2016, SAS Institute Inc., Cary, North Carolina, USA. ALL RIGHTS RESERVED.

Match-Merging: Sorting the Data Sets

The data sets in a match-merge must be sorted by the common variable or variables that are being matched.

```
PROC SORT DATA=input-SAS-data-set
          <OUT=output-SAS-data-set>;
   BY <DESCENDING> by-variable(s);
RUN;
```

50

10.03 Multiple Choice Poll

Which of the following BY statements correctly sorts by descending **salary** within **gender**?

a. by descending salary within gender;
b. by descending salary gender;
c. by gender descending salary;
d. by gender salary descending;

51

Copyright © 2016, SAS Institute Inc., Cary, North Carolina, USA. ALL RIGHTS RESERVED.

Business Scenario

Merge the Australian employee data set with a phone data set to obtain each employee's home phone number. Store the results in a new data set.

empsau

First	Gender	EmpID

\+

phoneh

EmpID	Phone

empsauh

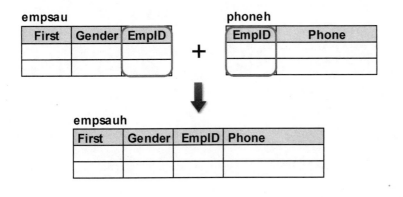

First	Gender	EmpID	Phone

53

Match-Merging

The *MERGE statement* in a DATA step joins observations from two or more SAS data sets into single observations.

```
data empsauh;
   merge empsau phoneh;
   by EmpID;
run;
```

MERGE *SAS-data-set1 SAS-data-set2 . . .*;
BY <DESCENDING> *BY-variable(s)*;

A *BY statement* indicates a match-merge and lists the variable or variables to match.

54

p110d04

Copyright © 2016, SAS Institute Inc., Cary, North Carolina, USA. ALL RIGHTS RESERVED.

MERGE and BY Statements

Requirements for match-merging:

- Two or more data sets are listed in the MERGE statement.
- The variables in the BY statement must be common to all data sets.
- The data sets must be sorted by the variables listed in the BY statement.

55

One-to-One Merge

One observation in **empsau** matches exactly one observation in **phoneh**.

empsau

First	Gender	EmpID
Togar	M	121150
Kylie	F	121151
Birin	M	121152

phoneh

EmpID	Phone
121150	+61(2)5555-1793
121151	+61(2)5555-1849
121152	+61(2)5555-1665

The data sets are sorted by **EmpID**.

56

Copyright © 2016, SAS Institute Inc., Cary, North Carolina, USA. ALL RIGHTS RESERVED.

Final Results

empsau

First	Gender	EmpID
Togar	M	121150
Kylie	F	121151
Birin	M	121152

phoneh

EmpID	Phone
121150	+61(2)5555-1793
121151	+61(2)5555-1849
121152	+61(2)5555-1665

empsauh

First	Gender	EmpID	Phone
Togar	M	121150	+61(2)5555-1793
Kylie	F	121151	+61(2)5555-1849
Birin	M	121152	+61(2)5555-1665

57

10.04 Short Answer Poll

Complete program **p110a01** to match-merge the sorted SAS data sets referenced in the PROC SORT steps.

Submit the program. Correct and resubmit it, if necessary.

What are the modified, completed statements?

58

Copyright © 2016, SAS Institute Inc., Cary, North Carolina, USA. ALL RIGHTS RESERVED.

10.3 Merging Data Sets One-to-Many

Objectives

- Merge SAS data sets one-to-many based on a common variable.

62

Business Scenario

Merge the Australian employee information data set with the **phones** data set to obtain the phone numbers for each employee.

63

Copyright © 2016, SAS Institute Inc., Cary, North Carolina, USA. ALL RIGHTS RESERVED.

Considerations

In this one-to-many merge, one observation in **empsau** matches one or more observations in **phones**.

empsau

First	Gender	EmpID
Togar	M	121150
Kylie	F	121151
Birin	M	121152

phones

EmpID	Type	Phone
121150	Home	+61(2)5555-1793
121150	Work	+61(2)5555-1794
121151	Home	+61(2)5555-1849
121152	Work	+61(2)5555-1850
121152	Home	+61(2)5555-1665
121152	Cell	+61(2)5555-1666

The data sets are sorted by **EmpID**.

64

Match-Merging

Merge the two data sets by **EmpID** and create a new data set named **empphones**.

```
data empphones;
   merge empsau phones;
   by EmpID;
run;
```

65

p110d05

Copyright © 2016, SAS Institute Inc., Cary, North Carolina, USA. ALL RIGHTS RESERVED.

Match-Merging

BY variable

BY group

empsau

First	Gender	EmpID
Togar	M	121150
Kylie	F	121151
Birin	M	121152

phones

EmpID	Type	Phone
121150	Home	+61(2)5555-1793
121150	Work	+61(2)5555-1794
121151	Home	+61(2)5555-1849
121152	Work	+61(2)5555-1850
121152	Home	+61(2)5555-1665
121152	Cell	+61(2)5555-1666

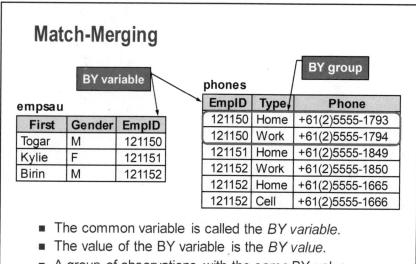

- The common variable is called the *BY variable*.
- The value of the BY variable is the *BY value*.
- A group of observations with the same BY value is a *BY group*.

66

Execution

empsau

First	Gender	EmpID
Togar	M	121150
Kylie	F	121151
Birin	M	121152

phones

EmpID	Type	Phone
121150	Home	+61(2)5555-1793
121150	Work	+61(2)5555-1794
121151	Home	+61(2)5555-1849
121152	Work	+61(2)5555-1850
121152	Home	+61(2)5555-1665
121152	Cell	+61(2)5555-1666

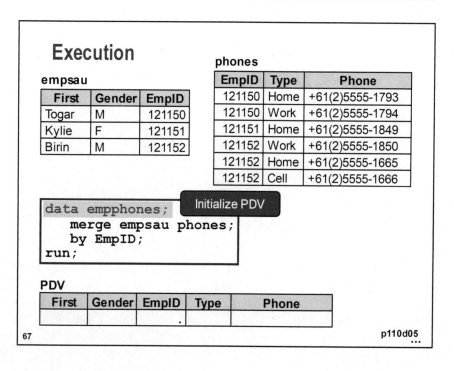

```
data empphones;
   merge empsau phones;
   by EmpID;
run;
```

Initialize PDV

PDV

First	Gender	EmpID	Type	Phone
		.		

67

p110d05

...

Copyright © 2016, SAS Institute Inc., Cary, North Carolina, USA. ALL RIGHTS RESERVED.

Execution

empsau

First	Gender	EmpID
Togar	M	121150
Kylie	F	121151
Birin	M	121152

phones

EmpID	Type	Phone
121150	Home	+61(2)5555-1793
121150	Work	+61(2)5555-1794
121151	Home	+61(2)5555-1849
121152	Work	+61(2)5555-1850
121152	Home	+61(2)5555-1665
121152	Cell	+61(2)5555-1666

```
data empphones;
   merge empsau phones;
   by EmpID;
run;
```

Do the **EmpID** values match?

Yes

PDV

First	Gender	EmpID	Type	Phone
		.		

68 ...

Execution

empsau

First	Gender	EmpID
Togar	M	121150
Kylie	F	121151
Birin	M	121152

phones

EmpID	Type	Phone
121150	Home	+61(2)5555-1793
121150	Work	+61(2)5555-1794
121151	Home	+61(2)5555-1849
121152	Work	+61(2)5555-1850
121152	Home	+61(2)5555-1665
121152	Cell	+61(2)5555-1666

```
data empphones;
   merge empsau phones;
   by EmpID;
run;
```

Reads both observations into the PDV.

PDV

First	Gender	EmpID	Type	Phone
Togar	M	121150	Home	+61(2)5555-1793

69 ...

Copyright © 2016, SAS Institute Inc., Cary, North Carolina, USA. ALL RIGHTS RESERVED.

Execution

empsau

First	Gender	EmpID
Togar	M	121150
Kylie	F	121151
Birin	M	121152

phones

EmpID	Type	Phone
121150	Home	+61(2)5555-1793
121150	Work	+61(2)5555-1794
121151	Home	+61(2)5555-1849
121152	Work	+61(2)5555-1850
121152	Home	+61(2)5555-1665
121152	Cell	+61(2)5555-1666

```
data empphones;
   merge empsau phones;
   by EmpID;
run;
```

Implicit OUTPUT;
Implicit RETURN;

PDV

First	Gender	EmpID	Type	Phone
Togar	M	121150	Home	+61(2)5555-1793

70 ...

Execution

empsau

First	Gender	EmpID
Togar	M	121150
Kylie	F	121151
Birin	M	121152

phones

EmpID	Type	Phone
121150	Home	+61(2)5555-1793
121150	Work	+61(2)5555-1794
121151	Home	+61(2)5555-1849
121152	Work	+61(2)5555-1850
121152	Home	+61(2)5555-1665
121152	Cell	+61(2)5555-1666

```
data empphones;
   merge empsau phones;
   by EmpID;
run;
```

Data set variables are not reinitialized.

PDV

First	Gender	EmpID	Type	Phone
Togar	M	121150	Home	+61(2)5555-1793

71 ...

Copyright © 2016, SAS Institute Inc., Cary, North Carolina, USA. ALL RIGHTS RESERVED.

Execution

empsau

First	Gender	EmpID
Togar	M	121150
Kylie	F	121151
Birin	M	121152

phones

EmpID	Type	Phone
121150	Home	+61(2)5555-1793
121150	Work	+61(2)5555-1794
121151	Home	+61(2)5555-1849
121152	Work	+61(2)5555-1850
121152	Home	+61(2)5555-1665
121152	Cell	+61(2)5555-1666

```
data empphones;
   merge empsau phones;
   by EmpID;
run;
```

Do the **EmpID** values match?

No

PDV

First	Gender	EmpID	Type	Phone
Togar	M	121150	Home	+61(2)5555-1793

72 ...

Execution

empsau

First	Gender	EmpID
Togar	M	121150
Kylie	F	121151
Birin	M	121152

phones

EmpID	Type	Phone
121150	Home	+61(2)5555-1793
121150	Work	+61(2)5555-1794
121151	Home	+61(2)5555-1849
121152	Work	+61(2)5555-1850
121152	Home	+61(2)5555-1665
121152	Cell	+61(2)5555-1666

```
data empphones;
   merge empsau phones;
   by EmpID;
run;
```

Did **EmpID** change?

No

PDV

First	Gender	EmpID	Type	Phone
Togar	M	121150	Home	+61(2)5555-1793

73 ...

Copyright © 2016, SAS Institute Inc., Cary, North Carolina, USA. ALL RIGHTS RESERVED.

Execution

empsau

First	Gender	EmpID
Togar	M	121150
Kylie	F	121151
Birin	M	121152

phones

EmpID	Type	Phone
121150	Home	+61(2)5555-1793
121150	Work	+61(2)5555-1794
121151	Home	+61(2)5555-1849
121152	Work	+61(2)5555-1850
121152	Home	+61(2)5555-1665
121152	Cell	+61(2)5555-1666

```
data empphones;
   merge empsau phones;
   by EmpID;
run;
```

Reads the matching observation into the PDV.

PDV

First	Gender	EmpID	Type	Phone
Togar	M	121150	Work	+61(2)5555-1794

74

...

Execution

empsau

First	Gender	EmpID
Togar	M	121150
Kylie	F	121151
Birin	M	121152

phones

EmpID	Type	Phone
121150	Home	+61(2)5555-1793
121150	Work	+61(2)5555-1794
121151	Home	+61(2)5555-1849
121152	Work	+61(2)5555-1850
121152	Home	+61(2)5555-1665
121152	Cell	+61(2)5555-1666

```
data empphones;
   merge empsau phones;
   by EmpID;
run;
```

Implicit OUTPUT;
Implicit RETURN;

PDV

First	Gender	EmpID	Type	Phone
Togar	M	121150	Work	+61(2)5555-1794

75

...

Copyright © 2016, SAS Institute Inc., Cary, North Carolina, USA. ALL RIGHTS RESERVED.

Execution

empsau

First	Gender	EmpID
Togar	M	121150
Kylie	F	121151
Birin	M	121152

phones

EmpID	Type	Phone
121150	Home	+61(2)5555-1793
121150	Work	+61(2)5555-1794
121151	Home	+61(2)5555-1849
121152	Work	+61(2)5555-1850
121152	Home	+61(2)5555-1665
121152	Cell	+61(2)5555-1666

```
data empphones;
   merge empsau phones;
   by EmpID;
run;
```

Do the **EmpID** values match?

Yes

PDV

First	Gender	EmpID	Type	Phone
Togar	M	121150	Work	+61(2)5555-1794

76 ...

Execution

empsau

First	Gender	EmpID
Togar	M	121150
Kylie	F	121151
Birin	M	121152

phones

EmpID	Type	Phone
121150	Home	+61(2)5555-1793
121150	Work	+61(2)5555-1794
121151	Home	+61(2)5555-1849
121152	Work	+61(2)5555-1850
121152	Home	+61(2)5555-1665
121152	Cell	+61(2)5555-1666

```
data empphones;
   merge empsau phones;
   by EmpID;
run;
```

Did **EmpID** change?

Yes

PDV

First	Gender	EmpID	Type	Phone
Togar	M	121150	Work	+61(2)5555-1794

77 ...

Copyright © 2016, SAS Institute Inc., Cary, North Carolina, USA. ALL RIGHTS RESERVED.

Execution

empsau

First	Gender	EmpID
Togar	M	121150
Kylie	F	121151
Birin	M	121152

phones

EmpID	Type	Phone
121150	Home	+61(2)5555-1793
121150	Work	+61(2)5555-1794
121151	Home	+61(2)5555-1849
121152	Work	+61(2)5555-1850
121152	Home	+61(2)5555-1665
121152	Cell	+61(2)5555-1666

```
data empphones;
   merge empsau phones;
   by EmpID;
run;
```

Reinitialize PDV

PDV

First	Gender	EmpID	Type	Phone
		.		

78 ...

SAS reinitializes the entire program data vector before processing a different BY group.

Execution

empsau

First	Gender	EmpID
Togar	M	121150
Kylie	F	121151
Birin	M	121152

phones

EmpID	Type	Phone
121150	Home	+61(2)5555-1793
121150	Work	+61(2)5555-1794
121151	Home	+61(2)5555-1849
121152	Work	+61(2)5555-1850
121152	Home	+61(2)5555-1665
121152	Cell	+61(2)5555-1666

```
data empphones;
   merge empsau phones;
   by EmpID;
run;
```

Reads both observations into the PDV.

PDV

First	Gender	EmpID	Type	Phone
Kylie	F	121151	Home	+61(2)5555-1849

79 ...

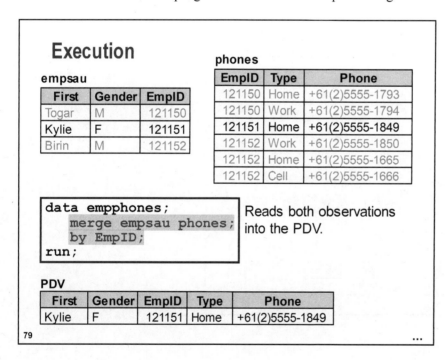

Copyright © 2016, SAS Institute Inc., Cary, North Carolina, USA. ALL RIGHTS RESERVED.

Execution

empsau

First	Gender	EmpID
Togar	M	121150
Kylie	F	121151
Birin	M	121152

phones

EmpID	Type	Phone
121150	Home	+61(2)5555-1793
121150	Work	+61(2)5555-1794
121151	Home	+61(2)5555-1849
121152	Work	+61(2)5555-1850
121152	Home	+61(2)5555-1665
121152	Cell	+61(2)5555-1666

```
data empphones;
   merge empsau phones;
   by EmpID;
run;
```

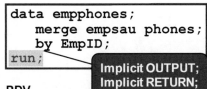

Implicit OUTPUT;
Implicit RETURN;

PDV

First	Gender	EmpID	Type	Phone
Kylie	F	121151	Home	+61(2)5555-1849

80 ...

Execution

empsau

First	Gender	EmpID
Togar	M	121150
Kylie	F	121151
Birin	M	121152

phones

EmpID	Type	Phone
121150	Home	+61(2)5555-1793
121150	Work	+61(2)5555-1794
121151	Home	+61(2)5555-1849
121152	Work	+61(2)5555-1850
121152	Home	+61(2)5555-1665
121152	Cell	+61(2)5555-1666

```
data empphones;
   merge empsau phones;
   by EmpID;
run;
```

Do the **EmpID** values match?

Yes

PDV

First	Gender	EmpID	Type	Phone
Kylie	F	121151	Home	+61(2)5555-1849

81 ...

Copyright © 2016, SAS Institute Inc., Cary, North Carolina, USA. ALL RIGHTS RESERVED.

Execution

empsau

First	Gender	EmpID
Togar	M	121150
Kylie	F	121151
Birin	M	121152

phones

EmpID	Type	Phone
121150	Home	+61(2)5555-1793
121150	Work	+61(2)5555-1794
121151	Home	+61(2)5555-1849
121152	Work	+61(2)5555-1850
121152	Home	+61(2)5555-1665
121152	Cell	+61(2)5555-1666

```
data empphones;
   merge empsau phones;
   by EmpID;
run;
```

Did **EmpID** change?

Yes

PDV

First	Gender	EmpID	Type	Phone
Kylie	F	121151	Home	+61(2)5555-1849

82 ...

Execution

empsau

First	Gender	EmpID
Togar	M	121150
Kylie	F	121151
Birin	M	121152

phones

EmpID	Type	Phone
121150	Home	+61(2)5555-1793
121150	Work	+61(2)5555-1794
121151	Home	+61(2)5555-1849
121152	Work	+61(2)5555-1850
121152	Home	+61(2)5555-1665
121152	Cell	+61(2)5555-1666

Reinitialize PDV

```
data empphones;
   merge empsau phones;
   by EmpID;
run;
```

PDV

First	Gender	EmpID	Type	Phone
		.		

83 ...

Copyright © 2016, SAS Institute Inc., Cary, North Carolina, USA. ALL RIGHTS RESERVED.

Execution

empsau

First	Gender	EmpID
Togar	M	121150
Kylie	F	121151
Birin	M	121152

phones

EmpID	Type	Phone
121150	Home	+61(2)5555-1793
121150	Work	+61(2)5555-1794
121151	Home	+61(2)5555-1849
121152	Work	+61(2)5555-1850
121152	Home	+61(2)5555-1665
121152	Cell	+61(2)5555-1666

```
data empphones;
   merge empsau phones;
   by EmpID;
run;
```

Reads both observations into the PDV.

PDV

First	Gender	EmpID	Type	Phone
Birin	M	121152	Work	+61(2)5555-1850

84 ...

Execution

empsau

First	Gender	EmpID
Togar	M	121150
Kylie	F	121151
Birin	M	121152

phones

EmpID	Type	Phone
121150	Home	+61(2)5555-1793
121150	Work	+61(2)5555-1794
121151	Home	+61(2)5555-1849
121152	Work	+61(2)5555-1850
121152	Home	+61(2)5555-1665
121152	Cell	+61(2)5555-1666

```
data empphones;
   merge empsau phones;
   by EmpID;
run;
```

Implicit OUTPUT;
Implicit RETURN;

PDV

First	Gender	EmpID	Type	Phone
Birin	M	121152	Work	+61(2)5555-1850

85 ...

Copyright © 2016, SAS Institute Inc., Cary, North Carolina, USA. ALL RIGHTS RESERVED.

Execution

empsau

First	Gender	EmpID
Togar	M	121150
Kylie	F	121151
Birin	M	121152

EOF

phones

EmpID	Type	Phone
121150	Home	+61(2)5555-1793
121150	Work	+61(2)5555-1794
121151	Home	+61(2)5555-1849
121152	Work	+61(2)5555-1850
121152	Home	+61(2)5555-1665
121152	Cell	+61(2)5555-1666

```
data empphones;
   merge empsau phones;
   by EmpID;
run;
```

Did **EmpID** change?

No

PDV

First	Gender	EmpID	Type	Phone
Birin	M	121152	Work	+61(2)5555-1850

86 ...

Execution

empsau

First	Gender	EmpID
Togar	M	121150
Kylie	F	121151
Birin	M	121152

EOF

phones

EmpID	Type	Phone
121150	Home	+61(2)5555-1793
121150	Work	+61(2)5555-1794
121151	Home	+61(2)5555-1849
121152	Work	+61(2)5555-1850
121152	Home	+61(2)5555-1665
121152	Cell	+61(2)5555-1666

```
data empphones;
   merge empsau phones;
   by EmpID;
run;
```

Reads the matching observation into the PDV.

PDV

First	Gender	EmpID	Type	Phone
Birin	M	121152	Home	+61(2)5555-1665

87 ...

Copyright © 2016, SAS Institute Inc., Cary, North Carolina, USA. ALL RIGHTS RESERVED.

Execution

phones

EmpID	Type	Phone
121150	Home	+61(2)5555-1793
121150	Work	+61(2)5555-1794
121151	Home	+61(2)5555-1849
121152	Work	+61(2)5555-1850
121152	Home	+61(2)5555-1665
121152	Cell	+61(2)5555-1666

empsau

First	Gender	EmpID
Togar	M	121150
Kylie	F	121151
Birin	M	121152

EOF

```
data empphones;
   merge empsau phones;
   by EmpID;
run;
```

Implicit OUTPUT;
Implicit RETURN;

PDV

First	Gender	EmpID	Type	Phone
Birin	M	121152	Home	+61(2)5555-1665

88 ...

Execution

phones

EmpID	Type	Phone
121150	Home	+61(2)5555-1793
121150	Work	+61(2)5555-1794
121151	Home	+61(2)5555-1849
121152	Work	+61(2)5555-1850
121152	Home	+61(2)5555-1665
121152	Cell	+61(2)5555-1666

empsau

First	Gender	EmpID
Togar	M	121150
Kylie	F	121151
Birin	M	121152

EOF

```
data empphones;
   merge empsau phones;
   by EmpID;
run;
```

Did **EmpID** change?

No

PDV

First	Gender	EmpID	Type	Phone
Birin	M	121152	Home	+61(2)5555-1665

89 ...

Copyright © 2016, SAS Institute Inc., Cary, North Carolina, USA. ALL RIGHTS RESERVED.

Execution

empsau

First	Gender	EmpID
Togar	M	121150
Kylie	F	121151
Birin	M	121152

EOF

phones

EmpID	Type	Phone
121150	Home	+61(2)5555-1793
121150	Work	+61(2)5555-1794
121151	Home	+61(2)5555-1849
121152	Work	+61(2)5555-1850
121152	Home	+61(2)5555-1665
121152	Cell	+61(2)5555-1666

```
data empphones;
   merge empsau phones;
   by EmpID;
run;
```

Reads the matching observation into the PDV.

PDV

First	Gender	EmpID	Type	Phone
Birin	M	121152	Cell	+61(2)5555-1666

90 ...

Execution

empsau

First	Gender	EmpID
Togar	M	121150
Kylie	F	121151
Birin	M	121152

EOF

phones

EmpID	Type	Phone
121150	Home	+61(2)5555-1793
121150	Work	+61(2)5555-1794
121151	Home	+61(2)5555-1849
121152	Work	+61(2)5555-1850
121152	Home	+61(2)5555-1665
121152	Cell	+61(2)5555-1666

```
data empphones;
   merge empsau phones;
   by EmpID;
run;
```

Implicit OUTPUT;
Implicit RETURN;

PDV

First	Gender	EmpID	Type	Phone
Birin	M	121152	Cell	+61(2)5555-1666

91 ...

Copyright © 2016, SAS Institute Inc., Cary, North Carolina, USA. ALL RIGHTS RESERVED.

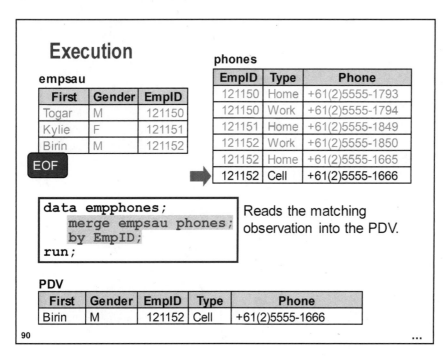

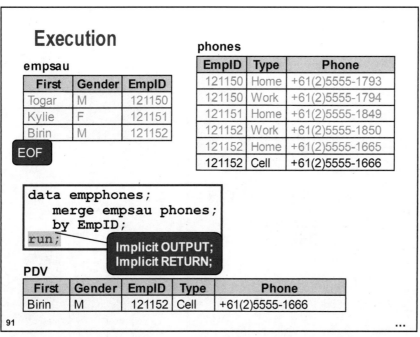

Execution

empsau

First	Gender	EmpID
Togar	M	121150
Kylie	F	121151
Birin	M	121152

EOF

phones

EmpID	Type	Phone
121150	Home	+61(2)5555-1793
121150	Work	+61(2)5555-1794
121151	Home	+61(2)5555-1849
121152	Work	+61(2)5555-1850
121152	Home	+61(2)5555-1665
121152	Cell	+61(2)5555-1666

EOF

```
data empphones;
   merge empsau phones;
   by EmpID;
run;
```

PDV

First	Gender	EmpID	Type	Phone
Birin	M	121152	Cell	+61(2)5555-1666

92

Final Results

empphones

First	Gender	EmpID	Type	Phone
Togar	M	121150	Home	+61(2)5555-1793
Togar	M	121150	Work	+61(2)5555-1794
Kylie	F	121151	Home	+61(2)5555-1849
Birin	M	121152	Work	+61(2)5555-1850
Birin	M	121152	Home	+61(2)5555-1665
Birin	M	121152	Cell	+61(2)5555-1666

93

Copyright © 2016, SAS Institute Inc., Cary, North Carolina, USA. ALL RIGHTS RESERVED.

10.05 Short Answer Poll

In a one-to-many merge, does it matter which data set is listed first in the MERGE statement?

- Open **p110a02** and submit the program.
- Reverse the order of the data sets and submit it again.
- Observe the results. How are they different?

95

Many-to-One Merge

One or more rows in one data set match exactly one row in the other data set.

phones

EmpID	Type	Phone
121150	Home	+61(2)5555-1793
121150	Work	+61(2)5555-1794
121151	Home	+61(2)5555-1849
121152	Work	+61(2)5555-1850
121152	Home	+61(2)5555-1665
121152	Cell	+61(2)5555-1666

empsau

EmpID	First	Gender
121150	Togar	M
121151	Kylie	F
121512	Birin	M

```
data phones;
   merge phones empsau;
   by EmpID;
run;
```

97 p110d06

Copyright © 2016, SAS Institute Inc., Cary, North Carolina, USA. ALL RIGHTS RESERVED.

Viewing the Output

PROC PRINT Output

Obs	EmpID	Type	Phone	First	Gender
1	121150	Home	+61(2)5555-1793	Togar	M
2	121150	Work	+61(2)5555-1794	Togar	M
3	121151	Home	+61(2)5555-1849	Kylie	F
4	121152	Work	+61(2)5555-1850	Birin	M
5	121152	Home	+61(2)5555-1665	Birin	M
6	121152	Cell	+61(2)5555-1666	Birin	M

- The results are the same as the one-to-many merge.
- The order of variables is different.

98

Copyright © 2016, SAS Institute Inc., Cary, North Carolina, USA. ALL RIGHTS RESERVED.

Exercises

> If you restarted your SAS session since the last exercise, open and submit the **libname.sas** program that can be found in the data folder.

Level 1

4. Merging Two Sorted Data Sets in a One-to-Many Merge

a. Retrieve the starter program **p110e04**.

b. Submit the two PROC CONTENTS steps or explore the data sets interactively to determine the common variable among the two data sets.

c. Add a DATA step after the two PROC CONTENTS steps to merge **orion.orders** and **orion.order_item** by the common variable to create a new data set, **work.allorders**. A sort is not required because the data sets are already sorted by the common variable.

d. Submit the program and confirm that **work.allorders** was created with 732 observations and 12 variables.

e. Add a statement to subset the variables. The new data set should contain six variables: **Order_ID**, **Order_Item_Num**, **Order_Type**, **Order_Date**, **Quantity**, and **Total_Retail_Price**.

f. Write a PROC PRINT step to create the report below. Include only those observations with a value for **Order_Date** in the fourth quarter of 2011. The results should contain 35 observations.

Order_ID	Order_ Type	Order_ Date	Order_ Item_Num	Quantity	Total_Retail_ Price
1243515588	1	01OCT2011	1	1	$251.80
1243515588	1	01OCT2011	2	1	$114.20
1243568955	1	07OCT2011	1	1	$172.50
1243643970	1	16OCT2011	1	1	$101.50
1243644877	3	16OCT2011	1	1	$14.60

Level 2

5. Merging a Sorted Data Set and an Unsorted Data Set in a One-to-Many Merge

a. Sort **orion.product_list** by **Product_Level** to create a new data set, **work.product_list**.

b. Merge **orion.product_level** with the sorted data set. Create a new data set, **work.listlevel**, which includes only **Product_ID**, **Product_Name**, **Product_Level**, and **Product_Level_Name**.

c. Create the report below. Include only those observations with **Product Level** equal to *3*. The results should contain 13 observations.

Partial PROC PRINT Output

Product_ Level	Product_Level_ Name	Product_ID	Product_Name

Copyright © 2016, SAS Institute Inc., Cary, North Carolina, USA. ALL RIGHTS RESERVED.

```
3    Product Category    210100000000    Children Outdoors
3    Product Category    210200000000    Children Sports
3    Product Category    220100000000    Clothes
3    Product Category    220200000000    Shoes
3    Product Category    230100000000    Outdoors
```

Challenge

6. Using the MERGENOBY Option

a. Use the SAS Help facility or online documentation to explore the MERGENOBY system option.

What is the purpose of this option and why is it used? ______________________________

____

b. Complete the following table to include the values that this option can assume:

Value	Description	Default (Y/N)

End of Exercises

Copyright © 2016, SAS Institute Inc., Cary, North Carolina, USA. ALL RIGHTS RESERVED.

10.4 Merging Data Sets with Nonmatches

Objectives

- Control the observations in the output data set by using the IN= data set option.

102

Business Scenario

An Orion Star manager in Australia requested an inventory of company phone numbers.

103

Copyright © 2016, SAS Institute Inc., Cary, North Carolina, USA. ALL RIGHTS RESERVED.

Merge with Nonmatches

There are observations in **empsau** that do not have a match in **phonec**, and some in **phonec** that do not match any observations in **empsau**.

empsau

First	Gender	EmpID
Togar	M	121150
Kylie	F	121151
Birin	M	121152

phonec

EmpID	Phone
121150	+61(2)5555-1795
121152	+61(2)5555-1667
121153	+61(2)5555-1348

The data sets are sorted by **EmpID**.

104

Match-Merging

Merge **empsau** and **phonec** by **EmpID** to create a new data set named **empsauc**.

```
data empsauc;
   merge empsau phonec;
   by EmpID;
run;
```

105

p110d07

Copyright © 2016, SAS Institute Inc., Cary, North Carolina, USA. ALL RIGHTS RESERVED.

Execution

empsau

First	Gender	EmpID
Togar	M	121150
Kylie	F	121151
Birin	M	121152

phonec

EmpID	Phone
121150	+61(2)5555-1795
121152	+61(2)5555-1667
121153	+61(2)5555-1348

```
data empsauc;
   merge empsau phonec;
   by EmpID;
run;
```

Initialize PDV

PDV

First	Gender	EmpID	Phone
		.	

106 ...

Execution

empsau

First	Gender	EmpID
Togar	M	121150
Kylie	F	121151
Birin	M	121152

phonec

EmpID	Phone
121150	+61(2)5555-1795
121152	+61(2)5555-1667
121153	+61(2)5555-1348

```
data empsauc;
   merge empsau phonec;
   by EmpID;
run;
```

Do the **EmpID** values match?

Yes

PDV

First	Gender	EmpID	Phone
		.	

107 ...

Copyright © 2016, SAS Institute Inc., Cary, North Carolina, USA. ALL RIGHTS RESERVED.

Execution

empsau

First	Gender	EmpID
Togar	M	121150
Kylie	F	121151
Birin	M	121152

phonec

EmpID	Phone
121150	+61(2)5555-1795
121152	+61(2)5555-1667
121153	+61(2)5555-1348

```
data empsauc;
   merge empsau phonec;
   by EmpID;
run;
```

Reads both observations into the PDV.

PDV

First	Gender	EmpID	Phone
Togar	M	121150	+61(2)5555-1795

108 ...

Execution

empsau

First	Gender	EmpID
Togar	M	121150
Kylie	F	121151
Birin	M	121152

phonec

EmpID	Phone
121150	+61(2)5555-1795
121152	+61(2)5555-1667
121153	+61(2)5555-1348

```
data empsauc;
   merge empsau phonec;
   by EmpID;
run;
```

Implicit OUTPUT;
Implicit RETURN;

PDV

First	Gender	EmpID	Phone
Togar	M	121150	+61(2)5555-1795

109 ...

Copyright © 2016, SAS Institute Inc., Cary, North Carolina, USA. ALL RIGHTS RESERVED.

Execution

empsau

First	Gender	EmpID
Togar	M	121150
Kylie	F	121151
Birin	M	121152

phonec

EmpID	Phone
121150	+61(2)5555-1795
121152	+61(2)5555-1667
121153	+61(2)5555-1348

```
data empsauc;
   merge empsau phonec;
   by EmpID;
run;
```

Do the **EmpID** values match?

No

PDV

First	Gender	EmpID	Phone
Togar	M	121150	+61(2)5555-1795

110 ...

Execution

empsau

First	Gender	EmpID
Togar	M	121150
Kylie	F	121151
Birin	M	121152

phonec

EmpID	Phone
121150	+61(2)5555-1795
121152	+61(2)5555-1667
121153	+61(2)5555-1348

```
data empsauc;
   merge empsau phonec;
   by EmpID;
run;
```

Did **EmpID** change?

Yes

PDV

First	Gender	EmpID	Phone
Togar	M	121150	+61(2)5555-1795

111 ...

Copyright © 2016, SAS Institute Inc., Cary, North Carolina, USA. ALL RIGHTS RESERVED.

Execution

empsau

First	Gender	EmpID
Togar	M	121150
Kylie	F	121151
Birin	M	121152

phonec

EmpID	Phone
121150	+61(2)5555-1795
121152	+61(2)5555-1667
121153	+61(2)5555-1348

Reinitialize PDV

```
data empsauc;
   merge empsau phonec;
   by EmpID;
run;
```

PDV

First	Gender	EmpID	Phone
		.	

112 ...

Execution

empsau

First	Gender	EmpID
Togar	M	121150
Kylie	F	121151
Birin	M	121152

phonec

EmpID	Phone
121150	+61(2)5555-1795
121152	+61(2)5555-1667
121153	+61(2)5555-1348

```
data empsauc;
   merge empsau phonec;
   by EmpID;
run;
```

Which **EmpID** value sequentially comes first?

`121151`

PDV

First	Gender	EmpID	Phone
		.	

113 ...

Copyright © 2016, SAS Institute Inc., Cary, North Carolina, USA. ALL RIGHTS RESERVED.

Execution

empsau

First	Gender	EmpID
Togar	M	121150
Kylie	F	121151
Birin	M	121152

phonec

EmpID	Phone
121150	+61(2)5555-1795
121152	+61(2)5555-1667
121153	+61(2)5555-1348

```
data empsauc;
   merge empsau phonec;
   by EmpID;
run;
```

Reads that observation into the PDV.

PDV

First	Gender	EmpID	Phone
Kylie	F	121151	

114 ...

Execution

empsau

First	Gender	EmpID
Togar	M	121150
Kylie	F	121151
Birin	M	121152

phonec

EmpID	Phone
121150	+61(2)5555-1795
121152	+61(2)5555-1667
121153	+61(2)5555-1348

```
data empsauc;
   merge empsau phonec;
   by EmpID;
run;
```

Implicit OUTPUT;
Implicit RETURN;

PDV

First	Gender	EmpID	Phone
Kylie	F	121151	

115 ...

Copyright © 2016, SAS Institute Inc., Cary, North Carolina, USA. ALL RIGHTS RESERVED.

Execution

empsau

First	Gender	EmpID
Togar	M	121150
Kylie	F	121151
Birin	M	121152

phonec

EmpID	Phone
121150	+61(2)5555-1795
121152	+61(2)5555-1667
121153	+61(2)5555-1348

```
data empsauc;
   merge empsau phonec;
   by EmpID;
run;
```

Do the **EmpID** values match?

Yes

PDV

First	Gender	EmpID	Phone
Kylie	F	121151	

116 ...

Execution

empsau

First	Gender	EmpID
Togar	M	121150
Kylie	F	121151
Birin	M	121152

phonec

EmpID	Phone
121150	+61(2)5555-1795
121152	+61(2)5555-1667
121153	+61(2)5555-1348

```
data empsauc;
   merge empsau phonec;
   by EmpID;
run;
```

Did **EmpID** change?

Yes

PDV

First	Gender	EmpID	Phone
Kylie	F	121151	

117 ...

Copyright © 2016, SAS Institute Inc., Cary, North Carolina, USA. ALL RIGHTS RESERVED.

Execution

empsau

First	Gender	EmpID
Togar	M	121150
Kylie	F	121151
Birin	M	121152

phonec

EmpID	Phone
121150	+61(2)5555-1795
121152	+61(2)5555-1667
121153	+61(2)5555-1348

Reinitialize PDV

```
data empsauc;
   merge empsau phonec;
   by EmpID;
run;
```

PDV

First	Gender	EmpID	Phone
		.	

118 ...

Execution

empsau

First	Gender	EmpID
Togar	M	121150
Kylie	F	121151
Birin	M	121152

phonec

EmpID	Phone
121150	+61(2)5555-1795
121152	+61(2)5555-1667
121153	+61(2)5555-1348

```
data empsauc;
   merge empsau phonec;
   by EmpID;
run;
```

Reads both observations into the PDV.

PDV

First	Gender	EmpID	Phone
Birin	M	121152	+61(2)5555-1667

119 ...

Copyright © 2016, SAS Institute Inc., Cary, North Carolina, USA. ALL RIGHTS RESERVED.

Execution

empsau

First	Gender	EmpID
Togar	M	121150
Kylie	F	121151
Birin	M	121152

phonec

EmpID	Phone
121150	+61(2)5555-1795
121152	+61(2)5555-1667
121153	+61(2)5555-1348

```
data empsauc;
   merge empsau phonec;
   by EmpID;
run;
```

Implicit OUTPUT;
Implicit RETURN;

PDV

First	Gender	EmpID	Phone
Birin	M	121152	+61(2)5555-1667

120 ...

Execution

empsau

First	Gender	EmpID
Togar	M	121150
Kylie	F	121151
Birin	M	121152

EOF

phonec

EmpID	Phone
121150	+61(2)5555-1795
121152	+61(2)5555-1667
121153	+61(2)5555-1348

```
data empsauc;
   merge empsau phonec;
   by EmpID;
run;
```

Did **EmpID** change?

Yes

PDV

First	Gender	EmpID	Phone
Birin	M	121152	+61(2)5555-1667

121 ...

Copyright © 2016, SAS Institute Inc., Cary, North Carolina, USA. ALL RIGHTS RESERVED.

Execution

empsau

First	Gender	EmpID
Togar	M	121150
Kylie	F	121151
Birin	M	121152

EOF

phonec

EmpID	Phone
121150	+61(2)5555-1795
121152	+61(2)5555-1667
121153	+61(2)5555-1348

Reinitialize PDV

```
data empsauc;
   merge empsau phonec;
   by EmpID;
run;
```

PDV

First	Gender	EmpID	Phone
		.	

122

...

Execution

empsau

First	Gender	EmpID
Togar	M	121150
Kylie	F	121151
Birin	M	121152

EOF

phonec

EmpID	Phone
121150	+61(2)5555-1795
121152	+61(2)5555-1667
121153	+61(2)5555-1348

```
data empsauc;
   merge empsau phonec;
   by EmpID;
run;
```

Reads the observation into the PDV.

PDV

First	Gender	EmpID	Phone
		121153	+61(2)5555-1348

123

...

Copyright © 2016, SAS Institute Inc., Cary, North Carolina, USA. ALL RIGHTS RESERVED.

Execution

empsau

First	Gender	EmpID
Togar	M	121150
Kylie	F	121151
Birin	M	121152

EOF

phonec

EmpID	Phone
121150	+61(2)5555-1795
121152	+61(2)5555-1667
121153	+61(2)5555-1348

```
data empsauc;
   merge empsau phonec;
   by EmpID;
run;
```

Implicit OUTPUT;
Implicit RETURN;

PDV

First	Gender	EmpID	Phone
		121153	+61(2)5555-1348

124 ...

Execution

empsau

First	Gender	EmpID
Togar	M	121150
Kylie	F	121151
Birin	M	121152

EOF

phonec

EmpID	Phone
121150	+61(2)5555-1795
121152	+61(2)5555-1667
121153	+61(2)5555-1348

EOF

```
data empsauc;
   merge empsau phonec;
   by EmpID;
run;
```

PDV

First	Gender	EmpID	Phone
		121153	+61(2)5555-1348

125

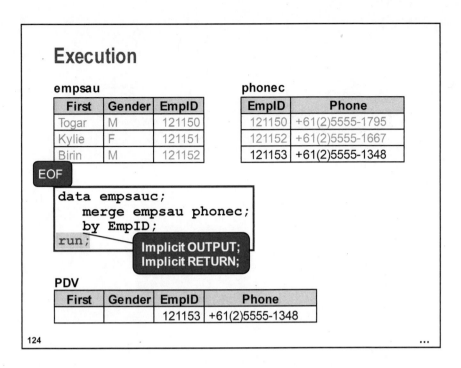

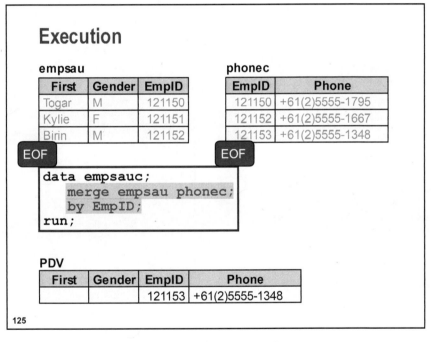

Copyright © 2016, SAS Institute Inc., Cary, North Carolina, USA. ALL RIGHTS RESERVED.

Final Results

empsauc

First	Gender	EmpID	Phone
Togar	M	121150	+61(2)5555-1795
Kylie	F	121151	
Birin	M	121152	+61(2)5555-1667
		121153	+61(2)5555-1348

The final results include both matches and nonmatches.

126

10.06 Short Answer Poll

Consider the data set **empsauc** created by the program in the previous example. Which input data sets contributed information to the last observation?

a. empsau
b. phonec
c. both empsau and phonec
d. There is insufficient information.

empsauc

First	Gender	EmpID	Phone
Togar	M	121150	+61(2)5555-1795
Kylie	F	121151	
Birin	M	121152	+61(2)5555-1667
		121153	+61(2)5555-1348

127

Copyright © 2016, SAS Institute Inc., Cary, North Carolina, USA. ALL RIGHTS RESERVED.

Business Scenario

An Orion Star manager requested three phone inventory reports.

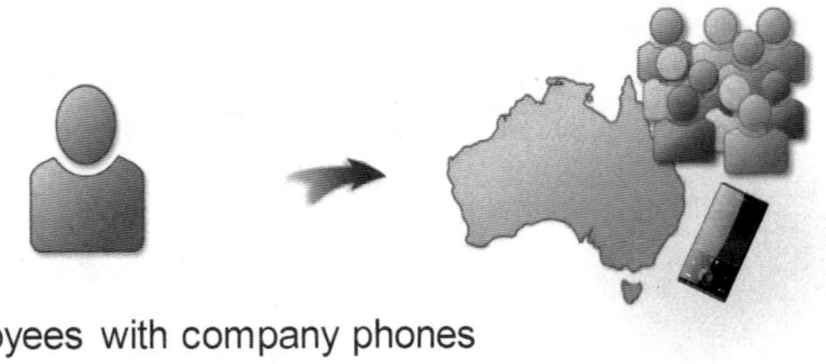

- employees with company phones
- employees without company phones
- phones with an invalid employee ID

130

IN= Data Set Option

The *IN= data set option* creates a variable that indicates whether the data set contributed to building the current observation.

MERGE *SAS-data-set* **(IN=***variable***) ...**

variable is a temporary numeric variable that has two possible values:

0	Indicates that the data set did ***not*** contribute to the current observation.
1	Indicates that the data set ***did*** contribute to the current observation.

131

Copyright © 2016, SAS Institute Inc., Cary, North Carolina, USA. ALL RIGHTS RESERVED.

IN= Data Set Option

MERGE statement examples:

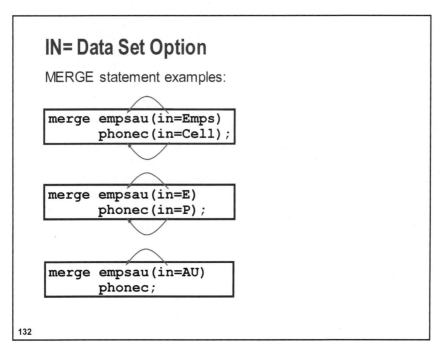

```
merge empsau(in=Emps)
      phonec(in=Cell);
```

```
merge empsau(in=E)
      phonec(in=P);
```

```
merge empsau(in=AU)
      phonec;
```

132

Execution

empsau

First	Gender	EmpID
Togar	M	121150
Kylie	F	121151
Birin	M	121152

phonec

EmpID	Phone
121150	+61(2)5555-1795
121152	+61(2)5555-1667
121153	+61(2)5555-1348

```
data empsauc;
   merge empsau(in=Emps)
         phonec(in=Cell);
   by EmpID;
run;
```

match

PDV

First	Gender	EmpID	D Emps	Phone	D Cell
Togar	M	121150	1	+61(2)5555-1795	1

133

p110d08

...

Copyright © 2016, SAS Institute Inc., Cary, North Carolina, USA. ALL RIGHTS RESERVED.

Execution

empsau

First	Gender	EmpID
Togar	M	121150
Kylie	F	121151
Birin	M	121152

phonec

EmpID	Phone
121150	+61(2)5555-1795
121152	+61(2)5555-1667
121153	+61(2)5555-1348

```
data empsauc;
   merge empsau(in=Emps)
         phonec(in=Cell);
   by EmpID;
run;
```

nonmatch

PDV

First	Gender	EmpID	D Emps	Phone	D Cell
Kylie	F	121151	1		0

134

...

Execution

empsau

First	Gender	EmpID
Togar	M	121150
Kylie	F	121151
Birin	M	121152

phonec

EmpID	Phone
121150	+61(2)5555-1795
121152	+61(2)5555-1667
121153	+61(2)5555-1348

```
data empsauc;
   merge empsau(in=Emps)
         phonec(in=Cell);
   by EmpID;
run;
```

match

PDV

First	Gender	EmpID	D Emps	Phone	D Cell
Birin	M	121152	1	+61(2)5555-1667	1

135

Copyright © 2016, SAS Institute Inc., Cary, North Carolina, USA. ALL RIGHTS RESERVED.

10.07 Short Answer Poll

What are the values of **Emps** and **Cell**?

empsau

First	Gender	EmpID
Togar	M	121150
Kylie	F	121151
Birin	M	121152

EOF

phonec

EmpID	Phone
121150	+61(2)5555-1795
121152	+61(2)5555-1667
121153	+61(2)5555-1348

```
data empsauc;
   merge empsau(in=Emps)
         phonec(in=Cell);
   by EmpID;
run;
```

PDV

First	Gender	EmpID	D Emps	Phone	D Cell
		121153		+61(2)5555-1348	

136

PDV Results

PDV

First	Gender	EmpID	D Emps	Phone	D Cell
Togar	M	121150	1	+61(2)5555-1795	1
Kylie	F	121151	1		0
Birin	M	121152	1	+61(2)5555-1667	1
		121153	0	+61(2)5555-1348	1

The variables created with the IN= data set option are available only during DATA step execution.

- They are not written to the SAS data set.
- Their value can be tested using conditional logic.

138

Copyright © 2016, SAS Institute Inc., Cary, North Carolina, USA. ALL RIGHTS RESERVED.

Matches Only

Add a subsetting IF statement to select the employees that have company phones.

```
data empsauc;
   merge empsau(in=Emps)
         phonec(in=Cell);
   by EmpID;
   if Emps=1 and Cell=1;
run;
```

empsauc

First	Gender	EmpID	Phone
Togar	M	121150	+61(2)5555-1795
Birin	M	121152	+61(2)5555-1667

139 p110d08

Nonmatches from empsau

Select the employees that do not have company phones.

```
data empsauc;
   merge empsau(in=Emps)
         phonec(in=Cell);
   by EmpID;
   if Emps=1 and Cell=0;
run;
```

empsauc

First	Gender	EmpID	Phone
Kylie	F	121151	

140 p110d08

Copyright © 2016, SAS Institute Inc., Cary, North Carolina, USA. ALL RIGHTS RESERVED.

Nonmatches from phonec

Select the phones associated with an invalid employee ID.

```
data empsauc;
   merge empsau(in=Emps)
         phonec(in=Cell);
   by EmpID;
   if Emps=0 and Cell=1;
run;
```

empsauc

First	Gender	EmpID	Phone
		121153	+61(2)5555-1348

141 p110d08

All Nonmatches

```
data empsauc;
   merge empsau(in=Emps)
         phonec(in=Cell);
   by EmpID;
   if Emps=0 or Cell=0;
run;
```

empsauc

First	Gender	EmpID	Phone
Kylie	F	121151	
		121153	+61(2)5555-1348

⚠ Use the OR operator, not the AND operator.

142 p110d08

Copyright © 2016, SAS Institute Inc., Cary, North Carolina, USA. ALL RIGHTS RESERVED.

Alternate Syntax

When checking a variable for a value of *1* or *0* as in the previous scenario, you can use the following syntax:

Instead of	You can use
if Emps=1 and Cell=1;	if Emps and Cell;
if Emps=1 and Cell=0;	if Emps and not Cell;
if Emps=0 and Cell=1;	if not Emps and Cell;
if Emps=0 or Cell=0;	If not Emps or not Cell;

143

Alternate Syntax

Both programs create a report of employees without cell phones.

```
data empsphone;
   merge empsact(in=inEmps)
         phoneact(in=inCell);
   by EmpID;
   if inEmps=1 and inCell=0;
run;
```

```
data empsphone;
   merge empsact(in=inEmps)
         phoneact(in=inCell);
   by EmpID;
   if inEmps and not inCell;
run;
```

p110d09

144

Copyright © 2016, SAS Institute Inc., Cary, North Carolina, USA. ALL RIGHTS RESERVED.

Business Scenario

Merge Orion Star customer information with customer type data to obtain a customer description. The new data set should include only US customers.

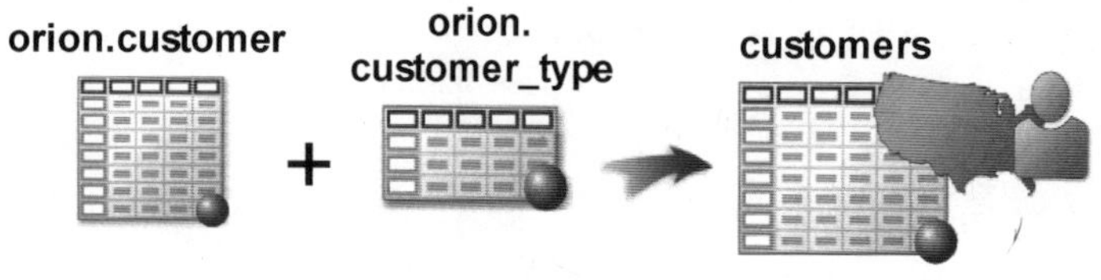

146

Considerations

The **orion.customer** data set is not sorted by **Customer_Type_ID**, the common variable. The subsetting variable, **Country**, is defined in only one data set.

orion.customer

Customer_ ID	Country	Customer_ Name	...	Birth_ Date	Customer_Type_ ID

orion.customer_type

Customer_ Group	Customer_Group_ ID	Customer_ Type	Customer_Type_ ID

147

Copyright © 2016, SAS Institute Inc., Cary, North Carolina, USA. ALL RIGHTS RESERVED.

10.08 Short Answer Poll

Open and submit **p110a03**. Correct the program and resubmit. What change is needed to correct the error?

```
proc sort data=orion.customer
          out=cust_by_type;
   by Customer_Type_ID;
run;

data customers;
   merge cust_by_type orion.customer_type;
   by Customer_Type_ID;
   where Country='US';
run;
```

148

Subsetting IF

Use a subsetting IF statement when the subsetting variable is not in all data sets that are named in the MERGE statement.

```
proc sort data=orion.customer
          out=cust_by_type;
   by Customer_Type_ID;
run;

data customers;
   merge cust_by_type  orion.customer_type;
   by Customer_Type_ID;
   if Country='US';
run;
```

150

p110a03s

Copyright © 2016, SAS Institute Inc., Cary, North Carolina, USA. ALL RIGHTS RESERVED.

Viewing the Output

Partial SAS Log

```
407  proc sort data=orion.customer
408            out=cust_by_type;
409     by Customer_Type_ID;
410  run;
NOTE: There were 77 observations read from the data set ORION.CUSTOMER.
NOTE: The data set WORK.CUST_BY_TYPE has 77 observations and 12 variables.

411
412  data customers;
413     merge cust_by_type orion.customer_type;
414     by Customer_Type_ID;
415     if Country='US';
416  run;

NOTE: There were 77 observations read from the data set WORK.CUST_BY_TYPE.
NOTE: There were 8 observations read from the data set ORION.CUSTOMER_TYPE.
NOTE: The data set WORK.CUSTOMERS has 28 observations and 15 variables.
```

151

WHERE versus Subsetting IF Statement

Step and Usage	WHERE	IF
PROC step	Yes	No
DATA step (source of variable)		
SET statement	Yes	Yes
assignment statement	No	Yes
INPUT statement	No	Yes
SET/MERGE statement (multiple data sets)		
Variable in ALL data sets	Yes	Yes
Variable not in ALL data sets	No	Yes

152

Copyright © 2016, SAS Institute Inc., Cary, North Carolina, USA. ALL RIGHTS RESERVED.

Exercises

> If you restarted your SAS session since the last exercise, open and submit the **libname.sas** program that can be found in the data folder.

Level 1

7. Merging Using the IN= Option

a. Retrieve the starter program **p110e07**. Add a DATA step after the PROC SORT step to merge **work.product** and **orion.supplier** by **Supplier_ID** to create a new data set, **work.prodsup**.

b. Submit the program and confirm that **work.prodsup** was created with 556 observations and 10 variables.

c. Modify the DATA step to output only those observations that are in **work.product** but not **orion.supplier**. A subsetting IF statement that references IN= variables listed in the MERGE statement must be added.

d. Submit the program and confirm that **work.prodsup** was created with 75 observations and 10 variables.

e. Submit the PROC PRINT step to create the report below. The results should contain 75 observations.

Supplier information is missing in the output.

```
                                                              Supplier_
Obs    Product_ID      Product_Name                Supplier_ID    Name

  1    210000000000    Children                          .
  2    210100000000    Children Outdoors                 .
  3    210100100000    Outdoor things, Kids              .
  4    210200000000    Children Sports                   .
  5    210200100000    A-Team, Kids                      .
```

Level 2

8. Merging Using the IN= and RENAME= Options

a. Write a PROC SORT step to sort **orion.customer** by **Country** to create a new data set, **work.customer**.

b. Write a DATA step to merge the resulting data set with **orion.lookup_country** by **Country** to create a new data set, **work.allcustomer**.

In the **orion.lookup_country** data set, rename **Start** to **Country** and rename **Label** to **Country_Name**.

Include only four variables: **Customer_ID**, **Country**, **Customer_Name**, and **Country_Name**.

Copyright © 2016, SAS Institute Inc., Cary, North Carolina, USA. ALL RIGHTS RESERVED.

c. Create the report below. The results should contain 308 observations.

Partial PROC PRINT Output

Obs	Customer_ID	Country	Customer_Name	Country_Name
1	.	AD		Andorra
2	.	AE		United Arab Emirates
...				
306	3959	ZA	Rita Lotz	South Africa
307	.	ZM		Zambia
308	.	ZW		Zimbabwe

d. Modify the DATA step to store only those observations that contain both customer information and country information. A subsetting IF statement that references the IN= variables in the MERGE statement must be added.

e. Submit the program to create the report below. The results should contain 77 observations.

Partial PROC PRINT Output

Obs	Customer_ID	Country	Customer_Name	Country_ Name
1	29	AU	Candy Kinsey	Australia
2	41	AU	Wendell Summersby	Australia
3	53	AU	Dericka Pockran	Australia
4	111	AU	Karolina Dokter	Australia
5	171	AU	Robert Bowerman	Australia

Challenge

9. Merging and Creating Output in Multiple Data Sets

a. Write a PROC SORT step to sort **orion.orders** by **Employee_ID** to create a new data set, **work.orders**.

b. Write a DATA step to merge **orion.staff** and **work.orders** by **Employee_ID** and create two new data sets: **work.allorders** and **work.noorders**.

- The **work.allorders** data set should include all observations from **work.orders**, regardless of matches or nonmatches from the **orion.staff** data set.
- The **work.noorders** data set should include only those observations from **orion.staff** that do not have a match in **work.orders**.
- Both new data sets should include only **Employee_ID**, **Job_Title**, **Gender**, **Order_ID**, **Order_Type**, and **Order_Date**.

c. Submit the program and confirm that **work.allorders** was created with 490 observations and six variables and **work.noorders** was created with 324 observations and six variables.

d. Create a detailed listing report for each new data set with an appropriate title.

End of Exercises

Copyright © 2016, SAS Institute Inc., Cary, North Carolina, USA. ALL RIGHTS RESERVED.

10.5 Solutions

Solutions to Exercises

1. **Concatenating Like-Structured Data Sets**

   How many observations in **work.thirdqtr** are from **orion.mnth7_2011**? **10 observations**

   How many observations in **work.thirdqtr** are from **orion.mnth8_2011**? **12 observations**

   How many observations in **work.thirdqtr** are from **orion.mnth9_2011**? **10 observations**

```
data work.thirdqtr;
   set orion.mnth7_2011 orion.mnth8_2011 orion.mnth9_2011;
run;

proc print data=work.thirdqtr;
run;
```

2. **Concatenating Unlike-Structured Data Sets**

   What are the names of the two variables that are different in the two data sets?

orion.sales	orion.nonsales
First_Name	First
Last_Name	Last

```
proc contents data=orion.sales;
run;

proc contents data=orion.nonsales;
run;

data work.allemployees;
   set orion.sales
       orion.nonsales(rename=(First=First_Name Last=Last_Name));
   keep Employee_ID First_Name Last_Name Job_Title Salary;
run;

proc print data=work.allemployees;
run;
```

Copyright © 2016, SAS Institute Inc., Cary, North Carolina, USA. ALL RIGHTS RESERVED.

3. Concatenating Data Sets with Variables of Different Lengths and Types

a. Open **p110e03**. Submit the PROC CONTENTS steps or explore the data sets interactively to complete the table below. Fill in attribute information for each variable in each data set.

	Code		Company		ContactType	
	Type	Length	Type	Length	Type	Length
orion.charities	Char	6	Char	40	Char	10
orion.us_suppliers	Char	6	Char	30	Char	1
orion.consultants	Char	6	Char	30	Num	8

```
proc contents data=orion.charities;
run;
proc contents data=orion.us_suppliers;
run;
proc contents data=orion.consultants;
run;

data work.contacts;
   set orion.charities orion.us_suppliers;
run;
proc contents data=work.contacts;
run;

data work.contacts2;
   set orion.us_suppliers orion.charities;
run;
proc contents data=work.contacts2;
run;

data work.contacts3;
   set orion.us_suppliers orion.consultants;
run;
```

c. Submit a PROC CONTENTS step to examine **work.contacts**. From which input data set were the variable attributes assigned? **the first data set in the set statement, orion.charities**

e. Submit a PROC CONTENTS step to examine **work.contacts2**. From which input data set were the variable attributes assigned? **the first data set in the set statement, orion.us_suppliers**

f. Write a DATA step to concatenate **orion.us_suppliers** and **orion.consultants**, and creating a temporary data set, **contacts3**.

Why did the DATA step fail? **ContactType was defined as both character and numeric.**

4. Merging Two Sorted Data Sets in a One-to-Many Merge

```
proc contents data=orion.orders;
run;
```

Copyright © 2016, SAS Institute Inc., Cary, North Carolina, USA. ALL RIGHTS RESERVED.

```
proc contents data=orion.order_item;
run;

data work.allorders;
   merge orion.orders
         orion.order_item;
   by Order_ID;
   keep Order_ID Order_Item_Num Order_Type
        Order_Date Quantity Total_Retail_Price;
run;

proc print data=work.allorders noobs;
   where Order_Date between '01Oct2011'd and '31Dec2011'd;
run;

  /* alternate solution */
proc print data=work.allorders noobs;
   where Order_Date>='01Oct2011'd and Order_Date<='31Dec2011'd;
run;

proc print data=work.allorders noobs;
   where qtr(Order_Date)=4 and year(Order_Date)=2011;
run;
```

5. **Merging a Sorted Data Set and an Unsorted Data Set in a One-to-Many Merge**

```
proc sort data=orion.product_list
          out=work.product_list;
   by Product_Level;
run;

data work.listlevel;
   merge orion.product_level work.product_list ;
   by Product_Level;
   keep Product_ID Product_Name Product_Level Product_Level_Name;
run;

proc print data=work.listlevel noobs;
   where Product_Level=3;
run;
```

6. **Using the MERGENOBY Option**

   a. What is the purpose of this option and why is it used? **This option is used to issue a warning or an error when a BY statement is omitted from a merge. Performing a merge without a BY statement merges the observations based on their positions. This is almost never done intentionally and can lead to unexpected results.**

Copyright © 2016, SAS Institute Inc., Cary, North Carolina, USA. ALL RIGHTS RESERVED.

b. Complete the following table to include the values that this option can assume.

Value	Description	Default (Y/N)
NOWARN	Performs the positional merge without warning.	N
WARN	Performs the positional merge but writes a warning message to the log.	Y
ERROR	Writes an error message to the log and the DATA step terminates.	N

7. Merging Using the IN= Option

```
proc sort data=orion.product_list
          out=work.product;
   by Supplier_ID;
run;

data work.prodsup;
   merge work.product(in=P)
         orion.supplier(in=S);
   by Supplier_ID;
   if P=1 and S=0;
run;

proc print data=work.prodsup;
   var Product_ID Product_Name Supplier_ID Supplier_Name;
run;
```

8. Merging Using the IN= and RENAME= Options

```
proc sort data=orion.customer
          out=work.customer;
   by Country;
run;

data work.allcustomer;
   merge work.customer(in=Cust)
         orion.lookup_country(rename=(Start=Country
                                      Label=Country_Name)
in=Ctry);
   by Country;
   keep Customer_ID Country Customer_Name Country_Name;
   if Cust=1 and Ctry=1;
run;

proc print data=work.allcustomer;
run;
```

9. Merging and Creating Output in Multiple Data Sets

```
proc sort data=orion.orders
          out=work.orders;
```

Copyright © 2016, SAS Institute Inc., Cary, North Carolina, USA. ALL RIGHTS RESERVED.

```
   by Employee_ID;
run;

data work.allorders work.noorders;
   merge orion.staff(in=Staff) work.orders(in=Ord);
   by Employee_ID;
   if Ord=1 then output work.allorders;
   else if Staff=1 and Ord=0 then output work.noorders;
  /* alternate statement */
  /* else output work.noorders; */
   keep Employee_ID Job_Title Gender Order_ID Order_Type
Order_Date;
run;

proc print data=work.allorders;
run;

proc print data=work.noorders;
run;
```

End of Solutions

Copyright © 2016, SAS Institute Inc., Cary, North Carolina, USA. ALL RIGHTS RESERVED.

Solutions to Student Activities (Polls/Quizzes)

10.01 Short Answer Poll – Correct Answer

How many variables will be in **empsall2** after concatenating **empscn** and **empsjp**?

empscn

First	Gender	Country
Chang	M	China
Li	M	China
Ming	F	China

empsjp

First	Gender	Region
Cho	F	Japan
Tomi	M	Japan

Four variables: First, Gender, Country, and Region

30

10.02 Short Answer Poll – Correct Answer

Which statement has correct syntax?

a.

```
set empscn(rename(Country=Location))
    empsjp(rename(Region=Location));
```

(b.)

```
set empscn(rename=(Country=Location))
    empsjp(rename=(Region=Location));
```

c.

```
set empscn rename=(Country=Location)
    empsjp rename=(Region=Location);
```

38

Copyright © 2016, SAS Institute Inc., Cary, North Carolina, USA. ALL RIGHTS RESERVED.

10.03 Multiple Choice Poll – Correct Answer

Which of the following BY statements correctly sorts by descending **salary** within **gender**?

a. by descending salary within gender;
b. by descending salary gender;
c. by gender descending salary; (circled)
d. by gender salary descending;

The keyword "descending" is placed before the variable to which it applies.

52

10.04 Short Answer Poll – Correct Answer

What are the modified, completed statements?

```
proc sort data=orion.employee_payroll
          out=work.payroll;
   by Employee_ID;
run;

proc sort data=orion.employee_addresses
          out=work.addresses;
   by Employee_ID;
run;

data work.payadd;
   merge work.payroll work.addresses;
   by Employee_ID;
run;
```

p110a01s

59

Copyright © 2016, SAS Institute Inc., Cary, North Carolina, USA. ALL RIGHTS RESERVED.

10.05 Short Answer Poll – Correct Answer

In a one-to-many merge, does it matter which data set is listed first in the MERGE statement?

- Open **p110a02** and submit the program.
- Reverse the order of the data sets and submit it again.
- Observe the results. How are they different?

The results are the same, but the order of the variables is different.

96

10.06 Short Answer Poll – Correct Answer

Consider the data set **empsauc** created by the program in the previous example. Which input data sets contributed information to the last observation?

a. empsau
(b.) phonec
c. both empsau and phonec
d. There is insufficient information.

empsauc

First	Gender	EmpID	Phone
Togar	M	121150	+61(2)5555-1795
Kylie	F	121151	
Birin	M	121152	+61(2)5555-1667
		121153	+61(2)5555-1348

128

Copyright © 2016, SAS Institute Inc., Cary, North Carolina, USA. ALL RIGHTS RESERVED.

10.07 Short Answer Poll – Correct Answer

What are the values of **Emps** and **Cell**?

empsau

First	Gender	EmpID
Togar	M	121150
Kylie	F	121151
Birin	M	121152

EOF

phonec

EmpID	Phone
121150	+61(2)5555-1795
121152	+61(2)5555-1667
121153	+61(2)5555-1348

```
data empsauc;
   merge empsau(in=Emps)
         phonec(in=Cell);
   by EmpID;
run;
```

nonmatch

PDV

First	Gender	EmpID	Emps	Phone	Cell
		121153	0	+61(2)5555-1348	1

137

10.08 Short Answer Poll – Correct Answer

What change is needed to correct the error?

```
proc sort data=orion.customer
          out=cust_by_type;
   by Customer_Type_ID;
run;
NOTE: There were 77 observations read from the data set ORION.CUSTOMER.
NOTE: The data set WORK.CUST_BY_TYPE has 77 observations and 12 variables.

data customers;
   merge cust_by_type orion.customer_type;
   by Customer_Type_ID;
   where Country='US';
ERROR: Variable Country is not on file ORION.CUSTOMER_TYPE.
run;

NOTE: The SAS System stopped processing this step because of errors.
WARNING: The data set WORK.CUSTOMERS may be incomplete.  When this step
was stopped there were 0 observations and 15 variables.
```

Country is not defined in both data sets. Replace the WHERE statement with a subsetting IF statement.

149

Copyright © 2016, SAS Institute Inc., Cary, North Carolina, USA. ALL RIGHTS RESERVED.

Copyright © 2016, SAS Institute Inc., Cary, North Carolina, USA. ALL RIGHTS RESERVED.

Chapter 11 Creating Summary Reports

Copyright © 2016, SAS Institute Inc., Cary, North Carolina, USA. ALL RIGHTS RESERVED.

11.1 The FREQ Procedure

Objectives

- Produce one-way and two-way frequency tables with the FREQ procedure.
- Enhance frequency tables with options.
- Use PROC FREQ to validate data in a SAS data set.

3

Business Scenario

Orion Star management wants to know the number of male and female sales employees in Australia.

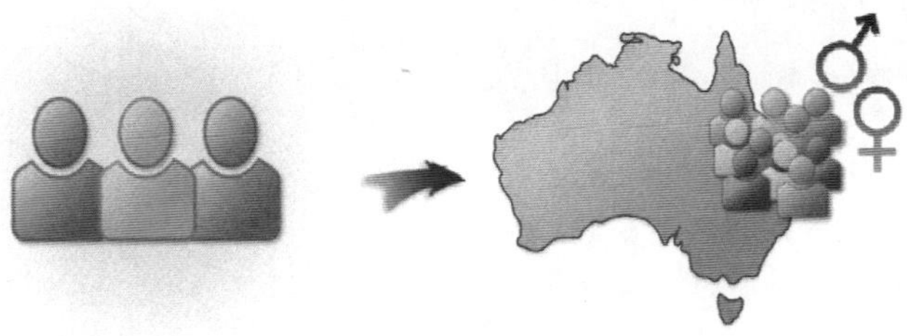

4

Copyright © 2016, SAS Institute Inc., Cary, North Carolina, USA. ALL RIGHTS RESERVED.

Considerations

Use the FREQ procedure to analyze the **Gender** variable in a subset of **orion.sales**.

```
          The FREQ Procedure

Gender      Frequency         Percent
--------------------------------------
 F              XX             XX.XX
 M              XX             XX.XX
```

5

FREQ Procedure

The FREQ procedure produces a one-way frequency table for each variable named in the TABLES statement.

```
proc freq data=orion.sales;
   tables Gender;
   where Country='AU';
run;
```

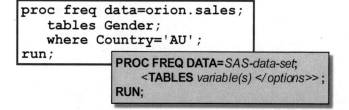

PROC FREQ DATA=*SAS-data-set*;
   <TABLES *variable(s) </ options>>* ;
RUN;

⚠ If the TABLES statement is omitted, a one-way frequency table is produced for ***every*** variable in the data set. This can produce a large amount of output and is seldom preferred.

6 **p111d01**

PROC FREQ displays a report by default. The output can be saved in a SAS data set.

The procedure can compute the following:

- chi-square tests for one-way to *n*-way tables
- tests and measures of agreement for contingency tables
- tests and measures of association for contingency tables and more

Copyright © 2016, SAS Institute Inc., Cary, North Carolina, USA. ALL RIGHTS RESERVED.

Viewing the Output

A one-way frequency table was created for **Gender**. It lists the discrete values found in the data set and the number of observations in which the variable has that value.

The FREQ Procedure

Gender	Frequency	Percent	Cumulative Frequency	Cumulative Percent
F	27	42.86	27	42.86
M	36	57.14	63	100.00

The default output includes frequency and percentage values, including cumulative statistics.

7

Options to Suppress Statistics

Use options in the TABLES statement to suppress the display of selected default statistics.

```
TABLES variable(s) / options ;
```

Option	Description
NOCUM	Suppresses the cumulative statistics.
NOPERCENT	Suppresses the percentage display.

8

Cumulative frequencies and percentages are useful when there are at least three levels of a variable in an ordinal relationship. When this is not the case, the NOCUM option produces a simpler, less confusing report.

Copyright © 2016, SAS Institute Inc., Cary, North Carolina, USA. ALL RIGHTS RESERVED.

Options to Suppress Statistics

NOCUM suppresses

The FREQ Procedure

Gender	Frequency	Percent	Cumulative Frequency	Cumulative Percent
F	27	42.86	27	42.86
M	36	57.14	63	100.00

NOPERCENT suppresses

9

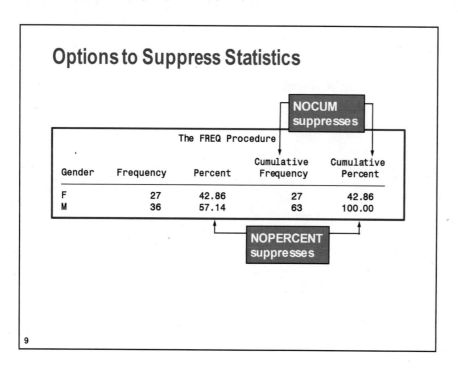

11.01 Short Answer Poll

Open and submit **p111a01**. Review the log to determine the cause of the error. Correct and resubmit the program. What change was needed?

```
proc freq data=orion.sales;
   tables country nocum nopercent;
run;
```

10

Copyright © 2016, SAS Institute Inc., Cary, North Carolina, USA. ALL RIGHTS RESERVED.

Idea Exchange

This step creates a table for every variable in the data set:

```
proc freq data=orion.sales;
run;
```

- **Employee_ID**
- **First_Name**
- **Last_Name**
- **Gender**
- **Salary**
- **Job_Title**
- **Country**
- **Birth_Date**
- **Hire_Date**

Which variables are most appropriate for a frequency analysis? Why?

12

Business Scenario

Orion Star management wants to know how many sales employees are in each country, as well as the count of males and females.

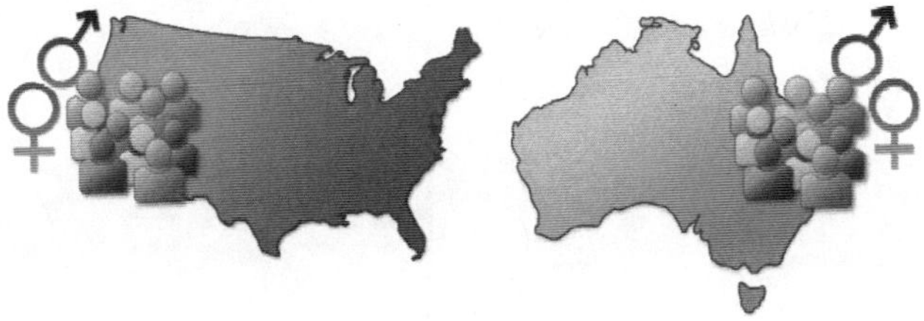

14

Copyright © 2016, SAS Institute Inc., Cary, North Carolina, USA. ALL RIGHTS RESERVED.

TABLES Statement

You can list multiple variables in a TABLES statement. A separate table is produced for each variable.

```
proc freq data=orion.sales;
   tables Gender Country;
run;
```

PROC FREQ Output

The FREQ Procedure

Gender	Frequency	Percent	Cumulative Frequency	Cumulative Percent
F	68	41.21	68	41.21
M	97	58.79	165	100.00

Country	Frequency	Percent	Cumulative Frequency	Cumulative Percent
AU	63	38.18	63	38.18
US	102	61.82	165	100.00

15 p111d02

BY Statement

The BY statement is used to request separate analyses for each BY group.

```
proc sort data=orion.sales out=sorted;
   by Country;
run;

proc freq data=sorted;
   tables Gender;
   by Country;
run;
```

The data set must be sorted or indexed by the variable (or variables) named in the BY statement.

16 p111d02

Copyright © 2016, SAS Institute Inc., Cary, North Carolina, USA. ALL RIGHTS RESERVED.

Viewing the Output

Each group appears on a separate page with a BY line.

```
----------------------- Country=AU -----------------------

                    The FREQ Procedure

                                        Cumulative    Cumulative
Gender     Frequency       Percent      Frequency      Percent

F                 27         42.86             27        42.86
M                 36         57.14             63       100.00
```

```
----------------------- Country=US -----------------------

                    The FREQ Procedure

                                        Cumulative    Cumulative
Gender     Frequency       Percent      Frequency      Percent

F                 41         40.20             41        40.20
M                 61         59.80            102       100.00
```

17

Crosstabulation Table

An asterisk between two variables generates a two-way frequency table, or *crosstabulation table*.

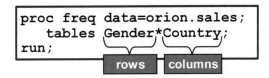

```
proc freq data=orion.sales;
   tables Gender*Country;
run;
```

rows columns

A two-way frequency table generates a single table with statistics for each distinct combination of values of the selected variables.

18 p111d02

Copyright © 2016, SAS Institute Inc., Cary, North Carolina, USA. ALL RIGHTS RESERVED.

Viewing the Output

PROC FREQ Output

```
                The FREQ Procedure

            Table of Gender by Country

Gender       Country

Frequency|
Percent  |
Row Pct  |
Col Pct  |AU      |US      |  Total
---------+--------+--------+
F        |     27 |     41 |     68
         |  16.36 |  24.85 |  41.21
         |  39.71 |  60.29 |
         |  42.86 |  40.20 |
---------+--------+--------+
M        |     36 |     61 |     97
         |  21.82 |  36.97 |  58.79
         |  37.11 |  62.89 |
         |  57.14 |  59.80 |
---------+--------+--------+
Total          63      102      165
            38.18    61.82   100.00
```

19

Options to Suppress Statistics

Use options in the TABLES statement to suppress the display of selected default statistics.

TABLES *variable(s) / options* ;

Option	Description
NOROW	Suppresses the display of the row percentage.
NOCOL	Suppresses the display of the column percentage.
NOPERCENT	Suppresses the percentage display.
NOFREQ	Suppresses the frequency display.

20

Copyright © 2016, SAS Institute Inc., Cary, North Carolina, USA. ALL RIGHTS RESERVED.

Options to Suppress Statistics

Table of Gender by Country

Gender / Frequency / Percent / Row Pct / Col Pct	Country: AU	US	Total
F	27	41	68
	16.36	24.85	41.21
	39.71	60.29	
	42.86	40.20	
M	36	61	97
	21.82	36.97	58.79
	37.11	62.89	
	57.14	59.80	
Total	63	102	165
	38.18	61.82	100.00

NOFREQ suppresses

NOPERCENT suppresses

21

Options to Suppress Statistics

Table of Gender by Country

Gender / Frequency / Percent / Row Pct / Col Pct	Country: AU	US	Total
F	27	41	68
	16.36	24.85	41.21
	39.71	60.29	
	42.86	40.20	
M	36	61	97
	21.82	36.97	58.79
	37.11	62.89	
	57.14	59.80	
Total	63	102	165
	38.18	61.82	100.00

NOROW suppresses

NOCOL suppresses

22

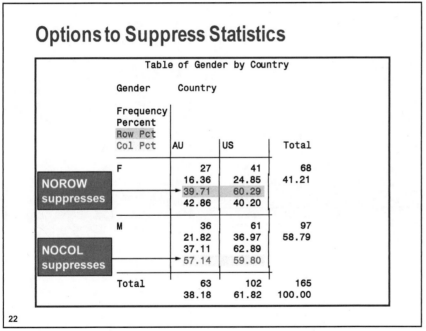

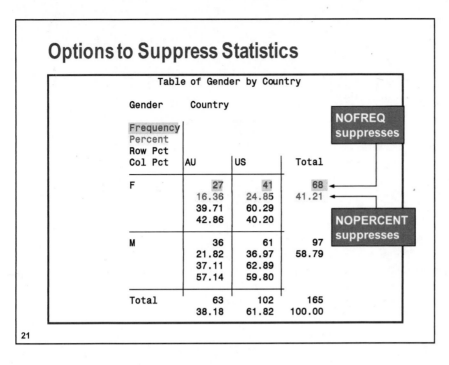

Copyright © 2016, SAS Institute Inc., Cary, North Carolina, USA. ALL RIGHTS RESERVED.

LIST and CROSSLIST Options

You can use the LIST and CROSSLIST options in the TABLES statement to "flatten" the output.

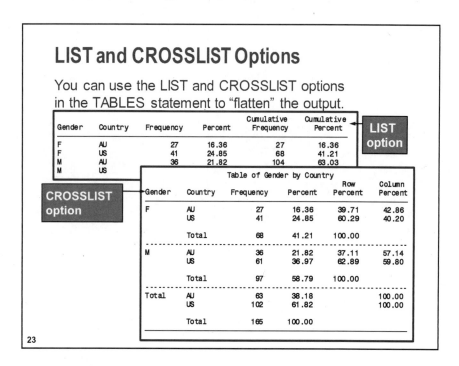

LIST option

Gender	Country	Frequency	Percent	Cumulative Frequency	Cumulative Percent
F	AU	27	16.36	27	16.36
F	US	41	24.85	68	41.21
M	AU	36	21.82	104	63.03
M	US				

CROSSLIST option

Table of Gender by Country

Gender	Country	Frequency	Percent	Row Percent	Column Percent
F	AU	27	16.36	39.71	42.86
	US	41	24.85	60.29	40.20
	Total	68	41.21	100.00	
M	AU	36	21.82	37.11	57.14
	US	61	36.97	62.89	59.80
	Total	97	58.79	100.00	
Total	AU	63	38.18		100.00
	US	102	61.82		100.00
	Total	165	100.00		

23

Business Scenario

A new data set, **orion.nonsales2**, must be validated. It contains information about non-sales employees and might include invalid and missing values.

Partial **orion.nonsales2**

Employee_ID	First	Last	Gender	Salary	Job_Title	Country
120101	Patrick	Lu	M	163040	Director	AU
120104	Kareen	Billington	F	46230	Admin Mgr	au
120105	Liz	Povey	F	27110	Secretary I	AU
120106	John	Hornsey	M	.	Office Asst II	AU
120107	Sherie	Sheedy	F	30475	Office Asst II	AU
120108	Gladys	Gromek	F	27660	Warehouse Asst II	AU

25

Copyright © 2016, SAS Institute Inc., Cary, North Carolina, USA. ALL RIGHTS RESERVED.

Considerations

Use the FREQ procedure to screen for invalid, missing, and duplicate data values.

Requirements of non-sales employee data:

- **Employee_ID** values must be unique and not missing.
- **Gender** must be *F* or *M*.
- **Job_Title** must not be missing.
- **Country** must have a value of *AU* or *US*.
- **Salary** values must be in the numeric range of 24000 to 500000.

26

11.02 Short Answer Poll

What problems exist with the data in this partial data set?

Employee_ID	First	Last	Gender	Salary	Job_Title	Country
120101	Patrick	Lu	M	163040	Director	AU
120104	Kareen	Billington	F	46230	Administration Manager	au
120105	Liz	Povey	F	27110	Secretary I	AU
120106	John	Hornsey	M	.	Office Assistant II	AU
120107	Sherie	Sheedy	F	30475	Office Assistant III	AU
120108	Gladys	Gromek	F	27660	Warehouse Assistant II	AU
120108	Gabriele	Baker	F	26495	Warehouse Assistant I	AU
120110	Dennis	Entwisle	M	28615	Warehouse Assistant III	AU
120111	Ubaldo	Spillane	M	26895	Security Guard II	AU
120112	Ellis	Glattback	F	26550		AU
120113	Riu	Horsey	F	26870	Security Guard II	AU
120114	Jeannette	Buddery	G	31285	Security Manager	AU
120115	Hugh	Nichollas	M	2650	Service Assistant I	AU
.	Austen	Ralston	M	29250	Service Assistant II	AU
120117	Bill	Mccleary	M	31670	Cabinet Maker III	AU
120118	Darshi	Hartshorn	M	28090	Cabinet Maker II	AU

Hint: There are seven data problems.

27

Copyright © 2016, SAS Institute Inc., Cary, North Carolina, USA. ALL RIGHTS RESERVED.

FREQ Procedure for Data Validation

The FREQ procedure lists all discrete values for a variable and reports missing values.

```
proc freq data=orion.nonsales2;
   tables Gender Country / nocum nopercent;
run;
```

29

p111d03

Viewing the Output

PROC FREQ Output

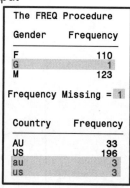

The FREQ Procedure

Gender	Frequency
F	110
G	1
M	123

Frequency Missing = 1

Country	Frequency
AU	33
US	196
au	3
us	3

30

Copyright © 2016, SAS Institute Inc., Cary, North Carolina, USA. ALL RIGHTS RESERVED.

NLEVELS Option

The *NLEVELS option* displays a table that provides the number of distinct values for each analysis variable.

```
proc freq data=orion.nonsales2 nlevels;
   tables Gender Country / nocum nopercent;
run;
```

```
PROC FREQ DATA=SAS-data-set NLEVELS;
    TABLES variable(s) ;
RUN;
```

31 p111d03

Viewing the Output

PROC FREQ Output

The FREQ Procedure

Number of Variable Levels

Variable	Levels	Missing Levels	Nonmissing Levels
Gender	4	1	3
Country	4	0	4

Gender	Frequency
F	110
G	1
M	123

Frequency Missing = 1

Country	Frequency
AU	33
US	196
au	3
us	3

32

Copyright © 2016, SAS Institute Inc., Cary, North Carolina, USA. ALL RIGHTS RESERVED.

Check for Uniqueness

The values of **Employee_ID** must be unique and not missing. PROC FREQ can be used to check for duplicate or missing values.

```
proc freq data=orion.nonsales2 order=freq;
   tables Employee_ID / nocum nopercent;
run;
```

The ORDER=FREQ option displays the results in descending frequency order.

33 p111d04

Viewing the Output

Partial PROC FREQ Output

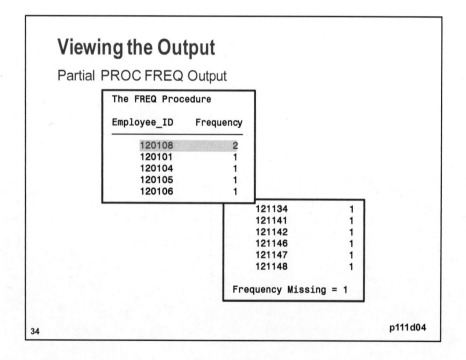

The FREQ Procedure

Employee_ID	Frequency
120108	2
120101	1
120104	1
120105	1
120106	1

121134	1
121141	1
121142	1
121146	1
121147	1
121148	1

Frequency Missing = 1

34 p111d04

Copyright © 2016, SAS Institute Inc., Cary, North Carolina, USA. ALL RIGHTS RESERVED.

NLEVELS Option

NLEVELS can also be used to identify duplicates, when the number of distinct values is known.

```
proc freq data=orion.nonsales2 nlevels;
   tables Employee_ID / noprint;
run;
```

This example uses the NOPRINT option to suppress the frequency table. Only the Number of Variable Levels table is displayed.

35 p111d04

Viewing the Output

Partial PROC FREQ Output

The FREQ Procedure

Number of Variable Levels

Variable	Levels	Missing Levels	Nonmissing Levels
Employee_ID	234	1	233

There are 235 employees, but there are only 234 distinct **Employee_ID** values. Therefore, there is one duplicate value and one missing value for **Employee_ID**.

36

Copyright © 2016, SAS Institute Inc., Cary, North Carolina, USA. ALL RIGHTS RESERVED.

NLEVELS Option

The _ALL_ keyword with the NOPRINT option displays the number of levels for all variables without displaying frequency counts.

```
proc freq data=orion.nonsales2 nlevels;
   tables _all_ / noprint;
run;
```

37

p111d04

Viewing the Output

PROC FREQ Output

The FREQ Procedure
Number of Variable Levels

Variable	Levels	Missing Levels	Nonmissing Levels
Employee_ID	234	1	233
First	204	0	204
Last	228	0	228
Gender	4	1	3
Salary	230	1	229
Job_Title	125	1	124
Country	4	0	4

No frequency tables were displayed.

38

Copyright © 2016, SAS Institute Inc., Cary, North Carolina, USA. ALL RIGHTS RESERVED.

11.03 Short Answer Poll

Modify **p111a02** to analyze **Job_Title**. Display the NLEVELS table listing the frequency counts in decreasing order.

How many unique, nonmissing job titles exist?
Which job title occurs most frequently?
What is the frequency of missing job titles?

39

Identifying Observations with Invalid Data

PROC FREQ uncovered the existence of invalid data values for **Gender**, **Country**, and **Employee_ID**. Use PROC PRINT to display the observations with invalid values.

```
proc print data=orion.nonsales2;
   where Gender not in ('F','M') or
         Country not in ('AU','US') or
         Job_Title is null or
         Employee_ID is missing or
         Employee_ID=120108;
run;
```

41

Copyright © 2016, SAS Institute Inc., Cary, North Carolina, USA. ALL RIGHTS RESERVED.

Viewing the Output

PROC PRINT Output

Obs	Employee_ID	First	Last	Gender	Salary	Job_Title	Country
2	120104	Kareen	Billington	F	46230	Administration Manager	au
6	120108	Gladys	Gromek	F	27660	Warehouse Assistant II	AU
7	120108	Gabriele	Baker	F	26495	Warehouse Assistant I	AU
10	120112	Ellis	Glattback	F	26550		AU
12	120114	Jeannette	Buddery	G	31285	Security Manager	AU
14	.	Austen	Ralston	M	29250	Service Assistant II	AU
84	120695	Trent	Moffat	M	28180	Warehouse Assistant II	au
87	120698	Geoff	Kistanna	M	26160	Warehouse Assistant I	au
101	120723	Deanna	Olsen		33950	Corp. Comm. Specialist II	US
125	120747	Zashia	Farthing	F	43590	Financial Controller I	us
197	120994	Danelle	Sergeant	F	31645	Office Administrator I	us
200	120997	Mary	Donathan	F	27420	Shipping Administrator I	us

original observation numbers

42

Business Scenario

The manager of Human Resources requested a report that shows the number and percent of sales employees who are hired each year.

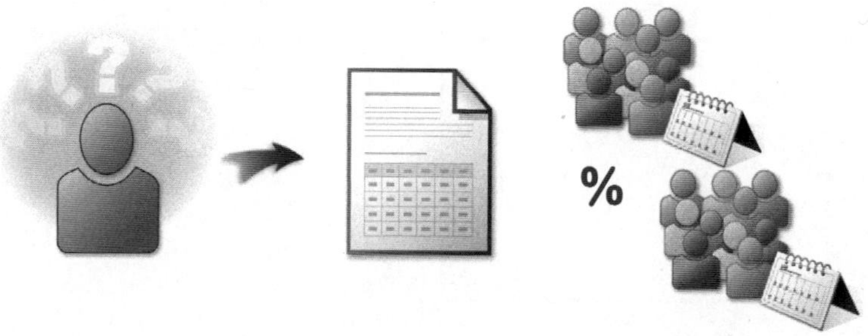

44

Copyright © 2016, SAS Institute Inc., Cary, North Carolina, USA. ALL RIGHTS RESERVED.

Using Formats in PROC FREQ

A FORMAT statement can be used in PROC FREQ to format data values.

```
proc freq data=orion.sales;
   tables Hire_Date / nocum;
   format Hire_Date date9.;
run;
```

Partial PROC FREQ Output

The FREQ Procedure

Hire_Date	Frequency	Percent
01JAN1978	17	10.30
01FEB1978	2	1.21
01APR1978	1	0.61
01JUL1978	1	0.61
01AUG1978	1	0.61

many discrete values, and not what the manager requested

45

p111d05

Using Formats in PROC FREQ

A FORMAT statement can also be used in PROC FREQ to group the data.

```
proc freq data=orion.sales;
   tables Hire_Date / nocum;
   format Hire_Date year4.;
run;
```

Partial PROC FREQ Output

The FREQ Procedure

Hire_Date	Frequency	Percent
1978	23	13.94
1979	2	1.21
1980	4	2.42
1981	3	1.82
1982	7	4.24

fewer discrete values

46

p111d05

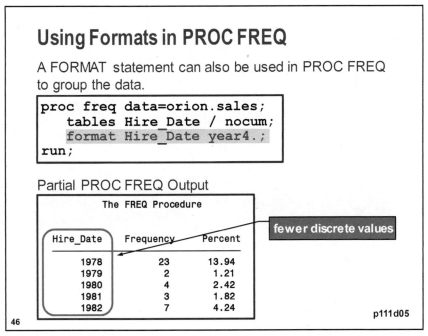

If a format is permanently assigned to a variable, PROC FREQ automatically groups the report by the formatted values.

Copyright © 2016, SAS Institute Inc., Cary, North Carolina, USA. ALL RIGHTS RESERVED.

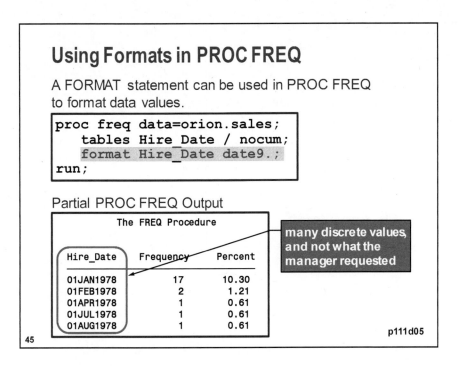

11.04 Short Answer Poll

Open and submit **p111a03** and view the output.
Add a statement to apply the TIERS format to **Salary** and resubmit the program.

Can user-defined formats be used to group data?

47

FORMAT Statement

User-defined formats can also be used to display levels with alternate text in a frequency table.

```
proc freq data=orion.sales;
   tables Gender*Country;
   format Country $ctryfmt.
          Gender $gender.;
run;
```

49 p111d06

Copyright © 2016, SAS Institute Inc., Cary, North Carolina, USA. ALL RIGHTS RESERVED.

Viewing the Output

Partial PROC FREQ Output

Table of Gender by Country

Gender Frequency Percent Row Pct Col Pct	Country Australi a	United S tates	Total
Female	27 16.36 39.71 42.86	41 24.85 60.29 40.20	68 41.21
Male	36 21.82 37.11 57.14	61 36.97 62.89 59.80	97 58.79
Total	63 38.18	102 61.82	165 100.00

Labels are wrapped.

50

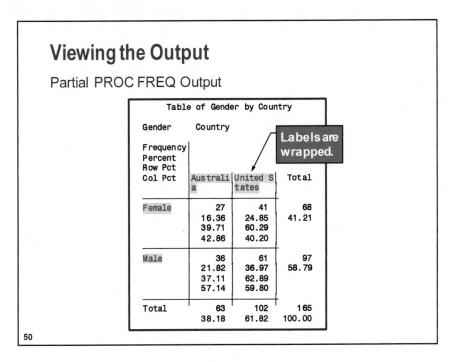

The default format for cell statistics is 8.*d*, where *d* is 0 for frequencies and 2 for percentages. Eight print positions are sometimes not enough for column headings.

FORMAT= Option

Use the *FORMAT= option* in the TABLES statement to format the frequency value and to change the width of the column.

```
proc freq data=orion.sales;
   tables Gender*Country / format=13.;
   format Country $ctryfmt.
          Gender $gender.;
run;
```

51

p111d06

Copyright © 2016, SAS Institute Inc., Cary, North Carolina, USA. ALL RIGHTS RESERVED.

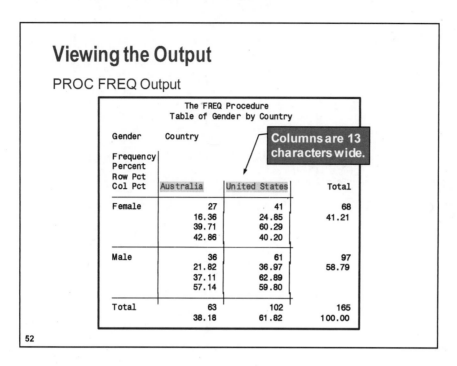

Viewing the Output

PROC FREQ Output

```
                 The FREQ Procedure
              Table of Gender by Country

Gender      Country

Frequency|
Percent  |
Row Pct  |
Col Pct  |Australia    |United States|  Total
---------+-------------+-------------+
Female   |           27|           41|     68
         |        16.36|        24.85|  41.21
         |        39.71|        60.29|
         |        42.86|        40.20|
---------+-------------+-------------+
Male     |           36|           61|     97
         |        21.82|        36.97|  58.79
         |        37.11|        62.89|
         |        57.14|        59.80|
---------+-------------+-------------+
Total             63           102      165
               38.18         61.82   100.00
```

Columns are 13 characters wide.

52

The FORMAT= option applies only to the frequency. Percentage values are always displayed with two decimal places.

Copyright © 2016, SAS Institute Inc., Cary, North Carolina, USA. ALL RIGHTS RESERVED.

Exercises

> If you restarted your SAS session since the last exercise, open and submit the **libname.sas** program that can be found in the data folder.

Level 1

1. **Counting Levels of a Variable with PROC FREQ**

   a. Retrieve the starter program **p111e01**.

   b. Submit the program without making changes to analyze **Customer_ID** and **Employee_ID** in **orion.orders**. Would you expect to see frequencies of 1 for customers and sales employees? ____

   c. Modify the program to produce two separate reports.

   1) Display the number of distinct levels of **Customer_ID** and **Employee_ID** for retail orders.

   a) Use a WHERE statement to limit the report to retail sales (**Order_Type=***1*).

   b) Do not display the frequency count tables.

   c) Display the title **Unique Customers and Salespersons for Retail Sales**.

   d) Submit the program to produce the following report:

   PROC FREQ Output

```
            Unique Customers and Salespersons for Retail Sales

                          The FREQ Procedure

                      Number of Variable Levels

               Variable       Label             Levels
               -------------------------------------------
               Customer_ID    Customer ID           31
               Employee_ID    Employee ID          100
```

   2) Display the number of distinct levels for **Customer_ID** for catalog and Internet orders.

   a) Use a WHERE statement to limit the report to catalog and Internet sales by selecting observations with **Order_Type** values other than *1*.

   b) Specify an option to display the results in decreasing frequency order.

   c) Specify an option to suppress the cumulative statistics.

   d) Display the title **Catalog and Internet Customers**.

   e) Submit the program to produce the following report:

Copyright © 2016, SAS Institute Inc., Cary, North Carolina, USA. ALL RIGHTS RESERVED.

Partial PROC FREQ Output

```
                Catalog and Internet Customers

                      The FREQ Procedure

                         Customer ID

        Customer_ID      Frequency        Percent
        -----------------------------------------
                 16             15           6.52
                 29              9           3.91
                  5              8           3.48
                ...
              26148              1           0.43
              70059              1           0.43
```

2. Validating orion.shoes_tracker with PROC FREQ

a. Retrieve the starter program **p111e02**.

b. Complete the PROC FREQ step to create one-way frequency tables for **Supplier_Name** and **Supplier_ID** in **orion.shoes_tracker**. Include the NLEVELS option.

The data in **orion.shoes_tracker** should meet the following requirements:

- **Supplier_Name** must be *3Top Sports* or *Greenline Sports Ltd.*
- **Supplier_ID** must be *2963* or *14682*.

What invalid data exists for **Supplier_Name** and **Supplier_ID**? ______________________________

Level 2

3. Producing Frequency Reports with PROC FREQ

a. Retrieve the starter program **p111e03**.

b. Add statements to the PROC FREQ step to produce three frequency reports.

1) Number of orders in each year: Apply a format to the **Order_Date** variable to combine all orders within the same year.

2) Number of orders of each order type: Apply the ORDERTYPES. format that is defined in the starter program to the **Order_Type** variable. Suppress the cumulative frequency and percentages.

3) Number of orders for each combination of year and order type: Suppress all percentages that normally appear in each cell of a two-way table.

Copyright © 2016, SAS Institute Inc., Cary, North Carolina, USA. ALL RIGHTS RESERVED.

c. Submit the program to produce the following output:

PROC FREQ Output

```
                Order Summary by Year and Type

                    The FREQ Procedure

              Date Order was placed by Customer

                                             Cumulative    Cumulative
Order_Date    Frequency     Percent           Frequency       Percent
----------------------------------------------------------------------
      2007         104        21.22                104          21.22
      2008          87        17.76                191          38.98
      2009          70        14.29                261          53.27
      2010         113        23.06                374          76.33
      2011         116        23.67                490         100.00


                        Order Type

                Order_
                  Type    Frequency      Percent
               ---------------------------------
               Retail          260         53.06
               Catalog         132         26.94
               Internet         98         20.00
              Table of Order_Date by Order_Type

        Order_Date(Date Order was placed by Customer)
                Order_Type(Order Type)

           Frequency|Retail   |Catalog |Internet|  Total
           ---------+---------+--------+--------+
                2007|      45 |     41 |     18 |    104
           ---------+---------+--------+--------+
                2008|      51 |     20 |     16 |     87
           ---------+---------+--------+--------+
                2009|      27 |     23 |     20 |     70
           ---------+---------+--------+--------+
                2010|      67 |     33 |     13 |    113
           ---------+---------+--------+--------+
                2011|      70 |     15 |     31 |    116
           ---------+---------+--------+--------+
           Total         260      132       98       490
```

4. Validating orion.qtr2_2011 with PROC FREQ

Write a PROC FREQ step to validate the data in **orion.qtr2_2011**.

a. Create frequency tables for **Order_ID** and **Order_Type**. Include the **Number of Variable Levels** table.

b. Submit the program.

The data in **orion.qtr2_2011** should meet the following requirements:

- **Order_ID** must be unique (36 distinct values) and not missing.

Copyright © 2016, SAS Institute Inc., Cary, North Carolina, USA. ALL RIGHTS RESERVED.

- **Order_Type** must have a value of *1*, *2*, or *3*.

What invalid data exists for **Order_ID** and **Order_Type**? ______________________________

Challenge

5. Creating an Output Data Set with PROC FREQ

Write a program to perform a frequency analysis on **Product_ID** in **orion.order_fact**.

a. Create an output data set that contains the frequency counts based on **Product_ID**. Explore the SAS Help Facility or online documentation for information about creating an output data set of counts from PROC FREQ results.

b. Combine the output data set with **orion.product_list** to obtain the **Product_Name** value for each **Product_ID** code. Output only those products that were ordered.

c. Sort the combined data so that the most frequently ordered products appear first in the resulting data set. Print the first five observations—that is, those that represent the five products ordered most often. Use the OBS= data set option to limit the number of observations that are displayed.

d. Submit the program to produce the following report:

PROC PRINT Output

```
                    Top Five Products by Number of Orders

                      Product
      Orders           Number    Product

         6       230100500056    Knife
         6       230100600030    Outback Sleeping Bag, Large,Left,Blue/Black
         5       230100600022    Expedition10,Medium,Right,Blue Ribbon
         5       240400300035    Smasher Shorts
         4       230100500082    Lucky Tech Intergal Wp/B Rain Pants
```

End of Exercises

Copyright © 2016, SAS Institute Inc., Cary, North Carolina, USA. ALL RIGHTS RESERVED.

11.2 The MEANS and UNIVARIATE Procedures

Objectives

- Calculate summary statistics and multilevel summaries with the MEANS procedure.
- Enhance summary tables with options.
- Identify extreme and missing values with the UNIVARIATE procedure.

56

Business Scenario

The payroll manager would like to see the average salary for all employees.

57

Copyright © 2016, SAS Institute Inc., Cary, North Carolina, USA. ALL RIGHTS RESERVED.

MEANS Procedure

The MEANS procedure produces summary reports with descriptive statistics.

```
proc means data=orion.sales;
run;
```

PROC MEANS DATA=*input-data-set <options statistics>*;
<**VAR** *analysis-variable(s)*;>
<**CLASS** *classification-variable(s)*;>
RUN;

- *Analysis variables* are the ***numeric*** variables for which statistics are to be computed.
- *Classification variables* are variables whose values define subgroups for the analysis. They can be character or numeric.

58 p111d07

Viewing the Output

PROC MEANS Output

The MEANS Procedure

Variable	N	Mean	Std Dev	Minimum	Maximum
Employee_ID	165	120713.90	450.0866939	120102.00	121145.00
Salary	165	31160.12	20082.67	22710.00	243190.00
Birth_Date	165	3622.58	5456.29	-5842.00	10490.00
Hire_Date	165	12054.28	4619.94	5114.00	17167.00

Default statistics are displayed for all numeric variables.

59

Copyright © 2016, SAS Institute Inc., Cary, North Carolina, USA. ALL RIGHTS RESERVED.

VAR Statement

The VAR statement identifies the analysis variable (or variables) and their order in the output.

```
proc means data=orion.sales;
   var Salary;
run;
```

VAR *variable(s)*;

The MEANS Procedure

Analysis Variable : Salary

N	Mean	Std Dev	Minimum	Maximum
165	31160.12	20082.67	22710.00	243190.00

60

p111d07

Business Scenario

Analyze **Salary** by **Country** within **Gender**.

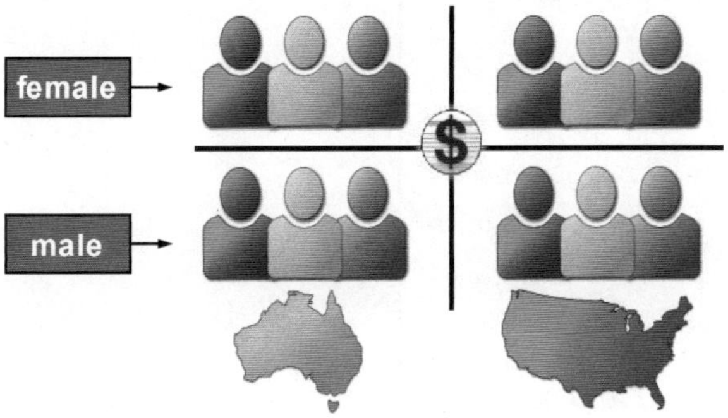

61

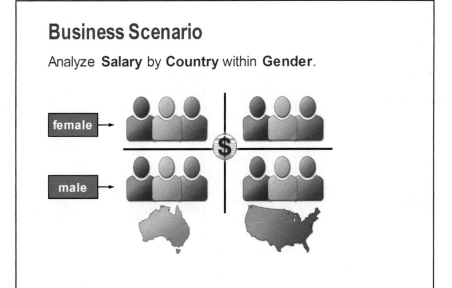

Copyright © 2016, SAS Institute Inc., Cary, North Carolina, USA. ALL RIGHTS RESERVED.

CLASS Statement

The *CLASS statement* identifies variables whose values define subgroups for the analysis.

```
proc means data=orion.sales;
   var Salary;
   class Gender Country;
run;
```

CLASS *classification-variable(s)*;

- Classification variables are character or numeric.
- They typically have few discrete values.
- The data set does ***not*** need to be sorted or indexed by the classification variables.

62 p111d08

Viewing the Output

Statistics are produced for each combination of values of the classification variables.

The MEANS Procedure
Analysis Variable : Salary

Gender	Country	N Obs	N	Mean	Std Dev	Minimum	Maximum
F	AU	27	27	27702.41	1728.23	25185.00	30890.00
	US	41	41	29460.98	8847.03	25390.00	83505.00
M	AU	36	36	32001.39	16592.45	25745.00	108255.00
	US	61	61	33336.15	29592.69	22710.00	243190.00

- *N Obs* – the number of observations with each unique combination of class variables
- *N* – the number of observations with nonmissing values of the analysis variable (or variables)

63

Copyright © 2016, SAS Institute Inc., Cary, North Carolina, USA. ALL RIGHTS RESERVED.

11.05 Short Answer Poll

For a given data set, there are 63 observations with a **Country** value of *AU*. Of those 63 observations, only 61 observations have a value for **Salary**.

Which output is correct?

a.

Analysis Variable : Salary

Country	N Obs	N
AU	63	61

b.

Analysis Variable : Salary

Country	N Obs	N
AU	61	63

64

Business Scenario

Analyze **Salary** by **Country** within **Gender**. Generate a report that includes the number of missing **Salary** values, as well as the minimum, maximum, and sum of salaries.

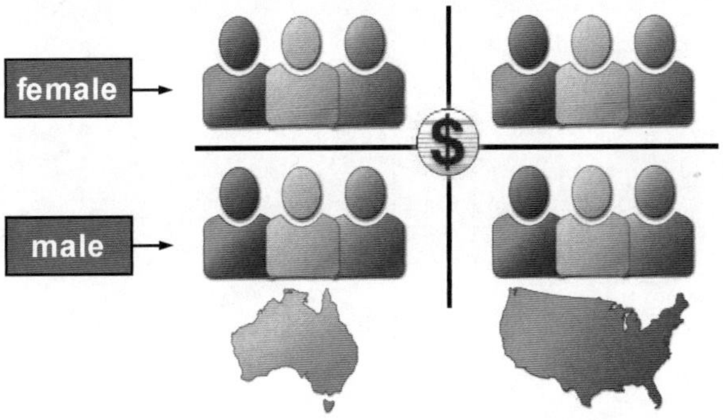

66

Copyright © 2016, SAS Institute Inc., Cary, North Carolina, USA. ALL RIGHTS RESERVED.

PROC MEANS Statistics

Use options in the PROC MEANS statement to request specific statistics.

```
proc means data=orion.sales nmiss min max sum;
   var Salary;
   class Gender Country;
run;
```

The requested statistics override the default statistics.

67 p111d09

PROC MEANS Statistics

The statistics are displayed in the order in which they are requested.

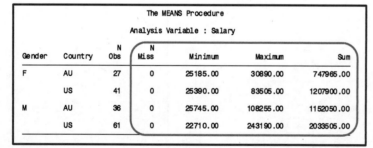

The MEANS Procedure

Analysis Variable : Salary

Gender	Country	N Obs	N Miss	Minimum	Maximum	Sum
F	AU	27	0	25185.00	30890.00	747965.00
	US	41	0	25390.00	83505.00	1207900.00
M	AU	36	0	25745.00	108255.00	1152050.00
	US	61	0	22710.00	243190.00	2033505.00

68

Copyright © 2016, SAS Institute Inc., Cary, North Carolina, USA. ALL RIGHTS RESERVED.

PROC MEANS Statement Options

Options can also be placed in the PROC MEANS statement.

Option	Description
MAXDEC=	Specifies the number of decimal places to display.
NONOBS	Suppresses the N Obs column.

69

MAXDEC= Option

MAXDEC=0

The MEANS Procedure
Analysis Variable : Salary

Country	N Obs	N	Mean	Std Dev	Minimum	Maximum
AU	63	63	30159	12699	25185	108255
US	102	102	31778	23556	22710	243190

MAXDEC=1

The MEANS Procedure
Analysis Variable : Salary

Country	N Obs	N	Mean	Std Dev	Minimum	Maximum
AU	63	63	30159.0	12699.1	25185.0	108255.0
US	102	102	31778.5	23555.8	22710.0	243190.0

p111d10

70

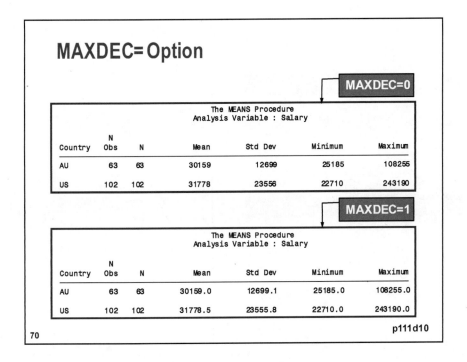

Copyright © 2016, SAS Institute Inc., Cary, North Carolina, USA. ALL RIGHTS RESERVED.

NONOBS Option

N Obs included by default

The MEANS Procedure
Analysis Variable : Salary

Country	N Obs	N	Mean	Std Dev	Minimum	Maximum
AU	63	63	30158.97	12699.14	25185.00	108255.00
US	102	102	31778.48	23555.84	22710.00	243190.00

NONOBS option

The MEANS Procedure
Analysis Variable : Salary

Country	N	Mean	Std Dev	Minimum	Maximum
AU	63	30158.97	12699.14	25185.00	108255.00
US	102	31778.48	23555.84	22710.00	243190.00

71 p111d10

Other PROC MEANS Statistics

Descriptive Statistic Keywords				
CLM	CSS	CV	LCLM	MAX
MEAN	MIN	MODE	N	NMISS
KURTOSIS	RANGE	SKEWNESS	STDDEV	STDERR
SUM	SUMWGT	UCLM	USS	VAR

Quantile Statistic Keywords				
MEDIAN | P50	P1	P5	P10	Q1 | P25
Q3 | P75	P90	P95	P99	QRANGE

Hypothesis Testing Keywords				
PROBT	T			

72

Copyright © 2016, SAS Institute Inc., Cary, North Carolina, USA. ALL RIGHTS RESERVED.

Idea Exchange

Which PROC MEANS statistics would you request when you are validating numeric variables?

73

Business Scenario

Validate salary data in **orion.nonsales2**. **Salary** must be in the numeric range of 24000 to 500000.

Partial **orion.nonsales2**

Employee ID	First	Last	Gender	Salary	Job_Title	Country
120101	Patrick	Lu	M	163040	Director	AU
120104	Kareen	Billington	F	46230	Admin Mgr	au
120105	Liz	Povey	F	27110	Secretary I	AU
120106	John	Hornsey	M	.	Office Asst II	AU
120107	Sherie	Sheedy	F	30475	Office Asst II	AU
120108	Gladys	Gromek	F	27660	Warehouse Asst II	AU

75

Copyright © 2016, SAS Institute Inc., Cary, North Carolina, USA. ALL RIGHTS RESERVED.

UNIVARIATE Procedure

PROC UNIVARIATE displays extreme observations, missing values, and other statistics for the variables included in the VAR statement.

```
proc univariate data=orion.nonsales2;
   var Salary;
run;
```

```
PROC UNIVARIATE DATA=SAS-data-set;
     <VAR variable(s);>
RUN;
```

If the VAR statement is omitted, PROC UNIVARIATE analyzes all numeric variables in the data set.

76

p111d11

Viewing the Output: Extreme Observations

The *Extreme Observations* section includes the five lowest and five highest values for the analysis variable and the corresponding observation numbers.

Partial PROC UNIVARIATE Output

Extreme Observations

-----Lowest----		-----Highest----	
Value	Obs	Value	Obs
2401	20	163040	1
2650	13	194885	231
24025	25	207885	28
24100	19	268455	29
24390	228	433800	27

Obs is the observation number, not the count of observations with that value.

77

Copyright © 2016, SAS Institute Inc., Cary, North Carolina, USA. ALL RIGHTS RESERVED.

NEXTROBS=Option

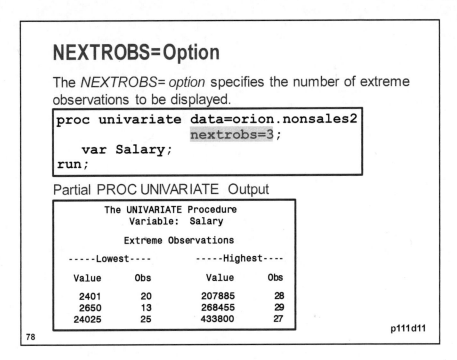

The *NEXTROBS= option* specifies the number of extreme observations to be displayed.

```
proc univariate data=orion.nonsales2
                nextrobs=3;
   var Salary;
run;
```

Partial PROC UNIVARIATE Output

```
         The UNIVARIATE Procedure
            Variable:  Salary

           Extreme Observations

 -----Lowest----        -----Highest----

 Value      Obs           Value       Obs

  2401       20          207885        28
  2650       13          268455        29
 24025       25          433800        27
```

78 p111d11

The default value for NEXTROBS= is 5, and *n* can range between 0 and half the maximum number of observations. You can specify NEXTROBS=0 to suppress the table of extreme observations.

ID Statement

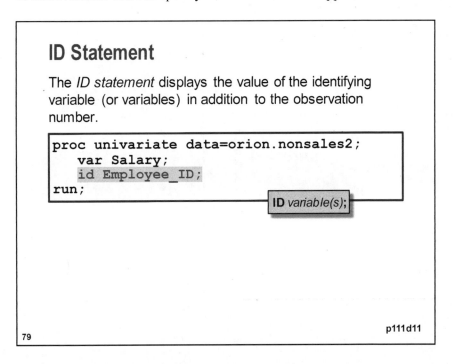

The *ID statement* displays the value of the identifying variable (or variables) in addition to the observation number.

```
proc univariate data=orion.nonsales2;
   var Salary;
   id Employee_ID;
run;
```

ID *variable(s)*;

79 p111d11

Copyright © 2016, SAS Institute Inc., Cary, North Carolina, USA. ALL RIGHTS RESERVED.

Viewing the Output

Partial PROC UNIVARIATE Output

```
                         The UNIVARIATE Procedure
                            Variable:  Salary

                          Extreme Observations

------------Lowest---------          -----------Highest---------

 Value     Employee_ID     Obs           Value     Employee_ID     Obs

  2401          120191      20          163040          120101       1
  2650          120115      13          194885          121141     231
 24025          120196      25          207885          120260      28
 24100          120190      19          268455          120262      29
 24390          121132     228          433800          120259      27
```

80

Viewing the Output: Missing Values Section

The *Missing Values* section displays the number and percentage of observations with missing values for the analysis variable.

Partial PROC UNIVARIATE Output

```
                          Missing Values

                                     -----Percent Of-----
          Missing                                 Missing
            Value        Count       All Obs          Obs

                .            1          0.43       100.00
```

81

Copyright © 2016, SAS Institute Inc., Cary, North Carolina, USA. ALL RIGHTS RESERVED.

11.06 Short Answer Poll

PROC UNIVARIATE identified two observations with **Salary** values less than 24,000.

What procedure can be used to display the observations that contain the invalid values?

82

Copyright © 2016, SAS Institute Inc., Cary, North Carolina, USA. ALL RIGHTS RESERVED.

Exercises

> If you restarted your SAS session since the last exercise, open and submit the **libname.sas** program that can be found in the data folder.

Level 1

6. **Creating a Summary Report with PROC MEANS**

   a. Retrieve the starter program **p111e06**.

   b. Display only the SUM statistic for the **Total_Retail_Price** variable.

   c. Add a CLASS statement to display separate statistics for each combination of **Order_Date** and **Order_Type**.

   d. Apply the ORDERTYPES format so that the order types are displayed as text descriptions. Apply the YEAR4. format so that order dates are displayed as years.

   e. Submit the program to produce the following report:

   Partial PROC MEANS Output

```
                       Revenue from All Orders

                        The MEANS Procedure

   Analysis Variable : Total_Retail_Price Total Retail Price for This Product

                  Date
                 Order
                   was
                placed
                    by     Order            N
              Customer     Type           Obs                Sum
              ----------------------------------------------------
                  2007     Retail          53            7938.80

                           Catalog         52           10668.08

                           Internet        23            4124.05

                  2008     Retail          63            9012.22

                           Catalog         23            3494.60

                           Internet        22            3275.70
```

7. **Validating orion.price_current with the UNIVARIATE Procedure**

   a. Retrieve the starter program **p111e07**.

   b. Add a VAR statement to analyze **Unit_Sales_Price** and **Factor** and submit the program.

Copyright © 2016, SAS Institute Inc., Cary, North Carolina, USA. ALL RIGHTS RESERVED.

c. View the Extreme Observations output.

How many values of **Unit_Sales_Price** are over the maximum of 800? ____________

How many values of **Factor** are under the minimum of 1? ____________

How many values of **Factor** are over the maximum of 1.05? ____________

Level 2

8. Analyzing Missing Numeric Values with PROC MEANS

a. Retrieve the starter program **p111e08**.

b. Display the number of missing values and the number of nonmissing values present in the **Birth_Date**, **Emp_Hire_Date**, and **Emp_Term_Date** variables.

c. Add a CLASS statement to display separate statistics for each value of **Gender**.

d. Suppress the column that displays the total number of observations in each classification group.

e. Submit the program to produce the following report:

PROC MEANS Output

```
                Number of Missing and Non-Missing Date Values

                          The MEANS Procedure

Employee                                                          N
Gender       Variable         Label                            Miss        N
-----------------------------------------------------------------------------
F            Birth_Date       Employee Birth Date                 0      191
             Emp_Hire_Date    Employee Hire Date                  0      191
             Emp_Term_Date    Employee Termination Date         139       52

M            Birth_Date       Employee Birth Date                 0      233
             Emp_Hire_Date    Employee Hire Date                  0      233
             Emp_Term_Date    Employee Termination Date         169       64
-----------------------------------------------------------------------------
```

9. Validating orion.shoes_tracker with the UNIVARIATE Procedure

a. Write a PROC UNIVARIATE step to validate **Product_ID** of **orion.shoes_tracker**. A valid **Product_ID** value must have exactly 12 digits.

b. Submit the program and view the Extreme Observations output.

How many values of **Product_ID** are too small? ____________

How many values of **Product_ID** are too large? ____________

Copyright © 2016, SAS Institute Inc., Cary, North Carolina, USA. ALL RIGHTS RESERVED.

Challenge

10. Creating an Output Data Set with PROC MEANS

a. Retrieve the starter program **p111e10**.

b. Modify the PROC MEANS step to create an output data set that contains the sum of **Total_Retail_Price** values for each value of **Product_ID**. (Creating an output data set from PROC MEANS results is discussed in the SAS Help Facility and in the online documentation.)

c. Combine the output data set with **orion.product_list** to obtain the **Product_Name** value for each **Product_ID** code.

d. Sort the combined data so that the products with higher revenues appear at the top of the resulting data set.

e. Apply the OBS= data set option in a PROC PRINT step to display the first five observations—that is, those that represent the five products with the most revenue.

f. Display the revenue values with a leading euro symbol (€), a period that separates every three digits, a comma that separates the decimal fraction, and two decimal places.

g. Submit the program to produce the following report:

PROC MEANS Output

```
                    Top Five Products by Revenue

                                 Product
  Obs     Revenue                 Number    Product

    1     €3.391,80         230100700009    Family Holiday 6
    2     €3.080,30         230100700008    Family Holiday 4
    3     €2.250,00         230100700011    Hurricane 4
    4     €1.937,20         240200100173    Proplay Executive Bi-Metal Graphite
    5     €1.796,00         240200100076    Expert Men's Firesole Driver
```

11. Selecting Only the Extreme Observations Output from the UNIVARIATE Procedure

a. Write a PROC UNIVARIATE step to validate **Product_ID** in **orion.shoes_tracker**.

b. Before the PROC UNIVARIATE step, add the following ODS statement:

```
ods trace on;
```

c. After the PROC UNIVARIATE step, add the following ODS statement:

```
ods trace off;
```

d. Submit the program and notice the trace information in the SAS log.

What is the name of the last output added in the SAS log? ______________________________

e. Add an ODS SELECT statement immediately before the PROC UNIVARIATE step to select only the Extreme Observation output object. Documentation about the ODS TRACE and ODS SELECT statements can be found in the SAS Help Facility and in the online documentation.

Copyright © 2016, SAS Institute Inc., Cary, North Carolina, USA. ALL RIGHTS RESERVED.

f. Submit the program to create the following PROC UNIVARIATE report:

```
                    The UNIVARIATE Procedure
                Variable:  Product_ID  (Product ID)

                      Extreme Observations

        --------Lowest-------          -------Highest------
              Value       Obs                 Value       Obs

        2.20200E+10         4            2.2020E+11         6
        2.20200E+11         1            2.2020E+11         7
        2.20200E+11         2            2.2020E+11         9
        2.20200E+11         3            2.2020E+11        10
        2.20200E+11         5            2.2020E+12         8
```

End of Exercises

Copyright © 2016, SAS Institute Inc., Cary, North Carolina, USA. ALL RIGHTS RESERVED.

11.3 Using the Output Delivery System

Objectives

- Define the Output Delivery System and ODS destinations.
- Create HTML, PDF, RTF, and LISTING files with ODS statements.
- Use the STYLE= option to specify a style template.
- Create files that can be viewed in Microsoft Excel.

87

Business Scenario

Generate reports in various formats for distribution within Orion Star.

88

Copyright © 2016, SAS Institute Inc., Cary, North Carolina, USA. ALL RIGHTS RESERVED.

Interactive Method

Each SAS interface creates a specific report format by default and has an interactive method for changing the type of report format.

	Default Report Formats	Interactive Method for Changing Report Format	Possible Interactive Report Formats
SAS Studio	HTML, PDF, and RTF	More Application Options ⇨ Preferences ⇨ Results	HTML, PDF, and RTF
SAS Enterprise Guide	SASREPORT	Tools ⇨ Options ⇨ Results General ⇨ Results	SASREPORT, HTML, PDF, RTF, and LISTING (text)
SAS Windowing Environment	HTML	Tools ⇨ Options ⇨ Preferences ⇨ Results	HTML and LISTING (text)

89

SAS Studio:

- creates HTML output based on HTML5.
- creates PDF and RTF output in addition to HTML output. The PDF and RTF output is not visible on the Results tab. A download button must be clicked so that you can see the PDF or RTF output.

SAS Enterprise Guide:

- creates HTML output based on HTML4.

SAS windowing environment:

- creates HTML output based on HTML4.
- Prior to SAS 9.3, the SAS windowing environment created LISTING (text) output.

Copyright © 2016, SAS Institute Inc., Cary, North Carolina, USA. ALL RIGHTS RESERVED.

Programming Method

Alternatively, a user can add ODS statements to a SAS program to control the report formats that are created.

```
ods html file="&path\myreport.html";

proc freq data=orion.sales;
   tables Country;
run;

ods html close;
```

ODS *destination* **FILE="*filename*"** *<options>*;
<SAS code to generate the report>
ODS *destination* **CLOSE;**

In addition, the ODS statements are used to control the names and locations of the files that are created.

90 p111d12

Output Delivery System (ODS)

Use the Output Delivery System to create different report formats by directing output to various ODS destinations.

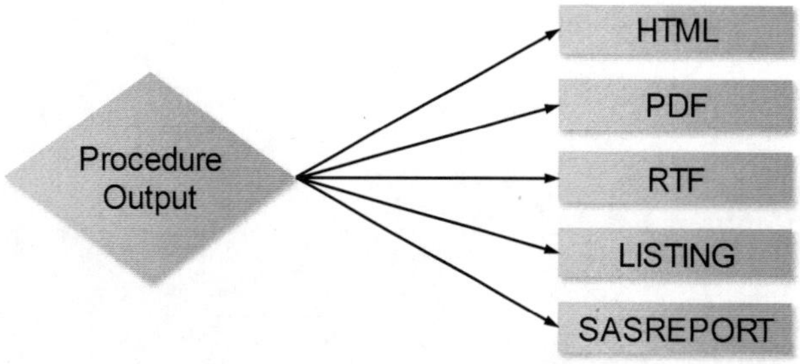

ODS destinations and statements can be used regardless of the operating environment, processing mode, or SAS interface.

91

Copyright © 2016, SAS Institute Inc., Cary, North Carolina, USA. ALL RIGHTS RESERVED.

ODS Destinations

The following are some of the common ODS destinations:

Destination	Type of File	Extension	Viewed In
HTML	Hypertext Markup Language	.html	Web browser such as Internet Explorer
PDF	Portable Document Format	.pdf	Adobe product such as Adobe Reader
RTF	Rich Text Format	.rtf	Word processor such as Microsoft Excel
LISTING	Text	.txt	Text editor such as Notepad
SASREPORT	Extensible Markup Language	.xml	SAS product such as SAS Enterprise Guide

92

ODS Statements

With ODS statements, output from multiple procedures can be sent to multiple ODS destinations.

```
ods html file="&path\example.html";
ods pdf file="&path\example.pdf";
ods rtf file="&path\example.rtf";

proc freq data=orion.sales;
   tables Country;
run;
proc means data=orion.sales;
   var Salary;
run;

ods html close;
ods pdf close;
ods rtf close;
```

93 p111d13

Copyright © 2016, SAS Institute Inc., Cary, North Carolina, USA. ALL RIGHTS RESERVED.

ODS Statements

ALL can be used in the ODS CLOSE statement to close all open destinations.

```
ods html file="&path\example.html";
ods pdf file="&path\example.pdf";
ods rtf file="&path\example.rtf";

proc freq data=orion.sales;
   tables Country;
run;
proc means data=orion.sales;
   var Salary;
run;

ods _all_ close;
ods html;
```

A good habit is to open a destination such as HTML after you close all destinations.

94 p111d13

11.07 Short Answer Poll

What is the problem with this program?

```
ods listing file="&path\myreport.txt";

proc print data=orion.sales;
run;

ods close;
```

95 p111a05

Copyright © 2016, SAS Institute Inc., Cary, North Carolina, USA. ALL RIGHTS RESERVED.

ODS Results

An ODS statement with the FILE= option creates a physical file that can be viewed outside of SAS.

```
ods html file="&path\example.html";
ods pdf file="&path\example.pdf";
ods rtf file="&path\example.rtf";
```

For example, double-click the file in Windows Explorer to open the file in the appropriate application.

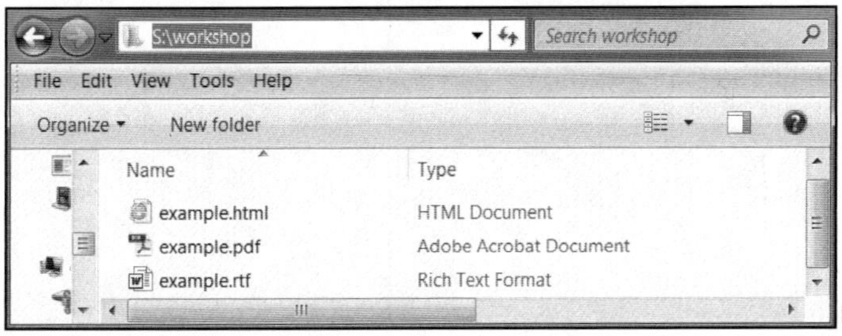

97 p111d13

ODS Results

In addition, the SAS interface can be used to access the file that was created with ODS statements.

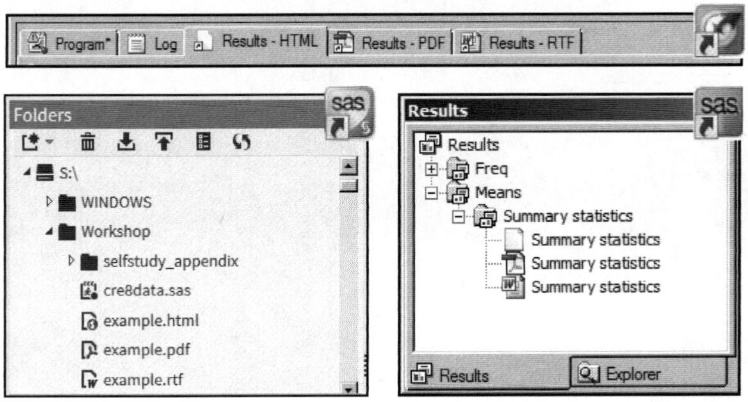

98

To access the ODS file, do the following:

- In SAS Enterprise Guide, click the download button on the Results tab.
- In SAS Studio, double-click the file in the Folders section of the navigation pane.
- In the SAS windowing environment, double-click the file in the expanded Results window.

Copyright © 2016, SAS Institute Inc., Cary, North Carolina, USA. ALL RIGHTS RESERVED.

STYLE=Option

Use a STYLE= option in the ODS statement to specify a style template.

```
ODS destination FILE="filename"
                STYLE=style-template;
```

- A *style template* sets presentation aspects including colors and fonts.

✎ STYLE= has no effect in the LISTING destination.

99

HTML Examples

The FREQ Procedure

Country	Frequency	Percent	Cumulative Frequency	Cumulative Percent
AU	63	38.18	63	38.18
US	102	61.82	165	100.00

STYLE=HTMLBLUE

STYLE=DEFAULT

The FREQ Procedure

Country	Frequency	Percent	Cumulative Frequency	Cumulative Percent
AU	63	38.18	63	38.18
US	102	61.82	165	100.00

The FREQ Procedure

Country	Frequency	Percent	Cumulative Frequency	Cumulative Percent
AU	63	38.18	63	38.18
US	102	61.82	165	100.00

STYLE=SASWEB

100 p111d14

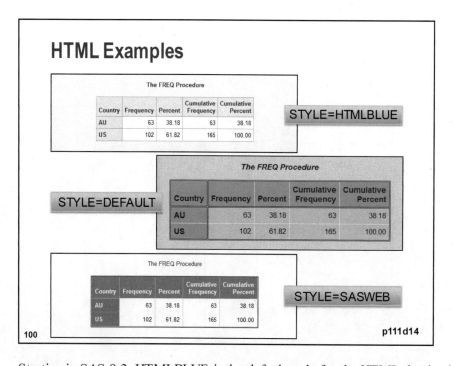

Starting in SAS 9.3, HTMLBLUE is the default style for the HTML destination.

Prior to SAS 9.3, DEFAULT is the default style for the HTML destination.

Copyright © 2016, SAS Institute Inc., Cary, North Carolina, USA. ALL RIGHTS RESERVED.

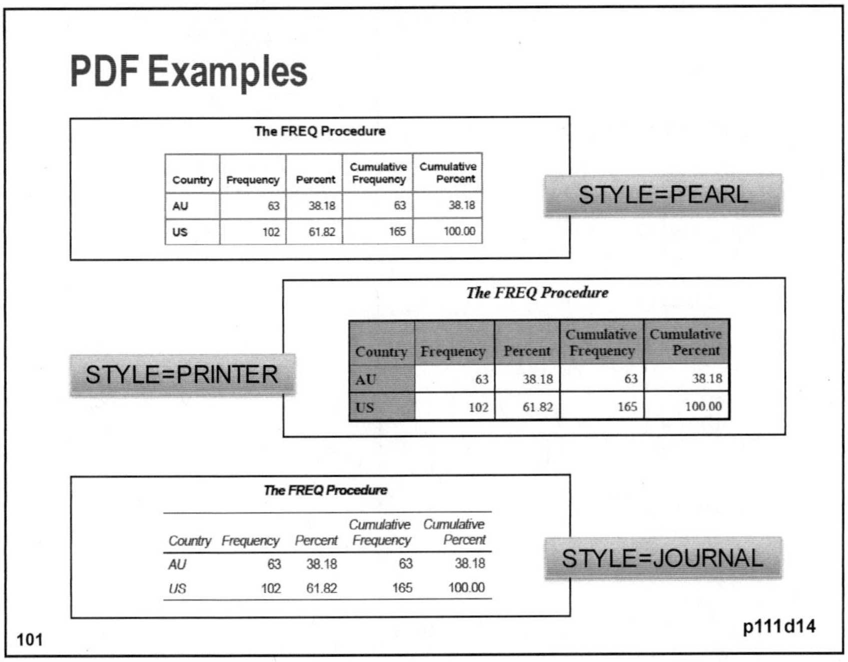

Starting in SAS 9.4, PEARL is the default style for the PDF destination.

Prior to SAS 9.4, PRINTER is the default style for the PDF destination.

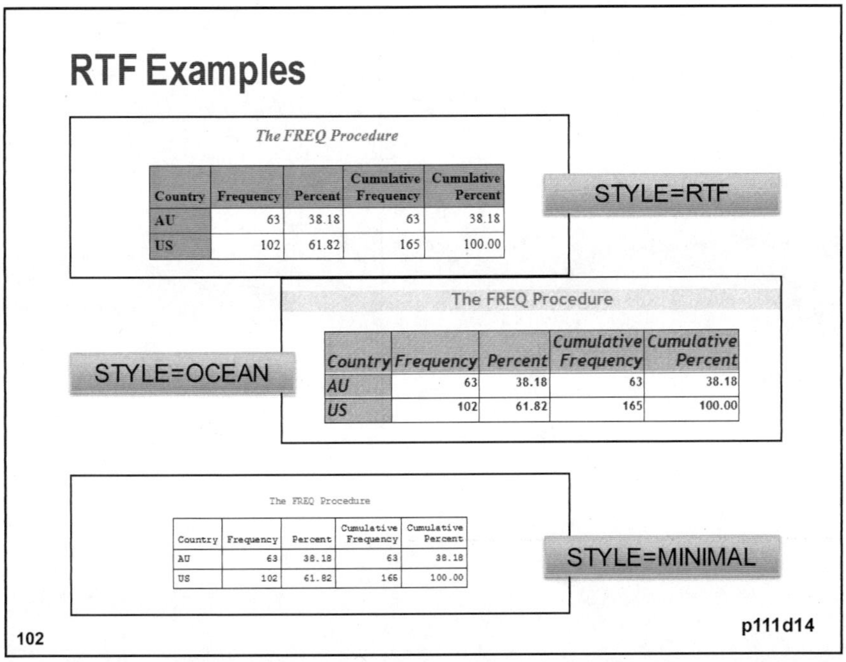

RTF is the default style for the RTF destination.

Copyright © 2016, SAS Institute Inc., Cary, North Carolina, USA. ALL RIGHTS RESERVED.

Available Styles

Use the TEMPLATE procedure to see a list of the available styles.

```
proc template;
   list styles;
run;
```

Partial Output

```
Listing of: SASHELP.TMPLMST
Path Filter is: Styles
Sort by: PATH/ASCENDING

Obs    Path                        Type
----------------------------------------
  1    Styles                      Dir
  2    Styles.Analysis             Style
  3    Styles.BarrettsBlue         Style
  4    Styles.BlockPrint           Style
  5    Styles.DTree                Style
  6    Styles.Daisy                Style
  7    Styles.Default              Style
```

103 p111d14

Business Scenario

Create SAS reports that can be opened in Microsoft Excel. Use the CSVALL, MSOFFICE2K, and EXCELXP destinations.

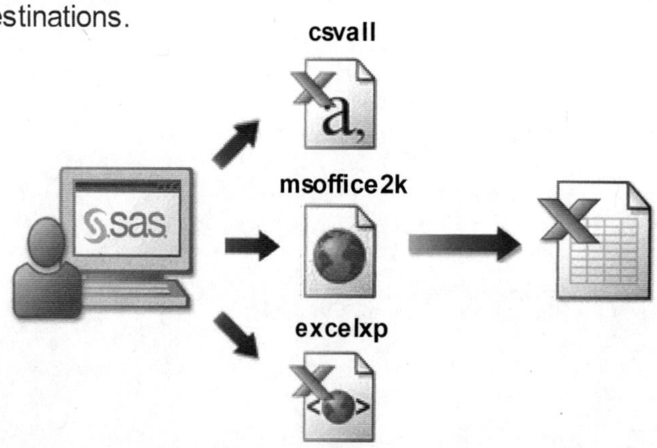

105

Copyright © 2016, SAS Institute Inc., Cary, North Carolina, USA. ALL RIGHTS RESERVED.

ODS Destinations Used with Excel

The following ODS destinations are used to create files that can be opened in Excel:

Destination	Type of File	Extension	Viewed In
CSVALL	Comma-Separated Value	.csv	Text Editor or Microsoft Excel
MSOFFICE2K	Hypertext Markup Language	.html	Microsoft Word or Microsoft Excel
TAGSETS. EXCELXP	Extensible Markup Language	.xml	Microsoft Excel

106

11.08 Short Answer Poll

Complete the ODS statements below to send the output to a CSVALL destination.

```
ods ______ file="&path\myexcel.___";

proc freq data=orion.sales;
   tables Country;
run;

proc means data=orion.sales;
   var Salary;
run;

ods ______ close;
```

107

Copyright © 2016, SAS Institute Inc., Cary, North Carolina, USA. ALL RIGHTS RESERVED.

CSVALL Destination

CSVALL does not include any style information.

example.csv

	A	B	C	D	E	F
1	The FREQ Procedure					
2	Country	Frequenc	Percent	Cumulativ	Cumulative Percent	
3	AU	63	38.18	63	38.18	
4	US	102	61.82	165	100	
5						
6	The MEANS Procedure					
7	Analysis Variable : Salary					
8	N	Mean	Std Dev	Minimum	Maximum	
9	165	31160.12	20082.67	22710	243190	

example

109 p111d15

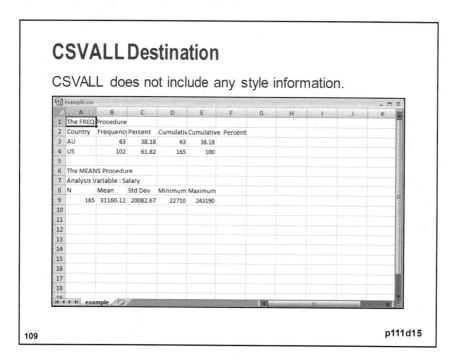

MSOFFICE2K Destination

MSOFFICE2K keeps the style information, including spanning headers.

example.html

The FREQ Procedure

Country	Frequency	Percent	Cumulative Frequency	Cumulative Percent
AU	63	38.18	63	38.18
US	102	61.82	165	100

The MEANS Procedure

Analysis Variable : Salary				
N	Mean	Std Dev	Minimum	Maximum
165	31160.12	20082.67	22710	243190

example

110 p111d15

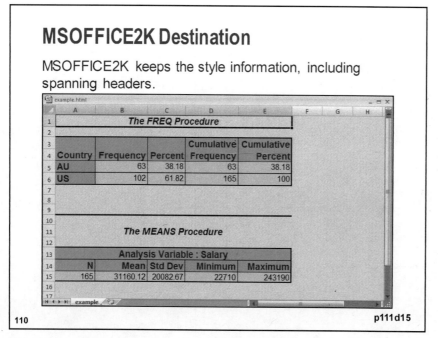

Copyright © 2016, SAS Institute Inc., Cary, North Carolina, USA. ALL RIGHTS RESERVED.

EXCELXP Destination

EXCELXP keeps the style information. Output from each procedure is on a separate sheet.

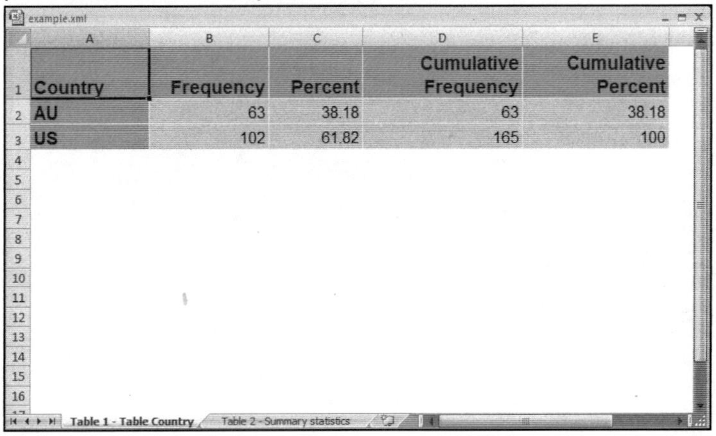

Country	Frequency	Percent	Cumulative Frequency	Cumulative Percent
AU	63	38.18	63	38.18
US	102	61.82	165	100

111 p111d15

XLS Extension

An XLS extension can be used in place of the CSV, HTML, or XML extension in order to open the file in Excel from within SAS.

```
ods csvall file="&path\myexcela.xls";
ods msoffice2k file="&path\myexcelb.xls";
ods tagsets.excelxp file="&path\myexcelc.xls";
```

Excel warns you that the file is not an XLS file.

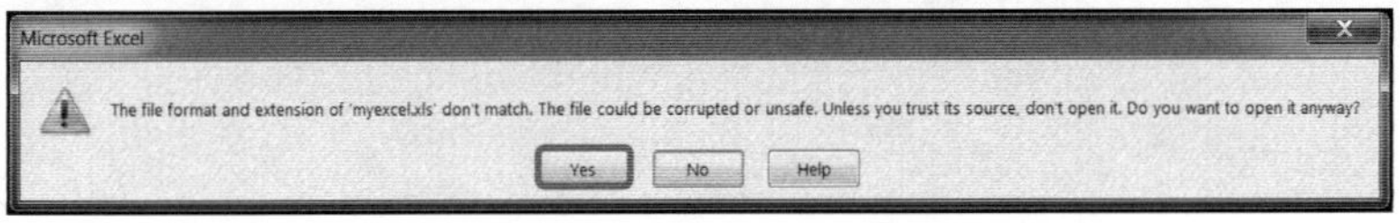

112

Copyright © 2016, SAS Institute Inc., Cary, North Carolina, USA. ALL RIGHTS RESERVED.

Using the Output Delivery System

Creating HTML, PDF, and RTF Files

1. Open and submit **p111d16**.

```
options nodate nonumber;
title; footnote;

ods listing; /* Output window in SAS Windowing Environment */
ods html file="&path\myreport.html";
ods pdf file="&path\myreport.pdf";
ods rtf file="&path\myreport.rtf";

title 'Report 1';
proc freq data=orion.sales;
   tables Country;
run;

title 'Report 2';
proc means data=orion.sales;
   var Salary;
run;

title 'Report 3';
proc print data=orion.sales;
   var First_Name Last_Name
       Job_Title Country Salary;
   where Salary > 75000;
run;

ods _all_ close;
ods html; /* SAS Windowing Environment */
```

2. View the HTML, PDF, and RTF files in the appropriate application outside of your SAS session. The LISTING file can be viewed in the Output window of the SAS windowing environment.

Creating CSV, HTML, and XML Files That Open in Excel

1. Open and submit **p111d17**.

```
options nodate nonumber;
title; footnote;

ods csvall file="&path\myexcela.xls";
ods msoffice2k file="&path\myexcelb.xls";
ods tagsets.excelxp file="&path\myexcelc.xls";

title 'Report 1';
proc freq data=orion.sales;
```

Copyright © 2016, SAS Institute Inc., Cary, North Carolina, USA. ALL RIGHTS RESERVED.

```
   tables Country;
run;

title 'Report 2';
proc means data=orion.sales;
   var Salary;
run;

title 'Report 3';
proc print data=orion.sales;
   var First_Name Last_Name
       Job_Title Country Salary;
   where Salary > 75000;
run;

ods _all_ close;
ods html; /* SAS Windowing Environment */
```

2. View the CSV, HTML, and XML files in Microsoft Excel. Select **Yes** to open the files when you are prompted about the file format and extension not matching.

End of Demonstration

Copyright © 2016, SAS Institute Inc., Cary, North Carolina, USA. ALL RIGHTS RESERVED.

Exercises

Level 1

12. Directing Output to PDF and RTF Destinations

a. Retrieve the starter program **p111e12**.

b. Add ODS statements to create a PDF file with the following naming convention:

Windows	"&path\p111e12.pdf"
UNIX	"&path/p111e12.pdf"

c. Submit the program and view the PDF output in Adobe Reader.

d. Add additional ODS statements to create an RTF file with the following naming convention:

Windows	"&path\p111e12.rtf"
UNIX	"&path/p111e12.rtf"

e. Submit the program and view the RTF output in Microsoft Word.

f. Add the STYLE= option to the ODS PDF statement to use the Curve style template, and add the STYLE= option to the ODS RTF statement to use the Journal style template.

g. Submit the program and view the output in Adobe Reader and Microsoft Word.

Level 2

13. Directing Output to the EXCELXP Destination

a. Retrieve the starter program **p111e13**.

b. Add ODS statements to create an XML output with the following naming convention:

Windows	"&path\p111e13.xls"
UNIX	"&path/p111e13.xls"

c. Add the STYLE= option to the ODS statement to use the Listing style template.

d. Submit the program and view the XML output in Microsoft Excel. Select **Yes** to open the files when you are prompted about the file format and extension not matching.

Challenge

14. Adding Options to the EXCELXP Destination

a. Retrieve the starter program **p111e14**.

Copyright © 2016, SAS Institute Inc., Cary, North Carolina, USA. ALL RIGHTS RESERVED.

b. Submit the program and view the XML output in Microsoft Excel. Select **Yes** to open the files when you are prompted about the file format and extension not matching.

c. In the log, view the documentation for the EXCELXP destination.

d. Add EMBEDDED_TITLES= and SHEET_NAME= options to create the following output:

p111e14.xls

	A	B	C	D	
1			Customer Type Definitions		
2					
3	Obs	Customer_Type_ID	Customer_Type	Customer_Group_ID	Cust
4	1	1010	Orion Club members inactive	10	Orior
5	2	1020	Orion Club members low activity	10	Orior
6	3	1030	Orion Club members medium activity	10	Orior
7	4	1040	Orion Club members high activity	10	Orior
8	5	2010	Orion Club Gold members low activity	20	Orior
9	6	2020	Orion Club Gold members medium activity	20	Orior
10	7	2030	Orion Club Gold members high activity	20	Orior
11	8	3010	Internet/Catalog Customers	30	Intern
12					
13					

First Report | Second Report

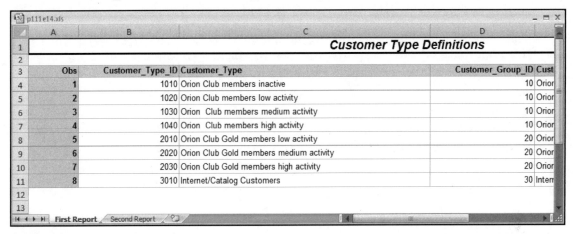

End of Exercises

Copyright © 2016, SAS Institute Inc., Cary, North Carolina, USA. ALL RIGHTS RESERVED.

11.4 Solutions

Solutions to Exercises

1. **Counting Levels of a Variable with PROC FREQ**

   Would you expect to see frequencies of 1 for customers and sales employees? **No. This file contains all customer orders, and the ID of the employee who helped with the sale. Employee_ID is likely to have higher frequency counts, as would frequent customers.**

```
title1 'Unique Customers and Salespersons for Retail Sales';
proc freq data=orion.orders nlevels;
   where Order_Type=1;
   tables Customer_ID Employee_ID / noprint;
run;
title;
title1 'Catalog and Internet Customers';
proc freq data=orion.orders order=freq;
   where Order_Type ne 1;
   tables Customer_ID / nocum;
run;
title;
```

2. **Validating orion.shoes_tracker with PROC FREQ**

```
proc freq data=orion.shoes_tracker nlevels;
   tables Supplier_Name Supplier_ID;
run;
```

   What invalid data exists for **Supplier_Name** and **Supplier_ID**?

   - **two observations with invalid values for Supplier_Name (*3op Sports*)**
   - **one observation with a missing value for Supplier_ID**

3. **Producing Frequency Reports with PROC FREQ**

```
proc format;
   value ordertypes
         1='Retail'
         2='Catalog'
         3='Internet';
run;

title 'Order Summary by Year and Type';
proc freq data=orion.orders;
   tables Order_Date;
   tables Order_Type / nocum;
   tables Order_Date*Order_Type / nopercent norow nocol;
   format Order_Date year4. Order_Type ordertypes.;
run;
title;
```

Copyright © 2016, SAS Institute Inc., Cary, North Carolina, USA. ALL RIGHTS RESERVED.

4. **Validating orion.qtr2_2011 with PROC FREQ**

```
proc freq data=orion.qtr2_2011 nlevels;
   tables Order_ID Order_Type;
run;
```

What invalid data exists for **Order_ID** and **Order_Type**?

- **two observations with missing values for Order_ID**
- **one observation with a value of *0* for Order_Type**
- **one observation with a value of *4* for Order_Type**

5. **Creating an Output Data Set with PROC FREQ**

```
proc freq data=orion.order_fact noprint;
   tables Product_ID / out=product_orders;
run;

data product_names;
   merge product_orders orion.product_list;
   by Product_ID;
   keep Product_ID Product_Name Count;
run;

proc sort data=product_names;
   by descending Count;
run;

title 'Top Five Products by Number of Orders';
proc print data=product_names(obs=5) label noobs;
   var Count Product_ID Product_Name;
   label Product_ID='Product Number'
         Product_Name='Product'
         Count='Orders';
run;
title;
```

6. **Creating a Summary Report with PROC MEANS**

```
proc format;
   value ordertypes
      1='Retail'
      2='Catalog'
      3='Internet';
run;

title 'Revenue from All Orders';
proc means data=orion.order_fact sum;
   var Total_Retail_Price;
   class Order_Date Order_Type;
   format Order_Date year4. Order_Type ordertypes.;
run;
title;
```

7. **Validating orion.price_current with the UNIVARIATE Procedure**

Copyright © 2016, SAS Institute Inc., Cary, North Carolina, USA. ALL RIGHTS RESERVED.

```
proc univariate data=orion.price_current;
   var Unit_Sales_Price Factor;
run;
```

Find the Extreme Observations output.

- How many values of **Unit_Sales_Price** are over the maximum of 800? **one (*5730*)**
- How many values of **Factor** are under the minimum of 1? **one (*0.01*)**
- How many values of **Factor** are over the maximum of 1.05? **two (*10.20* and *100.00*)**

8. Analyzing Missing Numeric Values with PROC MEANS

```
title 'Number of Missing and Non-Missing Date Values';
proc means data=orion.staff nmiss n nonobs;
   var Birth_Date Emp_Hire_Date Emp_Term_Date;
   class Gender;
run;
title;
```

9. Validating orion.shoes_tracker with the UNIVARIATE Procedure

```
proc univariate data=orion.shoes_tracker;
   var Product_ID;
run;
```

How many values of **Product_ID** are too small? **one (*2.20200E+10*)**

How many values of **Product_ID** are too large? **one (*2.2020E+12*)**

10. Creating an Output Data Set with PROC MEANS

```
proc means data=orion.order_fact noprint nway;
   class Product_ID;
   var Total_Retail_Price;
   output out=product_orders sum=Product_Revenue;
run;

data product_names;
   merge product_orders orion.product_list;
   by Product_ID;
   keep Product_ID Product_Name Product_Revenue;
run;

proc sort data=product_names;
   by descending Product_Revenue;
run;

title 'Top Five Products by Revenue';
proc print data=product_names(obs=5) label;
   var Product_Revenue Product_ID Product_Name;
   label Product_ID='Product Number'
         Product_Name='Product'
         Product_Revenue='Revenue';
   format Product_Revenue eurox12.2;
```

Copyright © 2016, SAS Institute Inc., Cary, North Carolina, USA. ALL RIGHTS RESERVED.

```
run;
title;
```

11. Selecting Only the Extreme Observations Output from the UNIVARIATE Procedure

```
ods trace on;
ods select ExtremeObs;
proc univariate data=orion.shoes_tracker;
   var Product_ID;
run;

ods trace off;
```

What is the name of the last output added in the SAS log? **ExtremeObs**

12. Directing Output to PDF and RTF Destinations

```
ods pdf file="&path\p111e12.pdf" style=curve;
ods rtf file="&path\p111e12.rtf" style=journal;

title 'July 2011 Orders';
proc print data=orion.mnth7_2011;
run;

ods pdf close;
ods rtf close;
```

13. Directing Output to EXCELXP Destination

```
ods tagsets.excelxp file="&path\p111e13.xls" style=Listing;

title 'Customer Type Definitions';
proc print data=orion.customer_type;
run;

title 'Country Definitions';
proc print data=orion.country;
run;

ods tagsets.excelxp close;
```

Copyright © 2016, SAS Institute Inc., Cary, North Carolina, USA. ALL RIGHTS RESERVED.

14. Adding Options to the EXCELXP Destination

```
ods tagsets.excelxp file="&path\p111e14.xls"
                    style=Listing
                    options(doc='help'
                            embedded_titles='yes'
                            sheet_name='First Report');

title 'Customer Type Definitions';
proc print data=orion.customer_type;
run;

ods tagsets.excelxp options(sheet_name='Second Report');

title 'Country Definitions';
proc print data=orion.country;
run;

ods tagsets.excelxp close;
```

End of Solutions

Copyright © 2016, SAS Institute Inc., Cary, North Carolina, USA. ALL RIGHTS RESERVED.

Solutions to Student Activities (Polls/Quizzes)

11.01 Short Answer Poll – Correct Answer

What change was needed? **A slash is required before the options in the TABLES statement.**

```
31   proc freq data=orion.sales;
32        tables country nocum nopercent;
ERROR: Variable NOCUM not found.
ERROR: Variable NOPERCENT not found.
33   run;
```

```
proc freq data=orion.sales;
   tables country / nocum nopercent;
run;
```

```
The FREQ Procedure
Country    Frequency

AU                63
US               102
```

11

p111a01s

11.02 Short Answer Poll – Correct Answer

What problems exist with the data in this partial data set?

Employee_ID	First	Last	Gender	Salary	Job_Title	Country
120101	Patrick	Lu	M	163040	Director	AU
120104	Kareen	Billington	F	46230	Administration Manager	au
120105	Liz	Povey	F	27110	Secretary I	AU
120106	John	Hornsey	M	.	Office Assistant II	AU
120107	Sherie	Sheedy	F	30475	Office Assistant III	AU
120108	Gladys	Gromek	F	27660	Warehouse Assistant II	AU
120108	Gabriele	Baker	F	26495	Warehouse Assistant I	AU
120110	Dennis	Entwisle	M	28615	Warehouse Assistant III	AU
120111	Ubaldo	Spillane	M	26895	Security Guard II	AU
120112	Ellis	Glattback	F	26550		AU
120113	Riu	Horsey	F	26870	Security Guard II	AU
120114	Jeannette	Buddery	G	31285	Security Manager	AU
120115	Hugh	Nichollas	M	2650	Service Assistant I	AU
.	Austen	Ralston	M	29250	Service Assistant II	AU
120117	Bill	Mccleary	M	31670	Cabinet Maker III	AU
120118	Darshi	Hartshorn	M	28090	Cabinet Maker II	AU

Hint: There are seven data problems.

28

Copyright © 2016, SAS Institute Inc., Cary, North Carolina, USA. ALL RIGHTS RESERVED.

11.03 Short Answer Poll – Correct Answer

How many unique, nonmissing job titles exist? **124**

Which job title occurs most frequently? **Trainee**

What is the frequency of missing job titles? **1**

```
proc freq data=orion.nonsales2 nlevels
          order=freq;
   tables Job_Title /nocum nopercent;
run;
```

40 p111a02s

11.04 Short Answer Poll – Correct Answer

Can user-defined formats be used to group data? **yes**

The FREQ Procedure

Salary	Frequency	Percent	Cumulative Frequency	Cumulative Percent
Tier1	1	0.61	1	0.61
Tier2	158	95.76	159	96.36
Tier3	4	2.42	163	98.79
Tier4	2	1.21	165	100.00

48 p111a03s

Copyright © 2016, SAS Institute Inc., Cary, North Carolina, USA. ALL RIGHTS RESERVED.

11.05 Short Answer Poll – Correct Answer

For a given data set, there are 63 observations with a **Country** value of *AU*. Of those 63 observations, only 61 observations have a value for **Salary**.

Which output is correct?

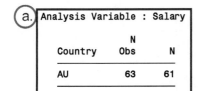

(a.) Analysis Variable : Salary

Country	N Obs	N
AU	63	61

b. Analysis Variable : Salary

Country	N Obs	N
AU	61	63

65

11.06 Short Answer Poll – Correct Answer

PROC UNIVARIATE identified two observations with **Salary** values less than 24,000.

What procedure can be used to display the observations that contain the invalid values? **PROC PRINT**

```
proc print data=orion.nonsales2;
   where Salary<24000;
run;
```

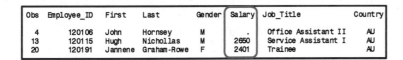

Obs	Employee_ID	First	Last	Gender	Salary	Job_Title	Country
4	120106	John	Hornsey	M	.	Office Assistant II	AU
13	120115	Hugh	Nichollas	M	2650	Service Assistant I	AU
20	120191	Jannene	Graham-Rowe	F	2401	Trainee	AU

p111a04s

83

Copyright © 2016, SAS Institute Inc., Cary, North Carolina, USA. ALL RIGHTS RESERVED.

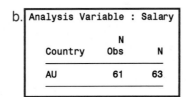

11.07 Short Answer Poll – Correct Answer

What is the problem with this program?

```
ods listing file="&path\myreport.txt";

proc print data=orion.sales;
run;

ods listing close;
```

96 p111a05s

11.08 Short Answer Poll – Correct Answer

Complete the ODS statements below to send the output to a CSVALL destination.

```
ods csvall file="&path\myexcel.csv";

proc freq data=orion.sales;
   tables Country;
run;

proc means data=orion.sales;
   var Salary;
run;

ods csvall close;
```

108 p111a06s

Copyright © 2016, SAS Institute Inc., Cary, North Carolina, USA. ALL RIGHTS RESERVED.

Chapter 12 Learning More

Copyright © 2016, SAS Institute Inc., Cary, North Carolina, USA. ALL RIGHTS RESERVED.

12.1 Introduction

Objectives

- Identify the areas of support that SAS offers.
- Identify the next steps after the completion of this course.

2

Customer Support

SAS provides a variety of resources to help customers.

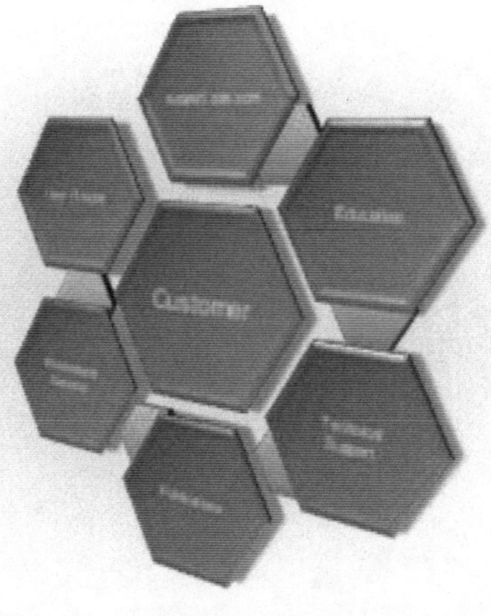

http://support.sas.com/resourcekit/

3

Copyright © 2016, SAS Institute Inc., Cary, North Carolina, USA. ALL RIGHTS RESERVED.

Education

SAS Education provides comprehensive training, including

- more than 200 course offerings
- world-class instructors
- multiple delivery methods
- worldwide training centers.

http://support.sas.com/training/

4

SAS Global Certification Program

SAS Education also provides

- globally recognized certifications
- preparation materials
- practice exams.

http://support.sas.com/certify/

5

Copyright © 2016, SAS Institute Inc., Cary, North Carolina, USA. ALL RIGHTS RESERVED.

Networking

Social media channels and user group organizations enable you to

- interact with other SAS users and SAS staff
- learn new programming tips and tricks
- get exclusive discounts.

For training-specific information:

http://support.sas.com/training/socialmedia

6

The following icons are identified from top left to right, and then bottom left to right:

Twitter, RSS, Myspace, YouTube, Facebook, Technorati, and sasCommunity.org

SAS Books

Convenient. Practical. Enlightening.
Valuable insight with solid results.

Available in a variety of formats to best meet your needs:

- hard-copy books
- e-books
- PDF

www.sas.com/store/books

7

Copyright © 2016, SAS Institute Inc., Cary, North Carolina, USA. ALL RIGHTS RESERVED.

Beyond This Course

To grow your SAS skills, remember to activate the ***extended learning page*** for this course.

Individual learning software is available.

8

Next Steps

To learn more about this:	Enroll in this course:
Programming techniques, including DATA and PROC steps to manipulate data	SAS® Programming 2: Data Manipulation Techniques
How to use SQL to manipulate and merge data files	SAS® SQL 1: Essentials
Creating reports using the REPORT and TABULATE procedures, plus the Output Delivery System (ODS)	SAS® Report Writing 1: Essentials
Performing statistical analysis using SAS/STAT software	Statistics 1: Introduction to ANOVA, Regression, and Logistic Regression
How to use many of the most popular SAS functions	SAS® Functions by Example
A variety of techniques to find errors in your data	Data Cleaning Techniques

9

Copyright © 2016, SAS Institute Inc., Cary, North Carolina, USA. ALL RIGHTS RESERVED.

Appendix A Self-Study Topics

Copyright © 2016, SAS Institute Inc., Cary, North Carolina, USA. ALL RIGHTS RESERVED.

A.1 Submitting Programs in UNIX and z/OS

Objectives

- Use the SAS windowing environment in UNIX to open and submit a SAS program and browse the results.
- Use the SAS windowing environment on a z/OS mainframe to open and submit a SAS program and browse the results.

3

Copyright © 2016, SAS Institute Inc., Cary, North Carolina, USA. ALL RIGHTS RESERVED.

Submitting a Program in the SAS Windowing Environment: UNIX

p102d01

- Start a SAS session.
- Open and submit a SAS program.
- Examine the results.

Starting a SAS Session

In your UNIX session, enter the appropriate command to start a SAS session. The method that you use to invoke SAS varies by your operating environment and any customizations that are in effect at your site.

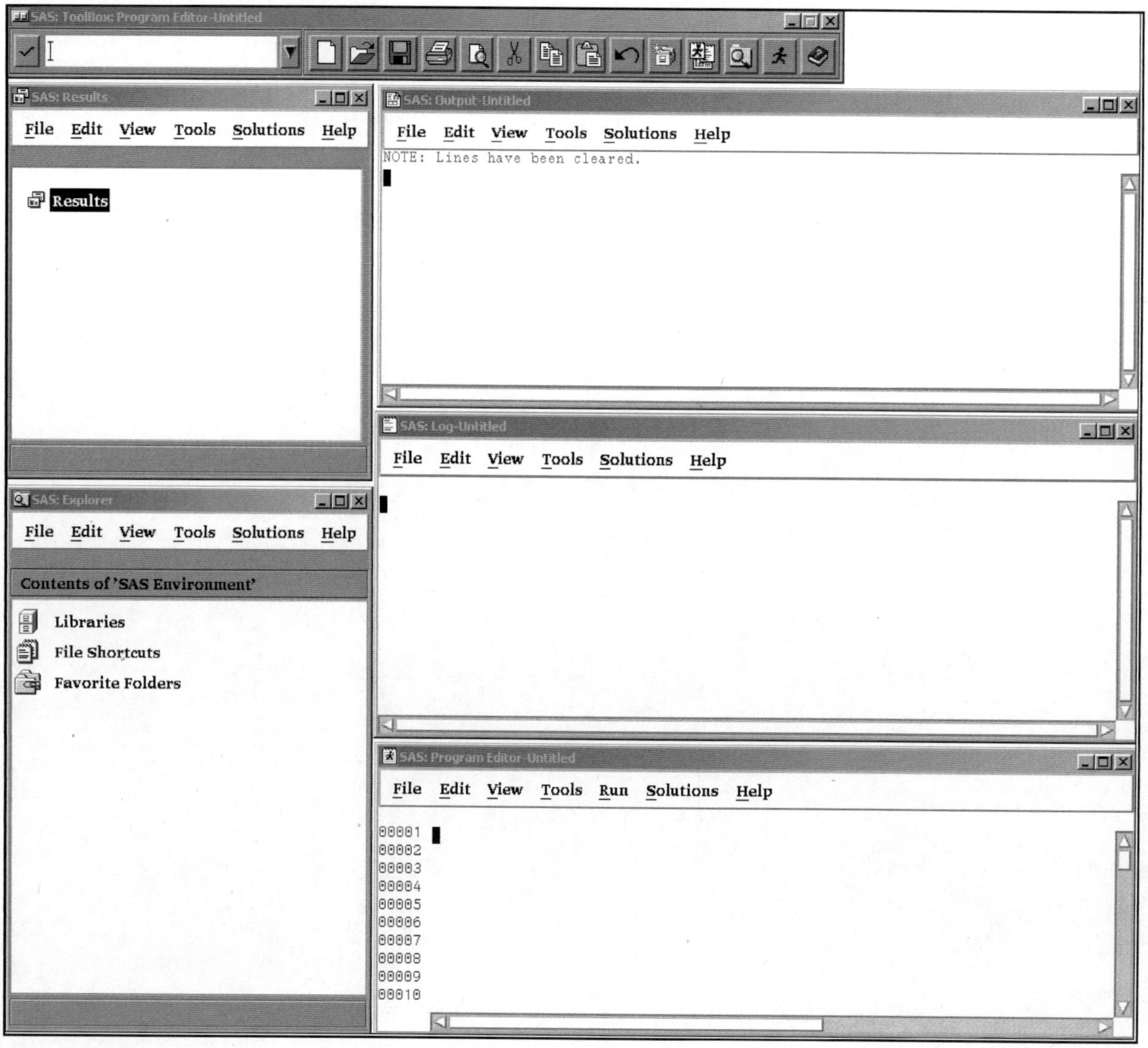

Copyright © 2016, SAS Institute Inc., Cary, North Carolina, USA. ALL RIGHTS RESERVED.

Including and Submitting a SAS Program

1. To open a SAS program, select **File** ⇨ **Open** or click and then select the file that you want to open.

   To open a program, your Program Editor must be active.

   You can also issue the INCLUDE command to open (include) a SAS program into your SAS session.

   With the Program Editor active, on the command bar, enter **include** and the name of the file that contains the program. Press Enter.

   The program is included in the Program Editor window.

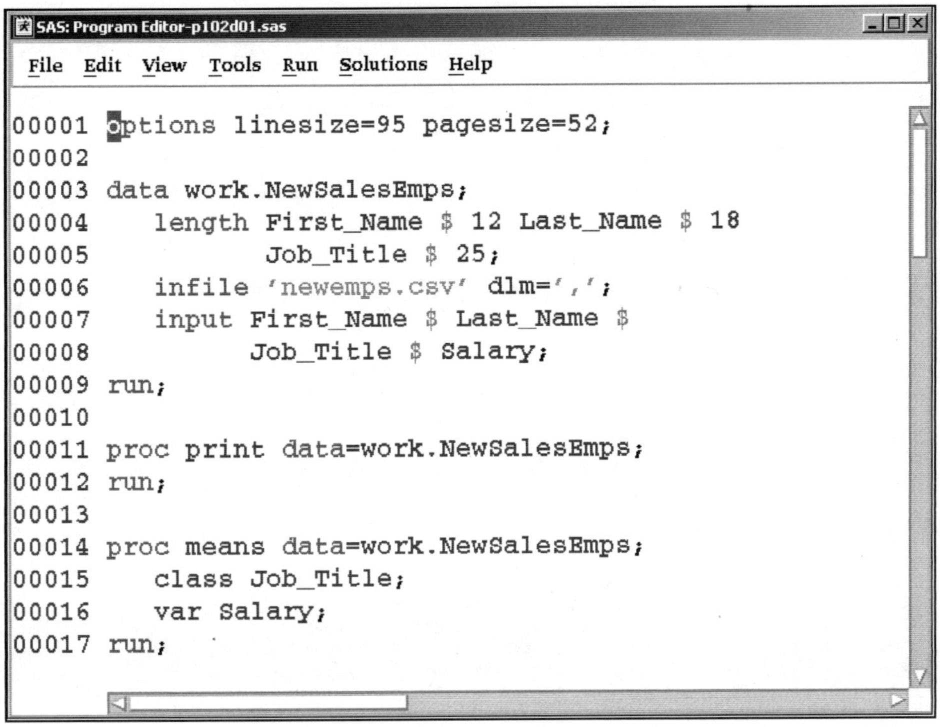

   You can use the Program Editor window to access and edit existing SAS programs, write new programs, submit programs, and save programs to a file.

   Within the Program Editor, the syntax in your program is color-coded to show step boundaries, keywords, and variable and data set names

2. To submit the program for execution, issue the SUBMIT command, click , or select **Run** ⇨ **Submit**. The output from the program is displayed in the Output window.

Examining the Results

The Output window is one of the primary windows and is open by default. It becomes the active window each time it receives output. Output automatically accumulates in the order in which it is generated.

To clear the contents of the window, issue the CLEAR command, select **Edit** ⇨ **Clear All**, or click .

Copyright © 2016, SAS Institute Inc., Cary, North Carolina, USA. ALL RIGHTS RESERVED.

To scroll horizontally in the Output window, use the horizontal scroll bar or issue the RIGHT and LEFT commands.

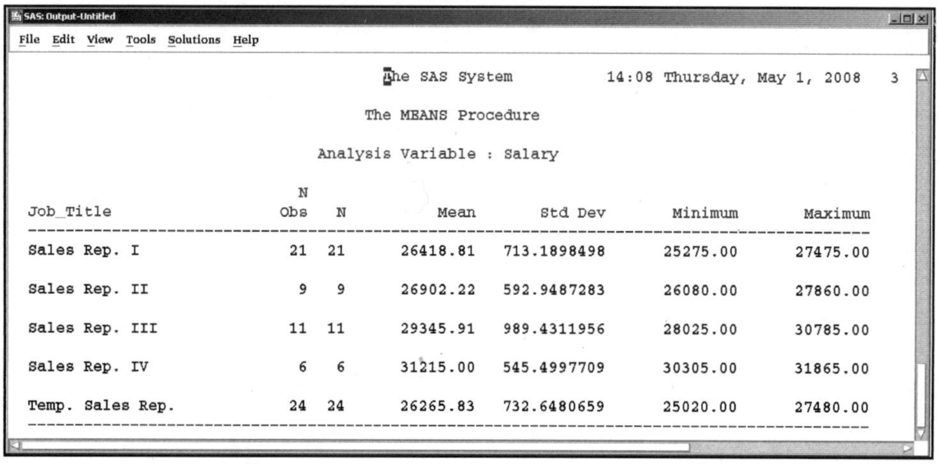

Job_Title	N Obs	N	Mean	Std Dev	Minimum	Maximum
Sales Rep. I	21	21	26418.81	713.1898498	25275.00	27475.00
Sales Rep. II	9	9	26902.22	592.9487283	26080.00	27860.00
Sales Rep. III	11	11	29345.91	989.4311956	28025.00	30785.00
Sales Rep. IV	6	6	31215.00	545.4997709	30305.00	31865.00
Temp. Sales Rep.	24	24	26265.83	732.6480659	25020.00	27480.00

To scroll vertically within the Output window, use the vertical scroll bar or issue the FORWARD and BACKWARD commands. The TOP and BOTTOM commands can also be used to scroll vertically.

1. Scroll to the top to view the output from the PRINT procedure.

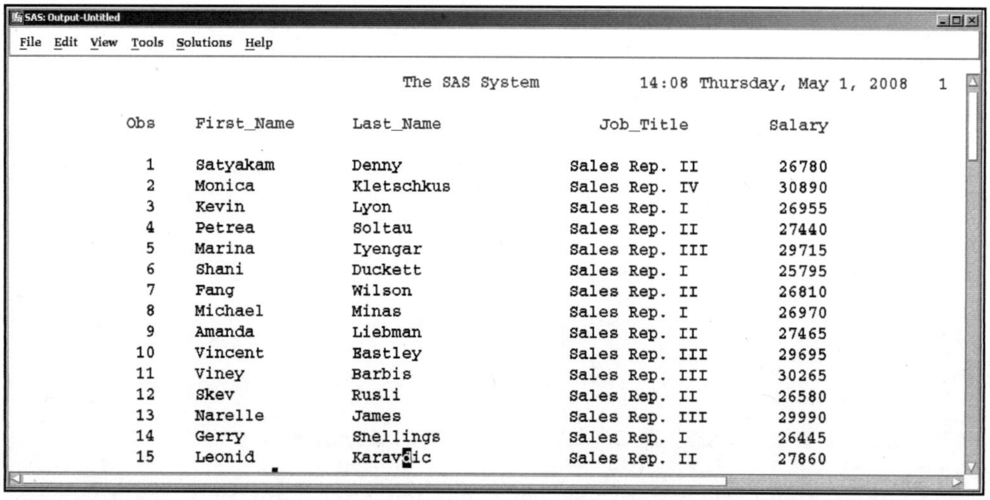

Obs	First_Name	Last_Name	Job_Title	Salary
1	Satyakam	Denny	Sales Rep. II	26780
2	Monica	Kletschkus	Sales Rep. IV	30890
3	Kevin	Lyon	Sales Rep. I	26955
4	Petrea	Soltau	Sales Rep. II	27440
5	Marina	Iyengar	Sales Rep. III	29715
6	Shani	Duckett	Sales Rep. I	25795
7	Fang	Wilson	Sales Rep. II	26810
8	Michael	Minas	Sales Rep. I	26970
9	Amanda	Liebman	Sales Rep. II	27465
10	Vincent	Eastley	Sales Rep. III	29695
11	Viney	Barbis	Sales Rep. III	30265
12	Skev	Rusli	Sales Rep. II	26580
13	Narelle	James	Sales Rep. III	29990
14	Gerry	Snellings	Sales Rep. I	26445
15	Leonid	Karavdic	Sales Rep. II	27860

2. To open the Log window and browse the messages that the program generated, issue the LOG command or select **View ⇨ Log**.

   The Log window is one of the primary windows and is open by default. It acts as a record of your SAS session. Messages are written to the log in the order in which they are generated by the program.

Copyright © 2016, SAS Institute Inc., Cary, North Carolina, USA. ALL RIGHTS RESERVED.

3. To clear the contents of the window, issue the CLEAR command, select **Edit** ⇨ **Clear All**, or click .

   The Log window contains the program statements that were most recently submitted. It also includes notes about the files that were read, the records that were read, and the program execution and results.

   In this example, the Log window contains no warning or error messages. If your program contains errors, relevant warning and error messages are also written to the SAS log.

4. Issue the END command or select **View** ⇨ **Program Editor** to return to the Program Editor window.

End of Demonstration

Copyright © 2016, SAS Institute Inc., Cary, North Carolina, USA. ALL RIGHTS RESERVED.

Submitting a Program in the SAS Windowing Environment: z/OS

workshop.sascode(p102d01)

- Start a SAS session.
- Open and submit a SAS program.
- Examine the results.

Starting a SAS Session

Enter the appropriate command to start your SAS session. The method that you use to invoke SAS varies by your operating environment and any customizations that are in effect at your site.

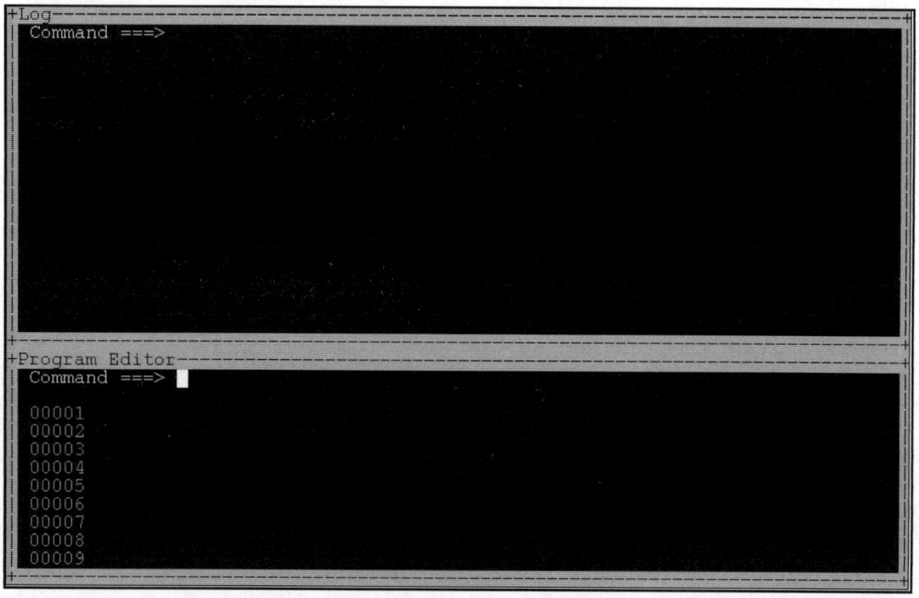

Including and Submitting a SAS Program

1. To include (copy) a SAS program into your SAS session, issue the INCLUDE command.

   a. Enter **include** and the name of the file that contains your program on the command line of the Program Editor.

   ```
   inc '.workshop.sascode(p102d01)'
   ```

   b. Press Enter.

Copyright © 2016, SAS Institute Inc., Cary, North Carolina, USA. ALL RIGHTS RESERVED.

```
+Program Editor----------------------------------------------------------+
 Command ===> inc '.workshop.sascode(p102d01)'
```

The program is included in the Program Editor.

```
+Program Editor----------------------------------------------------------+
 Command ===>

options linesize=95 pagesize=52;

data work.NewSalesEmps;
   length First_Name $ 12 Last_Name $ 18
          Job_Title $ 25;
   infile '.workshop.rawdata(newemps)' dlm=',';
   input First_Name $ Last_Name $
         Job_Title $ Salary;
run;

proc print data=work.NewSalesEmps;
run;

proc means data=work.NewSalesEmps;
   class Job_Title;
   var Salary;
run;
```

You can use the Program Editor to access and edit existing SAS programs, write new programs, submit programs, and save programming statements in a file.

This program contains three steps: a DATA step and two PROC steps.

2. Issue the SUBMIT command to execute your program.

   The first page of the output from your program is displayed in the Output window.

```
+Output--------------------------------------------------PROC PRINT suspended-+
 Command ===>
 NOTE: Procedure PRINT has created 1 page(s) of output so far.
                21     Alena          Moody                 Sales Rep. II
                22     Andrew         Conolly               Sales Rep. I
                23     Koavea         Pa                    Sales Rep. I
                24     Lorian         Cantatore             Temp. Sales Rep.
                25     Geok-Seng      Barreto               Temp. Sales Rep.
                26     Brig           Blanton               Temp. Sales Rep.
                27     Ari            Moore                 Temp. Sales Rep.
                28     Sharon         Bahlman               Temp. Sales Rep.
                29     Merryn         Quinby                Temp. Sales Rep.
                30     Reyne          Catenacci             Temp. Sales Rep.
                31     Shanmuganath   Baran                 Temp. Sales Rep.
                32     Mihailo        Lachlan               Temp. Sales Rep.
                33     Meera          Body                  Sales Rep. III
                34     Terrill        Jaime                 Sales Rep. IV
                35     William        Smades                Sales Rep. I
                36     Nasim          Smith                 Sales Rep. IV
                37     David          Anstey                Sales Rep. I
                38     Roger          Mandzak               Sales Rep. I
                39     Karen          Grzebien              Sales Rep. I
                40     Lawrie         Clark                 Sales Rep. I
                41     Perrior        Bataineh              Sales Rep. I
                42     Patricia       Capristo-Abramczyk    Sales Rep. II
                43     Richard        Fay                   Sales Rep. II
                44     Clement        Davis                 Sales Rep. III
                45     Debra          Armant                Sales Rep. IV
                46     Corneille      Malta                 Sales Rep. III
                47     Jeanilla       Macnair               Sales Rep. IV
                48     Agnieszka      Holthouse             Sales Rep. III
```

Copyright © 2016, SAS Institute Inc., Cary, North Carolina, USA. ALL RIGHTS RESERVED.

Examining the Results

The Output window is one of the primary windows and is open by default. It becomes the active window each time it receives output. Output automatically accumulates in the order in which it is generated.

You can issue the CLEAR command or select **Edit** ⇨ **Clear All** to clear the contents of the window.

To scroll horizontally in the Output window, issue the RIGHT and LEFT commands.

To scroll vertically in the Output window, issue the FORWARD and BACKWARD commands. The TOP and BOTTOM commands can also be used to scroll vertically within the Output window.

1. Issue the END command. If the PRINT procedure produces more than one page of output, you are taken to the last page of output. If the PRINT procedure produces only one page of output, the END command enables the MEANS procedure to execute and produce its output.

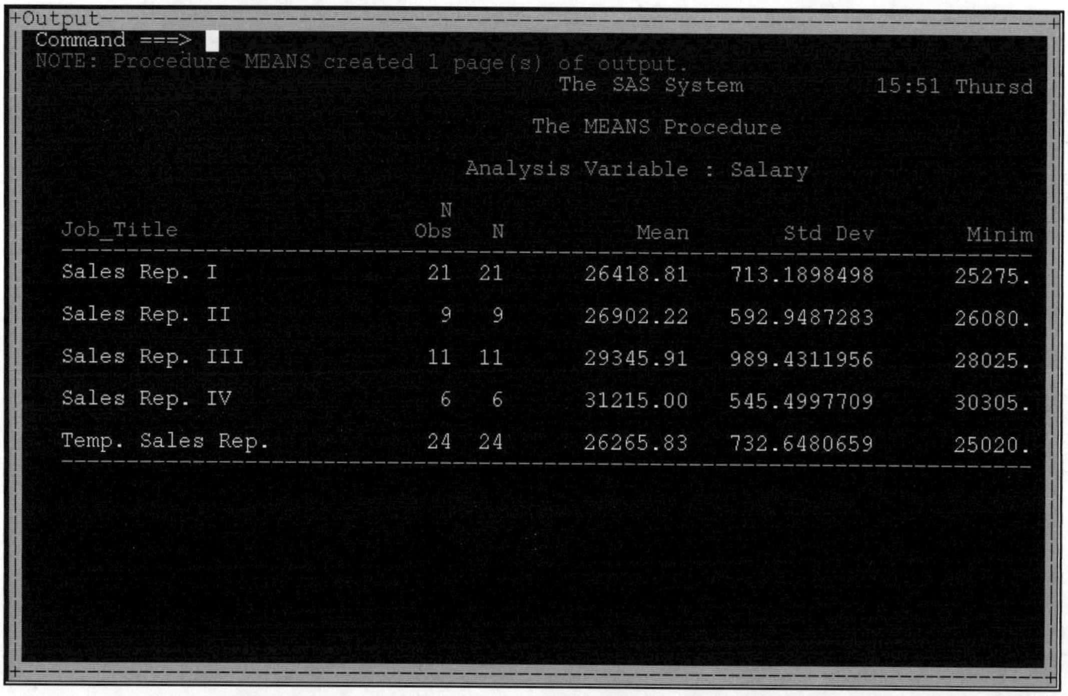

```
Output
Command ===>
NOTE: Procedure MEANS created 1 page(s) of output.
                                   The SAS System               15:51 Thursd

                                 The MEANS Procedure

                             Analysis Variable : Salary

                                  N
Job_Title                       Obs    N        Mean         Std Dev       Minim
--------------------------------------------------------------------------------
Sales Rep. I                     21   21    26418.81     713.1898498      25275.

Sales Rep. II                     9    9    26902.22     592.9487283      26080.

Sales Rep. III                   11   11    29345.91     989.4311956      28025.

Sales Rep. IV                     6    6    31215.00     545.4997709      30305.

Temp. Sales Rep.                 24   24    26265.83     732.6480659      25020.
--------------------------------------------------------------------------------
```

> You can issue an AUTOSCROLL 0 command on the command line of the Output window so that all of your SAS output from one submission is placed in the Output window at one time. This eliminates the need to issue an END command to run each step separately.
>
> The AUTOSCROLL command is in effect for the duration of your SAS session. If you want this every time you invoke SAS, you can save this setting by entering **autoscroll 0; wsave** on the command line of the Output window.

2. Issue the END command to return to the Program Editor.

   After the program executes, you can view messages in the Log window. The Log window is one of the primary windows and is open by default. It acts as a record of your SAS session. Messages are written to the log in the order in which they are generated by the program.

   You can issue the CLEAR command to clear the contents of the window.

Copyright © 2016, SAS Institute Inc., Cary, North Carolina, USA. ALL RIGHTS RESERVED.

The Log window contains the programming statements that were recently submitted, as well as notes about the files and records that were read, and the program execution and results.

In this example, the Log window contains no warning or error messages. If your program contains errors, relevant warning and error messages are also written to the SAS log.

3. Issue the END command to return to the Program Editor.

End of Demonstration

Copyright © 2016, SAS Institute Inc., Cary, North Carolina, USA. ALL RIGHTS RESERVED.

A.2 Accessing Data

Objectives

- Write to an Excel workbook as if it were a SAS library.
- Use the COPY procedure to copy an Excel worksheet to a SAS data set.
- Use the Import and Export Wizards and the IMPORT and EXPORT procedures to read and write external data.

7

Business Scenario

Use a DATA step to create an Excel worksheet from a SAS data set.

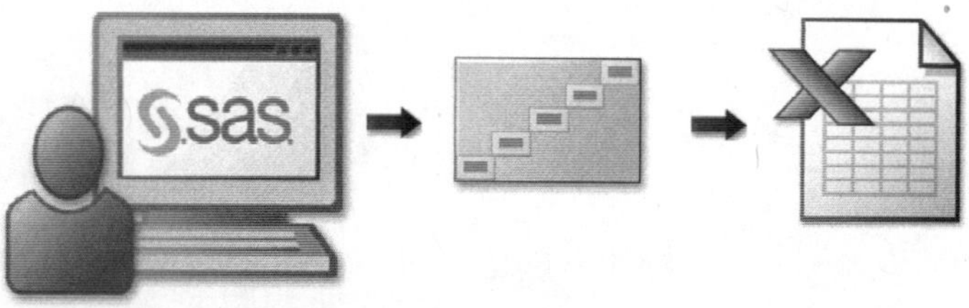

8

Copyright © 2016, SAS Institute Inc., Cary, North Carolina, USA. ALL RIGHTS RESERVED.

Creating Excel Worksheets

A SAS/ACCESS LIBNAME statement can be used in a program to create an Excel worksheet.

```
libname orionxls pcfiles
        path="&path\qtr2007a.xls";

data orionxls.qtr1_2007;
   set orion.qtr1_2007;
run;

data orionxls.qtr2_2007;
   set orion.qtr2_2007;
run;

proc contents data=orionxls._all_;
run;

libname orionxls clear;
```

workbook

Two worksheets are created.

9

p1aad01

⚠ Delete **qtr2007a.xls** if it already exists.

Creating Excel Worksheets

Partial SAS Log

```
70    data orionxls.qtr1_2007;
71       set orion.qtr1_2007;
72
73    run;

NOTE: SAS variable labels, formats, and lengths are not written to DBMS tables.
NOTE: There were 22 observations read from the data set ORION.QTR1_2007.
NOTE: The data set ORIONXLS.qtr1_2007 has 22 observations and 5 variables.

74    data orionxls.qtr2_2007;
75       set orion.qtr2_2007;
76    run;

NOTE: SAS variable labels, formats, and lengths are not written to DBMS tables.
NOTE: There were 36 observations read from the data set ORION.QTR2_2007.
NOTE: The data set ORIONXLS.qtr2_2007 has 36 observations and 6 variables.
```

10

Copyright © 2016, SAS Institute Inc., Cary, North Carolina, USA. ALL RIGHTS RESERVED.

Creating Excel Worksheets

Partial PROC CONTENTS Output

```
                The CONTENTS Procedure

                      Directory

    Libref            ORIONXLS
    Engine            EXCEL
    Physical Name     qtr2007a.xls
    User              Admin

                                  DBMS
                       Member     Member
    #   Name           Type       Type

    1   qtr1_2007      DATA       TABLE
    2   qtr1_2007$     DATA       TABLE
    3   qtr2_2007      DATA       TABLE
    4   qtr2_2007$     DATA       TABLE
```

workbook

worksheets

named ranges

11

Creating Excel Worksheets

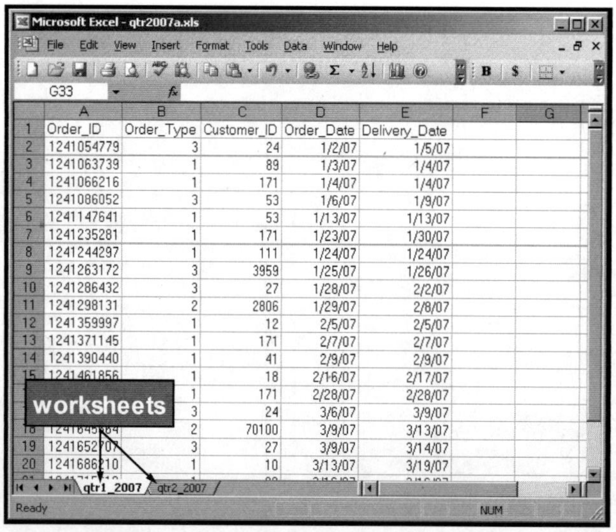

	A	B	C	D	E	F	G
1	Order_ID	Order_Type	Customer_ID	Order_Date	Delivery_Date		
2	1241054779	3	24	1/2/07	1/5/07		
3	1241063739	1	89	1/3/07	1/4/07		
4	1241066216	1	171	1/4/07	1/4/07		
5	1241086052	3	53	1/6/07	1/9/07		
6	1241147641	1	53	1/13/07	1/13/07		
7	1241235281	1	171	1/23/07	1/30/07		
8	1241244297	1	111	1/24/07	1/24/07		
9	1241263172	3	3959	1/25/07	1/26/07		
10	1241286432	3	27	1/28/07	2/2/07		
11	1241298131	2	2806	1/29/07	2/8/07		
12	1241359997	1	12	2/5/07	2/5/07		
13	1241371145	1	171	2/7/07	2/7/07		
14	1241390440	1	41	2/9/07	2/9/07		
15	1241461856	1	18	2/16/07	2/17/07		
[illegible]	[illegible]	1	171	2/28/07	2/28/07		
[illegible]	[illegible]	3	24	3/6/07	3/9/07		
18	[illegible]	2	70100	3/9/07	3/13/07		
19	[illegible]	3	27	3/9/07	3/14/07		
20	1241686210	1	10	3/13/07	3/19/07		

12

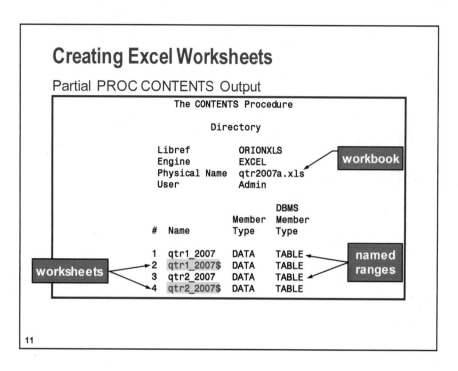

Copyright © 2016, SAS Institute Inc., Cary, North Carolina, USA. ALL RIGHTS RESERVED.

Business Scenario

Use the COPY procedure to create an Excel worksheet from a SAS data set.

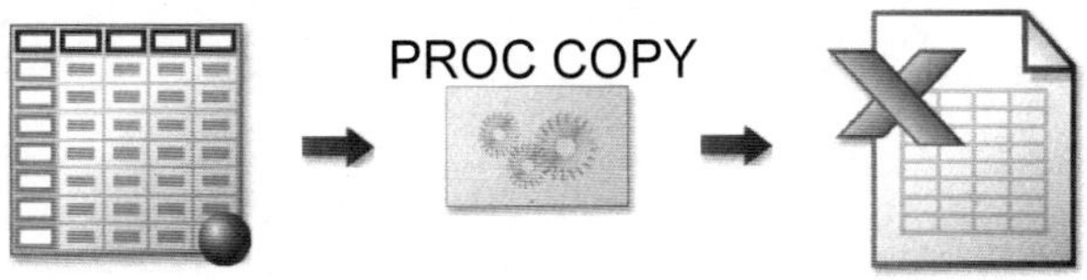

13

Creating Excel Worksheets

As an alternative to the DATA step, the COPY procedure can be used to create an Excel worksheet.

```
libname orionxls pcfiles
         path="&path\qtr2007b.xls";

proc copy in=orion out=orionxls;
   select qtr1_2007 qtr2_2007;
run;

proc contents data=orionxls._all_;
run;

libname orionxls clear;
```

14 p1aad01

⚠ Delete **qtr2007b.xls** if it already exists.

Copyright © 2016, SAS Institute Inc., Cary, North Carolina, USA. ALL RIGHTS RESERVED.

Creating Excel Worksheets

Partial SAS Log

```
82   proc copy  in=orion out=orionxls;
83      select qtr1_2007 qtr2_2007;
84   run;

NOTE: Copying ORION.QTR1_2007 to ORIONXLS.QTR1_2007 (memtype=DATA).
NOTE: SAS variable labels, formats, and lengths are not written to DBMS tables.
NOTE: There were 22 observations read from the data set ORION.QTR1_2007.
NOTE: The data set ORIONXLS.QTR1_2007 has 22 observations and 5 variables.
NOTE: Copying ORION.QTR2_2007 to ORIONXLS.QTR2_2007 (memtype=DATA).
NOTE: SAS variable labels, formats, and lengths are not written to DBMS tables.
NOTE: There were 36 observations read from the data set ORION.QTR2_2007.
NOTE: The data set ORIONXLS.QTR2_2007 has 36 observations and 6 variables.
```

15

Business Scenario

Use the Import and Export Wizards and the IMPORT and EXPORT procedures to read and create Microsoft Excel worksheets in SAS Enterprise Guide and in the SAS windowing environment.

16

Copyright © 2016, SAS Institute Inc., Cary, North Carolina, USA. ALL RIGHTS RESERVED.

Import and Export Wizards and Procedures

The Import and Export Wizards and the IMPORT and EXPORT procedures enable you to read and write data between SAS data sets and external files.

- The wizards and procedures are part of Base SAS.
- They enable access to delimited files.

17

Import and Export Wizards and Procedures

The SAS/ACCESS products enable the Import and Export Wizards and procedures to access other external file types.

For example, a license to SAS/ACCESS Interface to PC Files enables you to access Microsoft Excel, Microsoft Access, dBASE, JMP, Lotus 1-2-3, SPSS, Stata, and Paradox files.

18

Copyright © 2016, SAS Institute Inc., Cary, North Carolina, USA. ALL RIGHTS RESERVED.

Import and Export Wizards and Procedures

The Import and Export Wizards and procedures have similar capabilities. The wizards are point-and-click interfaces and the procedures are code based.

- To invoke the Import or Export Wizard in the SAS windowing environment, select **File** ⇨ **Import Data** or **File** ⇨ **Export Data**.
- To invoke the Import Wizard in SAS Enterprise Guide, select **File** ⇨ **Import Data** or select **Open** ⇨ **Data** and select the Excel workbook.
- To export a data set, open the data set and select the **Export** task from the Data Grid menu.

19

Import Wizard: SAS Windowing Environment

The Import Wizard enables you to read data from an external data source and write it to a SAS data set.

Follow these steps:

1. Select the type of file that you are importing.
2. Locate the input file.
3. Select the table range or worksheet from which to import data.
4. Select a location to store the imported file.

In the SAS windowing environment, you can save the generated PROC IMPORT code.

20

Select your data source from the drop-down list. If the installed versions of SAS and Microsoft Office have the same bit count, as described in the course notes, the default engine can be used. If the bit count is different, then you must use the PC Files Server. In this case, select **Microsoft Excel Workbook on PC Files Server** and enter **localhost** in the **Server Name** field. If your installation uses a remote PC Files Server, then you must enter the name of that server instead of **localhost**.

Copyright © 2016, SAS Institute Inc., Cary, North Carolina, USA. ALL RIGHTS RESERVED.

Import Wizard: SAS Enterprise Guide

The Import Wizard opens automatically when you select the file to import.

Follow these steps:

1. Specify the output data set name and location.
2. Specify the spreadsheet or named range and options for column names.
3. Modify column attributes and select columns.
4. Select advanced options if appropriate.

✎ SAS Enterprise Guide generates a DATA step that reads from the data source and creates a SAS data set.

21

Import Wizard

A note is written to the log and indicates success or failure.

Partial SAS Log

```
NOTE: WORK.SUBSET2A data set was successfully created.
```

Submit a PROC PRINT step to display the new data set.

```
proc print data=work.subset2a;
run;
```

Partial PROC PRINT Output

Obs	Employee_ID	First_Name	Last_Name	Gender	Salary	Job_Title	Country	Birth_Date	Hire_Date
1	120102	Tom	Zhou	M	108255	Sales Manager	AU	11AUG1969	01JUN1989
2	120103	Wilson	Dawes	M	87975	Sales Manager	AU	22JAN1949	01JAN1974
3	120121	Irenie	Elvish	F	26600	Sales Rep. II	AU	02AUG1944	01JAN1974
4	120122	Christina	Ngan	F	27475	Sales Rep. II	AU	27JUL1954	01JUL1978
5	120123	Kimiko	Hotstone	F	26190	Sales Rep. I	AU	28SEP1964	01OCT1985

22 p1aad02

Copyright © 2016, SAS Institute Inc., Cary, North Carolina, USA. ALL RIGHTS RESERVED.

Import Wizard

Use PROC CONTENTS to view the descriptor portion of the new data set.

```
proc contents data=work.subset2a;
run;
```

Partial PROC CONTENTS Output

Alphabetic List of Variables and Attributes

#	Variable	Type	Len	Format	Informat	Label
8	Birth_Date	Num	8	DATE9.	DATE9.	Birth Date
7	Country	Char	2	$2.	$2.	Country
1	Employee_ID	Num	8			Employee ID
2	First_Name	Char	10	$10.	$10.	First Name
4	Gender	Char	1	$1.	$1.	Gender
9	Hire_Date	Num	8	DATE9.	DATE9.	Hire Date
6	Job_Title	Char	14	$14.	$14.	Job Title
3	Last_Name	Char	12	$12.	$12.	Last Name
5	Salary	Num	8			Salary

23 p1aad02

IMPORT Procedure

The PROC IMPORT step below was created and saved using the Import Wizard and the PCFILES server in the SAS windowing environment.

```
PROC IMPORT OUT= WORK.subset2a
            DATAFILE="S:\Workshop\sales.xls"
            DBMS=EXCELCS REPLACE;
   SERVER="localhost";
   PORT=9621;
   SSPI=YES;
   RANGE="Australia$";
   SCANTEXT=YES;
   USEDATE=YES;
   SCANTIME=YES;
RUN;
```

24

The Import Wizard used the path that was in effect when this program was created. Your path might be different.

OUT=<*libref.*>*SAS-data-set*

identifies the output SAS data set.

DATAFILE="*filename*"

specifies the complete path and filename or a fileref for the input PC file, spreadsheet, or delimited external file.

Copyright © 2016, SAS Institute Inc., Cary, North Carolina, USA. ALL RIGHTS RESERVED.

DBMS=*identifier*

specifies the type of data to import. To import a DBMS table, you must specify DBMS= using a valid database identifier. For example, DBMS=EXCELCS specifies to import a Microsoft Excel worksheet.

REPLACE

overwrites an existing SAS data set. If you do not specify REPLACE, PROC IMPORT does not overwrite an existing data set.

RANGE="*range-name* | *absolute-range*"

subsets a spreadsheet by identifying the rectangular set of cells to import from the specified spreadsheet.

GETNAMES=YES | NO

for spreadsheets and delimited external files, determines whether to generate SAS variable names from the column names in the input file's first row of data. If a column name contains special characters that are not valid in a SAS name, such as a blank, SAS converts the character to an underscore.

MIXED=YES | NO

converts numeric data values into character data values for a column that contains mixed data types. The default is NO, which means that numeric data is imported as missing values in a character column. If MIXED=YES, then the engine assigns a SAS character type for the column and converts all numeric data values to character data values.

SCANTEXT=YES | NO

scans the length of text data for a data source column and uses the longest string of data that is found as the SAS column width.

USEDATE=YES | NO

specifies which format to use. If USEDATE=YES, then the DATE. format is used for date/time columns in the data source table when importing data from an Excel workbook. If USEDATE=NO, then a DATETIME. format is used for date/time.

SCANTIME=YES | NO

scans all row values for a DATETIME data type field and automatically determines the TIME data type if only time values (that is, no date or datetime values) exist in the column.

⚠ The GETNAMES= and MIXED= options are not supported by all SAS/ACCESS engines. See SAS Usage Note *41060* (**http://support.sas.com/kb/41/060.html**) for more information.

Copyright © 2016, SAS Institute Inc., Cary, North Carolina, USA. ALL RIGHTS RESERVED.

Export Wizard in SAS Windowing Environment

The Export Wizard reads data from a SAS data set and writes it to an external file source.

Follow these steps:

1. Select the data set from which you want to export data.
2. Select the type of data source to which you want to export the files.
3. Assign the output file.
4. Assign the table name.

In the SAS windowing environment, you can save the generated PROC EXPORT code.

25

Select your data source from the drop-down list. If the installed versions of SAS and Microsoft Office have the same bit count as described in the course notes, accept the default. If the bit count is different, then use the PC Files Server by selecting **Microsoft Excel Workbook on PC Files Server** and entering **localhost** in the **Server Name** field. If your installation uses a remote PC Files Server, then you need to enter the name of that server instead of **localhost**.

Export Wizard in SAS Enterprise Guide

Open the data set to be exported and select **Export** ⇨ **Export *name* As A Step In Project**.
The wizard starts automatically.

Follow these steps:

1. Select the file to export.
2. Select a file type for the output file.
3. Select a location and name for the output file.
4. Confirm the selections that you made and click **Finish**.

26

Copyright © 2016, SAS Institute Inc., Cary, North Carolina, USA. ALL RIGHTS RESERVED.

Export Wizard

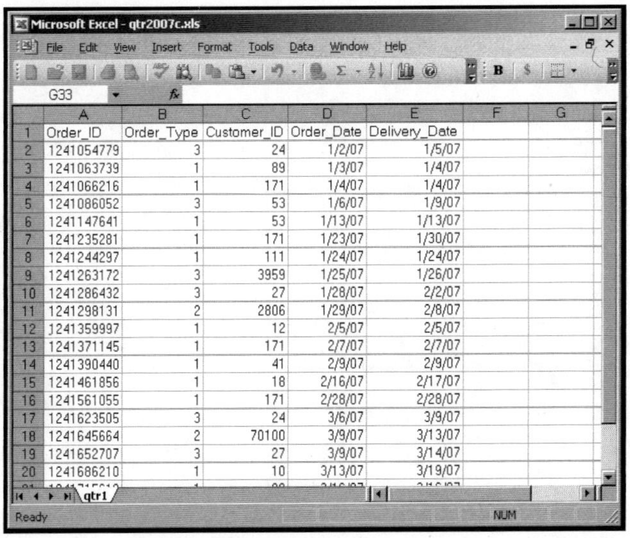

	A	B	C	D	E
1	Order_ID	Order_Type	Customer_ID	Order_Date	Delivery_Date
2	1241054779	3	24	1/2/07	1/5/07
3	1241063739	1	89	1/3/07	1/4/07
4	1241066216	1	171	1/4/07	1/4/07
5	1241086052	3	53	1/6/07	1/9/07
6	1241147641	1	53	1/13/07	1/13/07
7	1241235281	1	171	1/23/07	1/30/07
8	1241244297	1	111	1/24/07	1/24/07
9	1241263172	3	3959	1/25/07	1/26/07
10	1241286432	3	27	1/28/07	2/2/07
11	1241298131	2	2806	1/29/07	2/8/07
12	1241359997	1	12	2/5/07	2/5/07
13	1241371145	1	171	2/7/07	2/7/07
14	1241390440	1	41	2/9/07	2/9/07
15	1241461856	1	18	2/16/07	2/17/07
16	1241561055	1	171	2/28/07	2/28/07
17	1241623505	3	24	3/6/07	3/9/07
18	1241645664	2	70100	3/9/07	3/13/07
19	1241652707	3	27	3/9/07	3/14/07
20	1241686210	1	10	3/13/07	3/19/07

27

Copyright © 2016, SAS Institute Inc., Cary, North Carolina, USA. ALL RIGHTS RESERVED.

PROC EXPORT: SAS Windowing Environment

The PROC EXPORT step below was created and saved using the Export Wizard and the PCFILES server in the SAS windowing environment.

```
PROC EXPORT DATA= ORION.QTR1_2007
            OUTFILE="S:\Workshop\qtr2007c.xls"
            DBMS=EXCELCS REPLACE;
   SERVER="localhost";
   PORT=9621;
   SSPI=YES;
   SHEET="qtr1";
RUN;
```

The Export Wizard in SAS Enterprise Guide does not generate PROC EXPORT code.

28

The Export Wizard used the path that was in effect when this program was created. Your path might be different.

DATA=<*libref.*>*SAS-data-set*

identifies the input SAS data set.

OUTFILE="*filename*"

specifies the complete path and filename or a fileref for the output PC file, spreadsheet, or delimited external file.

DBMS=*identifier*

specifies the type of data to export. To export a DBMS table, you must specify DBMS= by using a valid database identifier. For example, DBMS=EXCELCS specifies to export a table into a Microsoft Excel worksheet.

Copyright © 2016, SAS Institute Inc., Cary, North Carolina, USA. ALL RIGHTS RESERVED.

Exercises

1. Using PROC COPY to Create an Excel Worksheet

a. Write a LIBNAME statement to create a libref named **mnth** that references a new Excel workbook named **mnth2011.xls**.

b. Write a PROC COPY step that copies **orion.mnth7_2011**, **orion.mnth8_2011**, and **orion.mnth9_2011** to the new Excel workbook.

c. Write a PROC CONTENTS step to view all of the contents of **mnth**.

d. Write a LIBNAME statement to clear the **mnth** libref.

2. Using the Import Wizard to Read an Excel Worksheet

a. Use the Import Wizard to read the **products.xls** workbook.

1) Select the worksheet that contains the children data.

2) Name the new data set **work.children**.

3) Save the generated PROC IMPORT code to a file named **children.sas**.

b. Write a PROC PRINT step to create a report of the new data set.

c. Open **children.sas** to view the PROC IMPORT code.

3. Using the EXPORT Procedure to Create an Excel Worksheet

a. Write a PROC EXPORT step to export the data set **orion.mnth7_2011** to an Excel workbook named **mnth7.xls**.

b. Submit the program and confirm in the log that the **mnth_2007** worksheet was successfully created in **mnth7.xls**.

End of Exercises

Copyright © 2016, SAS Institute Inc., Cary, North Carolina, USA. ALL RIGHTS RESERVED.

A.3 Manipulating Data

Objectives

- Create multiple data sets in a single DATA step.
- Explore the DROP= and KEEP= data set options.
- Use the APPEND procedure to combine two data sets.
- Interleave two or more data sets.
- Eliminate duplicate observations using PROC SORT.
- Compare a many-to-many merge with an SQL inner join.

31

Business Scenario

Write a DATA step that creates two data sets: one for valid observations and one for invalid observations. Direct observations to the appropriate data set based on **_ERROR_**.

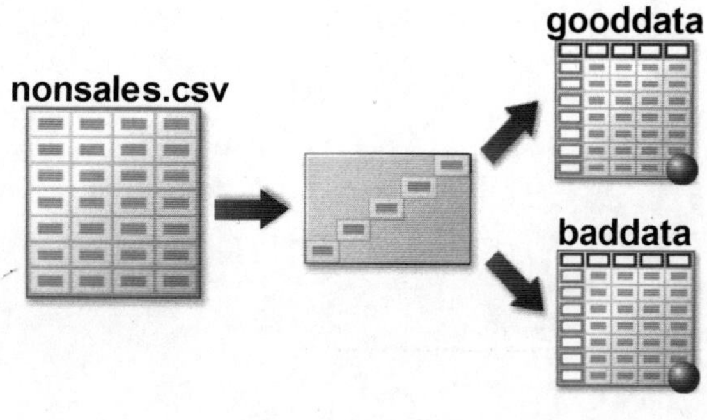

32

Copyright © 2016, SAS Institute Inc., Cary, North Carolina, USA. ALL RIGHTS RESERVED.

Creating Multiple Data Sets

The DATA statement can specify multiple output data sets.

```
data work.baddata work.gooddata;
   length Employee_ID 8 First $ 12 Last $ 18
          Gender $ 1 Salary 8 Job_Title $ 25
          Country $ 2 Birth_Date Hire_Date 8;
   infile "&path\nonsales.csv" dlm=',';
   input Employee_ID First $ Last $
         Gender $ Salary Job_Title $ Country $
         Birth_Date :date9.
         Hire_Date :date9.;
   format Birth_Date Hire_Date ddmmyy10.;
   if _error_=1 then output work.baddata;
   else output work.gooddata;
run;
```

33 p1aad03

Creating Multiple Data Sets

An *OUTPUT statement* writes the current observation to a specific data set that is listed in the DATA statement.

```
data work.baddata work.gooddata;
   length Employee_ID 8 First $ 12 Last $ 18
          Gender $ 1 Salary 8 Job_Title $ 25
          Country $ 2 Birth_Date Hire_Date 8;
   infile "&path\nonsales.csv" dlm=',';
   input Employee_ID First $ Last $
         Gender $ Salary Job_Title $ Country $
         Birth_Date :date9.
         Hire_Date :date9.;
   format Birth_Date Hire_Date ddmmyy10.;
   if _error_=1 then output work.baddata;
   else output work.gooddata;
run;
```

34 p1aad03

Copyright © 2016, SAS Institute Inc., Cary, North Carolina, USA. ALL RIGHTS RESERVED.

Creating Multiple Data Sets

Partial SAS Log

```
NOTE: Invalid data for Salary in line 4 23-29.
RULE:      ----+----1----+----2----+----3----+----4----+----5----+----6
4          120106,John,Hornsey,M,unknown,Office Assistant II,AU,23DEC19
      61  44,01JAN1974 72
Employee_ID=120106 First=John Last=Hornsey Gender=M Salary=.
Job_Title=Office Assistant II Country=AU Birth_Date=23/12/1944
Hire_Date=01/01/1974 _ERROR_=1 _N_=4
NOTE: Invalid data for Hire_Date in line 9 63-71.
9          120111,Ubaldo,Spillane,M,26895,Security Guard II,AU,23JUL194
      61  9,99NOV1978 71
Employee_ID=120111 First=Ubaldo Last=Spillane Gender=M Salary=26895
Job_Title=Security Guard II Country=AU Birth_Date=23/07/1949
Hire_Date=. _ERROR_=1 _N_=9
NOTE: 235 records were read from the infile
      's:\workshop\nonsales.csv'.
      The minimum record length was 55.
      The maximum record length was 82.
NOTE: The data set WORK.BADDATA has 2 observations and 9 variables.
NOTE: The data set WORK.GOODDATA has 233 observations and 9 variables.
```

35

Business Scenario

Explore the DROP= and KEEP= data set options and how they can be used instead of a DROP or KEEP statement.

36

Copyright © 2016, SAS Institute Inc., Cary, North Carolina, USA. ALL RIGHTS RESERVED.

DROP= and KEEP= Options

The DROP= and KEEP= data set options are alternatives to the DROP and KEEP statements. They can be specified in the DATA statement.

- The DROP= data set option in the DATA statement lists the variables to exclude from the output data set.

```
DATA output-SAS-data-set (DROP=variable-list);
```

- The KEEP= data set option in the DATA statement specifies the variables to write to the output data set.

```
DATA output-SAS-data-set (KEEP=variable-list);
```

37

DROP= and KEEP= Options

The DROP= and KEEP= data set options can also be placed in the SET statement to control which variables are read from the input data set.

- The DROP= data set option in the SET statement excludes the variables for processing in the PDV.

```
SET input-SAS-data-set (DROP=variable-list);
```

- The KEEP= data set option in the SET statement specifies the variables for processing in the PDV.

```
SET input-SAS-data-set (KEEP=variable-list);
```

38

Copyright © 2016, SAS Institute Inc., Cary, North Carolina, USA. ALL RIGHTS RESERVED.

DROP= and KEEP= Options

```
data work.comp(drop=Salary Hire_Date);
   set orion.sales(keep=Employee_ID First_Name
                         Last_Name Salary Hire_Date);
   Bonus=500;
   Compensation=sum(Salary,Bonus);
   BonusMonth=month(Hire_Date);
run;
```

orion.sales

Employee_ ID	First_ Name	Last_ Name	Gender	Salary	Job_ Title	Country	Birth_ Date	Hire_ Date

PDV

Employee_ ID	First_ Name	Last_ Name	Salary	Hire_ Date	Bonus	Compensation	BonusMonth

work.comp

Employee _ID	First_ Name	Last_ Name	Bonus	Compensation	BonusMonth

39 p1aad04

DROP= and KEEP= Options

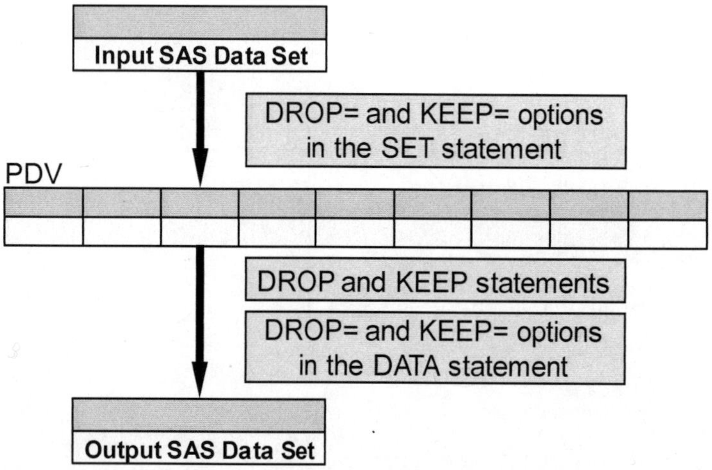

40

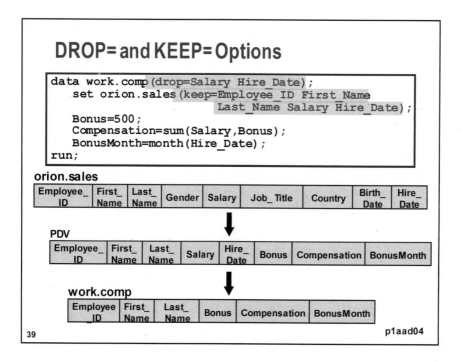

Copyright © 2016, SAS Institute Inc., Cary, North Carolina, USA. ALL RIGHTS RESERVED.

Business Scenario

Use the DELETE statement to select employees hired in December.

41

DELETE Statement

Use the DELETE statement in an IF-THEN statement as an alternative to a subsetting IF statement.

```
data work.december;
   set orion.sales;
   where Country='AU';
   BonusMonth=month(Hire_Date);
   if BonusMonth ne 12 then delete;
   Bonus=500;
   Compensation=sum(Salary,Bonus);
run;
```

IF ***expression*** **THEN DELETE;**

The *DELETE statement* stops processing the current observation.

42 p1aad04a

Copyright © 2016, SAS Institute Inc., Cary, North Carolina, USA. ALL RIGHTS RESERVED.

IF-THEN DELETE

```
data work.december;
   set orion.sales;
   where Country='AU';
   BonusMonth=month(Hire_Date);
   if BonusMonth ne 12 then delete;
   Bonus=500;
   Compensation=sum(Salary,Bonus);
run;
```

equivalent

```
data work.december;
   set orion.sales;
   where Country='AU';
   BonusMonth=month(Hire_Date);
   if BonusMonth=12;
   Bonus=500;
   Compensation=sum(Salary,Bonus);
run;
```

43 p1aad04a

Copyright © 2016, SAS Institute Inc., Cary, North Carolina, USA. ALL RIGHTS RESERVED.

Exercises

4. Using an IF-THEN/DELETE Statement to Subset Observations

a. Create a temporary data set named **work.bigdonations**. Use **orion.employee_donations** as input.

b. Create a new variable named **Total** that is equal to the sum of **Qtr1**, **Qtr2**, **Qtr3**, and **Qtr4**.

c. Create a new variable named **NoDonation** that is equal to the count of missing values in **Qtr1**, **Qtr2**, **Qtr3**, and **Qtr4**. Use the NMISS function.

d. The final data set should contain only observations that meet the following two conditions:
- **Total** values greater than or equal to 50
- **NoDonation** values equal to 0

Use an IF-THEN/DELETE statement to eliminate the observations when the conditions are not met.

e. Write a PROC PRINT step to create the report below. The results should contain 50 observations.

Partial PROC PRINT Output

Obs	Employee_ID	Qtr1	Qtr2	Qtr3	Qtr4	Total	No Donation
1	120267	15	15	15	15	60	0
2	120269	20	20	20	20	80	0
3	120271	20	20	20	20	80	0
4	120275	15	15	15	15	60	0
5	120660	25	25	25	25	100	0

End of Exercises

Copyright © 2016, SAS Institute Inc., Cary, North Carolina, USA. ALL RIGHTS RESERVED.

A.4 Combining Data Sets

Objectives

- Append one SAS data set to another. Use the APPEND procedure.
- Append unlike-structured data sets. Use the FORCE option.
- Compare the APPEND procedure to the SET statement.
- Interleave two or more data sets. Use the SET and BY statements in a DATA step.
- Eliminate duplicate observations with the SORT procedure.
- Create multiple data sets based on matches and nonmatches during a merge.
- Compare the results of a many-to-many merge with a DATA step and the SQL procedure.

46

Business Scenario

Update a master data set by appending observations from other data sets.

emps

First	Gender	HireYear
Stacey	F	2006
Gloria	F	2007
James	M	2007

Append observations to an existing data set.

47

Copyright © 2016, SAS Institute Inc., Cary, North Carolina, USA. ALL RIGHTS RESERVED.

APPEND Procedure

The *APPEND procedure* adds the observations from one SAS data set to the end of another SAS data set.

```
PROC APPEND BASE=SAS-data-set
            DATA=SAS-data-set;
RUN;
```

BASE= names the data set to which observations are added.

DATA= names the data set containing observations that are added to the base data set.

48

APPEND Procedure

Requirements:

- Only two data sets can be used at a time in one step.
- The observations in the base data set are not read.
- The variable information in the descriptor portion of the base data set cannot change.

49

Copyright © 2016, SAS Institute Inc., Cary, North Carolina, USA. ALL RIGHTS RESERVED.

Business Scenario

emps is a master data set that contains employees hired in 2006 and 2007.

emps

First	Gender	HireYear
Stacey	F	2006
Gloria	F	2007
James	M	2007

50

Business Scenario

emps is a master data set that contains employees hired in 2006 and 2007.

emps

First	Gender	HireYear
Stacey	F	2006
Gloria	F	2007
James	M	2007

The employees hired in 2008, 2009, and 2010 need to be appended.

emps2008

First	Gender	HireYear
Brett	M	2008
Renee	F	2008

emps2009

First	HireYear
Sara	2009
Dennis	2009

emps2010

First	HireYear	Country
Rose	2010	Spain
Eric	2010	Spain

51

Copyright © 2016, SAS Institute Inc., Cary, North Carolina, USA. ALL RIGHTS RESERVED.

Like-Structured Data Sets

emps

First	Gender	HireYear
Stacey	F	2006
Gloria	F	2007
James	M	2007

emps2008

First	Gender	HireYear
Brett	M	2008
Renee	F	2008

The data sets contain the same variables.

```
proc append base=emps
            data=emps2008;
run;
```

52

p1aad05

Like-Structured Data Sets

```
84   proc append base=emps
85               data=emps2008;
86   run;

NOTE: Appending WORK.EMPS2008 to WORK.EMPS.
NOTE: There were 2 observations read from the data set
      WORK.EMPS2008.
NOTE: 2 observations added.
NOTE: The data set WORK.EMPS has 5 observations and 3 variables.
```

emps

First	Gender	HireYear
Stacey	F	2006
Gloria	F	2007
James	M	2007
Brett	M	2008
Renee	F	2008

53

Copyright © 2016, SAS Institute Inc., Cary, North Carolina, USA. ALL RIGHTS RESERVED.

Unlike-Structured Data Sets

emps

First	Gender	HireYear
Stacey	F	2006
Gloria	F	2007
James	M	2007
Brett	M	2008
Renee	F	2008

emps2009

First	HireYear
Sara	2009
Dennis	2009

The BASE= data set has a variable that is not in the DATA= data set.

```
proc append base=emps
            data=emps2009;
run;
```

54 p1aad05

Unlike-Structured Data Sets

```
90   proc append base=emps
91               data=emps2009;
92   run;

NOTE: Appending WORK.EMPS2009 to WORK.EMPS.
WARNING: Variable Gender was not found on DATA file.
NOTE: There were 2 observations read from the data set
      WORK.EMPS2009.
NOTE: 2 observations added.
NOTE: The data set WORK.EMPS has 7 observations and 3 variables.
```

emps

First	Gender	HireYear
Stacey	F	2006
Gloria	F	2007
James	M	2007
Brett	M	2008
Renee	F	2008
Sara		2009
Dennis		2009

55

Copyright © 2016, SAS Institute Inc., Cary, North Carolina, USA. ALL RIGHTS RESERVED.

Unlike-Structured Data Sets

emps

First	Gender	HireYear
Stacey	F	2006
Gloria	F	2007
James	M	2007
Brett	M	2008
Renee	F	2008
Sara		2009
Dennis		2009

emps2010

First	HireYear	Country
Rose	2010	Spain
Eric	2010	Spain

The DATA= data set has a variable that is not in the BASE= data set.

```
proc append base=emps
            data=emps2010;
run;
```

56 p1aad05

Unlike-Structured Data Sets

```
96   proc append base=emps
97               data=emps2010;
98   run;

NOTE: Appending WORK.EMPS2010 to WORK.EMPS.
WARNING: Variable Country was not found on BASE file. The
         variable will not be added to the BASE file.
WARNING: Variable Gender was not found on DATA file.
ERROR: No appending done because of anomalies listed above.
       Use FORCE option to append these files.
NOTE: 0 observations added.
NOTE: The data set WORK.EMPS has 7 observations and 3 variables.
NOTE: Statements not processed because of errors noted above.

NOTE: The SAS System stopped processing this step because of
      errors.
```

57

Copyright © 2016, SAS Institute Inc., Cary, North Carolina, USA. ALL RIGHTS RESERVED.

Unlike-Structured Data Sets

The *FORCE option* forces the observations to be appended when the DATA= data set contains variables that are not in the BASE= data set.

```
proc append base=emps
            data=emps2010 force;
run;
```

PROC APPEND BASE=*SAS-data-set*
DATA=*SAS-data-set* **FORCE;**
RUN;

The FORCE option causes the extra variables to be dropped and issues a warning message.

58 p1aad05

The FORCE option is needed when the DATA= data set contains variables that either

- are not in the BASE= data set
- do not have the same type as the variables in the BASE= data set
- are longer than the variables in the BASE= data set.

If the length of a variable is longer in the DATA= data set than in the BASE= data set, SAS truncates values from the DATA= data set to fit them into the length that is specified in the BASE= data set.

If the type of a variable in the DATA= data set is different than in the BASE= data set, SAS replaces all values for the variable in the DATA= data set with missing values and keeps the variable type of the variable specified in the BASE= data set.

Copyright © 2016, SAS Institute Inc., Cary, North Carolina, USA. ALL RIGHTS RESERVED.

Unlike-Structured Data Sets

```
100  proc append base=emps
101              data=emps2010 force;
102  run;

NOTE: Appending WORK.EMPS2010 to WORK.EMPS.
WARNING: Variable Country was not found on BASE file. The
         variable will not be added to the BASE file.
WARNING: Variable Gender was not found on DATA file.
NOTE: FORCE is specified, so dropping/truncating will occur.
NOTE: There were 2 observations read from the data set
      WORK.EMPS2010.
NOTE: 2 observations added.
NOTE: The data set WORK.EMPS has 9 observations and 3 variables.
```

59

Unlike-Structured Data Sets

emps

First	Gender	HireYear
Stacey	F	2006
Gloria	F	2007
James	M	2007
Brett	M	2008
Renee	F	2008
Sara		2009
Dennis		2009
Rose		2010
Eric		2010

60

Copyright © 2016, SAS Institute Inc., Cary, North Carolina, USA. ALL RIGHTS RESERVED.

Unlike-Structured Data Sets

Situation	Action
The BASE= data set contains a variable that is not in the DATA= data set.	The observations are appended, but the observations from the DATA= data set have a missing value for the variable that was not present in the DATA= data set. The FORCE option is not necessary in this case.
The DATA= data set contains a variable that is not in the BASE= data set.	Use the FORCE option in the PROC APPEND statement to force the concatenation of the two data sets. The statement drops the extra variable and issues a warning message.

61

Appending to a Master File

Submitting this program once appends six observations to the **emps** data set, which results in a total of nine observations.

```
proc append base=emps
            data=emps2008;
run;
proc append base=emps
            data=emps2009;
run;
proc append base=emps
            data=emps2010 force;
run;
```

3 obs + 2 obs = 5 obs

5 obs + 2 obs = 7 obs

7 obs + 2 obs = 9 obs

62

Copyright © 2016, SAS Institute Inc., Cary, North Carolina, USA. ALL RIGHTS RESERVED.

Appending to a Master File

If the program is submitted a second time, there are 15 observations in **emps**.

```
proc append base=emps
            data=emps2008;
run;
proc append base=emps
            data=emps2009;
run;
proc append base=emps
            data=emps2010 force;
run;
```

9 obs + 2 obs = 11 obs

11 obs + 2 obs = 13 obs

13 obs + 2 obs = 15 obs

⚠ Observations are added to the BASE= data set every time you submit the program.

63

APPEND Procedure versus SET Statement

- The data set that results from concatenating two data sets with the SET statement is the same data set that results from concatenating them with the APPEND procedure if the two data sets contain the same variables.
- The APPEND procedure concatenates much faster than the SET statement because the APPEND procedure does not process the observations from the BASE= data set.
- The two methods are significantly different when the variables differ between data sets.

64

Copyright © 2016, SAS Institute Inc., Cary, North Carolina, USA. ALL RIGHTS RESERVED.

APPEND Procedure versus SET Statement

Criterion	APPEND Procedure	SET Statement
Number of data sets that you can concatenate	Uses two data sets	Uses any number of data sets
Handling of data sets that contain different variables	Uses all variables in the BASE= data set and assigns missing values to observations from the DATA= data set where appropriate; cannot include variables found only in the DATA= data set	Uses all variables and assigns missing values where appropriate

65

Business Scenario

Interleave two sorted data sets vertically so that the resulting data set is also sorted.

empscn

First	Gender	Country
Chang	M	China
Li	M	China
Ming	F	China

+

empsjp

First	Gender	Region
Cho	F	Japan
Tomi	M	Japan

→

empsall2

First	Gender	Country
Chang	M	China
Cho	F	Japan
Li	M	China
Ming	F	China
Tomi	M	Japan

66

Copyright © 2016, SAS Institute Inc., Cary, North Carolina, USA. ALL RIGHTS RESERVED.

Interleaving

Interleaving intersperses observations from two or more data sets, based on one or more common variables.
The SET statement with a BY statement in a DATA step interleaves SAS data sets.

```
DATA SAS-data-set;
    SET SAS-data-set1 SAS-data-set2 . . .;
    BY <DESCENDING> BY-variable(s);
    <additional SAS statements>
RUN;
```

⚠ The data sets must be sorted by the BY variable.

67

Typically, it is more efficient to sort small SAS data sets and then interleave them rather than concatenating several SAS data sets and then sorting the resultant larger file.

Interleaving

empscn

First	Gender	Country
Chang	M	China
Li	M	China
Ming	F	China

empsjp

First	Gender	Region
Cho	F	Japan
Tomi	M	Japan

Which value comes first?

Chang

```
data empsall2;
   set empscn empsjp(rename=(Region=Country));
   by First;
run;
```

BY <DESCENDING> *BY-variable(s)*;

PDV

First	Gender	Country
Chang	M	China

68 p1aad06 ...

Copyright © 2016, SAS Institute Inc., Cary, North Carolina, USA. ALL RIGHTS RESERVED.

Interleaving

empscn

First	Gender	Country
Chang	M	China
Li	M	China
Ming	F	China

empsjp

First	Gender	Region
Cho	F	Japan
Tomi	M	Japan

Which value comes first?

Cho

Reinitialize PDV

```
data empsall2;
   set empscn empsjp(rename=(Region=Country));
   by First;
run;
```

The PDV is reinitialized when switching to a different data set.

PDV

First	Gender	Country

69 ...

Interleaving

empscn

First	Gender	Country
Chang	M	China
Li	M	China
Ming	F	China

empsjp

First	Gender	Region
Cho	F	Japan
Tomi	M	Japan

Which value comes first?

Cho

```
data empsall2;
   set empscn empsjp(rename=(Region=Country));
   by First;
run;
```

PDV

First	Gender	Country
Cho	F	Japan

70 ...

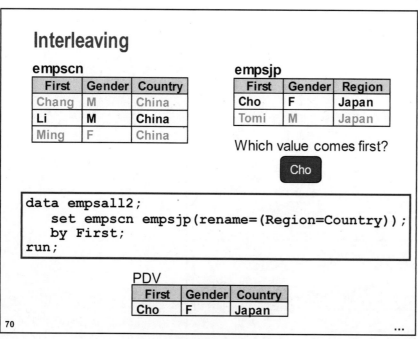

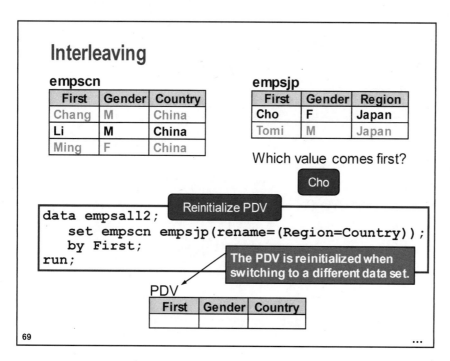

Copyright © 2016, SAS Institute Inc., Cary, North Carolina, USA. ALL RIGHTS RESERVED.

Interleaving

empscn

First	Gender	Country
Chang	M	China
Li	M	China
Ming	F	China

empsjp

First	Gender	Region
Cho	F	Japan
Tomi	M	Japan

Which value comes first?

Li

Reinitialize PDV

```
data empsall2;
   set empscn empsjp(rename=(Region=Country));
   by First;
run;
```

PDV

First	Gender	Country

71 ...

Interleaving

empscn

First	Gender	Country
Chang	M	China
Li	M	China
Ming	F	China

empsjp

First	Gender	Region
Cho	F	Japan
Tomi	M	Japan

Which value comes first?

Li

```
data empsall2;
   set empscn empsjp(rename=(Region=Country));
   by First;
run;
```

PDV

First	Gender	Country
Li	M	China

72 ...

Copyright © 2016, SAS Institute Inc., Cary, North Carolina, USA. ALL RIGHTS RESERVED.

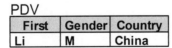

Interleaving

empscn

First	Gender	Country
Chang	M	China
Li	M	China
Ming	F	China

empsjp

First	Gender	Region
Cho	F	Japan
Tomi	M	Japan

Which value comes first?

Ming

```
data empsall2;
   set empscn empsjp(rename=(Region=Country));
   by First;
run;
```

PDV

First	Gender	Country
Ming	F	China

73

...

Interleaving

empscn

First	Gender	Country
Chang	M	China
Li	M	China
Ming	F	China

EOF

empsjp

First	Gender	Region
Cho	F	Japan
Tomi	M	Japan

Which value comes first?

Tomi

Reinitialize PDV

```
data empsall2;
   set empscn empsjp(rename=(Region=Country));
   by First;
run;
```

PDV

First	Gender	Country

74

...

Copyright © 2016, SAS Institute Inc., Cary, North Carolina, USA. ALL RIGHTS RESERVED.

Interleaving

empscn

First	Gender	Country
Chang	M	China
Li	M	China
ng	F	China

EOF

empsjp

First	Gender	Region
Cho	F	Japan
Tomi	M	Japan

Which value comes first?

Tomi

```
data empsall2;
   set empscn empsjp(rename=(Region=Country));
   by First;
run;
```

PDV

First	Gender	Country
Tomi	M	Japan

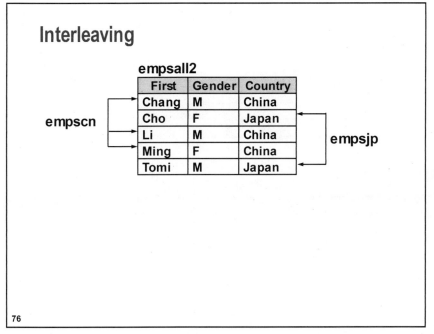

75 ...

Interleaving

empsall2

First	Gender	Country
Chang	M	China
Cho	F	Japan
Li	M	China
Ming	F	China
Tomi	M	Japan

empscn (Chang, Li, Ming) — empsjp (Cho, Tomi)

76

If the data values are equal, the observation is always read first from the first data set that is listed in the SET statement.

Copyright © 2016, SAS Institute Inc., Cary, North Carolina, USA. ALL RIGHTS RESERVED.

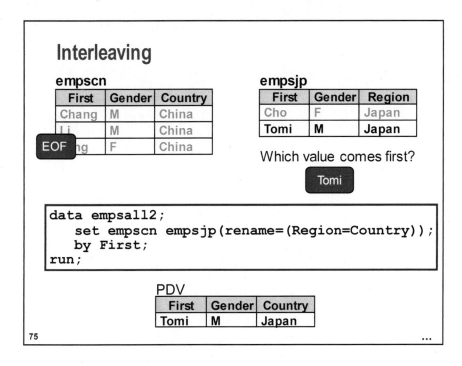

Business Scenario

Use the SORT procedure to eliminate duplicate observations from a SAS data set.

77

Eliminating Duplicates with the SORT Procedure

The following options control which observations are eliminated:

Option	Description
NODUPKEY	Deletes observations with duplicate BY values.
NODUPRECS	Deletes duplicate observations.
DUPOUT=	Specifies the output data set to which duplicate observations are to be written.

When you remove consecutive duplicate observations in the output data set with NODUPRECS, the choice of EQUALS or NOEQUALS can have an effect on which observations are removed.

78

Copyright © 2016, SAS Institute Inc., Cary, North Carolina, USA. ALL RIGHTS RESERVED.

Eliminating Duplicates with the SORT Procedure

The EQUALS/NOEQUALS options specify the order of the observations in the output data set.

Option	Description
EQUALS (Default)	For observations with identical BY-variable values, EQUALS maintains the relative order of the observations within the input data set in the output data set.
NOEQUALS	NOEQUALS does not necessarily preserve this order in the output data set.

79

Eliminating Duplicates with the SORT Procedure

```
proc sort data=empsdup
          out=empsdup1 nodupkey equals;
   by EmpID;
run;
```

empsdup

First	Gender	EmpID
Matt	M	121160
Julie	F	121161
Brett	M	121162
Julie	F	121161
Chris	F	121161
Julie	F	121163

empsdup1

First	Gender	EmpID
Matt	M	121160
Julie	F	121161
Brett	M	121162
Julie	F	121163

80

p1aad07

Copyright © 2016, SAS Institute Inc., Cary, North Carolina, USA. ALL RIGHTS RESERVED.

Business Scenarios

Write a DATA step that merges two data sets and creates three output data sets. Direct observations to a specific data set based on data set contributors.

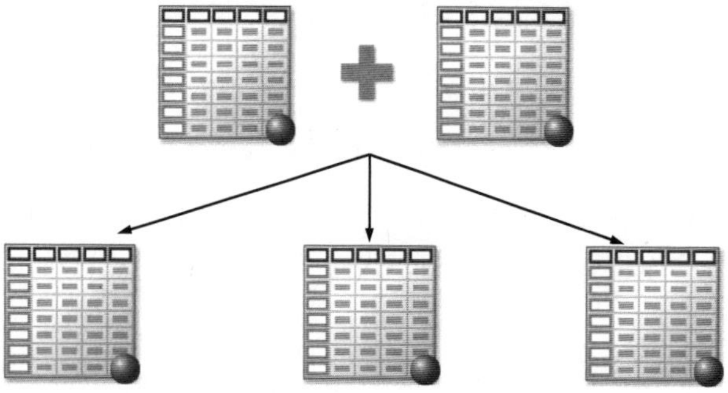

81

Creating Output to Multiple Data Sets in a Merge

The DATA statement can specify multiple output data sets.

```
data empsauc empsonly phoneonly;
   merge empsAU(in=emps) phoneC(in=Cell);
   by EmpID;
   if emps=1 and Cell=1
        then output empsauc;
   else if emps=1 and Cell=0
        then output empsonly;
   else if emps=0 and Cell=1
        then output phoneonly;
run;
```

82 p1aad08

Copyright © 2016, SAS Institute Inc., Cary, North Carolina, USA. ALL RIGHTS RESERVED.

Creating Output to Multiple Data Sets in a Merge

An OUTPUT statement can be used in a conditional statement to write the current observation to a specific data set that is listed in the DATA statement.

```
data empsauc empsonly phoneonly;
   merge empsAU(in=emps) phoneC(in=Cell);
   by EmpID;
   if emps=1 and Cell=1
        then output empsauc;
   else if emps=1 and Cell=0
        then output empsonly;
   else if emps=0 and Cell=1
        then output phoneonly;
run;
```

83

p1aad08

Creating Output to Multiple Data Sets in a Merge

empsauc

First	Gender	EmpID	Phone
Togar	M	121150	+61(2)5555-1795
Birin	M	121152	+61(2)5555-1667

empsonly

First	Gender	EmpID	Phone
Kylie	F	121151	

phoneonly

First	Gender	EmpID	Phone
		121153	+61(2)5555-1348

84

Copyright © 2016, SAS Institute Inc., Cary, North Carolina, USA. ALL RIGHTS RESERVED.

Business Scenario

Examine the results of a many-to-many merge. Compare those results to the results of a PROC SQL inner join.

85

Many-to-Many Merge

Merge **emps_auus** and **phone_o** by **Country** to create a new data set named **emps_ofc**.

emps_auus

First	Gender	Country
Togar	M	AU
Kylie	F	AU
Stacey	F	US
Gloria	F	US
James	M	US

phone_o

Country	Phone
AU	+61(2)5555-1500
AU	+61(2)5555-1600
AU	+61(2)5555-1700
US	+1(305)555-1500
US	+1(305)555-1600

```
data emps_ofc;
   merge emps_auus phone_o;
   by Country;
run;
```

The data sets are sorted by **Country**.

86 p1aad09

In a many-to-many merge, this note is issued to the log:

```
NOTE: MERGE statement has more than one data set with repeats of BY values.
```

This message is meant to be informational. A DATA step that performs a many-to-many merge does not produce a Cartesian product.

Copyright © 2016, SAS Institute Inc., Cary, North Carolina, USA. ALL RIGHTS RESERVED.

Many-to-Many Merge

DATA Step Results

emps_ofc

First	Gender	Country	Phone
Togar	M	AU	+61(2)5555-1500
Kylie	F	AU	+61(2)5555-1600
Kylie	F	AU	+61(2)5555-1700
Stacey	F	US	+1(305)555-1500
Gloria	F	US	+1(305)555-1600
James	M	US	+1(305)555-1600

87

Many-to-Many Merge

The SQL procedure creates different results than the DATA step for a many-to-many merge.

emps_auus

First	Gender	Country
Togar	M	AU
Kylie	F	AU
Stacey	F	US
Gloria	F	US
James	M	US

phone_o

Country	Phone
AU	+61(2)5555-1500
AU	+61(2)5555-1600
AU	+61(2)5555-1700
US	+1(305)555-1500
US	+1(305)555-1600

```
proc sql;
   create table emps_ofc as
   select First, Gender, phone_o.Country,
          Phone
   from emps_auus, phone_o
   where emps_auus.Country=phone_o.Country;
```

88 p1aad09

The SQL procedure is the SAS implementation of Structured Query Language. PROC SQL is part of Base SAS software, and you can use it with any SAS data set. Often, PROC SQL can be an alternative to other SAS procedures or the DATA step.

Copyright © 2016, SAS Institute Inc., Cary, North Carolina, USA. ALL RIGHTS RESERVED.

Many-to-Many Merge

PROC SQL Results

emps_ofc

First	Gender	Country	Phone
Togar	M	AU	+61(2)5555-1500
Togar	M	AU	+61(2)5555-1600
Togar	M	AU	+61(2)5555-1700
Kylie	F	AU	+61(2)5555-1500
Kylie	F	AU	+61(2)5555-1600
Kylie	F	AU	+61(2)5555-1700
Stacey	F	US	+1(305)555-1500
Stacey	F	US	+1(305)555-1600
Gloria	F	US	+1(305)555-1500
Gloria	F	US	+1(305)555-1600
James	M	US	+1(305)555-1500
James	M	US	+1(305)555-1600

89

Copyright © 2016, SAS Institute Inc., Cary, North Carolina, USA. ALL RIGHTS RESERVED.

Exercises

5. **Appending Like-Structured Data Sets**

   a. Retrieve the starter program **p1aae05**.

   b. Submit the two PROC CONTENTS steps to compare the variables in the two data sets.

      How many variables are in **orion.price_current**? ____________________

      How many variables are in **orion.price_new**? ____________________

      Does **orion.price_new** contain any variables that are not in **orion.price_current**? __________

   c. Add a PROC APPEND step after the PROC CONTENTS steps to append **orion.price_new** to **orion.price_current**. The FORCE option is not needed.

      Why is the FORCE option not needed? ____________________

   d. Submit the program and confirm that 88 observations from **orion.price_new** were added to **orion.price_current**, which should now have 259 observations (171 original observations plus 88 appended observations).

6. **Appending Unlike-Structured Data Sets**

   a. Write and submit two PROC CONTENTS steps to compare the variables in **orion.qtr1_2011** and **orion.qtr2_2011**.

      How many variables are in **orion.qtr1_2011**? ____________________

      How many variables are in **orion.qtr2_2011**? ____________________

      Which variable is not in both data sets? ____________________

   b. Write a PROC APPEND step to append **orion.qtr1_2011** to a non-existing data set named **work.ytd**.

   c. Submit the PROC APPEND step and confirm that 22 observations were copied to **work.ytd**.

   d. Write another PROC APPEND step to append **orion.qtr2_2011** to **work.ytd**. The FORCE option is needed.

      Why is the FORCE option needed? ____________________

   e. Submit the second PROC APPEND step and confirm that 36 observations from **orion.qtr2_2011** were added to **work.ytd**, which should now have 58 observations.

7. **Using the APPEND Statement**

   a. Write and submit three PROC CONTENTS steps to compare the variables in **orion.shoes_eclipse**, **orion.shoes_tracker**, and **orion.shoes**.

   b. Write a PROC DATASETS step with two APPEND statements to append **orion.shoes_eclipse** and **orion.shoes_tracker** to **orion.shoes**. Use SAS Help or product documentation to explore PROC DATASETS.

Copyright © 2016, SAS Institute Inc., Cary, North Carolina, USA. ALL RIGHTS RESERVED.

c. Submit the PROC DATASETS step and confirm that **orion.shoes** contains 34 observations (10 original observations plus 14 observations from **orion.shoes_eclipse** and 10 observations from **orion.shoes_tracker**).

8. **Interleaving Data Sets**

   a. Open the starter program **p1aae08**.

   b. Add a PROC SORT step after the PROC SORT step to sort **orion.shoes_tracker** by **Product_Name** and create a new data set named **work.trackersort**.

   c. Add a DATA step after the two PROC SORT steps to interleave the two sorted data sets by **Product_Name** and create a new data set named **work.e_t_shoes**. Include only the following variables: **Product_Group**, **Product_Name**, and **Supplier_ID**.

   d. Create the report shown below. The results should contain 24 observations.

   Partial PROC PRINT Output

```
Obs    Product_Group    Product_Name                                    Supplier_ID

  1    Eclipse Shoes    Atmosphere Imara Women's Running Shoes                 1303
  2    Eclipse Shoes    Atmosphere Shatter Mid Shoes                           1303
  3    Eclipse Shoes    Big Guy Men's Air Deschutz Viii Shoes                  1303
  4    Eclipse Shoes    Big Guy Men's Air Terra Reach Shoes                    1303
  5    Eclipse Shoes    Big Guy Men's Air Terra Sebec Shoes                    1303
```

   The order of the observations is different for z/OS (OS/390).

9. **Merging and Creating Output to Multiple Data Sets**

   a. Sort **orion.orders** by **Employee_ID** to create a new data set named **work.orders**.

   b. Merge **orion.staff** and **work.orders** by **Employee_ID**.

   c. Create two new data sets, **work.allorders** and **work.noorders**.

   The data set **work.allorders** should include all observations from **work.orders**, regardless of matches or nonmatches from the **orion.staff** data set.

   The data set **work.noorders** should include the observations from **orion.staff** that do not have a match in **work.orders**.

   Include only the following six variables: **Employee_ID**, **Job_Title**, **Gender**, **Order_ID**, **Order_Type**, and **Order_Date**.

   d. Using the new data sets, write two PROC PRINT steps to create two reports.

   e. Submit the program and confirm that **work.allorders** was created with 490 observations and six variables and **work.noorders** was created with 324 observations and six variables.

End of Exercises

Copyright © 2016, SAS Institute Inc., Cary, North Carolina, USA. ALL RIGHTS RESERVED.

A.5 Advanced Reporting Techniques

Objectives

- Enhance listing output. Use SAS system options and macro variables.
- Create an output data set. Use the FREQ procedure.
- Create an output data set. Use the MEANS procedure.
- Create multi-way tables. Use the TABULATE procedure.
- Create an output data set. Use PROC TABULATE.

92

Business Scenario

Use SAS system options in the SAS windowing environment to enhance reports in LISTING output.

93

Copyright © 2016, SAS Institute Inc., Cary, North Carolina, USA. ALL RIGHTS RESERVED.

Enhancing Reports with SAS System Options

The OPTIONS statement is a global statement.

- Global statements can be specified anywhere in a SAS program.
- They remain in effect until canceled or changed or until your SAS session ends.

94

OPTIONS Statement

The *OPTIONS statement* changes the value of one or more SAS system options.

OPTIONS *option(s)*;

- Some SAS system options change the appearance of a report.
- The OPTIONS statement is ***not*** usually included in a PROC or DATA step.

95

Copyright © 2016, SAS Institute Inc., Cary, North Carolina, USA. ALL RIGHTS RESERVED.

SAS System Options for Reporting

Selected SAS System Options

DATE (default)	Displays the date and time that the SAS session began at the top of each page of SAS output.
NODATE	Does not display the date and time that the SAS session began at the top of each page of SAS output.
DTRESET	Updates date and time at the top of each page of SAS output.
NODTRESET (Default)	Does not update date and time at the top of each page of SAS output.
CENTER (default)	Centers output.
NOCENTER	Left-aligns output.

96

continued...

SAS System Options for Reporting

Selected SAS System Options

NUMBER (default)	Prints page numbers at the top of each page of output.
NONUMBER	Does not print page numbers top of each page of output.
PAGENO=*n*	Sets the page number (*n*) for the next page of output. It is a best practice to specify the NUMBER option when you set the PAGENO= option.
PAGESIZE=*n* PS=*n*	Defines the number of lines (*n*) displayed per page of output.
LINESIZE=*width* LS=*width*	Defines the line size (*width*) for the SAS log and SAS output.

97

Copyright © 2016, SAS Institute Inc., Cary, North Carolina, USA. ALL RIGHTS RESERVED.

SAS System Options for Reporting

```
options ls=80 date number;

proc means data=orion.sales;
   var Salary;
run;
```

09:11 Monday, January 14, 2008 35

The MEANS Procedure

Analysis Variable : Salary

N	Mean	Std Dev	Minimum	Maximum
165	31160.12	20082.67	22710.00	243190.00

80 characters wide

98 p1aad10

SAS System Options for Reporting

```
options nodate number pageno=1;

proc freq data=orion.sales;
   tables Country;
run;
```

1

The FREQ Procedure

Country	Frequency	Percent	Cumulative Frequency	Cumulative Percent
AU	63	38.18	63	38.18
US	102	61.82	165	100.00

80 characters wide

99 p1aad10

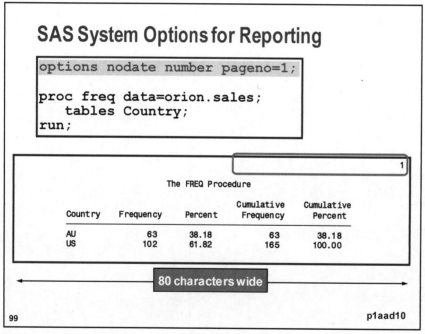

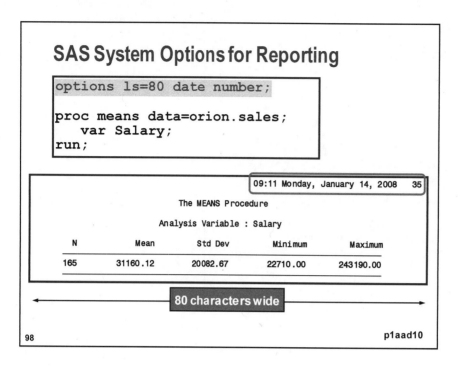

Copyright © 2016, SAS Institute Inc., Cary, North Carolina, USA. ALL RIGHTS RESERVED.

Business Scenario

Include the current date and time in report titles.

100

Titles with Dates and Times

Use the %LET statement with %SYSFUNC and the TODAY function or the TIME function to create a macro variable with the current date or time.

%LET *macro-variable* **= %SYSFUNC(today(),** *date-format***);**

%LET *macro-variable* **= %SYSFUNC(time(),** *time-format***);**

- %LET is a macro statement that creates a macro variable and assigns it a value without leading or trailing blanks.
- %SYSFUNC is a macro function that executes SAS functions outside of a step.

101

Copyright © 2016, SAS Institute Inc., Cary, North Carolina, USA. ALL RIGHTS RESERVED.

Titles with Dates and Times

```
%let currentdate=%sysfunc(today(),worddate.);
%let currenttime=%sysfunc(time(),timeampm.);

proc freq data=orion.sales;
   tables Gender Country;
   title1 'Orion Star Employee Listing';
   title2 "Created &currentdate";
   title3 "at &currenttime";
run;
```

Example Title Output

```
Orion Star Employee Listing
  Created March 11, 2008
      at 4:09:43 PM
```

102

p1aad11

Business Scenario

Use the FREQ procedure to produce an output data set that contains counts and percentages.

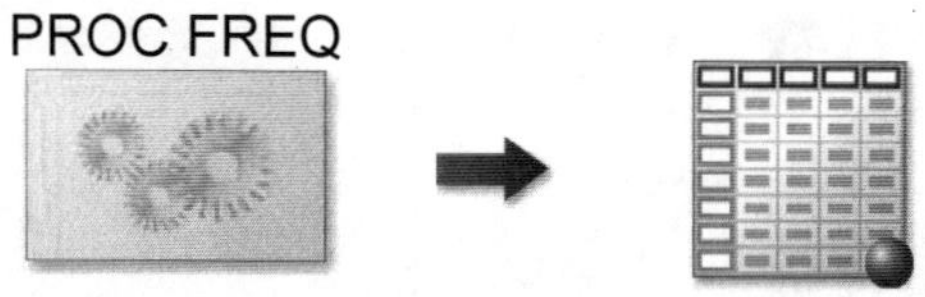

103

Copyright © 2016, SAS Institute Inc., Cary, North Carolina, USA. ALL RIGHTS RESERVED.

Output Data Sets

PROC FREQ can use two different methods to produce output data sets.

- The TABLES statement with an OUT= option is used to create a data set with frequencies and percentages.

TABLES *variables* **/ OUT=***SAS-data-set* *<options>*;

- The OUTPUT statement with an OUT= option is used to create a data set with specified statistics such as the chi-square statistic.

OUTPUT OUT=*SAS-data-set* *<options>*;

104

If there are multiple TABLES statements, the contents of the data set corresponds to the last TABLES statement.

TABLES Statement OUT= Option

The OUT= option in the TABLES statement creates an output data set with the following variables:

- BY variables
- TABLES statement variables
- the automatic variables **COUNT** and **PERCENT**
- other frequency and percentage variables requested with options in the TABLES statement

TABLES *variables* **/ OUT=***SAS-data-set* *<options>*;

If more than one table request appears in the TABLES statement, the contents of the data set correspond to the last table request.

105

Copyright © 2016, SAS Institute Inc., Cary, North Carolina, USA. ALL RIGHTS RESERVED.

TABLES Statement OUT= Option

```
proc freq data=orion.sales noprint;
   tables Gender Country / out=work.freq1;
run;

proc print data=work.freq1;
run;
```

PROC PRINT Output

Obs	Country	COUNT	PERCENT
1	AU	63	38.1818
2	US	102	61.8182

The NOPRINT option suppresses the display of all output.

106 p1aad12

TABLES Statement OUT= Option

```
proc freq data=orion.sales noprint;
   tables Gender*Country / out=work.freq2;
run;

proc print data=work.freq2;
run;
```

PROC PRINT Output

Obs	Gender	Country	COUNT	PERCENT
1	F	AU	27	16.3636
2	F	US	41	24.8485
3	M	AU	36	21.8182
4	M	US	61	36.9697

107 p1aad12

Copyright © 2016, SAS Institute Inc., Cary, North Carolina, USA. ALL RIGHTS RESERVED.

TABLES Statement OUT= Option

Options can be added to the TABLES statement after the forward slash to control the additional statistics added to the output data set.

Option	Description
OUTCUM	Includes the cumulative frequency and cumulative percentage in the output data set for one-way frequency tables.
OUTPCT	Includes the percentage of column frequency and row frequency in the output data set for *n*-way frequency tables.

108

TABLES Statement OUT= Option

```
proc freq data=orion.sales noprint;
   tables Gender Country / out=work.freq3
                            outcum;
run;

proc print data=work.freq3;
run;
```

PROC PRINT Output

Obs	Country	COUNT	PERCENT	CUM_FREQ	CUM_PCT
1	AU	63	38.1818	63	38.182
2	US	102	61.8182	165	100.000

109 p1aad12

Copyright © 2016, SAS Institute Inc., Cary, North Carolina, USA. ALL RIGHTS RESERVED.

TABLES Statement OUT= Option

```
proc freq data=orion.sales noprint;
   tables Gender*Country / out=work.freq4
                           outpct;
run;

proc print data=work.freq4;
run;
```

PROC PRINT Output

Obs	Gender	Country	COUNT	PERCENT	PCT_ROW	PCT_COL
1	F	AU	27	16.3636	39.7059	42.8571
2	F	US	41	24.8485	60.2941	40.1961
3	M	AU	36	21.8182	37.1134	57.1429
4	M	US	61	36.9697	62.8866	59.8039

110 p1aad12

Business Scenario

Use the OUT= option in the MEANS procedure to produce an output data set.

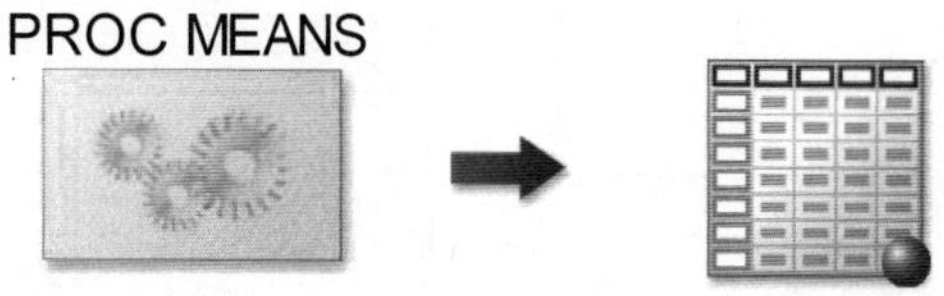

111

Copyright © 2016, SAS Institute Inc., Cary, North Carolina, USA. ALL RIGHTS RESERVED.

Output Data Sets

PROC MEANS uses the following method to produce output data sets:

OUTPUT OUT=*SAS-data-set <options>*;

The output data set contains the following variables:

- BY variables
- class variables
- the automatic variables **_TYPE_** and **_FREQ_**
- the variables requested in the OUTPUT statement

112

OUTPUT Statement OUT= Option

The statistics in the PROC statement impact only the MEANS report, not the data set.

```
proc means data=orion.sales sum mean range;
   var Salary;
   class Gender Country;
   output out=work.means1;
run;
```

113 p1aad13

Copyright © 2016, SAS Institute Inc., Cary, North Carolina, USA. ALL RIGHTS RESERVED.

OUTPUT Statement OUT= Option

```
proc print data=work.means1;
run;
```

Partial PROC PRINT Output

Obs	Gender	Country	_TYPE_	_FREQ_	_STAT_	Salary
1			0	165	N	165.00
2			0	165	MIN	22710.00
3			[illegible]	[illegible]	MAX	243190.00
4			[illegible]	[illegible]	MEAN	31160.12
5			0	165	STD	20082.67
6		AU	1	63	N	63.00
7		AU	1	63	MIN	25185.00
8		AU	1	63	MAX	108255.00
9		AU	1	63	MEAN	30158.97
10		AU	1	63	STD	12699.14
11		US	1	102	N	102.00
12		US	1	102	MIN	22710.00
13		US	1	102	MAX	243190.00
14		US	1	102	MEAN	31778.48
15		US	1	102	STD	23555.84
16	F		2	68	N	68.00
17	F		2	68	MIN	25185.00

default statistics

114

OUTPUT Statement OUT= Option

The OUTPUT statement can also do the following:

- specify the statistics for the output data set
- select and name variables

```
proc means data=orion.sales noprint;
   var Salary;
   class Gender Country;
   output out=work.means2
          min=minSalary max=maxSalary
          sum=sumSalary mean=aveSalary;
run;

proc print data=work.means2;
run;
```

The NOPRINT option suppresses the display of all output.

115 p1aad13

Copyright © 2016, SAS Institute Inc., Cary, North Carolina, USA. ALL RIGHTS RESERVED.

OUTPUT Statement OUT= Option

PROC PRINT Output

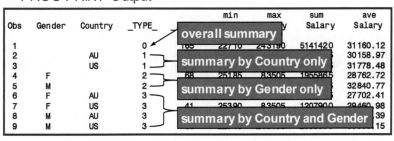

Obs	Gender	Country	_TYPE_	_FREQ_	min Salary	max Salary	sum Salary	ave Salary
1			0	165	22710	243190	5141420	31160.12
2		AU	1	63	25185	108255	1900015	30158.97
3		US	1	102	22710	243190	3241405	31778.48
4	F		2	68	25185	83505	1955865	28762.72
5	M		2	97	22710	243190	3185555	32840.77
6	F	AU	3	27	25185	30890	747965	27702.41
7	F	US	3	41	25390	83505	1207900	29460.98
8	M	AU	3	36	25745	108255	1152050	32001.39
9	M	US	3	61	22710	243190	2033505	33336.15

116

OUTPUT Statement OUT= Option

TYPE is a numeric variable that shows which combination of class variables produced the summary statistics in that observation.

PROC PRINT Output

Obs	Gender	Country	_TYPE_	sum Salary	ave Salary
1			0	5141420	31160.12
2		AU	1		30158.97
3		US	1		31778.48
4	F		2		28762.72
5	M		2		32840.77
6	F	AU	3		27702.41
7	F	US	3		
8	M	AU	3		
9	M	US	3		

- _TYPE_ 0: overall summary
- _TYPE_ 1: summary by Country only
- _TYPE_ 2: summary by Gender only
- _TYPE_ 3: summary by Country and Gender

117

Copyright © 2016, SAS Institute Inc., Cary, North Carolina, USA. ALL RIGHTS RESERVED.

OUTPUT Statement OUT= Option

Obs	Gender	Country	_TYPE_	_FREQ_	min Salary	max Salary	sum Salary	ave Salary
1			0	165	22710	243190	5141420	31160.12
2		AU	1	63	25185	108255	1900015	30158.97
3		US	1	102	22710	243190	3241405	31778.48
4	F		2	68	25185	83505	1955865	28762.72
5	M		2	97	22710	243190	3185555	32840.77
6	F	AU	3	27	25185	30890	747965	27702.41
7	F	US	3	41	25390	83505	1207900	29460.98
8	M	AU	3	36	25745	108255	1152050	32001.39
9	M	US	3	61	22710	243190	2033505	33336.15

TYPE	Type of Summary	_FREQ_
0	Overall summary	165
1	Summary by **Country** only	63 AU + 102 AU = 165
2	Summary by **Gender** only	68 F + 97 M = 165
3	Summary by **Country** and **Gender**	27 F AU + 41 F US + 36 M AU + 61 M US = 165

118

OUTPUT Statement OUT= Option

Options can be added to the PROC MEANS statement to control the output data set.

Option	Description
NWAY	Specifies that the output data set contain only statistics for the observations with the highest **_TYPE_** value.
DESCENDTYPES	Orders the output data set by descending **_TYPE_** value.
CHARTYPE	Specifies that the **_TYPE_** variable in the output data set is a character representation of the binary value of **_TYPE_**.

119

Copyright © 2016, SAS Institute Inc., Cary, North Carolina, USA. ALL RIGHTS RESERVED.

OUTPUT Statement OUT= Option

without options

Obs	Gender	Country	_TYPE_	_FREQ_	min Salary	max Salary	sum Salary	ave Salary
1			0	165	22710	243190	5141420	31160.12
2		AU	1	63	25185	108255	1900015	30158.97
3		US	1	102	22710	243190	3241405	31778.48
4	F		2	68	25185	83505	1955865	28762.72
5	M		2	97	22710	243190	3185555	32840.77
6	F	AU	3	27	25185	30890	747965	27702.41
7	F	US	3	41	25390	83505	1207900	29460.98
8	M	AU	3	36	25745	108255	1152050	32001.39
9	M	US	3	61	22710	243190	2033505	33336.15

with NWAY

Obs	Gender	Country	_TYPE_	_FREQ_	min Salary	max Salary	sum Salary	ave Salary
1	F	AU	3	27	25185	30890	747965	27702.41
2	F	US	3	41	25390	83505	1207900	29460.98
3	M	AU	3	36	25745	108255	1152050	32001.39
4	M	US	3	61	22710	243190	2033505	33336.15

120 p1aad13

OUTPUT Statement OUT= Option

with DESCENDTYPES

Obs	Gender	Country	_TYPE_	_FREQ_	min Salary	max Salary	sum Salary	ave Salary
1	F	AU	3	27	25185	30890	747965	27702.41
2	F	US	3	41	25390	83505	1207900	29460.98
3	M	AU	3	36	25745	108255	1152050	32001.39
4	M	US	3	61	22710	243190	2033505	33336.15
5	F		2	68	25185	83505	1955865	28762.72
6	M		2	97	22710	243190	3185555	32840.77
7		AU	1	63	25185	108255	1900015	30158.97
8		US	1	102	22710	243190	3241405	31778.48
9			0	165	22710	243190	5141420	31160.12

121 p1aad13

Copyright © 2016, SAS Institute Inc., Cary, North Carolina, USA. ALL RIGHTS RESERVED.

OUTPUT Statement OUT= Option

with CHARTYPE

Obs	Gender	Country	_TYPE_	_FREQ_	min Salary	max Salary	sum Salary	ave Salary
1			00	165	22710	243190	5141420	31160.12
2		AU	01	63	25185	108255	1900015	30158.97
3		US	01	102	22710	243190	3241405	31778.48
4	F		10	68	25185	83505	1955865	28762.72
5	M		10	97	22710	243190	3185555	32840.77
6	F	AU	11	27	25185	30890	747965	27702.41
7	F	US	11	41	25390	83505	1207900	29460.98
8	M	AU	11	36	25745	108255	1152050	32001.39
9	M	US	11	61	22710	243190	2033505	33336.15

122 p1aad13

Subset the Results

A WHERE statement can be added to the PROC PRINT step to subset observations based on **_TYPE_**.

```
proc print data=work.means2;
   where _type_ = '10';
run;
```

Obs	Gender	Country	_TYPE_	_FREQ_	min Salary	max Salary	sum Salary	ave Salary
4	F		10	68	25185	83505	1955865	28762.72
5	M		10	97	22710	243190	3185555	32840.77

123 p1aad14

Copyright © 2016, SAS Institute Inc., Cary, North Carolina, USA. ALL RIGHTS RESERVED.

OUTPUT Statement OUT= Option

Program **p112d07** merges a PROC MEANS output data set with a detail data set to create the following report:

Partial PROC PRINT Output

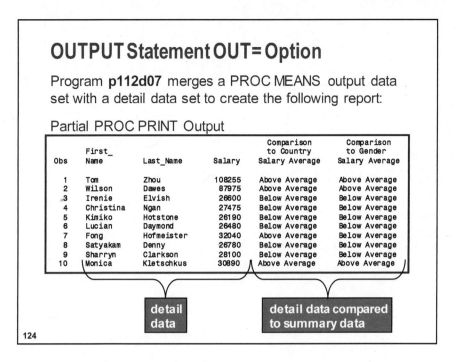

Obs	First_ Name	Last_Name	Salary	Comparison to Country Salary Average	Comparison to Gender Salary Average
1	Tom	Zhou	108255	Above Average	Above Average
2	Wilson	Dawes	87975	Above Average	Above Average
3	Irenie	Elvish	26600	Below Average	Below Average
4	Christina	Ngan	27475	Below Average	Below Average
5	Kimiko	Hotstone	26190	Below Average	Below Average
6	Lucian	Daymond	26480	Below Average	Below Average
7	Fong	Hofmeister	32040	Above Average	Below Average
8	Satyakam	Denny	26780	Below Average	Below Average
9	Sharryn	Clarkson	28100	Below Average	Below Average
10	Monica	Kletschkus	30890	Above Average	Above Average

detail data

detail data compared to summary data

124

Business Scenario

Use the TABULATE procedure to create one-, two-, and three-dimensional tabular reports.

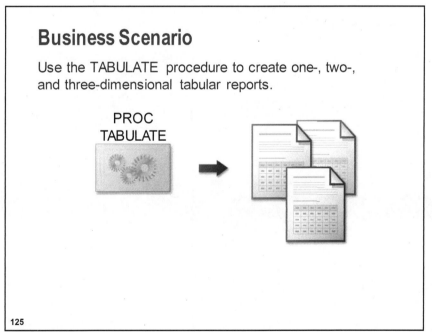

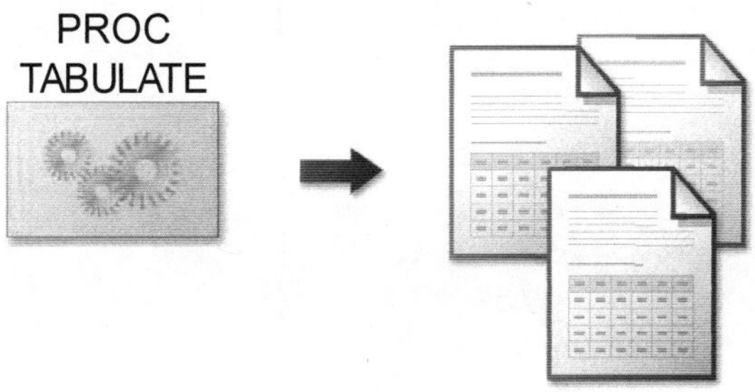

125

Copyright © 2016, SAS Institute Inc., Cary, North Carolina, USA. ALL RIGHTS RESERVED.

TABULATE Procedure

The TABULATE procedure displays descriptive statistics in tabular format.

General form of the TABULATE procedure:

```
PROC TABULATE DATA=SAS-data-set <options>;
      CLASS classification-variables;
      VAR analysis-variables;
      TABLE  page-expression,
             row-expression,
             column-expression </ options>;
RUN;
```

126

The TABULATE procedure computes many of the same statistics that are computed by other descriptive statistical procedures such as PROC MEANS and PROC FREQ.

A CLASS statement or a VAR statement must be specified, but both statements together are not required.

Dimensional Tables

The TABULATE procedure produces one-, two-, or three-dimensional tables.

	page dimension	row dimension	column dimension
one-dimensional			✓
two-dimensional		✓	✓
three-dimensional	✓	✓	✓

127

Copyright © 2016, SAS Institute Inc., Cary, North Carolina, USA. ALL RIGHTS RESERVED.

One-Dimensional Table

Country	
AU	US
N	N
63.00	102.00

- **Country** is in the column dimension.

128

Two-Dimensional Table

	Country	
	AU	US
	N	N
Gender		
F	27.00	41.00
M	36.00	61.00

- **Country** is in the column dimension.
- **Gender** is in the row dimension.

129

Copyright © 2016, SAS Institute Inc., Cary, North Carolina, USA. ALL RIGHTS RESERVED.

Three-Dimensional Table

Job_Title Sales Rep. I

	Country	
	AU	US
	N	N
Gender		
F	8.00	13.00
M	13.00	29.00

- **Country** is in the column dimension.
- **Gender** is in the row dimension.
- **Job_Title** is in the page dimension.

130

TABLE Statement

The TABLE statement describes the structure of the table.

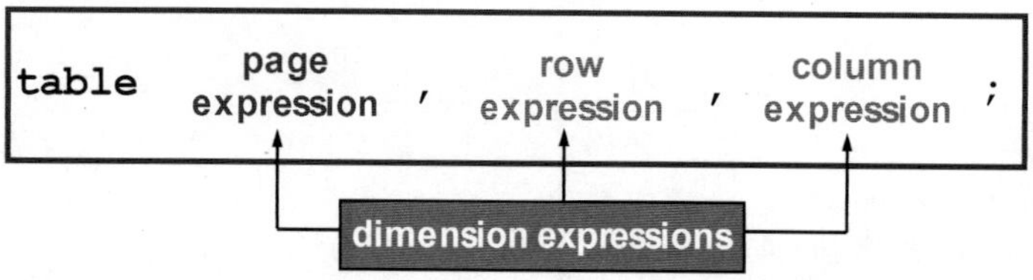

- Commas separate the dimension expressions.
- Every variable that is part of a dimension expression must be specified as a classification variable (CLASS statement) or an analysis variable (VAR statement).

131

Copyright © 2016, SAS Institute Inc., Cary, North Carolina, USA. ALL RIGHTS RESERVED.

TABLE Statement

```
table  page expression , row expression , column expression ;
```

Examples:

```
table Country;
```

```
table Gender, Country;
```

```
table Job_Title, Gender, Country;
```

132

CLASS Statement

The CLASS statement identifies variables to be used as classification, or *grouping*, variables.

General form of the CLASS statement:

CLASS *classification-variables*;

- N, the number of nonmissing values, is the default statistic for classification variables.
- Examples of classification variables are as follows: **Job_Title**, **Gender**, and **Country**

133

Class variables can be numeric or character. They identify classes or categories on which you can perform calculations. Numeric class variables represent discrete categories (for example, **Year**).

Copyright © 2016, SAS Institute Inc., Cary, North Carolina, USA. ALL RIGHTS RESERVED.

VAR Statement

The VAR statement identifies the numeric variables for which statistics are calculated.

General form of the VAR statement:

```
VAR analysis-variable(s);
```

- SUM is the default statistic for analysis variables.
- Examples of analysis variables are as follows: **Salary** and **Bonus**

134

Analysis variables are always numeric. They tend to be continuous and are appropriate for calculating averages, sums, or other statistics.

One-Dimensional Table

```
proc tabulate data=orion.sales;
   class Country;
   table Country;
run;
```

Country	
AU	US
N	N
63.00	102.00

135 p1aad15

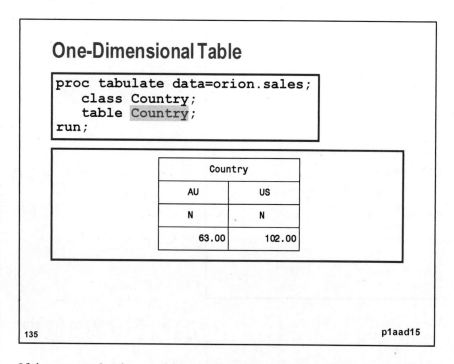

If there are only class variables in the TABLE statement, the default statistic is N, which is the number of nonmissing values.

Copyright © 2016, SAS Institute Inc., Cary, North Carolina, USA. ALL RIGHTS RESERVED.

Two-Dimensional Table

```
proc tabulate data=orion.sales;
   class Gender Country;
   table Gender, Country;
run;
```

	Country	
	AU	US
	N	N
Gender		
F	27.00	41.00
M	36.00	61.00

136 p1aad15

Three-Dimensional Table

```
proc tabulate data=orion.sales;
   class Job_Title Gender Country;
   table Job_Title, Gender, Country;
run;
```

137 p1aad15

Copyright © 2016, SAS Institute Inc., Cary, North Carolina, USA. ALL RIGHTS RESERVED.

Three-Dimensional Table

Partial PROC TABULATE Output

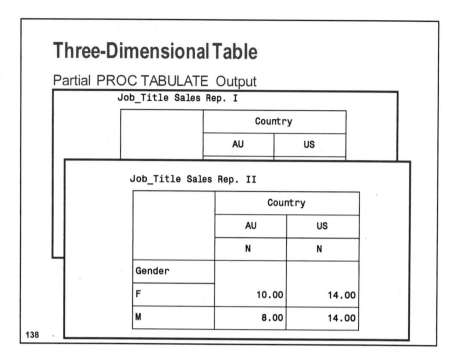

Job_Title Sales Rep. I

	Country	
	AU	US

Job_Title Sales Rep. II

	Country	
	AU	US
	N	N
Gender		
F	10.00	14.00
M	8.00	14.00

138

Dimension Expression

Elements that can be used in a dimension expression:

- classification variables
- analysis variables
- the universal class variable **ALL**
- keywords for statistics

Operators that can be used in a dimension expression:

- blank, which concatenates table information
- asterisk *, which crosses table information
- parentheses (), which group elements

139

Other operators include the following:

- brackets < >, which name the denominator for row or column percentages
- equal sign =, which changes the label for a variable or a statistic

Copyright © 2016, SAS Institute Inc., Cary, North Carolina, USA. ALL RIGHTS RESERVED.

Dimension Expression

```
proc tabulate data=orion.sales;
   class Gender Country;
   var Salary;
   table Gender all, Country*Salary;
run;
```

	Country	
	AU	US
	Salary	Salary
	Sum	Sum
Gender		
F	747965.00	1207900.00
M	1152050.00	2033505.00
All	1900015.00	3241405.00

140 p1aad15

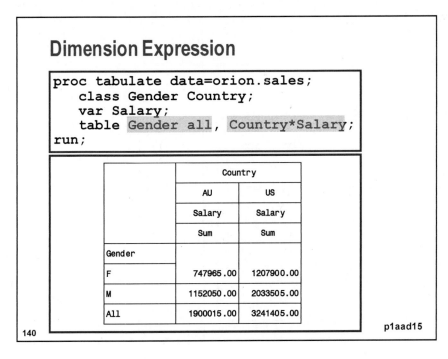

If there are analysis variables in the TABLE statement, the default statistic is SUM.

PROC TABULATE Statistics

Descriptive Statistic Keywords				
	CSS	CV	LCLM	MAX
MEAN	MIN	MODE	N	NMISS
KURTOSIS	RANGE	SKEWNESS	STDDEV	STDERR
SUM	SUMWGT	UCLM	USS	VAR
PCTN	REPPCTN	PAGEPCTN	ROWPCTN	COLPCTN
PCTSUM	REPPCTSUM	PAGEPCTSUM	ROWPCTSUM	COLPCTSUM

Quantile Statistic Keywords				
MEDIAN | P50	P1	P5	P10	Q1 | P25
Q3 | P75	P90	P95	P99	QRANGE

Hypothesis Testing Keywords				
PROBT	T			

141

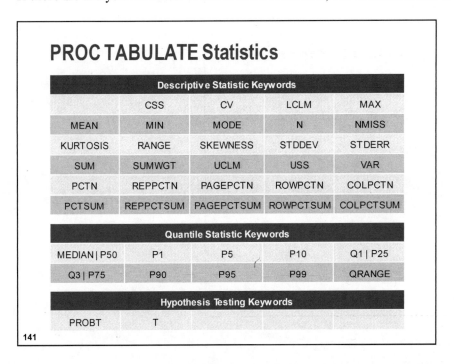

Copyright © 2016, SAS Institute Inc., Cary, North Carolina, USA. ALL RIGHTS RESERVED.

PROC TABULATE Statistics

```
proc tabulate data=orion.sales;
   class Gender Country;
   var Salary;
   table Gender all, Country*Salary*(min max);
run;
```

	Country			
	AU		US	
	Salary		Salary	
	Min	Max	Min	Max
Gender				
F	25185.00	30890.00	25390.00	83505.00
M	25745.00	108255.00	22710.00	243190.00
All	25185.00	108255.00	22710.00	243190.00

142 p1aad15

Business Scenario

Use the OUT= option in the TABULATE procedure to produce an output data set.

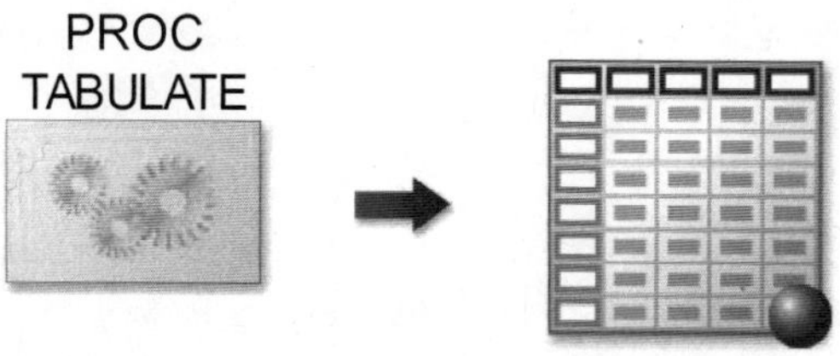

143

Copyright © 2016, SAS Institute Inc., Cary, North Carolina, USA. ALL RIGHTS RESERVED.

Output Data Sets

PROC TABULATE uses the following method to produce output data sets:

PROC TABULATE DATA=*SAS-data-set*
OUT=*SAS-data-set <options>*;

The output data set contains the following variables:

- BY variables
- class variables
- automatic variables **_TYPE_**, **_PAGE_**, and **_TABLE_**
- calculated statistics

144

PROC Statement OUT= Option

```
proc tabulate data=orion.sales
              out=work.tabulate;
   where Job_Title contains 'Rep';
   class Job_Title Gender Country;
   table Country;
   table Gender, Country;
   table Job_Title, Gender, Country;
run;

proc print data=work.tabulate;
run;
```

145 p1aad16

Copyright © 2016, SAS Institute Inc., Cary, North Carolina, USA. ALL RIGHTS RESERVED.

PROC Statement OUT= Option

Partial PROC PRINT Output

Obs	Job_Title	Gender	Country	_TYPE_	_PAGE_	_TABLE_	N
1			AU	001	1	1	61
2			US	001	1	1	98
3		F	AU	011	1	2	27
4		F	US	011	1	2	40
5		M	AU	011	1	2	34
6		M	US	011	1	2	58
7	Sales Rep. I	F	AU	111	1	3	8
8	Sales Rep. I	F	US	111	1	3	13
9	Sales Rep. I	M	AU	111	1	3	13
10	Sales Rep. I	M	US	111	1	3	29

146

PROC Statement OUT= Option

TYPE is a character variable that shows which combination of class variables produced the summary statistics in that observation.

Partial PROC PRINT Output

Obs	Job_Title	Gender	Country	_TYPE_	_PAGE_	_TABLE_	N
1			AU	001	1	1	61
2			US	001	1	1	98
3		F	AU	011	1	2	27
4		F	US	011			
5		M	AU	011			
6		M	US	011			

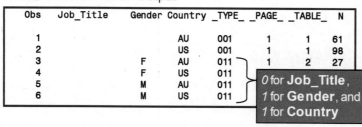

0 for **Job_Title**, *1* for **Gender**, and *1* for **Country**

147

Copyright © 2016, SAS Institute Inc., Cary, North Carolina, USA. ALL RIGHTS RESERVED.

PROC Statement OUT= Option

PAGE is a numeric variable that shows the logical page number that contains that observation.

Partial PROC PRINT Output

Obs	Job_Title	Gender	Country	_TYPE_	_PAGE_	_TABLE_	N
7	Sales Rep. I	F	AU	111	1	[illegible]	[illegible]
8	Sales Rep. I	F	US	111	1	[illegible]	[illegible]
9	Sales Rep. I	M	AU	111	1	[illegible]	[illegible]
10	Sales Rep. I	M	US	111	1	3	29
11	Sales Rep. II	F	AU	111	2	[illegible]	[illegible]
12	Sales Rep. II	F	US	111	2	[illegible]	[illegible]
13	Sales Rep. II	M	AU	111	2	[illegible]	[illegible]
14	Sales Rep. II	M	US	111	2	[illegible]	[illegible]
15	Sales Rep. III	F	AU	111	3	[illegible]	[illegible]
16	Sales Rep. III	F	US	111	3	[illegible]	[illegible]
17	Sales Rep. III	M	AU	111	3	[illegible]	[illegible]
18	Sales Rep. III	M	US	111	3	[illegible]	[illegible]

Page 1 for Sales Rep. I

Page 2 for Sales Rep. II

Page 3 for Sales Rep. III

148

PROC Statement OUT= Option

TABLE is a numeric variable that shows the number of the TABLE statement that contains that observation.

Partial PROC PRINT Output

Obs	Job_Title	Gender	Country	_TYPE_	_PAGE_	_TABLE_	N
1						1	61
2						1	98
3		F	AU	011	1	2	27
4						2	40
5						2	34
6		M	US	011	1	2	58
7	Sales Rep. I	F	AU	111	1	3	8
8	Sales Rep. I					3	13
9	Sales Rep. I					3	13
10	Sales Rep. I	M	US	111	1	3	29

1 for first TABLE statement

2 for second TABLE statement

3 for third TABLE statement

149

Copyright © 2016, SAS Institute Inc., Cary, North Carolina, USA. ALL RIGHTS RESERVED.

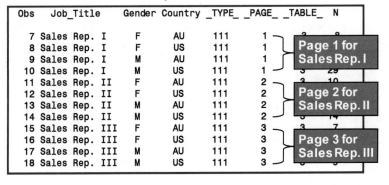

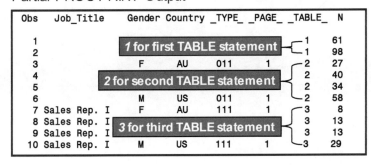

Exercises

10. Specifying Titles, Footnotes, and System Options

a. Retrieve the starter program **p1aae10**.

b. Use the OPTIONS statement to establish these system options for the PROC MEANS report:

1) Suppress the page numbers that appear at the top of each output page.

2) Suppress the date and time that appear at the top of each output page.

3) Limit the number of lines per page to 18 for the report.

c. Specify the following title for the report: **Orion Star Sales Report**.

d. Specify the following footnote for the report: **Report by SAS Programming Student**.

e. After the PROC MEANS step finishes, reset the number of lines per page to 52 and cancel the title and footnote.

f. Submit the program to create the following PROC MEANS report:

PROC MEANS Output

```
                         Orion Star Sales Report

                          The MEANS Procedure

   Analysis Variable : Total_Retail_Price Total Retail Price for This Product

        N            Mean         Std Dev         Minimum         Maximum
      ---------------------------------------------------------------------
      617     162.2001053     233.8530183       2.6000000         1937.20
      ---------------------------------------------------------------------





                   Report by SAS Programming Student
```

11. Specifying Multiple Titles and System Options

a. Retrieve the starter program **p1aae11**.

b. Limit the number of lines per page to 18 and then reset that option to 52 after both reports are complete.

c. Request that each report contain page numbers starting at 1.

d. Use the DTRESET option to include the ***current*** date and time at the top of each page; not the date and time that the SAS session began.

Copyright © 2016, SAS Institute Inc., Cary, North Carolina, USA. ALL RIGHTS RESERVED.

e. Specify the following title to appear in both reports: **Orion Star Sales Analysis**.

f. Specify a secondary title to appear in the first report with a blank line between the titles: **Catalog Sales Only**.

g. Specify the following footnote for the first report: **Based on the previous day's posted data**.

> The text specified for a title or footnote can be enclosed in single quotation marks or double quotation marks. Use double quotation marks when the text contains an apostrophe.

h. Specify the following secondary title to appear in the second report with a blank line between the titles: **Internet Sales Only**.

i. Cancel all footnotes for the second report.

j. Submit the program to create the PROC MEANS reports shown below.

k. Cancel all titles and footnotes after the second report.

PROC MEANS Output

```
                         Orion Star Sales Analysis                         1
                                          16:30 Monday, January 28, 2013
                            Catalog Sales Only

                           The MEANS Procedure

     Analysis Variable : Total_Retail_Price Total Retail Price for This Product

       N            Mean         Std Dev         Minimum         Maximum
     ------------------------------------------------------------------
     170     199.5961765     282.9680817       2.6000000         1937.20
     ------------------------------------------------------------------



                  Based on the previous day's posted data
```

```
                         Orion Star Sales Analysis                         1
                                          16:30 Monday, January 28, 2013
                            Internet Sales Only

                           The MEANS Procedure

     Analysis Variable : Total_Retail_Price Total Retail Price for This Product

       N            Mean         Std Dev         Minimum         Maximum
     ------------------------------------------------------------------
     123     174.7280488     214.3528338       2.7000000         1542.60
     ------------------------------------------------------------------
```

12. Inserting Dates and Times into Titles

Copyright © 2016, SAS Institute Inc., Cary, North Carolina, USA. ALL RIGHTS RESERVED.

a. Use the OPTIONS procedure to display the current value of the DATE option. Verify that the date and time are not automatically displayed at the top of each page. If the option is not set correctly, change it. Use SAS Help or product documentation to explore the OPTIONS procedure.

b. Open the starter program **p1aae12**.

c. Add a title with the below text. Use macro functions and variables to substitute the current date and time.

Sales Report as of *4:57 PM* on *Monday, January 28, 2013*

d. Submit the program to create the report below. Cancel the title.

PROC MEANS Output

```
                Sales Report as of 4:57 PM on Monday, January 28, 2013

                                The MEANS Procedure

      Analysis Variable : Total_Retail_Price Total Retail Price for This Product

           N            Mean         Std Dev         Minimum         Maximum
      ------------------------------------------------------------------------
         617     162.2001053     233.8530183       2.6000000         1937.20
      ------------------------------------------------------------------------
```

13. Creating an Output Data Set with PROC FREQ

a. Open the starter program **p1aae13**.

b. Create an output data set that contains the frequency counts based on **Product_ID**.

c. Merge the output data set with **orion.product_list** to obtain the **Product_Name** value for each **Product_ID** code. Include only **Product_ID**, **Product_Name**, and **Count** in the new data set.

d. Sort the merged data so that the most frequently ordered products appear at the top of the resulting data set. Print the first 10 observations—that is, those that represent the 10 products that are ordered most often. To limit the number of observations that are displayed by PROC PRINT, apply the OBS= data set option, as in the following:

```
proc print data=work.mydataset(obs=10);
```

e. Submit the program to produce the report below. Cancel the title.

PROC PRINT Output

```
                     Top Ten Products by Number of Orders

                              Product
      Obs     Orders           Number    Product

        1        6       230100500056    Knife
        2        6       230100600030    Outback Sleeping Bag, Large,Left,Blue/Black
        3        5       230100600022    Expedition10,Medium,Right,Blue Ribbon
        4        5       240400300035    Smasher Shorts
        5        4       230100500082    Lucky Tech Intergal Wp/B Rain Pants
        6        4       230100600005    Basic 10, Left , Yellow/Black
        7        4       230100600016    Expedition Zero,Medium,Right,Charcoal
```

Copyright © 2016, SAS Institute Inc., Cary, North Carolina, USA. ALL RIGHTS RESERVED.

8	4	230100600028	Expedition 20,Medium,Right,Forestgreen
9	4	230100700008	Family Holiday 4
10	4	230100700011	Hurricane 4

14. Creating an Output Data Set with PROC MEANS

a. Open the starter program **p1aae14**.

b. Create an output data set that contains the sum of **Total_Retail_Price** values for each **Product_ID**.

c. Merge the output data set with **orion.product_list** to obtain the **Product_Name** value for each **Product_ID** code. Include only **Product_ID**, **Product_Name**, and **Product_Revenue** in the new data set.

d. Sort the merged data so that the products with higher revenues appear at the top of the resulting data set. Print the first 10 observations, that is, those that represent the 10 products with the most revenue. To limit the number of observations displayed by PROC PRINT, apply the OBS= data set option, as in the following:

```
proc print data=work.mydataset(obs=10);
```

e. Display the revenue values with a leading euro symbol (€), a period that separates every three digits, and a comma that separates the decimal fraction.

f. Submit the program to produce the report below. Cancel the title.

PROC PRINT Output

Top Ten Products by Revenue

Obs	Revenue	Product Number	Product
1	€3.391,80	230100700009	Family Holiday 6
2	€3.080,30	230100700008	Family Holiday 4
3	€2.250,00	230100700011	Hurricane 4
4	€1.937,20	240200100173	Proplay Executive Bi-Metal Graphite
5	€1.796,00	240200100076	Expert Men's Firesole Driver
6	€1.561,80	240300300090	Top R&D Long Jacket
7	€1.514,40	240300300070	Top Men's R&D Ultimate Jacket
8	€1.510,80	240100400098	Rollerskate Roller Skates Ex9 76mm/78a Biofl
9	€1.424,40	240100400129	Rollerskate Roller Skates Sq9 80-76mm/78a
10	€1.343,30	240100400043	Perfect Fit Men's Roller Skates

15. Creating a Tabular Report with PROC TABULATE

a. Open the starter program **p1aae15**.

b. Add a CLASS statement to define **Customer_Group** and **Customer_Gender** as classification variables.

c. Add a VAR statement to define **Customer_Age** as an analysis variable.

d. Add a TABLE statement to create a report with the following characteristics:

1) **Customer_Group** defines the rows.

Copyright © 2016, SAS Institute Inc., Cary, North Carolina, USA. ALL RIGHTS RESERVED.

2) Add an extra row that combines all groups and appears at the bottom of the table.

3) **Customer_Gender** defines the columns.

4) The N and MEAN statistics based on **Customer_Age** are displayed for each combination of **Customer_Group** and **Customer_Gender**.

e. Submit the program to produce the report below. Cancel the title.

PROC TABULATE Output

Ages of Customers by Group and Gender

	Customer Gender			
	F		M	
	Customer Age		Customer Age	
	N	Mean	N	Mean
Customer Group Name				
Internet/Catalog Customers	4.00	49.25	4.00	54.25
Orion Club Gold members	11.00	35.36	10.00	38.90
Orion Club members	15.00	32.53	33.00	47.03
All	30.00	35.80	47.00	45.91

16. Creating a Three-Dimensional Tabular Report with PROC TABULATE

a. Open the starter program **p1aae16**.

b. Define a tabular report with the following characteristics:

1) **Customer_Gender** defines the page dimension.

2) **Customer_Group** defines the row dimension.

3) The column dimension should display the number of customers and the percentage of customers in each category (COLPCTN).

> ✎ Use a KEYLABEL statement to change the headers for the statistic columns. Documentation about the KEYLABEL statement can be found in the SAS Help or product documentation.

Copyright © 2016, SAS Institute Inc., Cary, North Carolina, USA. ALL RIGHTS RESERVED.

c. Submit the program to produce the two-page report below. Cancel the title.

PROC TABULATE Output

```
Customers by Group and Gender

Customer Gender F
```

	Number	Percentage
Customer Group Name		
Internet/Catalog Customers	4.00	13.33
Orion Club Gold members	11.00	36.67
Orion Club members	15.00	50.00

```
Customers by Group and Gender

Customer Gender M
```

	Number	Percentage
Customer Group Name		
Internet/Catalog Customers	4.00	8.51
Orion Club Gold members	10.00	21.28
Orion Club members	33.00	70.21

17. Creating a Customized Tabular Report with PROC TABULATE

a. Retrieve the starter program **p1aae17**.

b. Modify the label for the **Total_Retail_Price** variable.

c. Suppress the labels for the **Order_Date** and **Product_ID** variables.

d. Suppress the label for the SUM keyword.

e. Insert this text into the box above the row titles: **High Cost Products (Unit Cost > $250)**. Suppress all titles.

f. Display all calculated cell values with the DOLLAR12. format.

g. Display **$0** in all cells that have no calculated value.

> Use SAS Help or product documentation to explore the PROC TABULATE statement, the TABLE statement, and the KEYLABEL statement that can perform the requested actions.

Copyright © 2016, SAS Institute Inc., Cary, North Carolina, USA. ALL RIGHTS RESERVED.

h. Submit the program to produce the report below. Cancel the title.

PROC TABULATE Output

High Cost Products (Unit Cost > $250)	Revenue for Each Product			
	230100700008	230100700009	240300100028	240300100032
2003	$0	$0	$0	$1,200
2005	$2,057	$2,256	$0	$0
2006	$0	$1,136	$0	$0
2007	$519	$0	$1,066	$0

18. Creating an Output Data Set with PROC TABULATE

a. Open the starter program **p1aae18**.

b. Create an output data set from the PROC TABULATE results. The output data set should contain average salaries for each combination of **Company** and **Employee_Gender**, plus overall averages for each **Company**.

c. Sort the data set by **Average Salary**.

d. Print the sorted data set. Assign a format and column heading to the **Average Salary** column.

e. Submit the program to produce the report below. Results should contain 24 observations. Cancel the title.

Partial PROC PRINT Output

Average Employee Salaries

Obs	Company	Employee Gender	Average Salary
1	Orion Australia	F	$27,760
2	Orion USA	F	$29,167
3	Orion Australia		$30,574
4	Orion USA		$31,226
5	Orion USA	M	$32,534

End of Exercises

Copyright © 2016, SAS Institute Inc., Cary, North Carolina, USA. ALL RIGHTS RESERVED.

A.6 Introduction to SAS/GRAPH

Objectives

- Create bar charts and pie charts.
- Create plots.
- Use options to enhance reports.

152

What Is SAS/GRAPH Software?

SAS/GRAPH software is a component of SAS software that enables you to create the following types of graphs:

- bar, block, and pie charts
- two-dimensional scatter plots and line plots
- three-dimensional scatter and surface plots
- contour plots
- maps
- text slides
- custom graphs

153

Copyright © 2016, SAS Institute Inc., Cary, North Carolina, USA. ALL RIGHTS RESERVED.

Bar Charts (GCHART Procedure)

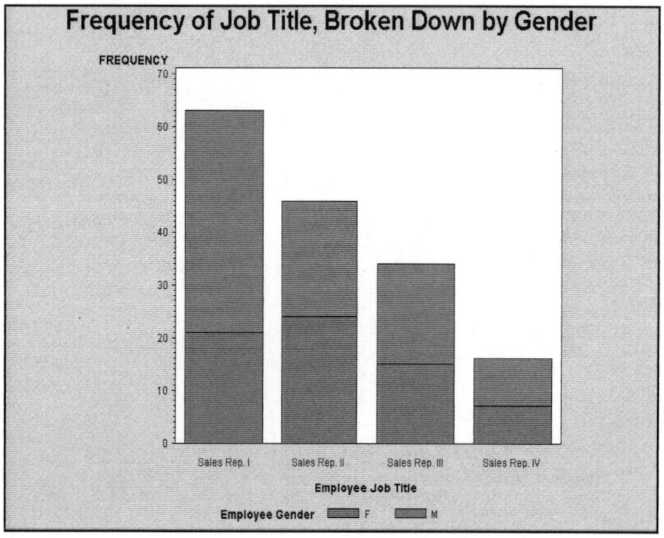

154

Pie Charts (GCHART Procedure)

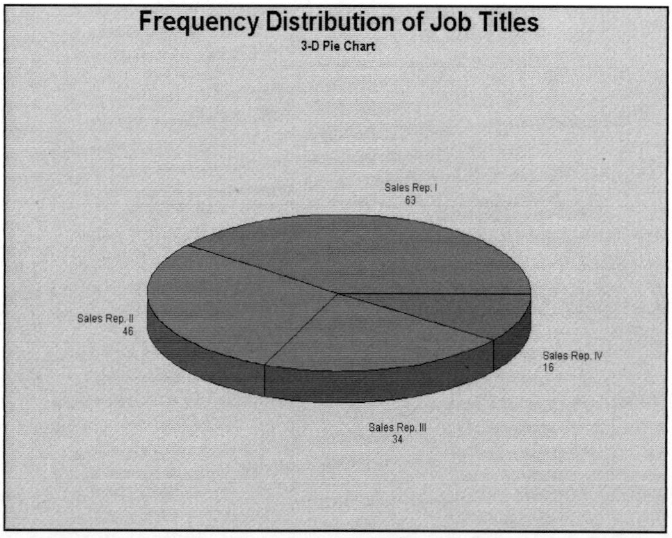

155

Copyright © 2016, SAS Institute Inc., Cary, North Carolina, USA. ALL RIGHTS RESERVED.

Scatter and Line Plots (GPLOT Procedure)

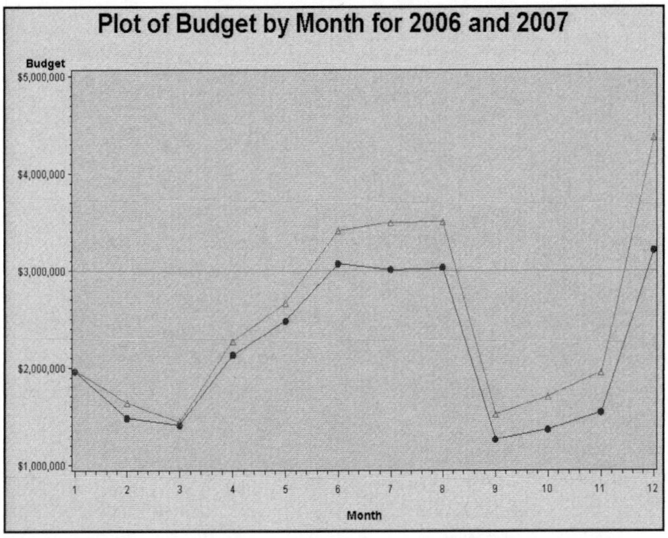

156

Bar Charts with Line Plot Overlay (GBARLINE Procedure)

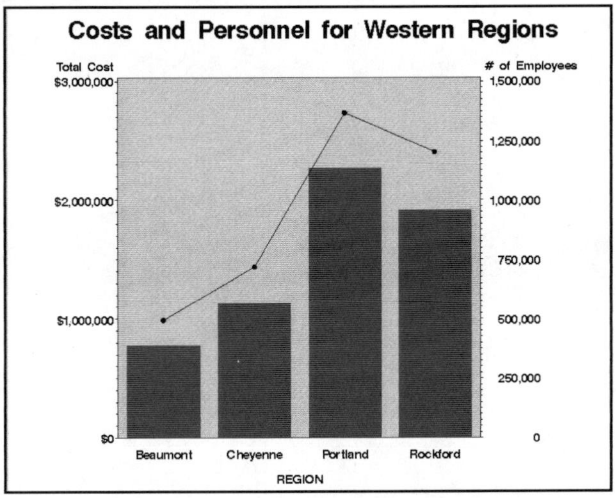

157

Copyright © 2016, SAS Institute Inc., Cary, North Carolina, USA. ALL RIGHTS RESERVED.

Three-Dimensional Surface and Scatter Plots (G3D Procedure)

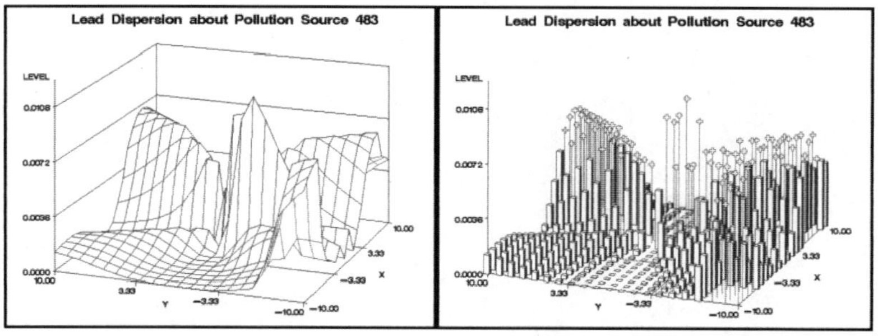

158

Three-Dimensional Contour Plots (GCONTOUR Procedure)

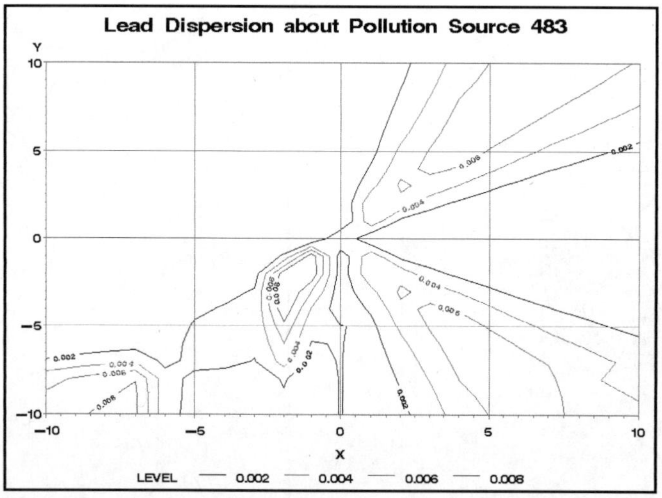

159

Copyright © 2016, SAS Institute Inc., Cary, North Carolina, USA. ALL RIGHTS RESERVED.

Maps (GMAP Procedure)

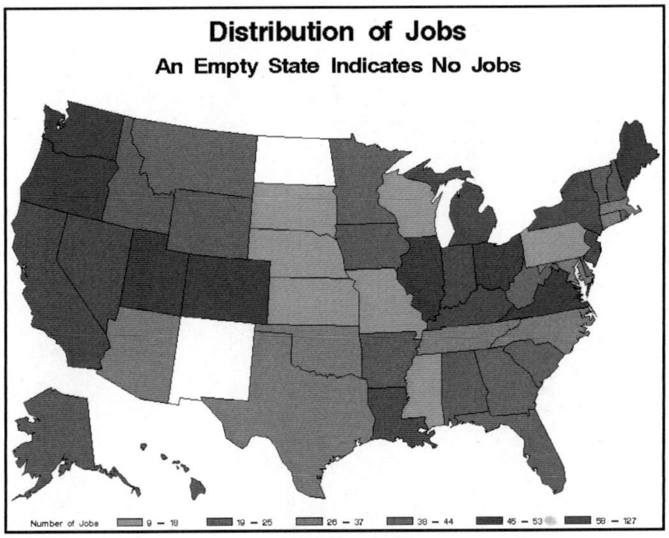

160

Multiple Graphs on a Page (GREPLAY Procedure)

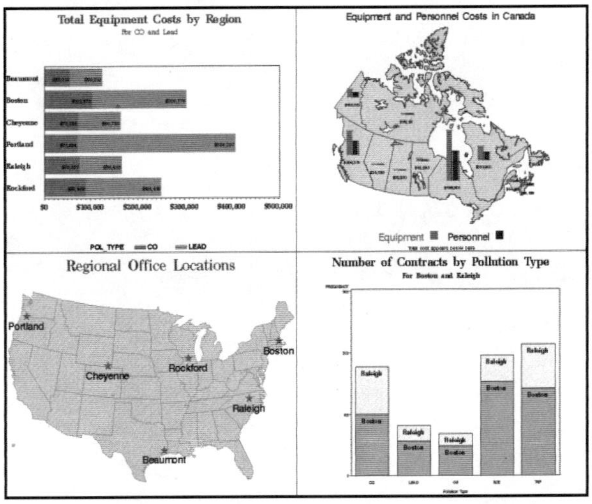

161

Copyright © 2016, SAS Institute Inc., Cary, North Carolina, USA. ALL RIGHTS RESERVED.

SAS/GRAPH Programs

A typical SAS/GRAPH program starts by setting graphic options, followed by global statements such as titles and footnotes, and then the PROC steps.

```
goptions cback=white;
title 'Number of Employees by Job Title';
proc gchart data=orion.staff;
   vbar Job_Title;
   where Job_Title contains 'Rep';
run;
quit;
title;
```

GOPTIONS *options*;
global statements
graphics procedure steps

162 p1aad17

RUN-Group Processing

To use RUN-group processing, you start the procedure and then submit multiple RUN groups.

- A RUN group is a group of statements that contains at least one action statement and ends with a RUN statement.
- As long as you do not terminate the procedure, it remains active and you do not need to resubmit the PROC statement.
- To end RUN-group processing and terminate the procedure, submit a QUIT statement or start a new procedure.

163

Copyright © 2016, SAS Institute Inc., Cary, North Carolina, USA. ALL RIGHTS RESERVED.

Example of RUN-Group Processing

- **Start PROC GCHART.** → `proc gchart data=orion.staff;`
- **first run group** → `vbar Job_Title; where Job_Title contains 'Rep'; title 'Bar Chart of Job Titles'; run;`
- **second run group** → `pie Job_Title; title 'Pie Chart of Job Titles'; run;`
- **Terminate PROC GCHART.** → `quit;`

```
proc gchart data=orion.staff;
   vbar Job_Title;
   where Job_Title contains 'Rep';
   title 'Bar Chart of Job Titles';
run;
   pie Job_Title;
   title 'Pie Chart of Job Titles';
run;
quit;
title;
```

164 p1aad17

Business Scenario

Create bar and pie charts that represent the number of employees by job title.

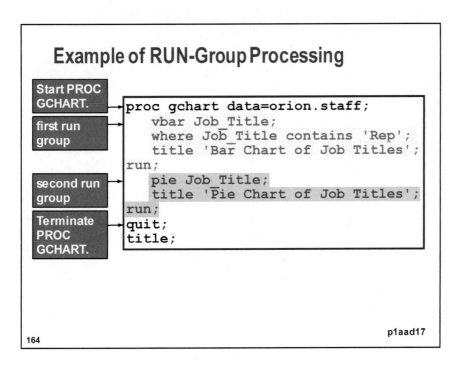

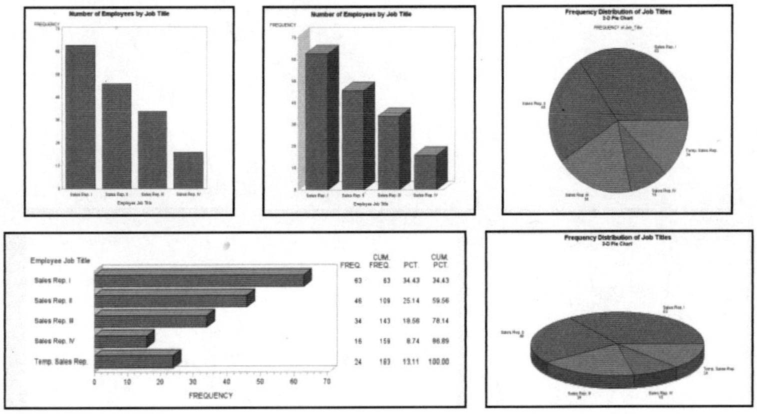

165

Copyright © 2016, SAS Institute Inc., Cary, North Carolina, USA. ALL RIGHTS RESERVED.

VBAR Statement

The VBAR statement requests a vertical bar chart.

```
goptions reset=all;
proc gchart data=orion.staff;
   vbar Job_Title;
   where Job_Title contains 'Rep';
   title 'Number of Employees by Job Title';
run;
quit;
title;
```

VBAR *chart-variable . . . </ options>*;

- The chart variable determines the number of bars in the graph.
- The height of the bar represents the frequency count of the values of the chart variable.

166 p1aad18

Viewing the Results

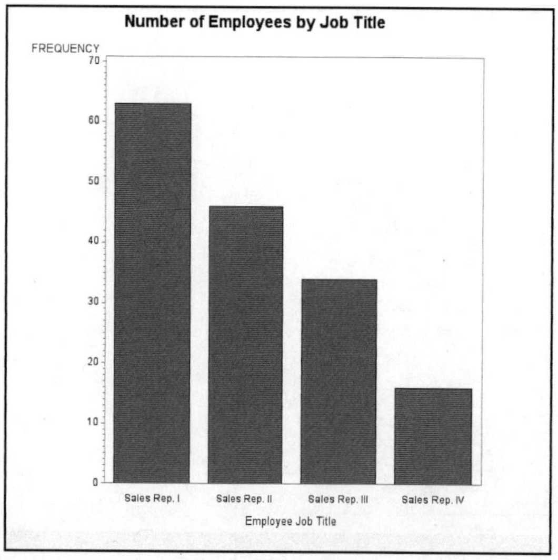

167

Copyright © 2016, SAS Institute Inc., Cary, North Carolina, USA. ALL RIGHTS RESERVED.

VBAR3D Statement

The VBAR3D statement requests a three-dimensional vertical bar chart.

```
goptions reset=all;
proc gchart data=orion.staff;
   vbar3d Job_Title;
   where Job_Title contains 'Rep';
   title 'Number of Employees by Job Title';
run;
quit;
title;
```

VBAR3D *chart-variable . . . </ options>*;

168

p1aad18

Viewing the Results

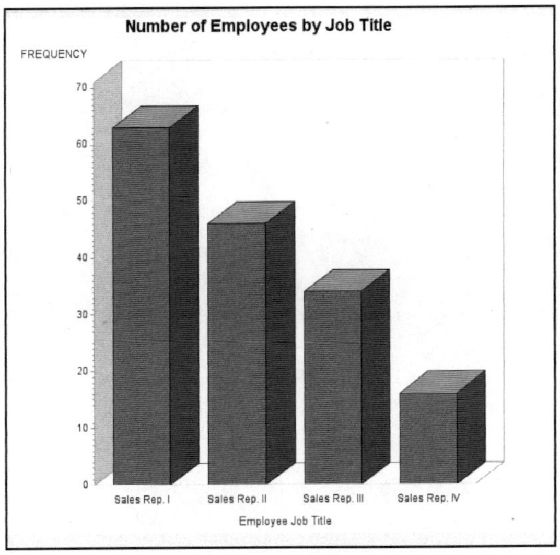

169

Copyright © 2016, SAS Institute Inc., Cary, North Carolina, USA. ALL RIGHTS RESERVED.

Producing Bar and Pie Charts

Use one of these statements to specify the chart type:

VBAR *chart-variable* . . . </ *options*>;
VBAR3D *chart-variable* . . . </ *options*>;

HBAR *chart-variable* . . . </ *options*>;
HBAR3D *chart-variable* . . . </ *options*>;

PIE *chart-variable* . . . </ *options*>;
PIE3D *chart-variable* . . . </ *options*>;

170

The chart variable determines the number of bars or slices produced within a graph. The chart variable can be character or numeric. By default, the height, length, or slice represents a frequency count of the values of the chart variable.

Copyright © 2016, SAS Institute Inc., Cary, North Carolina, USA. ALL RIGHTS RESERVED.

Creating Bar and Pie Charts

p1aad18

1. Submit the first PROC GCHART step to create a vertical bar chart that represents a frequency count.

   The VBAR statement creates a vertical bar chart that shows the number of sales representatives for each value of **Job_Title** in the **orion.staff** data set. **Job_Title** is referred to as the *chart variable*. Because the chart variable is a character variable, PROC GCHART displays one bar for each value of **Job_Title**.

```
goptions reset=all;
proc gchart data=orion.staff;
   vbar Job_Title;
   where Job_Title=:'Sales Rep';
   title 'Number of Employees by Job Title';
run;
quit;
title;
```

   The RESET=ALL option resets all graphics options to their default settings and clears any titles or footnotes that are in effect.

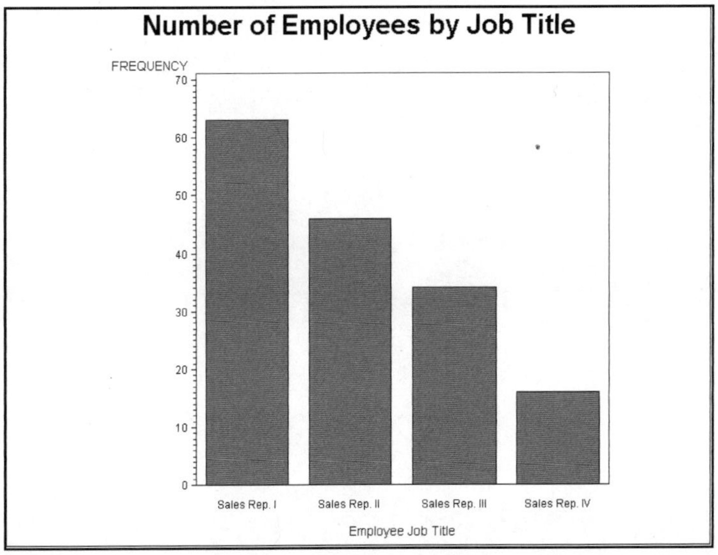

2. Submit the second PROC GCHART step to create a three-dimensional horizontal bar chart.

   The HBAR3D statement creates a three-dimensional horizontal bar chart, which shows the same information as the previous bar chart. Notice that the HBAR and HBAR3D statements automatically display statistics to the right of the chart.

```
goptions reset=all;
proc gchart data=orion.staff;
   hbar3d Job_Title;
   title 'Number of Employees by Job Title';
   where Job_Title=:'Sales Rep';
```

Copyright © 2016, SAS Institute Inc., Cary, North Carolina, USA. ALL RIGHTS RESERVED.

```
run;
quit;
title;
```

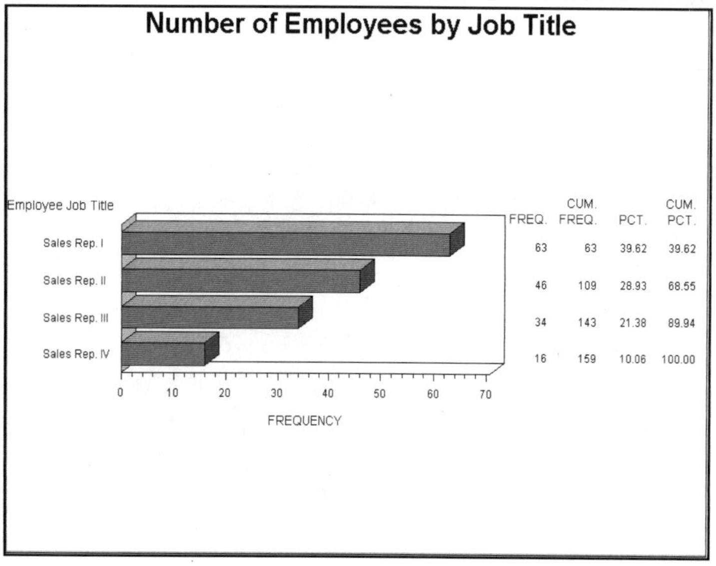

3. Submit the third PROC GCHART step to suppress the display of statistics on the horizontal bar chart.

   The NOSTATS option in the HBAR3D statement suppresses the display of statistics on the chart.

```
goptions reset=all;
proc gchart data=orion.staff;
   hbar3d Job_Title / nostats;
   title 'Number of Employees by Job Title';
   where Job_Title =:'Sales Rep';
run;
quit;
title;
```

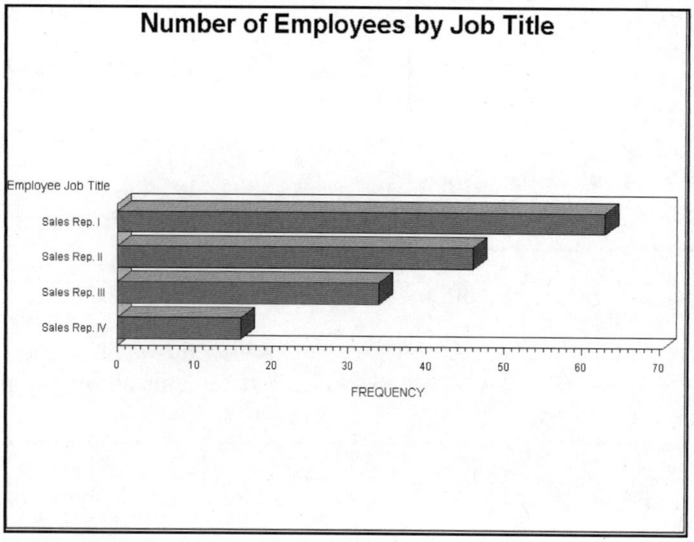

4. Submit the fourth PROC GCHART step to use a numeric chart variable.

Copyright © 2016, SAS Institute Inc., Cary, North Carolina, USA. ALL RIGHTS RESERVED.

The VBAR3D statement creates a vertical bar chart that shows the distribution of values of the variable **Salary**. Because the chart variable is numeric, PROC GCHART divides the values of **Salary** into ranges and displays one bar for each range. The value under the bar represents the midpoint of the range. The FORMAT statement assigns the DOLLAR9. format to **Salary**.

```
goptions reset=all;
proc gchart data=orion.staff;
   vbar3d salary / autoref;
   where Job_Title=:'Sales Rep';
   format salary dollar9.;
   title 'Salary Distribution Midpoints for Sales Reps';
run;
quit;
title;
```

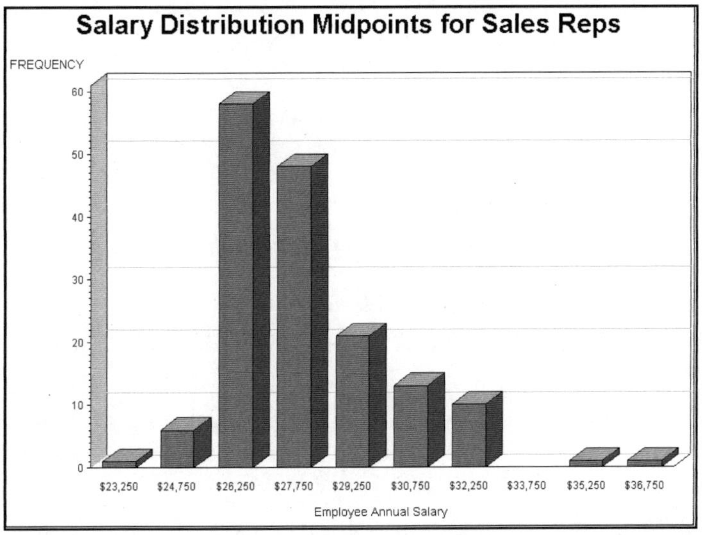

5. Submit the fifth PROC GCHART step to specify ranges for a numeric chart variable and add reference lines.
   - The HBAR3D statement creates a three-dimensional horizontal bar chart.
   - The LEVELS= option in the HBAR3D statement divides the values of **Salary** into five ranges and displays a bar for each range of values.
   - The RANGE option in the HBAR3D statement displays the range of values, rather than the midpoint, under each bar.
   - The AUTOREF option displays reference lines at each major tick mark on the horizontal (response) axis.

```
goptions reset=all;
proc gchart data=orion.staff;
   hbar3d salary / levels=5 range autoref;
   where Job_Title=:'Sales Rep';
   format salary dollar9.;
   title 'Salary Distribution Ranges for Sales Reps';
run;
quit;
title;
```

Copyright © 2016, SAS Institute Inc., Cary, North Carolina, USA. ALL RIGHTS RESERVED.

To display a bar for each unique value of the chart variable, specify the DISCRETE option instead of the LEVELS= option in the VBAR, VBAR3D, HBAR, or HBAR3D statement. The DISCRETE option should be used only when the chart variable has a relatively small number of unique values.

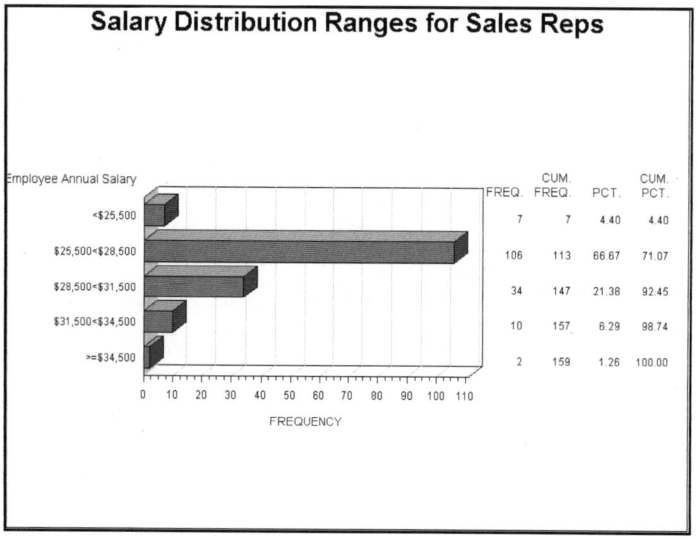

6. Submit the sixth PROC GCHART step to create bar charts based on statistics.
   - A vertical bar chart displays one bar for each value of the variable **Job_Title** by specifying **Job_Title** as the chart variable in the VBAR statement. The height of the bar should be based on the mean value of the variable **Salary** for each job title.
   - The SUMVAR= option in the VBAR statement specifies the variable whose values control the height or length of the bars. This variable (**Salary**, in this instance) is known as the *analysis variable.*
   - The TYPE= option in the VBAR statement specifies the statistic for the analysis variable that controls the height or length of the bars. Possible values for the TYPE= option are SUM and MEAN.
   - A LABEL statement assigns labels to the variables **Job_Title** and **Salary**.

```
goptions reset=all;
proc gchart data=orion.staff;
   vbar Job_Title / sumvar=salary type=mean;
   where Job_Title =:'Sales Rep';
   format salary dollar9.;
   label Job_Title='Job Title'
         Salary='Salary';
   title 'Average Salary by Job Title';
run;
quit;
title;
```

If the TYPE= option is not specified, the default value of the TYPE= option is SUM.

Copyright © 2016, SAS Institute Inc., Cary, North Carolina, USA. ALL RIGHTS RESERVED.

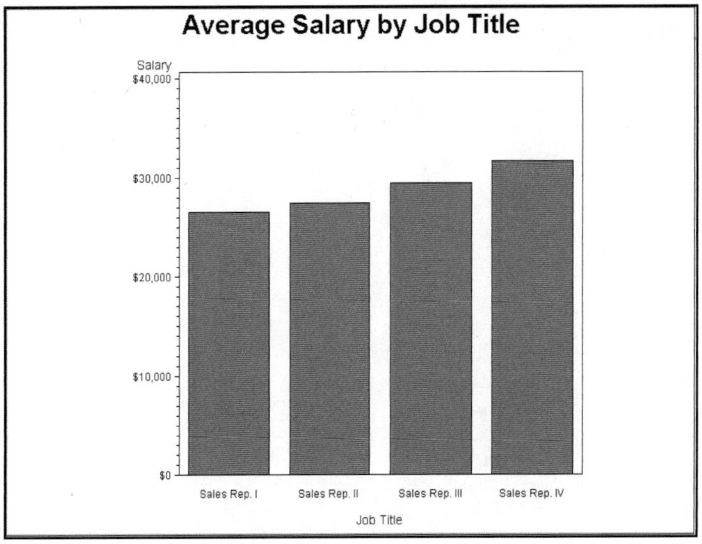

7. Submit the seventh PROC GCHART step to assign a different color to each bar and display the mean statistic on the top of each bar.
   - The PATTERNID=MIDPOINT option in the VBAR statement causes PROC GCHART to assign a different pattern or color to each value of the midpoint (chart) variable.
   - The MEAN option in the VBAR statement displays the mean statistic on the top of each bar. Other options such as SUM, FREQ, and PERCENT can be specified to display other statistics on the top of the bars.

```
goptions reset=all;
proc gchart data=orion.staff;
   vbar Job_Title / sumvar=salary type=mean patternid=midpoint
mean;
   where Job_Title=:'Sales Rep';
   format salary dollar9.;
   title 'Average Salary by Job Title';
run;
quit;
title;
```

Only one statistic can be displayed on top of each vertical bar. For horizontal bar charts, you can specify multiple statistics, which are displayed to the right of the bars.

Copyright © 2016, SAS Institute Inc., Cary, North Carolina, USA. ALL RIGHTS RESERVED.

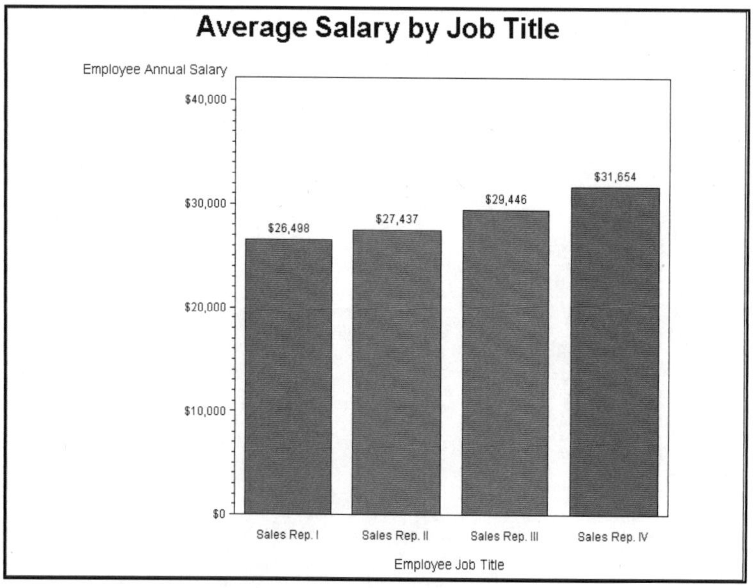

8. Submit the eighth PROC GCHART step to divide the bars into subgroups.
   - A VBAR statement creates a vertical bar chart that shows the number of sales representatives for each value of **Job_Title**.
   - The SUBGROUP= option in the VBAR statement divides the bar into sections. Each section represents the frequency count for each value of the variable **Gender**.

```
goptions reset=all;
proc gchart data=orion.staff;
   vbar Job_Title / subgroup=Gender;
   where Job_Title=:'Sales Rep';
   title 'Frequency of Job Title, Broken Down by Gender';
run;
quit;
title;
```

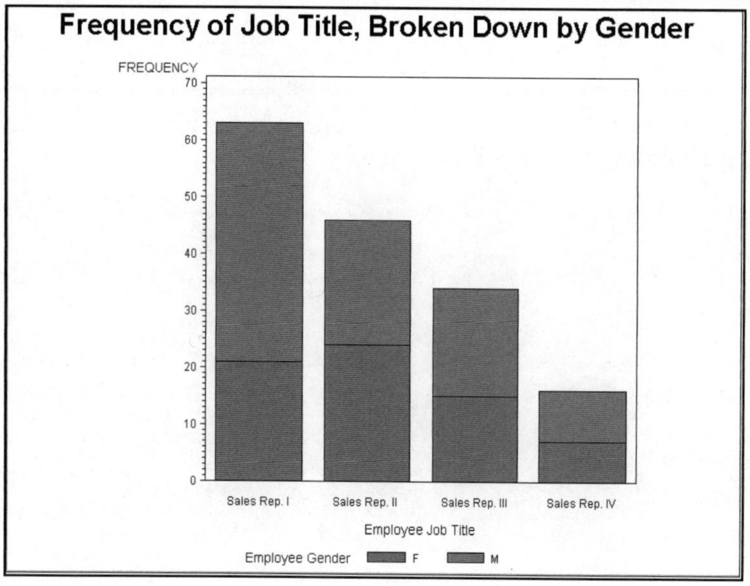

Copyright © 2016, SAS Institute Inc., Cary, North Carolina, USA. ALL RIGHTS RESERVED.

9. Submit the ninth PROC GCHART step to group the bars.
   - A VBAR statement creates a vertical bar chart that shows the frequency for each value of **Gender**.
   - The GROUP= option in the VBAR statement displays a separate set of bars for each value of **Job_Title**.
   - The PATTERNID=MIDPOINT option in the VBAR statement displays each value of **Gender** (the midpoint or chart variable) with the same pattern.

```
goptions reset=all;
proc gchart data=orion.staff;
   vbar gender / group=Job_Title patternid=midpoint;
   where Job_Title=:'Sales Rep';
   title 'Frequency of Job Gender, Grouped by Job Title';
run;
quit;
title;
```

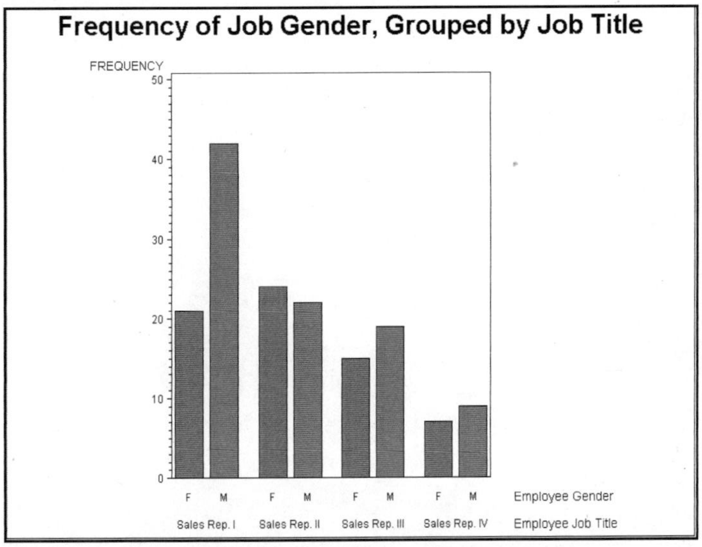

Submitting the following statements (reversing the chart and group variables) produces a chart with two groups of four bars:

```
proc gchart data=orion.staff;
   vbar gender/group=Job_Title patternid=midpoint;
```

10. Use RUN-group processing to submit the final PROC GCHART step and create multiple pie charts.
    - A PIE statement and a PIE3D statement in the same PROC GCHART step produce both a two-dimensional pie chart and a three-dimensional pie chart that show the number of sales representatives for each value of **Job_Title**.
    - The TITLE2 statements specify different subtitles for each chart. The NOHEADING option in the PIE3D statement suppresses the **FREQUENCY of Job_Title** heading.

    Because RUN-group processing is in effect, notice the following:
    - It is not necessary to submit a separate PROC GCHART statement for each graph.
    - The WHERE statement is applied to both charts.
    - The TITLE statement is applied to both charts.
    - A separate TITLE2 statement is used for each chart.

Copyright © 2016, SAS Institute Inc., Cary, North Carolina, USA. ALL RIGHTS RESERVED.

```
goptions reset=all;
proc gchart data=orion.staff;
   pie Job_Title;
   where Job_Title=:'Sales Rep';
   title 'Frequency Distribution of Job Titles';
   title2 '2-D Pie Chart';
run;
   pie3d Job_Title / noheading;
   title2 '3-D Pie Chart';
run;
quit;
title;
```

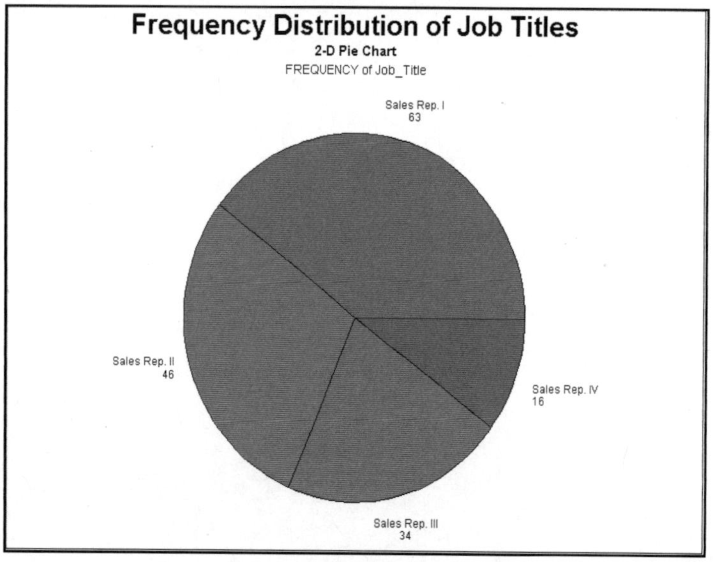

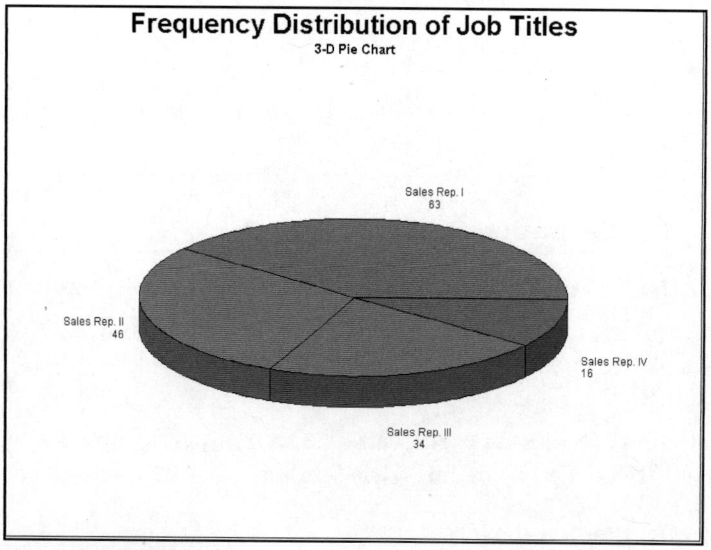

End of Demonstration

Copyright © 2016, SAS Institute Inc., Cary, North Carolina, USA. ALL RIGHTS RESERVED.

Business Scenario

Use the GPLOT procedure to plot one variable against another within a set of coordinate axes.

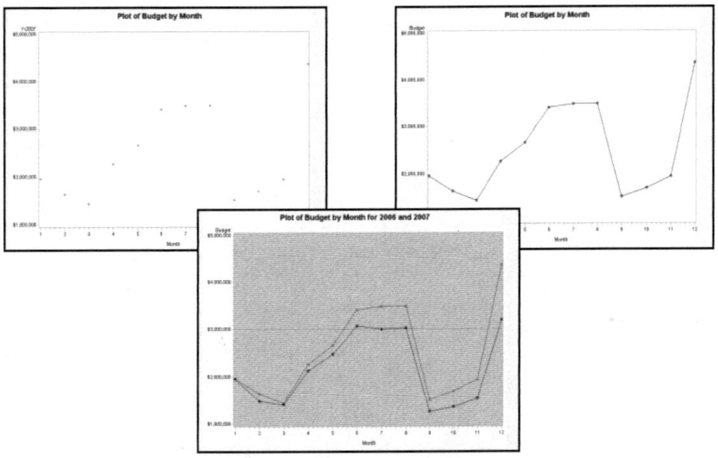

172

Producing Plots with the GPLOT Procedure

Plot one variable against another within a set of coordinate axes.

```
goptions reset=all;
proc gplot data=orion.oldbudget;
   plot Yr2007*Month;
   format Yr2007 dollar12.;
   title 'Plot of Budget by Month';
run;
quit;
title;
```

PROC GPLOT DATA=*SAS-data-set*;
  PLOT *vertical-variable*horizontal-variable* </ *options*>;
RUN;
QUIT;

173 p1aad19

Copyright © 2016, SAS Institute Inc., Cary, North Carolina, USA. ALL RIGHTS RESERVED.

Viewing the Output

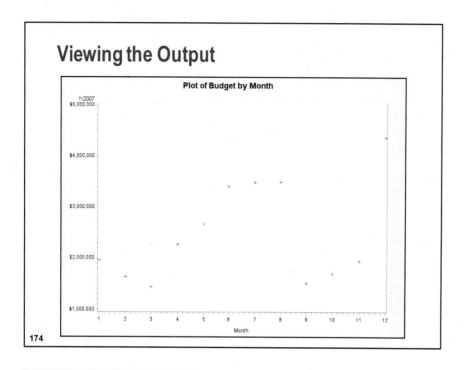

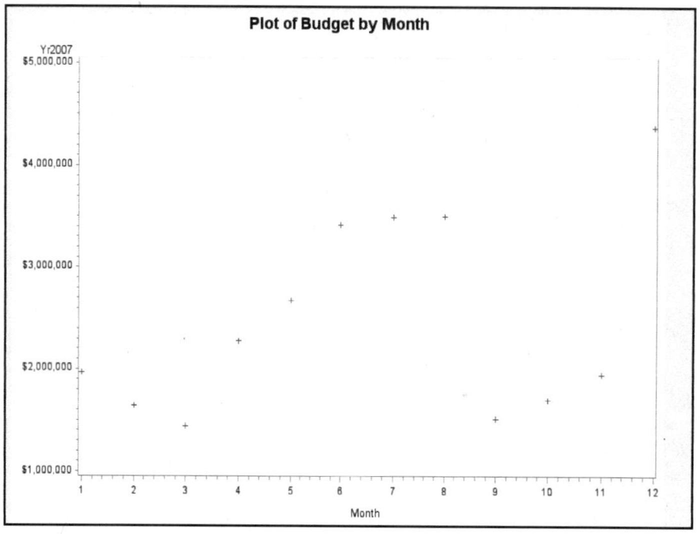

174

Plot Options

Use options and statements to specify plot symbols and interpolation lines.

```
goptions reset=all;
proc gplot data=orion.oldbudget;
   plot Yr2007*Month / haxis=1 to 12;
   label Yr2007='Budget';
   format Yr2007 dollar12.;
   title 'Plot of Budget by Month';
   symbol1 v=dot i=join cv=red ci=blue;
run;
quit;
title;
```

175 p1aad19

Copyright © 2016, SAS Institute Inc., Cary, North Carolina, USA. ALL RIGHTS RESERVED.

Viewing the Output

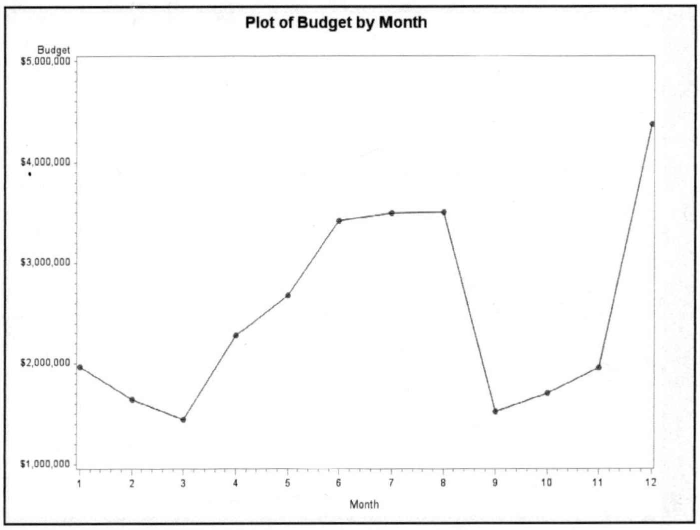

176

Copyright © 2016, SAS Institute Inc., Cary, North Carolina, USA. ALL RIGHTS RESERVED.

Creating Plots

plaad19

1. Submit the first PROC GPLOT step to create a simple scatter plot.
   - The PROC GPLOT step creates a plot that displays the values of the variable **Yr2007** on the vertical axis and **Month** on the horizontal axis. The points are displayed with the default plotting symbol (a plus sign).
   - A FORMAT statement assigns the DOLLAR12. format to **Yr2007**.

```
goptions reset=all;
proc gplot data=orion.oldbudget;
   plot Yr2007*Month;
   format Yr2007 dollar12.;
   title 'Plot of Budget by Month';
run;
quit;
title;
```

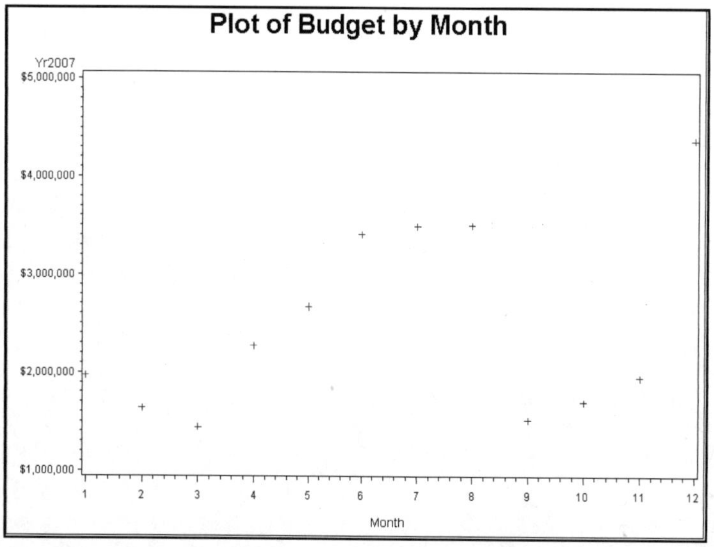

2. Submit the second PROC GPLOT step to specify plot symbols and interpolation lines.

   The SYMBOL statement specifies an alternate plotting symbol and draws an interpolation line that joins the plot points. The options in the SYMBOL statement are as follows:
   - V= specifies the plotting symbol (a dot).
   - I= specifies the interpolation method to be used to connect the points (join).
   - CV= specifies the color of the plotting symbol.
   - CI= specifies the color of the interpolation line.

   The LABEL statement assigns a label to the variable **Yr2007**.

```
goptions reset=all;
proc gplot data=orion.oldbudget;
```

Copyright © 2016, SAS Institute Inc., Cary, North Carolina, USA. ALL RIGHTS RESERVED.

```
   plot Yr2007*Month / haxis=1 to 12;
   label Yr2007='Budget';
   format Yr2007 dollar12.;
   title 'Plot of Budget by Month';
   symbol1 v=dot i=join cv=red ci=blue;
run;
quit;
title;
```

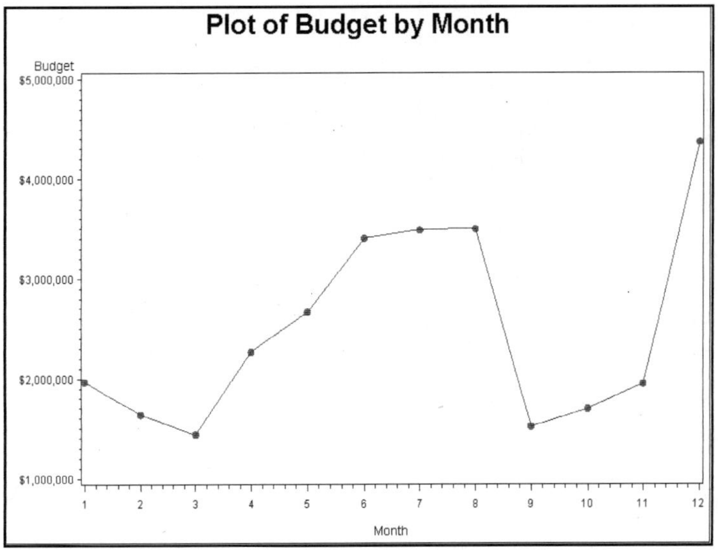

3. Submit the third PROC GPLOT step to overlay multiple plot lines on the same set of axes.

   The PLOT statement specifies two separate plot requests (**Yr2006*Month** and **Yr2007*Month**). This results in an overlay plot with the variables **Yr2006** and **Yr2007** on the vertical axis and **Month** on the horizontal axis.

   The options in the PLOT statement are as follows:

   - The OVERLAY option causes both plot requests to be displayed on the same set of axes.
   - The HAXIS= option specifies the range of values for the horizontal axis. (The VAXIS= option can be used to specify the range for the vertical axis.)
   - The VREF= option specifies a value on the vertical axis where a reference line should be drawn.
   - The CFRAME= option specifies a color to be used for the background within the plot axes.

```
goptions reset=all;
proc gplot data=orion.oldbudget;
   plot Yr2006*Month yr2007*Month / overlay haxis=1 to 12
   vref=3000000
   cframe="very light gray";
   label Yr2006='Budget';
   format Yr2006 dollar12.;
   title 'Plot of Budget by Month for 2006 and 2007';
   symbol1 i=join v=dot ci=blue cv=blue;
   symbol2 i=join v=triangle ci=red cv=red;
run;
quit;
```

Copyright © 2016, SAS Institute Inc., Cary, North Carolina, USA. ALL RIGHTS RESERVED.

```
title;
```

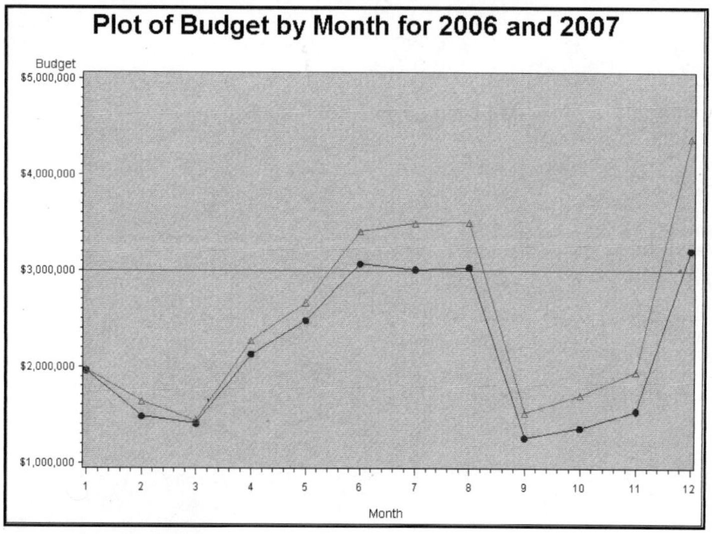

End of Demonstration

Copyright © 2016, SAS Institute Inc., Cary, North Carolina, USA. ALL RIGHTS RESERVED.

Business Scenario

Use options and global statements to enhance SAS/GRAPH output.

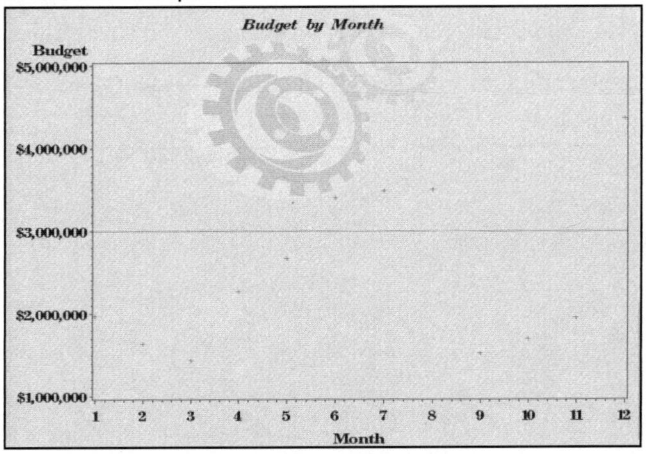

178

Enhancing SAS/GRAPH Output

SAS/GRAPH uses default values for colors, fonts, text size, and other graph attributes. You can override these defaults using the following methods:

- specifying an ODS style
- specifying default attributes in a GOPTIONS statement
- specifying attributes and options in global statements and procedure statements

179

Copyright © 2016, SAS Institute Inc., Cary, North Carolina, USA. ALL RIGHTS RESERVED.

Enhancing Output

p1aad20

1. Submit the first PROC GPLOT step. Use ODS styles to control the appearance of the output.

   Specifying the style in the ODS LISTING statement with the STYLE= option produces a different ODS style.

```
ods listing style=gears;
goptions reset=all;
proc gplot data=orion.oldbudget;
   plot Yr2007*Month;
   format Yr2007 dollar12.;
   label Yr2007='Budget';
   title 'Plot of Budget by Month';
run;
quit;
title;
```

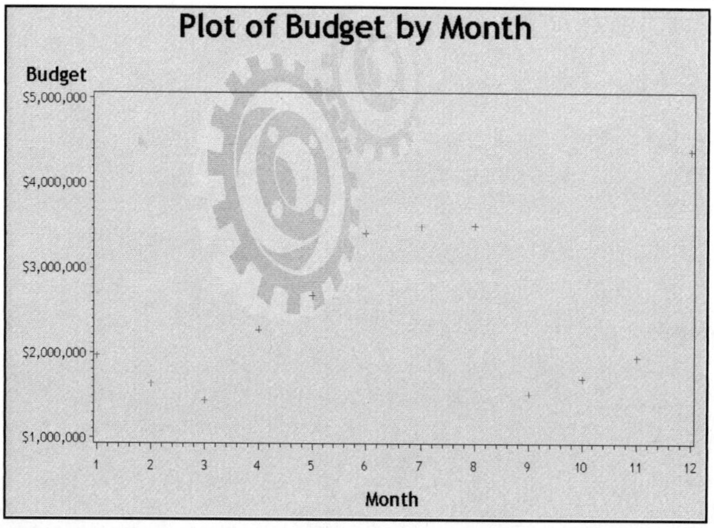

2. Submit the second PROC GPLOT step. Specify the options in the TITLE and FOOTNOTE statements to control the text appearance.

   The TITLE and FOOTNOTE statements override the default fonts, colors, height, and text justification. The following options are used:

   - F= (or FONT=) specifies a font.
   - C= (or COLOR=) specifies text color.
   - H= (or HEIGHT=) specifies text height. Units of height can be specified as a percent of the display (PCT), inches (IN), centimeters (CM), cells (CELLS), or points (PT).
   - J= (or JUSTIFY=) specifies text justification. Valid values are LEFT (L), CENTER (C), and RIGHT (R).

   All options apply to the text that follows the option.

Copyright © 2016, SAS Institute Inc., Cary, North Carolina, USA. ALL RIGHTS RESERVED.

```
ods listing style=gears;
goptions reset=all;
proc gplot data=orion.oldbudget;
   plot Yr2007*Month / vref=3000000;
   label Yr2007='Budget';
   format Yr2007 dollar12.;
   title f=centbi h=5 pct 'Budget by Month';
   footnote c=green j=left 'Data for 2007';
run;
quit;
title;
```

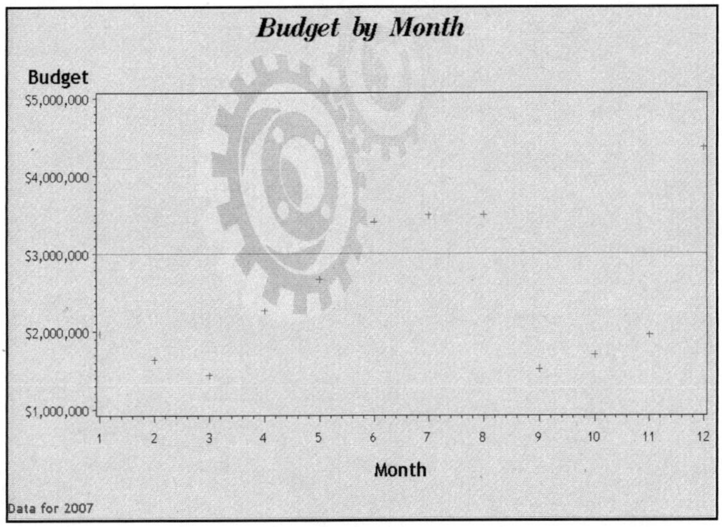

3. Submit the third PROC GPLOT. It uses a GOPTIONS statement.

   A GOPTIONS statement specifies options to control the appearance of all text in the graph. The following options are used:

   - FTEXT= specifies a font for all text.
   - CTEXT= specifies the color for all text.
   - HTEXT= specifies the height for all text.

   If a text option is specified both in a GOPTIONS statement and in a TITLE or FOOTNOTE statement, the option specified in the TITLE or FOOTNOTE statement overrides the value in the GOPTIONS statement for that title or footnote only.

```
ods listing style=gears;
goptions reset=all ftext=centb htext=3 pct ctext=dark_blue;
proc gplot data=orion.oldbudget;
   plot Yr2007*Month / vref=3000000;
   label Yr2007='Budget';
   format Yr2007 dollar12.;
   title f=centbi 'Budget by Month';
run;
quit;
title;
```

Copyright © 2016, SAS Institute Inc., Cary, North Carolina, USA. ALL RIGHTS RESERVED.

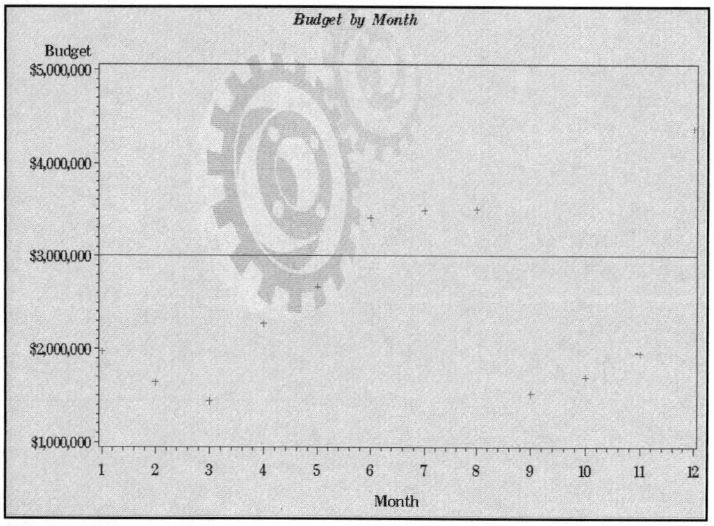

End of Demonstration

Copyright © 2016, SAS Institute Inc., Cary, North Carolina, USA. ALL RIGHTS RESERVED.

A.7 Solutions

Solutions to Exercises

1. **Using PROC COPY to Create an Excel Worksheet**

```
libname mnth pcfiles path="&path\mnth2011.xls";

proc copy in=orion out=mnth;
   select mnth7_2011 mnth8_2011 mnth9_2011;
run;

proc contents data=mnth._all_;
run;

libname mnth clear;
```

2. **Using the Import Wizard to Read an Excel Worksheet**

This solution uses the SAS windowing environment.

Select **File** ⇨ **Import Data**. Accept the default type or select **Microsoft Excel Workbook on PC Files Server**. Browse your data folder and select the workbook **products.xls**.

If you selected the PC Files Server, then you must enter a server name. Enter **localhost** or the name of your remote PC Files Server.

1) Select the worksheet to import.

2) Enter a SAS library and data set name for the new data set.

3) Enter a filename for the generated PROC IMPORT code.

4) Click **Finish**.

```
proc print data=work.children;
run;
```

```
PROC IMPORT OUT= WORK.CHILD
            DATAFILE= "S:\workshop\products.xls"
            DBMS=EXCELCS REPLACE;
   SERVER="localhost";
   PORT=9621;
   SSPI=YES;
   RANGE="Children$";
   SCANTEXT=YES;
   USEDATE=YES;
   SCANTIME=YES;
RUN;
```

3. **Using the EXPORT Procedure to Create an Excel Worksheet**

```
proc export data=orion.mnth7_2011
```

Copyright © 2016, SAS Institute Inc., Cary, North Carolina, USA. ALL RIGHTS RESERVED.

```
              outfile="&path\mnth7.xls"
              dbms=excelcs replace;
run;
```

4. **Using IF-THEN/DELETE to Subset Observations**

```
data work.bigdonations;
   set orion.employee_donations;
   Total=sum(Qtr1,Qtr2,Qtr3,Qtr4);
   NoDonation=nmiss(Qtr1,Qtr2,Qtr3,Qtr4);
   if Total<50 or NoDonation>0 then delete;
run;

proc print data=work.bigdonations;
   var Employee_ID Qtr1 Qtr2 Qtr3 Qtr4 Total NoDonation;
run;
```

5. **Appending Like-Structured Data Sets**

   How many variables are in **orion.price_current**? **6**

   How many variables are in **orion.price_new**? **5**

   Does **orion.price_new** contain any variables that are not in **orion.price_current**? **no**

```
proc contents data=orion.price_current;
run;

proc contents data=orion.price_new;
run;

proc append base=orion.price_current
            data=orion.price_new;
run;
```

   Why is the FORCE option not needed? **The variables in the DATA= data set are all in the BASE= data set.**

6. **Appending Unlike-Structured Data Sets**

   How many variables are in **orion.qtr1_2011**? **5**

   How many variables are in **orion.qtr2_2011**? **6**

   Which variable is not in both data sets? **Employee_ID**

```
proc contents data=orion.qtr1_2011;
run;

proc contents data=orion.qtr2_2011;
run;

proc append base=work.ytd
            data=orion.qtr1_2011;
run;

proc append base=work.ytd
            data=orion.qtr2_2007 force;
```

Copyright © 2016, SAS Institute Inc., Cary, North Carolina, USA. ALL RIGHTS RESERVED.

```
run;
```

Why is the FORCE option needed? **The variable Employee_ID in the DATA= data set is not in the BASE= data set.**

7. **Using the APPEND Statement**

```
proc contents data=orion.shoes_eclipse;
run;

proc contents data=orion.shoes_tracker;
run;

proc contents data=orion.shoes;
run;

proc datasets library=orion nolist;
   append base=shoes data=shoes_eclipse;
   append base=shoes data=shoes_tracker force;
quit;
```

8. **Interleaving Data Sets**

```
proc sort data=orion.shoes_eclipse
          out=work.eclipsesort;
   by Product_Name;
run;

proc sort data=orion.shoes_tracker
          out=work.trackersort;
   by Product_Name;
run;

data work.e_t_shoes;
   set work.eclipsesort work.trackersort;
   by Product_Name;
   keep Product_Group Product_Name Supplier_ID;
run;

proc print data=work.e_t_shoes;
run;
```

9. **Merging and Creating Output to Multiple Data Sets**

```
proc sort data=orion.orders
          out=work.orders;
   by Employee_ID;
run;

data work.allorders work.noorders;
   merge orion.staff(in=Staff) work.orders(in=Ord);
   by Employee_ID;
   if Ord=1 then output work.allorders;
```

Copyright © 2016, SAS Institute Inc., Cary, North Carolina, USA. ALL RIGHTS RESERVED.

```
   else if Staff=1 and Ord=0 then output work.noorders;
   keep Employee_ID Job_Title Gender Order_ID Order_Type
Order_Date;

proc print data=work.allorders;
run;

proc print data=work.noorders;
run;
```

10. Specifying Titles, Footnotes, and System Options

```
options nonumber nodate pagesize=18;

title 'Orion Star Sales Report';
footnote 'Report by SAS Programming Student';

proc means data=orion.order_fact;
   var Total_Retail_Price;
run;

options pagesize=52;
title;
footnote;
```

11. Specifying Multiple Titles and System Options

```
options pagesize=18 number pageno=1 date dtreset;
title1 'Orion Star Sales Analysis';

proc means data=orion.order_fact;
   where Order_Type=2;
   var Total_Retail_Price;
   title3 'Catalog Sales Only';
   footnote "Based on the previous day's posted data";
run;

options pageno=1;
proc means data=orion.order_fact;
   where Order_Type=3;
   var Total_Retail_Price;
   title3 'Internet Sales Only';
   footnote;
run;
options pagesize=52;
title;
```

12. Inserting Dates and Times into Titles

```
proc options option=date;
run;
options nodate;

%let currentdate=%sysfunc(today(),weekdate.);
%let currenttime=%sysfunc(time(),timeampm8.);
```

Copyright © 2016, SAS Institute Inc., Cary, North Carolina, USA. ALL RIGHTS RESERVED.

```
proc means data=orion.order_fact;
   title "Sales Report as of &currenttime on &currentdate";
   var Total_Retail_Price;
run;
title;
```

13. Creating an Output Data Set with PROC FREQ

```
proc freq data=orion.order_fact noprint;
   tables Product_ID / out=product_orders;
run;

data product_names;
   merge product_orders orion.product_list;
   by Product_ID;
   keep Product_ID Product_Name Count;
run;

proc sort data=product_names;
   by descending Count;
run;

proc print data=product_names(obs=10) label;
   var Count Product_ID Product_Name;
   label Product_ID='Product Number'
         Product_Name='Product'
         Count='Orders';
   title 'Top Ten Products by Number of Orders';
run;
title;
```

14. Creating an Output Data Set with PROC MEANS

```
proc means data=orion.order_fact noprint nway;
   class Product_ID;
   var Total_Retail_Price;
   output out=product_orders sum=Product_Revenue;
run;

data product_names;
   merge product_orders orion.product_list;
   by Product_ID;
   keep Product_ID Product_Name Product_Revenue;
run;

proc sort data=product_names;
   by descending Product_Revenue;
run;

proc print data=product_names(obs=10) label;
   var Product_Revenue Product_ID Product_Name;
   label Product_ID='Product Number'
```

Copyright © 2016, SAS Institute Inc., Cary, North Carolina, USA. ALL RIGHTS RESERVED.

```
         Product_Name='Product'
         Product_Revenue='Revenue';
   title 'Top Ten Products by Revenue';
run;

proc print data=product_names(obs=10) label;
   var Product_Revenue Product_ID Product_Name;
   label Product_ID='Product Number'
         Product_Name='Product'
         Product_Revenue='Revenue';
   format Product_Revenue eurox12.2;
   title 'Top Ten Products by Revenue';
run;
title;
```

15. **Creating a Tabular Report with PROC TABULATE**

```
proc tabulate data=orion.customer_dim;
   class Customer_Group Customer_Gender;
   var Customer_Age;
   table Customer_Group all,
         Customer_Gender*Customer_Age*(n mean);
   title 'Ages of Customers by Group and Gender';
run;
title;
```

16. **Creating a Three-Dimensional Tabular Report with PROC TABULATE**

```
proc tabulate data=orion.customer_dim;
   class Customer_Gender Customer_Group;
   table Customer_Gender, Customer_Group, (n colpctn);
   keylabel colpctn='Percentage' N='Number';
   title 'Customers by Group and Gender';
run;
title;
```

17. **Creating a Customized Tabular Report with PROC TABULATE**

```
proc tabulate data=orion.order_fact format=dollar12.;
   where CostPrice_Per_Unit > 250;
   class Product_ID Order_Date;
   format Order_Date year4.;
   var Total_Retail_Price;
   table Order_Date=' ', Total_Retail_Price*sum*Product_ID=' '
         / misstext='$0'
           box='High Cost Products (Unit Cost > $250)';
   label Total_Retail_Price='Revenue for Each Product';
   keylabel Sum=' ';
run;
```

18. **Creating an Output Data Set with PROC TABULATE**

```
proc tabulate data=orion.organization_dim format=dollar12.
              out=work.salaries;
   class Employee_Gender Company;
```

Copyright © 2016, SAS Institute Inc., Cary, North Carolina, USA. ALL RIGHTS RESERVED.

```
   var Salary;
   table Company, (Employee_Gender all)*Salary*mean;
   title 'Average Employee Salaries';
run;

proc sort data=work.salaries;
   by Salary_Mean;
run;

proc print data=work.salaries label;
   var Company Employee_Gender Salary_Mean;
   format Salary_Mean dollar12.;
   label Salary_Mean='Average Salary';
   title 'Average Employee Salaries';
run;
title;
```

End of Solutions

Copyright © 2016, SAS Institute Inc., Cary, North Carolina, USA. ALL RIGHTS RESERVED.

Copyright © 2016, SAS Institute Inc., Cary, North Carolina, USA. ALL RIGHTS RESERVED.